TARAS KUZIO

# PUTIN'S
# WAR
# AGAINST
# UKRAINE

## REVOLUTION, NATIONALISM, AND CRIME

*PUBLISHED IN ASSOCIATION WITH THE*
*CHAIR OF UKRAINIAN STUDIES*
*UNIVERSITY OF TORONTO*

The photograph of a Ukrainian soldier in combat on the front cover is reproduced courtesy of Noah Brooks who is a documentary photographer from Point Pleasant, New Jersey, USA. Noah began his photography taking photos of the ocean along the New Jersey Shore, then moved on to photograph protests around the United States. After the war broke out in Ukraine, Noah felt compelled to document the story of Euromaidan Revolution protesters leaving the barricades in Kyiv to fight in combat on the front line in Donbas. He can be reached at noahbrooks99@gmail.com.

The remaining photographs were taken by Taras Kuzio and Natali Prylutska (Dziuba). After her brother-in law Dmytro Kuzmin was killed in combat in July 2014, Natali decided to become a civil society volunteer and since then has been delivering food, uniforms, boots, medicines, night vision, and sleeping bags 2-3 times each month to Ukrainian soldiers on the front line. When the photograph was taken is given in brackets.

Printed by CreateSpace, An Amazon.com Company

First Printing, 2017

Published in association with the
Chair of Ukrainian Studies
University of Toronto

www.betweeneuropeandrussia.com

*There is no doubt as to the Austro-German origin of the legend of the existence of a separate Ukrainian nation.*

Prince Alexandre Wolkonsky, The Ukraine Question (1920)

*Modern Ukraine's borders also do not correspond to historic ethnographic limits. Seven million Russians and, probably, no less Russianised Ukrainians live in Ukraine, and it would be more appropriate to transfer several Ukrainian oblasts to Russia. We are not even talking about the flagrant injustice of giving Crimea to Ukraine...If a question about the independence of Ukraine really arose, its boundaries should be revised. In such a case, Ukraine should cede the following territories to Russia: (a) Crimea, (b) Kharkiv, Donetsk, Luhansk, and Zaporizhzhya oblasts (where the Russian population dominates), and (c) Odesa, Mykolayiv, Kherson, Dnipropetrovsk (Dnipro), and Sumy oblasts (where the population is Russified enough and which were historically developed by the Russian state).*

Russian Patriots, *A Nation Speaks* (1970)

*Maybe it will be necessary to have a referendum in each region and then ensure preferential and delicate treatment of those who would want to leave. Not the whole of Ukraine in its current formal Soviet borders is indeed Ukraine. Some regions on the left bank (of the river Dnipro) clearly lean more towards Russia. As for the Crimea, Khrushchev's decision to hand it over to Ukraine was totally arbitrary.*

Alexander Solzhenitsyn, *Rebuilding Russia* (1990)

*The outcome of the referendum should be calculated separately in each region and each region must decide for itself where it stands.*

Alexander Solzhenitsyn, Appeal on the Ukrainian Referendum on Independence (1991)

*Our concerns are understandable because we are not simply close neighbours but, as I have said many times already, we are one people. Kyiv is the mother of Russian cities. Ancient Rus is our common source and we cannot live without each other.*

President Vladimir Putin (2014)

# CONTENTS

# TABLES AND BOXES

# MAPS

# ABBREVIATIONS, ACRONYMS, AND KEY PERSONALITIES

## ABREVIATIONS AND ACRONYMNS

ATO – Anti-Terrorist Operation is the official name for Ukraine's military operations in the separatist-controlled Donbas territories.

Banderite – follower of OUN leader Stepan Bandera, but extensively used by Russia for all supporters of Ukrainian patriotism and nationalism.

Batkivshchyna – Fatherland party led by Yulia Tymoshenko (1999-2011, since 2014).

Berkut – riot police in the Ministry of Interior and the snipers who murdered protesters on the Euromaidan, disbanded in spring 2014.

BYuT – Bloc of Yulia Tymoshenko (2002-2011).

CIS – Commonwealth of Independent States, successor organisation to the USSR established in December 1991.

Colour revolutions – the term used to denote democratic revolutions after opposition groups used colours to differentiate themselves (e.g. orange in Ukraine in 2004).

Cyborg – the term applied to Ukrainian troops fighting for a long period of time against Russian and separatist forces in Donetsk Airport.

DCFTA – Deep and Comprehensive Free Trade Agreement, part of the EU-Ukraine Association Agreement.

Dnipro - the new name for Dnipropetrovsk which this book continues to use.

DNR – Donetsk People's Republic, separatist Russian satellite region in Donetsk *oblast*.

EaP – Eastern Partnership policy established by the EU in 2009 for six former Soviet republics.

Euromaidan – Revolution of Dignity between November 2013-February 2014.

EU – European Union.

GRU – Russian military intelligence whose *spetsnaz* became known as 'little green men' because they lacked country insignia on their uniforms. *Zelyonye chelovechki* also refers to outer space humanoids who came from nowhere and nobody knows who they are, a sarcastic response to Russia's stubborn denial that these military forces had anything to do with Russia.

Gubernia – administrative region of the Tsarist Russia Empire.

Holodomor – artificial terror-famine unleashed by Joseph Stalin in 1933 that murdered five million people in the Soviet Ukrainian republic and the Ukrainian-populated Kuban region of the northern Caucasus.

Homo Sovieticus – Soviet person used to denote somebody with a Soviet ('Sovok') mentality.

ICC – International Criminal Court.

IRI – International Republican Institute.

Khazayin – Lord of the manor, the unbridled sovereign of a region.

KHRPG – Kharkiv Human Rights Protection Group.

KIIS – Kyiv International Institute of Sociological Studies.

Night Wolves – Pro-Vladimir Putin Russian Hells Angels led by Aleksandr ('Surgeon') Zaldonstanov whose units are fighting for the separatists in the LNR.

Komsomol – Communist Party of the Soviet Union youth league.

Krysha – a roof, but used as criminal slang to denote political protection for corrupt and criminal activities.

KPRF – Communist Party of the Russian Federation.

KPRS – Communist Party of the Soviet Union.

KPU – Communist Party of Ukraine, banned in 1991, revived in 1993, and *de facto* defunct since 2014.

Little Green Men – the term used to describe Russian *spetsnaz* without country insignia who invaded Ukraine's Crimea and eastern Ukraine in 2014.

LNR – Luhansk People's Republic, separatist Russian satellite region of Luhansk *oblast*.

Maskirovka - Russian military deception or hybrid war.

Mejlis – Crimean Tatar unofficial parliament banned by the Russian occupation authorities in April 2016.

Minsk Accords – negotiated in September 2014 and February 2015 by Ukraine, Russia, France and Germany.

MVS – Ministry of Interior.

Nashi – Ours, a pro-Putin youth movement established in 2005.

NKVD – People's Commissariat for Internal Affairs, Stalin's secret police (1934-1946).

Nomenklatura – Soviet ruling class.

NovoRossiya – New Russia, Tsarist Russian term for eastern and southern Ukraine revived by President Putin in spring 2014.

NTS – National Alliance of Solidarists, Russian neo-fascist émigré organisation established in 1930 by young Russian White émigrés and funded by the US government after World War II until 1991.

Okhrana – Tsarist Russian secret police.

Oplot (Stronghold) – pro-Russian and pro-separatist vigilante group with ties to organised crime that moved to the DNR after it was defeated in its home base of Kharkiv.

OSCE – Organisation for Security and Cooperation in Europe, which has a Special Monitoring Mission to Ukraine based in the Donbas since March 2014.

OUN – Organisation of Ukrainian Nationalists, Ukrainian nationalist organisation active in Poland (1930s), USSR (1940s) and the Ukrainian diaspora (1945-1991).

RFERL – Radio Free Europe and Radio Liberty.

RNBO – Ukrainian) National Security and Defence Council.

RNE – All-Russian Public Patriotic Movement Russian National Unity, Russia's first neo-Nazi political party.

RUE – RosUkrEnergo gas intermediary organised by Gazprom and Ukrainian oligarchs Dmytro Firtash and Ivan Fursin (2004-2008).

Rukh – Ukrainian Popular Movement for Restructuring.

Russkiy Mir – Russian World, Russian government organisation created to spread Moscow's influence among Russian speakers in the former USSR.

Samizdat/Samvydav – unofficial writings and publications in the USSR.

SBU – Security Service of Ukraine, successor to the Soviet Ukrainian KGB.

Shistdesyatnyky – generation of the 1960s's writers and cultural activists.

Spetsnaz – military and intelligence special forces.

SVR – Foreign Intelligence Service of the Russian Federation.

UDAR – Ukrainian Democratic Alliance for Reforms, political party led by Vitaliy Klitschko.

Ukrainian (Russian) Orthodox Church – Ukrainian branch of the Russian Orthodox Church under the jurisdiction of the Moscow Patriarch.

Ukrop – derogatory separatist term for Ukrainians, drawing on the word for dill.

UNA-UNSO – Ukrainian National Assembly-Ukrainian Peoples Self Defence Forces (1990-).

UNHCR – United Nations High Commission for Refugees.

UNHCHR – United Nations High Commission for Human Rights.

UOC-KP – Ukrainian Orthodox Church-Kyiv Patriarch, pro-autocephalous Orthodox Church led by Patriarch Filaret (1992-).

UPA – Ukrainian Insurgent Army, nationalist partisan movement which fought Nazi and Soviet security forces (1942-1952).

VAAD – Association of Jewish Organisations and Communities (of Ukraine).

Vatniks – derogatory term for separatists used by Ukrainian forces that draws on the word for cotton padded jacket worn by common labourers.

## KEY PERSONALITIES

Rinat Akhmetov – wealthiest oligarch in Ukraine and leading financier of the Party of Regions and Opposition Bloc.

Yuri Andropov – first Secretary of the KPRS (1982-1984).

Sergey Aksyonov – former organised crime leader (nickname 'the Goblin'), leader of the (Crimean) Russian Party of Unity and prime minister of the Crimea (spring 2014-).

Nikolai Azarov – Head of the State Tax Administration (1996-2002) and Ukrainian prime minister (2010-2014). In exile in Moscow where he heads a government in exile (2014).

Stepan Bandera – leader of one of three wings of OUN. Aleksandr Barkashov – leader of the RNE.

Oleksandr Bazylyuk – leader of the Civic Congress which became the Party of Slavic Unity and Party of Regions deputy.

Akhat ('the Greek') Brahin – leading Donetsk organised crime leader and Akhmetov's mentor who was assassinated in 1995.

Leonid Brezhnev – first Secretary of the KPRS (1964-1982).

Igor ('Strelkov [Shooter]') Girkin – Russian GRU officer who led *spetsnaz* special forces into eastern Ukraine in April 2014.

Sergey Glazyev – born in Zaporizhzhya, Soviet Ukraine and a senior adviser to Putin on Ukraine.

Mikhail Gorbachev – first Secretary of the KPRS (1985-1991) and Soviet president (1990-1991).

Ramzan Kadyrov – pro-Putin President of Chechnya whose security forces have fought alongside Donbas separatists.

Hennadiy Kernes – Mayor of Kharkiv and until 2014, a staunch pro-Yanukovych ally.

Nikita Khrushchev – General Secretary of the KPRS (1953-1964).

Borys Kolesnykov – Donetsk oligarch and key Akhmetov ally. In exile in Moscow (2014-).

Ihor Kolomoyskyy – joint owner of the Pryvat business empire, Dnipro oligarch and Dnipro governor (2014-2015). Funded volunteer battalions in 2014.

Vadym Kolesnichenko - Pan-Slavic ideologist, leading member of the Party of Regions and joint author of the controversial 2012 language law.

Dmitriy Kozak – known for submitting the 'Russian Draft Memorandum on the Basic Principles of the State Structure of a United State in Moldova' ('Kozak Memorandum') to the Moldovan government in 2003 laying out plans for a confederation of the Trans-Dniestr, Gagauzia and Moldova. Currently head of the 'Inter-Ministerial Commission for the Provision of Humanitarian Aid for the Affected Areas in the South East of the Regions of Donetsk and Luhansk, Ukraine' (shadow Russian government of the DNR-LNR).

Leonid Kravchuk – Ukrainian president (1991-1994).

Leonid Kuchma - Ukrainian president (1994-2004).

Pavlo Lazarenko – Ukrainian prime minister (1996-1997), in exile (1998-) and imprisoned in the US (2006-2012).

Vladimir I. Lenin – Soviet leader (1917-1922).

Alyaksandr Lukashenka – Belarusian president (1994-).

Ihor Markov – leader of the Odesa-based Rodina (Motherland) party and Party of Regions deputy.

Viktor Medvedchuk – leader of the Social Democratic united party and Ukrainian Way NGO.

Dmitriy Medvedev – Russian president and prime minister.

Viktor Pinchuk – Ukrainian-Jewish oligarch from Dnipro and head of the Interpipe business group.

Petro Poroshenko – oligarch and head of the Roshen confectionary business, elected Ukrainian president after the Euromaidan (2014-).

Volodymyr Shcherbytskyy – First Secretary of the Soviet Ukrainian Communist Party (1972-1989).

Petro Shelest – national communist and First Secretary of the Soviet Ukrainian Communist Party (1963-1972).

Radosław ('Radek') Sikorski – Polish Foreign Minister (2007-2014).

Yevhen Shcherban – leading Donetsk oligarch who was assassinated in 1996.

Alexander Solzhenitsyn – Soviet political prisoner, writer and Russian nationalist.

Joseph Stalin – Soviet dictator and General Secretary of the KPRS (1924-1953).

Vladislav Surkov – senior adviser and political technologist to President Putin, kurator of the DNR and LNR.

Dmytro Tabachnyk – Minister of Education (2010-2014).

Yulia Tymoshenko – Batkivshchyna party leader and political prisoner (2011-2014).

Arseniy Yatsenyuk – Prime Minister of Ukraine (2014-2016).

Boris Yeltsin – Russian president (1991-1999).

Viktor Yanukovych – Ukrainian president (2010-2014) who fled to Moscow (2014).

Viktor Yushchenko – Ukrainian president (2005-2010).

Aleksandr Zakharchenko – Prime Minister of the DNR.

# ACKNOWLEDGEMENTS

This book came into existence because of generous financial support provided by the Ukrainian Studies Fund (USF) of the US and the enthusiastic encouragement of Bohdan Vitvitsky and Roman Procyk. The USF grant was provided through the Canadian Institute of Ukrainian Studies (CIUS) at the University of Alberta. As always, Professor Paul R. Magocsi, Chair of Ukrainian Studies at the University of Toronto, provided invaluable intellectual advice and guidance. I am grateful to Peter Shutak, formerly at the BBC, who edited the manuscript.

The idea for a book on the Donbas was envisaged mid way through Yanukovych's presidency after I returned from a visiting fellowship at the Slavic Research Centre in Hokkaido University, Japan. In three-way discussions between the USF, CIUS and me, we came to strongly believe there was a need to increase Western scholarship about the Donbas which barely existed in the English language. The Donetsk clan, through the Party of Regions and President Yanukovych, had created a formidable political machine and were seeking the state capture of Ukraine.

The three-year research project was launched in September 2013 at an opportune moment in Ukrainian history to incorporate the tumultuous events that were about to shake the country and Europe only a few months later. World-wide interest in Europe's worst crisis since World War II was evident in the author's 300 interviews on the Euromaidan Revolution, Crimea and the Donbas during the course of 2013-2015 for television, radio and print media. I am grateful to the USF for its understanding and extension of the research project from three to four years.

In 2013-2016, the author conducted 15 research visits to cities, villages and military front-lines in eastern and southern Ukraine and the ATO conflict zone (see Interviews Conducted in Ukraine). This extensive field research and discussions in Ukraine and within Western academic and policy making seminars provided the basis for this book and scholarly articles on the Donbas, Ukraine-Russia conflict and the Crimea (see Further Reading).

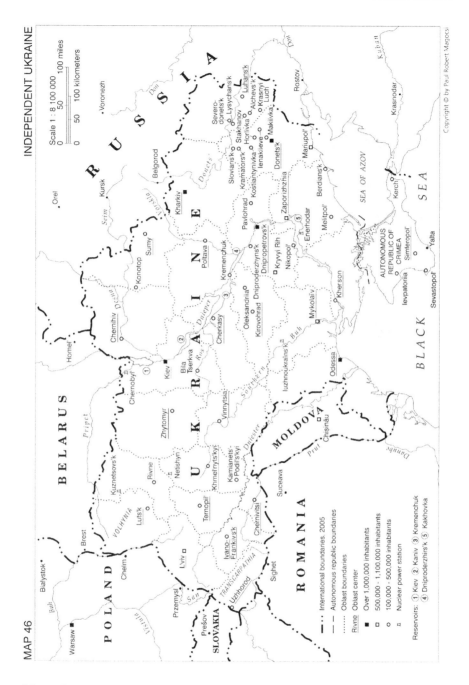

*Map of Independent Ukraine. Courtesy of Paul Robert Magocsi, Chair of Ukrainian Studies, University of Toronto.*

## The situation in the Eastern regions of Ukraine*

Legend:
— Demarcation Line at the time of signing Minsk Agreements
▨ Territory seized by pro-Russian separatists after the Minsk Agreements had been signed

* *Source* – the website of the Information Analysis Center of the NSDC, *www.mediarnbo.org*

FOREWORD

# RUSSIA IS AT WAR
# WITH THE WEST AND UKRAINE

*If the message wasn't clear to all then it sure is now. We didn't know it at the time
but Putin's Munich speech was a declaration of war*
Brian Whitmore

In late 2016 and early 2017, just as this book was going to press, the US and
Europe were waking up to the fact that Russia had long believed it was at war
with the West. It had taken a long time coming. The EU (European Union)
and particularly Germany, could no longer continue to ignore reality.[1]

In a move not seen since the Cuban Missile crisis, on 29 December 2016
the US expelled 35 Russian intelligence agents and diplomats. A report published on the same day by the FBI and the Department for Homeland Security's
Cybersecurity and Communications Integration Center said there had been
'spearphishing, campaigns targeting government organisations, critical infrastructure, think-tanks, universities, political organisations, and corporations;
theft of information from these organisations; and the recent public release of
some of this stolen information.'

These expulsions and report coupled with earlier think tank reports and
media articles have taken the lid off what has hitherto been clouded by diplomatic obfuscation in what was described as a 'decade-long campaign' of Russian 'behaviour unprecedented in the post-Cold War era.'[2] The West has
awoken to the unpleasant fact that it is living through the first world cyberwar
but had not wanted to call it that.[3] Russia's interference in the US presidential

elections forced Western policymakers to acknowledge the reality that Russia believes it is at war with the West.

Over the last decade, Russia has used Estonia, Georgia and especially Ukraine as testing grounds for developing its hybrid, information and cyber warfare capabilities which have in the last few years spread to NATO and EU members.[4] Ukraine is on the frontline of Russia's war with the West and the International Criminal Court (ICC) recognised in November 2016 that Ukraine and Russia are *de facto* at war.

Russia – unlike the West – never believed the Cold War had ended. It is Western diplomats and policymakers who have been unwilling to acknowledge that Russian leaders believe they are in a state of undeclared war with the West. Russia's turn to the right came sharply into the open in President Vladimir Putin's 2007 speech to the Munich security conference but was ignored. The angry Russian leader resembled the producer in the 1976 American satirical black comedy-drama 'Network' where he shouts on screen during a live performance 'I'm mad as Hell and I'm not going to take this anymore.'

The Russian public are in tune with Russian leaders that the onus for an improvement of relations lies with the West. Russia has nothing to apologise for because it is the aggrieved party that has been forced to defend itself against Western malfeasance. Russia was allegedly forced to react in the Crimea and Ukraine because a Western-backed 'putsch' overthrew a legitimately elected president that brought 'fascists' to power who threatened Russian speakers. In December 2016, the Russian State Duma adopted a resolution to this effect. Russian leaders and public opinion does not comprehend why they have been punished with sanctions over Ukraine.

Western leaders have twice failed to reset relations with Russia. President George W. Bush sought an alliance with Putin following the 9/11 attacks but soon found that the US and Russia viewed terrorism very differently. President Barack Obama had illusions about the 'liberal' Russian President Dmitriy Medvedev and a belief that Russia inside the G8 would eventually come to resemble 'us' and become a 'normal' country. This flatly contradicted the reports of Western foundations and human rights organisations such as Freedom House who have described Russia as a 'consolidated authoritarian state' since the mid 2000's. If Russian leaders do not follow the rules or the letter of the law inside Russia why will they do so in the international arena?

Russia believes the West launched its war against Russian interests as long ago as the late 1990s when NATO and the US orchestrated a democratic revolution in Serbia and supported an independent Kosovo. In Moscow's eyes it was the West that tore up the rule book when it militarily attacked Serbia and four years later in Iraq - both without UN authorisation. Russia's hacking and cyber warfare can be similarly traced back over a decade. In 2007, Russia orchestrated violent riots and a month-long massive cyber attack against NATO and EU member Estonia after it decided to move the Soviet World War II memorial. The cyber attack targeted computer networks, banks and the media. A year after the attacks, NATO opened a Cooperative Cyber Defence Centre in Tallinn. During Viktor Yanukovych's presidency, Russian and Ukrainian hackers accessed files from *Batkivshchyna* and Yulia Tymoshenko's Western political consultants and published them on-line during her trial on trumped-up charges. During the Euromaidan Revolution, the Security Service (SBU), then heavily infiltrated by Russian intelligence, raided *Batkivshchyna's* Kyiv headquarters and confiscated servers.

Russia's hacking of the 2016 US elections is far more than simply revenge for Secretary of State Hilary Clinton's support for Russians protesting at election fraud in 2011 and 2012 that brought United Russia and Putin to power. Russian asymmetric warfare is viewed by Moscow as a strategic tool to respond to decades of Western support for regime change stretching back to the disintegration of the USSR and coloured revolutions in eastern Europe and Eurasia. The West believed, Putin said, that 'after the Soviet Union has fallen apart, we need to finish Russia off.'

Putin and other post-Soviet authoritarian leaders have always understood colour revolutions in Serbia, Georgia, and twice in Ukraine not as genuine public protests standing up for human rights and democracy but as CIA and EU conspiracies seeking to undermine what President Medvedev coined as Russia's 'zone of privileged interests.' Colour revolutions are viewed as Western soft enlargement complimenting the hard expansion of NATO and the EU. The Euromaidan Revolution was, Russian leaders said in spring 2014, cover for the Black Sea Fleet bases becoming NATO bases when Ukraine joins NATO and the EU.

When the EU's Eastern Partnership was launched in 2009 for post-Soviet countries such as Ukraine and Georgia, Russia responded with a competing CIS Customs Union becoming in 2015 the Eurasian Economic Union. The EU never took Putin's plans and rhetoric seriously and in the 2014 crisis the EU was therefore flabbergasted to realise that Russia views the EU as an expansionist Western project in the same way as it has always understood NATO.

EU leaders were even more shocked to find that Putin had evolved from offering competing integration models to seeking to bring down the EU and NATO. NATO, the European Parliament and Organisation for Security and Cooperation in Europe (OSCE) have suffered major cyber attacks. In 2016, France blocked 24,000 cyber attacks targeting its military. Ukraine experienced 24, 000 cyber attacks in only the last two months of 2016.

US realists, who now have the ear of President Donald Trump, were always wrong to claim that Putin was not interested in moving beyond non-NATO members such as Ukraine. Russia has launched hybrid, information and cyber warfare against NATO members Estonia, Britain, Germany, Norway, Netherlands, France, Greece, Hungary, Bulgaria, Turkey and prospective NATO member Montenegro.[5] German intelligence has revealed that the parliament has been cyber attacked and they have publicly aired concerns that Russia will cyber attack its 2017 elections. The Czech Republic in response to fears of Russian information warfare aimed at discrediting its October elections has set up an 'anti-fake' news unit. In January 2016, Russia was behind a fake story alleging a German girl had been raped by migrants fueling support for the anti-EU far right. After the US expulsions an official said 'Russia is not going to stop. We have every indication that they will continue to interfere in democratic elections in other countries.'[6]

Estonian security services officer Eston Kohver was kidnapped by Russian intelligence agents in a direct snub to the US coming only two days after President Obama's visit to that country. In NATO member Hungary, Russian agents were behind the training of a neo-Nazi militia that sought to take power. Russian diplomats and paramilitaries had openly trained with the group.

Moscow was behind a coup attempt and assassination plot against Montenegrin Prime Minister Milo Djukanovic using nationalist Serbs and Russian Cossacks who had fought for the separatists in the Donbas. Cossack General Viktor Zaplatin, a Russian citizen, told a rally in Montenegro 'The Orthodox world is one world. Here we see Serbs, Montenegrins, Russians, and Belarusians.' Aleksandr Borodai, former editor of the Russian nationalist *Zavtra (Tomorrow)* newspaper and 'Prime Minister' of the Donetsk People's Republic, sent greetings.[7] Twenty Serbs and Russians are in custody in Montenegro and Montenegro has issued an international warrant for a further two Russians and three Serbs. One of the Serbs sought by Montenegro, Nemanja Ristic, was photographed next to Russian Minister of Foreign Affairs Sergei Lavrov during his 12 December 2016 visit to Belgrade.[8]

Russia actively intervened in Ukraine's 2004 elections and 2013-2014 Euromaidan Revolution in support of presidential candidate and President Yanukovych respectively. After the Orange Revolution, Russia launched a 'technology of preventive counterrevolution' against Western-backed regime change and revolution in Russia. *Nashi (Ours)*, launched in 2005, mobilised young Russians against the West and became a thorn in the side of US and British Ambassadors.

Russian leaders and media have recently made disparaging remarks questioning Belarusian independence and threatening it to not follow Ukraine's path of breaking out of Moscow's sphere of influence. In Russia's eyes, Belarusians and Ukrainians are branches of a single 'Russian' people and their statehood cannot exist outside Russia's 'zone of privileged interests.' Russian leaders have never respected and have long refused to view Ukraine as a sovereign country taking the entire decade of the 1990s to recognise its borders. Putin has long sought to transform Ukraine into a Belarusian-style dominion ruled by a pro-Russian satrap believing he had achieved this goal by turning President Yanukovych away from Europe. Putin was again foiled by Western-backed regime change. If there had been no Euromaidan Revolution, Russia would have intervened to assist in Yanukovych's 2015 re-election and in gratitude he would have taken Ukraine into the Eurasian Economic Union.

In April 2008 – a full six years before the 2014 crisis – President Putin speaking to the NATO-Russia Council at the Bucharest summit described Ukraine as an 'artificial' country and questioned its eastern and southern borders. The following year, Ukraine's relations with Russia sharply deteriorated after two Russian diplomats accused of fomenting Crimean separatists were expelled. President Medvedev responded with a bellicose open letter to Viktor Yushchenko outlining a host of demands that was tantamount to brazen interference in Ukraine's domestic affairs.

In the same year as Putin laid out territorial demands against Ukraine, Russia invaded Georgia and recognised the independence of South Ossetia and Abkhazia. Russia claimed a moral equivalence between their 'right' to independence and Kosovo – just as it did in the case of Crimea's 'right to self determination.' No Western sanctions ensued for Russia's actions and the following year the US launched a re-set of relations with Russia that sent a signal to Putin there would be no repercussions if he again undertook military intervention in other neighbouring states.

In 2007, the *Russkiy Mir (Russian World)* organisation was created with the aim of supporting Russian speakers in the former USSR. Although touted as analogous to the British Council the Russian World organisation was in reality very different. Through close ties to Russian intelligence and extreme Russian nationalists and Eurasianists such as Aleksandr Dugin it provided paramilitary training and ideological indoctrination for extremist groups in Ukraine and elsewhere. Marginal extremist groups and parties, such as the Donetsk Republic in the Donbas and Russian Unity in the Crimea who had received paramilitary training in Russia, were installed into power by Russian troops in 2014. Russia's support for extremist Russian nationalists in Ukraine and elsewhere in Eurasia has been replicated in the financial and paramilitary support Moscow has provided to anti-EU nationalist populists. In December 2016, the 'anti-fascist' United Russia party signed a cooperation agreement with Austria's neo-fascist Freedom Party.

In the last decade, Russia has resumed the Soviet practice of 'wet operations' (assassinations) abroad and at home. In 2004, opposition leader Yushchenko was poisoned by dioxin in the Ukrainian presidential elections. Two years later radioactive polonium was used to murder FSB defector Aleksandr Litvinenko in London only a month after journalist Anna Polikovskaya was gunned down in Moscow on Putin's birthday. The dioxin and radioactive polonium is produced in Russian laboratories inherited from the USSR and run by the secret services. Countless Chechen nationalists have been murdered in Europe, Turkey and the Middle East since 2004, with Russian agents going on trial in Qatar.

Russia has always had a Janis faced policy towards separatism condemning separatism inside Russia while promoting it in its neighbours. Russia has hosted annual congresses of separatist movements from around the world. Like its Soviet predecessor, Russia is known to have supported Kurdish separatist groups in Turkey and elsewhere and other reports claim Russia is secretly supporting Islamic State, at the very least by permitting supporters to leave Russia and join the terrorist organisation.

Western policymakers have slowly and hesitantly begun to take at face value what Putin and Russian leaders have been saying and acting upon for over a decade. Putin believes Russia is at war with the West in a conflict that it did not begin and has been forced to respond to. Putin is defending Russian and Eurasian civilisation against a Western onslaught, that the EU is a puppet of the US, and Ukraine is a Western fifth column that naturally belongs to Russia's 'zone of privileged interests.'

Putin is seeking from a third attempt at resetting relations with the US a new Yalta agreement that would divide up Europe and Eurasia into nineteenth century-style spheres of influence. Henry Kissinger is said to have advised Trump 'to roll out a plan to end sanctions on Moscow that would "recognise Russia's dominance" in the former Soviet states of Belarus, Ukraine, Georgia and Kazakhstan.'[9] Great powers are living in a delusional world if they believe that countries assigned to spheres of influence will passively accept their fate and in the case of Russia they wrongly assume it has the economic, financial and military resources to control a large country such as Ukraine.

Kissinger's proposal would be unable to repeal legislation adopted by the US Congress and pit him against the Republicans in both houses of Congress who believe that Russia hacked into the US elections. Speaker of the House and senior Republican in Congress Paul Ryan, applauded the expulsions which although overdue 'were an appropriate way to end eight years of failed policy with Russia.' It would also put President Trump at odds with NATO and could never be delivered by the EU. Putin and Russians are convinced of their innocence and no reset can succeed if it is only undertaken by one side of the relationship.

In 2016-2017, Europe and North America, the EU and NATO, woke up to the fact that Russia believes it is at war with the West and its 'proxy state' – Ukraine. This book explains why and how President Putin launched a war against Ukraine.

# CHAPTER 1

# UNDERSTANDING THE UKRAINE-RUSSIA CRISIS AND THE DONBAS

*Only Ukraine can save the Donbas as it needs it. It is not needed by Russia*
President Leonid Kravchuk, 1994[10]

There is limited room to analyse all of the multi-faceted factors within the Russia-Ukraine crisis that began in 2014 and therefore not all of these are covered in this book. In contrast to the majority of what has been published on the causes of the crisis this book focuses upon Russian-Ukrainian identity relations and the Donbas. Mikhail Zygar writes that Putin was from the onset of his first term as Russian president fixated on the 'Ukrainian question'. 'We must do something or we'll lose it' Putin repeatedly said to his staff.[11]

The first section of this chapter discusses scholarly literature on the Ukraine-Russia crisis by dividing it into nine groups. The next section discusses the Donbas region through its political culture, concept and identity. Finally, the remaining ten chapters of the book are detailed.

## THE RUSSIA-UKRAINE CRISIS IN SCHOLARLY LITERATURE

Elias Götz presents a framework that divides scholarly work on the Ukraine-Russia crisis into four main themes. These include Putin's career and worldview, domestic politics (fear of contagion, prevention of internal unrest and nationalism used to turn public attention away from internal failures), ideas (national identity, spheres of influence and recognition as a great power), geopolitics and great power competition. What is missing from his framework are

*Trade Union building burnt out after a raid by SBU Aplha spetsnaz during the Euromaidan Revolution (January 2014)*

scholarly works depicting Russia as the victim of Western policy mistakes or deliberate malfeasance. Ukraine is also largely treated in this body of literature as a side show to that of the West and Russia.[12] This book divides published scholarly work (occasional and research think tank papers, academic articles and books) on the Ukraine-Russia crisis by dividing them into nine themes. These include the Euromaidan Revolution of Dignity, Russia as a victim, geo-political explanations, Russia as a troublemaker and aggressor, domestic factors in Russia, Russian-Ukrainian identity relations, national minorities, regionalism and identity and the Donbas and eastern Ukraine.

The first group of scholarly work deals with the Euromaidan Revolution which was different to the 2004 Orange Revolution in five ways. The first difference is that it lasted for three months which was far longer than the seventeen-day Orange Revolution. The second was that unlike earlier 'colour revolutions' in Serbia, Georgia and Ukraine the Euromaidan did not take place within an election cycle. The third factor, following on from the previous, was that the Euromaidan was driven as much by national liberation as it was by European integration and human rights. Political repression, the creation of a

*Post-Euromaidan Revolution Khreshchatyk Street (spring-summer 2014)*

'mafia state' and return to neo-Soviet nationality and language policies culminated in an angrier population and, as Petro Poroshenko's former Chief of Staff Borys Lozhkin wrote, 'gave the protests a national liberation bent.'[13] The fourth was that the Euromaidan was violent with the deaths of over one hundred protestors and nearly 20 law enforcement officers. Earlier 'colour revolutions' had been led by NGOs and opposition leaders committed to nonviolent strategies and in 2004, Leonid Kuchma was leaving office and was not contemplating using violence to cling to power. Yanukovych acted as though he would be president for the long term and most certainly expected that he would win a second term in 2015. The fifth factor was that opposition leaders led the Orange Revolution while the Euromaidan was driven by NGOs, civil society and journalists. Opposition leaders had become discredited during the decade following the Orange Revolution and there was no popular opposition leader such as Yushchenko.

The second group of published materials portrays Russia as a victim and being forced to react to NATO and EU enlargement and democracy promotion into its 'privileged zone of interests.' This analysis can be described as 'out-

*Early makeshift shrine to the Heavenly Hundred (spring-summer 2014)*

in' because it prioritises external factors. Left-wing anti-Americanism influences this scholarly analysis through its critique of Washington's democracy promotion and regime change strategies. Russia had been allegedly humiliated and wronged by the West since the collapse of the USSR in 1991 and in intervening in Ukraine, Putin drew a 'red line.' An added argument is Putin allegedly believed that Ukraine would join NATO (which was not on the cards) and that the Black Sea Fleet would be evicted from Sevastopol. Mark Galeotti and Andrew Bowen point out that Putin does not see himself as an empire builder but as 'defending a civilisation against the 'chaotic darkness' that will ensue if he allows Russia to be politically encircled abroad and culturally colonised by Western values at home.'[14]

Many claims of victimhood are sympathetic to Russia's poor treatment by the West, its search for security and demand for the recognition of its great power status. This group of scholars is diverse and includes left-wing academics and right-wing realists who blame the West for the crisis. Fundamentally, both groups propose the same prescriptions for Ukrainian leaders of coming to terms with the reality that their country lies geographically within Russia's sphere of influence. They thereby propose that Kyiv drops its goal of European integration and agrees to a neutral status similar to Austria or Finland during the Cold War. They also ignore the huge pressure exerted by Putin on Yanukovych to drop the EU Association Agreement in favour of integration within Eurasia, a region dominated by undemocratic and kleptocratic regimes. Left-wing and realist policy prescriptions naively assume that Russia would agree to a neighbouring country remaining democratic in an authoritarian neighbourhood. In addition, 'Leaving Ukraine in limbo between the West and Russia is not a solution that is fair to Ukraine or to any other interested party.'[15]

The third and by far largest group of scholarly and think tank published material can be defined as Russia in geopolitical competition with the EU and the West and the West's response to Russia's re-assertion as a great power. This collection of scholarly work can also be described as 'out-in' where Ukraine is a pawn competed over by Russia and the West. This body of literature includes relations between the EU and Russia, international sanctions against Russia and the manner in which Russia's aggression has infringed international law. Nuclear proliferation is included within this section because of Russia's abrogation of the 1994 Budapest Memorandum where it, together with the US and UK, provided security assurances in return for Ukraine's nuclear disarmament.

The fourth group of published work focuses upon Russia as a troublemaker and can be defined as 'in-out-in' because of the complex inter-relationship between national identity, the search for great power status and Russian imperialism. This body of scholarly literature incorporates analyses of Russia's creation of frozen conflicts since the disintegration of the USSR in 1991. The Crimea is briefly analysed but the main focus of this book is the Donbas and eastern and southern Ukraine. Prior to the crisis, scholarly treatment of the Crimea focused primarily upon the Tatars rather than on politics and separatism in the autonomous republic. An exception was a think tank monograph published by this author in 2010 that predicted Russia's annexation five years later. Two other areas this group of publications analyses are Russian empire building and Russian imperialism. Putin and Russian leaders lament the disintegration of the USSR and some scholars see in his actions a desire for revenge. The CIS Customs Union and Eurasian Union are the latest attempts by Russia to integrate CIS states which some scholars believe reflect Putin's desire to rebuild an empire or a new Soviet Union. Although the EU and Russia can be both criticised for competing over Ukraine's allegiance it was only Russia that ultimately resorted to military force.

*Huge numbers of flowers on Instytutska Street where the Heavenly Hundred were gunned down by Berkut snipers (spring-summer 2014)*

The fifth group of scholarly work is that of Russia as an aggressor state and can be defined as 'in-out.' This body of scholarly literature analyses Russian military activities and hybrid (non-military) and informational warfare techniques. Despite the growing interest in hybrid warfare, many of the key aspects of Russia's non-military activities in the pursuit of its security policies are not new and were not invented by Putin. The USSR had undertaken 'wet actions' (assassinations) abroad since the 1920s, murdering four Ukrainian nationalist leaders in France, Netherlands and Germany in 1926-1959. The USSR had deployed special forces in developing countries in advance of invasions or to train local forces and rebel groups. The Soviet Union was very active in the field of disinformation.[16]

Nevertheless, the existence of satellite and cable television, 24-hour news and social media provides contemporary Russia with greater possibilities to pursue hybrid and information warfare. Russian television propaganda deserves full-length analytical studies in of itself and in one of the first by Stephen Hutchings and Vera Tolz they describes it as confrontational, crude, and producing a 'frenzy of anti-Western Cold War rhetoric.'[17]

*Memorial to the Heavenly Hundred (2016)*

Modern technology and social media, as well as growing cynicism and populist nationalism in Western democracies, provides Russia with greater opportunities to influence European politics and foreign policies. Although much is new, the USSR long practiced 'Subversion, disinformation and forgery, combined with the use of special forces' and the KGB 'had a special department responsible for "active measures", designed to weaken and undermine the West.'[18] Russia's post-modern approach to propaganda is a new approach whereby many narratives are broadcast on multiple media to undermine the entire concept of a single truthful narrative. Russia does not offer an alternative truth, as the Soviet Union did, but deconstructs the very idea of objective reporting. This post-modern approach to propaganda has been attached to an increasingly effective use of digital media.

The sixth group of publications analyses Russia's domestic scene and can be defined as 'in-out.' This scholarly literature incorporates definitions of Putin's regime and how the type of regime influences military aggression against Ukraine and elsewhere. Alexander Motyl persuasively argues that the Russian regime is fascist and that this provides much of the explanation for Putin's militarised and 'macho' foreign policy. Some scholars define Russia as a militocracy where the *siloviki* (security forces, particularly the intelligence services) are in control and their 'chekisty' and Soviet KGB operating culture is at

*Author at a 'United Ukraine' rally in Kyiv (May 2014)*

the root of Russia's military aggression. Added to this is the growing view of Russia as a mafia state and kleptocracy where pursuit of money is as important as the pursuit of Russia recognised by the West as a great power. Galeotti points out that it is wrong to believe there is an inconsistency between widespread corruption and nationalism because the biggest organised crime group in Russia is the Kremlin. Kleptocrats in many parts of the world are nationalists. There is often the 'thinnest of lines'[19] between organised crime and paramilitaries, as in Ulster and the DNR and LNR (Donetsk and Luhansk People's Republics respectively).

Putin's personality is analysed by many scholars seeking to understand his actions after Yanukovych fled from power. Can Putin be best understood as an improviser and gambler who is spontaneous and emotional or a cold calculating strategist? Did Putin act decisively in the Crimea because of a power vacuum or because he implemented long-term plans? The Russian parliament and political parties have laid territorial claims against the Crimea and Sevastopol throughout the post-Soviet era but only under Putin did they find support at the executive level.

The scholarly publications within this group largely ignore the role of Russian nationalism. Some scholars downplay Putin's nationalism by arguing he is an instrumental nationalist and cynic who only draws upon it during elections and to undermine domestic protests, such as those that rocked Russia in 2011-2012. Western biographies of Putin barely touch upon Russian nationalism and national identity and how this influences his policies and attitudes towards Ukraine.[20] Robert Horvath argues that Russian nationalism went into crisis in response to the Euromaidan and Putin's aggression against Ukraine but many of the political groups and leaders he discusses are marginal and most are electorally unpopular.[21] Richard Sakwa completely ignores Russian nationalism in his book on the Ukraine crisis while exaggerating the influence of Ukrainian nationalism by using language that at times resembles contemporary Russian and Soviet propaganda. Opposition Russian nationalists buy into the regime's anti-Americanism, xenophobia and conspiracy theories because Russian nationalism has always included a 'strong mood of anti-Westernization.'[22] All Russian political forces, whether democrat or nationalist, support Russia's annexation of the Crimea while the majority of Russians believe that eastern and southern Ukraine was wrongly included inside Ukraine. Pro-Putin *and* opposition nationalists, such as Alexei Navalny, believe that Ukraine is an artificial and failed state, Ukrainians and Russians are one people and Ukrainian is a dialect of the Russian language.

The seventh group of scholarly publications analyses external aspects of Ukraine and can be defined as 'in-out-in.' Ukrainian-Russian identity relations and Russian chauvinism towards Ukrainians features in only a minority of the scholarly and think tank publications on the crisis. Scholarly experts on Russia do not always appreciate the importance of this question and prefer to focus on other factors, such as geopolitics, Putin's personality and the *siloviki*. Scholarly articles that have shed new light on Ukrainian-Russian identity questions have been written by historians and political scientists who have an expertise on Ukraine. And yet, as Ivan Krastev writes, 'It is Putin the conservative and not Putin the realist who decided to violate Ukraine's sovereignty. His march on Crimea is not realpolitik it is kulturkampf.'[23]

The eighth group of publications analyses national minorities, regionalism, and economics in Ukraine and can be defined as 'in-out.' Only a small minority of Western scholars who have written about the crisis use Ukrainian language sources and an even smaller number have visited the country and the

ATO conflict zone. Their analyses and subjective interpretations can be influenced by their expertise on Russia which provides them with an 'out-in' view of the crisis. Sakwa, similar to Western historians of Russia, sees the Crimea as returning to its 'natural' home within Russia, begging the question whether the Crimea had no history prior to the 1780s. Using a similar analogy, we could argue that North America's history began in the 1600's. Sakwa's only Ukrainian sources are sixteen citations of the *Kyiv Post*; if a book was written about Russia citing only the *Moscow Times* it could not be defined as a scholarly work. Sakwa on no occasion cites Ukrainian President Poroshenko while quoting Putin on 31 occasions and the overwhelming majority of his 75 primary sources are from Russia, including the highly biased Russian Ministry of Foreign Affairs White Book.

Four myths have emerged in scholarly discussions of the Donbas conflict. These are language, religion, Ukrainian nationalism and nationality.

Language is by far the biggest myth in the crisis and yet it played little role in Russia's annexation of the Crimea and is not playing an important role in the Donbas conflict. A November-December 2016 survey asked respondents to chose what were the three most important national issues they believed Ukraine was facing. Only one percent believed gaining official status for the Russian language was important coming second from the bottom of seventeen issues.[24] International human rights organisations reported there was no threat to Russian speakers in the Crimea in spring 2014. Ukrainian opinion polls provide added confirmation that language is not an important issue in eastern Ukraine. Minister of Information Policy Yuriy Stets said 'In Ukraine there will not be xenophobia towards the Russian language and literature.'[25] Two thirds of Ukrainian troops in the ATO are Russian speakers and nationalist battalions *Pravyy Sektor (Right Sector)* and *Azov* include Russian language speakers. Ukraine's largely Russian-language speaking Jewish community has provided resources for Ukrainian forces fighting Russian and separatist proxies. The preponderance of Russian speakers among Ukrainian troops and nationalist battalions undercuts the myth of the Donbas conflict being an outgrowth of a 'nationalist' state unwilling to be inclusive enough to accommodate its Russian speakers.

Language is an important marker of identity in every country and that is also the case in Ukraine but just as important is a citizen's relationship to competing languages as well as their attitudes to the historical past and country's future trajectory. Russian and separatist leaders continue to harbour Soviet stereotypes of the primacy of the Russian language and they glorify the 'great leader' Joseph Stalin and the myth of the Great Patriotic War. Meanwhile, they continue to denigrate the Ukrainian language as a peasant and uncouth language that is unfit for the modern and industrialised world. Soviet and Russian chauvinism towards Ukrainian is reflected in the closure of all Ukrainian schools and media in the Crimea and in the two separatist enclaves. In contrast, the majority of Russian speaking Ukrainians do not harbour Soviet style chauvinism towards the Ukrainian language, they support de-Stalinisation and de-Sovietisation and among them can be found the soldiers and nationalist volunteers I met during my frequent visits to eastern Ukraine and the ATO. Serhiy Kudelia writes that language use played a role because 'Most of the towns and villages in Donetsk and Luhansk *oblasts* with the share of native Ukrainian speakers over eighty percent never came under rebel control.'[26] While Kudelia is certainly correct to emphasise the importance of language use it does not represent a fundamental determinant of attitudes towards Ukraine and the separatists. This is clearly borne out in the fact that the majority of Ukrainian soldiers and even some members of nationalist battalions are Russian language speakers.

Although Russian leaders find it impossible to comprehend the concept of a Russian speaking Ukrainian patriot it is not a new concept. Petro Shelest and Leonid Kravchuk, both considered national communists but born in opposite sides of Ukraine (the former was from Kharkiv and the latter from Volyn), spoke Russian at home while publicly promoting the Ukrainian language and opposing Russian chauvinism.[27] Hiroaki Kuromiya writes that Volodymyr Shcherbytskyy, although traditionally viewed as synonymous with Russification and political repression, was an 'ardent Ukrainian patriot.'[28]

Russian Jews in Ukraine supported the Euromaidan and showed their patriotism to the Ukrainian state during its war with Russia. The Jewish minority in the separatist enclaves fled to Ukrainian territory. Soviet, Russian and Donbas anti-Zionism (all of which are camouflaged forms of anti-Semitism) are analysed in a separate chapter of the book.[29]

A second myth of the Donbas conflict is Ukrainian nationalism which has long been the bug bear of the Tsarist Russian Empire, USSR and contemporary Russia where 'Ukrainian nationalist' was conflated with 'Nazi collaborator' and 'fascism' was the term used against all shades of political opinion that opposed Russia's domination of Ukraine. In Putin's Russia the term 'fascism' is used against a multitude of different subjects (i.e. those imposing a ban on Russia participating in the Olympics, NATO, the US, Ukraine, liberal opposition, etc.).[30] In the Soviet Union a 'bourgeois nationalist' could be a national communist such as Ivan Dzyuba, author of the well-known book *Internationalism or Russification?* or liberal democratic dissidents in the Ukrainian Helsinki Group. In claiming that 'radicalised Ukrainian nationalist elites' control the Ukrainian parliament,[31] Sakwa reveals his Moscow-centric approach to Ukrainian politics by also defining all Ukrainian politicians who seek a future in Europe as 'nationalists' and 'fascists.'

Ukraine's nationalist right has always been unpopular and has only once entered parliament in 2012. In the 2014 elections, nationalists received a combined six percent of the vote. The Communist Party of Ukraine (KPU) and the Party of Regions won pluralities in five out of seven of Ukraine's parliamentary elections and four out of five Ukrainian presidents have been from eastern and southern Ukraine.

A third myth is that of religion, specifically the alleged suppression of the Russian Orthodox Church by 'Ukrainian nationalists.'[32] Ukraine has a relatively high number of religious believers and although Ukraine's population is only a third of the size of Russia's population it has a similar number of Orthodox parishes. The majority of these are to be found in Ukrainian-speaking central and western Ukraine, two regions which supported the Orange and Euromaidan Revolutions.

The stereotype of an 'Orthodox east' versus a 'Catholic' West' has always been misplaced because Catholics have a majority in only three Galician out of seven western Ukrainian *oblasts*. Adherence to Orthodoxy in the Donbas is the same as that in western Ukraine (54 percent) which is lower than in central, southern and eastern Ukraine where it ranges from 72-76 percent.[33]

Driving around the Donbas one sees very few Churches of any religious confession and Protestantism is as prevalent, and some sources say more popular, than Russian Orthodoxy. Protestants in the Donbas and eastern Ukraine are Ukrainian patriots.[34] Senior DNR and LNR leaders are not Orthodox activists. The Russian Orthodox Church and extremist Russian Orthodox nationalist paramilitaries claim to be defending 'Orthodoxy' in a region of Ukraine which was heavily Sovietised, where the Church was weak and the Russian Orthodox Church only opened eparchies in 1944. Historically, the Donbas was a region with high levels of atheism[35] and religion was never influential in the Donbas where 'organised religion was weak.'[36]

A fourth myth relates to national identity and the revival of chauvinistic depictions of Russians and Ukrainians as *'odin narod' (one people)*. President Putin and Russian leaders have adopted the rhetoric of extreme Russian nationalists and fascists to describe Russians and Ukrainians as constituting one people. They belittle Ukrainian sovereignty by describing Ukaine as an 'artificial' and 'failed' state which is propped up by Western malfeasance and conspiracies to weaken Russia. Igor ('Strelkov [Shooter]') Girkin, who credits himself with launching the Donbas conflict, believes Ukrainians are really Russians who speak 'a different dialect.'[37] Putin's fondness for White émigré writers and Eurasianist ideology only compounds his chauvinism towards Ukrainians because this school of thought has never believed Ukrainians are a separate people. At the heart of Putin's policies towards Ukraine are age-old Russian stereotypes of Ukrainians, Soviet conspiracy theories and anti-Western xenophobia coupled with a profound misunderstanding of the internal dynamics of Ukrainian politics and identity.

Important for our understanding of the Donbas conflict is that it was not Ukrainian nationalism that tipped the Donbas into mass violence but Russia's massive interference and (from August 2014) invasion. Radical Ukrainian Pan-Slavists and Soviet nationalists had received training in Russian camps since 2006-2007.[38] Russian intelligence, which had taken control of the SBU during Yanukovych's presidency, was active on the ground throughout the Euromaidan when it provided funding and training for anti-Maidan vigilantes. Andrew Wilson argues that the Donbas would have certainly experienced civil strife but not mass violent conflict if Russia had not tipped the balance.[39]

Nikolay Mitrokhin divides the war in 2014 into three phases. In the first phase in April, *spetsnaz*, Cossacks, Orthodox activists, neo-Nazis, and Dugin's Eurasianists assisted 'criminals from the Donbas region' and transition losers who were seeking to enrich themselves by removing local oligarchs. Mitrokhin defines the second phase as beginning in May when 'fanatics, adventurers and soldiers', including large numbers of Russian veterans and 'politicised supporters of Russian neo-imperialist organisations,' intervened in the conflict. Mitrokhin's third phase begins in August when Russian regular forces in tactical battalion groups of 3-4, 000 combatants invaded the Donbas.[40]

The ninth group of scholarly publications analyses the Donbas and eastern Ukraine and these can be defined as 'in-out.' Scholarly literature about the Party of Regions, the violent political culture and conspiracy mind-set of Donbas leaders and corruption and criminality in the region during the 1980s and

1990s has grown in recent years.[41] This book provides extensive analysis of the history, political culture and politics of the Donbas based on primary sources and field work. Although crime and organised crime groups in post-Soviet Russia have been extensively analysed by scholars, this field of enquiry as pertaining to Ukraine remains in its infancy. The historic and contemporary importance of corruption and crime in the Donbas and the separatist enclaves are analysed in a separate chapter.

Yuriy M. Zhukov believes that where the opportunity costs of rebellion were lower, conflict was more likely in the Donbas. Support for the separatists was higher in regions of the Donbas where industries were dependent on trade with Russia and Zhukov believes this factor was more important than culture and language.[42] There are important nuances to Zhukov's analysis. Although there continues to be mistrust of Kyiv and 'Ukrainian nationalists,' the DNR and LNR do not have broad public support throughout the regions they control and the inhabitants of the city of Donetsk are equally divided into pro-Ukrainian and pro-separatist groups of people. The strongest support for the separatists is to be found among pensioners, villagers and unskilled workers and the lowest support with the middle classes, businesspersons and Ukrainians with a higher education.[43] The separatists attracted those who had been marginalised by the post-Soviet transition who were often people with lower education, unemployed and poor who had nostalgia for the USSR.[44]

In contrast to the diverse range of published scholarly literature, this book places Russian nationalism and Russian-Ukrainian identity relations at the centre of the crisis. Russian military aggression in 2014 was preceded during the previous decade by the growth of popularity of Russian nationalism and a growing chauvinistic view towards Ukrainians. Fascist ideologies, such as Eurasianism and the views and world outlooks of White Russian émigré writers, moved from the margins to the centre of Russian political life. This book emphasises the importance of Ukrainian-Russian identity relations, regional identity, language and culture to explain the sources of the Ukraine-Russia crisis.

## THE SUBJECT

The bulk of the Donbas lies within Ukraine and encompasses Donetsk and Luhansk *oblasts*. A small part of the Donbas is located in Russia adjacent to the border with Ukraine. The Donbas was a sparsely populated no-mans land until the late nineteenth century when industrialisation and urbanisation attracted large numbers of settlers from Russia. Ukrainian peasants were more reluctant to move into coal mining and industry in the Donbas until the USSR launched the polices of indigenisation and Ukrainianisation in the 1920s. Following World War II, the Donbas became a melting pot for Soviet nationalities when workers were sent or encouraged to migrate to the region to work in its growing economy. The Donbas therefore straddled Ukraine and Russia and its common border and was always a frontier that bridged two worlds.

There are three ways to analyse the Donbas. These include political culture, concept and identity.

The political culture of the Donbas has been gritty, proletarian and violent in nature since the industrialisation of the region began in the late nineteenth century. Human life had little value. Crime has always played a prominent part in Donbas life because of the frontier nature of the region, preponderance of young males among migrants seeking work and the high number of criminal prisoners who settled there in return for early release from confinement.

On the eve of the crisis, the Donbas contributed 16 percent of Ukraine's GDP and 25 percent of the sales of industrial products. $14.1 billion of Ukraine's $68.8 billion exports originated in the Donbas, accounting for 27 percent of total Ukrainian exports. The mythology of the Donbas as an economic powerhouse and its net contribution to the Ukrainian budget ignores deep fundamental problems that would have become exacerbated over time. The Donbas was the equivalent of southern Yorkshire (Sheffield and Donetsk are twinned) and southern Wales which were also two British regions dominated by old metallurgical industries and coalmining. Metallurgy accounted for 63 percent of Donetsk and 37 percent of Luhansk exports in 2012 (28 percent of Ukraine's total exports). These industries had been in decline since the 1980s and were major pollutants of the environment, particularly in Mariupol. Ukraine was second to China in the number of coalmining accident fatalities and the mines were unprofitable and subsidised by the central government. On the grounds of their threat to life and financial burden on the budget, Ukraine's coalmines would have been closed down if they had been located in Europe and North America. The importance of Russia for the final destination of regional exports has been exaggerated and they accounted for 43 percent of Luhansk and 22 percent of Donetsk exports (compared to 26 and 21 percent respectively exported to the EU).

In terms of concept, the population of the Donbas believed the economic power of their region 'fed' Ukraine and therefore their economic clout gave them a right to be the 'natural' rulers of independent Ukraine. Although the old industries of the Donbas were important, the region's power and influence were in long-term decline. The capital city of Kyiv, for example, contributed more to the Ukrainian budget than the Donbas. In contrast to old industries in the Donbas, IT is the growing sector of the economy in Lviv on the opposite side of Ukraine and in neighbouring Kharkiv, the intellectual centre of eastern Ukraine.

Although widely believed by the region's population, it was always unclear whether the Donbas was a net contributor to the Ukrainian budget because it received large subsidies to its coalmining sector and taxes were usually not paid on the profits generated by its industrial sector. The Donbas Free Economic Zone, VAT refunds, and the preferential allocation of privatisations and government tenders benefited the region's oligarchs and their purchase of European real estate, rather than contributing to Ukraine's state budget.

Ukraine has had a perennial Donbas problem because of what Kuromiya describes as its fierce spirit of freedom and independence which made it a reluctant part of Ukraine. The Donbas was always a 'problem child for both Moscow and Kiev,'[45] he writes. On four occasions, the disintegration of central power led to anarchy, civil war and high levels of violence during the 1917-1920 Russian civil war, World War II, on the eve of the disintegration of the USSR in the late 1980s and first half of the 1990s and during the 2013-2014 Euromaidan. In the Russian civil war, the region established an independent Soviet republic that sought to become an autonomous region of Bolshevik Russia. The Donbas was alienated from the Soviet Union and alarmed at President Boris Yeltsin's anti-communism and it supported Ukrainian independence in the December 1991 referendum (although the majority was not high). In 2014, the Donbas was alienated from the Euromaidan Revolution, especially after they had toppled Yanukovych. In two out of three occasions the fate of the Donbas was decided by Russia's intervention because '…Kiev never succeeded in influencing the Donbas.'[46]

The population of the Donbas exhibited a deeply held regional identity that was more popular than Ukrainian civic (state) and especially ethnic Ukrainian identity. Residents of the region hold tremendous pride in the region's history as an industrial powerhouse of the Tsarist Russian Empire and the USSR. Donbas regional identity was combined with a high level of attachment to Soviet culture that was also found in the Crimea. Kuromiya wrote long before the Ukraine-Russia crisis that 'Whenever Kiev has attempted to build a nation, the Donbas has acted like an anti-metropolitan Cossack land, resisting Kiev nation-building.'[47] Lenin and Putin have both sought to maintain the Donbas within Ukraine through which Moscow could exert influence and maintain the country within Russia's sphere of influence.

The collapse of central power in 2014 led to a power vacuum filled by previously marginal political forces and Russian proxies. The Minsk Accords have not created a durable ceasefire and the conflict is on–going, rather than a frozen conflict similar to that of the Trans-Dniestr in Moldova.

Andras Racz and Arkady Moshes[48] point to ten differences that make Ukraine different to the Trans-Dniestr, a frozen conflict inside Moldova. The sizes of the populations of Ukraine and Moldova are vastly different and the Trans-Dniestr accounts for a higher proportion of the total population inside Moldova than the Donbas inside Ukraine. Since 1992, separatists have controlled the entire Trans-Dniestr region while the DNR and LNR only control a third to a half of Donetsk and Luhansk *oblasts*. The Trans-Dniestr and Donbas are both dominated by outdated heavy industry but Ukraine has other industries in different regions of the country. Russian energy pipelines cross Trans-Dniestr but not the Donbas.

In terms of identity, Racz and Moshes wrongly believe that the Trans-Dniestr has little in common with the Donbas as the former had been an autonomous republic inside inter-war Soviet Ukraine while the Donbas, in contrast, has always been administered from Kyiv. The identity of both regions was Soviet. In 1991-1992, right-bank Moldovan Russians fought against the 'Communist' Trans-Dniestr and today ethnic Russians fight against the 'Sovok' Donbas separatists. Artyom Shirobokov, a Russian citizen, has chosen to fight within the *Azov* battalion not against 'Russian separatists' but those who have a 'Soviet mind-set.' He therefore does not believe he is fighting 'my own people.'[49] The two separatist regions are different ethnically. The Trans-Dniestr has a majority Slavic population that contrasts with Romanian-speaking Moldova. The Russian and Ukrainian population of the Donbas is similar to the ethnic make-up of other regions of Ukraine.

In the early 1990s and in 2014, similar calamities befell the Russian-speaking leaders of the Trans-Dniestr and Donbas respectively when their ruling elites were removed from power by what they believed were 'nationalists' in the pay of the West. Trans-Dniestr regional elites had ruled Soviet Moldova since World War II but they were replaced by Moldovan nationalists when the USSR disintegrated and the Soviet republic became an independent state. Donbas elites had never ruled Soviet Ukraine but its regional elites felt their economic power entitled them to be the natural leaders of independent Ukraine. Therefore, the removal of Yanukovych (building on resentment at the prevention of him taking power a decade earlier) increased support in the Donbas for exit over voice. Paul D'Anieri writes that 'It made no sense for eastern Ukrainians to split off when it might control the entire country.'[50] The Ukrainian public on both sides of the political divide, pro-Western national democrats and the Party of Regions, had been radicalised in the decade between the Orange and Euromaidan Revolutions.

A major difference between the two conflicts is the size of the Moldovan and Ukrainian militaries. In 1992, the Moldovans were militarily defeated and they have never attempted to recapture the Trans-Dniestr. Ukraine has far larger security forces that defeated the separatists until a Russian invasion in August 2014 turned the tide. Since then, Ukrainian security forces have improved through training, re-organisation, reforms and the supply of new military equipment.

The Donbas conflict has produced large amounts of damage to industry, infrastructure and civilian residences and led to massive numbers of refugees and IDP's (Internally Displaced People). Even if Ukraine were to re-conquer the Donbas it would find it difficult to provide the technical, financial and personnel resources to rebuild the region. Continued low intensity conflict will inevitably mean the proliferation of soft security threats, the circulation of cheap priced weaponry and the growth of criminality inside Ukraine and Russia.

The conflict – as with all wars – is changing the identities of the Donbas, Ukraine and Russia. Putin's aggression against Ukraine has destroyed the Soviet myth of the 'brotherhood of people's.' After all, Russia cannot have it both ways. The transfer of the Crimea to Ukraine in 1954 was in commemoration of the three hundredth anniversary of the 're-union' of Ukraine and Russia and consequently, Russia's annexation of the Crimea ended the union.

The West's relations with Russia are at an all-time low last seen in the early 1980s during the height of the Soviet Union's confrontation with the US. Outside the country, particularly following Russia's war crimes in Syria, neither Putin nor Russia receive the respect or support they crave as a great power.[51] German-speaking Putin misjudged Germany's reaction to his aggression because his stationing in the GDR gave him no experience of Western Germany.

Putin completely misread the absence of sanctions and the West's passivity following Russia's invasion of Georgia six years earlier again leading to no sanctions after he invaded the Crimea. The threat from Ukraine's forces who were never militarily defeated will require a costly stationing of Russian forces and the continued provision of supplies, training and equipment to Russian proxy forces.

**Table 1.1. Chronology of the Ukraine-Russia Crisis**

| Date | Event |
| --- | --- |
| 2003-2012 | |
| 2003-2004 | Rose revolution in Georgia. Yanukovych's election fraud provokes the Orange Revolution and ends in a 'Russian 9/11' for Putin |
| 2005 | Pro-Putin youth groups *Nashi* and Walking Together are launched to prevent a colour revolution in Russia |
| March 2006 | Brokered by Russia, the Party of Regions establish an alliance with Russian nationalists in Crimean local elections |
| September 2006 | Prime Minister Yanukovych tells NATO that Ukraine does not want a Membership Action Plan (MAP) |
| June 2007 | Russkiy Mir founded |
| February 2007 | Putin gives a bombastic speech to the Munich security conference |
| April 2008 | Putin's speech to the NATO summit talks of an artificial Ukraine and makes territorial claims towards eastern and southern Ukrainian territory |
| August 2008 | Russia invades Georgia |
| September 2008 | Party of Regions loses a vote to support Russia's recognition of the independence of South Ossetia and Abkhazia but a similar vote in the Crimean Supreme Soviet is successful |
| May 2009 | EU launches the Eastern Partnership |
| Summer 2009 | Ukraine expels Russian diplomats in the Crimea and Odesa for espionage |

| | |
|---|---|
| August 2009 | President Medvedev sends an open address to President Viktor Yushchenko with tough demands |
| 21 April 2010 | Kharkiv Accords extends the basing treaty of the Russian Black Sea Fleet to 2042-2047. Russia lays out extensive economic and energy demands towards Ukraine |
| May 2010 | Ukraine permits the return of Russian intelligence services to the Black Sea Fleet |
| 16 July 2010 (annulled on 23 December 2014) | Ukrainian parliament adopts a non-bloc foreign policy that rules out NATO membership but maintains a course for EU membership |
| 2011-2012 | Russian mass protests against Putin |
| March 2012 | Putin is re-elected on a nationalist platform |
| 2013 | |
| May | Ukraine and the Eurasian Economic Commission sign a memorandum granting Ukraine observer status |
| July | Russia launches a trade war against Ukraine |
| 27 July | Putin visits Ukraine on the anniversary of the adoption of Christianity by Kyiv Rus |
| 27 October | Yanukovych meets Putin in Sochi |
| 9 November | Azarov visits Moscow. Yanukovych meets Putin on a Russian military base where he threatens to annex the Crimea and *NovoRossiya* |
| 12 November | Putin pressures Yanukovych to delay signing the EU Association Agreement at the Vilnius summit of the Eastern Partnership |
| 21 November | Prime Minister Azarov suspends Ukraine's bid for the EU Association Agreement |
| 22 November | Euromaidan Revolution begins |
| 28-29 November | Yanukovych attends the Vilnius summit of the Eastern Partnership |
| 30 November-1 December | Riot police attack protesters sparking larger protests |
| 6 December | Yanukovych and Putin meet in Sochi |

| | |
|---|---|
| 17 December | Ukraine and Russia sign economic treaties. Russia agrees to buy $15 billion of Ukrainian debt and reduce the price of gas paid by Ukraine by a third |
| 18 December | Yanukovych agrees that Ukraine receive observer status in the Eurasian Economic Union |
| 2014 | |
| 8 January | Yanukovych meets Putin in Valdai |
| 16 January | Ukrainian parliament adopts anti-democratic legislation on 'Black Thursday' |
| 22 January | 5 protesters are murdered |
| 18-20 February | Over 100 protesters are murdered |
| 21 February | Yanukovych signs a compromise agreement with opposition leaders brokered by the EU that keeps him in power until December. Euromaidan protestors reject the compromise and he flees in the evening from Kyiv to Kharkiv |
| 22 February | Euromaidan takes power and impeaches Yanukovych. The 2012 language law is annulled but acting head of state Oleksandr Turchynov vetoes the annulment |
| 27-28 February | Paramilitaries and Russian *spetsnaz* seize Crimean state and government buildings. Crimean Supreme Soviet votes to hold a referendum |
| 1 March | Pro-Russian protests led by Pavel Gubarev lead the first take-overs of state buildings in Donetsk. They describe the Euromaidan regime as 'illegitimate' and demand a referendum for the Donbas |
| 1 March | Yanukovych calls from exile for Russia to intervene in the Crimea |
| 16 March | 97% vote in favour of joining the Russian Federation in the Crimean Referendum |
| 17 March | The first Western sanctions are imposed on Russia |
| 18 March | Russian parliament votes to annex the Crimea |
| 20 March | Ukrainian parliament votes for a resolution 'On |

| | |
|---|---|
| | the Struggle for the Liberation of Ukraine' |
| 21 March | Russian Federal Assembly ratifies the incorporation of the Crimea |
| 27 March | UN votes to affirm Ukrainian territorial integrity and 11 countries voted against the motion and 5 abstained |
| 7 April | Russian *spetsnaz* invade eastern and southern Ukraine. Protesters capture buildings in Kharkiv, Odesa and Donbas. The DNR is established |
| 16 April | The ATO is launched against Donbas separatists |
| 28 April | The LNR is proclaimed |
| 2 May | Clashes between pro-Ukrainian and pro-Russian forces in Odesa lead to 48 dead |
| 5 May-1 July | Ukraine re-captures western and southern Donetsk and northern Luhansk |
| 11 May | DNR and LNR referendums are supported by 89%. The DNR and LNR declare independence |
| 24 May | The DNR and LNR unify into *NovoRossiya* |
| 25 May | Poroshenko is elected president and Vitaliy Klitschko elected mayor of Kyiv |
| 27 June (and partly on 21 March) | EU and Ukraine sign the Association Agreement and DCFTA |
| 17 July | MH17 is shot down by Russian troops manning a BUK missile |
| 22 August | First Russian 'humanitarian' convoy crosses into the Donbas |
| 24 August | Russia invades eastern Ukraine to assist separatists on the verge of defeat. Ukrainian forces are defeated at Ilovaysk |
| 16 September | Ukrainian and European parliaments ratify the EU Association Agreement |
| 5 and 19 September | Minsk-1 Accords are signed |
| 2 November | DNR and LNR hold elections |
| 4 November | Ukraine ends financial transactions with the DNR and LNR |
| 2015 | |

| 22 January | Russian and separatist proxies launch offensive and capture Donetsk Airport |
| --- | --- |
| 12 February | Minsk-2 Accords are signed |
| 18 February | Ukrainian forces are defeated at Debaltseve |
| May | Crimean Tatar media banned |
| September | Ukraine halts its participation in CIS structures |
| 20 September | Crimean Tatars and *Pravyy Sektor* launch a blockade of the Crimea |
| 2016 | |
| January | Ukrainian parliament votes to end supplies of food and electricity to the Crimea |
| February | Launch of blockade of Russian trucks crossing Ukraine |
| August | Russia claims to have foiled a plot by Ukrainian military intelligence to launch terrorist attacks in the Crimea |
| September | Dutch Safety Board issues its final report blaming Russia for supplying the BUK that shot down MH17 |
| October | Russia bans the Crimean Tatar *Mejlis* |
| October | DNR and LNR hold local elections |
| November-December | Russian and separatist attacks escalate against Ukrainian forces |

## OUTLINE OF THE BOOK

The book is divided into eleven chapters. Chapter 2 surveys Russian nationalism, chauvinism and imperialism and Russian attitudes towards Ukraine and Ukrainians. The chapter traces the evolution of Putin from KGB officer to a corrupt politician and Russian president to nationalist leader. This chapter describes in detail the growing influence of nationalism from the margins of Russian political life to centre stage and the revival of Russian imperialism and chauvinistic views of Ukrainians as 'Little Russians' whose 'natural home' is within the *Russkiy Mir*.

Chapter 3 analyses the long-term nature of Ukrainophobia within the Tsarist Russian Empire, Soviet Union and Russian Federation towards Ukraine and Ukrainians. The chapter investigates the role of the state manipulation of the media, particularly Russian television and its broadcasting of xenophobia and Western-backed conspiracies, and deception. Ukrainophobia divides Ukrainians into 'good Little Russians' and 'fascist' and 'Russophobic' supporters of the Euromaidan and European integration. Ukrainianophobia was historically high during periods of Russian and Soviet conservative retrenchment and counter-revolution alongside myths of the Great Patriotic War and the rehabilitation of totalitarian dictator Stalin.

Chapter 4 analyses anti-Semitism in Russian and Ukrainian political and social life during the course of the twentieth century and the Donbas conflict. The chapter investigates the long-term relationship of Russian nationalism with anti-Semitism and its influence over anti-Zionist ideological crusades in the Soviet Union. The legacies of Soviet anti-Zionism and Russian anti-Semitism provide the basis for the widespread xenophobia and anti-Semitism of DNR and LNR separatist leaders.

Chapter 5 investigates criminality and violence in the Donbas, the region with the highest proportion of people who were imprisoned in Soviet *and* independent Ukraine. Kuromiya has written about the culture of extreme levels of violence that have existed in the Donbas since the late nineteenth century which exploded during periods of chaos when there was no central authority in Moscow or Kyiv. Factory towns, prevalent in the Donbas, have contributed to atomisation of the population, low levels of efficacy and election fraud. During the 1990s the appointment of Yanukovych as regional governor helped solidify the Donetsk Clan and its oligarch-criminal nexus into the Party of Regions *krysha* and political machine.

Chapter 6 analyses the Donbas as a region that grew from that of a 'Welsh' outpost in the Tsarist Russian Empire to the emergence of a large metropolis in a region where Soviet identity had sunk deep roots through demographic changes brought about by Soviet nationality policies and Stalinist and Nazi crimes against humanity. The chapter provides an understanding of why Donbas Soviet identity reflects the importance not of language *per se* but that of culture and attitudes to history. This in turn, defines regional attitudes towards Russia, independent Ukraine and ethnic Ukrainian identity and language.

Chapter 7 analyses the significance of the rise of the Party of Regions as Ukraine's only political machine. The Party of Regions successfully brought together former state industrial 'Red Directors,' new oligarchic business interests, former Communists, criminal leaders, Pan-Slavic groups, and Crimean Russian nationalists. Using an efficiently organised, well financed, and thuggish and corrupt operating culture, the Party of Regions expanded from its Donbas home base to politically, economically and financially monopolise eastern-southern Ukraine. The attempted monopolisation of the entire Ukrainian state in 2004 and 2010-2013 provoked two democratic revolutions and Yanukovych's overthrow.

Chapter 8 investigates Russian policies towards Ukraine during the decade from the Orange Revolution to the Euromaidan. The chapter analyses the sources of Russia's inability to recognise an independent Ukraine and Putin's policies aimed at dismembering and subverting Ukraine through invasion, annexation, hybrid war and terrorism. The chapter analyses the treasonous policies of the Yanukovych presidency that laid the groundwork for Russia's plans.

Chapter 9 analyses Russia's hybrid War in the Donbas through the use of 'little green men' *spetsnaz* without country insignia, Russian volunteer nationalists, Tsarist monarchists, fascists, Cossacks and Orthodox zealots. The chapter investigates the separatist forces that have been built, trained and equipped by Russia and the Ukrainian security forces and volunteer battalions they have faced on the front-line. The chapter dissects the large number of casualties of Russian and Ukrainian military forces, nationalist volunteers on both sides, Russian separatist proxies and civilians as an outcome of a Russian-Ukrainian low intensity conflict rather than an ATO.

Chapter 10 investigates the sources of unprecedented levels of violence, widespread human rights abuses, and high levels of civilian casualties committed primarily by Russian occupation forces and their separatist proxy allies. The chapter surveys the reports of international institutions, human rights organisations, think tanks and NGOs on human rights and war crimes committed during the Donbas conflict.

Chapter 11 analyses the impact of the Ukrainian-Russian conflict upon national identity in Ukraine and how this is being transformed by conflict and war. The chapter investigates why Ukraine's Russophones outside the Donbas in eastern and southern Ukraine did not support Putin's *NovoRossiya* project. As with conflicts and wars throughout history, Ukrainian identity is undergoing rapid change domestically and vis-a-vis the outside world.

There cannot be a conclusion to the book because the Donbas is an unresolved conflict that is on-going. There will be no closure of the Ukraine-Russia crisis as long as Putin is Russian president which will be as long as he remains alive. To fully implement the Minsk-2 Accords would mean jettisoning the DNR-LNR which Putin will not do and therefore, a political resolution to the Donbas conflict is difficult to envisage.

# CHAPTER 2

# RUSSIAN NATIONALISM
# AND IMPERIALISM AND UKRAINE

*An independent Ukraine is an absurd concept simply because today's Ukraine is a free nation. It stands in brotherhood with the other nations of the Soviet Union.*
Soviet security service interrogator, 1952[52]

*The 'Ukrainian project' was established by Austria to tear you from Russia, from Rus. They divided us.*
Russian General Consul Yevgeniy Guzeyev, 2010[53]

Russian political thought in Tsarist Russia and the USSR, among émigrés and in independent Russia has traditionally adopted a negative attitude towards Ukrainian demands for autonomy and independence and a complete indifference and hostility to complaints of denationalisation and Russification. In Tsarist Russia and in the dissident movement in the USSR the proportion of Russian democrats who supported Ukrainian national goals were in a decided minority. In the Russian civil war, no Russian political forces supported Ukrainian autonomy within a new federalised democratic Russia (let alone independence). Liberal political parties such as the *Kadets (Constitutional Democratic Party)* who backed the provisional government were opposed to Ukrainian autonomy.[54] Russian émigrés from the Soviet Union were predominantly nationalist, imperialist and Eurasianist and admirers of fascism, ideological traditions that are dominant in Russian politics today. Among Russian democratic dissidents in the USSR, only Andrei Sakharov, Vladimir Bukovsky and Andrei Amalrik were sympathetic to Ukrainian national demands.

Two constants have therefore remained in Russian attitudes towards themselves and Ukraine. The first is a disinterest in establishing Russia as an independent state and a preference for being the centre of an empire. Hutchings and Tolz write how Eurasianism is a substitute for de-colonisation because it claims Russia has been more successful than the West in managing ethnic diversity. Even more so, 'Eurasianism treats Russia not as a colonial power, but as a community which is itself under threat of being colonized by the West.'[55] Russia's mythical success provides it with an excuse to maintain a Eurasian empire rather than build a nation-state. Russians have never been separatists and therefore they are better defined as imperialists rather than nationalists. It is no coincidence that the minority of Russians who have supported an independent state have also been positively inclined towards Ukrainian national aspirations. The second constant is Russia's unwillingness to accept that Ukrainians are a separate people, that Ukrainian is a bona fide language (and not a Russian dialect) who have an independent state and a right to decide their own geopolitical destiny.

These two constants in Russian history have been largely absent from Western analyses of the Ukrainian-Russian crisis because they hark back to the primordial nationalism, imperialism and great power spheres of influences in the inter-war era and earlier. Indeed, during the crisis, the post-modern EU came face to face with traditional nineteenth century imperialism and inter-war revanchism.

## THEORIES OF NATIONALISMS, RUSSIA AND UKRAINE

The theoretical literature defines a large variety of types of nationalism which can be applied to Russia and Ukraine. These range from civic nationalism that is often associated with patriotism and territorial nationalism, examples of which lie in eastern Ukraine, the Russian Federation and English-speaking Scotland. Other forms of patriotism are often attributed to immigrant settler countries such as the US, Canada and Australia. Portraying western states as 'civic' and eastern as 'ethnic' is a false dichotomy because all European and North American democracies combine both elements and all civic states have to make choices about the language(s), culture(s) and historical myths that would constitute their ethno-cultural core(s).[56] In Ukraine it was therefore a false dichotomy of choosing between an 'ethnic Ukrainian' and 'civic state' because the real choice was a state with an ethnic Ukrainian core or a state with Ukrainian-Russian ethnic cores. The latter approach would transform Ukraine into a state resembling Belarus which is built on a Belarusian-Russian core.

Ethnic forms of nationalism are discernible from the numerous conflicts in many parts of the world. Although ethnic nationalism is often viewed in solely negative terms because of these images of ethnic conflict this has not always been the case. Nationalism in the nineteenth century and in the first three decades following World War II was more often associated with liberal nationalism, a defensive anti-colonial movement against repression and assimilation and aimed at the break up of empires and establishment of independent states. Nevertheless, just as one person's terrorist is another person's freedom fighter, so too one person's patriotism is another person's nationalism. Ukrainians and Irish seeking to provide incentives to overcome denationalisation, Russification and Anglicisation would argue that this is an inherently liberal policy and affirmative action. Many Russians and English and particularly those Ukrainians and Irish who have become Russian and English speakers respectively will view these policies as anti-democratic and misplaced. The Russian language in the Tsarist Empire and USSR, English in Great Britain and French in France were promoted as the languages of contemporary 'civilisation' and modernity while Ukrainian, Irish, Welsh and Breton were derided as provincial peasant tongues (or dialects) unfit for use in a modern state. This chauvinism has a long history. Terry Martin writing about the 1920s pointed out that Russians 'still consider the Ukraine and the modern in fundamental opposition.'[57] A third of Russians in Ukraine lived in five major industrial *oblasts* (Luhansk, Donetsk, Kharkiv, Zaporizhzhya and Dnipro) with Russians 'highly associated and the Ukrainians highly negatively associated with modernization.'[58]

Nationalisms have different levels of mobilisation capitol. Ethnic nationalism, civil society and anti-colonial discourse worked together to mobilise against European Empires after World War I and their overseas empires after World War II. In the USSR in the late 1980s, examples of this occurred in western Ukraine, the three Baltic states, Moldova, Georgia and Armenia.[59] Anti-colonial and anti-Soviet mobilisation proved to be weak where territorial identities were more prominent in Russia, Belarus and eastern Ukraine, and in the five Central Asian republics.[60] In the early 1990s, ethnic Russian minorities living outside the independent Russian state did not mobilise when the USSR disintegrated, unlike Serbian minorities living outside Serbia within the former

Yugoslavia.[61] Until the Euromaidan Revolution, nationalist mobilisation in Ukraine remained confined to Ukrainian speakers and the Russian speaking population remained passive. Western Ukrainians led the way in mobilising against the Soviet regime in the late 1980s, during the 2000-2001 Kuchmagate crisis when President Kuchma was implicated in the murder of journalist Georgiy Gongadze, the Orange Revolution and Euromaidan. Ethnic Ukrainian national identity was more successful in mobilising Ukrainians because the identity of Russians and Russian speakers was grounded not in ethno-cultural resources but territorial, as in Russia itself, or in supra-national Pan-Slavic and Soviet identities.

The Russian SFSR was never a fully-fledged Soviet republic and Russians, similar to the English in Great Britain, were unlikely to therefore mobilise against their own empires or multi-national states. Russian and English nationalism would only arise in response to other nationalisms (i.e. Ukrainian and Scottish) and would always prefer a multi-national state to an independent state. Soviet nationality policies led to the emergence of a Soviet Belarusian territorial identity (as personified by President Alyaksandr Lukashenka) in a republic that had no nationalist or democratic dissident movement in the USSR. Russia *and* Belarus held no referendums on independence after the failed August 1991 putsch.

President Yeltsin pursued a civic territorial identity for independent Russia in the 1990s but this failed to find resonance among the Russian population.[62] President Putin's nation-building policies have promoted an alternative neo-Soviet and imperial-great power national identity that has been popular and has given him very high rates of popularity.

Ethno-cultural resources such as common identity, group solidarity, trust, and cultural and intellectual resources, are necessary for successful mobilisations of people. In eastern and southern Ukraine such resources were weak until four key developments took place. Firstly, Russian nationalism became increasingly ethno-culturally based and supportive of Russian speaking movements in neighbouring countries. Previously marginal nationalists such as Eurasianist ideologist Dugin became influential among policymakers in Moscow. Secondly, Russia reverted to traditional Soviet conspiracy theories in viewing the Serbian (2000), Georgian (2003), and Ukrainian democratic revolutions (2004, 2013-2014) as western-backed putsches directed against Russia's 'privileged interests' in Eurasia. Thirdly, Russia invested in the ideology of the *Russkiy Mir* that provided a group identity to Russian speakers and peoples who associate with Russian culture and language. As Russian and Soviet identities were irrevocably intertwined in the USSR it is not surprising the *Russkiy Mir* also mythologised the Great Patriotic War and Sevastopol as a 'hero city.'[63] It also presaged a return to Soviet ideological tirades against Ukrainian nationalists denounced as 'Nazi collaborators' and 'fascists.' Fourthly, Russia invested in its special forces ('little green men') who annexed the Crimea and unleashed hybrid warfare in the Donbas.

Russia built an empire before it built a nation-state and its national identity has always been more closely bound with multi-national Tsarist and Soviet empires. Russians in subsuming their national identity within a multi-national state were not alone, as the English had followed the same pattern inside Great Britain. The major difference was that England had created a nation-state before it had an empire. Nevertheless, Ireland, Ukraine and Algeria were comparable in that neither was viewed as lying within the broader British, Russian and French empires respectively but part of the metropolis. Ukraine belonged to what Moscow termed the 'Near Abroad' and therefore was different to real foreign countries (i.e. the 'Far Abroad').

In the USSR, Russians had viewed the entire country as their homeland by closely integrating Soviet and Russian identities and therefore making it difficult to disentangle them. Ukrainians and other non-Russians held Soviet republican *and* USSR identities and after the latter disintegrated a majority of the population transferred their allegiance to their newly independent republics. Soviet identities persisted up to the Euromaidan in eastern and southern Russian speaking Ukraine with the highest support for this cultural identity to be found in the Crimea and Donbas. Russians and Russophones living in Ukraine viewed the USSR – not Russia – as their homeland[64] and separatism therefore proved to be weak because Russians in Ukraine could not secede to the non-existent Soviet state and they were territorially loyal to the former boundaries of Soviet Ukraine that had become an independent state in 1991. Serbian minorities living outside Serbia took up arms to join a Greater Serbia and a similar armed rebellion by Russians and Russian speakers only took place in 2014 after Russia provided military and intelligence support.

Serbs were different to Russians because they had built an independent state prior to inter-war Yugoslavia and they had a robust ethnic identity going back to the nineteenth century; Serbian and Russian relationships to their multinational Soviet and Yugoslav states was therefore very different. The Russian

SFSR never possessed its own republican Communist Party and state institutions and there were only Soviet central institutions based in Moscow. In late 1991, Yeltsin took control of Soviet institutions that were reconstituted as those of the independent Russian Federation. Serbia in contrast, possessed a republican Communist Party, League of Communist Youth, Academy of Sciences and other institutions that were separate to those of Yugoslavia. These, after they were taken over by Slobodan Milosevic became vehicles promoting ethnic Serbian mobilisation and a Greater Serbia that would incorporate Serbian enclaves in Croatia and Bosnia-Herzegovina. In the late 1980s and early 1990s there were no Russian institutions in place to promote ethnic Russian nationalism and Yeltsin did not seek to build a Greater Russia. While Serbia sought to build a Greater Serbia from the ruins of Yugoslavia, Russia attempted to maintain the USSR and when that failed supported its transformation into the Commonwealth of Independent States (CIS) and in most recent times a Eurasian union.

## DEFINING RUSSIAN NATIONALISM AND IMPERIALISM

An important question that confuses scholarly studies of Russian politics is the misuse of the term 'nationalism' which, as David G. Rowley points out, is 'inaccurate and misleading.' Russians have 'expressed their national consciousness through the discourse of imperialism rather than discourse of nationalism.' Rowley writes that Tsars, Soviets, and Russian nationalists and liberals did not seek to build a nation-state and instead sought to preserve the empire. Up to the Bolshevik revolution not a singe Russian political party called for Russia to abandon its empire and build a nation-state; in other words, there was no Russian equivalent of Turkish leader Mustafa Kemal Ataturk who established a Turkish state from the Ottoman empire. Support for nationalism understood as separatism was not articulated in Russia. Rowley writes, 'Thus educated Russians particular sense of national identity contributed not to the creation of a nation-state, but to the maintenance of an empire.'[65]

In the 1990s, civic nation building failed to take hold among Russians because of the widespread influence of five beliefs that influenced Putin's nationalistic evolution and his imperialistic policies towards Ukraine:[66]

1. The Russian language is the main marker of identity as a community of Russian speakers, not civic citizenship of the Russian Federation.

2. The term 'Russian' is used inter-changeably with *Russkiy* that can mean both 'Great Russian' or eastern Slavic branches of the one Russian people.
3. Russians and Ukrainians are the same people.
4. Russians and Ukrainians should live closely bound, preferably in a union.
5. A Russian-speaking state should include the Crimea, Donbas, Kharkiv, and other regions in eastern and southern Ukraine.

In the USSR, the majority of Russian dissidents did not articulate nationalist-separatist demands because the Russian SFSR and the USSR were synonymous with one another. Russians were the 'awkward nationality.'[67] 'Russian national self-understanding was not firmly embedded in, or contained by, the territory and institutional frame of the Russian republic. The Russian republic was not for Russia what other national republics were for their corresponding nationalities.'[68] The Russian SFSR only began to build its republican institutions in 1990 less than a year before the USSR began to disintegrate which was too short a period of time. In the USSR, Russians had identified 'their national interests with Soviet interests,' where Russians were the first among equals.[69] The Russian SFSR was a 'comfortable home' 'but the Soviet Union was their motherland.'[70]

Rogers Brubaker provides an explanation as to why non-Russian republics such as Ukraine are defensive of their inherited republican borders while Russia views them as artificial, unjust and open to change. In 1990, the declaration of sovereignty of the Russian RSFSR was economic and political rather than national because the republic was a territory rather than the homeland for the Russian nation.[71] The Russian SFSR was therefore the least complete state in the USSR.[72]

Émigré political parties and Russian dissident groups and intellectuals traditionally ignored the nationalities question in the Russian empire and in the USSR. The grandiosely entitled Committee for the Liberation of the Peoples of Russia hardly mentioned the nationalities question and Ukraine in particular.[73] The neo-fascist NTS (National-Labour Solidarity) movement of young Russian émigré's heavily influenced General Vlasov's movement. Ukrainian leaders looked upon them 'with the utmost suspicion' because of their conflation of the Russian empire with a Russian nation-state.[74]

Of the 807 imprisoned dissidents in the USSR, Peter Reddaway found only 36 Russian nationalists, half of who were from the All-Russian Social Christian Union which was fewer in number than those from the far smaller Moldovan and Latvian populations. Only a handful of the imprisoned Russians were nationalist-separatists and the majority were best described as imperialist in their attitudes about Russia and towards the non-Russian republics; after all, liberals and conservatives had also supported the British and French empires.

Of the 942 dissidents arrested in Ukraine, only 0.5 percent were ethnic Russian, or less than the proportion of Crimean Tatars and Jews.[75] Motyl writes that Russian nationalists did not call for the secession of their republic from the USSR, the jettisoning of the empire or the building of a Russian nation-state.[76] Russian nationalists, chauvinists and imperialists were tolerated by the Soviet regime because they were not separatists and they called for the USSR to become more 'Russian' than it already was.

President Yeltsin could be described as one of the first Russian 'nationalists' because of his backing for an independent Russian state.[77] The Russian SFSR did not declare independence from the USSR and after the failed putsch in August 1991 absorbed Soviet institutions in Moscow. Soviet leader Mikhail Gorbachev asked 'Why did Russia need independence? From whom did they need to be independent? From itself?'[78]

The dismantling of the USSR in December 1991 was a product of the congruence of Yeltsin's and Kravchuk's desire to remove Gorbachev 'rather than a desire to dismantle the empire and create a Russian nation state.'[79] Geoffrey Hoskings writes that 'a civic definition of nationhood' 'runs counter to Russian traditions'[80] and empire 'is the historic and geopolitical determinant form of development of the Russian state.'[81] Weak attention devoted to civic nation building in the 1990s by President Yeltsin and Russian democratic political parties, coupled with their over-focus on marketisation and privatisation which were unpopular because of growing social problems and rise of a rapacious oligarch class, produced a vacuum into which ethnic, imperial and chauvinistic forms of national identity could again become dominant under Putin.[82] Democratic politics consequently failed to fill the post-Soviet and post-imperial void in 1990s Russia which was eventually taken over by nationalism and chauvinism in the 2000s. Cheng Chen writes that 'successful liberal nationalism in Russia remains a remote scenario'[83] and predicted nearly a decade before the 2014-2015 crisis that Russian nationalism would become expansionist.

Putin was socialised in the USSR in the 1960s-1970s when Russian nationalism was officially encouraged within the Soviet system because it was never viewed as a threat to the state. Russian official nationalism came to dominate the Communist Party of the Soviet Union (KPRS) and the KGB in which Putin was an officer.[84] The Soviet Union in which Putin was socialised, promoted and cultivated public expressions of Russian nationalism, chauvinism, national superiority[85], the cult of Stalin, extolling of military victories and the monopolisation of religion by the Russian Orthodox Church throughout the eastern Slavic world. Unlike the nationalisms of non-Russian nations, the nationalism of the 'Great Russians' was never criticised in the Soviet media and 'it is as if the phenomenon did not exist.'[86] The growth of official Russian nationalism in the USSR and in independent Russia under Putin made the possibility of ethnic conflict more likely, as borne out in Chechnya and eastern Ukraine.[87]

Soviet culture, which Putin extols, was a product of the Sovietisation of Russian society and Russification of Soviet culture. This created an inner contradiction in Russian national identity between Soviet ideological-political and Russian cultural-historical facets. During the last two decades of the USSR, the fusion of Russian and Soviet national identities produced a strong base for what Chen describes as 'illiberal nationalism' which has formed the basis for Putin's 'consolidated authoritarian regime' and the source of racism, xenophobia and chauvinism.[88]

Omnipresent in Russian and Soviet history is the xenophobic portrayal of the West as Russia's 'Other.' Liah Greenfeld writes that 'The West was an integral, indelible part of the Russian national consciousness. There simply would be no sense in being a nation if the West did not exist.' The rejection of the West and state pressure for unity within 'Holy Rus' were inseparable, she believes.[89] The election of 'anti-Russian' Yushchenko, overthrow of Yanukovych and official course for European integration made Ukraine into an outpost of the West and Euromaidan leaders as Russia's 'fascist' 'Other.' The Russian Orthodox Church has become the handmaiden of Putin's imperialism and nationalism towards Ukraine and supports anti-Western xenophobia and the concept of Russia as a bulwark against decadent Western values.[90] Yitzhak M. Brudny writes that 'anti-Western' ideology 'indirectly legitimised the Soviet regime'[91] and the same is true today when 70-80 percent of Russians harbour xenophobic feelings.[92]

## RUSSIAN MESSIANISM AND XENOPHOBIA

The tenets of Russian nationalism in the Tsarist, Soviet and contemporary eras as well as among the majority of émigrés and dissidents has been remarkably consistent in the following nine areas:[93]

1. Russia should be protected from foreign, particularly European influences.

2. Conspiracy theories abound with suspicion of the West plotting to undermine Russia. Secretary of the Russian National Security Council Nikolai Petrushev believes Ukrainian leaders are US stooges 'who are doing their masters' bidding to pull away from Russia.'[94] Conspiracies against Russia are ever present and today 'seems omnipresent in Russian discourse and state-controlled media.' As political scientists have noted, those who endorse conspiracy theories are more likely to support violence.[95]

3. The morally bankrupt West is in decline while morally superior Russia is ascendant.

4. Russia is proceeding along its unique path and development as the centre of a separate Eurasian civilisation.

5. The Russian Orthodox Church promotes Russian messianism and Russia is destined to save the world and Eurasia is to become the new centre of world culture

6. The Catholic and Protestant Churches are inferior to Orthodoxy.

7. An exaggerated fear of revolution that threatens the Russian state and political stability.

8. The intelligentsia are 'rootless cosmopolitan' traitors in the pay of the West. The KPRS (with the exception of the Gorbachev era) and Russia under Putin has viewed liberals as alien and potentially dangerous.[96] Pro-Western intellectuals were, and continue to be denigrated as alien to Russian values, cosmopolitan and agents of the West (as seen in legislation adopted under Putin that requires them to register as 'foreign agents').

9. Anti-Semitism was always central to Russian nationalism in the Tsarist Empire and in the USSR was camouflaged as anti-Zionism. The Jewish people were the target of deep hatred by Russian nationalists who believed that Russia was a colony of Israel, Zionists had dominated the *Cheka* and 'Jewish-Bolsheviks' controlled the USSR.[97] Anti-Zionism (anti-Semitism) was influential in Russian academic and cultural circles,

the intelligence services and military. Russian nationalists, fascists and neo-Nazis believed in the authenticity of the forged Protocols of the Elders of Zion.[98]

## RUSSIAN FASCISM, NAZISM AND EURASIANISM

Different forms of Russian nationalism have been influential since the nineteenth century and these have often developed into fascist and neo-Nazi ideologies. John J. Stephan writes that Vladimir Purishkevich, leader of the Black Hundred 'Union of Russian People, was the first Russian fascist.'[99] *Pamyat* in the late 1980s and RNE in post-Soviet Russia were Russia's first contemporary neo-Nazi political forces.

In the inter-war era, the older generation of émigrés was close to German Nazis while the younger generation (such as NTS, the Young Russia Movement and National Toilers [formerly National Union of the New Generation]) leaned towards Italian, Spanish and Portuguese fascism.[100] From the mid-1940s to the early 1970s the Russian diaspora was dominated by nationalists, fascists and chauvinists who did not recognise that Ukrainians were a people, let alone they had a right to an independent state, making it impossible for Ukrainian nationalist émigré's to cooperate with them. This picture only changed in the 1970s and 1980s with the expulsion of democratic dissidents from the USSR.

The NTS believed it was continuing the struggle of White Russian leaders such as General Lavr Kornilov and they were close to the Vlasov ROA (Russian Liberation Movement) collaborationist movement during World War II. Their Solidarist and *Sobornost* ideology was similar to that of Mussolini's Italy. After World War II the NTS propagated a so-called 'third force' of Russia neither with Stalin nor Hitler. Surprisingly they continued, like all Russian nationalists, to reject liberal democracy even while accepting US government support which provided them with the resources to covertly distribute anti-communist and Russian nationalist literature in the USSR.[101] But, the anti-communism of NTS made it unpopular in Russia, where National-Bolshevism and Eurasianism would always have greater influence, while its chauvinism ruled out cooperation with non-Russian émigrés.

Eurasianism was born among young Russian émigrés in inter-war Europe and was revived in the late Soviet Union where it became very influential in the General Staff, KGB, Communist Party, Ministry of Foreign Affairs and

Academy of Sciences. Eurasianism appealed to Russian grievances and frustrations and fanned chauvinistic and racial-supremacist attitudes over smaller neighbours. 'Great Russians,' Eurasianists believed, were a super ethnos whose destiny is to control the Eurasian heartland. Jews meanwhile, are a 'parasite ethnos.'[102] Charles Clover describes Eurasianism as therapy for three generations of Russians to explain the Bolshevik revolution and their exile, deal with Stalinist reality and to explain the disintegration of the USSR. 'The 'National Bolshevism' of Stalin, 'the imperial deal of a great power,'[103] began to look very much like the political programme of Eurasianists.'[104]

Dugin, its most visible public personification in contemporary Russia, was an admirer of Nazism since the early 1980s when he joined Soviet neo-Nazi and fascist groups. Since 1991, he has been described as the 'St. Cyril and Methodius of fascism.'[105] The influence of Soviet Nazi groups and *Pamyat* are visible in Dugin's Eurasianism and his major books, *The Foundation of Politics* (1997) and *The Fourth Political Theory* 2007) integrate Soviet Communism, Nazism, traditionalism and environmental concerns with the ideas promoted by rural writers in the Leonid Brezhnev era. Dugin's racist belief in Russians as the 'chosen people' and 'Aryan race' draws upon Nazi writings.[106] Dugin has been consistent in his thorough opposition to Ukraine's very existence which he demands should be dismembered and parts of it annexed by Russia.

Dugin's influence could be best seen in the military and security services. From the late 1990s he has taught at Russia's most prestigious military academy of the General Staff whose patrons assisted him in publishing four editions of *The Foundations of Politics* in large print runs. Clover writes that his fan club was 'in some of the darker recesses of post-Yeltsin Russia'[107] After the disintegration of the USSR, the *siloviki* needed to know who were the new enemy which Dugin explained to them. His writings 'would plant the seed of European extreme-right theory in the fertile ground of Russia's military nomenklatura, shorn of its status and privilege, and there it began to germinate.'[108] Twenty years before Dugin's Eurasianism became mainstream under Putin it 'began life in a series of discussions with the European right'[109] and in lectures given to Russia's senior military command.

Dugin's fingerprints are to be found on a range of party projects. The National Bolshevik party was the first and his brainchild whose alternative names had been National Socialism, National Fascism and National Communism. Its members saluted with a straight arm raised in the air in a fist. The flag was a black hammer and sickle in a white circle on a red-black background.[110] The second was the short-lived and unsuccessful Eurasia Party. The third project, the Russian *Rodina (Motherland)* party established together with Sergey Glazyev and backed by thirty far-right parties and organisations, was more successful because it received official state backing. In fact, becoming too popular in the 2003 elections when it received nine percent, *Rodina* was briefly banned and its leader Dmitriy Rogozin was 'exiled' to NATO as Russia's Ambassador; nevertheless, *Rodina* was permitted to fight the 2012 elections. Dugin's fourth project, the Eurasian International Movement, a successor to the Eurasia party, was more successful out of which emerged the 'culture warriors' of its youth wing whose inspiration was the *Oprichniki* feared secret police of Ivan the Terrible.[111] The youth wing of the International Eurasia Movement was formed at the same time as *Nashi,* United Russia-Young Guard and Young Russia after the Rose and Orange Revolutions which co-opted and united skinheads and football *ultras (fanatical football fans).*[112]

Eurasianism is an outgrowth of the National-Bolshevism that a large body of émigré Russians viewed positively and began emerging in Stalin's Soviet Union. Eurasianists and National-Bolshevik's integrate Soviet Communism with Tsarist Russian nationalism into a great power and imperialistic ideology where Russian culture, language and civilisation is elevated to a dominant position. A major facet of Eurasianism is the call for Russia to disassociate itself from the West and hence it is fundamentally xenophobic, suspicious and paranoid with a deep seated conspiracy mind-set. Although Walter Laqueur believes Eurasianism to be a 'nebulous idea from both a cultural and political point of view'[113] this has not prevented it from becoming dominant in Putin's Russia.

What was once wacky and extreme in Russian politics became mainstream by Putin's re-election in 2012. From 2007-2008, formerly marginal proponents of neo-fascist and Eurasianist ideologies such as Dugin moved from the fringes to central policymaking before the 2012 elections. Dugin welcomed the birth of fascism in Russia as a 'conservative revolution.' He became over the course of the decade prior to the 2014 crisis an 'influential pundit' who predicted a 'closer rapprochement between the rhetoric of Russia's extreme right and those at the very top, not least Putin himself.'[114] Ivan Demidov, head of the ideological directorate of United Russia, was a fan of Dugin's work. In an article published six years prior to the Russian Spring, Andreas Umland wrote:

'The Russian extreme right, including some of its crypto-fascist sections, is becoming an ever more influential part of Moscow mainstream public discourse. Its influence can be felt in Russia's mass media, academia, civil society, arts, and politics.'[115]

The same was true of Vladimir Zhirinovsky's misnamed Liberal Democratic Party of Russia, a 'nationalist' political party originally established by the KGB in 1990 and since then working in league with the ruling authorities.[116] Zhirinovsky, once portrayed as the clown of Russian politics, replied to the question what nationality were his parents with 'My mother was Russian, my father was a lawyer' to hide the fact his father was a Polish Jew.[117]

'Numerous studies reveal Dugin – with different degrees of academic cogency – as a champion of fascist and ultranationalist ideas, a geopolitician, an 'integral Traditionalist', or a specialist in the history of religions.'[118] Dugin threatened Ukraine would cease to exist as early as 2009, the year when the expulsion of Russian diplomats from Ukraine led to President Medvedev's open address to Yushchenko. Dugin said Russia was prepared to cease recognising Ukraine's territorial integrity and would enter into armed conflict with Ukraine over the Crimea.[119] In *The Fourth Political Theory* published in 2009, Dugin warned of 'a possibility of a direct military clash.'[120] During the 2014 crisis, Dugin called for 'genocide' to be committed against 'Ukrainians' because they are a 'race of bastards that emerged from the sewer manholes.'[121] Dugin's chauvinistic contempt for Ukraine is couched in similar terms as that of Putin's; namely, that Ukraine is an unnatural and artificial construct and Ukrainians are a branch of the Russian people.

The All-Russian Society for the Protection of Historical Monuments, established in 1965, and the *Rodina* society were the modern-day reincarnation of the Black Hundreds and, according to Laqueur, their programmes drew on Nazi ideology. *Pamyat* had support in the highest levels of the central committee of the KPRS, KGB and armed forces[122] which has continued to provide a basis for anti-Semitism in the contemporary FSB.[123] As with the Liberal Democratic Party of Russia, *Pamyat* was an example of the first attempts by the security services to channel and manage nationalism against the pro-Western democratic opposition (Zhirinovsky's father had been a KGB officer). Aleksandr Yakovlev credited the KGB with having given birth to Russian fascism.[124] *Pamyat's* rabid anti-Semitism had its roots in official Soviet anti-Zionist propaganda and the Russian nationalist conspiracy mind-set. In April 1987, *Pamyat* took control of The All-Russian Society for the Protection of Historical Monuments and cooperated closely with the similar Russian nationalist organisation *Otechestvo*. Their ideology was 'totally irrational;' while they were devoted to Soviet leader Lenin they believed his entourage was dominated by Jews and Masons.[125] *Pamyat* became a 'crypto-fascist street gang' and a 'boot camp' for a new generation of nationalists and fascists such as Dugin and Barkashov.[126]

From the 1960s, Russian *samizdat*[127] publications and foreign correspondents in the USSR confirmed the growth of neo-Nazis. Russian dissidents described prisoners who had moved from admiration for Stalinism to fascism and talked of the need for a 'Soviet fascist party.' The views of Gennadiy Shimanov, a Russian Orthodox dissident who supported a union of the Soviet totalitarian state and Russian Orthodoxy became popular. In the 1980s the Soviet media increasingly began to publish letters from neo-Nazi's and analyses of the activities of neo-Nazi groups. Neo-Nazi groups of the kind Dugin was a member were active in depressed working class districts of central Russia and western Siberia. In April 1982, on Adolf Hitler's birthday, neo-Nazis held a protest in Pushkin square in Moscow but these and other neo-Nazi and fascist activists were never detained or politically repressed.[128]

Russian nationalism, Stalinism and National-Bolshevism merged into a powerful and influential body of opinion opposed to the policies undertaken during the liberal Gorbachev and Yeltsin eras. As Laqueur writes, 'The presence of so many leading former party officials, army and KGB generals among the leaders of the right is as striking as the survival of so many of the old ideas.'[129] In 1992, Russian nationalists grouped in the National Salvation Front had disdain for the Communist Party of the Russian Federation (KPRF) but at the same time forged a 'common front with yesterday's party and state nomenklatura.'[130] They provided the bedrock upon which Putin could take power at the end of the decade and have remained popular at the same time as dismantling Russia's democratic gains and fighting three wars in Chechnya, Ukraine and Syria.

Marlene Laruelle points to evidence of fascism in Dugin's 'Russian Spring' in two areas. The first is the call for a totalitarian nationalist revolution to overthrow the regime and transform Russian society through the cult of violence, death and sacrifice. Russian nationalists and Eurasianists are disappointed by Putin's refusal to annex the Donbas and *NovoRossiya*, as part of the 'reassembly of Russian lands' which they believe should be invited to join the

Eurasian Union as a federal republic.[131] The RNE seek to use the Donbas conflict as a staging post to overthrow the Putin regime through an anti-oligarch, totalitarian national revolution.[132] Putin and Russian nationalists both view the incorporation of the Crimea as correcting a historical injustice. The dominance of ethno-cultural factors in Russia's identity underpins the ideological articulation of demands for the reunification of the *Russkiy* people who are allegedly faced by 'linguistic ethnocide' in the Crimea and eastern Ukraine.[133]

The second is the alignment of Russian fascist nationalist thought with extreme left-wing discourse hostile to oligarchs, big business, the EU, US and globalisation.[134] *The Nation* editor Stephen Cohen, *The Guardian* journalist Jonathan Steele, UK Labour Party leader Jeremy Corbyn, and academics such as Sakwa have blamed EU and NATO enlargement and democracy promotion for the crisis.[135] Corbyn meekly campaigned for the UK to remain within the EU during the June 2016 referendum.

An eclectic coalition of extreme left and extreme right volunteers are fighting on the Donbas separatist side who are motivated by hostility to the US, globalisation and the EU and have travelled to eastern Ukraine to fight 'CIA-backed Nazi scum.'[136] 'The region has become a hub for those who believe the world is in the grip of a conspiracy, with the CIA, the masons, corporate capitalism or Zionism to blame, and they believe the Kremlin and the Donbas rebels are the last line of defence.'[137] Extreme left-wing and right-wing volunteers with the separatists share similar beliefs they are fighting a government installed by a US backed putsch.[138] Volunteers from Serbian nationalist groups such as the Radical Party, many of whom have battle experience in Croatia and Bosnia-Herzegovina, are fighting on the separatist side, together with Hungarian, French and German fascists. Internationalist formations unite extreme left French, Spanish and Brazilian volunteers.[139]

Motyl believes that after sixteen years in power Putin's Russia has evolved into a fascist political system.[140] Ukrainian and Russian political cultures are fundamentally different over who has sovereignty in their political system. In Russia,[141] it is the macho supreme leader or Tsar whereas in Ukraine it is, as was shown in the Orange and Euromaidan Revolutions, the people. Motyl argues that Russia evolved from 'full (consolidated) authoritarianism' into fascism during the 2014-2015 Ukraine-Russia crisis. The trajectory was propelled by Putin's re-election in 2012 when he fully embraced nationalism, 'conservative values,' imperialism and xenophobia in what had become a fossilised 'Brezhnevite regime.'[142] Such views were not confined to official circles with members of the opposition such as Alexey Navalny also expressing nationalistic stances.[143] Putin's Russia became a 'consolidated authoritarian regime' after the Orange Revolution and his turn to the right in 2007-2008,[144] and the evolution of Russia towards fascism is therefore a logical progression that has culminated – as with all such regimes – in inflammatory propaganda, xenophobia, war and destruction. Marginal Russian nationalist and fascist rhetoric of the 1990s 'became the standard jargon of state policy a mere decade and a half later.'[145]

Russia fits the classification of a fascist regime, Motyl writes, because it has a 'popular fully authoritarian political system with a personalistic dictator and a cult of the leader and therefore is similar to Mussolini's Italy, Hitler's Germany, Franco's Spain and Ustasha-ruled Croatia. Russia's 'Tsarist' political system has an absolute monarch (Putin) as a supreme leader who determines which policies' he will adopt. Motyl lists ten characteristics of a fully authoritarian and fascist political system in Russia:

1. *Political institutions*: dominant ruling party, rigged elections, rubber-stamp parliament and semi-independent judiciary.
2. *Leader*: personalistic dictator.
3. *World view*: state, nation, and leader exaltation.
4. *Popular attitudes toward the regime*: mass support.
5. *Economy*: state alliance with oligarchs in a market economy.
6. *Opposition*: wholly or nearly completely repressed.
7. *Civil rights*: routinely violated.
8. *Coercive apparatus*: incorporated within the ruling elite (i.e. the *siloviki* in Russia's militocracy).
9. *Propaganda apparatus*: large resources.
10. *Violence and coercion*: targeted violence and widespread coercion.

Fascist and nationalistic regimes need and thrive by seeking domestic and foreign enemies.[146] The enemies of Putin's Russia include a 'treacherous' internal opposition in the pay of Western intelligence agencies (a charge that is taken directly from Soviet Communist and KGB propaganda) and Chechen separatists and externally, the traditional bogeyman of a perfidious 'Russophobe' West, US and EU promotion of democracy, 'fascist Ukraine' and Islamic terrorism. Ukraine, in Russia's eyes, should be 'a more reliable satrap'[147] in the manner of Belarus. Putin has plunged Russia into three wars and is viewed by NATO and the US as a major threat to their national security interests.

In 1990, the RNE became the first Nazi party to be established in Russia and its party symbol resembles a Nazi swastika. The RNE's ideological origins lie in the neo-Nazi and Black Hundred groups that had officially existed or acted semi-covertly in the USSR. RNE leader Aleksandr Barkashov espouses Nazi ideology and his supporters routinely salute each other with the Nazi-style raised arm. Like all Russian nationalists, the RNE views Ukrainians and Belarusians as branches of the *Russkiy ('Russian')* people. In the Russian Union that the RNE seek to build, Ukrainians and Belarusians would possess no national minority rights and would be treated as regional branches of 'Russians.'[148]

In the 1990s, the RNE became a large nationalist party with 350 regional branches in 100 Russian regions and an estimated 50-200, 000 supporters. By the second half of the 1990s the RNE had become the fourth largest political party in Russia after the KPRF, Liberal Democratic party and Democratic Choice. Its newspaper *Russkiy Poryadok* had a circulation in the tens of thousands. RNE was in opposition to Yeltsin throughout the 1990s and in October 1993 backed parliament in its armed standoff with him. Some RNE members were killed in the armed conflict, it was temporarily banned and Barkashov was briefly detained but released in February 1994. RNE's influence was evident among officers in the Ministry of Interior, the growth of racist attacks, and the sending of its paramilitaries to the Trans-Dniestr, South Ossetian, Chechen and Ukrainian conflicts. RNE had warm ties to the KPRF, Liberal Democratic Party and Congress of Russian Communities.

Although the RNE was dormant in 2006-2013, it immediately intervened in Ukraine's Donbas conflict where Pavel Gubarev, a leading RNE member, proclaimed himself the 'People's Governor' of the DNR. Girkin, Gubarev and Aleksandr Boroday are close to, or members of RNE. Girkin arrived in Ukraine with the neo-Nazi Cossack *Volchia Sotnia (Wolves Hundred [company])* who model themselves on Cossacks in the White Army and a Nazi collaborationist Cossack unit of the same name (see later).[149] Dmitriy Boitsov, leader of Orthodox Donbas and Mikhail Verin, commander of the Russian Orthodox Army, are RNE members.[150] The RNE has played both an influential role in the leadership of the Donbas separatist movement and in providing armed volunteers to fight the Ukrainian 'fascist junta' run by what it believes are 'Jewish oligarchs.'[151] The banned Movement Against Illegal Immigration

(DPNI) sent volunteers to the Donbas and one of its leaders, Sergey Vorotsev was killed in the battle for Donetsk airport.[152] Other Russian fascist, Nazi and imperialist organisations sent volunteers to the Donbas where they formed battalions entitled National Unity, *Varyag*, *Rusych*, Imperial Legion, Russian Orthodox Army, *Vostok*, *Sparta*, Viking, and Don Cossacks. By autumn 2015, 18 months into the conflict it was estimated that there were between 30-60, 000 Russian volunteers in eastern Ukraine.[153]

Russian Nazis participate in combat in eastern Ukraine, they train others, perform Nazi and Satanic rituals, give the Nazi raised arm salute and pose for selfies next to dead Ukrainian combatants. One study of Russian Nazis in eastern Ukraine posted on social media concluded 'In Russia's army the Nazis structurally and openly belong to the core and they train others.'[154] Former Ukrainian vigilantes and police officers joined *Oplot (Stronghold)* and units named after *Berkut*.

## OFFICIAL RUSSIAN NATIONALISM IN THE USSR

Russian National-Bolshevism and Stalinism dominated the majority of the USSR's 69 years of existence, or two thirds of the life of the Soviet state. The Soviet Union's turn to the right took place in the early 1930s after Ukrainian-isation was crushed and the *holodomor* was unleashed after which 'The Soviet past was becoming progressively more Russian and so were the upper echelons of the party and state.'[155] From the mid-1930s, it was 'imperative to advance Russian nationalism' in the USSR and although chauvinistic and racist in nature towards Ukrainians, national Bolshevism and the lesser evil theory (that incorporation into the Russian Empire was more preferable) was portrayed as beneficial.[156]

Russian nationalism and the rehabilitation of Stalin went hand in hand under Brezhnev and ex-KGB Chairman Yuriy Andropov in the USSR and in Putin's Russia. The biggest clampdown on dissent and national communism since the Stalin era took place in Ukraine in 1972 and because of its ferocity and Ukrainophobia was described by Ukrainian oppositionists as a *pogrom*. Under Andropov, repression of dissent and repression returned 'to the methods characteristic of the Stalin era.'[157] Soviet nationalities policies under Brezhnev and Andropov increased the promotion of the Russian language and the Sovietisation of non-Russian peoples following the 1979 all-Union conference in

Tashkent entitled 'The Russian Language, Language of Friendship and Collaboration among the Peoples of the USSR.[158] Andropov also adopted a tougher line on the fusion of Soviet nationalities into a Russian-speaking *Homo Sovieticus*.

By the Brezhnev era, the Soviet Communist Party was imbued with some facets of National-Bolshevism, chauvinism, racism and fascism, especially in the political directorate of the armed forces and KGB where Putin was employed. Laquer writes, 'The ideas propagated by the right appealed to the generals and marshals.'[159] Russian nationalism was 'deeply embedded' in the Soviet ruling elites and became 'the dominant element of the official Soviet system of values, Soviet culture, and of the required norms and patterns of social behaviour.'[160] Little wonder that post-Soviet Russians remained under the influence of their socialisation into Russian nationalism and chauvinism.

Russian dissident Amalrik[161] divided Russian nationalism during the Brezhnev era into three components:

(1) 'Neo-Stalinist' (national Bolshevism) which was influential in the Communist Party and government, as well as the RSFSR Union of Writers and literary journals. National-Bolshevism emerged in the second half of the 1930s and was highly influential during World War II when the vanguard of the revolution changed from the proletariat to the Russian nation.[162]

(2) 'Neo-Stalinist Marxism' was influential in the conservative bureaucracy.

(3) 'Neo-Slavophilism' was prevalent among official Russian village writers and dissidents.

Russian nationalism was integrated into Soviet communism from the early to mid 1930s and was heavily promoted after 1945 when 'The Soviet media waxed rhapsodic about the Russians having always been the greatest, wisest, bravest and most virtuous of all nations.'[163] The Soviet 'friendship of peoples' of the 1920s was refashioned in December 1935 as a dominant 'elder brother' guiding 'younger brothers.' The fashioning of the concept of 'friendship of people's' emerged at the same time as Russian nationalism became state policy and 'Russian history, culture, and tradition would became the new force uniting the Soviet peoples.'[164] By the eve of World War II the Soviet Union 'was propagating an extraordinary crude essentialist Russian nationalism.'[165]

The Tsarist Russian Empire was portrayed as a positive precursor to the USSR which had inherited the cultural unity of the eastern Slavs from the medieval state of Kyiv Rus. Russia's Consul in the Crimea said that the 1654 Treaty of Peryaslav 'reunion' of Ukraine and Russia created Russian-Ukrainian unity 'forever.'[166]

The Soviet regime had monopolised the history of Kyiv Rus on behalf of the 'elder Russian brother' and the Museum of *The Lay of the Host of Ihor*, a well-known text from that era, was opened in Yaroslavl and not in Kyiv.[167] Putin has revived an eclectic mix of Tsarist and Soviet historiography of Kyiv Rus in his chauvinistic appeal for the eternal unity of the eastern Slavic peoples because they are 'odin narod.' Unveiling a monument to 'Grand Prince Vladimir' in November 2016 on Russia Unity Day, Putin said, 'Today, our duty is to jointly stand up to modern challenges and threats, relying on the priceless traditions of unity and accord, moving forward and safeguarding the continuation of our 1,000-year history.' Putin's manipulation of history conveniently ignores the fact that Grand Prince Volodymyr ruled Kyiv Rus (980–1015) over a century before Moscow existed while showing his poor command of mathematics as the city was founded in 1147; that is, only 869 (not 1, 000) years ago.

Ukrainian historians, such as the doyen of national historiography Mykhaylo Hrushevskyy, provided an alternative scheme of eastern Slavic history but from the 1930s they were rabidly attacked in the Soviet media. The incorporation of non-Russians into the Tsarist Empire was described as progressive acts and therefore those who were opposed, such as Ukrainian nationalists, were denounced as 'traitors' in the pay of foreign powers. Such views have remained deeply imbedded in Russian political culture and heavily influence Putin's policies and attitudes towards Ukraine.

Serhiy Yekelchyk[168] writes that the Soviet thesis of 're-union' in 1654 was 'a refurbished imperial concept' that included claims of Russian entitlement to 'age-old possessions' and Ukrainians as not a separate people but simply 'Little Russians.' At the same time, Putin and Russians cannot have their cake and eat it. If the independence of Ukraine represented in Moscow's eyes the tearing apart of the union consummated by the Treaty of Peryaslav then Russia's annexation of the Crimea represented the end of the 'reunion' at Peryaslav. The 1654 Peryaslav Treaty was commemorated in 1954 on its 300th anniversary by the transfer of the Crimea to Soviet Ukraine, an 'error' which Putin corrected in 2014. An anti-Putin Russian nationalist fighting for the *Azov* battalion viewed this relationship differently, saying Ukrainians are our 'our brothers' and 'you don't steal the land of your brothers.'[169]

Official tolerance for Russian nationalism declined under Nikita Khrushchev but resumed under Brezhnev and was in full swing from the mid

1960s to the mid 1980s. During these two decades, myths of the Great Patriotic War and a Stalin cult became integral components of official and unofficial Russian nationalism.

Putin's glorification of the Great Patriotic War and re-Stalinisation closely resemble this period of Soviet history under Soviet leaders Brezhnev, Andropov and Konstantin Chernenko. Official Russian nationalism was tolerated and promoted in literary journals, theatre, film and the media. By the late 1960s, official Russian nationalists had aligned with 'National-Stalinists' in *Molodaya Gvardiya*, the central organ of the Soviet *Komsomol*, and their hostility was aimed at the 'unpatriotic' and 'anti-Communist' liberal intelligentsia ensconced in the journal *Novy Mir*. The fusion of Russian nationalism and rehabilitation of Stalin, so redolent of Putin's Russia, had emerged decades earlier into the public domain in the journals *Molodaya Gvardiya*, *Nash Sovremennik* and *Moskva* which appealed to a 'sizable group of Soviet readers who share Stalinist, anti-Western, and ultra-nationalist convictions.' The three journals had a combined mass circulation of 1.3 million. Readers of these journals and similarly ideologically inclined books and viewers of serialised television shows, theatre and cinema reached an audience in the millions who represented a major political constituency in Soviet society.[170]

The growing influence of official Russian nationalism came at the same time as Brezhnev's retreat from Khrushchev's de-Stalinisation. This reflected a similar retreat under Putin from the exposure of Stalin's crimes under Soviet President Gorbachev and Russian President Yeltsin. Russian nationalists in the Brezhnev and Putin eras view Stalin as the creator of the Soviet nuclear superpower which was feared by the world and they ignore and downplay his crimes against humanity. At a time of ideological stagnation, whether under Brezhnev or Putin, Russian nationalism became and remains a useful tool to legitimise the Soviet and Russian state; 'Great Russians' were, after all, 'the ethnic backbone of the Soviet state.'[171]

The hostility of official Russian nationalist journals to Gorbachev's policies of *perestroika* and *glasnost* were ultimately reflected in Putin's antipathy to Gorbachev's and Yeltsin's Russia. The influence of official Russian nationalism in the 1970s and 1980s was widespread and they cultivated a 'substitute state ideology' that came to power under Putin.[172]

Official Russian nationalists and Stalinists in the Soviet Union and Putin's Russia share the following ten beliefs:[173]

1. They downplay Stalin's crimes against humanity.

2. They claim some of Stalin's repressive acts were justified.

3. They believe that Stalin was not responsible because the crimes were the fault of his entourage and bureaucracy.

4. They condemn work exposing Stalin's crimes and have been virulently hostile to Ukraine's de-Stalinisation and its depiction of the *holodomor* as a genocide.

5. They promote Russian language and culture as superior to other languages and cultures.

6. They believe Sovietisation and Russification was progressive and Ukrainians and Belarusians speak dialects, not languages and they should speak the more cultured Russian language.

7. Communists, nationalists and the extreme right are integrated in an eclectic melange of ideologies. The KPRF is as much nationalist and imperialist as it is Marxist-Leninist and in the 1990s allied itself with Russian nationalists and neo-Nazis. As a National-Bolshevik and Stalinist political party, the KPRF led the National Patriotic Union of Russia and worked within the Union for the Spiritual Rebirth of the Fatherland and United Workers Front of Russia.[174] The KPRF, in a similar manner to Russian nationalists, supports a Russian union state of the three eastern Slavs.[175]

8. They are xenophobic towards internal enemies and external influence and rant against the imposition of Western values upon Russia that they believe will undermine and destroy it from within.[176]

9. The Russian extreme left and right believe the disintegration of the USSR was a great tragedy and a product of a Western conspiracy. In August 1991, the hard-line putsch was backed by Russian National-Bolsheviks in the KPRF and by Russian nationalist organisations and if it had been successful in crushing the non-Russian national movements, Russian nationalism would have become the official ideology of the Soviet state reconstituted as an empire.[177]

10. Strong authoritarian state structures are the ideal form of government for Russia. Greenfeld writes that Russian nationalism 'was ethnic, collectivist, and authoritarian.'[178]

## RUSSIAN DISSENT IN THE USSR

Unofficial, dissident Russian nationalism was never as organisationally strong as non-Russian nationalism in the three Baltic states, Ukraine, Georgia and Armenia. Non-Russian nationalists had a clear enemy which was Soviet and Russian rule while Russian nationalists never called for the separation of the Russian SFSR from the USSR and the majority of them never viewed the Soviet state as their enemy. China, Jews, and the West were the 'Other' most referred to by unofficial and official Russian nationalists. The gulf between nationalist and democratic dissidents was greater in Russia than in the non-Russian republics where national democracy bridged both groups. But, unofficial Russian nationalism was far weaker than its non-Russian counterpart because it possessed major avenues for its expression within the Soviet system and what was permissible for Russians to say in public was not the case for Ukrainians and other non-Russian peoples. A major gulf between Russian and non-Russian nationalists, particularly Ukrainians, were their attitudes to Stalin and this clash of history has continued to the present day. Although Stalin also murdered Russians this was and is overlooked by Russian nationalists, including by Putin. Meanwhile, for Ukrainian nationalists and patriots in Soviet and independent Ukraine, Stalin's massive crimes against humanity and organisation of the *holodomor* are defining moments in Ukrainian national identity.

In 1964 one of only a few Russian nationalist organisations, the All-Russian Social Christian Union, was launched by Igor Ogurtsov who was detained and sentenced in 1967. The weakness of unofficial nationalism in organisational form was evident in the USSR having to wait until 1977 for the creation of a second group, the Christian Committee for the Defence of the Rights of Religious Believers which was led by Gleb Yakunin. In 1970 the nationalistic *samizdat* manifesto *Slovo Natsii (A Nation Speaks)* appeared which Luydmilla Alexeyeva writes preached 'racism, state despotism, and imperialism.'[179] Unofficial Russian nationalists published the *samizdat* publications *Viche*, *Zemlya*, *Moscow Collection* and *From Under the Rubble* which provided platforms for a broad range of views ranging from Russian liberal nationalists, Christian nationalists and National-Bolsheviks. After the expulsion of Alexander Solzhenitsyn from the USSR in 1974 and the growth of émigré Russian nationalist publications, unofficial Russian nationalists and democratic dissidents parted ways.[180]

# RUSSIAN NATIONALISM IN COMPARATIVE PERSPECTIVE

Two issues are different today for Russian nationalists compared to their counterparts in the USSR. The first is Islam which was not an issue for Russian nationalists in the USSR whereas today Islamic terrorism is portrayed as an existentialist threat to Russia. Secondly, the issue of China and the prospect of war with a hugely populated country pre-occupied the Soviet authorities and Russian official and unofficial nationalists after seven months of undeclared military clashes in 1969 on the Sino-Soviet border. Today, China is courted by Russia as an ally in the creation of a 'multi-polar' world to counter American hegemony. Aside from Islam and China, Soviet Russian official and unofficial nationalists have ten areas in common with contemporary Russian nationalists:

1.  Support for a unified and indivisible Russia.
2.  Centrality of Russian Orthodoxy as the state Church. In the USSR, unofficial Russian nationalists propagated the replacement of the Communist Party by the Orthodox Church.
3.  They ignored, and continue to ignore, the nationality question and the national rights of the non-Russians in the USSR and in the post-Soviet republics. *Kadet* supporters of the Russian provisional government, Vlasov's ROA, the NTS and the All-Russian Social Christian Union devoted barely a few lines in their programmes to the nationality question.
4.  Anti-Semitism has always been present in Russian nationalism and Soviet National Bolshevism. Anti-Zionism, under which the 'crudest forms of government anti-Semitism' was promoted, became official policy during heightened periods of Stalinism (1947-1953) and re-Stalinisation under Soviet leader Brezhnev. In 1953-1964, during a period of de-Stalinisation and liberalisation, anti-Zionism played a marginal role in Soviet propaganda. In the late Stalin era, Judeophobia was so high there were fears of a second holocaust and Stalin's death prevented his planned mass exile of Jews to the Jewish autonomous *oblast* of Birobidzhan and the Siberian Gulag. The image of Jews as accomplices of the Nazis, anti-Communists, Freemasons, and Western imperialists 'could have been taken straight from the Protocols of the Elders of Zion…'[181]
5.  Propagation and extolling of Russian messianism and exceptionalism.
6.  Support for a fusion of communism, Leninism and Stalinism with Orthodox and monarchist Russian nationalism.

7. Glorification of Stalin, great patriotic war, great power imperialism and expansion of Soviet and Russian influence in the world. Syria is modern day Russia's equivalent of the Soviet Union's Cuba, Angola, Somalia, Vietnam and elsewhere.

8. Deeply-felt anti-Westernism, fear of dependence upon the West and a rejection of Western 'decadent values.' The West is a source of secularism while Russia is a font of spirituality. Such views were as common in the writings of Solzhenitsyn as they were in other Soviet Russian and post-Soviet Russian nationalist publications. They have led to an alliance with the anti-EU extreme right.

9. Strong anti-democratic tendencies and belief in authoritarianism as the political system for Russia. In Solzhenitsyn's 1973 open letter to Soviet leaders he posed the question whether Russia 'is nevertheless destined to have an authoritarian order?' The ensuing Russian nationalist debate was unanimous in replying in the affirmative, as is the case under Putin today.

10. Intellectuals are unpatriotic agents of Western influence and were described as *obrazovanshchina* by Solzhenitsyn.

## GATHERING OF 'RUSSIAN' LANDS AND NOSTALGIA FOR WHITES

As is often the case in Russian nationalist politics, politicians in Russia have sought to overcome their differences with émigrés. In 1919-1921, former Tsarist and White officers rallied to the Bolsheviks in their war against Ukraine and Poland. As early as 1920, White Russian émigré Prince Wolkonsky was writing with optimism about the 'Russian character' of Soviet power and the growth of Russian nationalism and he predicted that the words 'Bolshevism' and 'Russia' would soon become interchangeable. He added, 'There can be no doubt that victory will remain with the Russian language.'[182]

In the inter-war era, émigré nationalists, Eurasianists, fascists and neo-Nazis, looked approvingly at National Bolshevism under Stalin who they viewed with pride in the same manner as Putin today because they were building a 'Russian' great power. Stalin to them was the 'ultimate fascist' in 'resurrecting Russian national power through internal regimentation and external expansion.'[183] The growth of National-Bolshevism under Stalin increased the attraction of the USSR to hitherto anti-communist Russian émigrés who were willing, like Putin, to ignore his mass crimes against humanity by glorifying his advance of the Russian great power. Laquer writes, 'Even an extreme Russian nationalist could not have found fault with Soviet communism in 1950 as far as its patriotic fervour was concerned.'[184]

The growth of official and unofficial Russian nationalism in the Brezhnev era inevitably brought to the surface sympathy for the Whites, as it has under Putin. Nostalgia and a longing to bridge the gulf with émigré nationalists could only be possible for Russians in the Soviet Union; Ukrainian émigré nationalists would continue to be attacked as 'bourgeois nationalists' and 'Nazi collaborators' until 1990 on the eve of the disintegration of the USSR.

In 1982, nostalgia for the Whites first appeared in Soviet cinema productions at a time when 'White officers are increasingly becoming models of honour and nobility for us' while Bolshevik heroes 'are figures of fun, the subject of obscene jokes.'[185] Putin's nostalgia for the White movement is therefore part of a long tradition in Russian history. The Russian nationalist quest for unity has been promoted by Putin through the re-unification of the émigré and Russian Orthodox Churches, the open letter by 100 émigré Russian aristocrats in support of Putin and the reburial of White Russian leaders and writers in Russia.[186] *Komsomolskaya Pravda* published an article entitled 'White Russian Émigrés Support Mother Russia Again.'[187]

In 2005-2007, Putin began to reach out to White Russian émigrés and in one of the first gestures General Anton Deniken's remains were brought to Russia for reburial. In May 2015, the two and half hour propaganda film 'President' was released to celebrate his 15 years in power which surveyed the victories Putin had won for Russia. These included the 'reunification' of the Crimea with Russia and the exhumation and reburial of Denikin and white émigré and fascist sympathiser Ivan Ilyin. The film showed Putin laying flowers at their new Moscow graves.[188] Putin ensured that Ilyin's remains were repatriated from Switzerland and his archive was returned from Michigan. In addition to Putin, Medvedev, Vladislav Surkov, the head of Russia's Constitutional Court and the Russian Orthodox Patriarch are all admirers of Ilyin. Surkov cited Ilyin in his ideological platform of 'sovereign democracy' while Putin has cited Ilyin in support of his authoritarian centralised state. Communist Party leader Gennadiy Zyuganov praised the neo-fascist writer Ilyin for his 'development of the Russian state ideology of patriotism.'

Russian nationalist thought has become influential and popular in contemporary Russia through the writings of Ilyin who was an admirer of Eurasianism and fascist regimes in inter-war Europe.[189] For Ilyin, the Nazis, fascists and émigré Whites were 'spiritually close' and Ilyin never rejected fascist ideology even after its defeat in World War II. In the 1940s and 1950s, Ilyin provided the outlines for a constitution of a fascist Holy Russia governed by a 'national dictator' who would be 'inspired by the spirit of totality' in a highly centralised state.

Ilyin believed the West was seeking to destroy Russia and that one part of this strategy was to separate Ukraine, views that Putin continues to uphold. Ilyin *and* Putin believe the goal of the West's promotion of democracy and triumph of freedom are to make Russia a weak power and both Ilyin and Putin harbour an 'uncompromising hatred for the West.' 'The reasons that Ilyin gives as explanation for the West's supposed hatred of Russia are voiced daily on Russian television: the West does not know or understand Russia, and it fears it.'[190]

Contemporary Russian nationalist nostalgia for the White Guards can lead to support for neo-Nazi views, as in the case of nationalist volunteer Anton Rayevsky who fought in Girkin's unit. Describing himself as a 'Russian Orthodox monarchist' Rayevsky nevertheless has a tattoo of Hitler on his arm and upholds anti-Semitic views.[191] Girkin, a GRU officer since 1996, is a poster boy for nostalgia for the White Guard reflecting its influence within the Russian intelligence services and armed forces. Girkin participated in military re-enactments organised by the 'Tsarist Wolves' when he wore the uniform of a White Guard officer. He implemented his fantasies during military operations in Bosnia-Herzegovina, Trans-Dniestr, Chechnya, Crimea and the Donbas. Girkin believes that Russia should be an Orthodox empire headed by a totalitarian leader, a Czar or Stalin. Girkin, a self-confessed Russian Orthodox nationalist, monarchist and imperialist, believes that 'Ukraine is and remains a part of Russia' and that 'Kiev' is a Russian city.[192] The *Russkiy Mir*, Girkin believes, should include the three eastern Slavic peoples, Georgia and Armenia. Similar to all Russian nationalists, he does not recognise the borders of the Russian Federation and believes Russia's 'natural borders' are those it possessed in 1939 which excludes the three Baltic states and western Ukraine.

## RUSSIAN ORTHODOXY

Robert Conquest in one of his seminal works wrote 'Communism is a sort of religion' and nowhere is this more the case than in Russia where the Orthodox Church is recognised as a state Church. Ukrainian presidents have sought to balance between competing Orthodox confessions; the exception was Yanukovych who, following his Russian mentor, favoured the Russian Orthodox Church that became a 'state quasi religion.'[193] In summer 2013, Yanukovych and Putin, two unlikely religious believers celebrated the 1025th anniversary of the introduction of Christianity to Kyiv Rus. During his presidency Yanukovych never met other religious confessions and threatened to ban the Greek Catholic Church during the Euromaidan.

The Russian Orthodox Church split in the 1920s and a wing inside the USSR agreed to collaborate with the Communist regime in return for being permitted to flourish. The Russian Orthodox Church expanded its size at the expense of the Ukrainian and Belarusian Autocephalous Orthodox and Catholic Churches and participated in the destruction in 1946 of the Ukrainian Greek Catholic Church. The Russian Orthodox Church, as a state Church in the Soviet Union, was heavily infiltrated by the KGB.

In the Russian emigration, the Russian Orthodox Church supported extreme variants of Russian nationalism and chauvinism and cooperated with neo-Nazi political forces such as NTS. In post-Soviet Russia, the Russian Orthodox Church has again allied itself with Russian nationalist and xenophobic political forces and has been co-opted by Putin. Ivan Okhlobystin and member of the Russian Orthodox Church Supreme Council Archimandrite Tikhon are just some of the Russian Orthodox clergy who are cooperating with nationalist and fascist political forces.

In a similar manner to Putin's embrace of Tsars and Commissars, political Orthodoxy successfully united supporters of the Reds and Whites in their evocation of the 'historical destiny' of Russia as an empire. The unity of (Bolshevik) Reds, (Monarchist Orthodox) Whites and (fascist) Browns was evident in the ideological supporters of *NovoRossiya*. The red-white-brown coalition includes *Den* and *Zavtra* newspaper editor and extreme nationalist Aleksandr Prokhanov, author of the July 1991 'Word to the People' which became the manifesto for the State Emergency Committee a month later, Communist Party patriot Sergey Kurginyan and Eurasianist Dugin.[194]

Oligarch Konstantin Malofeyev is close to Dugin and the Russian Orthodox Church and provides philanthropy to nationalist causes in Russia and in the Crimea and Donbas. Malofeyev has supported the formation of a European, anti-EU nationalist and fascist international and welcomed the rise of anti-immigrant sentiment and xenophobia in Germany and the Dutch vote against the EU-Ukraine Association Agreement.[195] The influence of these three wings of Russian and Soviet nationalism and chauvinism accelerated from 2007, when Putin first publicly broadcast his nationalism and xenophobia. Their influence culminated in the officially funded Izborsk Club, opened in September 2012 just after Putin's re-election where Reds and Whites could meet, network and discuss policies. The Club provided input to Russia's Foreign Policy Concept that became official policy on the eve of the Ukraine-Russia crisis,[196] assisted in the drafting of the DNR constitution[197] and represents the core group 'behind the Kremlin's drive towards fascism, war and Eurasian empire.'[198]

The ideological principles of the Russian Orthodox Church are the same as those long supported by Russian nationalists, chauvinists and imperialists. Political Orthodoxy draws its inspiration from the Black Hundreds,[199] Soviet anti-Zionism and modern-day equivalents in Russia. The Russian Orthodox Church has backed the canonisation of empire builders, equated the *Russkiy* people with the three eastern Slavic peoples, does not recognise Ukrainians as a separate people, believes the entire former USSR is its 'canonical' territory (not just the Russian Federation) and glorifies tyrannical Russian leaders Ivan the Terrible, Stalin and others.[200] Russian Orthodox Church believers have laid flowers at monuments to Stalin.[201] The messianism of the Russian Orthodox Church backs the hunt for foreign agents and virulently opposes the presence of competing religious confessions on what it considers its 'canonical' territory.[202] Other confessions have been stamped out and repressed in the separatist DNR and LNR enclaves and in western Donetsk when it was briefly occupied by Russian forces in spring 2014.

Putin has used his poor grasp of history to claim title to Kyiv Rus, even though Moscow did not exist until the 12th century, by claiming he had been baptised in the Crimea and 'the Crimea and Sevastopol have invaluable civilisational and even sacred importance for Russia.'[203] The Russian Orthodox Church agrees with Putin that Ukraine is an artificial Bolshevik construct and believes that violence is justified when it is in defence of 'Holy Rus' which is a 'single spiritual community' composed of Russians, Ukrainians and Belarusians who are 'united in faith, history and culture.' The Russian Orthodox Church, an advocate of the unity of the eastern Slavs of 'Holy Rus,' viewed Russia's intervention in eastern Ukraine as justified because this is 'the historical southern borders of Rus.'[204] The Moscow Patriarchate is the 'mother Church' of all Orthodox Churches in the former USSR, a policy that closely resembles Soviet elucidations of Russians as the elder brother, and claims that Kyiv is our 'common Jerusalem.' These Russian Orthodox Church chauvinistic views are not deemed to be 'nationalistic' because that derogatory term is only applied to Ukrainian Orthodox Churches that seek autocephaly from Moscow.

The Russian Orthodox Church and Russian nationalists 'live in nostalgia for the days of old, the original unity of the "*Russkiy* nation."' Participants in Russia's Unity day in November 2015 held banners reading 'Russia, Ukraine and Belarus – together we are Holy Rus!' and 'Lets bring back the borders of the (Soviet) union!'[205] Russian Orthodox Church support for Putin's policies in the Crimea and Donbas are popular among Ukrainian (Russian) Orthodox Church believers in those two regions, but the Church is losing ground to the Ukrainian Orthodox Church-Kyiv Patriarch and Protestant confessions. The majority of Ukrainian (Russian) Orthodox Church parishes lie in 'orange' western and central Ukraine. The Ukrainian (Russian) Orthodox Church has only 2-3, 00 more parishes than its Ukrainian rivals and public opinion has long shown that more Ukrainians are supportive of them than the Russian Orthodox Church. If Ukraine's Orthodox Churches were to unite into an autocephalous Church, it would be the second largest in the world after Romania which would be a devastating blow to the Russian Orthodox Church because Ukraine is the heart of the Church, its people are more religiously devout than in Russia and it would lose half of its parishes.[206] The Ukrainian parliament sent an appeal to the synod of Orthodox Churches in June 2016 requesting that it consider the question of Ukrainian autocephaly.

The Russian Orthodox Church has a long tradition of ultra-conservatism and anti-modernism, distrust of Western democracy and human rights, opposition to globalisation, and anti-Semitism. Alexander Verkhovsky describes the Russian Orthodox Church's xenophobia towards the worldwide Jewish-Masonic conspiracy, anti-Semitism and rants against Western liberalism and globalisation as 'Russian Orthodox Church fundamentalism.'[207] Orthodox fundamentalist jihadist volunteers travelling to the Donbas to fight alongside the separatists have often been previously blessed in Russia or after they arrive by the Russian Orthodox Church.[208]

Laruelle writes that 'Positive memories of Russia's Tsarist past are thus experiencing an unprecedented boost from the *NovoRossiya* mythmaking process.'[209] The Russian Orthodox Army, Imperial Legion, Cossack companies and White Guard nationalists such as Girkin all have close relations with the

Russian Orthodox Church. The intellectual background to the rise of an influential Orthodox-Monarchist nationalism emerged in 2012-2013 through the Russian Institute of Strategic Research which until 2009 had been controlled by the SVR, Russia's external intelligence service. Funded by Russian Orthodox zealot and oligarch Malofeyev the think tank prepared the strategy document that was leaked to *Novaya Gazeta*.[210] Their influence can be found in television, the Russian parliament, presidential administration, armed forces and intelligence services. The Director of the Russian Institute of Strategic Research, Leonid Reshetnikov, and head of its 'Ukraine' department Tamara Guzenkova, are Orthodox-monarchist nationalists and Ukrainophobes and as is common with Orthodox nationalists they are also anti-Semites and homophobes.[211] Interestingly, Girkin worked as a security guard for Malofeyev who was also close to Sergey Aksyonov.[212]  For this nationalistic constituency 'there is no Ukraine, only Little Russia,' Ukraine is an artificial entity and a failed state or in the words of Prime Minister Medvedev 'Why should we compare ourselves with Ukraine? I mean they have neither industry nor a state.'[213] The Ukrainian language 'was artificially created by the Austrians and Poles to break up Russian unity.' Ukrainians are a *'kvazinarod' (quasi people)*. The Russian Institute of Strategic Research recommended many of the same policies as Dugin's Eurasianists, such as covertly funding pro-Russian groups in the CIS and infiltrating official state structures.

The analysis of Ukraine by Russian nationalists, intelligence services and nationalistic think tanks portrays a country, Russophones and 'Little Russians' who are eager to be under the paternalistic embrace of Mother Russia, a view that only exists in their own imagination which they gleaned from Russian and Soviet history books and their own publications. The Russian Institute of Strategic Research – like the FSB – wrongly believes Ukrainians and Russians are one people, downplayed Ukrainian resistance to Russian hybrid war, exaggerated pro-Putin and anti-Ukrainian sentiment in eastern and southern Ukraine and cynically believed that Europeans could be bought off with cheap energy.

Putin and the *siloviki* completely misread Ukraine because the advice they received claimed that pro-Western sentiment was marginal and 'provoked by a handful of pro-fascist immigrants from west Ukraine.' The same wrong analyses were provided by Russian political technologists about Ukraine in the 2004 elections but seemingly nobody learnt from their mistakes.

## VLADIMIR PUTIN AND RUSSIAN NATIONALISM

There is inordinate evidence of the influence of Russian nationalism on President Putin. Russia would, Putin and other Russian leaders assert, undertake a unique path of development because it is a Eurasian civilisation that is neither European nor Asian and is superior to the West. The idealisation of the West in the late 1980s and 1990s evolved into envy and hatred of a West that Putin promised to protect Russia from because it is seeking to impose its alien values upon them.[214]

Since the early 2000's there has been a takeover of the Russian state by the *siloviki* who are nostalgic for the USSR and Soviet power and yearning for respect in the world; they are termed by Kryshtanovskaya and White[215] as a 'militocracy.' 'The only people that Putin is listening to are the military and the intelligence,' Polish Foreign Minister Radek Sikorski said.[216] The *siloviki*, long admirers of Dugin, supported the growing influence of nationalism within the Russian political leadership.

Putin's counter-mobilisation during and since the 2012 elections has integrated 'conservative and nationalist intellectuals' such as Kurginyan and Dugin and united 'moderate patriots' and 'radical nationalists' on the basis of 'conservative values.' These ideological proponents of Russian messianism and anti-Western xenophobia were increasingly courted after Putin was re-elected through the Izborsk Club.[217] Russia's foreign policy 'fuelled the views of the imperialist character of contemporary Russia'[218] and empire-building and imperial rhetoric legitimised and entered the mainstream of Slavophile and Eurasianist ideologies.[219]

Putin came to power at the same time as NATO's bombardment of Yugoslavia, the detachment of Kosovo from Serbia into a future independent state,[220] and the bulldozer revolution in Serbia that was the first of what became called coloured or democratic revolutions. Kosovo had never been a Yugoslav republic and therefore unlike the 15 Soviet and six Yugoslav republics it had no right under international law to become an independent state. Russian leaders and the Party of Regions in 2008 raised the Kosovo precedent as justification for their recognition of the independence of South Ossetia and Abkhazia and the annexation of the Crimea.

Russian and Ukrainian leaders were socialised within a conspiracy mind set and they therefore viewed these developments as one chain of events. This worldview deepened with the Rose and Orange Revolutions in 2003 and 2004 leading to calls in their legislatures (which were successful in Russia, but unsuccessful in Ukraine) to clamp down on alleged Western intelligence support for NGOs, mass popular protests and regime change. In 2005, the pro-regime *Nashi* anti-colour revolution and 'anti-fascist' movement was officially launched in Russia. The United Russia party signed a cooperation agreement with the Party of Regions whose leader, Yanukovych, believed he had been prevented from becoming president by a Western-orchestrated Orange Revolution. Russian and eastern Ukrainian leaders saw little difference between NATO's intervention in Serbia and the US invasion of Iraq as both did not have UN authorisation.

The return to Soviet conspiracy mind sets was accompanied by a return to anti-Americanism first witnessed during Ukraine's 2004 presidential elections. Yanukovych's election campaign, led by Russian political technologists (such as Gleb Pavlovsky) on loan from Putin organised a 'directed chaos' strategy that portrayed Yushchenko, who has a Ukrainian-American spouse, as a US satrap and extreme nationalist. It was relatively easy to blame the Orange Revolution as a Western backed putsch following such a negative campaign. Ironically, Yanukovych's anti-Americanism took place while Ukrainians constituted the third largest military contingent in the US-led coalition in Iraq (and largest non-NATO force).

Needless to say, the Euromaidan in November 2013-February 2014 was also seen as a Western backed putsch that overthrew a democratically elected President and brought 'fascists' to power. Yanukovych and Putin could not comprehend the notion of individuals protesting as volunteers or unpaid civil society activists because their experience is of a world where people attend rallies when they are induced by the threat of losing their employment or they receive payment in cash or kind. Yanukovych drew on 'political tourists' (i.e. paid rally participants) in the 2004 elections and when he was Prime Minister and President (2006-2007, 2010-2014).

## *RUSSKIY MIR, NOVOROSSIYA* AND RUSSIAN FOREIGN POLICY

Not coincidentally, in 2007, the same year Putin gave his aggressive speech in Munich, the *Russkiy Mir* organisation was launched to unite and support ethnic Russians and Russian speakers living outside Russia.[221] Although this policy was pursued more vigorously under Putin, all Russian leaders since the disintegration of the USSR have, as Foreign Minister Andrei Kozyrev told the UN in September 1993, a 'special responsibility' to protect them. Kozyrev pre-empted

President Medvedev's description of Russia's right to a 'sphere of privileged interests' in Eurasia by 15 years when he called upon the UN to grant Russia a primacy in future peacekeeping on the territory of the former USSR.[222]

Stephen Blank points out: 'Moreover, Moscow subsidises and otherwise supports a large number of organisations and movements inside all of its neighbours, from Kazakhstan to the Baltic, to ensure that the pot is kept boiling over the issue of the purported discrimination against these minority Russian communities and the Russian diaspora. Although these tactics emerged most violently in Ukraine, their origin goes back at least to Peter the Great, who legitimised his military campaigns against the Ottomans by claiming Russia was protecting the Orthodox subjects of the Ottoman Empire from discrimination. Such methods have continued to the present day.'[223]

Foreign Minister Lavrov promised that 'Rendering comprehensive support to the *Russkiy Mir* is an unconditional foreign policy priority for Russia…we will keep enthusiastically defending the rights of compatriots, using for that the entire arsenal of available means envisioned by international law.'[224] As Catherine Wanner points out, Russia's definition of compatriots 'is very broad' and they are protected 'regardless of whether they want it or need it and irrespective of the fact that they live in another sovereign state.'[225]

Blank believes 'such speeches and articles indicate the utter politicisation in Russia of the ethnic card and diaspora for use as a state-breaking instrument abroad and a state-making one at home.'[226] Furthermore, 'The idea of the "Russian people" is today a fully politicised and state-propagated concept, usable for the purpose of destroying or building consolidated states in the former Soviet imperial space.'[227] President Putin told NATO in 2008 that eastern and southern Ukraine was populated by 'Russians' which justified his revival of the Tsarist designation for the region as 'New Russia' in spring 2014. Hutchings and Tolz criticise the term compatriots: 'There can be no more graphic illustration of the consequences of the confused ethnicization of national identity that our book has traced.'[228] The arbitrary conflation of ethnic Russians with Russian speakers was disproven by the high level of Ukrainian patriotism of its Russian speakers and was as unscientific as France claiming that all the world's French speaking 'compatriots' were ethnic French.

Six years prior to the Ukraine-Russia crisis, Putin told US President Bush at the 2008 NATO summit (see later) that Ukraine was not a real country, a view of Ukraine as an 'artificial' and 'failed' state that continues to be extensively promoted in the Russian media.[229] Putin was not striking out alone but merely echoing views that have long been commonly believed in Russia about Ukraine and especially among Russian nationalists. They, like Putin in Bucharest, talk of Ukraine within its borders as an artificial construct created by the Soviet regime, that Ukraine was never a 'historical state' within its current boundaries, it is composed of two different parts (a view central to Sakwa's framework) and because of these factors, was unsuccessful in forging a united nation after 1991. Ukraine's disintegration and fragmentation was therefore only a matter of time because of internal contradictions and threats to Russophones from Ukrainian 'nationalists' and 'fascists.' Such views did not just suddenly appear in 2014, or after 2012 when Putin supposedly discovered Russian nationalism, but were routinely expressed by the Russian media and Russian political technologists during and since the 2004 Ukrainian elections. [230]

Although Putin's territorial claims were alarming in the light of future Russian policies towards Ukraine they reflected a consensus in Russian nationalistic thinking about Ukraine as an artificial construct and more importantly, that eastern and southern Ukraine and Crimea should be 'returned' to Russia. Russian émigrés of all ideological persuasions, Russian Patriots in the Soviet Union, well-known Russian dissident Solzhenitsyn and Putin agreed on the need to dismember Ukraine with the east and south becoming part of Russia, the remaining rump remaining a quasi independent dominion under Russian control and western Ukraine allowed to go its own way or be annexed by Poland. Solzhenitsyn and Putin both believe Ukrainians and Russians are one people who have been artificially divided by the Mongols and Poles. 'The Ukrainians are very close to us. I see no differences at all between Ukrainians and Russian, and I consider on the whole that we are one people (*odin narod*),' Putin said. [231] To Russian nationalists, Ukraine and Russia should be compared to the relationship between Prussia and Bavaria. Russian National Security Council Secretary Nikolay Petrushev says 'One nation inhabits Ukraine and the Russian Federation which is for the time being divided (by the Russian-Ukrainian border).' [232] Putin's Chief of Staff Sergey Ivanov, talking of Ukrainians said, 'We are one people. Mentally, religiously, and culturally, between us there is infinitely a lot in common, including language. That we are a single Slavic people cannot be disputed.' [233]

Solzhenitsyn and Putin condemned the 'artificial' borders drawn up by Soviet leader Lenin and such views are widespread. In 1991, Yeltsin threatened to change the borders of all Soviet republics except the three Baltic states while Anatoly Sobchak, in whose office Putin worked in St. Petersburg, warned that

Ukrainian independence would lead to border conflict and assimilation of Russian speakers.[234] Throughout the 1990s, both houses of the Russian parliament adopted resolutions demanding the 'return' of the Crimea and Sevastopol.

Russian views of territories in Ukraine's east and south that had been wrongly included in that country were voiced by Russian nationalists long before the USSR disintegrated. In 1970 the nationalistic *samizdat* manifesto *Slovo Natsii* by Russian Patriots called it an historical injustice that 'the current frontiers of Ukraine did not correspond to its ethnography.'[235] 'Russian patriots' condemned the inclusion of 'seven million Russians as well as many Russified Ukrainians' living in Ukraine. Half a century later Putin condemned in similar terms the fact that 'seventeen million Russians' lived in eastern-southern Ukraine.

Solzhenitsyn had outlined his nationalist credentials only four years after that of the 'Russian patriots' in his Letter to Soviet Leaders. Solzhenitsyn writing in 1990 on the eve of the disintegration of the USSR, believed if Ukraine is to be an independent state it could only exist without regions that 'weren't part of old Ukraine...*NovoRossiya* or Crimea or Donbas and areas practically to the Caspian Sea' which should be allowed 'self-determination.'[236] On the eve of the December 1991 referendum on independence, Solzhenitsyn called for the addition of a question for each *oblast* as to whether it should remain inside Ukraine. Solzhenitsyn's nationalism was used by the Putin regime as part of its 'technology of preventive counterrevolution.'[237] Solzhenitsyn expressed his admiration for Putin's reassertion of Russian national pride. Putin reciprocated and signed a decree conferring on Solzhenitsyn the State Prize for his humanitarian work and personally visited the writer at his home in June 2007 to present him with the award.[238] Solzhenitsyn had, similar to other Russian nationalists, shown his preference for nationalism over democracy and had 'institutionalized an authoritarian regime.'[239]

At the 2008 NATO summit Putin outlined a historical right to Ukraine's eastern and southern regions which he wrongly claimed was solely inhabited by 'Russians.' Putin's discourse signalled his intention of future intervention in eastern Ukraine in support of *NovoRossiya*.[240] Putin ominously warned of his intentions six years ahead of his military intervention in Ukraine:[241]

'But in Ukraine, one third is ethnic Russians. Out of forty-five million people, in line with the official census, seventeen million are Russians. There are regions where only the Russian population lives, for instance, in the Crimea

90 percent are Russians. Generally speaking, Ukraine is a very complicated state. Ukraine, in the form it currently exists, was created in Soviet times, it received its territories from Poland – after the Second World war, from Czechoslovakia, from Romania – and at present not all of the problems have been yet resolved in the border region with Romania in the Black Sea. Then, it received huge territories from Russia in the east and south of the country. It is a complicated state formation. If we introduce NATO problems into it, other problems may put the state on the verge of its existence. …Well, seventeen million Russians currently live in Ukraine. Who may state that we do not have any interests there? In the south of Ukraine, there are only Russians living there.'

## RUSSIAN AND SOVIET NATIONALISM IN UKRAINE

Russian nationalist groups were always weak in Ukraine with the exception of the Crimea and to a far smaller extent in Odesa. In Donetsk in the 1990s Russian nationalism was to be found within Pan-Slavic organisations such as Civic Congress and the Party of Slavic Unity but it was only after the Orange Revolution that more overtly Russian nationalist organisations emerged such as the Donetsk Republic. Pan-Slavic and Russian nationalist organisations in Ukraine held similar outlooks and chauvinistic views of Ukrainians as those of nationalists in Russia. [242] In Ukraine they were divided by generation with older generation Pan-Slavists such as Oleksandr Bazylyuk integrated into the Party of Regions while the Donetsk Republic attracted the more aggressive and more overtly pro-Putin younger generation.

In the late 1990s, Anatoly Lieven[243] wrote of the 'weaknesses of Russian nationalism in Ukraine' where there had not been the kind of ethnic mobilisation that had taken place among Serbian minorities in Yugoslavia. Lieven was writing at a time when Crimean Russian nationalists had become marginalised through internal quarrels, a tough Ukrainian response from eastern Ukrainian President Kuchma and weak external Russian support. These three factors changed following the election of Putin and his pursuit of a Russian nationalist agenda, the monopolisation of power in eastern and southern Ukraine by the more overtly Russophile and Sovietophile Party of Regions and its alliance with Crimean Russian nationalists.

Pan-Slavists in Ukraine had never reconciled themselves to living in a state ruled by the ideology of 'western Ukrainian nationalism.' Two decades before the Ukraine-Russia crisis, Civic Congress leader and Deputy Mayor of

Donetsk Yuriy Boldyrev said that the outcome of the 1994 elections were a positive development because 'We lived for years on the basis of western Ukraine's ideology. Now it is time to implement the wishes of citizens of eastern Ukraine.'[244] Such views were revived by the Party of Regions during Yushchenko's presidency.

Russian nationalism in independent Ukraine has appeared in three different forms with only the first and second recognising Ukraine as an independent state:

*Liberal Democrats*: Constitutional Democratic Party (based on the tradition of the Russian *Kadets*), Inter-Regional Bloc of Reforms (MRB), the Social-Liberal Alliance (SLON) and *Viche* were liberal parties that targeted the urban Russian speaking population and middle class. They were electorally unsuccessful even in eastern Ukraine. In the 1998 elections, SLON received only 0.51 percent in Donetsk *oblast* which was slightly higher than the 0.39 it received in Ivano-Frankivsk.[245] These liberal Russophone parties were created as election projects and after losing the elections they disappeared from the political arena.

*Leftist Populists*: the KPU and the Party of Regions were successful in monopolising Russophone Ukraine in the 1990s in the former case and 2000s in the latter. In the 1990s, a Ukrainian scholar wrote that the 'main movement of the Russian great power idea in Ukraine is still the Communist Party.'[246] Both parties disintegrated after Yanukovych fled from office in spring 2014. Although these two parties recognised the Ukrainian state their bases of support in the Donbas and Crimea infused an anti-Ukrainian element into their political programmes and the national identities they propagated. Anti-Ukrainian sentiments had deep roots in a region where Stephen Crowley found that 'many in the Donbas claimed to be anti-nationalist, employing Soviet-era rhetoric against nationalism, with more than a few equating nationalism with fascism.'[247] Some members of the Party of Regions would routinely show their contempt for the Ukrainian language and Ukrainian history and many would use Soviet style denunciations of 'fascists' when referring to the political opposition.[248] Such chauvinistic views had deep roots in the Donbas where in the 1920s, the policy of Ukrainianisation (indigenisation) was already associated with 'nationalism.'[249]

*Russian Nationalists, Chauvinists and Imperialists*: in the 1990s, Pan-Slavic groups such as Civic Congress (renamed in 1998 the Party of Slavic Unity), Internationalist Movement of the Donbas, Movement for the Revival of the Donbas, Congress of Russian Organisations of Ukraine, Russian Movement of

Ukraine, Russia-Ukraine Union and Union of Soviet Officers were on the margins of political life where they cooperated with the KPU and the Progressive Socialist Party. The description of the Civic Congress as 'Russophile' was a misnomer as it rejected the very idea of a Ukrainian nation and therefore was best described as chauvinistic and extremist.[250] Ukraine, the Civic Congress claimed, was ruled by a 'nationalistic regime' that infringed upon the rights of two thirds of the Ukrainian population who are Russian speakers.[251] Such views, at one time on the margins of Ukrainian political life, became mainstream in Yanukovych's Ukraine and Putin's Russia. The ideologies of Russian nationalist groups are similar to those of Russian nationalists in Ukraine who 'attempt to maintain the hegemonic status of the minority in the linguistic-cultural sphere.' Bazylyuk believed the very existence of Ukraine was wrong because it was a 'nationalist' project that would become a 'Western satellite or colony.'[252] From 2000, the leaders of Russian nationalist and Pan-Slavic groups in Ukraine were integrated into the Party of Regions.

Openly Russian nationalist organisations such as Donetsk Republic emerged after the Orange Revolution and at the local level in the Donbas they cooperated with the Party of Regions, KPU and the Progressive Socialist party. The Donetsk Republic had the support of high ranking patrons 'who condoned their anti-Ukrainian and separatist activities.'[253] 'Several newspapers and magazines (of the Donetsk Republic) appeared out of nowhere, but everyone knew they were funded by Moscow. At around the same time, new NGOs of unclear origin set up operations. These were run from Russia by the "International Eurasian Movement" headed by chief ideologist Dugin.'[254]

In the decade prior to the Euromaidan, pro-Russian extremist and nationalist groups underwent training in the Crimea and in Russia without any hindrance from the SBU or interference from the Party of Regions and KPU.[255] Presidents Yanukovych and Lukashenka *both* tolerated Russian neo-Nazi groups like the RNE while opposing the 'fascist' pro-Western opposition.

The Donetsk Republic's call for a referendum on the independence of the Donbas led the Ukrainian authorities to ban it after which it continued to operate underground with the local Party of Regions providing a *krysha*. As with the entire range of Russian nationalist groups, the Donetsk Republic rejected the very concept of a Ukrainian nation as an 'artificially created community' believing the *Russkiy* 'super ethnos' included the three eastern Slavic peoples. It denounced 'forced Ukrainianisation' and 'genocide' of the 'indigenous

Russian people.' As Aleksandr Zakharchenko's party of power these chauvinistic views have become the official ideology of the DNR.

DNR activist Ilya Goryachev founded the Nazi organisation *Russkiy Obraz* when he was living in Makiyivka in Donetsk *oblast*. Prior to the Euromaidan, *Russkiy Obraz* and its paramilitary arm *BORN (Militant Organisation of Russian Nationalists)* used the Donbas as a base to recruit, collect financing and train as well as to launch attacks inside Russia against targets the authorities wished to injure or murder.[256] BORN had a relationship to *Russkiy Obraz* that was similar to the relationship between the IRA and Sinn Fein. In reality, the relationship was probably more akin to that between British intelligence and Ulster protestant paramilitaries who received files on IRA suspects from the former with the purpose of them undertaking the 'wet actions' that the British government could not be seen to be undertaking. BORN were given files by *Russkiy Obraz*, which had close ties to 'Leonid Simulin' in the Russian presidential administration, on anti-fascists who were targeted with violence and assassinations. BORN are credited with six assassinations. From 2008, the Kremlin both oppresses recalcitrant nationalists and co-opts nationalist and fascist groups in what Surkov describes as 'managed nationalism.'[257] 'Ilya Goryachev and his *Russkiy Obraz* were long considered a virtual 'Kremlin project,' that had been launched as part of the 'managed nationalism' programme[258] that sought to co-opt fascists and skinheads who had supported the Party of Slavic Union and Movement Against Illegal Immigration which had been banned.[259] *BORN* therefore acted in a similar manner to Kadyrov's security forces as the Kremlin's assassins for hire. The 'virulent nationalist opposition movement' in effect 'took the mainstream hostage.'[260] *BORN* added to the eclectic mix of Russian nationalists, imperialists, neo-Nazis and fascists that came to fight Ukrainian 'fascists' and NATO in the Donbas: 'Collected now in the Donbas are all manner of murderers, marginal and pathological people who were used by the Kremlin in recent years and who could not find a legal place in Russia's political system.'[261]

In 2009, on the eve of elections which they feared would again deny Yanukovych the presidency, the Donetsk Republic and pro-Russian organisations from Ukraine declared a Donetsk Federal Republic drawn from representatives of southern and eastern Ukraine in an analogy similar to plans for the Ukrainian Front in Kharkiv seven years later. The proposed Federal Republic incorporated the Donbas, Dnipro, Zaporizhzhya, Kharkiv and Kherson *oblasts* which were included in Putin's short-lived *NovoRossiya* project.

Russian nationalist parties in the Crimea were always separatist. Active in the first half of the 1990s they became marginalised by a combination of President Kuchma's astute and tough policies and weak Russian external support. From 2006 until the annexation of the Crimea they were allied domestically with the Party of Regions when they were energetically supported by Russia with financing, military equipment and training. In spring 2014, extremist Crimean Russian nationalist groups moved into the political vacuum with assistance from the Russian military and intelligence services.

*Soviet Nationalists*: The KPU and Progressive Socialist party never accepted an independent Ukrainian state and the former backed the revival of the USSR while the latter supported the union of the three eastern Slavic peoples. The Progressive Socialist party was the closest in Ukraine to a Russian-style National Bolshevik political force and was a member of Dugin's International Eurasian Movement. During the separatist takeover of the Donbas in spring 2014, both parties backed the separatists and the Progressive Socialist party, according to research by the anti-fascist magazine *Searchlight*, cooperated closely with the Nazi RNE. The KPU, Progressive Socialist and other extreme left political forces cooperated with Donbas separatists.[262] Volodymyr Marchenko, a close associate of Progressive Socialist party leader Natalia Vitrenko, was under investigation for his cooperation with the separatist information service Anna-News in Abkhazia. Valentyn Landyk revealed that in Luhansk the separatists were financed by the leadership of the Party of Regions and KPU, including Luhansk Communist leader Spyrydon Kilinkarov who received cash in the Kyiv office of KPU leader Petro Symonenko.[263] Dmytro Nikonov, the self-proclaimed and short-lived 'people's governor' of Mykolayiv, and Aleksandr Kharitonov, commander of the separatist Luhansk Guard, were local leaders of the Progressive Socialist party.[264] Progressive Socialist leader Vitrenko and the Crimean Russia Bloc, who were allies of the Party of Regions from 2006, were trained in camps run by Dugin's International Eurasian Movement and the pro-Putin youth movement *Nashi*.

## RUSSIAN CHAUVINISM TOWARDS UKRAINE

Mykola Riabchuk[265] places contemporary ukrainophobia in a historical context that stretches back to the eighteenth century where a historically informed Russian hegemonic view was first elaborated of Ukrainians as 'younger brothers' who should be both patronised and kept in their place. Russian attitudes towards Ukrainians are embedded in deeply held ethnic stereotypes in folklore and ideologically constructed in cultural and political discourses where Russians are the dominant group and Ukrainians the subjugated people.

Putin follows in a long line of Russian nationalists stretching back to the 1917 revolution who believe the West (Austrian-Hungarians, Nazi Germans, US intelligence and democracy promoting foundations, and more recently the EU) are seeking to break apart two branches of the 'Russian people.' In such a view, Ukrainian 'separatism' has no domestic roots and is being artificially propped up by Western conspiracies. Tolz writes, 'The majority of Russians saw Ukrainian nationalism as a result of intrigues either by the Poles or the Austrians' and 'Even some liberals began to see Ukrainian separatism solely as a result of intrigues of foreign powers aimed at dismembering Russia.'[266]

President Putin's warning during the 2008 NATO summit that Ukraine could disintegrate was a long standing view held by Russian nationalists who viewed Ukraine as an artificial construct. 'Practically throughout all of the years of Ukrainian independence our north-eastern neighbour harboured a fantasy about its imminent disintegration if not today then most definitely tomorrow.'[267] Worse still, the Ukrainian analyst wrote, 'Such views were once only those of uneducated marginal forces. But, now such views have become trendy and yesterday's marginal forces have become respectable representatives of the Russian elites who are listened to by senior persons in the country.'[268]

Putin's derogatory views of Ukraine and his conviction that eastern and southern Ukraine were wrongly given to the Soviet Ukrainian republic were discussed throughout the decade prior to the crisis. In the same month of Putin's speech to NATO, Russian political technologist Pavlovsky's *Russkiy Zhurnal* published an article entitled 'Clockwork Orange' which laid out a replica scenario of what took place six years later in the Crimea.[269] Dmitry Trenin revealed that in 2011, when Yanukovych was Ukrainian president and the country's alleged 'fascists' were in retreat, there was discussion in Moscow 'of a major geopolitical redesign of the northern Black Sea area, under which southern Ukraine, from the Crimea to Odesa, would secede from Kyiv and form a Moscow-friendly buffer state.'[270]

As the world has come to belatedly realise since the Ukraine-Russia crisis, Putin and his political and government allies are serial liars who practise the art of *maskirovka (Russian military deception)*. In 2008, Putin was asked if Russia had designs on the Crimea to which he responded that it is 'not a disputed territory.' This was because there had been no ethnic conflict, unlike in South Ossetia, and because 'Russia has long recognised the borders of modern-day

Ukraine.' Putin ended with the words, I think questions about such goals for Russia have provocative undertones.'[271]

Putin's description of Ukraine to President Bush as an 'artificial state' was echoed in over 50 Russian novels and books with huge print runs (some written by future separatist leaders) which were published in the decade prior to the Ukraine-Russia crisis. Such views were found in numerous films attacking Ukrainian-Nazi collaboration, depictions of Ukraine as a failed state and predictions of a future conflict with NATO and the US over Ukraine that leads to a 'civil war.'[272] From 2006-2007, books began to be published in Russia predicting in great detail fictional future wars with Ukraine and the disintegration of the Ukrainian state.

Luhansk-based novelist Serhiy Chebanenko was one of the first to predict the development of the 2014 crisis. Deputy Defence Minister of the DNR Fedor Berezin authored 24 science fiction ('historical fantasy') novels on Russian nationalist military  themes and science fiction, including *War 2010: the Ukrainian Front* (2009) and *Ukrainian Hell* (2011, reprinted in 2014).[273] In 2008, the Russian publishing house Folio issued *Independent Ukraine. Collapse of a Project* where Maksym Kalashnikov argued that Ukraine will follow Yugoslavia by splitting into two parts with the western part of the country fighting the eastern regions.[274] Such views were mixed with dire future scenarios of Ukraine's inevitable default on its sovereign debt and becoming a bankrupt state. Yuriy Savitsky's *Battleground Ukraine. The Broken Tryzub* is a fantasy novel that outlines a future war between Russia and Ukraine on Ukrainian territory. NATO troops, US aviation and western Ukrainian 'nationalist mercenaries' launch a campaign to destroy the Russophone population in the country that provokes an uprising in eastern-southern Ukraine and the Crimea. Russia intervenes in support of Russophones and together they destroy the 'damned (Stepan) Banderite Tryzub!' Savitsky is confidant that Ukraine will become Russia's 'last and most decisive struggle.'[275]

Fedor Berezin's novel *War in 2010. The Ukrainian Front* also describes a future fictional war on Ukrainian territory and again it is remarkably similar to real events in the 2014-2015 Ukraine-Russia crisis. Berezin writes of an uprising by 'fascists,' conflict in the Crimea, civil war and Russian intervention which then spreads to the remainder of Ukraine and Europe, eventually leading to a third world war. Both Savitsky and Berezin are from Donetsk and supporters of the separatists. Oleksandr Syevyer's novel *The Russian-Ukrainian War* denigrates orange political forces as 'Russophobic' and 'fascist' who are following in the footsteps of the 'traitor (Cossack Hetman Ivan) Mazepa, (followers of Symon) Petlura, (supporters of Stepan) Bandera and Ukrainian nationalists in the nineteenth and twentieth centuries.[276] If we substitute the word orange for Euromaidan, Syevyer's fiction becomes remarkably similar to real life developments in 2014-2015.

The Russian chauvinism that is to be found in these party political programme's, popular stereotypes and writings towards Ukraine is an outgrowth of two factors. Firstly, views of Ukraine as an 'artificial state' arise from the deeply held Russian view that Ukrainians are incapable of building an independent state. Russian chauvinism towards smaller peoples are nothing new and writing in the 1970s, then Moscow correspondent Hedrick Smith heard from Swedish diplomats how Soviet officials were disparaging of their country.[277] Ukrainian dissident Ivan Plyushch described the USSR as imbued with Russian chauvinism and 'white racists' who were fond of camouflaging their nationalism as 'internationalism.'[278] Council for Foreign and Defence Policy head Sergey Karaganov depicts Ukraine - alongside 'Pakistan' and 'African countries' - as a 'failed state' because of its inability to rule itself, 'immature elites' and political instability. 'Russian peacekeeping forces,' Karaganov believes, will have to intervene to stabilise a disintegrating Ukraine in order to protect the Russophone population, a scenario that took place six years later.[279] Reading Karaganov, a Ukrainian analyst concluded that 'Russia is already preparing a scenario for Ukraine's occupation.'[280] Russian chauvinistic politicians viewed Ukraine in five ways:

1. As a failed state.
2. Ukraine was in a process of 'de-sovereignisation' and was dysfunctional with its regions pulling away from each other.
3. Ukrainians are a 'degraded people' who cannot produce an effective ruling elite to run an independent state.
4. Ukraine cannot therefore be a subject of international relations.
5. For 'justice' to be restored, the 'Russian' lands in Ukraine should be returned to Russia.

Denigrating Ukraine as an 'artificial' country more than once landed Viktor Chernomyrdin in trouble for speaking his mind as a *Gubernator* rather than as Russia's Ambassador to Ukraine. It is impossible to negotiate with Ukraine's current leaders, Chernomyrdin said, but, 'Other people will appear and then we will see…It is imperative that other more sober, normal people will appear' which presumably was a reference to a figure akin to Yanukovych.[281] As to Yushchenko, the Russian Ambassador said 'He looks like an otherwise normal *muzhyk* (serf but here meaning pleb)' that likes to play with folklore but has not shown himself suited to high office.'[282] The Russian Ministry of Foreign Affairs believed that Chernomyrdin's views could 'not be classified as interference in Ukraine's internal affairs.'[283] In this and other statements, such as Medvedev's 2009 address to Yushchenko, Russia proved itself unable to accept Ukraine as a normal independent country to which international diplomatic norms should be applied.

## SOVIET AND RUSSIAN NATIONALISM IN THE DONBAS

The DNR and LNR espouse an eclectic mix of Russian and Soviet nationalism, Pan-Slavism (whereby the three eastern Slavs are understood as one 'Russian' people), Russian Orthodoxy, and 'anti-nationalism' and 'anti-fascism.' In other words, the DNR and LNR are mini replicas of Putin's Russia. Prime Minister Zakharchenko believes that the DNR should be built on Soviet identity: 'We thought, still think and will think of ourselves as part of the Soviet Union, of Russia.'[284] The integration of Soviet and Russian identities in the USSR has led to 'pro-Russian' being in effect the same as pro-Soviet for DNR-LNR separatist leaders and their supporters, as it is for Putin in Russia. The 'Russian imagined community' in the USSR was larger than the Russian SFSR and it remains greater in size than the Russian Federation today. The imagined community of 'Russia' in Tsarist Russia, the USSR and post-Soviet Russia was not the same as that of a Russian nation-state and those Russians supporting a civic Russian identity since the 1960s have been in a minority and they always have been heavily contested by imperialists and nationalists who imagine Russia as a multinational empire. Russians in all three historical periods identified with the empire, Soviet Union and the Eurasian CIS. [285]

The clash of civilisations between ethnic Ukrainian and east Slavic identities is reflected in the toppling and defence of Lenin monuments and de-Stalinisation and Stalin cult respectively in Ukraine and the separatist enclaves. Ukrainian identity is growing in Ukrainian controlled Donbas while re-Sovietisation and de-Ukrainianisation is taking place in the DNR and LNR. From 2015, Ukrainian identity became more popular than regional identity in the Ukrainian controlled Donbas.[286] From the nineteenth century to the 2014 Ukraine-Russia crisis, the Donbas was colonised by Ukrainians and Russians and became a frontier zone between both countries. The war has dramatically changed the Donbas which is no longer a united region and single political space.

Nostalgia for 'Russia' (USSR) is a reflection of the Soviet identity prevalent in the Donbas and low levels of attachment to Ukrainian identity. 'Soviet identity put down deep roots in the Donbas because nothing much came before it,' Wilson writes.[287] The proportion of Ukrainians with a Soviet and Russian identity was naturally in decline since 1991 and fell by half in the decade prior to the Ukraine-Russia crisis from 27 to 13 percent. But, Soviet identity remained doggedly persistent in the Donbas where it commanded the allegiance of a quarter of the population.[288]

Soviet nostalgia encapsulates a broader range of people than the proportion of Ukrainians who hold a Soviet identity. 88 percent of Galician's are positive about the disintegration of the USSR, which is the highest proportion in Ukraine. Only three regions had higher negative than positive feelings about this historical event and the highest of these was in the Donbas where 70 percent felt negatively about the collapse of the USSR and only 12 percent positively. In Kharkiv, more felt negatively than positively but the gulf between them was smaller with 52 percent negatively disposed and 31 percent positively. In *Prydniprovya* (Dnipro and Zaporizhzhya) the figures were similar with 49 percent feeling negative and 39 percent positive, or only a ten percent gulf.[289] Former SBU officer and DNR military commander Serhiy Zdrilyuk believes 'The Soviet Union was the most righteous country. It was built on communism. Then America told us we didn't have enough sex, drugs and rock-and-roll. And we've had all that up to here.'[290]

The Donbas possessed greater attachment to the Soviet past, weak support for Ukrainian identity and high levels of crime making it different even in comparison with neighbouring *oblasts*.[291] Destruction, migration and deaths from the conflict have deepened these differences, as all conflicts inevitably do. High school teacher Alla Andrievska said 'We don't have a road to return to Ukraine. We are too different.' This was, unemployed Vadim Marchenko, believes because 'We are part of the *Russkiy Mir*.'[292]

The rhetoric and propaganda broadcast by DNR and LNR television is a mirror image of the Soviet nostalgia and anti-western diatribe on Russian television with its mythologising of the Great Patriotic War and liberation from the fascists, and nostalgia for Soviet military parades, Soviet pioneer groups and Soviet sports festival amid virulent calls to 'protect our (eastern Slavic) roots.' Educational policies in the DNR and LNR reflect the above and are similar to those that remained in the Trans-Dniestr and were re-introduced by Lukashenka into Belarus. Geography classes would now emphasise the USSR and Russia, history classes would focus on the history of the Donbas (not Ukraine) and the Great Patriotic War and adopt the Russian view of the *holodomor* as a Soviet-wide famine. Similar to policies undertaken by Lukashenka that reintroduced Russification, learning the Ukrainian language would be reduced from 8 to 2 hours per week while Russian language instruction would be expanded.[293] School children are taught 'Fatherland History' that highlights the strong ties between the Donbas and Russia. DNR Minister of Education Ihor V. Kostenok talks of the need to inculcate 'an idea about socialism, about creating a cult, a cult of the Slavic world, for the *Russkiy Mir.*'[294] The ideology of the Soviet state was good because, Zakharchenko believes, children were raised on values that included 'family, loyalty, brotherhood, and love for the motherland.'[295]

Soviet nostalgia is combined with Ukrainophobia that is even included in children's magazines published by the LNR. One such magazine entitled *Polite Little People*, a pun on the 'little green men' specialises in diatribes against Ukrainian 'fascists' and evil Americans.[296] Quotations on billboards and posters by Zakharchenko 'read like posters of Lenin in Soviet times.' Television rhetoric and billboard propaganda rant against 'fascists' who 'always wanted to kill us,' 'Kyiv want to drag us into the EU and destroy our Orthodox Church' and 'The US wants to take our shale gas and disgrace our holy places.'[297]'Tanya,' a Ukrainian teacher working in a school in the DNR complained about edicts forcing them to use Russian nationalist books: 'We are an educational institution and we are allowing all kinds of fascists into our midst.'[298]

The cult of Stalin is paramount in both Russia and the DNR and LNR. Three large portraits of Stalin hang in the centre of Donetsk. A 22-year-old says 'I think the portraits of Stalin are a good thing. It's our history and a lot of people have forgotten he even existed.' Stalin portraits are fashionable in the offices of DNR and LNR officials. The LNR official symbol includes a sheaf of corn and a red star. DNR Deputy Minister of Defence Eduard Basurin proudly wears a Stalin badge on his uniform.[299] Portraits of Stalin hang in cars of separatist fighters, one of who told the *BBC*: 'I have adored him as a man since my childhood. Because he was a real man.'[300]

As in the Trans-Dniestr region of Moldova, the DNR and LNR separatist enclaves have re-created mini Soviet Unions. The cult of Alexey Stakhanov is in full swing. The Communist Party Pioneer youth group has been revived. Internal security forces have been renamed after Soviet security organs, as with the continued use of the KGB for Lukashenka's security service in Belarus. The justice system has returned to the Soviet system with the use of the death penalty for looting and other crimes.

In propagating 'Russian' and 'Slavic' values, DNR and LNR leaders are emulating Putin and turning their backs on Europe. The DNR constitution adopted in May 2014 states 'European values are alien to us, we should support our Russian traditions.'[301] In other words, the supporters of the DNR and LNR believe Yanukovych took the right decision to not sign the Association Agreement with the EU because the priority for Ukraine should be integration into the CIS Customs Union and the Eurasian Union. Anti-western xenophobia is as prevalent in the DNR and LNR as it is in Russia. Zakharchenko said that since 1991 the West had imposed its values upon them by exporting Coca-Cola, Mickey Mouse, blue jeans, and Playboy, as well as a 'democracy that implies that the family could have two dads or two moms.'[302] Western scholars have nearly exclusively focused on homophobia in nationalist parties such as *Svoboda (Freedom)* [303] while ignoring the more widespread prevalence of homophobia in the Party of Regions, Viktor Medvedchuk's Ukrainian Way, *Rodina* and *Oplot* whose pronouncements and policies mirrored those found in Putin's Russia and the DNR and LNR.

## WHO ARE THE REAL SEPARATISTS?

Russian nationalist and separatist history and identity has been turned on its head; it is not they who are separatists but the Ukrainians. Because Ukrainians and Russians are one people it is the former, the 'fascists' among them, who are the separatists in seeking to break away from 'Great Russians' and their natural home in the *Russkiy Mir*. Girkin turns the charge of separatism on its head when he says it is the Ukrainian authorities who are separatists because they wish to break away from the *Russkiy Mir*.[304] Girkin believes 'The real separatists are the ones in Kyiv because they want to split Ukraine from Moscow.'[305] Ukrainian separatism from Russia and the *Russkiy Mir* continues to be understood as artificially constructed and Western promoted, as it has been understood by all Russian nationalists since the nineteenth century.

If the Donbas is 'Russian,' as the separatists and Russian nationalists claim, they are not the invaders but the Ukrainians. Asked about a Russian invasion a separatist replied 'What invasion? This is Russian territory. We are liberating it.'[306] A Russian soldier in the Donbas said: 'People say we're in a foreign country, but we're not. This is our land. This war isn't just material, it's spiritual. It's a fight against the values of the western world.' He continued: 'Americans shouldn't be trying to build democracy in other places.'[307]

Russian nationalists commonly believe they are not going to fight in a foreign country and there is no Russian aggression because Ukraine and Belarus are part of 'Russia.' Belarusians are an artificial nation and Ukrainians are in fact Russians, the Russian Institute of Strategic Studies, the Kremlin's official think tank, wrote.[308] DNR Deputy Minister of Defence Basurin views Ukraine as an artificially created state.[309]

Aleksandr Matyushin explained that 'We are fighting for the liberation of all Russian lands and we are ready to march all the way to the Danube.' 'We need to take land which is ours by right and bring it back into the fold of Holy Rus,' he added, because like Putin he was angry that injustice had divided the 'Russian' people.[310] A volunteer of the Russian Imperial Movement explained to the BBC that he was travelling to fight in Ukraine 'to defend the Russian people, Russian nation whose ancestors lived there for centuries.' He was seeking to 'defend the people, their culture, language, and orthodox religion.' Russia imperialists such as these were recruited by posters calling for 'Help to the Russians of *NovoRossiya*.'[311] The Donbas conflict was a 'Holy War of the Russian People' fought for 'God, Tsar and the Nation.'[312]

## CONCLUSIONS

Putin's rise to power and establishment of a strong state, culminating in a fully authoritarian political system, was contrasted as the antithesis of the unstable and weak Russian state in the 1990s. Ukrainian identity was anti-imperial and liberation-seeking (i.e. national democratic). From 1991, nation-building was therefore an important aspect of Ukraine's quadruple transition of which the end goal was 'returning to Europe' which required a commitment to building a democratic system.[313] When the Donetsk clan attempted to come to power through election fraud in 2004 or emulate Russia's authoritarian system and re-Sovietisation in 2010-2013, Ukrainians mobilised two democratic revolutions.[314]

Aggressive and chauvinistic attitudes towards Ukraine emerged during Putin's leadership of Russia as a 'consensus that consolidates the Russian elite.' This 'unites otherwise antagonistic businessmen and security force personnel, liberals and patriots' that consolidates and mobilises the Russian population around

Putin.[315] In contrast to Russia, ethnic nationalism has always been electorally weak in Ukraine and the conflict and war has led to the growth of patriotism and hostility towards Putin and other Russian leaders, not ethnic hatred of the Russian people.

The evolution of Putin's nationalism took place during four Ukrainian presidents – Kuchma (2000-2004), Yushchenko (2005-2010), Yanukovych 2010-2014) and Poroshenko (2014-). Putin's best relations were with Kuchma, an eastern Ukrainian and therefore not ideologically suspect, who was a member of the senior Soviet *nomenklatura*. Yushchenko was anathema to Russian leaders who were 'probably' behind his September 2004 poisoning. Yanukovych was the most palatable because he came from the Donbas, the existence of Soviet *kompromat* on him held by Russia, his willingness to implement Russian demands, the Party of Regions cooperation with Crimean Russian nationalists and giving a green light to Russia's intelligence services to take over the SBU and have free reign in the Crimea.

Putin's evolution towards nationalism and Ukrainophobic chauvinism took place simultaneously with the transformation of Russia into a 'consolidated authoritarian regime' after the Rose and Orange Revolutions and these developments became evident in his ideological tirade to the 2007 Munich conference and speech to the 2008 NATO summit. Russia's demands for recognition of its hegemony in Eurasia clashed with its desire to develop productive relations with the West and this came to a head in the Ukraine-Russia crisis. The crisis came as a shock to Western policymakers because a body of scholars and 'experts' had 'sleepwalked' through the earlier decade when analysing, conducting and handling relations with Russia and ignoring the movement of extremist views from the margins of political life to the centre of policymaking in the Kremlin. In particular, there was little understanding of Russian attitudes to Ukraine that became progressively hostile and chauvinistic and which culminated in annexation and aggression.

All of Ukraine's presidents have experienced difficult relations with Russia and even Yanukovych, the most pro-Russian of them, was treated with contempt by Putin. In a US cable from Kyiv, then Ukrainian Ambassador to Russia Kostyantyn Hryshchenko is cited as saying 'No one' in the Russian government 'wants to listen to the Ukrainian side of things.' The Kremlin wants a 'regency' in Ukraine; that is, 'someone in power in Kyiv who is totally subservient.'[316] Putin thought he had succeeded in buying Yanukovych as his satrap regency in December 2013 but the Ukrainian people reminded the Russian president that Ukraine is not Russia. The next chapter analyses long-standing Soviet and Russian Ukrainophobia which through television propaganda, political technology and social media became an important component of Russia's hybrid war against Ukraine

.

# CHAPTER 3

# UKRAINOPHOBIA
# AND RE-STALINISATION

*Over the last one-and-a-half years, we witness rampant Neo-Nazism, Banderism,*
*and radical nationalism in Ukraine. This is one of the Russian foreign policy priorities.*
Russian Foreign Ministry's Commissioner for Human Rights, Democracy and
Supremacy of Law Konstantin Dolgov[317]

*Even speaking Ukrainian, two years ago the state language, can be dangerous,*
*sparking animosity from locals or suspicions of subversiveness from gun-toting rebels.*
Roman Olearchyk[318]

Russian campaigns against Ukrainian separatism and nationalism stretch as far
back as the 1709 Battle of Poltava where Ukrainian Cossack forces led by Hetman Mazepa forged an alliance with Sweden and were defeated by the Tsarist
Russian Empire. During the last three centuries the themes of 'betrayal' and
Western governments behind a Ukrainian conspiracy to weaken Russia have
been at the core of Ukrainian-Russian relations. In this discourse Ukrainians
have been positively depicted when they have supported the Tsarist, Soviet and
Russian hierarchy of nationalities and Russians the elder brother while those
who disagree have been denigrated as 'agents of Austria,' 'bourgeois nationalists' and 'fascists.' Loyalists believed Ukrainians were 'brotherly peoples' in
close union whether as a *gubernia* in Tsarist Russia, as a Soviet republic or a
dominion in the CIS, accepting of Ukraine's junior role in the *Russkiy Mir*[319] and

opposed to European integration. Loyalists held Soviet identities and constituted the largest identity group in the Crimea and Donbas. The Crimea has the highest levels of xenophobia in Ukraine which was further inflamed by Russian television propaganda in 2014-2015 and became expressed in repression of Ukrainian and Crimean Tatar language, culture and history.[320] In Russia, Ukrainian migrant workers became 'extremists' simply 'because they speak Ukrainian to one another.'[321] Ukrainians who did not accept the Russian hierarchy of nationalities policies and supported Ukraine's future in Europe were the 'betrayers' who had turned their back on the Russian 'brotherly people.' In the Soviet Union they were disparaged as 'bourgeois nationalists' and 'Nazi collaborators' and in contemporary Russia as 'fascists.' President Putin said in spring 2014, 'We see neo-Nazis, nationalists, and anti-Semites on the rampage in parts of Ukraine, including Kyiv.'

Ukrainians in the Tsarist, Soviet and Russian worldview have never been independent and sovereign actors but only the pawns of conspiracies by the Swedes (1709), Austrians during World War I,[322] Nazi Germany in World War II, Western and Israeli intelligence agencies during the Cold War and US and EU democracy promotion. Conspiracy theories remain deeply ingrained in post-Soviet political forces, such as United Russia and the Party of Regions. Yanukovych has always been convinced that the Orange and Euromaidan Revolutions were Western conspiracies to prevent him from taking power in the first instance and remove him from power in the second. Putin has a pathological fear of revolutions since he was stationed in the GDR where he witnessed people power overthrowing the Communist regime.[323] Putin told the UN that the Euromaidan capitalised on 'discontent of the population with the current authorities' and 'the military coup was orchestrated from outside,' which then 'triggered a civil war as a result,' thereby blaming Western governments for the ensuing conflict.[324] Russian media had long warned of the threat of 'civil war' in Ukraine[325] and depicted Ukraine as a 'failed state.'

The use of 'fascism' in this chapter has nothing in common with Western political science definitions of the term. 'Fascism' was a misused and abused term in the Soviet Union and this continues in contemporary Russia. In both cases this has been misused by denouncing all shades of political opinion ranging from national communist through to liberal democrat and nationalist in Ukraine.[326] Ivan Dzyuba in his masterful *Internationalism or Russification?'* wrote that 'nationalists' in the Soviet Union 'means any Ukrainian who has preserved the least trace of his nationality.'[327]

The terms 'fascist' and 'neo-Nazis' have been consistently used by the Soviet and Putin's regimes when describing pro-Western forces in Ukraine, whether dissidents or supporters of the Euromaidan.[328] Good 'non-fascist' Ukrainians see their country as naturally belonging within the *Russkiy Mir* and believe in the myth, as the web site http://we-are-one.ru/ on the pro-government *Komsomolskaya Pravda* extorts, of 'One people! One history!' Use of the term 'fascist' remains additionally problematical because many of the Russian nationalists supporting the annexation of the Crimea and the DNR-LNR's fight against 'Ukrainian fascists' 'are not that different in their ideology with the people that they proclaim to be struggling against.'[329]

This chapter analyses how conservative counter-liberalisation in the Brezhnev and Putin eras has drawn on the mythology of the Great Patriotic War and Generalissimo Stalin which led to re-Stalinisation in Brezhnev and Andropov's USSR, Putin's Russia and the DNR and LNR. Putin was socialised in the Brezhnev era and therefore, as somebody who believes the disintegration of the USSR was a tragedy, his reference points for building contemporary Russia are not surprisingly the conservatism of the Brezhnev 'era of stagnation' when official Russian nationalism was tolerated and encouraged.

The first section of this chapter explores Russia's information war and political technology as one element of Putin's hybrid war against Ukraine and the manner in which it fanned pernicious lies and hatreds which, in turn, fuelled vicious combat, huge civilian losses and human rights abuses and war crimes. The second section investigates the contemporary origins of anti-Ukrainian nationalism in the late 1920s with the rise of Stalin to power, curtailment of the indigenisation campaign, repression of national communists, *holodomor* and Great Terror. These reverses took place alongside a return to Tsarist Russian historiography and revival of a hierarchy of nationalities in the eastern Slavs with Russians designated as the 'elder brother.' The third section analyses the sources and internal contradictions of anti-(Ukrainian) nationalism in Ukraine and Russia.

## NOTHING IS TRUE AND EVERYTHING IS POSSIBLE: SOVIET COMMISSARS AND RUSSIAN POLITICAL TECHNOLOGY

Soviet use of television, newspaper, radio and Communist Party and Communist youth gatherings were exhaustive and a reflection of the totalitarian nature of Soviet rule. Nevertheless, ideological campaigns from the 1960s suf-

*Anti-fascist propaganda published in the Soviet Union as Mercenary of Fascism (Ukrainian Bourgeois Nationalists in the Service of Hitlerites in the Inter-War Period from 1921-1939) (1981) and Fascism in Ukraine: threat or reality? authored by Communist Heorhiy Kruchkov and President Viktor Yanukovych's Minister of Education Dmytro Tabachnyk (2008)*

fered from a decline in public acceptance as cynicism and careerism grew, corruption became more widespread and public backing for Communism declined. Soviet ideological campaigns were devoid of satellite broadcasting, the Internet and social media, let alone even fax machines which only appeared in the late 1980s, that are available to Putin's Russia.

The vitriolic level of Russia's television onslaught is reminiscent of Soviet propaganda barrages in the Cold War's pre-détente era but, with annual spending at $1.4 billion, modern technology, social media and political technology, it is on a completely different and expanded level.[330] Many commentators have pointed to Russia's xenophobic discourse and television propaganda as contributing to fanning conflict and violence during the Ukraine-Russia crisis through the propagation of stereotypes of 'Banderites,' 'fascists' and 'Ukrainian nationalists.'

Propaganda, as an increasingly important aspect of Putin's 'consolidated authoritarian regime,' is used to mobilise domestic support for his vitriolic xenophobia against domestic opponents, foreign funded NGOs and external enemies (the 'West,' particularly the US, 'Ukrainian fascists,' Islamic State terrorists and Turkey).[331] Massive propaganda onslaughts on Russian television[332] have been described as 'The most amazing information warfare blitzkrieg we have ever seen in the history of information warfare.'[333] Information in Putin's Russia is not merely a product of the state's control over mass media but an important component of hybrid warfare, or war by stealth and deceit. Putin's Russia has produced the 'weaponisation of information' alongside 'weaponisation' of organised crime, finance and business corruption, the Internet and refugees.'[334] Surkov described himself to Dugin as a 'state envoy to the organised crime world.'[335] Lies, deceit, blackmail and contradictions mixed together in a cocktail of spin doctoring on Russian television seeks to confuse and throw into disarray Russia's domestic and external enemies. Propaganda and 'weaponisation of information' have played a major part in fuelling the conflict in the Donbas, fanning xenophobia in the Crimea and brutalising treatment of the pro-Ukrainian and Crimean Tatar activists and Ukrainian prisoners of war. Ukrainian-language schools and classes, publications, television and Internet have been closed down in the Crimea and DNR-LNR.

Since Putin's re-election in 2012, television and other Russian media outlets depicted the Ukrainian opposition and later the Euromaidan as 'fascist' in propaganda diatribes that were last seen during the Brezhnev and Andropov eras. In Ukraine, the Party of Regions returned to Soviet era depictions of their opponents as 'fascists' after Yanukovych was elected president in 2010[336] and in 2012-2013 they began mobilising 'anti-fascist' rallies throughout Ukraine in anticipation of the upcoming presidential elections in 2015. Anti-fascist rhetoric encouraged violent attacks by pro-Russian vigilantes against Ukrainian patriots and nationalists; in January 2012 a vigil to commemorate the battle of Kruty was brutally attacked by thugs shouting 'Donbas is a Russian land!' and 'Death to Banderites and fascists!'[337] The January 1918 battle of Kruty, where Ukrainian military cadets died defending a social-democratic and pro-independence Ukrainian government against Bolshevik invaders, had nothing to do with Bandera, Ukrainian nationalism or western Ukraine.

The revival of Soviet era anti-nationalist rhetoric came into prominent display during the Ukraine-Russia crisis. Putin described the leaders of the Euromaidan as having 'resorted to terror, murder, and riots. Nationalists, neo-

Nazis, Russophobes, and anti-Semites executed this coup.'[338] Putin's stark language drew on decades of Soviet anti-nationalist propaganda where 'nationalists' are a 'group defined as irredeemable by nature' which 'allows for the construction of conspiracy narratives and excluded alternative ways of thinking.'[339]

The use of terror against such opponents in the USSR 'required no evidence of crimes;'[340] in a similar manner there is no need to find real crimes allegedly committed by Ukrainian 'nationalists' in contemporary Russia and the DNR-LNR. In the USSR, Ukrainian 'nationalists' were imprisoned for 'ordinary criminal offences'[341] and this has continued in contemporary Russia with the sentencing of Ukrainians on flimsy charges.[342] In 1967, the fifth directorate of the KGB was established with the task of surveillance of émigrés, foreign journalists and unofficial groups in the USSR and its soul and spirit was resurrected in Russian legislation combating 'extremism' and 'terrorism'.[343]

The hybrid war launched in the Donbas in the 'Russian Spring' of 2014 is an 'offshoot of political technology' where 'information warfare' plays a central role in the operation[344] and where 'Lies are part of the coin of the intelligence operative, and facts are fungible.' Putin spent 'a great deal of time in his professional life bending the truth, manipulating facts, and playing with fictions.'[345] Falsifications and propaganda have mobilised Russian and European neo-Nazi and Stalinist volunteers to travel to the Donbas to fight against 'fascists,' NATO and 'American mercenaries.' Not all Russian volunteers find 'fascists' and 'American imperialists' in the Donbas. Bondo Dorovskikh returned home disillusioned because instead of finding a contemporary re-enactment of the Great Patriotic War's fight against 'fascism' he found 'pure aggression' by the separatists and Russian forces.[346] Other Russian volunteers returned home complaining they were called 'occupiers' in the Donbas, as recounted by a group of 180 who had been hired by *spetsnaz* veteran Vladimir Yefimov.[347] Denys Deykin learnt about the aggression of *Pravyy Sektor* on Russian television programmes but during his participation on the separatist side he never encountered 'Ukrainian nationalists,' until he was captured.[348]

Russian television propaganda has specialised in churning out brazen lies. *Svoboda* was supposedly planning to print a *hryvnya* note with a portrait of Hitler.[349] Russian troll factories target EU and US leaders and 'Ukrainian nationalists' by inserting derogatory comments in on line media outlets reporting on the Crimea, the shooting down of the MH17 Malaysian airliner, Western sanctions and Euromaidan politicians. The Russian media and Foreign Minister

Lavrov have claimed Ukraine has been using phosphorous bombs which Russia's Ambassador to the UN demanded the international community condemn Ukraine for allegedly using. The pictures of these bombs were actually from Iraq. A *Reuters* photograph of a Ukrainian tank when rebroadcast on Russian television had a swastika on it. Photographs of 'Ukrainian soldiers' with Nazi tattoos turned out to be photographs of criminals in Russian prisons.[350]

The most outlandish of lies have included Ukrainian armed forces crucifying a 3-year old child in front of his mother who subsequently died after he was allegedly tied to a Ukrainian APC (Armoured Personnel Carrier) and dragged through the streets until he was dead. Two other pieces of disinformation were that *Aydar* had raped 12 orphans and President Poroshenko had authorised killings in the Donbas.[351] A Cossack told a journalist that he had come here to 'fight fascism and the Nazis' after reading such lies. These untruths fanned Ukrainophobia against the Euromaidan government and Ukrainian military: 'I read an article about how somewhere in the Luhansk region, the Ukrainian National Guard found a World War II veteran, put a uniform on him and slit his throat.'[352]

Lies are inculcated in children attending primary and high schools in Russia by visiting lecturers supposedly seeking to educate children about 'patriotism and family values.' Ivan Ogulov, a retired actor, told children in a Russian school about the fabricated story of the crucified child and added his own bias by alleging 'several months of rain could not wipe away the blood.' Despite protests from parents that these lectures led to their children being unable to sleep, the headmistress defended them and Ogulov said 'They (the children) need to know what is fascism and what it leads to.'[353] The Ukrainian soldiers allegedly undertaking these atrocities in areas of the Donbas they controlled are 'beasts and fascists.'[354]

Another brazen lie alleged a 'mass grave' had been found in Komunar of 80 victims with their ears chopped off which included a decapitated pregnant woman murdered by 'fascists' in the Ukrainian armed forces.[355] Although the figure of 80 victims was a 'widely accepted fact' that fuelled anger and suspicion it was completely false. Donbas residents are quoted on Russian television saying outrageous comments such as 'They (Kyiv fascists) want to exterminate us.'[356] A Russian Orthodox priest in the Urals blessed volunteers heading for Ukraine to fight 'fascist scum'[357] while other Russian Orthodox priests helped torture Ukrainian prisoners of war, beating them with crosses over their heads.[358] Former Swedish Foreign Minister Carl Bildt, an architect of the EU's

Eastern Partnership (EaP), was ludicrously described as a CIA agent in his youth driven by a desire for revenge against Russia because of Sweden's defeat in 1709.

Lies and deception emanating from Russian and Donbas separatist television channels serve to 'reinforce hatred and divisions.'[359] A young Ukrainian soldier driving an APC hit a landmine which blew his body parts high up on to a telegraph pole where his remains were left to rot by separatist forces.[360] A Donbas separatist remarked 'That's my favourite sight: a Nazi hanging from a wire. There's a God after all.'[361] Rabid Ukrainophobia and equating of the Euromaidan with the coming to power of 'fascists' fanned violent conflict in the swing cities of Kharkiv and Odesa in spring 2014. Pro-Russian activists guarding the large Lenin monument in Kharkiv held signs saying 'Fascists. Don't test Kharkiv's patience' and warning Kyiv not to unleash repression of Ukraine's Russian speakers.[362] Russian television promotion of hate propaganda became so intense that those protecting Kharkiv's Lenin monument told CBC 'How can I support a state which has declared war against me?'[363]The large Lenin monument in Kharkiv was pulled down in September 2014. Russian intelligence trained and paid local *Oplot* vigilantes to beat up 'fascists' (i.e. protestors in the Euromaidan Revolution) in Kharkiv and young supporters were dragged out of official buildings and savagely beaten by a crowd applauding such atrocious behaviour.[364]

17 Interior Ministry officers were killed on the Euromaidan, 7 from the *Berkut* and 10 from Internal Troops, and of these 3 were from the Crimea and 4 from Kharkiv. *Berkut* riot police officers who had participated in the murder of unarmed Euromaidan protesters were applauded when they returned to Donetsk and the Crimea.[365] Ten of the *Berkut* officers who are wanted for the sniper murders during the Euromaidan Revolution fled to Russia where they were given Russian citizenship.

Peaceful pro-Ukrainian protesters and supporters of the Euromaidan were violently attacked in Donetsk, Luhansk, Kharkiv and Odesa in spring 2014 when 'opponents of separatism were automatically branded as 'fascist,' 'Maidanut' (supporters of the Euromaidan Revolution), 'Banderovets' (supporters of OUN [Organisation of Ukrainian Nationalists] leader Bandera), and subhuman. Even if you had never been a fascist, did not support the Euromaidan protests, and were not a Bandera follower, it was all the same to them – you were an enemy.'[366] As the Donetsk commentator said, 'What is this, if not fascism?' when the millions of Ukrainians who participated in the Euromaidan 'were retroactively declared enemies and "sentenced to death."'[367]

A key figure in Putin's propaganda, political technology and ideological discourse is senior adviser Surkov who is well known for developing the concept of 'sovereign democracy' to describe Putin's regime. He is the master manipulator in a political system where 'Every politician was an actor, taking their script from Surkov.'[368] Russia's 'dramaturgia' had its own logic and 'long ago lost touch with reality or real world consequences' marching at high speed into Ukraine, Syria and elsewhere 'while drugged up to the eyeballs.'[369] Russian propaganda ties US foreign policies and democracy promotion in the Middle East to the Nazis and warns Russia not to retreat as 'Behind Syria lies the Russian border.'[370] Such a statement was made two years ahead of Russia's military intervention in Syria in 2015.

Propaganda espoused by Russian media, spin doctors and political technologists is believed by Russian leaders and the public because 'In place of politics, there is performance art. Instead of debate, there is spectacle. In lieu of issues, there is *dramaturgia*. And in place of reality, there is fantasy.'[371] Vitaliy Sych, editor of the Russian-language *Novoye Vremya* published in Kyiv, noted that Russian propaganda that looked 'ridiculous' in Kyiv was 'extremely effective' in some Russian-speaking regions of Ukraine and even more so in Russia where the Euromaidan Revolution was presented as 'an illegal rebellion of neo-Nazis financed and managed by Americans.'[372] The Euromaidan, which was an 'anti-criminal revolution,' was 'shown as an aggressive offensive on anything that is Russian-culture, language, identity.'[373] Sych is himself a Russian-language speaker.

Surkov promoted pro-Russian groups such as Ukrainian Choice headed by Medvedchuk, he facilitated funding for extreme right politicians and groups in Europe, and laid out the parameters for Russia's political technology towards Ukraine which is the 'life blood of the system.'[374] Surkov provided advice to President Yanukovych when he travelled to Ukraine during the Euromaidan Revolution and was the author of the infamous 'dictatorship laws' voted through on 16 January 2014 that became a major factor in Ukraine's deterioration into violence.[375] Hacked emails from Surkov's accounts provided extensive evidence of his and Malofeyev's support to separatists in the Russian Spring and showing high-level Russian involvement behind separatism in Ukraine. Surkov micromanaged the separatists and chose who would be included in the

DNR government.[376] A second batch of hacked emails from Surkov's accounts confirmed that senior Kremlin officials are supervising separatist leaders, funding separatist movements in Ukrainian cities outside the Donbas and guiding propaganda campaigns against Ukrainian leaders.

Surkov was also behind and attended the inaugural congress of the Slavic Anti-Fascist Front in February 2014 launched by thirty Russian nationalist organisations such as the ROK (Russian Community of the Crimea), Russian Unity and Congress of Russian Communities.[377] The Donbas separatists describe him as their 'political supervisor' who provided the ideological background to the 'New Russia' project.[378] Peter Pomerantsev describes Surkov as Putin's chief adviser on Ukraine 'For what is Russia's policy in Ukraine if not a war on reality?'[379] The separatist Luhansk and Donetsk enclaves 'began as fictions thought up by oligarchs in Ukraine's eastern regions and propagandists in the Kremlin.'[380]

Russia's 'war on reality' used political technology of a kind unimaginable to Soviet leaders and has inculcated a contradictory imagery of 'fascist' Ukrainians who are at the same time Russia's 'brothers' because they are the 'same people.' A Russian Aeroflot pilot on a flight from Moscow described Ukrainians over the intercom as 'filth,' 'scum' and 'killers'. Night Wolves, a hells angels gang led by Aleksandr ('Surgeon') Zaldostanov which receives the most funding of any group from the Russian presidential administration, had been holding annual biker shows in the Crimea since 2010 which had used the myth of the Great Patriotic War as its central message. Night Wolves leader Zaldostanov was the first to receive the state medal 'For the liberation of Sevastopol and the Crimea.'[381] In August 2014, the Night Wolves held a 'nationalist rock, pyrotechnics, Nazi and illumanti imagery and interpretive dance to portray Ukraine as a state overrun by fascists.' All of the usual ideological props were included: a US conspiracy against Russia, Western Russophobia, the Ukrainian state overrun by 'fascists' who are puppets of the West, Russian liberators of the Crimea, Ukrainian atrocities in the Donbas and Russian warriors defeating Ukrainian neo-Nazis and liberating its Russian brothers. The event, costing in the millions of dollars, was broadcast live on Russian-2 channel and set in Sevastopol from where 'We are celebrating our sacred victory at a time when fascism, like putrid, poisonous dough, has over filled its Kyiv trough and begun to spread across Ukraine.' Ukraine's leaders were placed in the same category as 'Enemies who hated us, killed the Soviet state, and took away its territory and its army.'[382]

'War on reality' political technology was explicit in the Party of Regions slogan 'To Europe without fascists!' promoted by a political force very far removed from European values. The most profound attempt at presenting an Orwellian claim was that it was Ukraine – not Russia – that was guilty of crimes against humanity in the Donbas when the evidence from international organisations and human rights groups points to Russia and the separatists as the main culprits.[383] Russia's Investigative Committee called for the punishment of Ukraine's 'genocide' against the Russian speaking population of eastern and southern Ukraine.[384] Such bombastic rhetoric from Moscow became mainstream before and under Putin: in July 2000; 345 deputies voted in the State Duma in support of a resolution denouncing the 'discrimination of the Russian language in Ukraine' blaming the authorities 'and the extreme nationalist forces of Ukraine' who deride 'our history' and seek to infuse 'spiritual alienation between the brother nations.'[385]

This spurious claim was contradicted by the fact the majority of Ukraine's Russophones backed Kyiv, not Moscow, in the Donbas conflict. Investigations by international organisations and reports by human rights groups into the Donbas conflict have not agreed with the falsehoods propounded by Russia's Investigative Committee which claimed Ukrainian forces 'issued orders aimed at the total annihilation of specific Russian speaking citizens' in the Donbas. They were allegedly deliberately murdered because 'they spoke Russian and did not want to descend into nationalist hysteria and allow fascist ideology in their native land.'[386] Russia expanded this mythology to claim that Ukrainian nationalists on the Euromaidan had earlier fought on the Chechen side in the 1990s. Russia's Investigation Committee head Aleksandr Bastrykin made a bizarre claim that former Prime Minister Arseniy Yatsenyuk had fought in Grozny in late 1994-early 1995, when he would have been 20 years old, and allegedly participated in 'the torture and execution of Russian army servicemen.'[387]

But, if this was not bizarre enough, the Russian media recycled a ludicrous story that had first appeared the year before claiming that the Ukrainian parliament was demanding compensation from the Mongolian government for the 'genocide of the Ukrainian people' carried out by the 13th century Mongolian ruler Batu Khan, grandson of Genghis Khan. After outlining details of the supposed compensation claim, Russian television and print media viewers were told that the chairman of the Mongolian parliament had responded to the

Ukrainian demand by saying his country would only compensate the actual victims of Batu Khan and members of their family. The bizarre allegations did not only appear on an X-Files type conspiratorial web site but on leading Russian news outlets *Rossiya 1*, state news channel *Rossiya 24*, the Moscow government owned Centre TV, the St Petersburg based Channel 5, the newspapers *Nezavisimaya Gazeta* and *Komsomolskaya Pravda*, state news agency RIA *Novosti* and numerous other Russian websites.[388] The purpose was to poke derision and Russian chauvinistic contempt at Ukraine as a failed state propped up by foreign assistance.

Russia's call for an international tribunal to investigate 'Ukrainian crimes' in the Donbas would never materialise and was disingenuous; after all, had not Russia voted against the formation of a UN tribunal to investigate the crime of shooting down MH17 that killed 298 innocent civilians. Russia's demands were not made more believable by the publication of a 'White Book of (Ukrainian) Crimes' that used fake photographs on its front cover.[389]

Demonisation of Ukrainian separatism rested on similar contemporary Russian stereotypes of Ukrainians, with Putin reminding the US President that they did not possess the attributes of a genuine 'nation.' If Ukrainian independence is artificial it only exists because it is propped up by the US, NATO and EU in order to weaken Russia.[390] Putin has claimed the separatists were not fighting the Ukrainian army but a 'foreign legion' supported by NATO and Russian television has repeatedly lied that NATO troops are embedded in Ukrainian armed forces.[391] Russian soldiers sent to fight in Ukraine are told what they are doing is assisting their 'Russian brothers' who are facing Ukrainian forces supplied with NATO weapons and fighting alongside Polish mercenaries.[392] A young woman from Kyiv asked Donbas separatists why they used the term 'fascist' and 'none could answer the question' except to repeat the stock phrase 'fascists and Banderists are one and the same!'[393]

*Pravyy Sektor* has been described in the Russian media as a 'US subunit' with the implication that it is a puppet organisation of Washington.[394] Interrogations of Ukrainian prisoners on Russian television repeat 3 allegations and 1 demand:[395]

1.  The majority of Ukrainian security forces are Nazi sympathisers.
2.  They are trained and supported by the West.
3.  They deliberately target civilians.
4.  Resistance to Russia is futile and Ukrainians should therefore surrender.

## SOVIET ANTI-(UKRAINIAN) NATIONALISM AND RESTALINISATION

Attacks on Ukrainian nationalism began in 1928-1932 during the revision by the Soviet state of its attitudes towards national communism and was followed by the rehabilitation of the Russian Empire, Russian nationalists, military leaders and Russian historians.[396] From the mid to late 1930s the Soviet regime increasingly pursued a blurring of Soviet and Russian identities and Russian nationalism with Soviet patriotism. The Russian people become the 'elder brother' and 'leading people' through the 'wartime restoration of an ethnic hierarchy.'[397]

Ukrainian historian and political leader Hrushevskyy, a social democrat, fell victim to this re-direction in Soviet nationalities policies when he was re-classified in the early 1930s as a 'bourgeois historian' and his views as 'national-fascist.'[398] World War II, when Russian great power nationalism was fully rehabilitated, depicted Ukrainians of all ideological persuasions (apart from supporters of Stalin) as 'fascist nationalists.'[399] Anti-nationalist tirades targeted Ukrainian historians and political leaders, Ukrainian military formations from the Cossacks to the present that had fought for independence, the Ukrainian Greek-Catholic Church and Ukrainians who celebrated 'the struggle for independence.'[400] Attacks on Ukrainian nationalism and glorification of Russian nationalism 'came down to re-educating the peoples of the USSR to identify with the Soviet present and the Russian imperial past.'[401]

From the 1940s, Soviet attacks on Ukrainian nationalism increasingly targeted western Ukrainians who, as in the Russian Empire, were seen as 'contaminated' and different to Russophones in eastern and southern Ukraine. 'Banderites' was simply a modern term for older derogatory depictions of Ukrainian nationalists as *Mazepintsy (Mazepists)* and 'Petliurites.' In the Russian Empire the choices open to Ukrainians were 'to face persecution as *Mazepintsy*, self-effacement as 'little Russians,' or contempt as *'khokhols.'*[402]

The Soviet tradition of targeting western Ukrainians as the most ideologically suspect of Ukrainians first emerged in the 1930s against Galician Ukrainians who had travelled to Soviet Ukraine to work for the Ukrainianisation (indigenisation) campaign.403 In the Great Terror of the late 1930s just speaking Ukrainian was sufficient to be arrested, tortured and executed by the NKVD and by the outbreak of World War II the Ukrainian intelligentsia had been decimated.404 The Yanukovych election campaign in 2004 and Party of Regions deputies in subsequent elections revived Soviet era tirades against, and stereotypes of, western Ukrainians. They demanded western Ukrainians stop imposing their values on eastern Ukraine and 'Galicians should understand they are spongers in this country and, like all spongers, they ought to know their place by not imposing their values on the rest of us while understanding who feeds them, who supports them and who has the right to their own values,' Party of Regions deputy Boldyrev said. Party of Regions and Nikolay Azarov government members castigated Galicians for allegedly not speaking 'literary Ukrainian.'405

Such doctrinaire views had deep roots in the Soviet era and were fanned by Russian television propaganda that fed into local support in the Donbas for violent counter-revolution against the 'fascist' Euromaidan. Boldyrev believes the Ukrainian diaspora in North America is 'organically tied to the collaborationist period of World War Two.'406 Senior Party of Regions deputy Borys Kolesnykov always portrayed the democratic opposition as 'Banderites' and 'bandits' and therefore implicitly hostile to Russophones, eastern Ukrainians and Russia. These Russophobes were portrayed as in the pay of the West to prevent Yanukovych being elected president in 2004 and remove him from power a decade later.407 Accusations such as these were directed not only at nationalist groups Pravyy Sektor and Svoboda, but as much at Yushchenko and national democrats as well as at centrists such as Klitschko and Poroshenko. Poroshenko is an example of the perversion of the term 'fascism' used by the Russian and separatist media as he was born in Odesa, is a founding member of the Party of Regions, was a cabinet member in the Azarov government and had business ventures in Russia.

Throughout the 1940s through to 1953, Soviet leaders  Zhdanov and Lazar Kaganovich sought 'To carry through the liquidation of bourgeois nationalist distortions in the history of Ukraine' and the 'cleansing' of Ukrainian culture and educational institutions.408 The 'Ukrainian problem' was an issue that had, and continues to, plague Soviet and Russian leaders; Khrushchev told the 1956 Communist Party congress that Ukrainians avoided the fate of smaller peoples such as Crimean Tatars at the end of World War II were not deported 'only because there were too many of them and there was no place to which to deport them.'409

During the late Stalin era, Soviet Ukrainian readers would send protests to newspapers criticising these Soviet nationalities policies and historiography that looked up to the Russian 'elder brother' and down at the Ukrainian 'peasant bumpkin.' Underground nationalist organisations printed and distributed leaflets and brochures throughout the 1940s and early 1950s condemning Soviet nationalities policies and Russian chauvinism towards Ukrainians.[410]

A respite from Russian chauvinistic depictions of Ukrainians only came following Khrushchev's 1956 secret speech and under Soviet Ukrainian Communist Party leader and national communist Shelest. But, he was deposed in 1971 after being accused of 'national deviationism' and his removal was followed by what was described as a *pogrom* of Ukrainian dissent, culture and scholarship, the biggest purge in any Soviet republic since the Stalin era. In 1972-1989, during Soviet Ukraine's rule by Communist Party leader Shcherbytskyy, Soviet nationality policies pursued a chauvinistic and paternalistic attitude toward the Ukrainian language and culture that reflected the Little Russian character of those who had come to power and paid ritualistic homage to the 'Great Russian elder brother.' 'Ethnic Ukrainians were thus pressed into the task of exorcising Ukrainian 'separatist nationalism' on behalf of Moscow and the Shcherbytskyy era began with widespread repression that continued through to 1987.[411]

After visiting Soviet Ukraine, Ukrainian-Canadian John Kolasky wrote, 'Russians are everywhere with their arrogant overbearing attitude; their contempt, sometimes veiled but often overt, for the Ukrainian language, their open display of a feeling of Russian superiority.'[412] If a Ukrainian dissident or national communist leader had said this, he or she would have been accused of being a 'bourgeois nationalist' and the irony is that Kolasky was not a member of one of the three wings of the émigré OUN but until then a pro-Soviet Ukrainian-Canadian communist. Ukrainian-Canadians represented a very large component of Canada's Communist Party and were especially influential among Ukrainian communities in the prairie provinces of Alberta, Manitoba and Saskatchewan.

From the 1960s, Soviet anti-nationalist tirades targeted émigré OUN groups, domestic nationalists, pro-democracy dissidents, and national communists who were defined collectively as 'bourgeois nationalists,' a depiction similar to today's elastic use of the term 'fascists.'[413] The Soviet understanding of 'bourgeois nationalists' was very broad and included individuals and groups in Soviet Ukraine and the West who promoted democracy and human rights, patriots who defended the Ukrainian language and culture, moderates who supported greater autonomy for Soviet Ukraine within a looser confederation of Soviet republics, and nationalists who demanded Ukrainian independence from the USSR.

The cult and myths of the Great Patriotic War were developed by Soviet Communist leader Brezhnev from the mid-1960s and under Putin have been promoted as the regime's new religion. The myth of the Great Patriotic War is essential to Russia's understanding of its self and national identity and cannot be utilised by the Brezhnev and Putinist regimes without recourse to praise for Generalissimo Stalin.[414] It is also a means to deflect attention from Stalin's crimes against humanity[415] by a regime whose ideological foundation is 'velvet Stalinism' which although disguised as patriotism is 'an old mix of Russian Orthodoxy, state nationalism and autocracy.'[416] 9 May has been a national holiday in the USSR and post-Soviet Russia since 1965 when Brezhnev ended the campaign of de-Stalinisation and began the cult of the Great Patriotic War.

Soviet identity was grounded in the Great Patriotic War. Intensive celebration of the Great Patriotic War between 1965-1985 is still within living memory of contemporary Russian and Ukrainian leaders, such as Putin and Yanukovych. The Great Patriotic War is reflected in medals on Soviet veterans, Soviet flags and emblems, portraits of Stalin and the Red Army, religious sanctification by the Russian Orthodox Church, and swastikas painted on *tryzubs* used in military attacks against Ukrainian 'fascists.' Separatist banners draw on these Soviet ideological motifs, which have been revived by Putin's Russia through slogans such as 'Beat the fascist beast!'[417] Donbas residents have been quoted as praying for Russian liberation from Ukrainian forces who are 'tyrants' and 'worse than fascists' with Russian viewers commenting on *Rossiya-1* channel afterwards that Nazi Germany treated Soviet peoples better than Ukraine did its own people. 'They are barbarians, true fascists!'[418] Russian leaders and veterans have called upon European leaders to halt the rise of 'new Banderas and Shukhevychs and to stop supporting the Euromaidan authorities because they are 'condoning Ukrainian Nazism.' These demands are Orwellian in nature in view of Putin supporting the coalition of anti-EU nationalists, fascists and neo-Nazis who have gained electoral popularity in many European countries. The French National Front, one of the most popular neo-Nazi parties in Europe, received a $11.7 million 'loan' (gift) from Russia at the end of 2014. In March 2015, *Rodina*, a nationalist party loyal to Putin, organised a meeting of 150 representatives of European nationalist and fascist parties at the 'International Russian Conservative Forum.'[419]

Re-Stalinisation then and today drew on deeply felt Soviet nostalgia, Russian great power nationalism, ambivalent attitudes towards democracy and the blending of Russian and Soviet identities.[420] A second important component of the cult was the eternal union of Ukrainians and Russians as 'fraternal peoples' and those 'nationalists' who fought against this union are therefore by definition 'Nazi hirelings' who betrayed the Soviet fatherland. Clifford G. Gaddy and Fiona Hill[421] write that for Putin this myth is very personal because his father was one of only a few who survived as a member of an NKVD unit sent into Nazi occupied Estonia. In Brezhnev's USSR and Putin's Russia, anti-(Ukrainian) nationalism has therefore gone hand in hand with the promotion of the cult of the Great Patriotic War and re-Stalinisation. In 2014, Putin expanded these links further by stating the Russian motherland had a right and duty over and above international law and existing treaties with Ukraine to protect ethnic Russians and Russophones in the Crimea against 'fascists' who had come to power with the assistance of the West. Such claims were nothing new. The USSR has repeatedly claimed it had been invited into countries to protect them; whether the Ukrainians from the Polish-Lithuanian Commonwealth, Georgians from the Ottoman Empire, Czechoslovaks from NATO in 1968, Afghans from Pakistan in 1979 and the population of the Crimea from pro-NATO Ukrainians in 2014.

Added to Russia's equivalent of the 'white man's burden' was the age-old Russian yearning for the re-gathering and reuniting of historic *Russkiy* lands; with Russians, Ukrainians and Belarusians branches of the Russian nation. Putin, in claiming the Crimea as Russian territory from historical, cultural and linguistic perspectives, laid claim to Kyiv Rus history alleging Grand Prince Volodymyr was baptised in the peninsula.[422]

From the 1930s to 1980s, Kyiv Rus was portrayed as the birthplace of the 'fraternal' Russian, Ukrainian and Belarusian peoples in Soviet historiography by incorporating the Russian Imperial succession theory of Kyiv Rus transferring the centre of power to Vladimir-Suzdal, Muscovy, Imperial Russia and the USSR. In Russian imperial historiography, Ukrainians have no historical origins except in union with Russia (a yearning allegedly demonstrated by the 1654 Treaty of Peryaslav) and no existence outside Russia's sphere of influence and the *Russkiy Mir*.[423]

The Great Patriotic War was the antidote for those Soviet and Russian leaders with Stalinist and Russian nationalist ideological sympathies who wished to end the de-Stalinisation campaigns of the mid-1950s to the mid-1960s and late 1980s. The cult of the Great Patriotic War in the Brezhnev era and Putin's Russia covers up Stalinist crimes against humanity and 'suppresses memory of the Gulag, to rename and suppress the memory of the irrational, unjustified sufferings of the victims of the Soviet system.'[424] Putin is heir to the Brezhnev tradition of covering up Stalinist crimes and instead focusing attention on how Generalissimo Stalin won the Great Patriotic War, defeated the Nazis and transformed the USSR into a nuclear superpower that was internationally respected and globally feared. Anti-Stalinist Soviet leaders in contrast, focused on the mass crimes and on the large number of casualties in World War II, why the Soviet army was unprepared, the causes of the defeats the Soviet army suffered, the Nazi-Soviet Molotov-Ribbentrop Pact, deportations to Siberia from western Ukraine and the three Baltic republics, and the massacre of Polish officers in the Katyn forest. Victory in the Great Patriotic War was from the anti-Stalinist viewpoint a product not just of Generalissimo Stalin but the efforts of all Soviet nationalities.[425]

In Brezhnev's USSR, the Great Patriotic War was used to mobilise 'increasingly disaffected, alienated, and alcohol-prone youth.'[426] Similar motivations lie behind Putin's turn to Russian nationalism and Great Patriotic War myths after he returned to power following mass pro-democracy protests in 2011-2012. In Brezhnev's USSR, the mythology of the Great Patriotic War attempted to shield Soviet youth from the Prague Spring, dissidents and stagnation in popular attitudes towards, and respect for, Communist ideology. The cult of the Great Patriotic War mobilised 'military-patriotic upbringing' that integrated young people with veterans and promoted respect for elders. The war was a 'reservoir of national suffering to be tapped and tapped again to mobilise loyalty, maintain order, and achieve a semblance of energy to counter the growing national apathy and loss of popular resilience of spirit.'[427] The same reasons could be found to explain Putin's extensive use of Great Patriotic War mythology in contemporary Russia.[428]

From 1965 until the 1980s the USSR mobilised an over-arching comprehensive cult of the Great Patriotic War. The full cult included a panoply of saints, sacred relics, and rigid master narrative of the war.'[429] During Putin's upbringing the Breznevite system militarised Soviet youth 'to an extraordinary degree'[430] within the Communist Party, All-Union Pioneer Organisation, the *Komsomol (Communist Youth League)*, and paramilitary DOSAFF (Voluntary Society For Cooperation with the Army, Air Force and Navy). They toured battle sites and war museums, met veterans, organised school exhibitions and commemorative evenings, attended war games and weapons study camps, participated in rituals with honour guards, took oaths, marched in uniforms and waved flags. Much of this cult 'exuded a profound falseness' where the history of the Great Patriotic War 'had been purposively manipulated, twisted, and tin-selled over to serve the political needs of those who ran the country.'[431] Ideo-logical castigation of Ukrainian nationalists became intricately tied to the Soviet (and today Russian) cult of the Great Patriotic War. Praise for Generalissimo Stalin and the cult of the Great Patriotic War portrayed the 1930s not as a decade of mass crimes but lauds it as one where industrialisation prepared the Soviet state for victory which saved Europe from 'fascism.' Stalin is described in current Russian school textbooks as an 'effective manager.'[432]

The Soviet Ukrainian Communist Party and KGB linked 'Ukrainian bourgeois nationalism' with fascism and World War II Nazi collaborators, Ukrainian émigrés, and fifth columnist anti-communists act with the support of Western intelligence agencies seeking to destroy the Soviet Union. From the late 1960s through to the late 1980s the Soviet Communist Party and KGB increasingly viewed support for the Ukrainian language and culture by dissi-dents and the political opposition as manifestations of 'Ukrainian nationalism.' Being publicly proud of speaking Ukrainian would lead the KGB to view a person suspiciously as an ideological subversive. Nationalist activist Anatoliy Lupynis recounted how the KGB had asked him during an interrogation 'Why do you converse exclusively in Ukrainian? What prompted you, one who had been speaking Russian during the first three years at the institute, to start speak-ing Ukrainian? Are you not aware that the official language of our country is Russian and that in the future all nations will speak Russian? Why did you grow a moustache?'[433] Bizarrely, we can only conclude that not only speaking Ukrain-ian but also growing a Cossack handlebar moustache had become a sign of 'bourgeois nationalism' in the eyes of the Soviet KGB. Fast forward 5 decades to the separatist Donbas where one could be detained for speaking Ukrainian, waving a Ukrainian flag and attending Euromaidan and pro-unity rallies.[434]

Contemporary derogatory views and stereotypes of the Ukrainian lan-guage, culture and history by the Party of Regions, KPU, Donbas separatists and Russian leaders has its origins in the Brezhnev 'era of stagnation.' Motyl pointed out that 'a frequent refrain in Ukrainian dissident writings was the com-plaint that fellow citizens would sneer at them when they spoke Ukrainian and tell them to speak 'human'—namely Russian.'[435] Such views have left an indel-ible imprint and in spring 2014, Ukrainian journalists who travelled to the Cri-mea and Donetsk found that using the Ukrainian language made them auto-matically suspect as supporters of the Euromaidan and 'Western Ukrainian Banderites.'[436] This tradition stretches back to the 1960s and 1970s in Soviet ideological denunciations of the Ukrainian language as a 'Bandera-ite tongue.'[437] A Luhansk resident told of his preference for joining Russia over 'fascist Kyiv,' one reason being that 'I don't speak the *telyacha mova (calf's language)*;' that is, Ukrainian.[438] Two decades into Ukrainian independent statehood, Anna Fournier found that Kyiv school students remained reluctant to speak Ukrainian in class for fear of appearing to be too 'nationalist.'[439]

Although far larger numbers of Russians volunteered for military service in Nazi military forces during World War II, the Soviet Communist Party and KGB did not unleash ideological tirades against émigré Russians and accusing them of collaboration with the Nazis. The Russian émigré NTS had grown out of the collaborationist Vlasov movement but émigré Russians were not targeted by the Soviet regime because they never constituted a separatist threat to the territorial integrity of the USSR. Russians were not separatist nationalists and had never sought to secede from the USSR and in August 1991 the Russian SFSR did not declare independence. Meanwhile, the privileged status of the Russian language and culture meant that Russian dissidents and anti-Communist émigrés had few grounds to complain about national discrimination. Russians opposed to the Soviet regime were therefore never accused of 'bourgeois nationalism' because Russians (similar to the English in the United Kingdom) did not seek a separate state. The Russian SFSR declared sovereignty in June 1990 and celebrates 'independence day' (Russia Day) based on this anniversary.[440] Ukraine declared sovereignty in July 1990 and independence in August 1991 and celebrates independence day on 24 August. Russian forces invaded eastern Ukraine at Ilovaysk and Novoazovsk on 24 August 2014, a coincidence of an important Ukrainian anniversary and Russian action taking place on the same day that has been repeated on more than one occasion (see Table 3.1).

**Table 3.1. Coincidence or Planned Insult? Significant Dates in Russia's War Against Ukraine**

| Date | Historical Significance | Modern Policies |
| --- | --- | --- |
| 21 November 2013 | Anniversary of the 2004 Orange Revolution celebrated as 'Freedom Day' (2006-2011) until the holiday was abolished by | Government decision to not sign the EU Association Agreement |

|  | Yanukovych |  |
|---|---|---|
| 22 January 2014 | Ukrainian independence day (1918) | First protesters murdered on the Euromaidan |
| 26 May 2014 | Ukrainian presidential elections | Russian forces attack Donetsk airport |
| 24 August 2014 | Ukrainian independence day (1991) | Russian invasion of Ukraine at Ilovaysk and Novoazovsk |
| 22 January 2015 | Ukrainian independence day (1918) | Russian offensive at Donetsk airport and Debaltseve |

The Soviet regime spent a large amount of resources condemning 'bourgeois nationalism' at home and abroad through to the late 1980s; indeed, some of the most vociferous tirades against Ukrainian émigrés were in the 1980s to assist with the international hunt for 'war criminals' in Canada, the UK and US. In 1960, the Soviet Union established the KGB-controlled Society for Cultural Relations with Ukrainians Abroad (commonly known as Tovarystvo Ukrayiny [The Ukrainian Society]) that specialised in attacks on Ukrainian 'nationalist' émigrés. Similar societies were established for Lithuanians, Latvians, and Estonians — but not for Russians. Tovarystvo Ukrayiny's two weekly newspapers *Visti z Ukrayiny* and its English-language equivalent *News from Ukraine*, both only available outside the USSR, became a major source of disinformation and accusations against individual members of the Ukrainian diaspora who were depicted as 'Nazi collaborators.' The newspapers contained information about trials of Ukrainian 'nationalists' in the USSR and analysis of the allegedly perfidious ways in which Ukrainian émigré organisations were seeking to undermine Soviet power with the support of Western intelligence through their local 'puppets.' The KGB specialised in linking 'nationalist' émigrés with Ukrainian dissidents and cultural activists in order to buttress their claim they were not authentic home grown movements but inspired by outside 'Nazi war criminals' and Western intelligence agencies. Linking home grown groups to Western-funded centres continues in Russian and Belarusian legislation that describes NGOs as 'foreign agents.' The Party of Regions and KPU failed to receive sufficient parliamentary support to adopt similar legislation in 2003-2004 in Ukraine.

## UKRAINOPHOBIA AND RE-STALINISATION IN PUTIN'S RUSSIA

Russian leaders who are nostalgic for the Soviet Union and Stalin's leadership are also believers of Russians and Ukrainians as one people (a view that is at odds with the Soviet recognition of Ukrainians as a separate people). Putin repeatedly says there are no differences between Ukrainians and Russians who are one people (*odin narod*).[441] Chauvinistic views that today are commonplace in the Russian leadership have received barely any analysis in Western scholarly studies of the Ukraine-Russia crisis.

The 'friendship of peoples' mythology formulated by Soviet nationalities policies propagandised this as 'a kind of supranational imagined community for the multi-ethnic Soviet people'[442] forged by Russia and which had existed for centuries. Such mythology ruled out objective appraisals of Ukrainian-Russian relations because it could not adequately deal with military conflicts between both countries, as in 1709 and 1917-1920, or Ukraine's cultural denationalisation and massive crimes against humanity. A history of Ukrainian-Russian relations therefore written from the viewpoint of 'friendship of peoples' cannot be classified as scholarly work because it implicitly glosses over problem areas where Ukraine and Russia were in conflict or when Russia adopted anti-Ukrainian policies.

A second contradiction lies in how Russia has to deal with uncomfortable facts on the ground that existed earlier but have changed since 2014. If Ukrainians and Russians are 'fraternal peoples' why do only a minority of Ukrainians support their country joining the CIS Customs Union and Eurasian Union? Are these uninterested Ukrainians really all 'fascist' because they, especially after the annexation of the Crimea and hybrid war in eastern Ukraine, do not want to be part of the *Russkiy Mir*? Ukrainians who seek independence from Russia are depicted as 'pro-fascist' and 'Russophobes.'[443] If such a large number of Ukrainians are indeed 'fascist' led by Euromaidan leaders brought to power through a 'Nazi coup d'état' why did so few of them vote for nationalist candidates and parties in the presidential and parliamentary elections held in 2014?[444] In the 2014 elections, Ukraine's extreme right received a third of the vote that it had received 3 years earlier. The *Svoboda* nationalist party has only once entered parliament and this was during Yanukovych's, not Yushchenko's or Poroshenko's, presidency. *Pravyy Sektor*, which is routinely demonised in the Russian media, has never been elected to the Ukrainian parliament. *Svoboda* and *Pravyy Sektor* are 'conservative nationalists' rather than fascist or Nazi parties.[445]

The greatest concentration of Nazis and fascists in the Donbas come from Russian nationalist groups such as RNE[446] and from European fascist groups. Russian nationalist volunteers deflect accusations they are Nazis, claiming swastika tattoos on their arms are 'ancient Slavic symbols.'[447] One anti-Semitic Russian Nazi fighting in the Donbas had a tattoo of Hitler on his arm.[448] Russian bona fide fascists travel to the Donbas to fight Russian-speaking Ukrainian 'fascists' in the army and National Guard. Aleksandr Kravtsov, one of the leaders of the separatist Luhansk Young Guard who had close ties to the Progressive Socialist party, posted on his *Facebook* and *VKontakte* pages 'neo-Nazi and pagan symbols' that are often taken 'from the website of the "Slavic Union", a neo-Nazi organisation.'[449] In the twentieth century the major atrocities committed in the Crimea were undertaken by Russia in the 1920s and 1944, not by mythical 'Ukrainian nationalists.' The Party of Regions, KPU and practically all Russian political parties, especially nationalists and communists support Stalin's charge of 'Nazi collaboration' used to justify his deportation in 1944 of Crimean Tatars to Central Asia. The annual May commemoration by Tatars of their deportation has been banned since Russia's annexation of the Crimea.[450]

Misconstrued Soviet and Russian mythology of 'friendship of peoples' has led to convoluted policies. Putin mistakenly told the US president of the large number of 'Russians' living in Ukraine by conflating Russian speakers and ethnic Russians to arrive at the figure of 'seventeen million.' Putin thereby erroneous claimed southern Ukraine is populated only by 'Russians.'[451] Russian speakers in Ukraine are not the same as ethnic Russians and not all ethnic Russians and Russian speakers support Putin, *NovoRossiya* or the *Russkiy Mir*.

With so many Russian speakers supporting Kyiv it would be therefore wrong to define the Donbas conflict as a 'civil war' between Ukrainian and Russian speakers but 'in reality, a Frankenstein-like conflict, created by the Russian government artificially and given life by the brute external shock of military force and invasion' with the GRU 'choreographing the takeover of eastern Ukraine.'[452] The conflict is more akin to a clash between competing Ukrainian/European and *Russkiy Mir* civilisational worlds[453] that Shulman[454] had earlier described as competition between 'ethnic Ukrainian' and 'east Slavic' identities.[455] 'East Slavic' herein incorporates the blending of ethnic and imperial Russian and Soviet identities. Ukrainians and Russians with Soviet nostalgia and those 'who wish the empire still stood' support the Donbas separatists.

Meanwhile, 'those who can no longer bear its lingering influence' have opposed them.[456]

## THE BATTLE OVER HISTORY

Soviet and Russian ideological tirades against 'Ukrainian nationalism' go together with glorification of Stalin. Contemporary Russian leaders fundamentally disagree with Ukraine's de-communisation,[457] commemoration of the *holodomor* as a major Soviet crime and genocide committed against the Ukrainian peoples and particularly rehabilitation of Ukrainian nationalist groups. In 2009-2012, Russian President Medvedev headed a Presidential Commission of the Russian Federation to Counter Attempts to Falsify History to the Detriment of Russia's Interests which would 'defend Russia against falsifiers of history and those who would deny Soviet contributions to the victory in World War II.'[458] In August 2009, Medvedev sent an 'address' (rather than a friendlier open letter) to President Yushchenko that claimed:

'Russian-Ukrainian relations have been further tested as a result of your administration's willingness to engage in historical revisionism, its heroisation of Nazi collaborators, exaltation of the role played by radical nationalists, and imposition among the international community of a nationalistic interpretation of the mass famine of 1932-1933 in the USSR, calling it the "genocide of the Ukrainian people."'[459]

Russia's campaign against the Ukrainian interpretation of the *holodomor* was so petty it included works by the highly respected Raphael Lemkin who coined the term 'genocide' on the Federal List of Extremist Materials. Yanukovych implemented Russia's demands to refrain from the Ukrainian position on the *holodomor* promoted by his three predecessors and took on board the Russian view of the 1933 famine as affecting the entire USSR. In Russian occupied Crimea, the very term *holodomor* has been banned and books on the famine have been classified as 'extremist.'

Rehabilitation of Stalin has led Putin to defend the Molotov-Ribbentrop Pact and blame Poland for having brought upon itself Nazi Germany's invasion when it earlier collaborated with the Nazis in the carve up of Czechoslovakia. Putin has alleged the USSR did not invade Poland in 1939 but merely took back lost territory, an argument also made in support of Russia's annexation of the Crimea. Putin never seemingly knows when to stop claiming that the holocaust was carried out by the Poles together with the Nazis.

Putin and Medvedev tread difficult ground when seeking to monopolise the Soviet victory in World War II. Putin claimed that Russia would have won the war even without Soviet Ukrainian troops, a curious claim when 8-10 million Ukrainians died and two million were slave labourers in Germany (including this author's father). The majority of the battles fought in the USSR were conducted in Soviet Ukraine and there were four Ukrainian military fronts, 2,072 Ukrainians were awarded 'Hero of the Soviet Union' and Ukrainian soldiers liberated Auschwitz and raised the victory flag in Berlin. In 2015, Poland justified its unwillingness to invite Putin to the commemoration of the liberation of Auschwitz by claiming it had been Ukrainian troops who had been its liberators, not Russians. The Polish Senate refused to jointly condemn nationalist groups in Ukraine whose popularity was growing, it pointed out, because of Russian policies. Another bone of contention has been Yushchenko and Poroshenko's preference for following Europe's example in celebrating 8 May as the end of World War II, not 9 May when the USSR celebrated the victory of the Great Patriotic War. In May 2015, Ukrainian television showed advertisements uniting Soviet veterans who had defended Soviet Ukraine with young soldiers who were defending Ukraine today. Russia's Victory Day has been 'packaged into patriotic-themed consumer entertainment.'[460]

## UKRAINOPHOBIA IN CONTEMPORARY UKRAINE
## YANUKOVYCH'S DONBAS AND THE CRIMEA

Soviet anti-nationalism was revived by post-Soviet Ukrainian leaders in the 2002 and 2004 elections in response to the new threat from Yushchenko and Our Ukraine who were dubbed as *'Nashism'* (from *Nasha Ukrayina [Our Ukraine]*) that was purposefully similar sounding to Nazism. Soviet style 'anti-fascist' labels against the opposition were revived in the 2004 elections[461] when an anti-American campaign was directed against opposition candidate Yushchenko.[462] Ukrainophobia did not therefore re-appear in 2013-2014 because the ideas, identity and chauvinism underlining it have deeper historical roots in Russia and the USSR. Putin adviser Glazyev described Ukraine led by eastern Ukrainian President Kuchma and Prime Minister Yanukovych as run by 'followers of Mazepa and Bandera.'[463]

During the 2004 elections, secret instructions sent to the media and regional governors from the presidential administration advised them to play up the threat of Yushchenko coming to power with the help of 'nationalists, oligarchs, and extremists.'[464] In October 2003, when Our Ukraine was to hold a congress in Donetsk, billboards were put up showing Yushchenko giving a Nazi salute. Television programmes funded by the Party of Regions integrated World War II Nazi parades with Yushchenko's election campaign. The Donetsk authorities depicted Yushchenko as a 'nationalist monster,' 'fascist' and 'Nazi,' Ukrainian writer Yuriy Andrukhovych recalled. In keeping with its Russian nationalist credentials the Russia bloc protested against the rehabilitation of Ukrainian nationalist groups as a 'provocation of ultra-right nationalist and extremist forces.'[465] The impact of 'anti-fascist (Yushchenko)' propaganda and fabrications in the 2004 elections could be seen in the fear of a pensioner who said 'If Yushchenko wins, the Nazis will return. I was in the west of Ukraine recently and saw columns of foreign troops, fascists. If war comes, I will fight until the last cartridge.'[466]

The destruction and defacing of monuments has a far greater track record in eastern than in western Ukraine. Ukrainian flags could be burnt prior to, or during, Ukrainian national holidays. 'Negative identity' in the Crimea and Donbas equating Kyiv with 'fascism' in the Orange Revolution and Euromaidan drew on conservative Russian Orthodox values, the cult of the Great Patriotic War, defence of Russian language and culture, mythology of the Donbas 'feeding Ukraine' and anti-Western and anti-American xenophobia. The Orange Revolution gave Russian commentators an early opportunity to link Ukrainian nationalism with Western conspiracies and colour revolutions. A Russian commentator said that the origins of the Orange Revolution should be traced further back than the US to Bandera's 'blueprint, the Prospects of a National Revolution.' If you compare the Orange Revolution and Bandera's text 'they match each other by 70 percent.'[467]

The growth of Russian nationalism and promotion of eastern Slavic Orthodox civilisation within the *Russkiy Mir* meant 'the rhetoric of the Kremlin was more or less congruent with the identity politics of the Party of Regions.'[468] Two of the most vociferous leaders of the anti-nationalist campaigns were Vadym Kolesnichenko and Minister of Education Dmytro Tabachnyk who began campaigning against Ukrainian nationalist leaders immediately after Yushchenko was elected president. Party of Regions deputy Kolesnichenko established a centre to investigate Nazi war criminals in Ukraine and an International Anti-Fascist Front, mirroring the World Without Fascism organisation established in Russia. Soviet Russian nationalist and homophobe[469] Kolesnichenko, co-author of the 2012 law on languages, demanded during the Euromaidan that 'neo-Nazis should be punished.' *Svoboda* and the opposition allegedly used 'extremist' and 'xenophobic' rhetoric calling for violence that tears apart Ukraine's national unity and incites hatred through the use of 'Nazi ideology.'[470]

Tabachnyk described the Yushchenko administration as 'fascism on the march' in a phrase that could have been taken from any Communist Party ideological manual. During Yushchenko's presidency, Tabachnyk, drawing on Soviet ideological propaganda, co-authored a book with a member of the KPU warning of the dangers of 'fascism' in Ukraine, a term which he applied to all supporters of the Orange Revolution.[471] Tabachnyk's new concept for school textbooks revived Soviet views on Ukrainian nationalists as 'murderers' and 'Nazi collaborators.' Tabachnyk forcibly asserted that 'Stepan Bandera and Roman Shukhevych will remain in history as nationalists, and organisers of mass murder and they will forever be stained by the brush of collaborationism.'[472]

'Anti-fascist' rhetoric was used extensively by the Party of Regions in opposition (2005–2010) and in power (2006-2007, 2010–2014) against the democratic and nationalist opposition. The Party of Regions had as its central concern how to manipulate and ensure Yanukovych's re-election in the 2015 elections:

1.  *Batkivshchyna* were restricted in their ability to fight elections through court decisions, bribing of parliamentary deputies to switch sides and the jailing of Tymoshenko to remove her from the 2015 and 2020 presidential and 2017 parliamentary elections.

2.  Klitschko and UDAR were co-opted by the gas lobby within the Azarov government where Poroshenko, a future ally of Klitschko, was a cabinet member.

3.  Oleh Tyahnybok and *Svoboda* were supported financially and given widespread access to television (especially *Inter* which is owned by the gas lobby). Yatsenyuk had been similarly courted in the 2010 elections when he was the moderate alternative to Tymoshenko. *Svoboda* thus entered parliament in 2012 with ten percent of the vote and aligned with UDAR and *Batkivshchyna*. The party's election in 2012, and earlier in local elections in 2009-2010, 'only fuels suspicion that covert support may have been given to *Svoboda*.'[473] The 'centrist' and 'pro-European' Yanukovych was to enter the second round of the 2015 elections against the 'fascist' Tyahnybok in a re-run of Ukraine's 1999 and Russia's 1996 elections when the incumbent was pitched against an extremist, that time on the far left. If the Euromaidan had not taken place

and the 'anti-fascist' scenario had been set in motion, Ukraine's democratic opposition would have faced a stark choice whether to support Tyahnybok or vote against both candidates, as some voters had done in the 2010 elections.

Vitriolic Party of Regions rhetoric was instrumental in raising the political temperature ahead of the Euromaidan and this contributed to the vicious conflict that followed. The following discourse was typically drawn upon in Party of Regions statements and publications:[474]

- 'fascist' fighters.
- atrocities and terror.
- political extremists.
- thugs, not people.
- brutality.
- crime, enmity and hatred.
- violence, chaos and riots.
- political terrorism.
- neo-Nazism, neo-fascism, fascists.
- To Europe without fascists!"

The Party of Regions statement issued during the 'anti-fascist' rallies in May 2013 were typical of the vitriol that was later spewed from Russian television. Everybody who opposed the Party of Regions was a 'fascist.'[475] Russian television which is widely viewed in the Donbas and Crimea went into overdrive in 2013-2014 in its Ukrainophobia blaming Ukrainian forces for all of the artillery and rocket fire damage to apartment buildings. A Ukrainian military officer witnessed separatists bombing civilian buildings and then showing up within minutes with Russian television crews 'to rescue people.'[476] The shelling of a trolleybus by separatists killing 13 civilians was blamed upon Ukrainian forces. When Ukrainian prisoners were brought to the scene and humiliated, Zakharchenko said 'I could not shoot them all unfortunately.'[477] Residents of the Donbas who receive their news from only Russian and DNR television channels (*NovoRossiya*, *Opora*) believed Russian propaganda that furthered their alienation from and hatred of the Ukrainian state.

The Party of Regions claimed for itself the monopoly of integrating Ukraine into Europe, a political party that had nothing in common with European values. Using Soviet era language, it described the opposition as 'radical political forces' who 'adhere to the principles of Nazi ideology' by 'promoting and inciting ethnic and inter-religious animosity' through 'destructive and provocative' actions. The Party of Regions called upon Ukrainians to remain vigilant against the 'revival of fascism' and warned that the opposition was colluding with 'aggressive nationalists' and 'becoming actually the accomplices of Ukrainian neo-Nazis.' This ideology was 'racist, anti-Semitic and xenophobic' and 'incompatible with the fundamental principles of the EU.' The Party of Regions called upon the EU to condemn Ukrainian politicians whose actions contributed to the 'revival of Nazism in Ukraine' and ended with the slogan 'Fascism will not succeed in Ukraine!'[478]

This vitriolic rhetoric was used in the build up to the launch of the 2015 presidential election campaign. In late October 2013, a month before the Euromaidan protests erupted, the Party of Regions commemorated the 69th anniversary of the liberation of Ukraine from the Nazis where – similar to Russia – past victories over Nazism were recalled in the battle against contemporary 'fascism' (i.e. the pro-Western opposition).

Violence against pro-Ukrainian activists in the Donbas was systematic because this was one of two regions where Russian chauvinists equated allegiance to Ukrainian national symbols and colours with 'fascism.' Soviet propaganda had linked Ukrainian national symbols, the blue and yellow flag and *tryzub* with 'fascism' and such stereotypes were revived in Putin's Russia. In the Donbas, years of attacks on 'fascists' by the KPU and Party of Regions culminated in 2014 in primitive stereotyping of Ukrainian patriots and Euromaidan supporters. Supporting the territorial unity of Ukraine was 'depicted as a sign of intolerance and nationalism' and it was dangerous to carry Ukrainian national symbols. Speaking in Ukrainian or carrying the national flag became a sign of 'fascism.'[479]

In November 2014, Russia's Supreme Court banned Ukrainian nationalist groups *Pravyy Sektor*, UNA-UNSO (Ukrainian National Assembly-Ukrainian People's Self Defence), and *Tryzub* in a country where they are not active. The Russian State Duma banned 'Bandera-ite' symbols that allegedly dominated the Euromaidan and were later used in the Donbas conflict because its supporters had called for 'genocide, in particular, against the Russian people.'

During the Euromaidan and Russia's hybrid war, 'It has become open hunting season for us, one Ukrainian activist said in Donetsk'[480] During the Euromaidan, vigilantes were coordinated by Andriy Kluyev, then secretary of

RNBO (National Security and Defence Council), trained on Ministry of Interior premises and led on the ground by the youth wing of the Party of Regions. Dressed in their customary track suits and often the *bratky (brothers)* of organised crime, they were used as stewards during 'anti-fascist' parades and for violent attacks against journalists and opposition activists.[481]These attacks brought out the irony of the slogan 'To Europe without fascists!'

During the Russian occupation of western Donetsk *oblast* in April-June 2014, Ukrainian speaking activists were targeted for abduction, torture and murder. The population of Slovyansk were advised to tell the *narodni druzhyny (people's volunteers)* about all suspicious people 'especially those who are speaking in Ukrainian.'[482] UDAR, *Svoboda* and *Batkivshchyna* parties were banned during the brief Russian occupation and Ukrainian political parties continue to be outlawed in the DNR and LNR. Prime Minister Zakharchenko has agreed to hold local elections but without the participation of Ukrainian parties. Residents of the DNR and LNR holding 'pro-Ukrainian' views are classified as 'spies' and 'terrorists.'[483]

Widespread Ukrainophobia and chauvinism in the Donbas and Crimea represented real vestiges of fascism. In the Crimea and DNR and LNR, the Russian occupation authorities and separatists have undertaken ethnic cleansing of Ukrainian and Tatar language, culture and history. A report by the Congress of National Communities of Ukraine, that includes Jewish organisations grouped in the Association of Jewish Organisations and Communities of Ukraine (VAAD), found that the only region where xenophobia had grown since 2014 was in the Crimea.[484] By 2015 there were two Donetsk Universities, one in Donetsk and another in exile in Vinnytsa – just as there are two parts of the Donbas with one controlled by Kyiv and another by Moscow. Dean of Donetsk National University Sergey Baryshnikov, who was appointed by the DNR, has long been associated with Ukrainophobic and chauvinistic views. In May 2015, a plaque to Ukrainian dissident Vasyl Stus, which had been unveiled in 2001 by Donetsk Governor Yanukovych, was destroyed by the DNR and replaced with a monument to Soviet secret agent Nikolay Kuznetsov. Stus was born in Vinnytsa but he studied in Donetsk in 1954-1959. Although Stus is no longer honoured in the Donetsk branch of the National University, the re-located University based now in his birthplace has been renamed after him. Stus died in the Soviet Gulag in 1985 just as Gorbachev was coming to power.

Anti-fascist rhetoric and playing the Jewish question was central to Yanukovych's preparations for the 2015 presidential elections.[485] Manipulation of anti-fascism was organically tied to a return to Soviet propaganda and myths about the Great Patriotic War and copying Russia's glorification of the 9 May celebration of the end of the war. An early experiment in fanning conflict was the presence of Russian nationalists wearing St. George ribbons in Lviv on 9 May 2011 which culminated in clashes with nationalists and the wounding of a *Svoboda* supporter.[486]

Anti-fascist rallies were organised throughout Ukraine in May 2013 by RNBO Secretary Kluyev and ideologically driven by Russian political technologists.[487] Rallies against 'fascists' and 'extremists' with slogans such as 'Fascism will not succeed!', 'Stop Extremism!' and 'Stop the Maidan!' continued through to and during the Euromaidan.[488] President Yanukovych and Prime Minister Azarov used similar language to Putin in describing the protesters as 'extremist forces' and 'Nazis, extremists and criminals.'[489]

The danger of fanning artificial 'anti-fascism' and claims of anti-Semitism was brought out in a statement issued by the VAAD and the Congress of National Communities. The two large Jewish organisations described the strategy as artificially dividing society and radicalising both sides with the aim of discrediting the entire opposition as 'fascists' and 'political extremists' in order to distract attention from the opposition's 'Arise Ukraine!' rallies. State employees were forced to join 'anti-fascist' rallies where students and pensioners were paid 100 *hryvnya* ($12) per day.[490] 'Anti-fascist' demonstrations were aimed exclusively at discrediting the political opposition by 'linking associations between historical fascism and the party *Svoboda* as well as all parties in opposition to the current regime.' They warned the organisers of the 'antifascist' political technology that they would bear responsibility for provocations and escalation in tensions, a poignant argument just head of the conflict in the Donbas.[491]

The four-year 'anti-fascist' struggle under Yanukovych, backed by incessant Russian television propaganda and covert operations, laid the ground for the Donbas conflict. In 2013, Lyudmilla Parasivka warned that the 'anti-fascist' discourse and other anti-Ukrainian activities of the Yanukovych regime and Party of Regions will lead to a bad ending because its widespread use would eventually come to be believed. The Party of Regions had nothing else to use in the 2015 elections.[492]

During Yanukovych's presidency a war of monuments was waged by both sides (the Party of Regions and Ukrainian patriots and nationalists). Between 2010-2012, three historic-cultural monuments were destroyed or damaged and in 2013 a monument to national heroes was severely damaged. Monuments of OUN leaders were attacked in Ukraine and abroad through to 2014-2015. Ukrainian nationalists responded by attacking Soviet monuments, including the first attempt at removing the Lenin monument in Kyiv (which was finally removed in December 2013).[493]

The tensions, violence and bitterness that were widely seen in 2014 did not appear out of nowhere but had been nurtured by decades of Soviet propaganda and at least a decade of prior rhetoric during election campaigns and published in Party of Regions literature. Warnings against the dangers of using such rhetoric had been made many years prior to the Euromaidan and Russian Spring.

## CONCLUSIONS

Russian campaigns against manifestations of different strands of Ukrainian nationalism have taken place since the early eighteenth century and became more pronounced and vociferous when the Russian state was in crisis in the early twentieth century, the Russian civil war, World War II, during the Cold War and the Brezhnev 'era of stagnation' and especially during the current Ukraine-Russia crisis. The Soviet and Russian concept of 'friendship of peoples' is premised on Russians and Ukrainians living in the same state or at a minimum within the same sphere of influence. This thoroughly primordial ethnic concept ignores the modern day reality of countries with the same languages nevertheless living in separate independent states. Scotland, Ireland and England speak English. Austria, parts of Switzerland and Germany speak German. Australia, New Zealand, the US, most of Canada and India, where English has become the lingua franca, all speak English. Should all central and South America except Brazil be united into one state because they speak the Spanish language? This would logically follow from Soviet and Russian doctrines of 'friendship of peoples.'

There are five components to Russian and Soviet anti-(Ukrainian) nationalist campaigns and re-Stalinisation. The first is these campaigns intensify during authoritarian and counterrevolutionary periods, such as in response to the Rose, Orange and Euromaidan Revolutions. Secondly, Russian and Soviet leaders behind the Ukrainophobic campaigns are allied to Russian great power nationalists, Stalinists and anti-Western xenophobes. Under Soviet and Russian leaders Brezhnev and Putin anti-(Ukrainian) nationalist campaigns have taken place at the same time as revivals of the mythology surrounding the Great Patriotic War and re-Stalinisation of the Soviet and Russian states. Thirdly, Ukrainian identity and autonomy have been more acceptable to Russian leaders during periods of liberalisation in the 1920s, mid 1950s to mid-1960s, and second half of the 1980s and 1990s. But, these have covered only a minority of Soviet history which was dominated by Stalin and Brezhnev for the majority of the USSR's 69 years of existence. Fourthly, Soviet and Russian nationalists and re-Stalinisers view Ukrainians in simplistic categories as compliant good Ukrainians or Russophobic 'bourgeois nationalists' and 'fascists' backed by foreign powers intent on weakening Russia.

Fifthly, Putin and Russian re-Stalinisers will remain increasingly frustrated because of their own undoing of the 'fraternal brotherhood' of Russians and Ukrainians for which they will deflect blame on to Western governments and foreign conspiracies. Putin has shattered illusions among some Russophone Ukrainians who had believed in such myths but came to view Russia's annexation of the Crimea as a stab in the back when Ukraine was down. Putin's military campaign against Ukraine has reduced feelings of 'fraternal brotherhood' with Russians living in the Russian Federation and thereby has contributed to Ukrainian nation building. Putin, in seeking to build a *Russkiy Mir,* has in fact promoted the opposite. Ukraine's European integration and history may come to show that Putin may have done more for Ukrainian nation building than his hated nemesis Bandera.

Ukrainianophobia and anti-Semitism may at first glance seem to be unrelated but this would be untrue. They germinate in the same roots of chauvinism, racism and xenophobia that has historically been central to Russian and Soviet great power nationalism. Ukrainianophobia and anti-Semitism are in fact the flip sides of the same Russian imperial national identity, as readers will come to understand in the next chapter.

# CHAPTER 4

# ANTI-ZIONISM AND ANTI-SEMITISM

*Ukraine is in the hands of homosexuals and Jewish oligarchs.*
Aleksandr Dugin[494]

Robert Conquest writes that anti-Semitism in the Soviet Union was fanned by the same people who had been undertaking massive state repression.[495] Indeed, anti-Semitism, anti-Zionism, the revival of the cult of Stalin and mythology of the Great Patriotic War have gone hand in hand with conservative and nationalist leaders when they have been in power in the Soviet Union *and* the Russian Federation. The Soviet Union's investment in anti-Zionism lasted for a quarter of a century and 'was to provide some continuity between the old anti-Semitism and the new.'[496]

Anti-Semitism under Stalin and from the mid-1960s to mid-1980s under Soviet leaders Brezhnev and Andropov masqueraded as 'anti-Zionism' which equated Judaism with world fascism. Anti-Zionist campaigns were also unfurled in Communist Poland and elsewhere in eastern Europe in the late 1960s. Belarusian President Lukashenka, whose regimes rests on a bedrock of Soviet Belarusian nationalism, continues to propagate 'Anti-Zionist' propaganda.[497] Anti-Semitism in the DNR and LNR draws on the legacy of Soviet anti-Zionism in its attacks on Jewish leaders and oligarchs who have come to power in Kyiv in an alliance with Ukrainian 'fascists.' Two strands of Soviet ideological propaganda campaigns against 'Zionism' and Ukrainian 'bourgeois nationalism' have been integrated within the Ukrainophobic and anti-Semitic rhetoric of the Donbas separatists and their Russian nationalist allies.

## ANTI-SEMITISM AND ANTI-ZIONISM

Anti-Semitism has always been central to Russian nationalism since the nineteenth century and this remains the case to the present-day. Vasiliy Grossman wrote in his well-known *Life and Fate* that anti-Semitism appeared in many forms in Russia. Russian serfs angry at their socio-economic plight blamed the Poles and Jews, not the Tsar or the Russian Empire. The Tsarist Russian Empire and the Soviet Union discriminated where Jews could live, the choice of professions that were open to them and their access to higher education in what Victor Zaslavsky describes as 'pragmatic anti-Semitism.'[498] Stalin had wanted to deport all Jews to the Artic Circle but instead created the autonomous *oblast* of Birobidzhan close to the Chinese border. [499]

Anti-Zionism in the USSR was a code-word for anti-Semitism. In the 1920s, Stalin encouraged anti-Semitism as a means to undermine Bolshevik Jewish leaders Leon Trotsky and Grigory Zinoviev and with the campaign against internal enemies in overdrive during the Great Terror, official anti-Semitism expanded from 1937 onwards. National communists in Ukraine and elsewhere viewed this as the inevitable outcome of Stalin's adoption of National Bolshevism that resembled Soviet style fascism.[500]

In the late 1940s, anti-Semitism 'became a part of Soviet state policy' that was a 'grass-roots phenomenon but also has adherents in the state-controlled media as well.'[501] The most well-known anti-Semitism took place towards the end of Stalin's rule during the 'anti-cosmopolitan' campaign which had 'thinly veiled, though unacknowledged, anti-Semitic overtones.' Jewish intellectuals were condemned for kowtowing to the West and being rootless[502] and being behind a fake 'Doctors Plot.'

Hostility to Israel and Zionism grew in the Soviet Union in the 1950s and 1960s when the promotion of 'anti-Zionism' gave an official and controlled outlet for Russian and Pan-Slavic anti-Semitism that fanned historical stereotypes. One such stereotype was that Jews lived better than Russians. Following World War II, official anti-Semitism (anti-Zionism) encouraged Russian nationalists and National Bolsheviks to align with the Soviet regime rather than go into opposition.[503]

In the 1970s, Valeriy Emelyanov's memorandum to the central committee of the KPRF and Presidium of the USSR Supreme Soviet made six ludicrously outrageous allegations:[504]

- Zionism controls the economy and media of the West.
- All peoples in the world are slaves of Jews.
- Jews have a target of achieving world domination by the year 2, 000.
- Jews will use freemasons to achieve their goal.
- The main Jewish conspiratorial organisation is B'nai B'rith.
- The human rights organisation Amnesty International, dissident groups in the USSR, Roy Medvedev, Solzhenitsyn and Sakharov are agents of Zionists and freemasons.

Emelyanov then goes on to make two recommendations:

- The Soviet authorities should publish the works of anti-Zionists Yuriy Ivanov (author of the infamous anti-Semitic tract *Caution Zionism*), Vladimir Begun, Dmitriy Zhukov, and Evgenii Evseev.
- Anti-Zionism should be promoted through military publications, such as the *Sovetsky Voin* newspaper.

The Soviet Union endured two decades of rabid anti-Zionism from the mid-1960s to the mid-1980s during which Jews were depicted as chauvinists, aggressors, and mass murderers who sought to destroy and subjugate others, especially Russians. Jews aimed to dominate the world through their deceit, corruption and mass murder.[505] Similar tenets of anti-Semitism were to be found in Russian nationalist *samizdat* which praised the anti-Zionist campaigns promoted by the Soviet authorities. Such support for anti-Semitism was not published in Ukrainian nationalist *samvydav*. In 1979, leaflets issued by the Russian Liberation Movement wrote approvingly of the influence of anti-Zionists in the Communist Party Politburo.[506]

Following Israel's invasion of Lebanon in 1982, Zionism was linked to fascism and Nazism. The following year in April a Soviet Public Anti-Zionist Committee was established that focused on attacking anti-Semitism in the US and Israeli policies.[507] The *Znanie (Knowledge)* Society held numerous public talks where Emelyanov spewed calls for a world-wide anti-Zionist front to fight Zionists and Freemasons. The Soviet Public Anti-Zionist Committee claimed that anti-Semitism flourished in the US, especially under President Ronald Reagan but that this was not the case in the USSR where Jewish culture was allegedly flowering in the Birobidzhan autonomous *oblast* in the Russian Federation.[508] A similar reverse 'rationale' is made today when the authoritarian 'anti-fascist' Russian state cooperates and finances fascist, racist and neo-Nazi political forces.[509]

The Soviet Public Anti-Zionist Committee and Association of Soviet Lawyers published a White Book in a print run of 150,000 to unmask the ideology and practices of 'international Zionism.'[510] The White Book and other examples of anti-Zionism were strongly condemned by the National Conference on Soviet Jewry for vilifying the Jewish people, Jewish religion and the state of Israel. The 302-page 'White Book' outlined five areas:[511]

- The horrors awaiting Jews who had emigrated from the USSR.
- Ideological subversion of the USSR by Zionists.
- Collaboration of Zionists with the Nazis.
- Israel's aggression against Lebanon.
- Widespread anti-Semitism in the US.

Soviet 'anti-Zionist' discourse was similar to the rabid anti-Semitism that had been propagated by Hitler and the Nazis. But, in many ways, Soviet anti-Zionism was worse as it made utterly bizarre claims such as the Nazis were 'puppets' of the Jews who connived with one another to murder poverty stricken Jews. Zionists and Nazis allegedly collaborated during World War II and both therefore have complicity in the holocaust. Although his family is Jewish, the grandfather of Ukrainian-Canadian Alex Shprintsen was accused of praising Nazi leader Hitler and he was convicted and executed for anti-Soviet activity.[512] The twisted 'rationale' of Soviet propaganda claimed Jews became virulent anti-communists to hide the fact they were behind the Bolshevik revolution and dominated the Communist Party, a twist of the inter-war anti-Semitic slogan 'Jew-Bolshevik.'

Soviet anti-Zionism followed in the path of Western revisionists with ties to European neo-Nazi and fascist political parties who alleged that the numbers of Jews murdered in the holocaust was exaggerated. Putin's Russia has aligned itself politically and in the case of France's National Front financially, with these political forces. The USSR portrayed itself as the only obstacle able to prevent world domination by the Jewish-led West and world capitalism.[513] Russian leaders continue to believe the US is seeking world domination by 'one undisputed leader who wants to remain such -- one who assumes that everything is allowed to him, but that others only need what he allows them and what meets his own interests.' Putin said, 'Russia will never be satisfied with this kind of world order' because 'it is perfectly clear that there is an attempt to hold back our development by various means.' Putin promised to fight back: 'Some may like living in a state of semi-occupation; we will not do this.'[514]

Anti-Semitism in the USSR took on one of its most grotesque forms in the cover up and downplaying of the holocaust. New administrative documents and city maps erased Jewish culture, history and cemeteries and maps in books showing Jewish historical sights were erased from maps.[515] In post-war Soviet city plans 'it was as if the Jewish people had never existed there, although some cities had 50 percent or 60 percent Jewish populations before the war.' Jewish schools and synagogues were closed and destroyed in a systematic manner. The Nazis and the Soviets used the materials from Jewish tombstones to build roads.

One of the largest Nazi atrocities in World War II took place at Babi Yar near Kyiv. This crime was ignored by the Soviet authorities and no memorial was ever erected to commemorate the atrocity. In an article in *Literaturna Gazeta* (19 September 1961) the well known Soviet Russian writer Yevgeniy Yevtushenko called for a memorial to be unveiled at Babi Yar but his call was denounced by Soviet leader Khrushchev. In the view of the KPRS, too much focus on the holocaust would deprive the Soviet regime of the ability to inflate the numbers of civilian and military casualties that play an important role in the mythology of the Great Patriotic War.[516] The holocaust and the massive crimes committed by the Nazis against Jews would, Soviet Communist leaders claim, lead to the growth of anti-Soviet feelings and anti-Semitism. Questions might arise about the role of the NKVD in destroying the Khreshchatyk main street in Kyiv and the Pecherska Lavra monastery. More importantly, Soviet leaders were wary of the possibilities of the growth of similarities in the public eye between Soviet communism and Nazism. In contemporary Russia, both Putin and Medvedev have condemned the equating of these two totalitarian ideologies and have condemned legislation in Ukraine that seeks to remove vestiges of the Nazi and Soviet past (e.g. monuments, plaques, street names, etc.,). The European Day of Remembrance for Victims of Stalinism and Nazism, known as the Black Ribbon Day in some countries, has been observed since 2009 on 23 August as the international day of remembrance for victims of totalitarianism; namely, Nazism, fascism, Stalinism and Communism. In September 2016, a new monument was unveiled in the presence of Israeli President Reuven Rivlin.

Although a film about the crimes of Babi Yar had been made in 1981 it was only in 1987, during Gorbachev's *glasnost*, that it could be publicly shown after the lobbying of Vitaliy Korotych who had been appointed editor of *Ogonyok* magazine. In October 1991, Parliamentary Chairman Kravchuk became the first Ukrainian leader to commemorate the victims on the 50th anniversary of Babi Yar when a new monument was unveiled.[517] A small monument had been erected 2 kilometres away from Babi Yar in 1976 but its inscription made no mention of the fact that the majority of the victims were Jews.[518]

Soviet anti-Zionist pamphlets and books were no less than coded anti-Semitic attacks on Jews. Propaganda works such as Trofim Kichko's *Judaism Without Embellishment* were published in millions of copies and influenced an entire generation of Soviet people who today are in power in Russia and the DNR and LNR. Anti-Zionism was prevalent in the political directorate of the armed forces, the KGB (where Putin was an officer between 1975-1991) and strongly influenced the Russian nationalist and conservative wing of the Soviet Communist Party.[519] In the 1970s and 1980s the publication of anti-Zionist books and articles dramatically increased and 'have been accorded rapturous reviews in the mass circulation media.'[520] In addition, anti-Zionism permeated large numbers of fictional books by authors such as Ivan Shevtsov where the villains were always Jews who were portrayed as murderers.

Anti-Zionist propaganda authors Yuriy Kolesnykov, Lev Korneev and Evseev focused on the alleged collaboration of Zionists and Nazis through a conspiracy between Jews, the SS and the Gestapo. V. V. Malyshev's *Behind the Screen of the Masons*, an expose of alleged freemason conspiracies, was published in a 100,000 print run in 1984. Zionism and Apartheid were alleged to be political collaborators because modern racism emerged from the Judaic-Christian tradition where Jews are God's chosen people and freemasons are basically secular Jews.[521] The influence of Korneev, the most prolific anti-Zionist and anti-Semitic propagandist in the USSR, was extensively cited by others. His large influence was evident throughout the USSR in published works such as *Klassovaya sushchnost sionizma* (Kyiv: Politizdat Ukrayiny, 1982) and *Sovremennyi yudaizm i sionism* (Frunze: 1983) in far away Kyrgyzstan.[522] Korneev published a particularly unpleasant anti-Semitic article in the Leningrad literary monthly *Neva* in May 1982 which was denounced by liberal authors. Korneev expanded on the traditional Jewish threat to Russia and its history and culture and the exploitation by wealthy Jews of Russian and Ukrainian workers through their control of banks and resources. He also expounded on the alleged ties between Zionists and Nazis, fascists, the mafia and freemasons.[523] These themes were expanded upon in Soviet anti-Zionist literature by Elena D. Modrzhinskaya and Vladimir F. Lapsky in their book *The Poison of Zionism* which added an additional conspiracy of Jews being behind the 1968 Prague Spring. Anti-Zionist authors blamed the Jewish-controlled Reagan administration and the US military-industrial complex for the deterioration in Soviet-US relations.[524]

Soviet anti-Zionist publications claimed that Jews had only been concerned with enrichment and emigration to Palestine and they had abandoned the poorer Jews to their fate under the Nazis. The most prolific of the Soviet anti-Zionist writers also made further bizarre allegations:[525]

- The claim of 6 million Jews murdered during the holocaust was an exaggeration because the figure was inflated 2-3 times.
- Zionists should be held responsible for the deaths of Jews during the holocaust.
- The number of Slavic, Jewish and Gypsy victims would be lower if there had not been a Zionist-Nazi alliance in place.
- The claim of the destruction of Jews by the Nazis was a legend that had been concocted.

Anti-Zionist publications were not completely halted after Gorbachev came to power in 1985 because they continued to receive the support of Russian National-Bolsheviks within the KPRS, Russian Writers Union and official Soviet Russian newspapers and journals.[526] In Soviet Ukraine, Communist Party leader Shcherbytskyy, a Russophile supporter of conservative Soviet leaders, also permitted anti-Zionist literature to be published during his seventeen year rule.

Soviet anti-Zionism left an indelible imprint on Russian and Donbas uneducated workers who harboured anger at their *nachalstvo (bosses* but also understood as oligarchs, Jews, Western capitalism, and IMF). Who should they blame for their conditions? Should this be the KPRS, Jews, the West, or perhaps themselves for accepting the brutal manner in which they were treated? It was always more convenient to blame somebody else. Soviet anti-Zionist propaganda directed anger away from Soviet ruling elites towards Jews and the West while contemporary Russian xenophobia lays the blame on the West, NATO and Ukrainian 'fascists' for all of Russia's ills.

Soviet anti-Zionist propaganda portrayed the Jews as parasites who had never created anything; they were pioneers of world capitalism and at the forefront of anti-communism who harboured a burning hatred for Russian culture. In the late 1980s, the impact of Soviet Anti-Zionist propaganda could be seen in the emergence of *Pamyat*, a modern incarnation of the Black Hundred Union of the Russian People. The *Protocols of the Elders of Zion,* a forgery invented by the *Okhrana* Tsarist secret police, became the theoretical basis of *Pamyat's* ideology. *Pamyat* recycled anti-Zionist propaganda from the 1970s and first half of the 1980s and its emphasis on the global domination of Zionism as an agent of imperialism showed 'how potent a force anti-Semitism is in the USSR.'[527]

*Refuseniks (Jews emigrating from the USSR)* were condemned in the vilest of anti-Semitic slogans by Anti-Zionist propagandists. A Jewish-Russian journalist recalled in the late 1980s that the Moscow City *Komsomol* Secretary told him 'Jews will at least leave, but Ukrainians want to destroy our great land.'[528] Jews and Ukrainians were lumped together then and today as anti-Russian and anti-Soviet troublemakers in the pay of the West.

Vladimir Begun, a prominent Anti-Zionist propagandist based in the Soviet Belarusian capital city of Minsk, was typical of National Bolsheviks who saw Zionist conspiracies and creeping counter-revolution everywhere that were striving for world domination. *Pogroms* had been historically justified, Begun claimed because they were undertaken by Russians in protest at the wealth accumulated from exploitation by 'Jewish oppressors.' In 1977, Begun's *Invasion Without Arms* was published by the official Soviet Russian nationalist *Molodaya Gvardiya* published house which continued in the vein of equating Jews and fascists as the greatest threat to world peace.[529] From the title of Begun's book the paranoia was evident of who was behind Communist Party ideological denunciations of dissidents and opposition leaders being in the pay of Western secret services who were seeking to ideologically subvert the Soviet state. Similar levels of paranoia permeated legislation on 'foreign agents' adopted in Russia and Belarus that linked domestic NGOs and opposition leaders, as in Soviet times, to Western intelligence agencies.

The heyday of Soviet anti-Zionism was from the mid-1960s to the mid-1980s during the same period of myth making of the Great Patriotic War and rehabilitation of the cult of Stalin. During Brezhnev's conservative 'era of stagnation,' Russian nationalists ranted about the Jewish Bolshevik plot in official

Soviet journals.[530] In the USSR, Jews were the main enemy of Russian nationalists and Laqueur believed that this would not 'radically change in the foreseeable future.'[531] Jews then and today were, and remain perceived as carriers of 'cosmopolitanism,' supportive of globalisation and international capitalism and unable to become spiritually Russian and therefore patriots of the Russian state. Understandably, they are therefore seen as the main beneficiaries of privatisation during the 1990s and the terms 'Jews' and oligarchs are used interchangeably. Jews provided a platform for world supremacy and Jews and Freemasons infiltrated Western intellectual circles.[532]

In contemporary Russia, 'international Jewry', the Euromaidan, its oligarchic and American supporters are lumped together in the diatribes of Russian nationalists who align with both extreme leftist anti-capitalist and anti-globalising movements *and* with the European neo-Nazi and nationalist populist right.[533] The KPRF are natural allies of Russian nationalists in their condemnation of Ukraine's Euromaidan government as dominated by oligarchs and portraying its puppet master Uncle Sam with Jewish facial features. Gaddy and Hill point to the roots of this rhetoric in the conspiracy mind-sets found on the extreme left and right in Russian politics and in the anti-Semitic forgery *The Protocols of the Elders of Zion*.[534]

In contemporary Russia, anti-Semitism is to be found among the same groups as in the Tsarist Empire and post-revolutionary Russian émigrés; that is, extreme Russian nationalists, White Guard imperialists, Eurasianists, Cossacks, and radical Russian Orthodox brotherhoods. Dugin as an admirer of fascism and 'conservative revolution' has pronounced anti-Semitic views. 'Nationalists, who were giving the tone on the Maidan, said they need to have a Ukrainian as a president. As a result, they elected a Jew and not a Slav, whoever he could be,'[535] Dugin said. The ideologies of Russian nationalist and neo-Nazi groups have political influence in the DNR and LNR. The Russian Orthodox Church and its Orthodox Brotherhoods in Ukraine have pronounced xenophobic and anti-Semitic tendencies.[536]

## ANTI-SEMITISM IN THE DONBAS AND CRIMEA

Anti-Semitism has a long tradition in the Donbas although this has not been the focus attention of scholars who have over-focused on anti-Semitism in western Ukraine. Jews comprised 15-25 percent of the population of the Donbas from the 1880s and they had a similar healthy dislike for coalmines and heavy industry as did Ukrainian peasants. Jews were not integrated into employment in the coalmines and factories and therefore they were viewed as outsiders who lived apart from the proletarian masses.[537] Donbas Jews were assimilated Russian speakers, rather than Yiddish speakers, and they lived in isolation from both their Ukrainian and Russian neighbours.

Anti-Semitism has been documented in the Donbas from the late nineteenth century through to the post-war Soviet era. During the Tsarist Empire, persecution of Jews and anti-Semitism was mobilised by the Russian Orthodox Church, schools, police and the *Okhrana* secret police. Common slogans included 'At the head of the Red Army stands a Jew!' 'Soviets but no Jews!' 'Death to the Jews and Communists!' and the most well known 'Beat the Jews and save Russia!' *Pogroms* of Jews took place throughout the later part of the Tsarist era. During the Russian civil war, Bolsheviks, Whites, and Nestor Makhno's anarchists committed *Pogroms* in southern and eastern Ukraine. 'Negative sentiments towards the Soviet government were often tinged with anti-Semitism,' Kuromiya writes.[538] The anarchist leader Makhno called for the killing of army generals, Jews, landowners and communists.

The factors lying behind these *pogroms* were not only ethnic and religious. Socio-economic factors played as important a role during a period of rapid transformation when Jews were perceived as agents of modernity and uprooted life, much as they are today by Donbas separatists who see Ukraine's Jews as agents of a pro-European Euromaidan leadership. Anti-Semitism was also a product of the popular culture in the Donbas of the *narod* versus the *nachalstvo*, a tradition that continues to be found in the anti-oligarch sentiments of Donbas separatists. Jews were accused of holding senior positions and dominating the Soviet secret police, they allegedly sent fewer numbers to fight in the Soviet armed forces during the Great Patriotic War, and were behind the arrests, torture, executions and *holodomor* undertaken by the Soviet regime.[539]

Anti-Semitism influenced how disgruntled workers in the Donbas directed their anger over their working conditions and how they were treated by the *nachalstvo*. One of the first anti-Soviet opposition groups in the post-war era, the Democratic Youth of Russia and Ukraine, was launched in the Donbas with the aim of improving workers lives. It attacked Jews as 'unjust people' who lived off the work undertaken by Ukrainians and Russian workers, a refrain no different to what had been behind all anti-Semitic attacks since the late nineteenth century.[540]

Blaming the *nachaltsvo* continues to influence contemporary separatist outlooks but leads to different conclusions to those made by protesters on the Euromaidan. The former seek in a traditional manner in Russia to circumvent the *nachaltsvo boyars* by requesting the assistance of the good Tsar (i.e. Putin) to resolve their problems. As late as spring 2016, I heard villagers in Ukrainian-controlled Donbas who believed that Putin would bring back the Soviet Union and then they would (again) live happily after. Meanwhile, Euromaidan supporters did not expect the 'good Tsar' (Poroshenko) to resolve their problems and instead participated in civil society NGOs, work in think tanks, write for independent publications and seek election to parliament and local councils. Clover writing about Russians says they continue to blame 'bad boyars' and 'blissfully assumed that the omnipresent tsar simply must not be aware of them.'[541]

Jews have migrated from the Donbas since the separatists took power to seek safe havens in Ukrainian controlled territory; in other words, the region's Jews have fled from the 'anti-fascist Donbas' to 'fascist Ukraine.' Eliyahu Zilberbord, a businessman and leader of the Jewish community in Donetsk, said that 'Jews are running from the *Russkiy Mir* to hide under the wing of the fascist Kiev junta. There is nothing more to say.'[542] Zilberbord was murdered after he attempted to stop a robbery of his neighbour's house.[543]

Anti-Semitism was commonplace among Russian nationalist, chauvinistic, anti-Maidan and Pan-Slavic groups in the Donbas, Odesa and Crimea who are nostalgic for the USSR. In Odesa, anti-Semitism was prevalent in the *Rodina* Party whose leaders were integrated into the Party of Regions after the 2007 elections. A US diplomatic cable from Kyiv noted the relatively high number of anti-Semitic incidents in Odesa.[544] Anti-Semitism was also prevalent in the Party of Slavic Unity and Odesa *militia*, some of who assisted pro-Russian separatists during the April-May 2014 violent confrontations in that city. A posting on *VKontakte* by the Odesa *militia* said 'Odesa is a hero-city. And only heroes, and not kikes and money grabbers, deserve to live in this city!'[545]

## ANTI-ZIONISM AND ANTI-SEMITISM IN THE DNR AND LNR

There is a 'high level of anti-Semitism in the public discourse of the DNR-LNR' coupled with anti-Tatar xenophobia in the Crimea.[546] Ukraine's foremost expert on anti-Semitism Vyacheslav Likhachev wrote that 'anti-Semitism has long become an important component of the official ideology of the puppet regimes declared on the territory of the Donetsk and Luhansk *oblasts*, occupied by Russia.'[547] Rabbi Pinchas Vishedski described Aleksandr Kriakov, the press secretary of Gubarev, as the most famous anti-Semite in the region' while the European Association of Jewish Culture said Major General Konstantin Petrov's former Conceptual Party Unity was a 'anti-Semitic neo-pagan nationalist-Stalinist sect.' Similar to the RNE, the Conceptual Party Unity have used the Donbas conflict to revive their popularity in Russia.[548]

Anti-Semitism and xenophobia exists alongside anti-Roma and racist attacks in the DNR and LNR. In the separatist enclaves, black foreign students have been detained and their separatist jailors have compared their captives to President Obama against who Russian trolls used racist language.[549] 32 foreign students, primarily from Nigeria, have been detained, kept for long periods of time in basements and forced to undertake slave labour for the separatists.[550] In 2013, on the eve of the Ukraine-Russia crisis, there were 21 racially and ethnically motivated attacks in Ukraine and between 199 or 205 (depending on the calculations of different NGOs ) in Russia. In Russia, 25 of those who were attacked died. In Ukraine there were 20 acts of 'xenophobic vandalism' compared to 70 in Russia.[551]

Anti-Semitism in the DNR and LNR has its origins in three sources. The first is the influence of Russian nationalist, chauvinistic and imperialist groups upon the separatists. RNE leader Barkashov has propagated anti-Semitic and Ukrainophobic texts and images on *VKontakte*.[552] The second is their anti-Western xenophobic, Soviet and Pan-Slavic ideology. The third important source of anti-Semitism comes from former supporters of the KPU and the Party of Regions who support 'order,' 'stability' and economic growth over democratic freedoms which surveys show is a predictor of anti-Jewish sentiments.[553]

Igor Plotnitsky and Zakharchenko, prime ministers of the LNR and DNR respectively, believe the Euromaidan is a 'Jewish Maidan' and they ridiculed the 'pathetic Jews in power in Ukraine.'[554] Zakharchenko said on *Rossiya-24* channel that Ukrainian leaders are 'miserable representatives of the great Jewish people.'[555] The anti-Semitic claims of the Kyiv government run by 'Jews' are fanned by separatist television channels.[556] Poroshenko has been labelled a 'secret Jew' whose real name is 'Valtsmen' which separatist media allege is his real name. Russian television has fanned anti-Semitism against Prime Minister Volodymyr Groysman over his Jewish roots.[557] These television channels have been 'allowed to employ fully anti-Semitic rhetoric on previous occasions.'

Tymoshenko (real Jewish name 'Kapitelman'), Yatsenyuk and even *Svoboda* leader Tyahnybok (real Jewish name 'Frontman') have similarly been attacked as Jews hiding their real identities. A poster in the LNR asked its readers 'The Jew (Savik) Shuster (a popular Ukrainian television host) should explain why Ukrainians must defend the interests of the Jew Yatsenyuk and Jewish oligarchs.'[558] DNR and LNR television propaganda has alleged that Ukraine's president, government and parliamentary coalition are run by Jews camouflaging as Ukrainians.

Boruch Gorin of the Federation of Jewish Communities of Russia when reading these bizarre allegations said 'Of course, it smells of anti-Semitism.' ADL (Anti-Defamation League) Chairman Abraham Foxman concurs, saying separatist rhetoric of a 'Jewish conspiracy' behind the anti-Yanukovych Euromaidan Revolution, which is the 'official ideology' of the DNR-LNR, is nothing less than anti-Semitism.[559]

LNR Prime Minister Plotnitsky spoke at a conference at Nekrasov State University entitled 'Contemporary Ukraine as a Fascist State of a New Type.' His speech deliberately intermingled 'Jews' ('Yevrey') with Yevro' to tie them to the Euromaidan. Plotnitsky told the conference:

'I have nothing against Valtsman, (Prime Minister) Groysman, and many others. I have nothing against the Jews as a people, as the 'Chosen People,' we can talk about this separately if we have the time. But the crux of the matter is that when we call what has happened a 'Euromaidan,' we infer that the leaders now are representatives of the people who have been harmed the most by Nazism.'

Russian nationalist volunteers from neo-Nazi political parties such as the RNE have brought their anti-Semitism to the Donbas[560] and, according to Jewish civic organisations monitoring anti-Semitism in Ukraine, these sentiments are becoming more influential in the DNR and LNR. There is a lot of evidence that 'pro-Russian extremists who terrorise eastern Ukrainian *oblasts* are rabid anti-Semites and racists.'[561] Russian nationalists with pronounced Nazi views such as Anton Rayevsky, who has a tattoo of Hitler on his arm and believes Jews are the main enemy of Russia, have fought on the side of the separatists in the Donbas.[562]

Kharkiv Partisans, which is responsible for numerous terrorist attacks in Kharkiv, is composed of members of the anti-Maidan vigilante group *Oplot*. The rhetoric of Kharkiv Partisan spokesman Filipp Ekozyants is laced with 'moody, anti-Semitic diatribes as the 'shameless yids' who have seized power in

Ukraine with the assistance of the West. In other words, his views are another replay of the old anti-Semitic claim going back to the Black Hundreds of a world Jewish conspiracy.[563]

In March 2014 in Luhansk, separatist leaders described the Euromaidan as a 'Zionist coup d'état' and pro-separatist crowds shouted back with 'Kikes!' The convoluted and bizarre manner in which this is rationalised is 'the anti-Semitic narrative of some elements of the anti-Maidan implies that Jews are 'fascists' (as in the USSR when 'Zionists' were accomplices of 'US imperialism') and 'anti-Semitism is interpreted as anti-fascism.' Separatist leaders claim they are fighting to liberate their 'Ukrainian brothers' 'from the Jews who are in power.'[564]

Key Euromaidan leaders such as Poroshenko, Yatsenyuk and Ihor Kolomoyskyy are routinely defamed as 'Kikes.' Anti-Maidan web sites have linked Jews and Ukrainian extreme nationalists with headlines screaming 'Death to Kike-Bandera' – a reference to Kolomoyskyy's iconic 'Jew-Bandera' tee-shirts and images.[565] 'Fedya,' a separatist, relieved himself on the corpse of a dead *Aydar* battalion soldier telling a journalist that 'His main argument against Ukraine is that "you are ruled by Jews.' Ilya Bogdanov, a Russian volunteer, explained his motivation for travelling to Ukraine was to help the Ukrainian people free themselves from Jewish rule and Western control.[566]

In 2014-2016, similar anti-Semitic articles, interviews and commentaries were published in mainstream Russian media, Russian nationalist publications and in media outlets in the DNR and LNR. Anti-Semitic slurs were also used during personality conflicts between separatist leaders. These publications provide us with the means to analyse contemporary Russian and Donbas separatist anti-Semitism and how it draws upon traditional Soviet anti-Zionism:[567]

1. Conflicts between separatist leaders, whether personality clashes or disputes over *biznes* and corruption, could lead to the use of anti-Semitic slurs. Aleksandr Khodakovskyy, for example, who defected from the SBU *Alpha spetsnaz* unit to the DNR and was appointed commander of the *Vostok* battalion, was accused of having being a specially trained Mossad (Israeli intelligence agency) agent planted in the DNR leadership to carry out sabotage and undermine military operations. 'Being a Jew and a citizen of Israel' he 'acted in accordance with the Torah.' Photographs of Khodakovskyy routinely had a Star of David imprinted upon his forehead.568

2. 'Jewish Bandera' is a term that first appeared in 2004 referring to Jews who supported the Orange Revolution. Jews are accused of being 'traitors' who sold themselves to the opposition and to Bandera. Russian nationalists claim that 'Jewish Banderas had captured power in Ukraine' and that the Euromaidan was a 'Jewish-Bandera coup d'état.'

3. Blaming 'freemasons' in Europe and the US for backing 'fascists' in Kyiv.

4. Fanning an image of Jewish enemies. DNR and LNR leaders in Moscow have said that the 'fifth column' in Russia is mainly composed of Jews.

5. The Jewish origins of Kyiv's Euromaidan leaders, in particular the claim that Poroshenko's real name is Valtsman. The alleged alliance of Zionists and Anti-Semites (termed the 'anti-Semitic Zionist political alliance') was created by Euromaidan leaders, most of who have 'Jewish roots.'

6. The Euromaidan was launched by Jews from Ukraine and abroad, including from Israel.

7. The revival of the Soviet anti-Zionist claim that Jews are unafraid of anti-Semitism and tolerant of Nazis if they did not hinder their business interests.

8. The Euromaidan was created by a 'radical Jewish fascist sect' led by Chabad Rabbis and Jews who plan to build a 'new Khazaria in Ukraine.'

9. A website of one of the Union of Writers of Russia published an article entitled 'Jewish Oligarchs as Hidden Engines behind the "Ukrainian Rebellion"' claiming the Euromaidan was mainly inspired by 'Jewish oligarchs' who seek to control the wealth of Ukraine. The overthrow of Yanukovych was led by Jews who wished to reclaim the property that they had lost to the Bolshevik regime.

10. The ATO was timed to coincide with Jewish festivals.

11. Describing a volunteer Jewish *Sotnya (a platoon of 100)* that was storming Donetsk: 'They are extremely bloodthirsty and they do not capture anyone but shoot everything that moves. They follow the ritual of eating the raw liver of the fighters (i.e. separatists) in order to make their rage burn before the battles.'569

12. Israeli agents were behind the fire in the Odesa Trade Union building on 2 May 2014 which was reminiscent of World War II when Jews were burnt alive.

**13.** A common theme is that volunteer battalions such as *Dnipro* and *Azov* were established with the 'money of the Jewish community of Dnipro.'

**14.** Comparisons of the Donbas and the Gaza strip are made to claim that supporters of Kolomoyskyy are also murdering Palestinians.

## ANTI-SEMITISM IN THE UKRAINIAN DIASPORA AND INDEPENDENT UKRAINE

Anti-Semitism remained on the margins of the Ukrainian diaspora until the expulsion of former Ukrainian nationalist dissidents Valentyn Moroz and Borys Terelya in the late 1970s and early 1980s. It is indicative that both quickly fell out with the émigré OUNb (Bandera wing of OUN) and launched marginal publications and organisations which had insignificant influence upon Ukrainian émigré politics. Anti-Semitism did not exist within mainstream Ukrainian dissident movements such as the *shistdesyatnyky*, national communists, the Ukrainian Helsinki Group and in the late 1980s the Ukrainian Helsinki Union and *Rukh*. Anti-Semitism was also not in evidence within underground Ukrainian Greek Catholic and nationalist groups, such as the UNF (Ukrainian National Front). The focus of these dissident groups, nationalist opposition movements and political parties was human rights, religious freedom and national liberation from Soviet and Russian rule. The enemies for these disparate groups were Communism, the Soviet state, and Russian chauvinism, not Jews. In fact, Jewish and Ukrainian dissidents closely synchronised their dissident and opposition activities and especially when they were incarcerated together in the Gulag.

The OUNb[570] dominated the Ukrainian post-war diaspora and their authoritarian ideology strove to monopolise Ukrainian communities. But, OUNb's monopolisation of the Ukrainian community became only possible in the UK where political émigrés only arrived in the late 1940s and alternative Ukrainian nationalist and democratic political groups were relatively weak. In Canada, where the first Ukrainians emigrated in the 1880s and Ukrainians dominated the Canadian Communist Party, it was always impossible for the OUNb to dominate KUK (Committee of Ukrainians in Canada). In the US, after the OUNb took control of the umbrella organisation UCCA (Ukrainian Canadian Congress Committee of America) other political and social groups left the organisation and launched their own umbrella body *UkrRada (Ukrainian Council)*.

While OUNb always remained an authoritarian, conservative nationalist organisation it did not propagate anti-Semitism in western Europe and North

America. OUNb was therefore certainly authoritarian but it was not anti-Semitic which places it (along with *Svoboda* and *Pravyy Sektor*) on the nationalist populist wing of the European political spectrum. The absence of anti-Semitism was the case even more for the other two wings of OUN, the conservative (original) wing led by Andrei Melnyk that is commonly known as OUNm[571] and the liberal and social democratic wing led by democratic Lev Rebet who led OUNz (OUN abroad). Lev Rebet and Bandera were assassinated by the KGB in Munich in 1957 and 1959 respectively. OUNz, the most democratically oriented of the three wings of OUN, was allied to zpUHVR (external representation of the Ukrainian Supreme Liberation Council) which cooperated with US intelligence since World War II in anti-Soviet activities. The US government funded the zpUHVR-led Prolog Research and Publishing Corporation from 1952 through to the disintegration of the USSR.[572] Prolog promoted Jewish-Ukrainian reconciliation and published Jewish-Ukrainian themes in books and articles in its monthly journal *Suchasnist* by Jewish-Ukrainian authors, Zionists and dissidents.

In comparison to high levels of support for nationalist and neo-Nazi political parties and movements in European states and in Russia, the nationalist right has never received widespread public support in Ukraine. In independent Ukraine, anti-Semitism has been limited and marginal, particularly when we compare the number of anti-Semitic incidents to those in Russia and in Europe. The peak of anti-Semitism in Ukraine occurred in 2005-2007 when the private university MAUP (Inter-Regional Academy of Personnel Management) received extensive foreign financing from Libya and Iran and published a large volume of anti-Semitic publications.573

Hannah Rosenthal, special envoy to monitor and combat anti-Semitism, believes anti-Semitism is not a widespread phenomenon in Ukraine: 'Ukraine's performance has also improved over the past five years. The number of anti-Semitic acts of vandalism has decreased by more than half in 2010. Moreover, due to joint pressure exerted by the Ukrainian government, NGOs and the Jewish community on MAUP, we have witnessed a sharp decline in the publication of anti-Semitic articles, proving that we can succeed if we work together.'574

A Ukrainian nationalist party was elected to the Ukrainian parliament on one occasion in 2012 when *Svoboda* received 10 percent as a protest vote against the Yanukovych regime's authoritarianism and Sovietophilia. As Table 4.1 shows, Ukraine's vote for the nationalist right is relatively low especially when compared to the support given to the nationalist populist right in Austria, Denmark, Switzerland, Poland and the Netherlands. Voters in the majority of European states give far higher levels of support and in Austria they nearly came to power in 2016. Nationalist political forces receive far greater support than in Ukraine the problem of anti-Semitism is also greater in Russia. Emigration of Jews from Russia to Israel is higher than from Ukraine, with a forty percent increase in 2015 over 2014 (compared to 16 percent for Ukraine) and 60 percent growth since 2013 (compared to less than 24 percent for Ukraine).[575]

**Table 4.1. Nationalist-Populists and Neo-Nazi Political Parties in European Parliamentary Elections**

| Country | Election Year | Vote (%) |
|---|---|---|
| Austria | 2016 | 46.2 |
| Macedonia | 2014 | 43.0 |
| Poland | 2015 | 37.6 |
| Switzerland | 2015 | 29.4 |
| Belgium (Flanders) | 2014 | 24.0 |
| Denmark | 2015 | 21.1 |
| Austria | 2013 | 20.5 |
| Hungary | 2014 | 20.2 |
| Finland | 2015 | 17.7 |
| Slovakia | 2012 | 16.68 |
| Norway | 2013 | 16.3 |
| Eire | 2016 | 13.8 |
| France | 2012 | 13.6 |
| Sweden | 2014 | 12.9 |
| Russian Federation | 2011 | 11.67* |
| Netherlands | 2012 | 10.1 |
| Bulgaria | 2013 | 7.3 |
| Germany | 2015 | 7.1 |
| Greece | 2014 | 6.99 |
| Ukraine | 2014 | 6.5** |

\* Liberal Democratic Party of Russia led by Vladimir Zhirinovsky.

\*\* Combined vote of *Svoboda* and *Pravyy Sektor*.

In the 1990s the predecessor to *Svoboda* was called the Social National Party of Ukraine (SNPU) that rallied under Nazi-like banners. In 2004, the SNPU transformed into a nationalist populist party and renamed itself Svoboda. Those who opposed the evolution of the SNPU into a nationalist populist party were mainly its Russian speaking eastern Ukrainian members who continued the traditions of the SNPU and its youth wing Patriot of Ukraine through the Social National Assembly. In 2014, some of these members and *ultras* volunteered to join the *Azov* battalion of the National Guard based in Mariupol.

Although *Svoboda* leader Tyahnybok was expelled from Our Ukraine in 2004 after he gave an anti-Semitic speech this was a rare occurrence that he did not repeat. In fact, *Svoboda* and *Pravyy Sektor* have not propagated anti-Semitism within their party political platforms and programmes. *Pravyy Sektor*, which has been subjected to a relentless barrage of Russian propaganda, has never received electoral support. One of 2 deputies that *Pravyy Sektor* elected to parliament in 2014 was in fact a Ukrainian Jew, Boryslav Bereza. Dmytro Yarosh, *Pravyy Sektor* leader in 2014-2015 has demonstrated a highly tolerant view of national minorities that would place him on the centre-right in European politics. Yarosh said that *Pravyy Sektor* are positively inclined towards those 'who join us in the fight for statehood of the Ukrainian nation' and we are 'tolerant to those who recognise our right to be masters of their own destiny in their own land.' At the same time, *Pravyy Sektor* is hostile to national minority groups who are opposed to Ukraine's right to statehood. *Pravyy Sektor* do not agree with some of the racist views found in *Svoboda* and *Azov*. The head of the *Pravyy Sektor* information office is an ethnic Russian from the Russian Federation and both *Pravyy Sektor* and *Azov* include Russian-speakers from Ukraine and Russia.

The Party of Regions is not above blame as its oligarchs provided financial assistance to and television coverage of *Svoboda*.[576] Provocations prepared by Russian intelligence services have also sought to exaggerate anti-Semitism in Ukraine. An example of this is a fraudulent November 2014 resolution by Rabbi Menachem Margolin, head of the European Jewish Association, to the EU which warned about the rise of anti-Semitism in Ukraine that cited a fake statement by *Pravyy Sektor* 'declaring war on Jews in Odesa.'[577] National democratic parties, the three largest of which were *Rukh* led by former dissident Vyacheslav Chornovil, Yushchenko's Our Ukraine and Tymoshenko's *Batkivshchyna* never exhibited anti-Semitism. Jews and Crimean Tatars have been elected to *Rukh*, Our Ukraine, *Batkivshchyna*, former Prime Minister Yatsenyuk's Popular Front and the Poroshenko bloc.

President Yushchenko focused excessively on the Ukrainian nationalist movement and *holodomor*, at the expense of contemporary politics and government, and this inflamed inter-regional relations within Ukraine, damaged relations with strategic ally Poland, and provided ammunition to Moscow for its 'fascist' accusations against pro-Western Ukrainian politicians. For Western experts and scholars who view Ukrainian nationalists as 'fascists' and anti-Semites, Yushchenko's glorification of them was immoral and a reflection of Ukraine's anti-Semitism. What has been often cited to back this allegation is the July 2008 list prepared by the SBU of 19 organisers of the *holodomor* who are mainly Jewish.

Yushchenko's zealousness in highlighting Soviet crimes against Ukrainians was reflected in the research and documentation of the Ukrainian Institute of National Memory which was established in May 2006. Unfortunately, his ignoring of Nazi crimes continued the Soviet tradition of largely side-lining the holocaust. 'Yushchenko appears to be unwilling to accept the holocaust as part of his country's history, or in any way to memorialise the holocaust for future generations of Ukrainians to understand.'[578] An inclusive Ukrainian history of World War II certainly needs to include all combatants on Ukrainian territory, and Nazi and Soviet crimes against humanity committed in Ukraine should be given equal prominence.

Jewish organisations in Ukraine supported the Euromaidan and 15 Jewish-Ukrainians, including five former members of the Israeli Defence Forces (IDF), joined its self defence forces. Former IDF soldier Shu'alei Shimshon described anti-Semitism on the Euromaidan as 'bullshit.' He had never seen anti-Semitism 'and the claims to the contrary were part of the reason I joined the (Euromaidan) movement.'[579] Five Jewish-Ukrainians, who wore *kippah's* under their helmets, led a *Sotnya* where the majority of volunteers were Ukrainians. 3 Jewish-Ukrainians were among the 100 protestors murdered by the *Berkut* riot police on the Euromaidan. One of those murdered, Oleksandr Shcherbatyuk was buried in his home region of Chernivtsi to a gun salute by *Pravyy Sektor*.[580]

When asked about anti-Semitism during and after the Euromaidan, Jewish-Ukrainian oligarch Viktor Pinchuk also replied 'It's bullshit.'[581] If a neo-Nazi junta is in power in Ukraine, as Russian propaganda claims, it would represent the first time in history that it has the support of Jews in the country and has given leading positions to Jews, including Prime Minister Groysman. Jewish-Ukrainians are among the many Russian speakers serving in the Ukrainian army and volunteer battalions, such as Orthodox Hassidic Jewish-Ukrainian Asher Cherkassky who serves in the *Dnipro* battalion.

The U.S. State Department's reports on human rights practices in Ukraine up to the Ukraine-Russia crisis of 2013-2014 recorded the highest numbers of anti-Semitic violence and vandalism in central, eastern, and southern Ukraine (Kyiv, Pavlohrad, Sumy, Kirovohrad, Dnipro, Cherkasy, Melitopol, and Mykolayiv) and the Crimea (Sudak and Sevastopol). VAAD's surveys of anti-Semitic publications showed that they were directed against opposition leaders as much as against the authorities and that anti-Semitic violence and desecrations of Jewish monuments and buildings had taken place as much in eastern-southern as in western Ukraine.582 Ukrainian surveys also showed higher levels of anti-Semitism in eastern and southern Ukraine and the Crimea than in western Ukraine.

The Odesa-based *Rodina* party routinely fanned anti-Semitism in the newspaper Nashe Delo sponsored by party leader and Party of Regions deputy Ihor Markov. Anti-Semitic inflammatory articles were published in local newspapers in Odesa against former mayor Eduard Hurvits who had allied with Our Ukraine and in 2012 was elected to parliament by UDAR. Anti-Semitic articles were published in the newspaper of the Russian nationalist and Pan-Slavic political party ZUBR (For the Union of Ukraine Belarus and Russia). Vitrenko's Progressive Socialist party and Pan-Slavic parties espoused anti-Semitism. Vitrenko and *Oplot* claimed, similar to the DNR and LNR, the Euromaidan was a conspiracy by Jews. In Sevastopol an underground skinhead organisation had planned to launch Pogroms against non-Slavic peoples in 2002.583 Anti-Semitism in eastern and southern Ukraine was propagated by skinheads with ties to Russian counterparts, Russian nationalists and Cossacks, all of whom have supported and sent volunteers to the DNR and LNR. Anti-Semitism in Sevastopol and the Crimea was prevalent among Russian Cossacks such as the Sobol company led by Vitaliy Khramov. Russian Cossacks have been based in the LNR since the outbreak of the conflict and they are some of the most xenophobic of Russian nationalist volunteers. The *Berkut* riot police were notorious on their social media for hosting anti-Semitic and homophobic attacks against the Euromaidan and the 'Jewish roots and connections of opposition leaders.'584

Anti-Semitic campaigns appeared during election campaigns, such as those directed at Hurvits in Odesa and against Tymoshenko in 2010.585 In the 2002 elections, the NDP (People's Democratic Party), usually classified within the moderate wing of pro-presidential centrist parties, published many anti-Semitic cartoons and articles in its publications. The Vinnitsa Jewish religious community wrote to the Organisation for Security and Cooperation in Europe (OSCE) Election Mission complaining that the NDP newspaper *Narodna Khvylya* (14 March 2002) 'represents the views of the *oblast* head and therefore places under question the absence of anti-Semitism in state policies.586 Centrist parties had ties to Ukraine's oligarchs and big business in eastern Ukraine and included Jews, such as Pinchuk and Kolomoyskyy but this did not mean that anti-Semitism was absent among eastern Ukrainian leaders. Presidential guard Mykola Melnychenko recorded President Kuchma as describing Yushchenko to Azarov, then head of the State Tax Administration, 'as a filthy Jew, a mother-fucker.' Azarov described with many similar epitaphs the Jews living in a Kyiv apartment who he asked Kuchma to forcibly evict so that he could take possession of it.587 Clearly, anti-Semitism was not an evil that was confined solely to western Ukraine but is given official support only in the DNR and LNR.

## CONCLUSIONS

Anti-Semitism has always been present in Russian nationalism and in the Soviet era was camouflaged as anti-Zionism. Anti-Semitism in the DNR-LNR draws upon these two strands in its rhetoric directed at the Euromaidan and its Jewish allies to explain an alleged Western and international capitalist conspiracy against the 'people's republics.' The separatist enclaves have become parodies of the Soviet Union where an official socialist ideology, anti-Zionism and anti-racism masks anti-Semitism and national and racial discrimination.

Anti-Semitism has not played a prominent role in Ukrainian political thought and Ukrainian nationalism that emerged in the second half of the nineteenth century and first 2 decades of the twentieth was federalist, social-democratic and national communist. This should not be surprising as Ukrainian nationalism was similar to its Irish counterpart in seeking to liberate the lower classes and an ethnic group from ruling classes and a foreign oppressor. It was only in the 1930s, as in the majority of European countries, that Ukrainian nationalism turned to the right and the OUN initially incorporated anti-Semitism until its evolution from 1943 when it returned to social democratic tendencies. Anti-Semitism has not been prominent in the Ukrainian diaspora or among Ukrainian dissidents and oppositionists who closely cooperated with Zionists outside and inside the Gulag. Jewish leaders in Ukraine supported the Euromaidan and patriotically rallied in defence of Ukraine in its war with Russia.[588] Anti-Semitic attacks in independent Ukraine are one of the lowest levels in Europe and the far right has been voted into parliament in only one out of seven elections. Anti-Semitic attacks in Ukraine are one of the lowest in Europe, particular in comparison to Germany, France and the UK.[589]

Historically, anti-Semitism and Russian nationalism have gone hand in hand in Tsarist Russia, the USSR (when it was disguised as anti-Zionism) and contemporary Russia. Political and cultural repression and violence towards Ukrainians and Jews has been central to Russian nationalism and part of everyday life in the frontier region of the Donbas, especially when central governments in Moscow and Kyiv have disintegrated. The next chapter explores the ties between crime, violence and the Donbas.

# CHAPTER 5

# CRIME AND VIOLENCE

*Ethnographic surveys of the speech of ethnic Russian Donbas miners was 'as if it were a thieves (blatnoy) language.'*
Terry Martin[590]

*Crime, especially organised crime, has been at the heart of the events in Ukraine from the start.*
Mark Galeotti[591]

Criminality, organised crime, violence and corruption have been largely absent from political science studies of Ukraine. One reason is because the Donbas and Crimea have been largely outside the Ukrainian 'imagined community' that has been taught, researched and written about in Ukrainian historiography in Ukraine and in the West. Yet, as Galeotti writes, no scholarly work on Russia's annexation of the Crimea and conflict in the Donbas would be complete without integrating criminality and violence into our analysis. The Crimea and the Donbas were major locations for large scale and systematic violence during the 1990s that drew upon a history of violence in these frontier regions. Their violent history in turn influenced two factors. Firstly, how the Crimea was annexed with the assistance of criminal *avtoritety* and their 'brigades' and who took power. Secondly, the prevalence of criminal networks in the Donbas and DNR and LNR.

## VIOLENT CULTURE IN THE DONBAS

Kuromiya writes that criminal gangs have existed in the Donbas from its beginnings.[592] One reason for this was the close connection between migration (specifically, the lack of rootedness) and crime. Crime increases due to the hard life of migrants, problems in finding suitable housing and employment, and adjusting to their new environment without their family.[593] In other countries, criminality has traditionally grown among recent arrivals into new cultures as testified to by the proliferation of ethnic-based gangs in the US in the late nineteenth and early twentieth centuries.

Migrants who came to work in the Donbas often did not possess identity papers while others were prisoners who had been released early in exchange for agreeing to work in the region's coalmines. In the decade immediately following World War II, 3.5 million workers and released prisoners migrated or were sent to the Donbas from other regions of the USSR to work in coalmines and factories. These included men with dubious pasts, those who wished to change their identities and hide their family ties, social undesirables and in 1939-1941 and following World War II, refugees, criminals, *Ostarbeitern* and former prisoners-of-war.[594] Criminals, adventurers and 'street waifs' contributed to the high levels of crime and Kuromiya writes that 'Everyone was said to participate in robbery' with gunfire at night a commonplace occurrence.[595]

Joseph Zisels, who was incarcerated in the USSR as a Zionist dissident, estimated that every third inmate he met was from the Donbas. Kuromiya estimates that one in ten of the population in the Donbas had a criminal record.[596] Every third coalminer had a criminal record, Mariupol Mayor Mykhaylo Pozhivanov said.[597] The Donbas region had a higher proportion of jails and camps than the size of its population.

Professional criminals (*vory v zakone*) despised collaborators with the prison guards who were nicknamed *kozly (goats but here a nickname for bitches)*.[598] Yanukovych was one of the inmates who collaborated with the authorities and was therefore one of the *kozly* in the eyes of the *pakhany*,[599] the name for leaders of the *vory v zakone*. He was denigrated even more as a *kham (boor)*. His collaboration with the prison guards laid the ground for the KGB to recruit Yanukovych to collect intelligence on criminal groups in the Donbas after his release from his second term in prison.

During the Stalin era, *vory v zakone* fought violent battles inside prisons and camps over the question of whether to remain committed to the criminal's code of not collaborating with the authorities or dropping this aspect of the

*President Viktor Yanukovych's scandalous Mezhyhirya palace, now a museum*

code. For obvious reasons, prison guards preferred to reduce their workload by bribing criminal leaders willing to cooperate with them. Incarcerated Ukrainian nationalists organised numerous uprisings in the Gulag camps in the late 1940s and early 1950s during which they targeted *vory v zakone* and *kozly*, but sometimes Ukrainian nationalists and *vory v zakone* would establish a temporary alliance against the hated collaborationist *kozly*.[600] Zisels recalls that political prisoners had good relations with those *vory v zakone* who continued to oppose cooperating with the prison authorities.[601] Memory is kept alive in the criminal world by generations of habitual offenders and professional criminals and it is not beyond the bounds of possibility that Yanukovych's loathing of Ukrainian nationalists was a product of stories he had heard about incarcerated nationalists targeting prisoner collaborators.

By the mid to late 1950s, the *vory v zakone* who supported cooperating with the authorities had overcome their old fashioned adversaries and during the Brezhnevite 'era of stagnation' and Gorbachev era the conditions were conducive for mutual enrichment and corruption of the *vory v zakone* and *siloviki*. During this same period of time, ethnic criminal groups became more established and wealthy from corruption, illicit trade and the underground economy. During the 1970s, Joseph D. Serio and Vyacheslav Razinkin write, the Georgian organised criminal world expanded out of the Soviet Georgian republic by capitalising on its massive underground economy.[602] The Nemsadze brothers, who were the most violent organised crime group in the Donbas and became the professional enforcers of Yanukovych and Akhmetov, emerged from this well established Georgian criminal milieu.

Extensive ties to the 'coal mafia' in the Kuzbas coal basin, second only to the Donbas as a coal producer in the USSR, led to strikes by coalminers in both regions in 1989. Akhmetov's family and other Volga Tatars migrated to the Donbas in the post-war period but maintained their networks to their home region. The city of Donetsk has a *rayon* with a large number of Volga Tatars two of whose most well known figures were mafia boss Brahin and his senior enforcer Akhmetov. Donbas Tatars differed from Crimean Tatars in their attitudes to Soviet history and their relations with Russians with the former holding a positive view and the latter a negative one. Donbas Tatars established an Islamic Party of Ukraine led by Brahin's brother with the goal to attract Muslim voters but its weak performance led to a merger with the Party of Regions.

Zisels, similar to other prisoners, found that people from the Donbas did not view imprisonment as shameful, one reason being because it included 'someone from each family.'[603] Imprisonment was an 'opportunity to enrich one's personal experience' and serving a sentence was 'the equivalent of serving in the military.'[604] This concurred with a generally held view of criminal culture throughout the USSR where 'The length of time in prison was a source of prestige and a sign of distinction among the criminals who aspired to be *vory*.'

Prison time was not dishonourable or detrimental to one's future criminal 'career'[605] and the negativity of a large majority of Ukrainians towards former criminal offenders serving in high state positions was therefore not shared by the population of the Donbas, or by large swathes of the Soviet population. Kuchma knew who he was appointing as prime minister and who he was choosing as his successor. First Deputy Prime Minister Vasyl Durdynets asked Kuchma after he appointed Yanukovych Donetsk governor: 'What are you doing?! He is a (criminal) bandit!'[606] In the 2004 elections, 66-69 percent of Ukrainians believed that a president should not have criminal convictions.[607] In anther poll, 61.8 percent of Ukrainian voters believed presidential candidates should not have past criminal records, a view upheld by two thirds of Yushchenko voters and, even half of those who would vote for Yanukovych.[608]

The Donbas was a magnet for labour and a haven for fugitives. Up to, and during World War II, the regions population was viewed with suspicion by Moscow and during the war the Communist underground was not extensive in the Donbas. The Stalino *oblast* underground Communist Party was poorly organised and infested with traitors and Nazi collaborators.[609] In 1942-1943, the OUNb nationalist underground led by Yevhen Stakhiv was more active in Stalino *oblast*, especially in Horlivka, Mariupol, and Staryy and Novyy Kramatorsk. The city of Mariupol, like much of the southern Donetsk region had been populated by Greek settlers escaping Ottoman rule. During World War II, Kuromiya writes, Mariupol was a stronghold of the OUNb, had an extensive Ukrainian nationalist underground - an ironic fact given that today it is the base of the *Azov* battalion.[610]

In the post-war era the Donbas became a showcase for Soviet industrialisation and the creation of a new Russian-speaking *Homo Sovieticus*. The Donbas had always been a 'hub of Russia's late industrial revolution,' a 'worker's city' and 'powerful proletariat core.' Importantly for the formulation of future Donbas myths, the Donbas was 'deeply imbued with the sense of status with which the Soviet regime endowed them from the earliest days of the revolution.' This arrogance translated in Ukraine into the demand that they be recognised as the 'natural rulers' of the country.

The ties between the Donbas and Moscow became as strong as those between the Donbas and Kyiv showing again the manner in which the region 'lived between Ukraine and Russia without a commitment to either.'[611] The Donetsk *oblast* branch of the Communist Party in Soviet Ukraine, the largest branch in the republic, was hostile to national communism, thought in 'All-Union' and 'centralist terms' and was 'eminently acceptable to Moscow.'[612] The Donets-Dnipro area was one of 19 strategic economic regions of the USSR and the Moscow-Donetsk 'corridor' provided regional Communist and government elites with a direct connection to Moscow.[613] John A. Armstrong described the party-state management in the Donbas as a 'partially distinct unit before 1953.'[614]

Towns and cities in the Donbas expanded in a massive way after World War II with migrants from all regions of the USSR who were attracted by the labour shortages. Social problems were massive and housing built in the

*In 1993, Donetsk organised crime boss Akhat Bragin ('Alik the Greek') had assisted in the founding of the Ibn Fadlan Donetsk Spiritual Centre of Muslims in the Kuy-byshevskyy rayon of the city of Donetsk where Volga Tatars from Russia live and many of them were brought to work in the Oktryabyrskyy coal mine. After Bragin's assassination in 1995 the Centre was renamed Akhat Jami and the mosque which opened in September 1999 was named in honour of 'Akhat Bragin.' Initially the project called for the construction of one minaret but financing from oligarch Rinat Akhmetov, also of Volga Tatar descent, made it possible to build two and the second was named in honour of him. On its first floor is a Ukrainian Islamic University, the first Muslim higher education institution to be opened in Ukraine (December 2013, Donetsk).*

Khrushchev and Brezhnev eras was usually inadequate and poorly built. Migrants lived in new, bland and impersonal surroundings without families and were distant from local customs. Housing was often scarce. Another factor why crime was high among migrants was because 'the Russian migrants are not moving to a foreign country and feel superior to the native population.'[615] Rapid urbanisation brought a larger numbers of Russians than Ukrainians to live and work in the Donbas. After World War II, there was an absolute decline in the number of ethnic Ukrainians who considered Ukrainian to be their native language at a time when urbanisation was expanding rapidly.[616] Theodore H. Friedgut writes that Donetsk 'has been predominantly Russian throughout its existence' and 'has remained Russian in ambience.'[617]

Russians (i.e. anybody who had migrated from the Russian SFSR) living in the Donbas felt 'perfectly at home, having long ago shed any sensation of foreignness.'[618] This was important in understanding the continuation of criminal, family, ethnic and old boy political and business networks. The Donbas had a large underground economy in the USSR with money laundering and illegal trade that had extensive ties through ethnic criminal groups with other Soviet republics. With assistance from the KGB, who hired him as a *stukach (informer)*, Yanukovych was given influential mentor's to facilitate his career and a position as director of the Donetsk Auto-Transportation Service which serviced the *oblasts* coalmines, opening up avenues for corruption and networks to local criminal groups.[619]

## PRISON CULTURE

High levels of crime had always been a feature of life in the Donbas and in Soviet Ukraine, a quarter of all penitentiaries and camps for criminals were located in the Donbas,[620] 20 in Stalino (Donetsk) and 16 in Voroshilovohrad (Luhansk). These prisons and camps held three times more inmates than their official capacities because Stalino and Voroshilovohrad experienced the largest number of criminal prosecutions in Ukraine.[621] Shcherban when asked why Donetsk had become well-known as 'the most criminalised city in Ukraine' replied 'You should recollect the city's history and consider its social structure.'[622]

In the Soviet and post-Soviet periods, the Donbas was one of three most criminalised regions of Ukraine along with the Crimea and Odesa. In 2005, long after the USSR had disintegrated and the Party of Regions had monopolised power, there were 44,000 crimes (of which 19, 000 were serious) and 395 murders.[623] This reflected the continued high level of violent culture in the Donbas during the 1990s when state assets were being carved up between rival business and criminal groups.

The Party of Regions had monopolised all facets of life in the Donbas by 2000 and 'The prison subculture is crucial to an understanding of the political-criminal nexus.' Prison sub-culture, or *urka*, spread into the senior ranks of the Donbas regional branch of the Communist Party and *silovi*ki during the last two decades of the USSR and took power in the 1990s.[624] Very few, if any, of the violent crimes committed in the 1980s and 1990s in the Donbas were resolved, especially those of senior figures, testifying to control of the *siloviki* by the local oligarchs. Many *siloviki* were attracted by offers of lucratively paid employment in oligarch business empires where they retained their old boy networks. The commander of the Donetsk *oblast* Ministry of Interior Volodymyr Malyshev became head of Systems Capital Management security and a Party of Regions deputy.

**Table 5.1. Illicit Financial Flows from Ukraine (in millions of U.S. dollars, nominal)**

| | |
|---|---|
| *2004* | *4,380* |
| 2005 | 5,626 |
| 2006 | 5,381 |
| 2007 | 7,175 |
| 2008 | 16,922 |
| 2009 | 10,574 |
| 2010 | 13,843 |
| 2011 | 17,949 |
| 2012 | 21,001 |
| 2013 | 13,911 |
| **Cumulative** | **116.762** |
| **Average** | **11.676** |

**Source**: Dev Kar and Joseph Spanjers, *Illicit Financial Flows from Developing Countries: 2004-2013* (Washington DC: Global Financial Integrity, December 2015), p.33. http://www.gfintegrity.org/wp-content/uploads/2015/12/IFF-Update_2015-Final-1.pdf

Former police officers Oleh Solodun and Mykhaylo Serbin, who had appeared three times on *Tor*, an independent television company based in Slovyansk, Donetsk, said that a close nexus existed between the Ministry of Interior, local prosecutor's office and organised crime groups in the Donetsk region.[625] In July 2001, Ihor Aleksandrov was murdered just ahead of the airing of a fourth programme that would have implicated Viktor Pshonka's son Artem with ties to organised crime in Kramatorsk.[626] Homeless person Yuriy

Veredyuk was framed by the Donetsk regional prosecutor's office with the murder and he tragically died from poisoning in prison in July 2002.[627] The murder of Aleksandrov was covered up by Governor Yanukovych and his political and business allies but this never became a moral issue for civil society in the Donbas, unlike the murder of Gongadze which spawned the Ukraine without Kuchma movement and demands for President Kuchma's impeachment.

Some of the Donbas *siloviki* moved to Kyiv when Yanukovych was elected president assisting him in asset stripping the country and covering up his illegal activities. When Yanukovych was in power 'organised crime felt safe that there would be no follow up from the authorities,' a US Embassy cable from Kyiv reported.[628] Under Yanukovych, Ukraine transitioned from a corrupt state to a mafia state[629] or in the words of an EU official, 'from an oligarchical economy to a mafia one.'[630] Oliver Bullough ruled out the use of the word 'corruption' to understand the Yanukovych presidency because the 'Entire state was a criminal enterprise.'[631] Ukrainian oligarchs and corrupt state officials had always sent illicitly accumulated capital to offshore tax havens but, as Table 5.1 shows, this massively expanded during Yanukovych's presidency.

Oligarch and Party of Regions control over the *siloviki* ensured their passivity or defection in spring 2014 during the Anti-Maidan and separatist revolt. The local administration and *militia* had long been controlled by the Party of Regions and 'They intersected with criminal groups like the (Armen) Sarkisian gang.' 'The police also had lists of criminals whom they had exploited (as vigilantes) and armed to attack pro-Maidan activists locally and in Kyiv.'[632] Sarkisian's organised crime group in Horlivka joined the separatists[633] while other organised crime groups remained passive and then resumed their illicit activities in the separatist enclaves.

## CRIME AND CRIMINALITY IN THE LATE SOVIET AND POST-SOVIET ERA

In the 1990s the Donbas region experienced one of the highest levels of criminality in Ukraine, particularly in 1990-1993 when it soared by 50 percent. Homicide and attempted homicide massively increased by a third and property offences by 55 percent.[634] In the year the USSR disintegrated there was a very large number of 2,186 criminal groups in the Donetsk region who committed 4, 000 crimes, including 33 known murders. 'The traditions of the criminal world have deeply entertained the language, culture and life of "Donetski."'[635]

In the 1990s these criminal groups reversed the hierarchy of power in comparison to the Soviet era and came out on top after taking control of the political and business worlds, *siloviki* and local government. Eventually, 'the emerging oligarchs came to depend on both the ex-KGB and organised crime to use targeted violence to control market entry, market share, and border control.'[636]

The 1990s were commonly described as a *bardak (mess)*, *durdom (nuthouse)* or simply *zakon dzhunhliv (law of the jungle)*.[637] Within the space of a decade, Ukrainians had transitioned from a relatively stable and domineering Soviet state to anarchy and civil war in the Donbas and Crimea where only the strong survived. To the average person on the street it seemed that organised crime had come to power (as reflected in opinion polls). Prison values and *ponyatta (how it is understood)* dominated the manner in which business and politics was undertaken.[638] To live by *ponyatta* signified that one lived according to the unwritten rules of the criminal world.

During Gorbachev's liberalisation in the late 1980s, criminal groups operated more freely and with a greater degree of impunity. By the close of the Soviet Union had come to dominate the region's cultural and social life, norms, customs and rituals as seen through the use of tattoos, nicknames (e.g. Brahin was known as 'Alek the Greek'), prison slang and the popularity of prison songs.[639]

Post-Soviet identity in the Donbas emerged out of the integration of regional identity, criminal culture, Sovietisation and the 1990s *zakon dzhunhliv*.

1.  Donbas regional identity as a frontier region had emerged since the late nineteenth century.

2.  Criminal and prison culture had always been present in the Donbas. During the 'era of stagnation,' criminal groups benefitted from greater tolerance of corruption, illicit trade, shortages, cynicism and alienation from Communist Party rule. Nevertheless, the Communist Party and KGB remained in control and Yanukovych worked for the prison guards and KGB as a *stukach*. During the late 1980s and 1990s, criminal groups reversed this power relationship and took power and from then on the KGB and its successor, the SBU, worked for them in regions such as the Donbas and the Crimea.

3.  Support for the Bolshevik party was high in the Russian civil war and this was a major reason behind Lenin's decision to include the Donbas within the Ukrainian SSR. Soviet identity came under competition from Ukrainianisation in the 1920s and opposition to Soviet economic

policies. The Donbas was one of the worst hit and affected by the *holodomor* and Great Terror and its emerging Ukrainian identity was destroyed. After World War II the Donbas was thoroughly Sovietised, Russified, and atomised. The region declined in the post-Soviet era and even more so in the DNR and LNR with high levels of alcoholism and narcotic abuse made worse by a general sense of despair.[640]

Since 1991, asset stripping of the Donbas and export of raw materials and industrial output has benefitted a small group of oligarchs and their cronies. As viewed by this author during field work in the Donbas, little was invested into basic infrastructure, education and social services. Writing from the town of Komunar, a *Guardian* journalist was shocked to find the absence of 'basic municipal improvements,' home telephones and gas pipelines. The main source of employment was the local coalmine where 'long shifts of backbreaking, dangerous work were rewarded with meagre wages.'[641] Low respect for human life was seen in the very high number of coalmining accidents.

Accidents were commonplace because of the age and depth of the coalmines, the lack of investment and because central government subsidies were largely stolen by coalmine directors. The coalmining mafia, led by senior 'Red Directors' united in the Labour Party, continued to cream huge rents in independent Ukraine from coal subsidies. Stealing coal subsidies to keep unprofitable coalmines open was a major source of revenue for old 'Red Directors' such as Yukhym Zvyahilskyy. Ninety percent of the subsidies were stolen and up to 6 million tonnes of coal was illegally extracted by shadow economic businesses controlled by Oleksandr Yanukovych, the president's eldest son.[642]

It has always baffled experts, whether in Ukraine or the West, why the local population would vote for crooks ensconced in the Party of Regions? Perhaps it was simply a case of the lesser of two evils, better 'our bandit' than western Ukrainian nationalists and 'fascists' in the pay of the West. Donetsk resident Elvira Serheyevna agreed that Yanukovych was a 'bandit' but she added that nevertheless 'he was our bandit.'[643] Another Donetsk resident, coalminer Volodymyr Kyyan agreed that the oligarchs were 'thieves and bandits' and added 'An honest man doesn't make billions just like that.' Regardless, he planned, like many of his colleagues, to vote for the Party of Regions in the hope their lives would improve. He reasoned his voting preference by saying 'Even though he's (Yanukovych) a criminal too he can sort out the other bandits.'[644]

Feeling betrayed by both Yanukovych and their 'bandits' on the one hand, and 'fascist' Kyiv and the Euromaidan on the other, a proportion of Donbas residents looked to Putin and the separatists as their local saviours. This fervour was dampened by the destruction and high number of civilian casualties during the war. Tom Coupe and Maksym Obrizan found that in Ukrainian-controlled areas of the Donbas which had experienced war damage there was low support for compromise with Russia and high support for keeping the region inside Ukraine.

Enthusiasm [645]also waned after it became clear that Putin did not plan to annex the Donbas as he had the Crimea, leaving an overall sense of resignation and despondency for those people living in the DNR and LNR. Between 2014-2015, support for separatism slumped in Dnipro from 7 to 1 percent, Zaporizhzhya from 6 to 2 percent, Odesa from 7 to 4 percent, Kharkiv from 16 to 5 percent and Mykolayiv from 7 to zero percent.[646] Of the three eastern Ukrainian regions of Dnipro, Zaporizhzhya and Kharkiv the first was the most Ukrainian in its identity and the latter had the highest level of Soviet identity. Russian traditions ranged from 3 in the first to 7 percent in the last of these regions. Fewer in Kharkiv (24 percent) blamed the war on Russia than in Dnipro and Zaporizhzhya (40-44 percent).[647]

The violent political culture found in the Donbas was evident in the criminal civil war from the mid 1980s to mid 1990s, attempts at stealing the 2004 presidential elections and during Yanukovych's presidency. The *zakon dzhunhliv* of the 1990s had 'produced not "free" but "feral citizens"' Fournier writes.[648] *The Economist* (11 October 2011) described Yanukovych as 'thuggish and vindictive.' Local thuggish culture rewards one's friends and publicly punishes one's enemies to demonstrate who is the *khazayin*. These traits produced a combustible mix that exploded into violence, chaos and anarchy when central authority - Moscow in 1917 and 1991 and Kyiv in 2014 – disintegrated.[649] This political culture included the following twelve characteristics:

1. Being oblivious to human suffering and not feeling responsible for the plight of others.
2. A history of wild economic exploitation and feral aggression to achieve objectives and a conviction that the end justifies the means.
3. Toughness and respect for the use of force, terror and brutality in everyday life.

4.  A love of extreme bling because of the need to show off one's wealth; this was clearly visible in Yanukovych's *Mezhyhirya* palace with its private zoo, collection of vintage cars and Spanish Galleon.
5.  They are street-wise but are not intellectual and have only completed lower levels of education. Higher degrees, such as Yanukovych's PhD, were bought to increase one's social standing.
6.  All types of theft are permissible, including plagiarism.
7.  Lacking in morals and decency.
8.  There are no limits to greed and willingness to steal. *Nashi Hroshi (Our Money)* NGO leader Oleksiy Shalayskyy said when talking about the Yanukovych presidency that 'We have never had such greed in Ukraine.'[650]
9.  Legal nihilism.
10. High levels of tolerance for corruption and illegality.
11. Limited popular support for liberal and national democratic political parties. The only two popular political parties in the Donbas have been the leftist-populist KPU and the Party of Regions.
12. Xenophobia, religious intolerance and anti-Semitism.

## OLIGARCHS AND POLITICAL *KRYSHY*: AKHMETOV AND MR. 50 PERCENT

Donetsk became peaceful only after a decade of rampant violence from the mid 1980s to mid 1990s was brought to a close by the Akhmetov-Yanukovych alliance that consolidated its power base.[651] Together, they formed a corrupt and highly lucrative *biznes* alliance that benefitted both of them through to spring 2014. As Akhmetov expanded his wealth and joined the top 50 wealthiest persons in the world he paid a percentage to Yanukovych, with some reports saying this was as high as half giving him the nickname 'Mr. 50 percent.'[652] Regardless, the relationship was, in the eyes of oligarch Serhiy Taruta, a unique business-political relationship that lasted a quarter of a century.[653]

The roots of this *biznes* alliance go back to the Soviet era when the former convicts who had agreed to work in the coalmines in exchange for early release transitioned into the vigilantes, brigadiers and enforcers of organised crime groups. Akhmetov's father, a Volga Tatar, arrived in Donetsk in the early 1960s and worked in the coalmines. Rinat and his brother Ihor Akhmetov did not seek employment in the coalmines because the Gorbachev era opened up criminal opportunities for enrichment.

Akhmetov's biography prior to 1995 does not exist, which is highly suspicious. From journalistic investigations and Ministry of Internal Affairs leaks we know that in 1986, Rinat and Ihor Akhmetov 'were involved in criminal activities' in gambling and illegal cloth trade. In one failed robbery, three people died and Ihor Akhmetov was arrested.[654] Although denied ever since by Akhmetov, local witnesses and *militia* confirmed the authenticity of the allegations to Tatyana Chornovol who undertook extensive interviews in the village of Pivnichne, near Donetsk, where the Akhmetov brothers spent their childhood. She published the investigation in *Obozrevatel* who were forced to remove it after Akhmetov took the publication to court in London.[655] Alone among Ukrainian oligarchs, Akhmetov has gone to great lengths and financial expense to cover up his past and his biography traditionally begins in 1995 while what he did prior to that 'remains controversial.'[656] If he has nothing to hide why is he so willing to spend millions of dollars on US lawyers blocking research by scholars and journalists into his past?[657]

Akhmetov was brought in for questioning in 1988 for being a member of an organised crime group in the Donetsk region after he had expanded his illicit activities into extortion. The allegations are supported by an internal 1999 document leaked by the Ministry of Interior Directorate on Combating Organised Crime which analyses organised crime groups in the Donetsk region.[658] 'Overview of the Most Dangerous Organised Crime Structures in Ukraine' listed seven organised crime groups in Donetsk *oblast*. The 'Renat' organised group, 'dealt with money laundering and financial fraud, and controlled a large number of both real and fictitious companies. It goes by the name Lyuksovska hrupa.' Underneath the report is written 'The leader is Akhmetov Renat Leonidovych born in 1966, and lives at 16 Udarnyy Street, Donetsk.'[659]

Akhmetov's criminal activities attracted the attention of Brahin who became his mentor and Akhmetov's right-hand man. But, as with all criminal enterprises there is no honour among thieves. In 1995, Akhmetov arrived late for a football game only to find Brahin blown to bits; if his car had not been 'stuck in traffic' he may have suffered the same fate. We will never know the answer to the question whether he knew in advance that it would be best for his health to take a route that would ensure he arrived late, which was probably the case. Akhmetov and Brahin had different views over whether the *vory v zakone* should cooperate with or ignore the authorities in a conflict of opinion that stretched back decades within the Soviet criminal milieu. Yanukovych had a long record of cooperation with the authorities and encouraged Akhmetov to 'go legit' by moving into and working with official structures, a step that required the removal of *vory v zakone* such as Brahin and others who were traditionalists.

In 1995, the city of Donetsk did not have an acute traffic problem and VIP's would be sped through any traffic hold ups by local *militia* who often provided escorts. Chornovol and other Ukrainian experts are convinced he knew of the planned assassination and deliberately arrived late for the football game.[660] A year later oligarch Yevhen Shcherban was assassinated by gunmen who managed to enter Donetsk airport and leave without any difficulties. Akhmetov claims he had nothing to do with both murders but suspicion is based on the fact he inherited their wealth and assets which means he personally gained from their deaths *Tserkalo Tyzhnya* editor Yulya Mostova said 'The majority of shares and Donetsk crown jewels ended up under the control of Akhmetov.'[661] Akhmetov owns the *Luks* palace in the former Donetsk Botanical Gardens which he inherited after the death of Brahin who in turn had taken it over from murdered organised crime boss Oleksandr Krantz.[662]

Sportsmen and former convicts, who acted as the lower level enforcers of criminal gangs and vigilantes during election campaigns, were often the first to control the new untaxed markets that became an important feature of the shadow economy.[663] Karen Dawisha writes that it was impossible to work in the black market in the USSR without having KGB connections.[664] In the late 1980s and early 1990s, the KGB assisted in the laundering of Communist Party funds and emerging criminal groups, such as those controlled by Brahin in Donetsk, 'had either KGB or *Komsomol* cover or *krysha*.'[665]

Yevhen Shcherban was a business partner of Brahin who was seen on many occasions in the Anton corporation offices that he owned. In 1994, the head of the Donetsk Ministry of Internal of Affairs Arkady Boldovskyy said in an interview for a local newspaper that Brahin was the 'head of the largest mafia clan in Donetsk.'[666]

The removal of Brahin was a reflection of the long-standing conflict within the criminal fraternity over whether they should cooperate with the authorities. The strategic goal of Yanukovych, Akhmetov and Kolesnykov to become legitimate political actors required the removal of those, such as the old fashioned *vor v zakone* Brahin, who opposed this evolution. The *vory v zakone* who opposed cooperation with the authorities lost the Donbas civil war to the young upstarts who believed that this represented the future.[667]

Yanukovych had long cooperated with prison guards during his two terms in prison in 1967 and 1969 when Serhiy Leshchenko and Dawisha[668] believe he was recruited as an informer by the KGB. Evidence of a collaborative relationship can be ascertained from the removal of Yanukovych's prison terms from his record, the support given to him by a famous cosmonaut, his rapid rise through the ranks of the Communist Party in the late 1970s and 1980s and the lucrative employment he was offered after two prison terms. His sentences were never included in his biographies until his appointment as prime minister in November 2002 and during the 2004 elections.[669] In the 1990s the Communist Party and KGB had lost power and Yanukovych needed to reinvent his usefulness to the new oligarchic power brokers as a political *krysha*. The assassination of Ukraine's then wealthiest oligarch Yevhen Shcherban was a baptism of fire for the Akhmetov-Yanukovych criminal alliance propelling them into the position of leaders of the Donetsk clan.

After old guard *vor v zakone* Brahin and oligarch Yevhen Shcherban were assassinated the division of responsibilities for the transition of the Donbas into some form of respectability and legitimacy was divided as follows:

1. *Khazayin (here understood as the criminal Lord of the manor)*: Akhmetov dealt with business affairs.
2. *Political krysha (regional governor, Party of Regions leader, prime minister and especially president)*: Yanukovych assisted criminals and oligarchs who wanted to become publicly legitimate in politics and *biznes*.
3. *Criminal World*: ties would not be cut completely to the former criminal world with Kolesnykov continuing to undertake 'other stuff' (i.e. criminal activities). There is no such thing as either a former spy or criminal *avtoritet*.

Akhmetov and Kolesnykov rose through the criminal ranks of the Donetsk region in the second half of the 1980s and first half of the 1990s and by the late 1990s were senior members of the wing of the Donetsk clan that had won the criminal civil war. Kolesnykov headed the Donetsk central *Oktyabrsk* market which was initially controlled by Brahin in the late 1980s and early 1990s. Other close business and political allies of Yanukovych's were Andriy and Serhiy Kluyev who are 'more family than (Yanukovych's) wife and kids.'[670] 'Hayduk and Andriy Klyuyev were both working under Yanukovych as deputy governors. Then Klyuyev provoked a change in the relationship by making Yanukovych his business partner, so he would get preferences,' a cable from the US Embassy in Kyiv reported.[671] Taruta described Andriy Kluyev and Yanukovych as enjoying a 'special relationship.'[672] The Donbas special economic zone was a black hole for illegal economic activity from which the Kluyev brothers benefited through the absence of import duties and tax evasion. Andriy Kluyev replaced Serhiy Lyovochkin as Chief of Staff in January 2014 and remained with him until he fled from Kyiv the following month.

Akhmetov successfully lobbied for the appointment of Yanukovych first as deputy governor and after Prime Minister Pavlo Lazarenko's fall from grace as Donetsk governor. In 2000 they completed their ascent to power and took control of the Donbas by uniting hitherto warring groups under them in the Party of Regions. Over the next 14 years, they established a dominant alliance with one providing political protection and the other financing for the Party of Regions political machine and in the process both becoming very wealthy.

From 1997, 'Akhmetov played a central role in establishing Viktor Yanukovych as a politician. He became an oligarch under President Leonid Kuchma.'[673]In the following two decades, the financial empire of Akhmetov grew 'under the protection of Yanukovych.' For Akhmetov, the golden eras were when Yanukovych was twice prime minister (2002-2004, 2006-2007) and president (2010-2014).[674] Akhmetov massively increased his business empire, taking control through insider sweetheart deals of regional thermal and power generators, the Mariupol Illich plant[675] and *UkrTelekom* 'ensuring Akhmetov's businesses flourished exponentially.'[676] Wilson writes that Yanukovych's political power 'provided political cover for Akhmetov's takeover of all local rackets' and they 'forged a natural partnership of business and political muscle.'[677]

The names of key organised crime enforcers have been well-known to the Ukrainian authorities but none of them have been criminally convicted. Many of them received parliamentary immunity as Party of Regions deputies, they were rehabilitated or their criminal charges were over-turned by prosecutors from Donetsk. First Deputy Prosecutor Renat Kuzmin had close ties to the Nemsadze criminal gang. During the Yanukovych presidency, eighteen Party of Regions deputies were members of organised crime.[678] Below are listed some of the well-known *vory v zakone* who had ties to organised crime groups in the Donetsk region, some of which were ethnically based:

1.   Nemsadze brothers, who are of Georgian ethnicity, were responsible for 57 murders,[679] according to a long investigation under President Yushchenko, which labelled Givi Nemsadze as Ukraine's most violent gangster. Under Interior Minister Yuriy Lutsenko, more than 30

corpses of businesspersons, judges, lawyers, investigators and others were exhumed who had been murdered in Donetsk in the 1990s. Givi Nemsadze returned to Ukraine under Yanukovych when his criminal convictions were closed by General Prosecutor Pshonka. A Kyiv court believed the lie that it was his (dead) brother Guram who had undertaken the murders (not Givi). Three witnesses to the murders died under mysterious circumstances in jail.[680]Lutsenko wrote that his rehabilitation was tantamount to returning Ukraine to 'the banditry of the 1990s.'[681]The Nemsadze gang worked on behalf of Yanukovych and Akhmetov for the purposes of eliminating rivals and establishing a monopoly of power in the Donbas.[682]

2.    Yuriy Ivanyushchenko was a killer enforcer for the Yevhen Kushnir gang in Yenakiyevo where he had undertaken illegal activities such as selling petrol stolen from the transportation depots run by Yanukovych. In the early 1990s he defected from the Dolidze brothers criminal gang to the Brahin-Akhmetov gang in Donetsk.[683] As a hit man in the late 1980s and first half of the 1990s he had been nicknamed 'Yuriy Yenakovo.' Ivanyushchenko has been dogged by allegations that he 'had a dodgy and even criminal past' that 'link him to an organised crime group allegedly involved in the assassination of Akhat Brahin' and 'to the 2005 assassination of Anatoliy Bandura, head of Mariupol-based Azov Shipping Company.'[684] His name was removed from Interpol's list of wanted Ukrainians, through an opaque deal with President Poroshenko, and he lives a comfortable life in his Monaco palace.

3.    There are two theories as to who was behind the assassinations of Brahin, Oleksandr Momot, and Yevhen Shcherban in 1995-1996 and Vadym Hetman in 1998. The first is that this was ordered by Lazarenko in a turf war between Dnipro and the Donbas. Lazarenko allegedly paid Oleksandr Mylchenko who in turn hired the Kushnir gang to undertake the assassinations. The improbability of this allegation is seen when President Yanukovych attempted to pin the blame for Shcherban's murder on Tymoshenko who had been Lazarenko's ally during most of the 1990s. The second and more likely theory is that this was the work of the 'young Turks' (Akhmetov-Yanukovych-Kolesnykov) who benefitted financially from their deaths. Ivanyushchenko switched sides and earned his place at Akhmetov's table as a reliable ally by undertaking the assassination of Brahin which broke the hold

of the old guard *vory v zakone*. Chornovol explained that 'In reality, all the major murders in the Donetsk region were very connected. This was because the people who ran the Donbas in the beginning of the 1990s and mid-1990s, who today are the masters of Donbas and even Ukraine, were closely tied.'[685]

4.  The Jewish-led Kushnir gang, which was heavily involved in all manner of criminal activities in the 1990s, was behind 27 murders and 17 attempted murders.[686]Kushnir worked with Liberal Party leader Volodymyr Shcherban. The Nemsadze gang destroyed their Kushnir gang rivals through 28 murders and arranging the imprisonment of eight using friendly members of the *siloviki* between 1997, when Yanukovych was appointed governor of Donetsk, to 1999. Anatoliy Rabin and Kushnir were assassinated in 1997 and 1998 respectively.[687]Yanukovych sought to 'conceal his role in the killings of the Kushnir-Rabin gang.'[688]

5.  The Krantz gang was allied to Brahin but was destroyed after its leaders, Yanush Krantz and Artur Yakov Bogdanov, were assassinated in 1992. Akhmetov and Brahin can be seen attending his funeral on a film leaked by the Ministry of Interior.[689]

6.  Party of Regions deputies Elbrus and Robert Tedeyev belonged to the Caucasian *Savlokhy* organised crime group.

7.  The *Seylem* organised crime gang was allied to the Party of Regions in the Crimea. *Seylem* had been responsible in the 1990s for 52 contract murders, including one journalist, two police officers, 30 business persons and 15 organised crime competitors. *Seylem* leader Oleksandr Melnyk represented Party of Regions and Akhmetov's and Vadim Novinsky's business interests in the Crimea.

In a 50:50 partnership with Donetsk Governor Yanukovych, Akhmetov replaced Yevhen Shcherban as Ukraine's wealthiest oligarch.[690] On the eve of the 2014-2015 Ukraine-Russia crisis, Akhmetov was ranked 38th richest person in the world and he was valued at $18.9 billion in Bloomberg's 200 wealthiest people in the world. His fortune was greater than Russia's two wealthiest oligarchs—Roman Abramovich (51st and valued at $14.7 billion) and Oleg Deripaska (90th and valued at $10.5 billion).[691]This is very surprising considering Ukraine was far poorer than Russia in raw material and energy resources.

The assassinations of Brahin and Yevhen Shcherban and the destruction of the Kushnir gang paved the way for the rise of the Akhmetov-Yanukovych-Kolesnykov trio and the 'legalisation' of organised crime as politicians.[692]Evidence of the integration of crime into the Party of Regions is available from US diplomatic cables from Kyiv and many other sources. A cable from the US Embassy in Kyiv quoted Taruta as dismissing the whole Donetsk-Regions group, saying 'they are all looters.'[693]Former RNBO Volodymyr Horbulin told US Ambassador to Ukraine John Herbst that the Party of Regions is 'notable for its inclusion of criminal and anti-democracy figures.' [694]Another cable from the US Embassy in Kyiv described the Party of Regions as, 'long a haven for DONETSK-based mobsters and oligarchs,' led by 'DONETSK CLAN godfather Rinat Akhmetov.'[695]

## VIGILANTES AND ENFORCERS

Vigilantes were drawn from sports clubs, Afghan veterans, police cadets, former coalminers and lower level criminal gang enforcers. Organised crime leaders were often heads of sports clubs.[696]They did not suddenly emerge out of nowhere during the Euromaidan but had a tradition stretching back to the late 1980s and early 1990s and were especially active in regions (such as the Donbas and the Crimea) where violence was endemic to the local culture. The violent culture of the Donbas was caught on the Melnychenko tapes when Yanukovych bragged about using vigilantes to smash up a rally of Tymoshenko supporters in Donetsk and when he demanded that Kuchma 'wipe' her out of the Yushchenko government.[697]

The violent methods used by the authorities on the Euromaidan and the ensuing separatist violence should not come as a surprise to those who have studied Party of Regions parliamentary deputies. Many of them had entered politics after careers in professional sports, security companies, *militia* and *biznes*. In these fields they had come into direct contact with 'mafia violence and physical elimination of competitors' when they had been targeting 'economically predatory business enterprises during the 1990s.'[698]They viewed violence as a necessary tool for use in politics based on their earlier experience of 'fighting' to keep their assets and protect their allies. A typical Party of Regions deputy possessed an attitude to violence that 'derived from his participation in the world of post-Soviet business and professional sports…'[699]

The use of vigilantes on a nation-wide scale took place for the first time during the 2004 elections when they were drawn upon for election fraud with the goal of achieving Yanukovych's election. The tried and tested methods of drawing upon state-administrative resources and criminal circles were transferred from the regional Donetsk to the national Ukrainian levels.[700]The use of vigilantes for corporate raiding was also transferred to the national level. In Mykolayiv, for example, Party of Regions deputy Artem Pshonka led corporate raiding of agro-businesses.[701] Sumy Governor Volodymyr Shcherban (no relation to assassinated Yevhen Shcherban) believed his main job description was asset stripping generating widespread hostility to carpet baggers from Donetsk and mobilising massive support in the *oblast* for Yushchenko in the 2004 elections.

Vigilantes dressed in standard appearances of short cut (skinhead-style) haircuts, leather jackets and sports trousers and spoke prison jargon.[702]The vigilantes had an appearance that was more 'characteristic of the 1990s' and they spoke 'like in the camps' head to head and quietly. Their brigadiers were better dressed with long leather coats and carrying mobile phones.[703]

During the 2004 elections, tens of thousands of vigilantes and coalminers were transported to Kyiv to be used against Orange Revolution protesters but President Kuchma forbade them from entering central Kyiv. The pro-Yanukovych vigilantes were organised by then Chief of Staff Medvedchuk and Akhmetov.[704] Bloodshed would have been widespread if they had been let loose on the unarmed protestors. But, Kuchma and his son-in-law oligarch Pinchuk, Parliamentary Chairman Volodymyr Lytvyn and the US Embassy worked behind the scenes for a peaceful outcome. Some violent attacks did nevertheless take place but these were not massive in scale and systematic, unlike during the Euromaidan.

The second mobilisation of vigilantes came ahead of the 2010 elections because Yanukovych was adamant he would not again permit a denial of his victory by what he believed was a Western-backed conspiracy similar to that believed to be behind the Orange Revolution. From 2007, anti-Maidan 'protesters' who were drawn from pro-Russian marginal groups (such as the Donetsk Republic) were trained in Russian and local camps in anticipation of him being again denied the presidency in 2010. The clear message was that Yanukovych 'would not accept defeat with anything resembling good grace.'[705]Paramilitary vigilante training was organised by Russian intelligence, condoned by the Party of Regions and ignored by the SBU. This training was part of Russia's soft power response to the coloured revolutions through the launch of *Russkiy Mir*, a Sovietised version of the British Council, and the Federal Agency for the

Commonwealth of Independent States, Compatriots Living Abroad, and International Humanitarian Cooperation.

Yanukovych was elected president in 2010 in a free and fair election and the vigilantes temporarily stood down but, following the 2012 elections preparations again went into full swing to ensure Yanukovych's re-election in 2015.[706] In 2013, the Party of Regions used the election of *Svoboda* the year before as the basis for tarnishing the opposition as 'fascists.' Nation-wide 'anti-fascist' rallies were mobilised where vigilantes were very much in evidence. In Kyiv, vigilantes attacked journalists and *Svoboda* supporters and were christened *titushky* after sportsman Vadym Titushko whose vigilante group of sportsmen was led by a regional leader of the youth wing of the Party of Regions. The unexpected Euromaidan Revolution, which Yanukovych was convinced Tymoshenko was manipulating from her prison cell such was his paranoia of her, forced the Party of Regions to mobilise vigilantes ahead of the 2015 election campaign.[707]

To counter the Euromaidan, vigilantes were mobilised from throughout eastern and southern Ukraine and the Crimea to operate alongside *Berkut* riot police and Ministry of Interior Internal Troops. The vigilantes who savagely beat Chornovol in December 2013 after she led an Automaidan column to Minister of Interior Vitaliy Zakharchenko's palace were from Dniprodzerzhinsk. In Dnipro, Party of Regions leaders Oleksandr Vilkul and Governor Dmytro Kolesnykov organised and armed anti-Euromaidan vigilantes. Vigilantes sent from the Crimea participated in this violence and Ukrainian nationalists counter-attacked them on their return home.

The main body of vigilantes were from Donetsk and Kharkiv with financing provided by Oleksandr Yanukovych, Ivanyushchenko and Oleksandr Yefremov.[708] Government *militia* resources were supplied by Zakharchenko who 'took care of coordinating, hiring and financing of vigilantes' with the full knowledge of President Yanukovych.[709] On 18-19 February 2014 the vigilantes were exceptionally brutal against Euromaidan protesters in Mariyinsky Park adjacent to parliament where they 'acted as a coordinated militarised unit together with law enforcement.'[710] A massive arsenal of weapons and bullets was stockpiled to be used against Euromaidan protestors on 20 February 2014 that would, if they had been used, have led to massive loss of life far higher than the number of protestors murdered that day.

In Kharkiv the hard-core vigilante group *Oplot* worked with Mayor Hennadiy Kernes who had himself emerged from organised crime groups and become a Party of Regions loyalist. *Oplot* was established by Party of Regions deputies Oleksandr Bobkov and Serhiy Arbuzov and since December 2014 is included on a list of organisations under US sanctions.[711] *Oplot* combined hardcore, pro-Russian violent thugs who ran businesses and rackets on the side and hung out in sports clubs. *Oplot* propagated a cult of violence and Pan-Slavic beliefs of common eastern Slavic roots, hostility to Ukrainian 'fascism,' anti-Western xenophobia and backing for Putin's 'conservative values' which made them natural allies of Russian nationalist volunteers. They were led by Ministry of Interior officer Yevhen Zhilin who fled to Russia after pro-Ukrainian forces won street battles in Kharkiv in spring 2014.[712]

*Oplot* took an active part in the Euromaidan as *militia* vigilantes and were 'believed to have been behind a number of abductions; torture; robbery; and threats to kill in Kyiv.'[713] *Oplot* acting as *titushky* were based in camps near Kyiv where kidnapped Euromaidan protesters were taken for interrogation and to be tortured. A Ukrainian court revealed the *Oplot titushky* to be behind kidnappings, beatings and torture of Automaidan and Euromaidan activists.[714] Kidnapped activists from western Ukraine, such as Yuriy Verbytskyy, were more likely to be murdered by vigilantes on the Euromaidan.

During the Euromaidan and Russian Spring, *Oplot* members were trained, financed and equipped by Russian intelligence, some of who had been covertly inserted on the ground as 'civilians' in eastern Ukraine a number of years earlier. GRU officer Igor ('Bes') Bezler, for example, had been living in Horlivka since 2012 and dropped his covert status in spring 2014 when he coordinated the separatist takeover of that city. Vigilantes and Russian intelligence facilitated the transportation of Russian political tourists into Kharkiv to beef up the pro-separatist rallies. "Igor" told *PBS Frontline* that 'We were recruited as pro-Russian *titushky*' and paid $40 per hour by Russian military and intelligence agencies operating in eastern Ukraine to beat up 'fascists.' The *PBS Frontline* documentary on Kharkiv shows Euromaidan supporters being dragged out of buildings and repeatedly beaten clearly petrified they were going to be killed.

*Oplot* members are also shown attacking a *Pravyy Sektor* office and two of them being killed by gunshots fired from inside the building. *Oplot* were outraged that Mayor Kernes allowed the *Pravyy Sektor* members to leave the building in order to defuse tensions, a decision that most likely led to its failed attempt to assassinate him a month later.[715] *Oplot* split from Kernes after he was

convinced by Kolomoyskyy, during a late February 2014 visit to his Swiss pa-
latial residence in Switzerland, to drop his backing for the collapsing Yanukovych regime and separatists.[716]

Included among DNR-LNR separatists are many members of *Oplot* such
as DNR Prime Minister Zakharchenko. They are the most ideologically zealot
of the locally recruited separatists and therefore have kindred spirits with Russian nationalist volunteers. *Vostok* battalion is composed largely of former *Oplot*
and similarly minded ideologically zealous separatists.

## SEPARATISTS, LOSERS AND CRIMINALITY

During the Euromaidan and in spring 2014 the Ukrainian state disintegrated in
the Donbas opening up a political and legal vacuum into which stepped hitherto marginal Russian nationalist and Pan-Slavic parties, paramilitary NGOs
and criminal groups. Since then, numerous testimonies and front line reports
have confirmed the presence of large numbers of criminals in an environment
where they could become quickly rich through looting, carjacking, kidnapping,
contraband of stolen goods, corporate raiding and theft from local businesses.
An epidemic of crime engulfed the LNR in an area where Russian Cossacks
became as notorious for their corruption as they did for their human rights
abuses. While some joined the separatists for ideological reasons, such as *Oplot*
vigilantes, many did so because it provided an income after their coalmines and
factories had closed or were destroyed in the conflict. In the DNR and LNR
there is no functioning economy and financial system making the separatist
enclaves a 'virtual mafia state.'[717]

Girkin described life for those living in the DNR and LNR as one of
being in a 'pigsty and a mess!' He described it as a caricature of the Russian
oligarchic system where the people had little say in running local affairs.[718] Although the standard of living has undoubtedly plummeted in the separatist enclaves since 2014, Girkin is wrong on three counts. The first is that the standard
of living was not a lot higher before the war under President Yanukovych. The
second is that an oligarchic system has long existed within a 'managed democracy' in the Donbas since 2000. The third is that the local inhabitants have never
had any say in the running of their affairs either when the Donbas was part of
Soviet Ukraine and the USSR or under the thumb of the Donetsk clan.

Russian soldiers and separatists have colluded in the looting of the
homes of what are already poor local people. Russian soldiers told a couple to
hide in the cellar from the battle that was about to begin in Debaltseve after

which separatists looted all of their possessions – pillows, blankets, gas stove, plasma television and even their teapots.[719] In the anarchic environment of the Donbas 'any person can become a victim of looting, torture, hostage-taking and execution.' Separatists and Russian forces can undertake crimes with complete impunity in an environment where there is no rule of law.[720] A Russian nationalist volunteer witnessed robberies, looting, the pillaging of scrap metal, and murders and his experience of the separatists led him to describe them as 'bandits' who had joined only to make money.[721]

Some reports testified to the instability of some volunteers who joined the separatists. James Sherr cites a separatist officer as saying 'mostly we have nut jobs.'[722] Those who joined the separatists were often the 'vengeful losers' and 'outcasts,' in Ben Judah's term, from post-Soviet economic transformations and the *zakon dzunhliv* of the 1990s. Those who had been on the fringes of society in Russia and in the Donbas became its mainstream in the separatist enclaves and Putin's Russia because the supporters of the separatists represented the 'more backward and ill-informed parts of society.'[723]

In Russia, former sportsmen, criminal enforcers and vigilantes, such as Vasily Yakemenko who had grown up in the gyms and gangs of the Lyubertsky working class district of Moscow, joined and led pro-Putin youth groups *Nashi* and Walking Together.[724] Yakemenko, who carried pictures of Hitler (as did many other Russian football *ultras*), had been typical of those who the KGB and its successor the FSB drew upon for important extra curricular work. They were the brutalised generation which had grown up at the end of the Brezhnev and Gorbachev eras and had experienced the criminal 1990s.

The justifications of these hardened men who joined the pro-Putin youth groups were akin to those who joined the separatists; that is, they wanted to fight 'fascism,' ward off Western-backed revolutions and regime change, and were paranoid about foreign agents who took advantage of Russia's weakness. Feelings of freedom in the late 1980s and early 1990s were replaced by those of fear and imminent disaster.[725] Such feelings were more common in Russia than in the Donbas and by the late 1990s more prevalent among Russian nationalist volunteers than locally recruited separatists. Girkin is disinterested in consumer materialism and for him the Crimea, Donbas conflict and fight for *NovoRossiya* was 'Russia's chance to avenge itself for losing the Cold War.'[726]

The nationalism and xenophobia of Putin's Russia and the DNR and LNR is popular among transition losers. Trump's 2016 election campaign ranted against globalisation, Mexicans and Muslims which mobilised white working class men. Socio-economically poorer people voted in far higher numbers for Britain's withdrawal from the EU in the June 2016 referendum. Paul Kubicek describes these losers in Ukraine as ethnic Russians, easterners, the elderly and those growing poorer who exhibit 'pro-Russian' attitudes and support closer ties with Russia 'perhaps even compromising Ukrainian sovereignty.'[727] Michael Gentile's research in the Donbas found that pro-Russian and Soviet identities were prevalent among older people, ethnic Russians, the lower educated, those less or not fluent in English, who hold intolerant attitudes and are generally unsatisfied with their lives.[728]

The middle classes tend to be more pro-Ukrainian in contrast with the working classes and transition losers who look to Russia as their substitute Soviet motherland and remain mired in Soviet nostalgia.[729] The middle classes prefer Ukraine 'because they identify with the freer political climate of the European Union' which is unattractive to the losers of the economic transition.[730] Many private businesses were forced to close after being looted by separatists leading to unemployment for those who had worked there.[731]

The Donbas war opened up class conflict with the middle class supporting Ukraine and some parts of the working classes, transition losers and pensioners backing the separatists. Separatists have recruited in cities that are economically depressed with many people reliant on subsidies and social welfare and where there is a large pool of pensioners. There is a difference between the 'simple people' who 'support the rebels' and the middle class who do not.[732] Middle class people had travelled outside the Donbas and often abroad, some of their children were enrolled in European schools and importantly, they had a lifestyle, businesses and expensive cars that they could lose from the conflict.

Pomerantsev describes 'local druggies and gangsters' among the separatists.[733] Many criminals were recruited and others joined after their local prisons were closed and emptied.[734] Local separatist leaders often came from criminal backgrounds. 'Aleksandr,' a Russian who participated in the annexation of the Crimea, said that the rebel groups in the Donbas 'turned into bands occupied with violence and looting' and 'People were taken hostage and released for ransom. Often they fought among themselves for spheres of influence.' 'In the pro-Russian zone (in the Donbas), weapons were handed out to criminals and drug addicts who robbed people, 'commandeered' businesses, homes, and cars,' he said. 'The situation for the Russian World project became more and more catastrophic. That romantic of the *Russkiy Mir*, Girkin, could not cope with the anarchy that was developing around him.'[735]

Denis Pushilin, self-declared 'governor' of the DNR had a 'reputation in Ukraine's criminal underworld'[736] from his involvement in the MMM pyramid scheme, among his other criminal activities. Well-known Russian singer Iosif Kobson, a frequent visitor to the DNR and LNR, has ties to organised crime since the 1990s, in many ways resembling those of Italian-American singer Frank Sinatra. Kobson and Otari Kvantrishvili, who was assassinated in 1994, had ties to the underworld and led social welfare charities and sportsmen clubs that were vehicles for money laundering.[737]

Asked if there would be support in Kharkiv if the separatists expanded their territory to that region, a local resident replied 'we also have plenty of rabble who will grab arms and run round: A person who was a nobody is given a rifle and he becomes a somebody.'[738] If an underemployed factory worker is given a weapon he receives a 'sense of purpose infused with history.'[739] There were many of these transition losers in the Donbas where machismo respect for toughness is commonplace. The view that the separatists brought with them criminality and lawlessness was commonplace. Former Mariupol Mayor Yuriy Khotlubey recalled the brief occupation of the city in April-June 2014 by pro-Russian separatists: 'they were simply criminals, who blackmailed and raped, so they aren't really welcome.'[740]

Donbas resident Viktor Alanov, an ethnic Russian, harboured negative feelings towards Ukrainian nationalism and the Euromaidan and supported the elevation of the Russian language to the status of a second state language. Nevertheless, he described many of the DNR and LNR separatists as 'morons' which was one of the reasons he did not support them[741]

Inevitably the character of those leading the separatists impacted upon their attitudes to human rights and the rule of law. In Luhansk, an alleged rapist was sentenced to death by a show of hands in a farce led by Aleksey Mozgovoy, the Russian commander of the Ghost Battalion.[742] Looters and drunk drivers were executed by Girkin's 'green men' in Slovyansk and by separatists elsewhere in the DNR and LNR.[743]

## THE CRIMEA

The Party of Regions integrated former and current criminal leaders to parliament, local government and the Crimean Supreme Soviet.[744] In the March 2006 elections to the Crimean Supreme Soviet and local councils, hundreds of candidates who had 'problems with the law,' according to then Interior Minister

Lutsenko, ran in the *Za Soyuz (For Union)*, For Yanukovych! and (Serhiy) Kunitsyn election blocs. Kunitsyn, who has close ties to gas tycoon Dmytro Firtash, was elected to parliament in 2012 by Vitaliy Klitschko's UDAR. Firtash, Russia's long-term agent of influence within Ukraine, who has business interests in the Crimea, financed Aksyonov's 2010 election campaign. After Russia's annexation, Rustam Temirgalyev, who also had long-term *biznes* ties to Firtash, joined the Crimean government.[745] The takeover of the Crimea was undertaken by 'Russian-speaking bureaucrats and criminals' who were supported by 'hired thugs.'[746]

Two organised crime bosses were elected in 2006 to the Crimean parliament by the Party of Regions. Oleksandr ('Sasha') Melnyk and Ihor Lukashev, who chaired the Crimean Parliaments budget committee and was known as the 'wallet' of the *Seylem* organised crime gang. Another *avtoritet,* leader of the *Bashmaki* organised crime gang Ruvim Aronov, was elected by the Kunitsyn bloc. Party of Regions parliamentary deputy Vasyl Kyselev condemned the presence of *Seylem* organised crime gang leader Melnyk in the For Yanukovych! parliamentary coalition in the Crimean Parliament. Yanukovych responded with the stern rebuke, 'I take responsibility for him!'[747] Melnyk 'is widely considered the protector of Rinat Akhmetov's interests in Crimea' which would point to Yanukovych providing a *krysha* for him on behalf of his business allies.[748] Deputy Prosecutor Kuzmin was responsible for Melnyk's evasion of justice after the Party of Regions lobbied the prosecutor's office to not press criminal charges.[749]

Russia relied on local organised crime to assist in its annexation of the Crimea. Russian 'little green men' organised a 'motley band of local activists and criminals'[750] and 'an ugly mixture of criminals, far-right radicals and nobodies.'[751] Putin's hybrid army in eastern Ukraine was not just 'little green men' but consisted of a ragtag band of mercenary Cossacks, pro-Kadyrov Chechens, organised crime vigilantes and extreme Russian nationalists. Organised crime groups involved in, for example cigarette smuggling on the Estonian-Russian border, were also involved in Russian espionage who when captured were sentenced by Estonian courts.[752] The collusion between the Russian state and its intelligence services and organised crime was even more prevalent in the Crimea and Donbas where organised crime transferred their criminal behaviour of kidnapping, theft, narcotic and people trafficking, and summary executions from the civilian to the military dimension.[753]

Close ties between criminal groups in the Donbas and Crimea were long evident in Crimean Prime Minister Aksyonov, local leader of the Russian Unity Party, who was head of the *Seylem* criminal 'brigade' in the 1990s when he had the criminal nickname 'Goblin.'[754] In the Crimea, organised crime groups had merged in the 1990s with Russian nationalists when Aksyonov 'was a rank and file 'brigadier' and was running criminal rackets.'[755] In taking over the Crimean parliament and government buildings they adopted similar corporate raiding techniques that had made organised crime leaders such as Aksyonov wealthy in the 1990s. On 27 February 2014, 60 armed Russia Unity party thugs, backed by Russian GRU *spetsnaz*, seized parliament and forced it at gun point to adopt a separatist resolution and appoint Aksyonov as prime minister. The Russian Unity party, a Crimean political ally of the neo-Nazi RNE, received a mere four percent in the 2010 elections and was merged into United Russia following the 2014 Crimean elections.

After the elections, Crimean organised crime received preferential access to former Ukrainian state and private assets in a massive 1990s style corporate raiding bonanza. Confiscations of state and private assets 'are being carried out in a widespread systematic fashion that has no recent precedent.' The use of corporate raiding has been dependent on the Ukrainian oligarch's past links to Putin and his attitudes to the Ukraine-Russia crisis. Firtash's businesses have not been touched in the Crimea. Kolomoyskyy meanwhile, had 83 assets (hotels, offices, apartments, tourist resorts and petrol stations) nationalised by the occupation authorities.[756]

## CONCLUSIONS

The 'Wild West' frontier nature of the Donbas was always associated with violence and inside the USSR with prison culture. The region attracted rootless people, was a place to go and conceal oneself and begin a new life, and convicted criminals were given reduced sentences in return for working in the coalmines. The region had a far higher rate of prisoner population than other regions of Soviet Ukraine. From the mid 1980s to the mid 1990s a criminal civil war pitted criminal groups against one another and turned the relationship on its head between *siloviki* and criminal groups. If in the USSR the *siloviki*, although corrupt, remained in control, that changed in the 1990s when criminal groups came to power in the Donbas and the Crimea.

With leading criminal and oligarch opponents eliminated by 1995-1999, Yanukovych and Akhmetov took control of the Donbas in a highly corrupt relationship where the former provided a political *krysha* for both of them to become wealthy. They drew on vigilante sportsmen for corporate raiding, election fraud and political violence, many of who naturally progressed into the separatist forces in the Donbas and the Crimea in spring 2014. These vigilante sportsmen attracted economic and social 'losers' (i.e. working classes, pensioners, and rural population) from the post-Soviet transition who were given training, weapons and financial support by Russian intelligence and military, which is analysed in subsequent chapters. This chapter's analysis of crime and violence provides the background for Chapters 5 and 6 on the past and current history of the Donbas region and the rise and fall of the Party of Regions political machine.

# CHAPTER 6

# THE DONBAS AND UKRAINE

*What, even the Donbas voted in favour (of the referendum on independence)?*
President Boris Yeltsin (December 1991)[757]

*A separate army is not necessary. Why do we need to defend ourselves against our brothers in Russia and Belarus?*
Former Army Colonel, Donetsk Mayor Viktor Vyichkov
(December 1991)[758]

The majority of nation-states are not ethnically or linguistically homogenous; for example, Alsace Lorraine is in France, Catalonia is in Spain, and South Tyrol is in Italy. But, these are long-established nation-states with a civic definition of nationhood and members of the European Union where borders have declined in importance under the Schengen zone. Russian identity remains primordial, ethnic and based on language and culture and therefore more closely resembles pre-1930s Europe. Countries with such definitions of their identity have sought to unite speakers of one language, whether German in the 1930s or Russian today.

The Donbas has always had an ambivalent relationship to Ukraine in a similar manner to the Crimea. Friedgut writing decades before the Donbas conflict said the question of the Donbas 'belonging to Russia rather than to an independent Ukraine were to play a central role in Donbas politics.'[759] During times of upheaval the question of the loyalty of the Donbas has always come under strain. During the Russian civil war, the Donbas created an independent pro-Bolshevik 'Donetsk-Kryviy Rih Soviet Republic' that sought to become an autonomous republic inside Bolshevik Russia but Lenin insisted the region be included within the Ukrainian SSR (Putin pointed to the absurdity of Lenin forcing the Donbas to join Soviet Ukraine to increase the proportion of Bolshevik support in the republic.[760] The Donbas had 33 monuments to 'Donetsk-Kryviy Rih Soviet Republican' leader Artem (Fyodor Sergeyev), including one in central Donetsk. In the first half of the 1990s coal miners' strikes organised by Donbas elites panicked Kravchuk into calling pre-term presidential elections in 1994 and in the same year's parliamentary elections held a local referendum on the region's status. The referendum produced 80 percent support for federalism, 87 percent backing for Russian to become a second state language and a very high 89 percent for Ukraine to join the CIS Economic Union and CIS Parliamentary Assembly. During the Orange Revolution, a separatist congress was held in Severdonetsk that demanded a federalised Ukraine with autonomous status for the east and south. During the Euromaidan, the region was at the forefront of anti-Maidan activities that evolved into an armed insurrection after Yanukovych fled from office.

From the 1870s the Donbas was heavily settled by Russians from Smolensk, Tula and Kursk because the local population 'is unwilling to engage in factory work.' In 1884, locals made up only a quarter of the inhabitants of Yuzovka (Stalino, Donetsk) while 71 percent were from Russia. The Russian village became the main source 'providing the human mass for a proletarian concentration second only to that in Russia's central industrial regions around Moscow and St. Petersburg.'[761] In the 1871 and 1897 censuses, Russians accounted for 82.5 and 73.1 percent respectively of the Donbas population. During the Russian civil war, Ukrainian peasants returned to their villages where they suffered from famine in the early 1920s. Donetsk 'has been predominantly Russian throughout its existence' and 'has remained Russian in ambience.'[762] Russians in the Donbas feel perfectly at home in the Donbas.[763]

In July 1917, Yuzovka had 32,000 Russians and 10,000 Jews with Ukrainians coming third with 7, 000. Between 1884-1923, the ethnic composition of Yuzovka changed from 87 to 54 percent Russian because of a growth of the Jewish population to 38 percent. In 1923, Ukrainians only accounted for only 7 percent of the city's population.

In the Russian civil war, the Donbas overwhelmingly supported the Bolsheviks who received 40 percent of the vote during the Constituent Assembly elections with the Socialist Revolutionaries (SR) and Mensheviks receiving 18 and 7 percent respectively. Although the Bolsheviks received high support in the Donbas, their support within Ukraine as a whole was low at 10 percent. High support for the Bolsheviks and the region accounting for two thirds of Bolshevik party members were important factors behind Lenin's decision to include the Donbas in Soviet Ukraine.[764]

Documented sources showed that in the Donbas there was 'no mention of the activities of any Ukrainian parties in the mines or factories.' Ukrainian parties were active in Kharkiv and other neighbouring provinces but the Donbas 'was a stronghold of Russian socialist activity rather than Ukrainian nationalism.'[765] This was also the case in independent Ukraine.

An intriguing aspect of the history of the Donbas is why Ukrainian peasants, unlike Russian peasants from central Russia, did not seek work in the coalmines and factories. Ukrainian political parties received some support in the district *zemstvo* but had no presence in the coal mines. Ukrainian peasants viewed the coalmines as 'foreign both ethically and ethnically.'[766] Ukrainian peasants viewed coal mines as dark, enclosed, dusty, full of smoke and blinding heat from furnaces.[767]

In Moscow's factories, local peasants were hired because 'they remained in a familiar surrounding that was Russian speaking, Orthodox Christian in its faith and based on a fairly uniform peasant sub-culture.'[768] In the Tsarist Russian Empire, Ukrainian peasants were used as strike breakers because they viewed coal miners as 'capable of any vileness.' Peasant women would scare their children with bed time stories of bogeymen miners. For Ukrainian peasants, the coalminers were dirty, not religious, liars and 'capable of killing a man for a few pennies.'[769] A century later similar stereotypes continue to exist on both sides of the Donbas conflict. In 1925, during the height of indigenisation, Ukrainians accounted for only 19.1 and 19.4 percent respectively of metallurgical workers and coal miners. The large number of Russian migrants in the Donbas made the Soviet policy of indigenisation unpopular. In the 1920s, Ukrainianisation made little headway in the Donbas where it was 'just above zero' and 'superficial' because the growth of the Ukrainian language met strong opposition and even hostility.[770]

The transformation of Soviet nationality policies in the early 1930s and the *holodomor*, 'brought an end of Ukrainianisation and the beginning of Russian rule.'[771] The Donbas was one of the hardest hit by Stalin's crimes against humanity and the Donbas political elite and *Komsomol* was decimated.[772] 40-50,

000 of the 267, 000 arrests during the Great Terror in Soviet Ukraine were made in the Donbas.[773] Kuromiya writes that by the 1930s any ethnic Ukrainian in the Donbas was a potential 'nationalist' and to Soviet Ukrainian First Secretary Kaganovich, one of the architects of the *holodomor*, 'every Ukrainian is potentially a nationalist.'[774]

Following World War II there was a 'dramatic decline in Ukrainian language affiliation'[775] in the Donbas that continued through to 1991 and was never reversed in independent Ukraine. Soviet nationality policies sought to 'solidify Ukraine's links to the RSFSR by strengthening the Russian character of Ukraine's border regions' and the Russian population of the Donbas surpassed that of the share of the Russian population in Latvia and Estonia.[776] Ukrainian became a minority language in Donetsk, Luhansk and Odesa and the proportion of ethnic Ukrainians was low in those three cities and in Kharkiv. The number of Ukrainians who gave Ukrainian as their native language in Soviet censuses declined and those who gave Russian rose to nearly 88 percent of the urban population of the Donbas.

'The Donets basin represents an extreme case'[777] of absolute decline in Ukrainian population, identity and language. During the same period, large number of Russians settled in eastern and southern Ukraine, particularly in the Donbas. Bohdan Krawchenko believes that unskilled Ukrainian workers could not compete with Russian migrants who received the best positions in the economy. Ukrainian identity was also threatened by inter-marriage and bilingualism and through pressure for assimilation.[778]

The city of Donetsk was so strategically important to be renamed Stalin in 1924 and Stalino in 1929, a name it carried until 1961. But, more importantly the Donbas was a 'corridor' with direct connection to Moscow.[779] Donetsk was a 'powerful proletariat core' that gave them high status within Soviet Communist mythology of the workers paradise.

Donetsk contributed the largest regional organisational membership to the Soviet Ukrainian Communist Party, and unusually the local Communist leader was an ethnic Russian. The Donbas faction in the Soviet Ukrainian Communist Party was 'eminently acceptable to Moscow' as it was from a region that was isolated from Ukrainian identity and culture. More importantly, Donbas regional elites 'are attuned to thinking in "All-Union", i.e. centralist terms.'[780] This remained the case in independent Ukraine where 'their views and assessments are shaped by Moscow rather than Kyiv.'[781] The Donbas related to other regions of Ukraine, Kirstin Zimmer writes, as if to foreign countries.[782] Russian print and electronic media, which became increasingly virulent, shrill and Ukrainophobic from 2012, dominated readers and viewers in the Donbas.

The Donbas Communist elites were hostile to national communism and supported the overthrow of Shelest in 1971 and his replacement by Brezhnevite Shcherbytskyy who returned to traditional Soviet nationality policies of assimilation, Russification and repression of dissent and opposition. They operated in 'an environment where the nationality problem is virtually non-existent.'[783] The Donbas produced few dissidents and even less *samizdat*; the one exception was the Free Trade Union Association of the Soviet Working People, an independent trade union established by Aleksey Nikitin and Volodymyr Klebanov.

The Donbas was never a source for Soviet Ukrainian first secretaries because this was reserved for the major cities of Dnipro, Kharkiv and Kyiv. But, the region was influential in government ministries such as coal and metallurgy. Yakiv Pohrebnyak, first secretary of the Donetsk Communist Party from 1969-1973, rose to become the chairman of the republic's Trade Union Council.

By the last two Soviet censuses the proportion of ethnic Russians had grown to 43.4 percent in the Donbas which was just under the 51.6 percent who were Ukrainians. [784] In the region ethnicity declared in censuses mattered far less than allegiance to Soviet and regional identity which cut across ethnic Ukrainian and Russian lines. The Soviet regime had facilitated the influx of Ukrainians into Donbas industry and coalmining although Ukrainians moving into the region came into an environment without Ukrainian-language schools and media and where Soviet and regional identity was expressed in the more 'civilised' Russian language used for urban modernity and industry. In 1989, Petro Poberezhnyy, deputy head of the Strike Committee of the Donbas Basin, said 'Well, it is not our fault that we do not know our symbols and the history of the Ukrainian people.'[785] By the late 1980s, Ukrainians in Horlivka, which experienced some of the first atrocities and conflict in spring 2014, had 'become similar to Indians of North America, and aboriginals of Australia and New Zealand. Ukrainian schools or kindergartens are absent. In the city you will not hear any Ukrainian language.'[786] There were no Ukrainian national cultural symbols and 'The town council places all emphasis to, so they say, prevent *Rukh* people or *Banderites* from coming here' while opposing steps to establish Ukrainian sovereignty. A quarter of a century on little had changed.

The Donbas, Crimea, Kharkiv and Odesa provided the lowest support for independence in the December 1991 referendum in a portend of the conflict that would erupt in the four regions. In the Crimea, support for independence was only a third (36.5 percent with 63.5 percent not participating), while in the three *oblasts* it was less than two thirds. In all of Ukraine's other *oblasts* the vote for independence received support in the 80s and 90s. With an average 'No' of 7.58 percent in Ukraine, the highest proportion of 'No' votes were in the Crimea (42.22 percent), Sevastopol (39.39), Luhansk (13.41), Donetsk (12.58), Odesa (11.6) and Kharkiv (10.43). The lowest turnout of voters was in Sevastopol (63.74 percent), Crimea (67.5), Donetsk (76.73), Odesa (75.01) and Kharkiv (75.68). Of these cities and regions, Sevastopol and the Crimea were annexed by Russia, Donetsk and Luhansk experienced separatist conflict and Kharkiv and Odesa were swing cities where pro-Ukrainian forces defeated Russian nationalists. In these two swing cities support for any form of separatism was far lower at 10.7 and 5.2 percent respectively than in the Donbas and the Crimea. Outside of these areas, support for separatism was even lower, with 86.2 and 93 percent respectively negatively disposed towards it in Dnipro and Zaporizhzhya.[787]

## INDEPENDENT UKRAINE

A majority of those who had identified as Ukrainians in the Soviet census nevertheless had a Russian-speaking eclectic Soviet and regional identity. This was expressed in the Donetsk coat of arms which 'is a bizarre mixture of Tsarist, Soviet and Ukrainian symbols.'[788] Since 1991, they have voted not for Ukrainian national democratic or social democratic political parties but for the pro-Russian and Sovietophile KPU, the Party of Regions and Progressive Socialist party. Separatists have received their greatest support in the most heavily industrialised regions and coalmines in eastern Donetsk and southern Luhansk.

Important for our understanding of the place of the Donbas and the Crimea in Ukrainian history and the crisis is that these regions were largely absent from what Benedict Anderson describes as a Ukrainian 'imagined community.' They never featured prominently in Ukrainian historiography, the programmes of political parties and in the research and publishing output of Ukrainian scholarly centres in Ukraine and especially the West. Western histories of Ukraine paid little attention to the Donbas. This was not the case for other eastern and southern Ukrainian regions such as Kharkiv, Dnipro and Zaporizhzhya.

The political culture that emerged from decades of Sovietisation in the Donbas created a set of nine discernable attributes:

1. The Soviet regime had stifled independent initiatives and 'installed habits of dependence' creating a deeply held culture of paternalism. A coalminer said in 1990, on the eve of the disintegration of the USSR, that they had 'learnt not to believe in anything.'[789] The population had a sense of 'excessive helplessness.'[790] Hans Van Zon writes 'Power is not used to facilitate but rather to block initiative coming from below.'[791] Small and medium businesses accounted for only 15 percent of the share of the economy in Donetsk *oblast*.[792] Pomerantsev found in the Donbas that opposition to the Euromaidan was also a product of injured male pride. Kyiv had stood up to a corrupt Donetsk president while Donetsk, which knew about the mafia culture of its regional clan, had not and in this way allowed them to get away with mass corruption.[793]

2. Donbas voters backed political parties propagating paternalistic populism (e.g. KPU, Party of Regions) and did not support former *Komsomol* leaders in the Liberal Party of Ukraine and Russophone intellectuals in SLON. Ihor Todorov believes the liberal idea failed in Donetsk because it could not compete with the left-populist KPU and Party of Regions.[794] Leftist populist parties with their bases in the Donbas promised a wide range of benefits if they were elected but there was no intention of ever implementing these because 'Distrust and cheating became rampant in society, at all levels.'[795]

3. The population of the Donbas has a 'syndrome of being captured by the past' in believing in their economic power and the growth of industry in the former USSR.[796] This myth was though, based on old and outdated industries of coal and metallurgy which have been in terminal decline in all industrialised countries.[797] The Ukrainian cultural intelligentsia on the other hand bemoaned industrialisation and urbanisation as destroying Ukrainian villages and therefore leading to denationalisation. First Secretary of the Soviet Ukrainian Communist Party Leonid Melnikov asked 'No, you tell me why (Ukrainian) writers are opposed to the Donbas and to industrialisation.'[798] After Ukraine became an independent state the myth of the Donbas as an industrial powerhouse of the USSR was transformed into the myth of the Donbas 'feeding' Ukraine (i.e. allegedly contributing the highest proportion towards its budget), especially the myth of the industrial Donbas 'feeding' rural,

agricultural western Ukraine.[799] The myth of the Donbas 'feeding' Ukraine translated into the right of Donbas leaders to be the 'natural rulers' of Ukraine. In reality, the Donbas received large subsidies, especially for coal mining, and a huge proportion of its profits were never taxed and did not contribute to the state budget.

4. A third of prisons in Soviet Ukraine were located in the Donbas and they held a higher than average proportion of felons. In the USSR, convicts were offered a reduction in their sentences if they agreed to become coalminers in the Donbas and every third coalminer had a criminal record.[800] Many small towns developed around coalmines with generations of families that included former convicted criminals.[801]

5. Low mobility of the Donbas population with few travelling outside their towns and region. When western Ukrainians wished to host children from the Donbas for a free vacation their parents refused to send them saying 'We'll never see them again; they will be used as organ donors!'[802] Many residents did not take the initiative to improve their standard of living by searching for work abroad or in other parts of Ukraine. Gentile found that those who were poor in the Donbas represented a stable group over the last three decades because they were resilient to change.[803] Western and southern Ukrainians have migrated in large numbers in search for employment throughout Europe and the income they have sent and brought home has built small and medium businesses in tourism and the hospitality trade.

6. Although the population were, and continue to be, treated with contempt, kept servile, provided with poor local services and impoverished they nevertheless voted for Ukraine's wealthiest oligarchs who purchased exorbitantly priced palaces and penthouses throughout Europe. The population of the Donbas blamed the 'mafia' for the high levels of corruption but could not see the 'mafia' on its own doorstep in the form of the oligarchs and the Party of Regions. A servile mentality and low feelings of efficacy was deeply ingrained and therefore continues to influence relations between the Donbas population and their new rulers, the separatists. A Ukrainian journalist held captive by the separatists was treated as a slave labourer alongside imprisoned locals. 'The rebels beat them up, take away their cars, rob them, and they still root for the LNR. It's a paradox I hadn't expected.'[804]

7. In going on strike in 1989, Donbas coalminers 'disavowed the source of their own privileged identity as a labour elite.'[805] Their standard of living dramatically declined in the 1990s and 2000's when coalmines became a dangerous source of employment and Ukraine had the second highest accident rate in the world after China.

8. The Russian language is viewed as the language of modernity and Soviet power. The expansion of Ukrainian-language education since 1991 did not take place in the Donbas and Crimea.

9. Soviet identity was the most popular of three cultural identities, the other two being Ukrainian and Russian. Very high levels of inter-marriage produced Soviet and regional identities, rather than identification with an ethnic group which would have required taking the side of one parent. Only one third of marriages in the Donbas were between two Ukrainians. The Donbas was both *more* Soviet in its identity than the Crimea and had a higher rate of inter-marriage, which by the 1970s reached 55 percent and by 1992 had slightly declined to 47.7 percent. The Crimea also had very high levels of inter-marriage.[806] Inter-marriage produced a large group of people who were bi-ethnically Ukrainian-Russian and who identified themselves as Soviet. 51 percent in Donetsk believed they were heirs of both Ukrainian and Russian cultures.[807] Soviet and regional identities were more popular than Ukrainian in the Donbas and this influenced the formation of a strong allegiance to a Donbas 'imagined community.'[808]

Nevertheless, the conflict showed to what degree it is difficult to define the contours of the Donbas as it does not perfectly ensconce the entire Donetsk and Luhansk *oblasts*. Separatism has been unpopular in northern Luhansk and western and southern Donetsk and even within these areas of Donetsk controlled by Kyiv there were sharp and unexplained differences. Although all of the schools in Slovyansk use Ukrainian (except one that uses Russian), Democratic Initiatives Foundation President Iryna Bekeshkina points out how it has a more pro-Russian orientation on domestic and foreign affairs than Kramatorsk which is only 10 miles away, which should caution scholars to make sweeping statements about language in Ukraine.[809] DNR Deputy Defence Minister Berezin admitted that although small towns support his 'republic' the population of the city of Donetsk is split 50: 50 into pro-Russian and pro-Ukrainian wings.[810] Evidence that Ukrainian identity was repressed can be found in the changes that have taken place in Ukrainian controlled Donbas since 2014 where for the first time Ukrainian civic (state) is more popular than regional identity. Identity in the Donbas can be analysed in three ways:

1. A third of the population supported some form of separatism, either as an independent Donbas (20 percent) or union of their region with Russia (15 percent).[811] Support for these two forms of separatism was highest among those holding a Soviet (16.2 percent) and Russian (31.9 percent) identity and lowest among Ukrainians (4.5 percent).[812] Russian nationalist-separatists were popular in the Crimea in the late 1980s and first half of the 1990s and their influence was revived by the Party of Regions during and after the 2006 elections. In the Donbas, separatist movements such as the Movement for the Rebirth of the Donbas, Civic Congress, Party of Slavic Unity, and Donetsk Republic were marginal but took power in the 2014-2015 crisis. In the 2014 DNR elections, the Donetsk Republic won first place with 68.35 percent of the vote and Free Donbas came second with 31.65 percent. Prior to the conflict the leaders of these marginal separatist and Pan-Slavic groups had been integrated into the KPU, Progressive Socialist Party and Party of Regions. Bazylyuk, a former leader of the Party of Slavic Unity, became an outspoken Ukrainophobe in the Party of Regions. The Party of Regions was different to centrist parties in having a noticeable Pan-Slavic and pro-Soviet wing led by deputies such as Kolesnichenko.

2. Decades of inculcation of hostility to western Ukrainians, 'bourgeois nationalists,' 'fascists' and 'Nazi hirelings.'

3. Distrust and xenophobia of the West, particularly the US and NATO. At the same time, Donbas oligarchs and regional elites lived a large proportion of their lives in western and southern Europe where they trusted banks with their cash, purchased real estate and sent their children to private schools. Ukraine was treated like a colony from where large rents were extracted on which taxes were not paid and the funds deposited in offshore tax havens.

The Donbas became associated with the rise of a rapacious oligarchic class in the 1990s that united after a decade of violence. Volodymyr Boyko, the former director of the Ilich plant in Mariupol said, the real *'khazayin'* in Donetsk *oblast* was the wealthiest oligarch and not Kyiv's governor.[813] In a December

2005 poll, 29.9 percent of Ukrainians viewed Akhmetov as a 'criminal authority (leader) of the Donetsk mafia' and another 28.4 percent the *khazayin* of Yanukovych and the Party of Regions. The remainder saw him as the wealthiest person in Ukraine and a businessman.[814] The *khazayin* is the equivalent of a feudal lord[815] and 'enlightened autocrat' who controls as much of the economy and the state as he can, is intolerant of dissent and harbours no mutual duties and rights towards his subjects.[816] Such a political culture is the antithesis of European values to which they allegedly claimed they aspired to. The greed of the Donetsk clan showed no bounds and was evident in Yanukovych's *Mezhyhirya* palace whose grounds were the size of Monaco and where he was serviced by hundreds of members of staff. Jaroslav Koshiw writes that, 'Not since serfdom was a landlord so well served.'[817]

In independent Ukraine, Donetsk elites sought economy autonomy in order that surpluses previously extracted by Moscow and Kyiv remained in Donetsk for the enrichment of emerging oligarchs and elites. The first attempt to extract autonomist concessions from Kyiv took place during the 1993 coal miner's strikes that led to the appointment of Donetsk 'Red Director' Zvyahilskyy (a long-term Party of Regions deputy who was elected by the Opposition Bloc in 2014). President Kravchuk agreed to pre-term presidential elections that were won by Kuchma. In 1996-1997, Kyiv and Donetsk negotiated a de facto 'non-aggression pact' of which Donetsk Governor Yanukovych was the intermediary, guarantor and *krysha*. In 1999, Donetsk became a Special Economic Zone, a black hole through which local oligarchs enriched themselves at the expense of the Ukrainian state.[818] Under the law, there was exemption from import duties and taxes for five years, exemption on income taxes for three years and exemption for half of income taxes for a further two years.

Similar to the USSR, the long-term competitors of the Donetsk clan were Dnipro and Kharkiv. The latter, an intellectual and student city without the feral culture of Donetsk, was relatively easy to co-opt. The former proved more difficult because it also produced 'strongmen' such as Lazarenko, Kolomoyskyy and Tymoshenko. The clash was present in assassinations and attempted assassinations in Donetsk and Dnipro in the 1990s and in 2014 when Governor Kolomoyskyy showed no quarter towards pro-Russian separatists in his native region.

Large Soviet era plants were perfect for machine politics and electoral fraud where workers, who felt little efficacy and fearful of unemployment, voted how the bosses instructed them – much as they had in the USSR.[819] But, a political machine could only appear after violence had subsided and the victorious side and governor brought together warring groups.

In 2000-2001, the Party of Regions was launched and cooperated with President Kuchma and pro-presidential centrist parties but from 2005 until 2014 the Party of Regions acted independently. In common with other authoritarian leaders in the Eurasian region, Yanukovych's cynicism believed that everybody had a price and that he could monopolise Ukraine by buying local elites, much as Putin had done in Chechnya; Putin had after all bribed him in December 2013 in gratitude for not signing the EU Association Agreement.[820] But, their mutual cynicism misunderstood the underlying dynamics of Ukraine as much as had Russian political technologists in 2004 and Russian intelligence services in 2013-2014. Yushchenko, his Chief of Staff Viktor Baloha, and Poroshenko could be bought, but Tymoshenko could not and she therefore had to be imprisoned. Importantly, millions of Ukrainians who are far from the feeding troughs of political power also could not be bought.

Post-Soviet transition in the Donbas deepened the dependence of workers on a patrimonial labour-boss relationship forged during a period of socioeconomic instability where workers were afraid of losing their jobs, unlike in the USSR where there was full employment. The deepened patrimonial dependence of workers on their bosses took place at the same time as the rise of a rapacious and kleptocratic elite that was unaccountable for all manner of crimes such as murder, wonton violence, massive theft, asset stripping, and corporate raiding.

The Donetsk elites, and other oligarchs, benefited from maintaining Ukraine in the twilight zone of 'partially reformed equilibrium'[821] The existence of Ukraine in a hybrid transition was best placed for oligarchs and corrupt state officials to financially benefit 'from arbitrage between the reformed and unreformed sectors of the economy.'[822] The Ukrainian state was on the verge of bankruptcy for much of its existence because oligarchs, as in the Donbas, were permitted to extract huge rents by 'abusing monopoly positions and privileged access to state resources,' price manipulation, tax evasion, asset stripping and high levels of criminalisation.[823]

## 'FRATERNAL PEOPLES'

Of all Ukrainian regions, the Donbas had the highest support of 72 percent for the statement that communities in Ukraine should have the right to honour their own heroes and traditions and the lowest of 20 percent agreeing with the statement there should be the same ones throughout Ukraine.[824] The Donbas was disinterested in participating in the Ukrainian national building project and celebrating its national heroes and myths.

The coming to power of the Donetsk clan in 2010 permitted them to introduce counter-nationality policies that had last been in place in the Soviet Union and which were popular in their home region. The Institute of National Memory was closed down and re-established as a research department within the Azarov government. The appointment of Communist Valeriy Soldatenko as its new director in February 2011 was a planned insult to patriotic Ukrainians as he had been the author of the 1990 statement of the Soviet Ukrainian Communist Party that denied the 1933 *holodomor* was artificial. The statement had claimed it was a consequence of bad weather and disorganisation arising from collectivisation. Soldatenko's long-running stance on the *holodomor* was the same as that of Yanukovych's and they were both in line with the demand by President Medvedev in his 2009 address to President Yushchenko to no longer pursue a policy at home and abroad of describing the *holodomor* as a 'genocide' committed against Ukrainians. Although Minister of Education Tabachnyk also adopted the Russian line on the *holodomor* this was a complete about turn with his international lobbying of the 'genocide' position when he had been in charge of the humanities in the Yanukovych government on the fiftieth anniversary of the *holodomor* in 2003.[825] It would be impossible to imagine an Israeli government minister remaining credible after moving from a position on the holocaust as an act of genocide to downplaying it some years later.

De-Stalinisation had been taking place over the course of the last two decades, beginning in the Ukrainian diaspora in 1983 on the fiftieth anniversary of the *holodomor* and from the late 1980s in Soviet and then independent Ukraine. The *holodomor* is a highly sensitive issue that any Ukrainian government would downplay or, worse still, adopt the Russian line at its own peril because it would be guaranteed to infuriate patriotic and nationalistic Ukrainians. Re-Stalinisation in Russia and under Yanukovych through the erection of monuments of Stalin, downplaying of his crimes and myths of the Great Patriotic War replacing the World War II narrative would contribute to the public anger bubbling under the surface that exploded into the open during the Euromaidan. In the eyes of patriotic and nationalistic Ukrainians, Putin and Yanukovych came to represent the revival of the Soviet Union's Ukrainianophobic policies.

Two other issues contributed to increasing public discontent. The first was a return to Soviet era denunciations of Ukrainian nationalism as 'fascism.' The second was steps to forge a common Ukrainian-Russian history which undermined the foundations of Ukrainian independence that Yanukovych was constitutionally required to uphold. A Russian-Ukrainian commission, led on the Russian side by the odious political technologist Sergey Markov (who is not a professional historian), on formulating a common approach to history found it difficult to deal with the origins of the Ukrainian state, the 1654 Pereyaslav Treaty and the Ukrainian national movement during the Russian civil war.

Radical changes in school textbooks began to be implemented that were different to the Ukrainian historiography that had been promoted since the late 1980s and especially in independent Ukraine. Such changes were obviously in line with those espoused in Putin's Russia and included the following historical myths.

1. Ukrainians and Russians are not different peoples. Putin and other Russian leaders have increasingly made this claim since 2012.
2. The Tsarist and Soviet myth of Kyiv Rus as the 'cradle' of three 'fraternal' eastern Slavic peoples.
3. Russification was no longer mentioned.
4. The myth of the Great Patriotic War replaced the history of World War II.
5. Return to Soviet denunciations of Ukrainian nationalists as 'fascists' and 'Nazi collaborators.'
6. Negative critical analysis of Soviet history was greatly reduced. Yanukovych had a decade earlier described the teaching of Ukrainian history as 'immoral' and 'one-sided, negative appraisals of the Soviet period in our history.' He added, 'to try to condemn all that legacy indiscriminately is simply to shamelessly insult the memory of our parents.'[826]
7. The importance of the Orange Revolution was minimised and election fraud in the 2004 elections was ignored.[827]

New attitudes to Ukrainian history reflected long-established views held in the Donbas where Ukrainian nationalist organisations, the disintegration of the USSR, Orange Revolution and EU Association Agreement were all viewed negatively. Hetman Mazepa, Bandera, Kravchuk, Yushchenko, and Poroshenko were perceived as negative political leaders. In contrast, Soviet leader Stalin was viewed positively in the Donbas, unlike in the remainder of eastern

Ukraine and especially in central and western Ukraine. Donbas residents positively viewed Hetman Bohdan Khmelnytskyy and the 1654 Treaty of Pereyaslav as a 'reunion' of Ukraine and Russia, Tsar Peter the 'Great' and the formation of the Russian Empire, Lenin and the creation of the USSR, and Soviet leader Brezhnev. Yanukovych is also viewed negatively by a quarter of the Donbas compared to over half of Ukrainians, although the reasons are likely to be different.[828]

The wholesale adoption of a Putinist historical narrative during Yanukovych's presidency coupled with a return to the use of the 'fascist' bogeyman would prepare the ground for conflict during the Euromaidan or, if this had not taken place, during the 2015 elections. In 'Putinising' Ukraine's history, President Yanukovych and Minister of Education Tabachnyk were playing with fire.

## THE DONETSK CLAN AND THE SEPARATISTS

The Donetsk clan were no strangers to separatism; they had, after all, threatened Kyiv every decade in 1994, 2004 and 2014. Because of this threat and the weakness of the Ukrainian state, successive Ukrainian presidents had delegated the running of the region to local oligarchs such as Akhmetov. Not all of the Party of Regions were separatists, and Valentyn Landyk, leader of the Labour Party, claimed in the late 1990s not to have met people clamouring for separatism in the Crimea and the Donbas.[829] Other Party of Regions leaders and activists had been willing to use the threat as leverage with Kyiv and while in 2004 this worked to their advantage, a decade later, when it was undertaken more forcibly alongside Russian intervention, it had slipped out from under their control. In a 2007 survey, 49 percent of Party of Regions voters were willing to back the separation of their region and the creation of an independent state. 45.4 percent of Party of Regions voters believed there were deep contradictions between the west and east of Ukraine that could lead to disintegrative consequences for Ukraine.[830]

Six factors should be considered when analysing the relationship between the Party of Regions and separatists. The first was the willingness to collude with and fan separatist inclinations in the Crimea from 2006 and in eastern and southern Ukraine from 2010. The Party of Regions sought to appeal to a wide audience ranging from centrist businessmen, leftist populists and Pan-Slavic and Sovietophile orientations, some of who are inclined towards supporting separatism. 'The Party of Regions believe that in this manner they can become a force that would attract the entire spectrum of pro-Russian voters ranging from the peaceful 'Little Russians' to the radical enemies of Ukrainian statehood.' Yanukovych and the Party of Regions believed that they could control the radical separatist movements and manipulate them. The Party of Regions had always integrated separatists (e.g. Bazylyuk, Viktor Tykhonov, Markov) into its ranks and worked alongside paramilitary separatist groups, such as the Donetsk Republic organisation (which had close ties to Kolesnykov). In September 2008, the Party of Regions, KPU and Crimean Russian nationalists supported separatism in South Ossetia and Abkhazia by backing Russia's recognition of their independence from Georgia. Six years later, Putin justified his annexation of the Crimea with reference to Kosovo, a false analogy that the Party of Regions had bought into with South Ossetia and Abkhazia.[831] Putin told the Russian Federal Assembly on 18 March 2018 that if Kosovo's secession from Serbia was justified than so too was the Crimea's from Ukraine.[832] The Party of Regions strategy of 'controlled separatism' through manipulation, co-opting and colluding with separatists and Ukrainophobic groups backfired because when it disintegrated it opened up a political vacuum into which hitherto marginal groups moved into taking control of large swathes of the Donbas.[833] After all, who is it to say whether separatists were co-opted by the Party of Regions or they themselves infiltrated the Party of Regions.

Yanukovych was typically deceitful when he said that he had not backed separatism in 2004, describing this as a 'political provocation.'[834] Nevertheless, what was autonomy and federalism on one side of a conflict could be interpreted as separatism by the other. All Donetsk political parties, including the Liberals, had championed 'local autonomy.'[835]

Secondly, the deeply embedded culture of violence in the Donbas and widespread use of vigilantes for election fraud, corporate raiding, attacks on journalists and the opposition in the Russian Spring, prepared the atmosphere for an escalation of violence. Leading Party of Regions oligarchs, such as Akhmetov, never condemned the violence unleashed by President Yanukovych against Euromaidan activists. Some of the vigilantes, such as from *Oplot*, joined separatist forces and formed the core of the *Vostok* battalion, a GRU *spetsnaz* force led by former SBU *Alpha* officer Khodakovskyy.

During the Orange Revolution and Euromaidan, the Party of Regions brought to Kyiv vigilantes who were members of sports clubs, lower level organised crime enforcers and mercenary coalminers. In 2014, unlike a decade earlier, there were no moderates inhibiting Yanukovych's use of violence and

President Putin, senior adviser Surkov and Russian intelligence was pressuring the Ukrainian president to take tough repressive measures against the protestors.[836]

Thirdly, Donbas oligarchs remained passive, neutral or colluded during the month and half from the time that Yanukovych fled from office in late February and the arrival of Girkin and Russian 'little green men' in early April. These undertook coordinated takeovers of Slovyansk, Horlivka, Krasnyy Lyman, Kramatorsk, Artemivsk, Kasnoarmiysk, Druzhkovke, Makeyvka and Yenakiyevo. Until their arrival, the separatists were not a professionally run military force.[837] Since 2010, Russian intelligence had been penetrating and taking over the commanding leadership of the SBU and was operating covertly during the Euromaidan in providing training and financing for 'anti-fascist' vigilantes and Russian nationalists.[838] It is not credible to believe that Akhmetov did not know of these Russian covert operations; after all, he had a massive business empire, a Party of Regions network in local government and had completely co-opted the security forces in Donetsk *oblast*.

Akhmetov declined the offer of Donetsk governor (with Taruta as governor of Luhansk) and he refused to support the formation of Ukrainian volunteer battalions,[839] taking a different stance to Kolomoyskyy on both counts. During these three months (February-April 2014), the separatists could have been pushed back by local elites and oligarchs through the mobilisation of pro-Ukrainian demonstrations. Workers and coalminers remained passive and only patrolled the streets in Mariupol when ordered to by Akhmetov, but much later.[840] Zvyahilskyy and other Party of Regions leaders controlled the largest coalmines and could have mobilised coalminers against the separatists.

Fourthly, Party of Regions leaders and oligarchs both encouraged anti-Maidan violence and, despite controlling local security forces, did not prevent their disintegration and defection to the separatists. The head of the Donetsk Ministry of Interior Roman Romanov, for example, was loyal to Oleksandr Yanukovych and his forces adopted passive, neutral or pro-separatist stances.

A fourth factor was that Donbas elites and Party of Regions leaders adopted the virulent rhetoric of Russia and the separatists towards the Euromaidan and the political opposition. Kolesnykov, close to Yanukovych and Akhmetov since the 1990s, issued shrill demands in terms no different to those broadcast by Russian television. Kolesnykov, similar to other Party of Regions leaders, had close ties to Russophile separatists such as the Donetsk Republic who went on to take a leading position in the DNR.[841] Claiming to speak on behalf of eastern Ukraine, Kolesnykov said: 'They don't want to see armed neo-fascists from western Ukraine and Kyiv in their region. They don't want all of their taxes going to Kyiv. And they don't want to be told what language to speak.'[842]

Sixth, oligarch control of local media was another avenue of influence that was not used to counter separatist propaganda. Akhmetov owned the popular *Donetskiy Kryazh* newspaper that became a leading mouthpiece of the separatist demands and published inflammatory rhetoric against the Ukrainian armed forces who were described as 'Nazis' and 'fascists.' The newspaper provided space on its web site for former members of *Berkut* to vent their hostility to the Euromaidan.

Finally, 'some local oligarchs' 'made tacit alliances with separatist leaders.' 'Quiet secession' in the Donbas 'was possible only because of the cooperation of local authorities and the non-formal allegiance of certain security forces to the Party of Regions and big business.' As Wilson points out, successful movements require resources for mobilisation, training and equipment and these were provided by local elites and Russia: 'elites and the resources were the keys to converting a marginal movement into a mass phenomenon.'[843]

The oligarch whose public image suffered the most from his mishandling of the separatist conflict was Akhmetov. In sitting on the fence he infuriated Ukrainian patriots while at the same time, in not fully backing the separatists he is tolerated by them only because he provides employment to many residents of the region.[844] As with many oligarchs, Akhmetov's concern was not Ukrainian national security but his business empire, and his industrial plants and palace in the Botanical Gardens have not been nationalised. Akhmetov's plants have continued to operate in the DNR and LNR to who they pay taxes.[845] Taruta and Kolomoyskyy, two oligarchs who agreed to become regional governors, have lost assets in the Donbas and the Crimea. Party of Regions local elites either actively supported the separatists or stayed neutral in an unwritten pact of non-aggression.

Akhmetov bided for time and sat on the fence seeking to play the same game the Donetsk clan had in November 2004 when they had threatened Kyiv with separatism and in so doing 'playing a duplicitous game' to maintain their influence.[846] Akhmetov's words and actions were again as duplicitous as when he had claimed to US Ambassador William Taylor that he supported transparent politics and business. Publicly Akhmetov called for 'calm and compromise' but behind the scenes he was negotiating a non-aggression pact with separatist leaders.[847] Denis Pushilin and his separatist allies were 'allegedly Akhmetov's puppet project' and two thirds of self declared DNR 'people's governor' Gubarov's activists were paid by Akhmetov's people.[848] Gubarev told a Russian newspaper that Akhmetov had provided the separatists with financing, which of course he denied.[849]

Akhmetov wanted to create a 'puppet government' in the Donbas 'to increase their bargaining power with Kyiv.'[850] Akhmetov therefore publicly upheld Ukraine's territorial integrity but did little to back this up. When head of the presidential administration Serhiy Pashynskyy asked Akhmetov for assistance he 'withdrew from the process, even though we asked him to assist us.'[851]

As the *khazayin* of the Donbas, Russian political tourists could have only travelled to the region with his neutrality or support and 'local thugs would not have organised themselves without his (at least) tacit approval.'[852] Instead, Akhmetov 'promised to prevent the dispersal of the separatist gangs, did not respond to looting and violence by the DNR militants in Donetsk, and urged the Kyiv authorities to listen to the Russian terrorist Girkin and Boroday, backing their demand to be the "Voice of Donbas."'[853] Akhmetov's double game could be also seen in his close ties to DNR Prime Minister Zakharchenko who 'has been part of the Donetsk clan for some time.' Akhmetov asked Surkov if he would agree to the appointment of Zakharchenko as head of the DNR as a way of guaranteeing the protection of his assets.[854] Since March 2014, when *Oplot* and Kharkiv Mayor Kernes parted ways, 'the financing of *Oplot* has been undertaken by people in Rinat Akhmetov's circle.'[855] It was perhaps not coincidental that Akhmetov met protesters on 8 April 2014 where he gave them his support at the same time as Girkin and the 'green men' arrived in the Donbas 'which leads one to think that he is well informed about what is happening.'[856] Long-term Russian analyst Trenin wrote that Ukrainian business-political leaders 'who had long been close to the Kremlin sponsored and encouraged early protests in the region against the central government in Kyiv.'[857]

Akhmetov's ally from the 1990s, former hit man Ivanyushchenko, has been directly implicated in supporting anti-Maidan vigilantes and Donbas separatists. Chornovol's investigations found evidence of Ivanyushchenko financing former organised crime leaders turned separatists in Horlivka and Yenakiyevo, where he has a palace.[858] Ivanyushchenko's second palace is in Monaco next door to palaces owned by former Minister of Energy Eduard Stavytskyy and Minister of Agriculture Mykola Prysyazhnyuk.

In Luhansk there was direct evidence of Party of Regions local *khazayin* Yefremov colluding with the separatists. Yefremov, who headed the Party of Regions parliamentary faction, 'fully controlled Luhansk and all decisions in the city were undertaken only in consultation with him.'[859] Landyk revealed that in February 2014, Yefremov met with Russian adviser Glazyev in his Luhansk palace and they agreed on the provision of support to a Russian takeover of the *oblast* in return for which he would remain as the local *khazayin*.[860] The LNR 'is a project of former governor Yefremov' where there were close ties between 'People's Governor' Valeriy Bolotovyy and Yefremov. The LNR was staffed by former members of the Luhansk state administration who were in turn appointed under the influence of Yefremov.[861] Bolotovyy was Yefremov's enforcer in illegal business activities and corporate raiding. The LNR leadership and 'government' included many old guard Party of Regions activists or from Yefremov placeman Luhansk Mayor Serhiy Kravchenko's office, who was installed into power by Yefremov. Luhansk *oblast* state television producer Radion Myroshnyk joined the LNR authorities.

## THE *NOVOROSSIYA* PROJECT

For a brief period in 2014-2015, Putin talked up the idea of *NovoRossiya* that he had first indirectly raised as far back as 2008 in his speech to NATO. But, Putin's history is rusty and he confused which territories had belonged to *NovoRossiya*. Putin has a poor grasp and malleable view of Russian history, whether he is talking about the Christianisation of Kyiv Rus (at a time when Moscow never existed) or *NovoRossiya*. There were two different *New Russias* in 1764-1802 and 1822-1874 and neither included Kharkiv (*Slobozhanshchyna*).

On 17 April 2014, Putin asked why the Soviet leaders had given Kharkiv, Luhansk, Donetsk, Kherson, Mykolayiv and Odesa to the Soviet Ukrainian republic? In the 1990s, Russian nationalists such as Moscow Mayor Yuri Luzhkov had asked a similar question about whether Khrushchev had been drunk when he had given the Crimea to Soviet Ukraine.' 'Russia lost these territories for various reasons, but the people remained' Putin said.

In fact, *NovoRossiya* was never inhabited by a majority of Russians but by Ukrainians, specifically Ukrainian peasants who moved there after its annexation by the Russian Empire and by the 1897 Tsarist census, Ukrainian peasants had become the majority of the population in all of the *NovoRossiya* regions.[862] The province was also populated by Jews, Romanians, and Tatars; Russians, to whom Putin always appeals, arrived much later during Soviet industrialisation.[863] The two *NovoRossiyas* never included Kharkiv which was an old centre of the *Slobozhanshchyna* province that had historical ties to Ukrainian Cossacks and since the opening of a University in 1804 had been the intellectual capital of eastern Ukraine. It was not until 1937 that a pedagogical institute was opened in Stalino (Donetsk) and not until three decades later in 1965 that this was transformed into Donetsk State University.

Following the failure to mobilise Russian speakers in the six *oblasts* outside the Donbas, the Kremlin project for a *NovoRossiya* was folded. By the spring of 2015, the Kremlin 'has effectively admitted defeat, no matter how it tries to spin it.' The 'dream of many Russian imperial nostalgists that great swathes of Russian-speaking Ukraine would flock to join Moscow has faded.'[864] The majority of Ukraine's Russian speakers flocked to Kyiv not to Moscow and the *NovoRossiya* project's leaders attributed the failure to the fact 'it has no active support in Ukraine's eastern regions.'[865] The *NovoRossiya* project never got off the ground because it is beyond the comprehension of Putin and Russian nationalists to understand Ukraine's Russian speakers as Ukrainian patriots. Girkin simplistically believes that *NovoRossiya* is a 'Russian state' that is inhabited by 'Russian' people 'the same people as you and me' who want to be part of Russia.[866] He and Putin were both very wrong.[867]

Russia's *NovoRossiya project* planned a civil war (with the assistance of hybrid activities) in the Russian Spring that could be turned to Russia's advantage. Kharkiv and Odesa were the strategic swing cities in which violence took place between February and May 2014 where there was some support for separatism, Putin and the *Russkiy Mir*. In four other *oblasts* – Dnipro, Zaporizhzhya, Kherson and Mykolayiv there was little public backing for separatism. Of these four, the most Sovietised was Mykolayiv which had a large military-industrial complex and greater economic ties to Russia; nevertheless, Oleksandr Senkevich, the candidate of *Samopomich (Self Reliance)*, a pro-Western political force in the Ukrainian parliament, defeated the Opposition Bloc to win the 2015 election for mayor of the city.[868]

## CONCLUSIONS

A century ago the Donbas had not wanted to be part of Soviet Ukraine and Ukrainian nationalists had not claimed it. The region was included by Lenin to bolster Bolshevik support inside Soviet Ukraine and during the history of the Soviet state the region remained a stronghold of conservative forces opposed to national communists. The Donbas was a strong supporter of Moscow's interests and Soviet nationality policies and Russification and disinterested in Ukrainian history, culture and language. Fast forward to independent Ukraine and little had changed. The Donbas emerged from a criminal civil war to negotiate semi-autonomy from Kyiv and after Yanukovych and the Donetsk clan moved to the national stage, sought on two occasions to capture the entire Ukrainian state which on both occasions provoked mass popular protests.

Ukrainian patriots have been willing to fight for the Donbas but not for the Crimea, a region which to an even greater degree has laid outside the Ukrainian 'imagined community.' Russian hybrid war and local separatists failed to establish a *NovoRossiya* and were only able to capture a minority of the Donbas region (accounting for thirteen percent of Ukrainian territory) showing how it is a misnomer to view Luhansk and Donetsk *oblasts* as uniformly similar. Three years into the Ukraine-Russia crisis the Parliamentary Assembly of the Council of Europe described Russian policies as 'hybrid annexation' of the DNR and LNR which had followed its hybrid war.[869]

The conflict had divided the Donbas into two with one part controlled by Kyiv and another by the DNR and LNR. On the side controlled by Kyiv, Ukrainian identity is growing and de-communisation is taking place while on the opposite side there are similar processes to those taking place in Russia of re-Sovietisation with a cult of Stalin and the Great Patriotic War. In the very near future the only place in the Donbas with monuments of Lenin will be the DNR and LNR as 'Donetsk is a city that feels increasingly Russified – politically, economically and socially.'[870]

The next chapter analyses the Party of Regions which in building a mafia and authoritarian state brought Ukraine to crisis.

CHAPTER 7

# THE PARTY OF REGIONS

*I say this as an academic, who devoted a lot of attention in his life to the question of investment. I researched in this field of science and for eight years headed a department at a university.*

Dr. Viktor Yanukovych, speaking during a 2010 visit to Berlin[871]

The Party of Regions was never a centrist political party but a leftist populist, paternalistic and authoritarian political force. 'Non-ideological authoritarian' political forces rule through powerful political machines and employ efficient repressive machines. But, as Krastev writes, 'Authoritarians are less likely to stay in power in states that are small and weak, that are located near the European Union or United States, need IMF loans, that are economically and culturally connected with the West, that lack a strong ruling party, and that cannot or will not shoot protesters.'[872] All of these factors applied to Ukraine which borders four NATO and EU members and is perennially in economic crisis and requires western financial assistance. Although the Party of Regions was a political machine it could never hope to monopolise Ukraine and in the 2006 and 2007 proportional elections it received a third of the vote. United Russia received twice the vote of the Party of Regions and Putin remained far more popular than Yanukovych. Unlike authoritarians in Eurasia, Yanukovych's regime was half hearted in its crackdown on the Euromaidan failing to find the same political will to murder hundreds of protesters on the scale of that carried out by Uzbek security forces in Andijon in May 2005.

Slavophile and Sovietophile orientations within the Party of Regions did not bring it the political stability and monopoly of power which great power imperial and Soviet nationalisms provided for Putin and Lukashenka respectively. In a regionally diverse country such as Ukraine these orientations were abhorrent to a majority of voters, many of who were active in civil society and nationalistic groups and mobilised their supporters *against* the 'Sovok' Yanukovych and Party of Regions 'Other' blocking Ukraine's integration into Europe. In Russia and Belarus, great power imperial and Soviet nationalisms respectively had majority appeal and pro-western liberals in the former and anti-Russian nationalists in the latter attracted minority support.

Yanukovych's 1997-2002 governorship of Donetsk established a managed democracy model that he sought to expand to the remainder of Ukraine during his presidency. Zimmer writes 'The Party of Regions cannot be viewed as an actor separate from the local and regional authorities. The local officials did not perceive this "fundamental" functional separation either. The resources of the city were used in a targeted and directed manner to fulfil the Party's "mandate".'[873] The Donetsk model of governance is a 'merging of political and economic power with total suppression of dissent and unbridled corruption' an 'extension of Soviet civilisation.' Van Zon describes this model as a 'semi-feudal oligarchic capitalism with a command-and-control approach to governance in which no dissent is tolerated.'[874] During his presidency, Yanukovych sought to build this model in the whole of Ukraine which failed because, as we know from Kuchma's book, *Ukraine is not Russia.*

But, could former criminals become respectable *biznesmeni* and play by the rules following the path of robber barons in the West? US Ambassador Taylor was typical of western policymakers and experts who naively wished to believe the words of Akhmetov that this was going to happen. They underestimated the unbridled greed of oligarchs, their narcissism, the need for the state (as in the West) to impose new rules of the game, their ability to continue to get away with massive rent seeking and the willingness of European states and offshore tax havens to accept their dirty money. Ambassador Taylor reported in cables from Kyiv that he had met Akhmetov many times when he had become convinced that he supported an open and transparent business environment. In a speech given in 2006, Akhmetov said 'I am of course for European choice. I am of course for European values.'[875] But, words are cheap and the proof was in the pudding. There was no evidence of Akhmetov going legit during Yanukovych's presidency when Akhmetov expanded his business empire through insider privatisations and government contracts during a time when 'Akhmetov's businesses flourished exponentially.'[876] Akhmetov's parliamentary group in the Party of Regions voted for anti-democratic legislation on 16 January 2014. Akhmetov was merely telling Western policymakers and Ambassadors what they wanted to hear and was, like Putin had for many years, practicing the Soviet game of hoodwinking naïve westerners, a diplomatic form of *maskirovka*.

Ambassador Taylor reported that Yanukovych wished to overcome his negative image after the 2004 elections and to shake off his image of authoritarianism and corruption. Taylor described him as the 'moderating centre of the party' who 'wants respect to polish his image, and to protect Ukrainian sovereignty.'[877] These were not Yanukovych's words, as he is a cynic, but those of US political consultant Paul Manafort whose talents for obfuscation made him attractive for US presidential candidate Trump who hired him to run his 2016 presidential election campaign. Manafort was successful in lobbying a softer image of Yanukovych in the US and European embassies in Kyiv.

Yanukovych never changed his operating style and during his presidency created a mafia state that ended in bloodshed and treason. Yanukovych had never had any intention of changing his image and if he had wanted to would have required a massive overhaul of his personality. Lyudmilla Pavlyuk showed how Yanukovych's 2004 election campaign had abused state-administrative resources, inflamed anti-western rhetoric and brought out his 'Soviet authoritarian style and local pattern in its most primordial version.'[878]

The kind of positive changes in the Donetsk clan that Western policymakers wished to find was impossible to achieve; after all, not all political leaders look up to and seek to emulate the West and the EU. Van Zon writes that parasitic elites, short-term corrupt perspectives, cynicism, contempt for the rule of law and human rights are 'pre-modern' and 'anti-modern practices" that 'are very resistant as they are rooted in a patrimonial world outlook.'[879]

## REGIONAL CAPTURE AND MONOLITHIC UNITY

The only centrist party of power in Ukraine to capture a region and mobilise a stable voter base was the Party of Regions. In the 1990s, the two strongholds of the NDP were Kharkiv and Dnipro, the two cities that had ruled Soviet Ukraine. Many of its members were drawn from the *Komsomol's* Democratic Platform and it therefore espoused a quasi-liberal ideology. The Inter-Regional Bloc of Reforms (MBR) had similar regional centers and *Komsomol* origins and also espoused a liberal but more Russian-speaking platform. The two parties

*One of a number of bizarre megalomaniac paintings, this of Viktor Yanukovych, found at the Mezhyhirya palace*

merged in 2000. In the late 1990s, the NDP suffered from a major split similar to that which the Soviet era Communist Party underwent dividing into *nomen-*

*klatura* and democratic platform wings. The former supported Prime Minister Valeriy Pustovoytenko and the latter split to launch the Reforms and Order Party led for most of its existence by Viktor Pynzenyk.

An important factor that worked against the resurgence of the Dnipro clan in post-Soviet Ukraine through the NDP was the inability of business elites to merge into a united regional clan. Divisions continue to hamper relations between Pinchuk and Kolomoyskyy, Lazarenko and Tymoshenko. Serhiy Tihipko, an ally of Pinchuk's, joined Prime Minister Azarov's government and his Strong Ukraine (formerly Labour Ukraine) party merged with the Party of Regions in 2012.

In the 1990s, Donetsk-based pro-business Liberal (created by former *Komsomol* leaders) and ('Red Director') parties were also electorally unsuccessful. Most of these parties were merged into Party of Regions or were co-opted by it. The Liberal Party emerged in Donetsk in October 1991 and was headed by unrelated former *Komsomol* leaders and oligarchs Volodymyr Shcherban and Yevhen Shcherban but it was never able to become the local party of power. In 1994-1998, the Liberal Party's Social Market Choice parliamentary faction was led by former SBU Chairman Yevhen Marchuk, testimony to the reversal of the relationship between *siloviki* and criminals discussed earlier. Liberal leader and parliamentary deputy Yevhen Shcherban was assassinated in November 1996 in Donetsk airport. The Liberals and the Labour Party joined forces in the *Razom (Together)* bloc in the 1998 elections but failed to enter parliament receiving only 1.89 percent of the vote. The Donetsk-based Party of Regional Revival of Ukraine (PRVU) obtained even less in that year with only 0.9 percent. The Party of Regions fifteenth anniversary in 2012 traced its roots to the PRVU and its founder, then Donetsk Mayor Volodymyr Rybak, was parliamentary chairman in 2012-2014.

Donetsk launched a regional party of power in 2000 through the unification of the PRVU, Labour Party, Party of Pensioners, Poroshenko's Party of Ukrainian Solidarity, and former Kyiv Mayor Leonid Chernovetskyy's for a Beautiful Ukraine party. The Party of Regional Revival-Labour Solidarity Ukraine was renamed the Party of Regions in March 2001 when it established the Regions of Ukraine parliamentary faction. After merging with (future Prime Minister) Azarov's European Choice faction the Regions of Ukraine became the second largest parliamentary faction (after Our Ukraine) in the 2002-2006 parliament.

The unification of the Donetsk clan ensured the Party of Regions received massive financial support from local oligarchs, such as Akhmetov and

*Prosecutor-General Viktor Pshonka painted as Napoleon with First
Deputy Prosecutor-General Renat Kuzmin on the left painted as one
of his commanders. Both are living in Russia and wanted by Interpol*

after 2006 from the 'gas lobby' headed by Firtash, Yuriy Boyko and Lyovochkin. Yanukovych used the entry of the 'gas lobby' to increase his autonomy
from Donetsk oligarchs and the merger of the Republican Party of Ukraine,
the party of the 'gas lobby,' with the Party of Regions provided him with an
alternative source of funding. In 2010-2012, 'gas lobby' leaders Lyovochkin,
Boyko and Hryshchenko held influential positions as chief of staff (head of the
presidential administration), Minister of Energy and Coal Industry and Minister
of Foreign Affairs respectively. Meanwhile, during Yanukovych's presidency,
Firtash, Akhmetov and Oleksandr Yanukovych who led 'The Family, the president's personal' clan, were awarded the greatest number of insider privatisation
deals. With high levels of distrust in Ukrainian society 'only the small circle of
family and friends can be trusted...'[880]

Yanukovych's four-year kleptocracy and corporate raiding facilitated the
rise of the president's 'Family' clan. State capture permitted Yanukovych to

strive to become the *khazayin* of Ukraine and towards this goal to become financially independent of both Donetsk oligarchs and the 'gas lobby' through accumulation of assets by 'The Family.' In 2011, Oleksandr Yanukovych, after being granted the lion's share of government tenders and corporate raiding, entered Ukraine's top 100 wealthiest people.[881] 'The Family' controlled state finances (Ministry of Finance, including the former State Tax Administration and National Bank of Ukraine) and the *siloviki* (Ministry of Interior, Ministry of Defence and SBU).

The Party of Regions provided a means of defence against what was perceived to be hostile political forces such as Yushchenko's Our Ukraine and the Bloc of Yulia Tymoshenko (BYuT). After Kuchma left office in 2004 the only powerful centrist party remained the Party of Regions and leading members of smaller centrist parties joined the Party of Regions to seek protection from possible criminal charges. The Party of Regions acted as an insurance policy for former state officials accused of abuse of office by giving them parliamentary seats and immunity from prosecution and therefore 'The Party of Regions is a kernel for the Kuchma elite.'[882] In 2005-2006, the former pro-Kuchma elites were fearful that the 'Bandits to Prison!' slogan of the Yushchenko election campaign would be put into practice and Kolesnykov's arrest in April 2005 was viewed by Donetsk elites as tantamount to a 'declaration of war.' When Yushchenko visited Donetsk he 'behaved like a conqueror that had come to a subjugated territory.'[883] In the process, the US Embassy in Kyiv reported, the Party of Regions has brought, 'together much of the political opposition to President Yushchenko.' Taras Chornovil, who played a leading role in the Party of Regions between 2005-2012, therefore does not describe it as a 'political party' but as a club of acquaintances who have come together to survive and defend their mutual interests.[884]

## STABLE VOTER BASE

A stable, disciplined and authoritarian voter base that prioritises the economy and stability over democracy facilitated the Donetsk clan in establishing a monolithic party machine and the Party of Regions monopolisation of power in eastern and southern Ukraine. The Donbas, during the decade after the collapse of the USSR, produced a neo-patrimonial institutional environment where no dissent was allowed and there was integration of politics, business, and crime, and the state and business empires resembled entire Soviet branches of government ministries.[885] Ukrainian experts had already begun describing the Donbas as the country's 'Belarus' as early as 2002, the year that Yanukovych was appointed prime minister.[886]

Patrimonial political culture perpetuates the Soviet paternalistic dependency of the working classes on elites, thereby elevating collectivism over individualism and personal efficacy. The Party of Regions had a stable election base of voters who comprise around a quarter to a third of the electorate who tend to be less educated, working class, pensioners and veterans, many of whom voted for the KPU when the Party of Regions did not exist (1994, 1998). Similar socio-economic voters have given President Lukashenka a stable base of support of Belarusian voters.

Party of Regions voters did not support political parties led by Russophone intellectuals, such as the MBR (1994), SLON (1998) and KOP (Winter Crop Generation, 2002). They would not have voted in such large numbers for middle class oligarchs, such as Tihipko if he had been the authority's candidate in the 2004 elections. In the 1998 elections, only 12, 400 out of 2.4 million voters in Donetsk *oblast* backed SLON. Ideologically liberal political parties that emerged from the *Komsomol* failed to find a large voter base at a time when the middle class had yet to emerge during Ukraine's transition to a market economy. The Party of Regions voter base was diametrically different and drew on big business and working class voters. Meanwhile, Donetsk elites were uninterested in 'the ideological, political and cultural aspects of independence nor with the idea of historical justice.'[887]

A large proportion of former KPU and Progressive Socialist Party voters defected to the Party of Regions and support for the KPU slumped from 20 in 2002 to 3 percent in the 2006 elections only growing again in 2012, at the expense of the Party of Regions, to twelve percent. Between two thirds to three quarters of Party of Regions voters held a socialist and communist orientation.[888] The Party of Regions replaced the KPU as the dominant regional political force and the Communists were gradually co-opted, joining Party of Regions-led parliamentary coalitions in 2006-2007 and 2010-2012. In the 1990s, the KPU and local business elites had closely cooperated when 'Donbas businessmen operated in the Communist Party's shadows' and after the launch of the Party of Regions, 'In 2002, Donetsk business completely moved out of the shadows of the KPU.'[889] The Party of Regions and Yanukovych remained loyal to Kuchma while he remained in power becoming an independent political force from 2005 after which it signed cooperation agreements with Putin's United Russia party and Crimean Russian nationalist parties.

## LEFTIST POPULIST AND AUTHORITARIAN

In the 'ideological' arsenal for Eurasian authoritarian leaders Yanukovych and Putin, *stability* represents discipline and the ability to get things done. Ukrainian Ambassador to Belarus Viktor Tikhonov, a senior Party of Regions leader, praised the Belarusian authoritarian regime for bringing 'stability.'[890] The Party of Regions abhors 'chaos' and described the Yushchenko presidency as 'orange lawlessness.'[891] Donetsk voters respect a strong power structure with a clearly defined hierarchy and a domineering *kerivnyk (boss) and khazayin.*[892] Stability is a key element of 'democracy,' Yanukovych adamantly believes.

As an authoritarian political party, its congresses felt like 'party congresses from Soviet times' that 'take place according to the best canons of CPSU congresses.'[893] In parliament, the Party of Regions and KPU were highly disciplined and uniform in their voting while Yanukovych 'still behaves like a Soviet era party boss.'[894] When the Party of Regions was in power in 2002, 2006-2007 and 2010-2014, it bribed, blackmailed or coerced opposition deputies into defecting to the government coalition. A 'black book' found in the Party of Regions headquarters during the fire on 18 February 2014 showed that it had spent $2 billion on bribing parliamentary deputies, government and state officials.[895] Bribes of as high as $6 million were offered, according to NU-NS (Our Ukraine-People's Self Defence) deputy Yuriy Hrymchak, for MPs to defect to Yanukovych. The 'black book' shed a spotlight on a massive programme of corrupting the state and its officials that began prior to the 2010 elections giving credence to views that Yanukovych came to power illegally through bribery.

When opponents could not be pressured to switch sides, they were denigrated in the media as 'fascists' and subjected to intimidation and repression. Tabachnyk, Education Minister in 2010-2014, wrote a book after the Orange Revolution denouncing his opponents as 'fascists.'[896]

The Party of Regions 2006 election programme prioritised 'stability, well-being and development perspectives' and Prime Minister Yanukovych promised he would install 'order' in the country. Yanukovych said on ICTV channel in the second round of the 2010 elections that 'democracy in the first instance is order.' 'We are going to install order in the nation, no matter what they call that process. If it is 'usurpation,' then let it be 'usurpation' You can hold us back, but to what benefit? I wouldn't advise that, neither to politicians nor to the president.'[897] Yanukovych had a similar view of unruly political processes as did Putin; the former saw 'anarchy' after the Orange Revolution while the latter described 1990s Russia as 'chaos.' The solution of both leaders was a managed democracy and authoritarian 'order' that would produce 'stability.' Yanukovych's election campaigns focused on providing stability and getting things done through discipline.[898] 'Stability' continues to be a buzzword in the Donbas and the separatists are fighting 'so there are no oligarchs, so we have stability.'[899]

The Party of Regions 2007 pre-term election programme was entitled 'Stability and Well Being' and during the elections, Yanukovych emphasised his party's principles as the 'renewal of justice and victory to the political forces which work for stability.' A US diplomatic cable from Kyiv reported, 'Yanukovych repeated again and again that the priority for the Party of Regions is stability.'[900] Pro-Yanukovych parliamentary coalitions were called Stability and Well Being (2006-2007) and Stability and Reforms (2010-2012). In the 2012 election campaign, the Party of Regions used billboards with the slogans 'From Stability to Prosperity,' 'Stability has been Achieved!' and 'Chaos has been Overcome. Stability has Been Achieved!'

Party of Regions election programmes emphasised the economy with little attention paid to the rule of law, media freedom, democracy, free elections and corruption. Yanukovych's election speeches and programmes and Akhmetov's statements stressed economic growth and higher standards of living while being conspicuously silent on democratisation and fighting corruption.[901] The Party of Regions by virtue of its reliance on former Communist voters and a working class base was one of the most populist parties in Ukraine. Yanukovych's 2010 election programme, drawn up in an alliance with the Soviet era, Federation of Trade Unions, made extravagant promises of higher social spending and pensions, tax-free breaks for small and medium businesses, and subsidised household utility prices.

Ukrainians who harbour eastern Slavic and Soviet identities that are commonly found in the Crimea and Donbas exhibit greater authoritarian tendencies and prioritise economics and stability over democracy.[902] 40 percent support for democratic governance in the Donbas was lower than 56 percent in western and central Ukraine.[903] Democratic values are more popular in western and central Ukraine. The highest numbers of Ukrainians who believe an opposition is necessary for a democracy are to be found in western Ukraine (81 percent) and the lowest in eastern Ukraine (46 percent).[904] Surveys by the Democratic Initiatives Foundation, Ukrainian Centre for Economic and Political Studies (Razumkov Centre) and the International Foundation for Electoral Systems (IFES) showed that a sizeable proportion of Ukrainians believe political stability and the economy are as important as democracy. Ukrainian preferences for democracy decline as one moves from the west to the east of the country. 47 percent believed (36 percent disagreed) that democracy is not a good political system to maintain order.[905]

The origins of preferences for stability, economic growth, standards of living and order over democracy are greater levels of Soviet nostalgia that are to be found in regions of eastern Ukraine, such as the Donbas. A survey by the All-Russian Center for Public Opinion (VTsIOM) showed that 64 percent of Russians would vote for the preservation of the USSR if a referendum was held today similar to the one held on 17 March 1991, which asked Soviet citizens if it was necessary to preserve the country in its current form. Voters who prioritise stability and economics over democracy were more likely to vote for the Party of Regions and the KPU and to be from eastern and southern Ukraine where there are very high levels of support for economic development (50 and 64 percent) over democratic rights (20 and 22 percent) respectively.

The opposite is true in 'orange' Ukraine where 41, 48 and 45 percent in western and central Ukraine and the city of Kyiv respectively supported democratic rights over economic development (32, 35 and 36 percent). A very high 55 percent of Ukrainians believed authoritarianism was better than democracy in certain situations (22 percent); it was unimportant if Ukraine was a democracy (17) or found it difficult to answer (14). 35 percent of Ukrainians believe the country needs a strong hand (compared to 43 in Russia).[906] Support for authoritarianism as more preferable than democracy in certain situations was highest among Party of Regions and KPU voters (23 and 36 percent respectively) and lowest for *Batkivshchyna* and even nationalist *Svoboda* party voters (16 and 20 percent).

IFES reported that apathy towards democratic development is highest in eastern, southern and northern Ukraine where 39 percent were ambivalent. Fewer eastern Ukrainians believe Ukraine is a democracy than western Ukrainians (47 compared to 36 percent). KPU voters (31 percent) gave the lowest support for democracy with the highest given by *Batkivshchyna* voters (59). A greater number of nationalist *Svoboda* voters supported democracy than Ukrainians who voted for the Party of Regions (55 and 51 percent respectively).

## STATE ADMINISTRATIVE RESOURCES AND ELECTION FRAUD

Donetsk machine politics rested on clientalism, violent coercion, and efficient use of state administrative resources for election fraud that had proven successful in local, parliamentary and presidential elections.[907] Wilson writes that the Party of Regions is a 'clientalistic and authoritarian organisation' that rewards friends and punishes enemies.'[908] Power translates into access to financial resources for patronage and clientalism, the ability to install 'order,' defeat ones *protyvnyky (mortal enemies)* and buy off one's opponents. 15 percent of Party of Regions voters believe financial and administrative resources are required to win elections, twice the number of Our Ukraine and BYuT voters.

The transition in Donetsk was one of 'may the strongest win' when competitors were pushed aside 'with unfair and often criminal methods.'[909] The strongest and most ruthless came out on top using unscrupulous methods. The 'Red Directors' took control of state enterprises through semi-criminal methods that provided them with the resources to 'secure the support of administrative, business and criminal structures.'[910] The primary manner in which ex-State Directors and criminals became oligarchs 'was based on plunder of state-owned companies with the complicity of public authorities.'[911] Donbas 'Red Directors' formed the Party of Labour headed by Landyk which although a lobby group for state subsidies to big business cooperated with the pan-Slavic Civic Congress and the Party of Slavic Unity.

State administrative resources were used in the Donetsk region from the 1999 elections, three years after Yanukovych was appointed regional governor, and in that year he bragged to Kuchma that his people were in total control of the *oblast*.[912] Greater access to state administrative resources facilitated an increase in turnout in Donetsk from an average of 66 percent in the 1994 and 1998 elections, 79 percent in the second round of the 1999 elections and an incredible 97 percent in the fraudulent second round of the 2004 elections. In December 1998, Governor Yanukovych established the Unity, Accord and Revival bloc that brought together seventeen Donetsk-based NGOs and parties to support Kuchma's re-election and joining the pro-Kuchma national movement *Zlahoda (Consensus)*. Governor Yanukovych never concealed the fact that district governors organised the Unity, Accord and Revival bloc under the aegis of the local state administration. State administrative resources supported Kuchma's re-election in 1999 and ZYU (For a United Ukraine) bloc in the 2002 elections.

In 1999, state administrative resources increased the vote for Kuchma between the first and second rounds by 21 percent. Kuchma came second to KPU leader Petro Symonenko in the first round of the 1999 elections but with the use of state administrative resources his vote massively jumped by 21 percent in the second round. The tapes made illicitly in the president's office by presidential guard Melnychenko recorded Governor Yanukovych reporting to President Kuchma, 'The boys who were put in place fulfilled what was asked of them. Moreover, in reality Socialist Party (SPU) leader Oleksandr Moroz came third. Basically he received 12-13 percent.' The official results only gave Moroz half of his real vote in Donetsk *oblast*.[913]

In the 2002 elections, Donetsk ensured the success of ZYU when it received 37 percent, the only region of Ukraine where the pro-Kuchma bloc received first place plurality.[914] 'Due to technology used in Donetsk Za Yedu entered parliament,'[915] Marchuk said. Kuchma repaid Donetsk for this loyalty by appointing Yanukovych as prime minister in 2002 and presidential candidate in 2004.

Eurasian authoritarian political culture cannot comprehend the illegality or very concept of election fraud and this was the case with the authoritarian Party of Regions. Yanukovych was a serial election fraudster who presided over election fraud as regional governor in the 1999 and 2002 elections, as prime minister in the 2004 elections and as president in the 2012 elections. In an interview given to three Ukrainian television channels in February 2012, Yanukovych reiterated his firm belief there had been no election fraud in 2004 and that he had won the second round of the elections.[916] The Orange Revolution and Euromaidan, in the view of Yanukovych and Putin, were western-backed coups that deprived a legitimate candidate of the presidency in the former and orchestrated a 'fascist-driven' coup against a legitimately elected president in the latter.

## MONOPOLISATION OF POWER

Between 2005-2007 the Party of Regions successfully removed competition from other 'centrist parties' by marginalising, merging with or co-opting them. The Party of Regions negotiated local alliances with Crimean Russian nationalist parties, in Odesa with Markov's *Rodina* party and in Trans-Carpathia with Baloha's United Centre party, three regions of Ukraine where it had been electorally and structurally weak. In March 2012, the merger of the Strong Ukraine party with the Party of Regions removed another threat to the Party of Regions in that year's parliamentary election and also from Tihipko, who received third place in 2010, to Yanukovych in the upcoming 2015 presidential elections. Strong Ukraine was the last centrist party in eastern and southern Ukraine to be removed in order to ensure the Party of Regions had a monopoly of power in that region.

The Party of Regions began as a merger of 'Red Directors' (PRVU – led by Rybak, Party of Labour – Landyk, Zvyahilskyy), and new oligarchs (Akhmetov, Kolesnykov, Andriy and Serhiy Kluyev) Donetsk elites. The Party of Regions integrated Donetsk and Crimean Pan-Slavists such as Kolesnichenko and Oleksiy Kostusyev of the Russian-speaking Movement and Party of Slavic Unity respectively. In 2006 and 2012, leaders of two Dnipro parties of power were absorbed: Labour Ukraine (Volodymyr Sivkovych, Valeriy Konovalyuk, Tabachnyk) and its successor, Strong Ukraine - with Tihipko becoming deputy party leader. Another three political parties were absorbed by the Party of Regions: New Generation of Ukraine (Yuriy Miroshnychenko), New Democratic party (Yevhen Kushnaryov), and the gas lobby's Republican Party of Ukraine.

In the Crimea the Party of Regions initially sought alliances with local political forces that had been marginalised under Kuchma. President Putin acting through political technologist Konstantin Zatulin brokered an alliance between the Party of Regions and local Russian nationalists who joined the For Yanukovych! bloc in the 2006 Crimean elections.[917] The US believed, 'Regions had given the Russian Bloc undue political prominence in 2006 by forming a single Crimean electoral list, providing them with  slots in the Crimean Rada they would not have won on their own.'[918] In the 2006-2010 Crimean Supreme Soviet, the Party of Regions cooperated with Russian nationalists (Party *Sojuz*) and the Progressive Socialist party, an alliance that President Kuchma would have never supported. The unholy alliance led to the Crimean Supreme Soviet adopting in September 2008 the only resolution in the CIS (outside Russia and frozen conflict enclaves) in support of the independence of South Ossetia and Abkhazia; an attempt to adopt a similar resolution in the Ukrainian parliament failed to receive sufficient votes. The Party of Regions Russian nationalist allies, such as the Russian Unity party led by Aksyonov, supported Russian's annexation of the Crimea.

## EUROMAIDAN REVOLUTION AND DISINTEGRATION OF THE PARTY OF REGIONS

Yanukovych fled from office on 22 February 2014 after he lost support from within the Party of Regions parliamentary faction and from the security forces. The Ukrainian military in the Orange and Euromaidan Revolution's refused to be dragged into repression of protesters. The regime disintegrated because of its unwillingness to compromise throughout the Euromaidan crisis, such as replacing Prime Minister Azarov in December 2013 (this only happened in late January) and never removing Minister of Interior Zakharchenko. Provocations such as the adoption of the 16 January 2014 anti-democratic legislation inflamed the political crisis. In the Donbas, 69 percent of the population held negative views of the Euromaidan (compared to 47 percent in Zaporizhzhya and Dnipro)[919] that reflected not only anger at what was perceived (and aggressively broadcast by Russian television) as an illegal putsch but also because they were convinced that Yanukovych's election a decade earlier had been 'stolen.' The Donbas, ensconced in its mythology of a region with industrial and economic power, was convinced that the east would always win elections and if they did not, as in 2004, this was because of a Western conspiracy.[920] The heavy handed use of *Berkut* riot police on 30 November 2013 and throughout the Euromaidan increased the numbers of protesters and made them more determined to stay until they achieved victory which they understood as Yanukovych's removal from power.

The Party of Regions distanced itself from Yanukovych two days after parliament had voted for a resolution calling for an end to bloodshed.[921] The Party of Regions began to implode after the number of murdered protesters became publicly known, their *khazayin* had fled and poltical leaders who had backed the Euromaidan Revolution had taken power. Zimmer writes, 'the *komanda (team)* is dependent on the patron in the political centre, and when he loses influence the *komanda* tends to dissolve.'[922] The first to leave the large Party of Regions faction were those who had been coopted and bribed to join as well as deputies who were from regions other than Donetsk, Luhansk and the Crimea, the party's three regional strongholds. In the course of the next nine months the Party of Regions faction shrunk to half its size from 206 to 105 deputies[923] while its popularity slumped in eastern and southern Ukraine.

In the Donbas the implosion of the Party of Regions opened up a political vacuum into which pro-Russian organisations stepped who been trained, funded and equipped by Russian intelligence since 2006-2007. Anti-Euro-maidan vigilantes, separatists, pro-Russian activists in the Donetsk Republic and former Party of Regions members felt doubly betrayed by Kyiv and local Donetsk clan leaders. They were also angry with their own Donetsk clan regional elites. As in the Crimea, they were perturbed at the manner in which the *Berkut*, three of who had been the first to be shot on 20 February 2014 had been mistreated by both sides.[924] They were given additional training by Russian intelligence and backed up by Russian *spetsnaz* 'little green men' who arrived in early April 2014. Their numbers were bolstered by the arrival of 'political tourists,' Russian nationalists and neo-Nazis who were of the belief that Putin intended to annex the Donbas or *NovoRossiya*, as he had undertaken in the Crimea.

Initially, Party of Regions leaders had hoped to use public protests in Donetsk to exert pressure on Kyiv in a similar manner to the Severdonetsk November 2004 congress. Party of Regions supporters of federalism and hostile opponents of the Euromaidan, such as Mykhaylo Dobkin and *NovoRossiya* supporter Oleh Tsaryov, hoped to ride the wave of regional discontent but were soon sidelined by hitherto marginal local and imported Russian nationalists bolstered by covert Russian intervention.[925]

Divisions within the Party of Regions undermined party discipline and it did not put forward a united candidate in the May 2014 pre-term elections. Of the 24 candidates who stood for election, seven had ties to the former Yanukovych regime of which seven were from or had close ties to the Party of Regions.[926] The popularity of the Party of Regions was further damaged by its backing of Dobkin's candidacy in the 2014 presidential elections.[927] Support for the Party of Regions further declined after Russia annexed the Crimea where 82 out of 100 deputies in the autonomous republic's parliament had been from the Party of Regions. United Russia elected a majority in the September 2014 Crimean elections.

The collapse of the Party of Regions was evident during the two pre-term elections held in 2014. In May, Dobkin received a paltry three percent coming in sixth place, a far cry from the 44 and 48 percent received by Yanukovych in the December 2004 and February 2010 elections respectively. Meanwhile in October, the Party of Regions took a wise decision to not participate but its leading members were elected in the Opposition Bloc that came fourth with 9.43 percent, again a far cry from the 30-34 percent the Party of Regions received in the 2006, 2007 and 2012 elections.

The Opposition Bloc was formed around two core groups – the Akhmetov-led Donetsk clan and the Lyovochkin-led gas lobby. The disintegration of the Party of Regions into disgrace followed revelations about the scale of the corruption during Yanukovych's mafia kleptocracy, murders of protestors on the Euromaidan and suspicion of its instigation of separatism. The forty-strong Opposition Bloc could not attract deputies elected in single mandate districts and its faction is a fifth of the size of that of the Party of Regions on the eve of Yanukovych fleeing from power.

## CONCLUSIONS

In Ukraine the creation of a united political machine was only successful in the Donbas. In Dnipro, local clans divided into three warring groups led by Pinchuk and Tihipko, Kolomoyskyy and Lazarenko and Tymoshenko. The SDPUo (Social Democratic United Party) could never establish its dominance in Kyiv, which has traditionally backed national democratic and 'orange' parties, and after Kuchma left office became a marginal political force. The Agrarian party failed to mobilise rural peasants and farmers. In the 1990s, 'centrist' parties formed by former *Komsomol* leaders targeted middle class and liberal voters but they failed to mobilise support in eastern and southern Ukraine where the leftist populist and oligarchic Party of Regions proved to be more successful.

Yanukovych and the Party of Regions successfully integrated 'Red Director' elites, budding oligarchs, Pan-Slavists, former Communists and criminal elements into an organisation that defended their interests from outside threats and provided extensive patronage to its members. Soviet historical myths and nostalgia, a stable voter base, aggressive and authoritarian operating culture and access to large amounts of finances and state administrative resources transformed the Party of Regions into a formidable, disciplined and united political machine which established a monopoly of power in eastern and southern Ukraine between the Orange and Euromaidan Revolutions. The Party of Regions was the only 'centrist' political party that survived the post-Kuchma era with two strong regional bases in the Donbas and in the Crimea. The satellite KPU added 5-12 percent support to the vote received by the Party of Regions.

The Yanukovych presidency negatively affected Ukraine's democratisation path and national integration in four ways. Firstly, support for Russophile and neo-Soviet culture and Ukrainophobia heightened regional and ethno-cultural tension, one example of which was the growth of support for the nationalist *Svoboda* party in the 2012 elections. Inter-regional tension had been high in the Orange Revolution and a barrage of Russian television and diplomatic propaganda painted 'orange' and Euromaidan supporters and leaders as 'fascists' and 'agents of the West.' The Donbas conflict began as a counter-revolution to the perceived illegitimate removal of an elected leader (Yanukovych) who had majority support in the Donbas but rapidly evolved into defence of Russian speakers from the 'fascist' Kyiv 'junta' put into power by a western–backed putsch. Donetsk separatists and Russian soldiers and Russian nationalist volunteers believed they were fighting 'NATO,' the 'Americans' and 'fascists.'

Secondly, the Yanukovych 'Family' never countenanced giving up power and this made bloodshed during the Euromaidan highly likely and a reason why it was different to the non-violent Orange Revolution when Kuchma was prepared to leave office.[928] Violence in the Euromaidan heightened tensions in the Crimea and Donbas and helped to escalate the conflict.

Thirdly, a culture of playing with the rules, and not by the rules impacted negatively on parliament and branches of the judiciary both of which were co-opted and corrupted.[929] Large amounts of cash were paid in bribes to opposition politicians, judges and state officials.

Fourthly, a penchant for monopolisation of economic and political power increased corruption, worsened the business climate, reduced foreign investment and left many non-Donetsk elites feeling ostracised and these were the first to defect during the Euromaidan and after Yanukovych fled from Ukraine. President Yanukovych and Prime Minister Azarov, who had built a mafia state, left behind a country economically in crisis and financially bankrupt that required billions of dollars in Western assistance to stave off default.

During the course of his presidency, Yanukovych had committed treason by permitting the Russians to capture the leadership of the SBU, degrade the military, and control his personal bodyguard and after his cabal had fled from Ukraine they publicly voiced their support for Russia's intervention in the Crimea. They and their allies had long been using vigilantes for elections and corporate raiding, supporting and protecting Russian nationalist and Pan-Slavic groups (such as Donetsk Republic) and during the Euromaidan had been providing resources for the Anti-Maidan. These three groups transformed into separatists in spring 2014 with the assistance of Putin and Russia, which is the subject of the next chapter.

# CHAPTER 8

# SUBVERTING AND DISMEMBERING UKRAINE

*The main problem, in my view, is Russia's heavy imperial heritage. Everybody thinks for some reason that Russia remains an empire and still treats it as an empire.*

Prime Minister Vladimir Putin (1999)[930]

*I don't know where the artificial stops and the real starts.*

Rusyn-American Pop Artist Andy Warhol

In the 2014-2015 Ukraine-Russia crisis, a Euromaidan Revolution seeking Ukraine's integration into post-modern Europe clashed with nineteenth century imperialist Russia. At the heart of the Ukraine-Russia crisis are three factors. The first is the inability of the majority of people living in the Russian Federation to recognise Ukrainians are a separate people. This fundamental question was not invented by Russian President Putin and if he were to be removed or replaced the issue would not go away. In 2000, just as Putin was first being elected, a survey found that the majority of Russians do not view Ukrainians as a separate people.[931] Stephen Kotkin writes that 'Unlike Stalin, Putin does not recognise the existence of a Ukrainian nation separate from a Russian one.'[932]

The second factor is the widely held view that Ukraine is not an independent and sovereign state and is propped up by the West to weaken Russia. Kotkin describes Putin as similar to Stalin with both viewing their neighbours 'as weapons in the hands of Western powers intent on wielding them against

Russia.'[933] Russia's views of Ukraine and other former Soviet republics as lacking sovereignty is incompatible with internationally understood norms of sovereignty. Russia's demand to be recognised as the first among 'unequals' and the primacy of Russian interests in Eurasia represents the 'pursuit of suzerainty.' The suzerain limits external sovereignty and permits the country to have complete internal autonomy while providing protection and aid.[934] An example of such a relationship is that between Russia and Belarus; Russian proposals for a resolution of the Donbas crisis aim to transform Ukraine into a similar Russian-Ukrainian client relationship. As argued in earlier chapters, this policy ignores the fact that Ukraine is not Belarus. E. Wayne Merry writes that 'much of the Russian elite is incapable of thinking about Ukraine other than as a suzerain client.'[935]

The third factor is the Russian view that the Crimea and Russian speaking eastern and southern Ukraine were wrongly included within Ukraine by the Soviet regime. Putin has repeated this claim on a number of occasions. Ukraine's ties to the Crimea are historically more tenuous than to the Donbas but such issues have nothing to do with the manner in which countries borders have been historically drawn. If this argument were to be used for Russia it should also hold referendums in the northern Caucasus, Kurile Islands and Kaliningrad. Indeed, the Crimea has historically greater ties to the Turkic and Tatar world, within which it lived from the thirteenth to the eighteenth centuries, than to Tsarist and Soviet Russia which ruled it for 170 years. The majority of the population of eastern and southern Ukraine were Ukrainian by the turn of the twentieth century and Russian claims are based on the chauvinistic designation of Russian speaking Ukrainians as *Russki* and *'compatriots' (sootechestvennyky)*.

## WESTERN HOPES CLASH WITH RUSSIAN EXCEPTIONALISM

A misplaced hope continued to exist until the 2013-2015 Ukraine-Russia crisis that the Russian Federation was an imperfect system but nevertheless in a convoluted transition to a political system that would come to eventually resemble Western democratic market economies. In 1998, on the eve of Putin being first elected president, Russia was invited to join the G7 even though it had a weak economy and imperfect democracy. Russia continued to be a member of the G7 from 2005-2014 when Freedom House defined it as 'not free' and a 'con-

*Belarusian volunteer fighting for Ukraine in the 128th brigade with author (Butivka coal mine, Avdyivka, May 2016).*

solidated authoritarian regime.' This was coupled with Western leaders and policymakers captivated by the allegedly more 'liberal' Russian President Medvedev[936] whose 'modernisation was an illusion.'[937]

Edward Lucas began writing his book *The New Cold War* after the assassination of Litvinenko in London in November 2006. He recalls that 'When it was published in 2008, it attracted acclaim from hawkish Russia-watchers, especially in eastern Europe. But the pinstriped consensus in London, Washington, Berlin and other capitals was that my book was alarmist nonsense.' This was because, 'Russia, the conventional wisdom maintained, was a capitalist country, albeit with some flaws. It had a pluralist political system, with elections, courts and institutions. Mr. Putin was unpleasant, but he had brought stability to his country and restored national pride. We could do business with him – both commercial and diplomatic.'[938]

The UK House of Lords reported that EU-Russian relations 'for too long had been based on the optimistic premise that Russia has been on a trajectory towards becoming a democratic 'European country' which they pointed out 'has not been the case.'[939] Russia's evolution towards a more nationalist, 'not free' and 'consolidated authoritarian regime' was therefore known for nearly a decade prior to the Ukraine-Russia crisis. Nevertheless, 'the West found it easier at the time to disregard this and indulge in the fantasy that Russia was progressing toward a liberal-hybrid model with which the West could feel comfortable.[940] Related to this was the assumption that Russian national identity was evolving in a normal way through decisions made by the rational choice of elites and therefore nothing out of the ordinary was taking place in Russia.[941]

A belief in a Russia in the midst of a convoluted transition but nevertheless heading in a Western direction could never have foreseen the impending Ukraine-Russia crisis. 'The war in Ukraine is, in part, the result of the West's laissez-faire approach to Russia,' a Chatham House report concluded.[942] The West fundamentally misread Russia ahead of the Ukraine-Russia crisis and 'failed to see that although few Russians longed for a return to Soviet communism, most were nostalgic for superpower status that Putin has tapped into.'[943] Domination of Ukraine is central to Russia seeking great power status and Ukraine's defence of its sovereignty wthin a European identity is viewed as a betrayal of an alleged 'age-old brotherly' relationship. Russian leaders are therefore in full agreement with Zbigniew Brzezinski's statement that Russia cannot be an empire without Ukraine.

Although the focus of this chapter is on Putin's relationship to Ukraine, we should not completely ignore Yeltsin who was Russia's president from 1990 to 2000 and is commonly viewed as more democratic than Putin. Kuchma differentiates between Yeltsin and Putin saying the former was friendlier towards Ukraine. Yeltsin was a democrat in 'his soul' and Kuchma recalls that at every meeting with him he was ready to 'capitulate and reverse his position.'[944] Kravchuk has a different viewpoint and believes there was not much to differentiate Yeltsin and Putin in their attitudes towards Ukraine.

Both Russian presidents did not respect a sovereign Ukraine and Yeltsin and Putin agreed with each other that Ukraine is part of Russia. Yeltsin asked Kravchuk: 'Do you really believe that Ukraine is going to move towards Europe?' and responded himself with words that could be taken from Putin's mouth: 'We have been together for 330 years. It is impossible to tear us apart.' Yeltsin was convinced that the majority of Russians believed that Russia would never permit Ukraine to leave Russia's orbit for Europe.[945] Four Ukrainian presidents living in Ukraine agreed that Putin's goal is 'To destroy the Ukrainian state' and Yeltsin was therefore only different in that he would not have taken Russia to war with Ukraine.

Putin's turn towards a nationalistic and revanchist foreign policy, his Ukrainophobia and xenophobia was clearly spelled out as early as in his addresses to the February 2007 Munich security conference and to the NATO-Russia Council at the April 2008 Bucharest NATO summit.[946] In that year Russia held its first massive military parade since Soviet times.[947] But, Judah believes the 'great turn,' as he describes it, in Putin's policies took place as early as 2003 because from then onwards he no longer pursued Yeltsin's policies.[948] A crucial factor in changing Putin's attitudes towards Ukraine and the West was the Orange Revolution which was the foreign policy equivalent of the 1998 default and was described by Russian political technologist Pavlovsky as Putin's '9/11.'[949]

In his two speeches in 2007 and 2008, Putin was signalling that Russia is now once again powerful and a great power and demands respect from the West. In 1918 and 1991, Russia had been weak and given up territory at Brest-Litovsk and permitted the USSR to disintegrate. Putins was saying 'Enough!' to the West and was signalling that he would defend Russian 'national interests' regardless of Western objections.[950]

The return to Soviet and KGB practices and revival of Russian nationalism could be readily seen in the assassination of Litvinenko that was described by a lawyer working for the London police as a 'nuclear attack on the streets of London.'[951] This dastardly deed:

'marked the point when Putin's Russia crossed the line. It was the point when Moscow went from troublesome partner of the West to international outlaw. Putin even stopped pretending it would play by international rules…It was the point when Putin's gangster state truly went international.'

Brian Whitmore continues:

'In the wake of this assassination of a British citizen, came the invasion of Georgia, annexation of the Crimea, intervention in Donbas, downing of MH17 and abduction of Estonian intelligence citizen Kohver and Ukrainian citizen Nadya Savchenko. In November 2006, Russia fully went rogue and got away with it…with virtually no consequences. And we have lived with the consequences ever since.'[952]

## DEMOCRATIC REVOLUTIONS AND SOVIET CONSPIRACIES

Putin came to power at the same time as NATO's bombardment of Yugoslavia, the detachment of Kosovo into an independent state, and the bulldozer revolution in Serbia that was the first of what became called coloured or democratic

*Georgian volunteer fighting for Ukraine in the OUN battalion (near Pisky, May 2016)*

revolutions. Russian and other post-Soviet leaders, including Yanukovych, were socialised within a conspiracy mind-set and they therefore viewed colour revolutions as one chain of events. But, these fears run even deeper with KGB officer Putin who witnessed first hand in 1989 a democratic revolution and collapse of the Communist regime in Dresden in the GDR. 'And all these old years come up inside him'[953] when he sees revolutions in what he considers Russia's exclusive neighbourhood.

The return to Soviet conspiracy mind-sets was accompanied by a revival of anti-Americanism, as witnessed during Ukraine's 2004 presidential elections. Yanukovych's election campaign, led by Russian political technologists on loan from Putin organised a 'directed chaos' strategy.

The Orange Revolution was viewed by Putin as his personal foreign policy defeat (or '9/11') and he plotted his counter-revolutionary revenge. A pro-European Ukraine would be a 'strategic defeat and humiliation' for Putin.[954] With Yanukovych elected in 2010, Putin was content that he had a potential satrap in the making; it was simply a matter of the price to offer him. Although Yanukovych implemented all of Russia's demands these were insufficient for Moscow to reduce the gas price and Ukraine continued to pay the highest price in Europe. Andrey Tsygankov[955] is therefore mistaken to argue that Yanukovych's relations with Putin were good as there continued to be tension because no matter what Ukrainian leaders did to satisfy Russian demands they never seemed to be enough.

Yanukovych's removal from power tipped Putin over the edge; one humiliation is one thing but two within a decade was too much. Putin had only himself to blame because the advice he was given by political technologists, intelligence services and nationalist allies and advisers drew on Tsarist and Soviet historical myths which failed him during the Orange and Euromaidan Revolutions. In 2004, Russian political technologists Pavlovsky, Konstantin Zatulin, Marat Gelman and Markov strongly believed that they understood Ukraine but in reality all of them got it completely wrong.[956] Pavlovsky ruled out a repeat of the Rose revolution in Ukraine.[957] The Russian belief that the majority of Ukrainians were pro-Russian and only a minority in western Ukraine did not want to be close to them, influenced their view that a pro-Russian candidate would always win a Ukrainian presidential election. In 2014, Russia's intelligence services and Rasputin-like grey eminences such as Surkov completely misunderstood the identity and loyalties of Ukraine's Russophone citizens. On the other hand, Putin is no different to other Russian citizens the majority of who were adamantly convinced that the Orange Revolution was US financed, Yushchenko was a US lackey, his wife was a CIA agent, and Ukrainian nationalists 'used bludgeons to herd the unfortunate Ukrainians to the main city square and force them to chant 'Yushchenko!' in front of the television cameras.'[958] A US conspiracy angle had to be included for Russians to make sense of the 'dumb *khokhly*' (derogatory term for Ukrainians which means country bumpkins) organising a revolution without the assistance of the 'elder brother,' the same 'brother' who has been incapable of organising a similar revolution in Russia.

Following the Rose and Orange Revolutions, Russia and other authoritarian states began preparing counter-revolutionary strategies in what Thomas Abrosio describes as 'resister states.'[959] Nebulous legislation against foreign funding of NGOs targeted them because their goals and objectives constituted a 'threat' to the 'sovereignty, political independence, territorial integrity, national unity, unique character, cultural heritage and national interests of the Russian Federation.'[960] Anti-NGO legislation was part of a range of policies that sought to pre-empt revolutions that could be used as justification for repression of opposition groups.[961] The opposition and civil society NGOs were placed in the same treasonous category as they had been in the USSR; that is, they are funded and supported from abroad without 'natural' roots at home. Only a year after the Orange Revolution, Putin said this kind of legislation was needed to safeguard Russia's political system 'against external interference and to protect our society and citizens from any terrorist or misanthropic ideology that could be spread under this or that sign.'[962]

In addition, Russian 'Public Diplomacy' 'draws strongly on the tradition of Soviet Public Diplomacy.'[963] They both have operated overtly to seek to convince and persuade and covertly through manipulation, disinformation and deceit. In the latter, the KGB and now FSB and SVR would operate covertly through agents of influence and front organisations and occasionally use 'active measures' (i.e. assassinations). The assassination of Litvinenko in London was in a long tradition of Soviet secret service assassinations that have included four Ukrainian nationalist leaders and other émigré leaders. Overt activities include the Russia Today channel, expanding news outlets such as *RIA Novosti* and *Sputnik*, Valdai Club discussions with foreign experts, setting up think tanks such as the Institute for Democracy and Cooperation and signing contracts with Western public relations firms such as Ketchum.

The Russian state has also funded pro-regime NGOs at home, such as the Eurasian Youth Union (the 'National-Bolshevik wing of the International Eurasia Movement'), *Nashi*, *Rossiya molodaya* and *Moloda gvardiya*. Pro-Russian NGOs abroad were funded, especially among Russian speakers and separatists, such as *Proryv* which has been active in Eurasian frozen conflicts.[964] Pro-Russian NGOs began to mushroom in Ukraine in 2009, just ahead of the elections, and especially from 2012 when Putin was re-elected.[965] In January 2015, the organisation Anti-Maidan was launched in Russia with a similar goal to earlier organisations such as *Nashi* to 'prevent colour revolutions, street unrest, chaos and anarchy' in Russia. Anti-Maidan, led by a ragbag collection of misfits, extremists and middle aged hells angels such as the Night Wolves provide paramilitary training for members in special camps. The ideology of Anti-Maidan drew on traditional Ukrainophobia and anti-Western xenophobia with slogans such as 'Maidan equals Fascism,' 'We won't forgive! We won't forget!' and 'Maidan benefits the enemies of Russia!' Anti-Maidan rallies are held under the banners of the flags of the DNR and LNR with Russian flags and banners of 'Donetskaya Rus.'[966]

Russian national minorities in the CIS became increasingly to be seen as 'active agents of influence.' The first mobilisation of these minorities was in

*Ukrainian Tatar volunteer fighting for Ukraine in the Kyiv Rus battalion with author (near Avdyivka, May 2016)*

Tallinn, Estonia in spring 2007 over the dismantling of a monument to Soviet soldiers in World War II. The Russian Orthodox Church, with its influence throughout the former USSR, became a key ally in Russia's Public Diplomacy. The *Russkiy Mir*, opened in 2007 with lavish state funding, is 'Putin' project.' The *Russkiy Mir* was meant to resemble the British Council although with a covert aspect to it because some of the support given to Russian minorities in neighbouring countries also went to separatist groups.

## GEORGIA AS A PRECEDENT FOR THE CRIMEA

Frozen conflicts were created under President Yeltsin through Russian overt and covert interventions in Georgia, Azerbaijan and Moldova. Putin has taken this further through Russian invasions of Georgia and Ukraine and annexation of regions in both countries. The West imposed belated and weak sanctions after Russia's invasion of Georgia in August 2008 and Moscow's recognition of the independence of South Ossetia and Abkhazia. Russia threatened to invade eastern Ukraine at that time if President Yushchenko had refused to permit the Black Sea Fleet, which had participated in the invasion, to return to its base in Sevastopol.[967] Six years later, Putin expected to be similarly treated in a lenient manner by the West after the annexation of the Crimea.

The framework for the annexation of the Crimea was developed by Russia as far back as 2008. Putin was not charting new territory in the Crimea 'He was circling around familiar territory' because the Crimean operation relied on the Georgian template' and, what Gaddy and Hill describe as 'contingency operations' were 'prepared in advance, ready to be used if needed — but only if needed.'[968] The contours of how Russia would annex the Crimea was long known but ignored by Kyiv and the West.[969] Moscow invested in the hybrid 'non-linear' war it unleashed in Ukraine which drew upon organised crime, intelligence services and military special forces.[970] Non-military linear warfare in Ukraine became 'a training exercise and training ground.'[971]

The West's weak reaction to the invasion of Georgia sent a signal to Putin that he could get away without consequences when Russia invaded and dismembered a neighbouring state. After the invasion, US President Obama sought to reset relations with Russia, a company headed by former German chancellor Gerhard Schroder built a gas pipeline from Russia to Germany and certain EU leaders courted and supplied military equipment to Russia. Germany built the training centre for Russian 'little green men'[972] who intervened in the Crimea in spring 2014.[973] Initial Western reaction to Russia's annexation of the Crimea and hybrid war in the Donbas was similarly feeble to that of the invasion of Georgia and tougher sanctions were only introduced after the shooting down of MH17 civilian airliner in July 2014 by a Russian BUK missile and Russia's overt military invasion of eastern Ukraine a month later.[974]

While sending wrong signals to Putin, Western policymakers and scholars who had ignored and played down Putin's nationalism did not appreciate that he was no longer only opposed to NATO enlargement but was also working against the expansion of EU influence into Eurasia, a region that President Medvedev had outlined in 2009 as Russia's 'zone of privileged interests.' Russia had claimed a right to intervene to protect Russians and compatriots throughout the former USSR since the 1990s during which it had acted covertly in Ukraine and overtly in 2014. Russian leaders and international organisations defined threats in very different ways. In March 2014, the same month that Russia invaded the Crimea ostensibly to protect Russian speakers, the Council of Europe concluded it 'did not observe an escalation of violence against the Russian speaking population in the east and south of Ukraine.'[975] Luke Harding writes that the threat to Crimea from neo-Nazis 'was a Kremlin fiction.'[976]

The clash over narratives between international organisations and Russia had deep roots. Contemporary Russia was continuing the "Brezhnev Doctrine' of intervening in neighbouring countries when it felt its interests were threatened. Soviet 'selective attitudes towards international law' were similar to those used by contemporary Russia, a country without the rule of law, which played with the rules and not by the rules at home and abroad. Soviet and Russian political culture prioritised 'justice' over legality – as seen in Putin's repeated references to *spravedlivost* when referring to the Crimea's incorporation into the Russian Federation. In addition to the above factors, traditional Russian chauvinism viewed most former Soviet republics as not truly sovereign states that allegedly justified Russia's 'pursuit of suzerainty.'[977] In Russia's eyes, Ukraine lacks the economic, military and cultural assertiveness as attributes of sovereignty and therefore Kyiv will always be dominated by a foreign power; the question is whether this will be the West or Moscow. Russian officials explained to Polish Foreign Minister Sikorski that Ukraine was 'sub-sovereign.'[978]

Ukrainians vehemently disagreed with the 'Medvedev/Putin Doctrine.' Only 2 percent believed the Russia should send its army to protect Russian speakers in Ukraine while 84 percent were somewhat or definitely opposed.[979] 80 percent of Ukrainians opposed Russia's annexation of the Crimea (10 percent agreed). With 71 percent believing the annexation was an illegal invasion and occupation (4 percent disagreed), 56 percent of Ukrainians supported the use of all means towards the return of the Crimea (20 percent disagreed).[980] Such polls showed to what extent Russia's actions had nothing to do with protecting the Russian language.

Ukraine's Russian speakers did not feel their language was under threat in 2014 or since. When asked if citizens whose native language was Russian felt it was threatened a whopping 82 percent said it was not (10 percent said yes).[981] Sych, editor of the weekly magazine *Novoye Vremya*, denied that Russian speakers such as himself are repressed. They can speak Russian freely in public, on television and in government and the media cater for their needs.[982] Of Ukraine's weekly political magazines, three are in Russian (*Novoye Vremya, Fokus, Korrespondent*) and two are in Ukrainian (*Krayina, Ukrayinskyy Tyzhden*).

*Ethnic Russian volunteer from Ukraine fighting in Pravyy Sektor with author (Butivka coal mine, Avdyivka, May 2016)*

Residents of large urban centres with better education and socio-economic professions buy these magazines and are tolerant towards language questions.

A year after the drawing of this red line, Russia launched the CIS Customs Union that was to become the Eurasian Economic Union in 2015. Yanukovych confided to Ukraine's oligarchs after the Vilnius summit that the dropping of the Association Agreement represented a 180-degree u-turn in Ukrainian foreign policy.[983] The EU's eastern neighbourhood was in reality a zone of rival competition with Russia in its western neighbourhood with only one side possessing hard power. In seeking to remove Ukraine from the Russian 'zone of privileged interests' the EU was not only encroaching into territory beyond the boundaries of the European Union but in Moscow's eyes was following an age-old strategy of seeking to divide the *Russkiy* people; that is, the EU and its US puppet master' was supporting 'Ukrainian separatism' from their natural home within the *Russkiy Mir*.

Russia's antagonism towards the EaP came as a shock to Brussels and the EU 'sleepwalked' into the biggest crisis since World War II in Europe and yet 'The EU should not have been taken by surprise. The evidence has been in plain view.'[984] Georgia and Moldova, two members of the EaP who seek to integrate into Europe, also lie in Russia's neighbourhood but Georgians and

*British and Italian Journalists Stefan Jajecznyk-Kelman, Mauro Voerzio and Marcello Tappo and author with Ukrainian soldiers (near Avdyivka, May 2016)*

Moldovans are not considered to belong to the 'one (Russian) people' and therefore Russian attitudes to them have never been as venomous as those towards Ukraine.

## PUTIN AND YANUKOVYCH

The Party of Regions and KPU were, outside the Crimea, the most pro-Russian and Sovietophile political parties in Ukraine and their base in the Donbas provided them with a historical, regional and ideological base for the mobilisation of a political machine and the capture and looting of the state. Yanukovych, first in the 2004 elections and the Party of Regions in subsequent elections, played the language card and opened up regional divisions in a manner that its earlier centrist allies under President Kuchma had never undertaken. As early as in the 2004 elections, Yanukovych and the Party of Regions called for a referendum to upgrade Russian to become a second state language thereby institutionalising Ukraine as a bilingual state.[985] This demand was coupled with additional incendiary rhetoric demanding an end to the alleged discrimination of the Russian language. This inflammatory rhetoric came before Putin's propaganda machine added its support.

During Kuchma's presidency, cooperation with Russia was managed by the president and the Party of Regions had to act as part of an uneasy coalition with centrist parties who were far less pro-Russian, some were sympathetic to Yushchenko and the majority of who – like Kuchma himself - did not support upgrading Russian to a second state language. In addition to the Russian language, Yanukovych and the Party of Regions also raised the question of extending the lease of the Black Sea Fleet base in Sevastopol beyond 2017 and they 'flirted rhetorically with the idea of joining the CIS Customs Union.'[986]

From 2005, the Party of Regions became an independent political actor with ambitions to monopolise Russophone eastern and southern Ukraine and destroy, integrate or buy off competitors. As an independent actor, the Party of Regions could show its true colours and forge a more determinedly pro-Russian line, first through a cooperation agreement with the United Russia party in 2005 and a year later in an election pact with Russian nationalist-separatists in the Crimea. Both agreements were brokered by Kremlin political technologist Zatulin. Azarov and Kolesnykov, the Godfather of the November 2004 Severdonetsk separatist congress, travelled to Moscow to sign the latter cooperation agreement.[987]

**Table 8.1. Viktor Yanukovych, Party of Regions (PofR) and Russia**

| Year | Event |
| --- | --- |
| 2004 | Russian Backing for Yanukovych's election, including supplying discounted gas through RUE. |
| September 2004 | Yushchenko is poisoned by biological agents. |
| 2005 | PofR and United Russia sign a cooperation agreement |
| January 2006 | Russian-Ukrainian gas crisis. |
| 2006 | PofR and Russian national-separatists create the For Yanukovych! election bloc for the Crimean local elections. |
| 2006 | Separatist Donetsk Republic paramilitary organisation launched. |
| 2008 | PofR, KPU and Crimean Russian nationalists support Russia's recognition of the independence of South Ossetia and Abkhazia |
| January 2009 | Russian-Ukrainian gas crisis. |

| 2009 | President Medvedev outlines Russian demands in an open address to President Yushchenko. |
|---|---|
| Spring 2010 | Yanukovych implements all of Russia's demands. |
| 2011 | Tymoshenko is imprisoned on trumped up charges. |
| 2012 | New language law raises the status of the Russian language. |
| May 2013 | Preparations begin for use of 'anti-fascist' campaign in the 2015 elections where Yanukovych would face *Svoboda* leader Tyahnybok. |
| July 2013 | Putin visits Ukraine to celebrate the 1025th anniversary of the Christianisation of Kyiv Rus. |
| October 2013 | Yanukovych and Putin meet in Sochi, Russia. |
| November 2013 | Ukrainian government refuses to sign EU Association Agreement. |
| December 2013 | Putin offers loans and discounted gas to beleaguered Yanukovych |
| January 2014 | Yanukovych and Putin meet in Valdai, Russia. |
| February 2014 | Yanukovych flees to Russia. Russian military forces invade the Crimea. |
| March 2014 | From Russian exile, Yanukovych calls for Russia to intervene in the Crimea. |

On 27 July 2013, on the eve of the Euromaidan, Putin visited Ukraine to celebrate alongside Yanukovych the 1025th anniversary of the baptism of Kyiv Rus. The following day Putin travelled to Sevastopol. Putin's rhetoric was in keeping with the Russian nationalist and Orthodox messaging of 'Holy Rus' as the cradle and eternal union of three eastern Slavic peoples as *odin Russkiy narod*. Putin used his visit to remind the Ukrainian 'younger brothers' that they and the Russians are 'one people' with 'common historical roots and common destiny, we have a common religion, a common faith, we have a very similar culture, language, traditions, and mentality…'[988] Agreeing to the concept of a single *Russkiy* people requires accepting a younger brother status, living in the *Russkiy Mir*, and accepting Russian and Soviet imperialistic mythology that life was good in both Empires. Putin, refusing to recognise any of the grievances

*Volunteer Natali Prylutska (Dziuba), British and Italian Journalists Stefan Jajecznyk-Kelman, Mauro Voerzio and Marcello Tappo and author (128th brigade forward base, Butivka coal mine, Avdyivka, May 2016)*

held by Ukrainians against Tsarist and Soviet rule (i.e. banning of the Ukrainian language and the *holodomor*), praised the association of Ukraine with Russia as having 'changed the lives of Ukraine's population and its elite for the better.'

In summer 2013, ahead of the Euromaidan Revolution, Putin adopted a three-track approach towards Yanukovych to pressure him to retreat from signing the EU Association Agreement which was more threatening and tougher than that from the EU.[989] Russia lunched a trade war against Ukraine in July 2013 that violated its obligations as a WTO member.

Firstly, he used the rhetoric of 'eastern Slavic brotherhood' to lobby Ukraine to abandon European integration and, after being re-elected in 2015, to join the Eurasian Union. Yanukovych met Putin on four occasions just before and during the Euromaidan. The first meeting was on 27 October 2013 in Sochi, Russia. On 9 November 2014, they met on a Russian military base where Putin threatened Yanukovych that if he went ahead and signed the Association Agreement, Russia would annex the Crimea and *NovoRossiya*. On 17 December 2013, Putin and Yanukovych signed an Action Plan where Russia would buy $15 billion of Ukrainian Eurobonds and the price of gas would be lowered to

*Volunteer Natali Prylutska (Dziuba), British and Italian Journalists Stefan Jajecznyk-Kelman, Mauro Voerzio and Marcello Tappo and author (128th brigade forward base, Butivka coal mine, Avdyivka, May 2016)*

$268 per 1, 000 cubic metres (similar to the price that Firtash's *Ostchem* gas intermediary had been paying throughout Yanukovych's presidency). Three billion was dispersed 'as payment for services rendered to Putin' before Yanukovych fled from office.[990] 'The bond was essentially a bribe to Viktor Yanukovych' *The Economist* reported.[991]

During Yanukovych's presidency, Russia had refused to reduce the highest price of gas in Europe that Ukraine was paying despite numerous concessions made by Ukraine. On 8 January 2014, they met at Valdai just ahead of the parliamentary vote on 16 January that transformed Ukraine into an authoritarian state which led to the first outbreak of violence on the Euromaidan.

Secondly, he began to turn the screws on Ukraine through an arsenal of tougher policies ranging from trade embargos, personal *kompromat*, blackmail, financial inducements and threats to annex the Crimea. Belarusian President Lukashenka had seen plans for Russia's annexation of eastern and southern Ukraine as early as May 2013,[992] the region that Putin described as *NovoRossiya* a year later. 'There have also been reports of Kremlin operatives openly discussing a project to annex the territory beginning in the summer of 2013,' Sikorski revealed.[993] He added 'alarm bells began to ring inside the Polish Foreign Ministry because "We learned Russia ran calculations on what provinces would be profitable to grab."'[994] The plans resembled those leaked to *Novaya Gazeta* in that they focused upon Russian annexation of Zaporizhzhya, Dnipro and Odesa but ruled out the Donbas as unprofitable.[995] In September 2013, Glazyev warned that if Ukraine signed the EU Association Agreement there would be fatal consequences; specifically, he threatened that Russia would no longer guarantee the existence of the Ukrainian state and could intervene 'if pro-Russian regions of the country appealed directly to Moscow,' which had been planned by Dobkin and Yanukovych through the Ukrainian Front in Kharkiv.

Thirdly, and the most personal, Russia had an additional lever of influence over Yanukovych, according to those who were in contact with him in 2013-2014. Polish Foreign Minister Sikorski believed Putin held some form of *kompromat* over Yanukovych that he could use to destroy him personally.[996] Sikorski said, 'my sense is that it was something Putin told him in Sochi. I think that Putin had *kompromat* on Yanukovych: we now know there was a weekly, biweekly truck taking out the cash (stolen from the Ukrainian budge) in a cash transfer. And I think he told him: 'Don't sign the Association Agreement; otherwise we'll seize Crimea.' That's why he cracked."[997]

Leshchenko finds a plausible sequence of events that points to a confidential relationship between Yanukovych and Putin. The first is the manner to which Yanukovych was willing to permit Russia to takeover and penetrate Ukrainian security forces. Leshchenko then raises Yanukovych's refusal to sign the Association Agreement, the January 2014 'dictatorship laws,' and his call for Russian intervention into the Crimea. Taken together, Leshchenko believes these factors point to Yanukovych's long-term collaboration with the KGB after he was twice imprisoned and had been recruited to provide intelligence on organised crime groups in the Donbas.

## PREPARING FOR COUNTER-REVOLUTION

The Rose and Orange Revolutions frustrated Putin's and Yanukovych's plans and made them invest in counter-revolutionary strategies for future elections. An important factor was to be prepared to counter protestors in the 2010 elections and after he was elected in 2015. In Ukraine, the Party of Regions could not draw on nationalism as a state ideology in the same manner as did Putin and instead he relied upon pro-Russian organised criminal and vigilante groups, such as *Oplot* in Kharkiv and *Rodina* in Odesa.

Russian nationalist organisations could not operate in authoritarian Russia without being either co-opted and/or infiltrated by Russian intelligence services. This was clearly evident in the case of GRU officer Girkin who participated in numerous military campaigns at home and abroad, was a re-enactor of military battles by White Russian forces during the Russian civil war and a member of monarchist nationalist organisations. Research by the anti-fascist magazine *Searchlight* found that every major neo-Nazi group in Russia included one or more members of the Russian secret services. Russia's far right was trained by Russian intelligence using *spetsnaz* officers from the FSB and GRU. The Russian authorities have permitted nationalists, Cossacks and others to train, advertise on the Internet, collect donations and cross the border unhindered into Ukraine. Little wonder Putin is refusing to implement the clause in Minsk-2 of returning control of the border to Ukraine. Russian Cossacks played a prominent role in the initial phases of the annexation of the Crimea when they pretended to be local self-defence units.[998] Aleksandr Mozhaev, a Wolves Hundred Cossack, said 'There's an open corridor for the Cossacks, for the Wolves' and 'They didn't even stamp my passport.'[999]

The nexus uniting the intelligence old boy network with far right groups was used in covert operations in Belarus and Ukraine; an example of which is Russian citizen Stanislav Markelov who was killed in an accidental explosion in Zaporizhzhya in 2011. Markulov 'was born in Moscow, served in a marine infantry unit in Sevastopol and held the rank of an FSB warrant officer. Several Nazi swastikas were tattooed on his body.'[1000]

In the Donbas, Pan-Slavic and pro-Russian groups had existed since the collapse of the USSR and they cooperated with the KPU, Progressive Socialist Party and the Party of Regions. These activists would earn money for themselves and attract funding for their organisations by working on the election campaigns of Yanukovych and the Party of Regions. Each summer the Donetsk Republic, the most notorious of these pro-Russian groups, sent its members to Russia to undertake paramilitary training alongside members of Dugin's Eurasian Youth Union where they were trained by the FSB and GRU in espionage, sabotage, and guerrilla tactics. Dugin and Surkov gave ideological lectures and seminars at these camps. Photographs of Donetsk Republic members at these Russian, Donbas and Crimean training camps holding weapons were posted on *VKontakte* social media.[1001] Future DNR Prime Minister Andrey Purgin and DNR parliamentary deputy Oleg Frolov attended the camps.

During Yanukovych's presidency the GRU 'created very covert but well-structured networks with agents, with pro-Russian organisations, involving illegal activities in many parts of Ukraine.' Former SBU Chairman Valentyn Nalyvaychenko said that Russian intelligence officers were 'recruiting and paying local organised crime' to join the separatist uprisings. 'They are very dangerous, well armed, and for years before preparing to do what they are doing now.'[1002]

Training of vigilantes was accelerated during Yanukovych's presidency with a view to preparing for the 2015 elections. Training programmes were assisted by the FSB's infiltration of the SBU and GRU of Ukrainian military intelligence. Paramilitary training took place at the annual 'Healthy Ukraine' summer camp in Sudak, Crimea and the Eurasian youth camp in Donuzlav. The Eurasian youth organisation had been holding its camp since 2006 under the noses of the SBU and next door to the former Ukrainian naval base; that is, it was held for four years without hindrance from President Yushchenko and the SBU then headed by Nalyvaychenko. From the Orange Revolution a network of different Russian nationalist organisations 'began working covertly and openly on the Crimean peninsula to agitate for re-joining Russia.' These included the ROK whose 'most prominent member' was Aksyonov, *Proryv* (with bases in frozen conflicts in Moldova and Georgia), paramilitary Cossacks, Dugin's Eurasian Youth Movement and the People's Front-Sevastopol-Crimea-Russia.[1003] The latter two were banned by the Ukrainian authorities and Dugin was banned from entering Ukraine. But, the Russia Bloc and Russian Unity, the party led by the future Crimean leader under Russia's occupation, were not banned until April 2014. During Yanukovych's presidency, growing networks of pro-Russian and extremist activists and radicals were facilitated and would go on to become a threat to Ukraine's territorial integrity. [1004]The SBU took no preventive measures against Crimean separatists throughout Yanukovych's presidency, including in 2013-2014 when Aksyonov's Russian Unity party was putting in place the final preparations for its paramilitary force.[1005]

The Eurasian youth camp was organised by the Russian Ministry of Foreign Affairs, *Russkiy Mir*, and the Institute of the CIS. With participants from Ukraine, Russia, Belarus, Moldova and frozen conflicts the speeches by Zatulin and Russian nationalists typically called for eastern Slavic unity and derided European integration. The web page of the 'Healthy Ukraine' camp posted anti-Semitic and Russian nationalist comments, posts and posters. Political support was given by the KPU, Progressive Socialist party, Medvedchuk's Ukrainian Way, and *Otpor* who, the anti-fascist magazine *Searchlight* writes, 'are balancing between neo-Nazism and neo-Stalinism.'[1006]

The duty of the GRU 'was to prepare (vigilante and paramilitary) gangs, and the job of the *spetsnaz* controlled by the GRU was to prepare an insurgency.'[1007] Training of pro-Russian paramilitaries and vigilantes in the run up to the 2015 elections was confirmed by *Oplot* fighter 'Igor' who told *PBS Frontline* in March 2014 that they would meet with Russian intelligence before rallies and protests to receive instructions. 'Igor' admitted that his 'supervisors are from the Russian military and intelligence agencies.'[1008]

During Yushchenko's presidency, the SBU launched a criminal investigation of the Donetsk republic and three leaders were charged with planning the forcible capture of the state, undermining Ukraine's territorial integrity and infringing racial and national equality. The charges were quietly dropped after Yanukovych came to power when the Donetsk Republic resumed its activities. In 2014, they cooperated with the RNE in forcibly capturing state institutions in the Donbas.[1009] Most other separatist and paramilitary groups were ignored and Andrey Kurkov writes 'Sometimes I have the impression that the SBU should not notice its own existence.'[1010]

Fighting separatists is the responsibility of the SBU and prosecutor's office and in the case of the latter organisation there has never been a commitment to anything other than enjoying the fruits of corruption. Presidents cannot escape responsibility for the inaction of the prosecutor's office against separatists because it is they who have appointed prosecutors. Under Yushchenko, the SBU undertook active measures for the first time against separatists in the Crimea, Sevastopol, Odesa and Donetsk leading to the expulsion of Russian 'diplomats.'[1011] But, these criminal cases were foiled because the prosecutor's office was permitted by Yushchenko to be controlled by the Party of Regions. Then SBU Chairman Nalyvaychenko said 'The blocking of the struggle against separatists in parliament and by the general prosecutor in 2008-2009 has led to the results we have now with the annexation of the Crimea and occupation of part of the Donbas.'[1012]

Nalyvaychenko seemed to not appreciate that it was president who appointed prosecutors and Yushchenko could have changed the Donetsk clan's agent of influence, General Prosecutor Oleksandr Medvedko. Ukraine had *never* taken resolute action against Crimean separatists except in 2008-2009; for example, Kuchma admitted that Russian consulates had been distributing Russian passports since 1994. In 2003, Kuchma returned early from a foreign visit and ordered Ukrainian forces to halt a Russian military advance on the island of Tuzla, just east of the Crimea. Kuchma said 'we will defend our territory as it is stated and outlined in our constitution.'[1013] Yanukovych in contrast supported Russia's annexation of the Crimea and intervention into eastern Ukraine.

## PRO-RUSSIAN FORCES IN THE YANUKOVYCH PRESIDENCY

In addition to the Donetsk clan, Yanukovych permitted leaders of the pro-Russian gas lobby to join the Party of Regions from 2006 and join the presidential administration and government when he was president. During Yanukovych's presidency, the gas lobby controlled foreign policy through Hryshchenko and Leonid Kozhara, energy relations with Moscow (Firtash and Minister of Fuel Boyko) with Lyovochkin Chief of Staff.[1014] Anatoliy Orel, with extensive ties to Moscow, was brought in as a senior presidential adviser. Chornovil, for many years a Party of Regions deputy, described Firtash, Lyovochkin, Valeriy Khoroshkovskyy and Boyko as the 'Moscow quartet.'[1015]

The Russian takeover and degrading of Ukraine's security forces during Yanukovych's presidency was largely missed or downplayed by Western experts of Ukraine and my description of this process at the time as the 'Putinisation' of Ukrainian forces was criticised as an 'exaggeration.'[1016] From evidence collected since Yanukovych's overthrow it can be ascertained that if anything I under-estimated the degree of Russian penetration of Ukraine's security forces.[1017] Russia's takeover of Ukrainian security forces and the practice of staffing security forces in the Crimea who were recruited locally, assisted Russia's annexation. The extent of Russian penetration could be seen when commanding officers such as Pavlo Lebedev fled to the Crimea and Rear Admiral Denis Berezovskyy defected to the Russians. Of the 18, 800 Ukrainian armed forces in the Crimea only 4, 300 re-joined the Ukrainian armed forces.[1018]

Leshchenko said, referring to Dmitriy Salamatin, that the 'Russian Minister of Defence of Ukraine destroys the defence capabilities of the armed forces in the interests of a neighbour-aggressor, and in parallel gives a gift to Yanukovych of American military technology from World War Two!'[1019] He was referring to the Studebaker US6-62 jeep, one of many vintage cars found at the *Mezhyhirya* palace.

The publication of the minutes of the RNBO meeting on 28 February 2014 confirms the depth of the treason undertaken during Yanukovych's presidency.[1020] Four aspects of the minutes are worth highlighting. The first is recognition of mass support for Russia among Crimean residents which is not surprising as pro-Russian sentiment was always high in this region. Secondly, recognition of mass defections and fears of betrayals among local Crimean security forces personnel. The defection of the majority of the officers and personnel in the Ministry of Interior, SBU, military and prosecutor's office constitutes one of the biggest single acts of treason in modern European history. In the Bakhchisaray *rayon* of the Crimea, 80 percent of the armed forces, 90 percent of prosecutors and 100 percent of the SBU and Ministry of Interior switched their allegiance overnight from Ukrainian to Russian.[1021] In the course of only 8 months up to March 2016, 30 SBU officers had been arrested for corruption and treason.[1022]

Third, a sense of disorientation on the part of the US coupled with an indecisive President Obama. Fourthly, recognition that armed resistance is futile because Ukraine had no large and well equipped security forces; in fact, the RNBO minutes confirm that Ukraine had only 6,000 troops that it could utilise in spring 2014.

Finally, weak political will by nearly most Euromaidan leaders with few voting for the imposition of martial law. Acting head of state Turchynov planned to visit the Crimea but Moscow advised him against, warning him that his plane would be shot down.[1023]

The RNBO minutes tell us much more as they point to the heart of the treason of Yanukovych's presidency making it incomprehensible why Poroshenko has been disinterested in pursuing criminal charges against Yanukovych and 'the Family.' President Yanukovych began his betrayal of Ukraine a month after he was elected when the Kharkiv Accords were railroaded through the Ukrainian parliament after they had been voted down by parliamentary committees and without any chance for parliamentary discussion.[1024] The voting was a charade and led to riots inside and outside parliament. The *de facto* loss of Ukrainian sovereignty over the Crimea began in spring 2010 when Yanukovych agreed to extend the Black Sea Fleet basing agreement in Sevastopol until 2042-2047. The 1997 Black Sea Fleet agreement had agreed on a 'temporary' 20-year basing agreement that would have expired in 2017. In addition to the Black Sea Fleet, Yanukovych agreed to the return of Russian intelligence units to the Black See Fleet who had been expelled under President Yushchenko. The Party of Regions, KPU and Lytvyn bloc[1025] voted unanimously for the Kharkiv Accords. The key persons behind the Kharkiv Accords are well known but none of them have been criminally charged and some were re-elected as Opposition Bloc deputies in 2014.[1026]

Five factors were put in place that facilitated Russia's later annexation:

1. The Party of Regions established an alliance with Crimean Russian separatist-nationalists.
2. Russian intelligence provided covert and overt operational assistance and training to their agents and informants.
3. Ukraine ended counter-intelligence operations against Russian intelligence services.
4. Russia increased its naval presence in the Crimea.
5. Russian naval personnel came to increasingly view Sevastopol and the Crimea as *de facto* Russian territory.[1027]

The seeds of the violence that led to the murder of over 100 and wounding of thousands of protesters in January and February 2014 can be traced to a May 2012 presidential decree 'On steps towards intensifying the struggle against terrorism in Ukraine'[1028] which listed the nebulous term 'extremism' alongside 'terrorism.'[1029] A government resolution five months later outlined steps to combat 'terrorism.'[1030] Early on during the Euromaidan senior Party of Regions leaders, such as Prime Minister Azarov and Kolesnykov, described protestors as 'extremists.'

The Ministry of Interior in the Donbas and Crimea was controlled by oligarchs and regional clans and the senior officers were more likely to obey their commands than those sent by Kyiv, particularly by a government led by political leaders who had supported the Euromaidan Revolution. In the Crimea and Donbas 'We had almost total betrayal' of Ministry of Interior personnel and the *militia* either abandoned their premises or defected to the separatists.[1031] Crimean Ministry of Interior senior officer Volodymyr Mertsalov described how he transformed his men into a pro-Russian paramilitary unit and cooperated with Russian airborne units in capturing Simferopil airport on 27 February 2014.[1032]

Under Minister of Defence Salamatin, who was a Russian citizen, the database of conscripts was destroyed.[1033] During the tenure's of Ministers of Defence Salamatin, Lebedev and Mykhaylo Yezhel, Ukraine's military budget was severely reduced and military equipment was sold or transferred to Russia. Salamatin planned to reduce Ukraine's armed forces to 75, 000 by 2017. Yezhel's daughter is married to an admiral of Russia's Pacific Fleet.[1034] During the spring 2014 invasion of the Crimea, the Ukrainian naval command did not destroy documentation which was captured by Russian intelligence. Since the Euromaidan, 40 percent of military officers have failed the polygraph and 15 out 25 senior army officers failed their re-certification test, including two generals and four colonels.[1035] Since 2014, some Ukrainian naval officers have continued to take their holidays in (Russian occupied) Crimea.[1036]

The president's bodyguards are the responsibility of a department in the SBU but Yanukovych did not use personnel from this structure for two reasons. Firstly, he had a fear of assassinations going back to the 1990s. In September 2004, his election campaign planned that he, wearing a bullet proof vest under his buttoned up coat, was to be shot by a blank and the 'assassination' would be blamed on 'Ukrainian nationalists.' His paranoia of assassination was so great that when he saw a projectile thrown by a student coming towards him he panicked and fell over feigning he had been shot.[1037] Murphy's law can sometimes get in the way of the best thought out plans, especially when students throw eggs. The second factor why he did not trust the SBU was during the Orange Revolution when it had supported Yushchenko. Yanukovych therefore turned to Russia and the head of Yanukovych's personal bodyguards, Vyacheslav Zanevskiy, was a Russian citizen.[1038]

During Yushchenko's presidency, Russia's intelligence services operated covertly and were tracked by the SBU and evicted from Ukraine. Under Yanukovych, Ukrainian intelligence services were ordered to end their operations against Russia and, in the words of the former Chairperson of the Foreign Intelligence Service Mykola Malomuzh 'the SBU, which was supposed to catch separatists and terrorists, almost completely stopped its monitoring in eastern Ukraine and in Crimea too.'[1039] Russian intelligence services were permitted to operate overtly in the Crimea, Donbas and elsewhere without hindrance.[1040] 90 percent of SBU activities were directed against the opposition in the form of illegal wiretapping, surveillance and organisation of vigilantes for election fraud, violence against opposition members and journalists.[1041] The FSB was given complete reign over the SBU and commandeered data on 22, 000 officials and informants. Hard drives and flash drives not taken to Russia were destroyed and the FSB took 'everything that forms a basis for a professional intelligence service.'[1042] The FSB reportedly introduced surveillance technology on Ukraine's mobile telephone network.[1043] SBU Chairman Aleksandr Yaky-menko, Russian citizen Igor Kalinin and four top intelligence chiefs fled to Russia.

The extent of Russian intelligence penetration came to light in spring-summer 2014 when Ukrainian missions in the ATO were compromised by in-telligence leaks that provided Russians and separatists with sufficient time to consolidate their positions in the crucial first months of the conflict.[1044] In spring 2016, the SBU published a list of the names of 1, 391 of its SBU officers who had defected to Russia in the Crimea, many of who have continued to work as FSB officers.[1045] The deputy commander of the ATO, a high ranking SBU officer, was a Russian agent.[1046] After the Euromaidan, 235 SBU agents were arrested of whom 25 were charged with high treason, including in absentia the counter-intelligence chief.

During the Euromaidan, 30 FSB officers visited Ukraine on 3 occasions between 13-15 December 2013, 26-29 January and 20-22 February 2014 using the SBU sanatorium at Koncha Zaspa, near Kyiv as their base of operations.[1047] Their main liaison was with SBU Counter-Intelligence Chief Volodymyr Buk. On each occasion their visits followed peaks of confrontation to replace Prime Minister Azarov and Minister of Interior Zakharchenko (10-11 December 2013), passage of anti-democratic legislation and first murders of protesters (16 and 22 January 2014) and the violent confrontation and victory of the Euro-maidan (18 and 20 February 2014).[1048] Their goals were to a) increase protection of their Russian assets; b) ensure continued access to SBU files, special com-munications and headquarters; c) provide training for 'anti-terrorism' exercises; and d) supply special equipment for a mass suppression of the protests. To-wards this goal, two military cargo planes with five tonnes of anti-terrorist and crowd control equipment arrived in Kyiv to be used by Ukraine's SBU *Alpha* special forces and Ministry of Interior *Berkut*.[1049]

An intriguing aspect of Yanukovych's relationship with Putin is his agreement to invite Russian forces into Ukraine. During a press conference from Rostov-on-Don, Yanukovych called upon Putin to 'restore order' because 'I think Russia should, and is obliged, to act.' Yanukovych defended Putin's intervention in the Crimea as the 'natural reaction to the bandit coup in Kyiv.' On 1 March 2014 from Russian exile, he appealed to Russian President Putin that 'The lives and security of people particularly in Crimea and the south-east are being threatened. Under the influence of Western countries there have been open acts of terror and violence. People have been persecuted for their language and political reasons. So in this regard I would call on the President of Russia, Mr. Putin, asking him to use the armed forces of the Russian Federation to establish legitimacy, peace, law and order, stability and defend the people of Ukraine.'[1050] Since then, Azarov has supported Russia's annexation of the Crimea arguing the region was never historically part of Ukraine. [1051]

In early February 2014, the Ukrainian Front, adopting the St. George ribbon as its symbol, was established in Kharkiv which was to become the stronghold of the anti-Maidan. Governor Dobkin told the congress 'Like their fathers and grandfathers in the 1940s, participants of the Ukrainian Front will liberate their lands.' The Ukrainian Front was set to hold a congress on 22 February attended by governors from eastern and southern Ukraine who would announce the launch of a territorial entity and declare autonomy from Euromaidan Ukraine. After Yanukovych fled from Kyiv for Kharkiv 'he was to convene a meeting of deputies of all levels of the Southeast and Crimea to repeat the scenario of 2004 to establish a Southeast Ukrainian Autonomous Republic.' This plan floundered because the following day Yanukovych did not show himself in the city.'[1052] The question of the Ukrainian Front inviting Russian troops into Ukraine was also raised using similar justification to that later used in the Crimea of the need to protect Russophones against 'fascists.' Events on the ground overtook these plans with the rapid disintegration of the Yanukovych regime after the cold blooded murders of protestors on the Euromaidan.

The plan to hold a separatist congress of the Ukrainian Front did not go ahead after Kharkiv Governor Dobkin told Yanukovych he could not guarantee his safety because the security situation in the city was deteriorating and local elites had begun to evacuate their families. Outside the Kharkiv Palace of Sport, young Kharkiv, Dnipro and Poltava *ultras* were in an aggressive mood following murders on the Euromaidan and they stormed through *militia* lines into the congress hall. After reading out on appeal on television that talked of 'banditry, vandalism, and a state coup' Yanukovych then tried to fly in his private 'Falcon' jet to Moscow but he was thwarted. His entourage drove to Donetsk, where he met oligarch Akhmetov who advised him to resign, and then he drove to the Crimea.[1053]

Yanukovych, backed by delegates from Russian speaking Ukraine, was meant to declare Kharkiv the new capital city of a 'Ukrainian Autonomous Republic' that would request Russian military support and which would be backed up on the ground by local pro-Russian groups. Dugin had written earlier about the coming 'Russian Spring' where the citizens of *NovoRossiya* would rise up against a 'punitive nationalist dictatorship' and 'Kyiv henchmen' leading to a bloody civil war with Moscow providing protection for Russian speakers while the West and NATO backed the 'fascists.' Dugin's 'Russian Spring' concluded with Russian and *NovoRossiya* forces liberating Ukraine up to the Dnipro river and eastern-southern Ukraine joining the Eurasian Union.[1054]

Leshchenko[1055] writes that there were no Russian plans for Yanukovych to leave Ukraine and Putin's claim that Russian forces helped him to escape from Kyiv is bizarre as why did they then leave him to find his own way to the Crimea? Two days prior to him fleeing from Kyiv, Prime Minister Azarov, who had always been negatively disposed towards European integration, was in St. Petersburg and Moscow. Ultimately, the kleptocratic and cowardly side of Yanukovych overruled other considerations.

Russia was therefore not acting in response to developments in the Euromaidan but had pre-planned for different contingencies and scenarios. Glazyev's threat of Russia intervening at the invitation of a Ukrainian leader was a reference to contingencies for Yanukovych retreating to eastern Ukraine where he would lead a congress of the Ukrainian Front, similar to that held in Severdonetsk in 2004, which would then send a request for Russian military assistance to protect Ukraine's Russian speakers.[1056] Yanukovych did flee to Kharkiv but two aspects of the Russian plan failed. The first was an inability to hold a congress of the Ukrainian Front in that city due to weak local support from eastern and southern Ukrainian elites and public. When asked if Russia had the right to intervene to protect Russian speakers, only five percent of Ukrainians said 'Yes' while 87 percent said 'No.' The highest number were to be found in the east but even there only 15 percent agreed while a far higher 66 percent disagreed.[1057] The second was the weak support given to separatists by Ukraine's Russian speakers outside the Donbas in the six Russian speaking *oblasts* of eastern and southern Ukraine.

## PUTIN AND UKRAINE'S COLOUR REVOLUTIONS

Reports fist surfaced in 2009 of Putin loathing Yanukovych. Although this may have something to do with his criminal background it would be mistaken to assume that this was entirely a product of this. Putin also reportedly takes a low view of Belarusian President Lukashenka who has not been linked to criminality and corruption scandals. Just as important is the nationalities question; Putin feels disdain for two regional *Russki* leaders who are viewed as disobedient freeloaders. As discussed earlier, Yanukovych's 'well-documented venality' and because he was 'relatively easy to buy off' made him vulnerable to blackmail that Putin could use as leverage.[1058]

Putin did though view both leaders differently. Lukashenka had always been tough in his response to threats to his regime and he was unfazed at Western criticism of his political repression. Lukashenka, like Putin, was decisive while Yanukovych dithered and wavered. Despite powerful Russian intelligence and security support, Yanukovych could not regain the initiative over Kyiv's streets in the way that Putin had successfully orchestrated in 2012 during mass protests in Moscow or Lukashenka six years earlier during the Jeans Revolution. In Russia's eyes, Yanukovych's crowd management skills were poor, he had permitted the authorities to lose control of the situation too early and small-scale violence had fuelled the protests and emboldened the population.[1059]

Putin covertly and overtly supported Yanukovych during the Orange Revolution *and* Euromaidan. In the former, he visited Kyiv in both rounds of the election to voice his support, a step that backfired and increased voter turnout in the capital city. Russia provided upwards of $300 million in support to his 2004 election campaign, although this was always denied.[1060] Further financial inducements were provided through a gas deal negotiated in summer 2004 with a very low price of $55 per 1,000 cubic metres that would be provided through the newly formed *RosUkrEnergo (RUE)* gas intermediary. Undoubtedly the most important support was provided through the loaning of Russian political technologists to Yanukovych's election campaign. Then Parliamentary Chairman Lytvyn said Ukraine was 'flooded with a host of political engineers who have no scruples' and who compete to undertake the 'blackest' of actions against the opposition election campaign.[1061]

Their activities backfired and provoked the Orange Revolution because of an inaccurate understanding of Ukrainian domestic politics and identity. Russian political technologists were as intellectually shallow as the FSB who had advised Putin that Russophone Ukrainians who would rise up against Kyiv. A leaked strategy discussion document prepared before Yanukovych's downfall focused on pro-Putin uprisings beginning in Kharkiv, not Donetsk, although its knowledge of eastern Ukraine was poor, as seen in *oblast* governor Dobkin described as the city's mayor.[1062] The document also showed a complete lack of understanding of the popular and widespread support given to the Euromaidan claiming organised crime and football fans with Western support were behind it. In Kharkiv the document claimed local elites were motivated towards meeting the 'new integration initiatives of Russia' which was also mistaken because Mayor Kernes's only motivation is rent seeking. Kharkiv was favoured in the document because of its symbolic importance as the first capital of Soviet Ukraine and would host an 'informal assembly' (i.e. the inaugural congress of the Ukrainian Front) to be attended by local elites from eastern and southern Ukraine. As with other leaked strategy documents, plans were laid out to covertly support civil disobedience, use of media propaganda, demands for referendums, federalisation and union of the east and south with Russia.

## PREPARING FOR THE CRIMEA'S ANNEXATION

International reaction to the annexation the Crimea has been more muted than that of Russia's hybrid war in the Donbas even though the former was a more brazen act of imperialism. There are close similarities in the agreements negotiated by the EU in 2008 and 2014-2015 to end Russia's wars against Georgia and Ukraine. EU negotiators omitted to mention Georgia's territorial integrity in 2008 while the Crimea question never appeared in the Minsk-1 and Minsk-2 Accords.[1063] Indeed, during the 2016 French presidential elections, Republican candidate Nicolas Sarkozy implicitly endorsed recognising the annexation of the Crimea - one important factor for the common perception among some Western experts that the Crimea has returned to its 'natural home.'[1064] Sakwa justifies Russia's annexation of the Crimea by describing it as 'the heartland of Russian nationhood' while Rajan Menon and Eugene Rumer describe it as 'an indisputably Russian territory.'[1065] Such statements assumes the Crimea had no history prior to the 1780s. From the mid-15th century to the 1780s (i.e. 330 years) the Crimean Khanate was a vassal state of the Ottoman Empire, it came under Russian and Soviet rule from 1783-1954 (i.e. 170 years) and following this it was part of Soviet and independent Ukraine for 60 years (1954-2014). Turkey ruled the Crimea for double the period of time of Russia and therefore has far more right to call itself the 'natural home.'

Russia's military plans to invade and annex the Crimea were not a reaction to the overthrow of Yanukovych because they required many months of preparation. Beginning in summer 2013, Putin had threatened Yanukovych with the dismemberment of Ukraine. The Russian state medal 'For the Return of the Crimea' is dated 20 February-18 March 2014 with a start date when Yanukovych was still Ukrainian president.[1066] Putin lied about the presence of Russian occupation troops but admitted in April 2014 they had been present. He justified the annexation as a response to an 'anti-constitutional takeover, an armed seizure of power' by 'reactionary, nationalist and anti-Semitic forces.' Putin's hypocrisy was all the more blatant because Russia had used Aksyonov's neo-fascist Russian Unity party to assist its 'little green men' in the takeover of the Crimea. Indeed, after three years of Euromaidan-ruled Ukraine, 81 percent (categorically or mainly) did not believe there was discrimination against native Russian language speakers in Ukraine with only 12 percent (categorically and mainly) disagreeing.[1067]

Russian intelligence planned 'long and meticulous preparations' for the invasion of the Crimea on the assumption that it would not meet Ukrainian resistance. The 'little green men' were small in number and lightly armed, a decision taken on the premise that Ukrainians would not fight; otherwise, 'it would have been a reckless undertaking.'[1068] Assisting lightly armed GRU 'green men' *spetsnaz* were former *Berkut* officers, angry at what had transpired in Kyiv where three of their colleagues had been killed and who had become heroes in the Crimea,[1069] Black Sea Fleet marines, Aksyonov's Russian Unity paramilitaries and organised criminals who joined 'self-defence' units. Ukrainian forces were demoralised, their equipment had been depleted during Yanukovych's presidency and the new Euromaidan authorities were not issuing any orders. Kyiv could have issued orders for ground troops to withdraw to Kherson and vessels to sail to Odesa or alternatively orders could have been given to defend their bases and fight back if they were attacked. Strategic retreat perhaps would have been a better option than the humiliation that ensued which resulted in further demoralisation of Ukraine's armed forces. Fighting back could have led to civilian casualties as Russian paramilitaries and 'little green men' used civilians as human shields, by placing them in front as they blockaded Ukrainian military bases.[1070]

Treason in the security domain was complimented by treason in the political realm. The Party of Regions, Russian Unity and Cossack organisations merged into a regional branch of the United Russia party. In the 2014 Crimean 'elections,' United Russia won 70 of the 75 seats with the Liberal Democratic Party of Russia winning the remaining five. 15, 000 of the Party of Regions 60,

000 members were accepted into United Russia with some of the former members who were rejected being permitted to join Just Russia and the Liberal Democratic Party of Russia.[1071] 'Aleksandr,' one of the Russians involved in the annexation of the Crimea and subsequent hybrid war in eastern Ukraine recalled that 'The entire Party of Regions organically merged into United Russia, while the people expected something completely different. They wanted new authorities.'[1072]

## SEEKING YALTA-2

Timothy Snyder explains the ideological thinking behind Putin's nostalgia for a new Yalta agreement and Grand Bargain.[1073] He compares Putin's justification for protecting Russian speakers to Hitler's rationale for protecting German speakers in the 1930s and his unwillingness to accept current borders, claiming – like Hitler in the 1930s – that they are 'unjust.'

Russian nationalists have always believed that Russia should unite with a Ukraine that has jettisoned its western region because it had not been part of the Tsarist Empire, was anti-Russian and therefore not culturally eastern Slavic and 'Russian.' Western Ukraine was the bogeyman in the Soviet Union which was routinely attacked for its alleged 'Nazi collaboration' during World War II. The solution to the 'Ukrainian question' proposed by the Putin regime and Russian nationalists was to jettison the troublesome and Russophobic western Ukraine and obtain Western recognition of the remainder of Ukraine as lying within the Russian sphere of influence. Although seemingly far fetched the arguments put forward by American realists,[1074] the most prominent of who is Kissinger,[1075] and far left scholars and journalists similarly support a Ukraine that would not join the EU or NATO and become a neutral state lying within Russia's sphere of influence.[1076] Kotkin argues that 'Distasteful as it might sound, Washington faces the prospect of trying to work out some negotiated larger territorial settlement' with Russia that would recognise Russia's sphere of influence.[1077] Sakwa and Menon and Rumer naively believe Russian leaders would accept a democratic system to operate in neutral Ukraine ignoring the widespread paranoia among them of contagion from its neighbours.

State Duma speaker Sergey Naryshkin, a member of Putin's St. Petersburg inner circle of former intelligence officers, praised the 1945 Yalta agreement because it kept peace for half a century. Instability had appeared when the West expanded NATO to Russia's border and promoted 'pro-Nazi forces in Ukraine.' Naryshkin used the anniversary of Yalta to lay out the reasons for a Yalta-2 that would include Ukraine within a Russian sphere of influence. Such a trade-off would halt the disintegration of Ukraine and reduce tension between Russia and the West.[1078]

In spring 2014, Russia made proposals for the great powers to sit down, as at Yalta in 1945, and recreate spheres of influence. Russian leaders dream of meeting European and US leaders and putting a map on the table where they would 'carve up Europe, Yalta-style, or Molotov-Ribbentrop-style.' 'In the Russian view, there should be a map and a line on the map' and 'they would want a secret appendix.'[1079]

Polish Foreign Minister Sikorski said, 'Putin wants Poland to commit troops to Ukraine…This was one of the first things that Putin said to my prime minister, Donald Tusk, when he visited Moscow. He went on to say Ukraine is an artificial country and that Lwow is a Polish city and why don't we just sort it out together.' Sikorski continued: 'This is why the Kremlin sent out feelers to Warsaw with a message from the clownish Russian speaker of parliament, Zhirinovsky, offering Poland five provinces of Western Ukraine. The belief in Warsaw was this message was a deniable feeler from the Kremlin's innermost circles.'[1080] Not surprisingly, Poland rejected the offer.

Russian leaders believe that the Russian state is the only real sovereign country in Eurasia and therefore other states, especially 'artificial' Ukraine, require a paternalistic elder brother to take care of them. Russia's over lordship of non-Russian states would stabilise Eurasia and therefore end the new Cold War between Russia and the West.[1081] Hill writing about 'What Putin Really Wants'[1082] describes him as the 'practitioner of realpolitik in its starkest form':

1. Respect for Russia in an old fashioned hard-power sense of the term.
2. Turn the clock back to Yalta 1945 'pushing for a new division of spheres of influence.'
3. The Russian sphere of influence coincides with the historic boundaries of the Russian Empire and USSR (i.e. without western Ukraine) where Russia would exercise a monopoly of power.
4. Russia is the only country in Eurasia with a unique orthodox and cultural civilisation, imperial history and robust economy, and with the capability to defend its territorial integrity and project power.
5. All former Soviet republics are 'appendages of Russia' that 'should pay fealty to Moscow.'
6. In the process of seeking a Yalta-2, Russia rejects the post-Cold War settlement, follows the traditional Soviet policy of dividing the US and

Europe and seeks a new European order run by the great powers and an end to the US unipolar world.

Russia seeks a 'grand bargain' with the US where the post-Cold War settlement would be renegotiated and towards this end seeks to undermine NATO and the EU. In early 2016, Western politicians woke up to these plans when they accused Russia of indiscriminate bombing of civilian targets in Syria to generate a mass refugee flow that would strain European resources and increase popular support for anti-EU far right parties some of who, like France's National Front, are funded by the Kremlin. Russia's proposals for a new European collective security treaty would create an umbrella council of NATO, the EU, OSCE and CSTO (CIS Collective Security Treaty) that would end NATO's domination of Europe and give Russia a say in European security.[1083] With Russia's zone of 'privileged interests' recognised the West would no longer 'interfere' in Eurasia through the promotion of democracy and NATO and EU enlargement.

## BOSNIANISATION

Unofficial Russian nationalists who flocked to support Putin's hybrid war in the Donbas expected and supported the annexation (in their eyes 'reunion') of the region and the other six *oblasts* of *NovoRossiya*; in other words, the Russian government would undertake the same steps as it took in the Crimea. In spring 2014, the pro-Russian crowds in Kharkiv, Odesa and elsewhere in eastern and southern Ukraine, although never large majorities, also expected a Russian annexation of their regions to follow that of the Crimea. Tape recordings of Glazyev and Zatulin from February-March 2014 reveal the extent of Putin's intervention in Ukraine. 'I have a direct order from the (Kremlin) leadership to mobilise the masses in Ukraine wherever we can,' Glazyev boasted, adding 'President (Putin) has signed the order (for military intervention in Ukraine). The operation has begun.' Protesters with the support of Russian intelligence officers were to take control of administrative buildings, force local officials to declare their loyalty to Russia and request Russia's intervention.[1084]

Hybrid wars require local support to camouflage the external country's intervention which failed to materialise outside the Donbas in eastern and southern Ukraine. Glazyev complained at the small numbers of protestors who took to the streets of the six *oblasts* of *NovoRossiya* outside the Donbas. 'Why is Zaporizhzhya silent?' 'Where are they? Where are the Cossacks?' Glazyev asked. In his home city of Zaporizhzhya a paltry 1,500 pro-Russian supporters gathered and they quickly dispersed after being pelted with eggs and flour by far larger pro-Ukrainian crowds.

Putin did not annex the Donbas and *NovoRossiya* for two reasons. The first because such a step would mean that he could no longer hide Russia's intervention through hybrid war. Their annexation would be viewed by the West in the same way as Russia's invasion of the Crimea. A second invasion and annexation of Ukrainian territory would trigger tougher international sanctions and create difficulties for some European countries to continue to oppose the provision of military support to Ukraine.

The annexation of *NovoRossiya* was never a serious option because there was too little public support in six of the eight *oblasts* outside the Donbas. But, if Russia had annexed the Donbas it would have made life perhaps easier for the Ukrainian authorities as it would have been a *fait d'accompli*. Leaving the Donbas inside Ukraine gave Kyiv three choices: (1) agreeing to demands for autonomous status for the DNR and LNR; (2) launching a military campaign to regain separatist controlled territories; or (3) agreeing to demands of separatist (but not Russian) leaders to hold a referendum on the region's status to remain inside Ukraine or join Russia.

Russia's commitment to defending its annexation of the Crimea is greater than Ukrainian willingness to fight for it. Only 18.5 percent of Ukrainians would fight to regain the Crimea compared to 62.8 percent for the Donbas.[1085] Ukrainian nationalists have not launched a partisan war against Russian occupation forces in the Crimea.

Ukraine demands that Russia first fulfil the following criteria:

1. Ensure the separatists abide by a ceasefire.
2. Withdraw military equipment.
3. Foreign troops and mercenaries should leave Ukraine.
4. Prisoners of War are exchanged.
5. Ukraine resumes control over its border with Russia.
6. After steps 1-5 are undertaken, Ukraine will hold elections under OSCE observation and Ukrainian law and adopt constitutional changes to establish a 'special status' for the DNR-LNR.

Russia disagrees with this sequencing and demands that Ukraine first:

1. Adopt constitutional changes for decentralisation and the 'federalisation' of Ukraine.

2. Hold local elections.
3. Adopt constitutional changes to establish a 'special status' of the DNR-LNR.
4. Russia will then implement the steps that Ukraine demands.

The Minsk-2 Accords are unachievable because Russia will not agree to Ukraine's sequencing of steps. Of the thirteen steps listed in the Minsk 2 Accords, the creation of a 'special status' for the DNR-LNR and holding of local elections come last just behind the handing over of the border to Kyiv and 'Withdrawal of all foreign armed forces, military equipment, and mercenaries and disarmament of all illegal groups.'

Not surprisingly, in Ukraine there is zero trust in Russia implementing its steps even if Ukraine went first. In his September 2016 state of the nation address President Poroshenko demanded that security issues be first taken care of: 'We must see a complete and sustainable cease-fire, the pull-out of Russian troops and military hardware, disarming of militants, and control over the whole Ukraine-Russian border (returned to Kyiv).' Poroshenko's view of Russia undertaking security measures before Ukraine adopts political reforms and holds elections is backed by the US and PACE (Parliamentary Assembly of the Council of Europe) which called upon Russia 'to withdraw its troops from the territory of Ukraine and stop military supplies to the separatists.'[1086]

In demanding Ukraine takes the first steps, Russian seeks to legitimise separatist rule over their territories. By empowering regions, Russia would 'veto Ukraine's possible NATO and EU integration' through 'a kind of Bosnianisation' that would render 'it a dysfunctional and divided state.'[1087] Poroshenko told the Ukrainian parliament: 'Russia wants to turn the territory it occupies in the Donetsk and Luhansk regions into a Donbas protectorate, and then infiltrate it back into Ukraine on its terms to destroy us from within.' He added 'we will not allow them to do this and it will not happen.'

The Minsk-2 Accords are also unachievable because they were signed under pressure and were not an outcome of negotiations. To many Ukrainians they feel unjust. Ukrainian parliamentary deputies do not view the Minsk Accords as international legal acts because they were never presented to parliament for ratification; indeed, it is unclear if Poroshenko had the legal right to sign them. Kuchma, the head of the Ukrainian negotiators, revealed that: 'We were effectively presented with an ultimatum. Either we accept his (Putin's) proposal and end all kinds of resistance or cease to exist as an independent state.'[1088] German Chancellor Angela Merkel asked Poroshenko during the Minsk negotiations if he was giving away too much.

Three policies have been put forward to revive or replace the impasse of the Minsk-2 accords.

Firstly, a proposal supported by Ukraine's most pro-Russian politician Medvedchuk, whose daughter has Putin as her godfather is to replace separatist enclave leaders Zakharchenko and Plotnitsky with oligarch Akhmetov and the leader of the Opposition Bloc and gas lobby oligarch Boyko.[1089]

A second more radical policy by *Batkivshchyna* is to accept Minsk-2 is not working, re-define the conflict from an ATO to that of a war with Russia and and to declare martial law in the Donbas. The *Samopomich* party calls for 'abandoning the Minsk deal and declaring rebel zones occupied territory, and for Russia to finance and feed, without a chance for integration until the Russian Army leaves.'[1090] 43 percent support recognising the DNR and LNR as 'temporarily occupied territories' with a similar number (44 percent) supporting a question on the future status of the two separatist enclaves being put to a national referendum.[1091] Motyl supports a policy of temporarily suspending Ukraine's sovereign over the Donbas separatist enclaves and deferring to the OSCE or the UN to organise and conduct elections. Alternatively, Ukraine could 'suspend' efforts to reintegrate the enclaves for ten years and then ask the OSCE or UN to oversee a referendum on self-determination in the occupied Donbas allowing the citizens to choose to return to Ukraine, remain independent, or join Russia.[1092] Motyl has long proposed jettisoning the Donbas,[1093] a policy which is growing in popularity.[1094]

A third policy proposal proposed by the *Batkivshchyna* party is to divide the security and political portions of the Minsk Accords.[1095] Resolving Ukraine's security questions first, such as the removal of Russian forces and equipment, returning the border to Ukraine and releasing political prisoners should be a pre-requisite. After these steps have been implemented, Ukraine could turn to political questions such as the holding of local elections and the adoption of a law defining the regional status of the Donbas. *Batkivshchyna* opposes the DNR and LNR having 'special status' and believes they should be included within Ukraine's overall plans for de-centralisation. *Batkivshchyna* also proposes changing the Normandy to a Budapest Format by expanding the members to include the US and UK alongside EU representatives Germany and France and Ukraine and Russia. In 1994, the Budapest Memorandum signed by the UK, US and Russia provided 'security assurances' on Ukraine's territorial integrity and sovereignty in return for its nuclear disarmament. A Budapest Format would cover Russia's occupation of the Crimea and Donbas separatist enclaves.

Separatist leaders and Russian nationalists support 're-union' with Mother Russia but they have little choice but to go along with Putin's strategy of keeping the Donbas inside Ukraine. Putin's proposals for the federalisation of Ukraine with 'autonomy' granted to the DNR and LNR is not a new concept. Russia proposed the '(Dmitriy) Kozak plan' to Moldova in 2003 to create a confederal union of Moldova, Trans-Dniestr and Gagauz which Communist President Vladimir Voronin rejected. No Ukrainian leader would accept a similar plan because Russian federalisation has nothing to do with internationally recognised concepts of federal political systems and everything to do with Bosnianisation.

Putin's strategy was to create the weak state that Russian nationalist literature and myth making had always claimed Ukraine was. In Russian nationalist eyes, Ukraine only existed because Russia permitted it to do so which signified that a Ukraine outside Russia's paternalistic embrace is a non-starter. Sergey Tsekov, leader of the Russian Community of the Crimea, said that the 1654 Treaty of Pereyaslav is important because without it 'then obviously today there would be no state which is called Ukraine.'[1096] In Russia's updated 'Kozak plan,' the DNR and LNR would be 'puppet provinces' and 'pro-Russian' voices inside Ukraine.[1097] Foreign Minister Lavrov said, in an echo of Putin's 2008 speech to NATO, 'only a non-aligned Ukraine may escape further territorial disintegration.'[1098] Separatist leader Pushilin warned, 'Any moves Kyiv may make towards NATO or any other anti-Russian alliance will be unacceptable to us.'[1099]

A weak Ukrainian state with no objectives of EU and NATO membership would be insufficient because Russia needed a guarantor of its influence; the bribing of Yanukovych to drop the EU Association Agreement was meant to have created such a Kadyrov-like satrap. Russian security expert Pavel Felgenhauer believes Putin's ultimate goal is to destroy Ukrainian independence through regime change that would end its plans for European integration:

'He wants to find a Ramzan Kadyrov who became Russia's proxy in Chechnya. He could have taken over Tbilisi. But he didn't. Instead he found Bidzina Ivanishvili who kind of changed Georgia. Ideally Russia would want to find an Ivanishvili for Ukraine, an interlocker who understands the old Kuchma policies that would let Ukraine be a Russian dominion, with limited sovereignty of some kind, without the Crimea, but with constitutional safeguards of power for the Donetsk guys to veto any attempt to move Ukraine to the West. Putin would want the leader to be controllable.'

## CONCLUSION

The roots of the Ukraine-Russia crisis do not lie in EU and NATO enlargement and democracy promotion, as left-wing scholars and realists would have us believe, but in two factors. The first is Russia's and specifically Putin's unwillingness to accept Ukrainians are a separate people and Ukraine is an independent state with a sovereign right to determine its geopolitical alliances. The second is Yanukovych and the Donetsk clan's penchant for the monopolisation of power, state capture, corporate raiding of the state and willingness to accommodate practically every demand made by Moscow that culminated in treason on a grand scale. This was coupled with a shift to Sovietophile and Ukrainophobic nationality policies and return to Soviet style treatment of political opponents. Taken together, these policies made popular protests inevitable in the 2015 elections but they came a year earlier after Yanukovych bowed to Russian pressure to back away from the EU Association Agreement. These protests, in turn, became violent and nationalistic in response to the Party of Regions and KPU's destruction of Ukraine's democracy through the passing of draconian legislation, the president's refusal to compromise and his use of vigilantes and police *spetsnaz* for political repression, torture, and murders of protestors.

Russia is unlikely to end its annexation of the Crimea in the near future and it will therefore remain a frozen conflict in Europe. While the West imposed sanctions for Russia's annexation of Ukrainian territory, the Crimean question was not included in the Minsk-1 and Minsk-2 negotiations. More importantly, it will be difficult for the EU and US to lift sanctions without, at the same time, rewarding Russia for invading a foreign country and annexing Ukrainian territory.

Russia will be searching for a 'Ukrainian Kadyrov' for a long time because of two factors. The first is that the pro-Russian camp has diminished significantly and it will be very difficult to find a Ukrainian leader willing to be Putin's satrap. The second is that Putin's policies have turned Ukrainians away from Russia and Eurasian integration. The Donbas conflict cannot be resolved while there is a President-for-life Putin[1100] in charge of Russia because, as assassinated Russian opposition leader Boris Nemtsov said, the war in the Donbas is 'Vladimir Putin's war.'[1101] With Russian demands for an outcome to the conflict unachievable, the unresolved Donbas conflict will continue indefi-nitely, which is analysed in the next chapter.

# CHAPTER 9

# INVASION, ANNEXATION
# AND HYBRID WAR

*What did Russia do? Russia grabbed (territory). Russia is financing the forces
fighting there, Russia is sending in weapons. Russia is spreading propaganda. Russia is doing everything. But, whose fault is it? America!*
Sardonic Humour in Kharkiv [1102]

*Of course, the Kremlin is sure that all its failures are the result of Western (US)
plotting and scheming to deprive Russia of its self-declared right to dominate Ukraine.*
Pavel Felgenhauer[1103]

The Russian Spring of 2014 was a synthesis of fascism, Stalinism, Russian nationalism and Russian Orthodoxy or what Laruelle describes as the red, white
and brown components of the *NovoRossiya* project.[1104] Boruch Gorin, head of
the Jewish Communities of Russia, said 'It is also no secret that, on the side of
the separatists, war is also being waged by real Russian Nazis.'[1105] In early 2014
in eastern Ukraine it was 'springtime for Russian ultranationalists and neo-Nazis.'[1106] Ideological influence for the Russian Spring was provided by Russian
émigré fascist and Eurasianist writers in the inter-war period whose ideas had
been incorporated into Russian nationalistic thought in the late Soviet Union
and in the Russian Federation.

There are three factors that united Russian *spetsnaz*, military, intelligence
services and Russian nationalist volunteers. The first was xenophobic contempt

## Box 9.1: Russian Military Policies towards Ukraine, 2014-2015

Russian military policies towards Ukraine can be divided into three components. The first was overt invasion and annexation of the Crimea, the second was a covert hybrid war in the Donbas and the third an even more secretive training of Ukrainians and Russians to undertake a terrorist campaign in *NovoRossiya*; that is, outside the DNR and LNR in the other six Russian speaking *oblasts* of *NovoRossiya*. The first was successful and met little resistance from Ukrainian security forces in the Crimea. The second was only partially successful in capturing a part of the Donbas that became the DNR and LNR. The latter, like the *NovoRossiya project*, became an abject failure. Russia's hybrid war in the Donbas evolved over four stages:

**1. January-March 2014, anti-Maidan and local revolt**: the separatists were primarily locals, some of who had been receiving training in Russian camps since 2006-2007 and were trained and financed by Russian intelligence during Yanukovych's presidency. They were bolstered by the arrival of Russian nationalists who took commanding positions in the revolt (e.g. RNE activist Gubarev).

**2. April-June 2014, Russian *Spetsnaz* and Nationalist Volunteers**: local separatists were provided with professional expertise after the arrival of Russian 'little green men' (e.g. Girkin) plus Russian nationalist volunteers. In May 2014, Russia began to take control of the military operations in three ways. Separatists were supplied with weapons to shoot down Ukrainian aircraft and helicopters, first man pads (shoulder-fired anti-aircraft missiles) and later more sophisticated surface to air missile systems. Russian GRU *spetsnaz* forces in the *Vostok* battalion attacked Donetsk airport on the day Poroshenko was inaugurated Ukrainian president. Putin issued a decree banning the disclosure of soldiers' deaths in 'special operations.'

**3. July-August 2014, Invasion and Prevention of Defeat** - a massive influx of weapons and tanks is accompanied by intense shelling of Ukraine from the Russian side of its border with Ukraine, forcing the Ukrainian forces to give up control of the border. An overt Russian invasion prevented the defeat of the separatists and inflicted a humiliating defeat on Ukrainian forces, forcing Poroshenko to negotiate the Minsk-1 Accords. Russia sent its first 'humanitarian convoy' that included military equipment and personnel.

**4. September 2014, Satellite State-Building:** Between the Minsk1 and Minsk 2 Accords (September 2014-February 2015) the DNR and LNR come under complete Russian economic and financial control and the separatist militias were transformed into a 35-40,000 armed force with modern equipment and Russian command and control.

and fear of the West because in Russia everybody believes the country is 'surrounded by imperialism that is aiming to crush the country.'[1107] The second was anti-democratic Soviet nostalgia and support for an authoritarian Russia, or what Surkov defined as 'sovereign democracy.' The third was they hold a chauvinistic view of Ukrainians as an artificial country and a racist view of Ukrainians as a branch of the *Russkiy* people.

The chapter is divided into six sections. The first two analyse Ukrainian and Russian security forces in Ukraine and in the latter case with reference to the annexation of the Crimea and hybrid war in the Donbas. The next two sections survey Russian nationalist volunteers, separatist forces and Russian Cossacks. The next section discusses Russia's little known terrorist campaign outside the Donbas in other parts of Ukraine. The final section analyses sources for Ukrainian and Russian casualties in a war that have surpassed those of Soviet forces in Afghanistan and US forces in Iraq.

## UKRAINIAN SECURITY FORCES AND THE ATO

The military component of the Donbas conflict should be divided into two phases. The first lasted from April-July 2014 when Ukraine with limited armed forces and volunteer battalions, many of which were composed of veterans of the Euromaidan, defeated the separatists and Russian forces and re-captured western and southern Donetsk *oblast* and northern Luhansk *oblast*. During this period, Russia had limited numbers of *spetsnaz* ('little green men') and intelligence officers on the ground and separatist forces were disorganised and badly led. The second phase began in summer 2014 when Putin, sensing his separatist proxies were on the verge of defeat, invaded Ukraine. At the Ilovaysk 'cauldron,' Russian and separatist militia's killed 366 Ukrainian soldiers in what became known as 'Ukraine's Stalingrad' with another 429 soldiers and volunteers wounded and 128 taken prisoner.[1108] Poroshenko signed the Minsk-1 Accords the following month. Between Minsk-1 and Minsk-2 (September 2014-February 2015), Putin increased the number of Russian security forces in Ukraine

*Destroyed APC on the road to Donetsk (March 2016)*

and placed Russian military and intelligence officers in control of the separatist forces which were re-organised and supplied with high-quality military equipment. The rag-tag separatist forces during the first phase of the conflict had become an organised force of between 35-40, 000 by the second, or larger than the armed forces of 14 of NATO's 28 members. Irrespective of the Minsk Accords, Putin has continued supplying arms and active service troops to the Donbas and building large new bases near the Ukrainian-Russian border.[1109]

Russian plans were laid from autumn 2014 for a fully fledged separatist force of seven infantry brigades, one artillery and one tank brigade and *spetsnaz* battalions. During the same period of time that Putin used the Minsk-1 and Minsk-2 Accords to build a separatist army; the US, Canada and the EU refused to supply Ukraine with defensive military equipment. Western governments and the OSCE argued that the Minsk Accords needed to be given time to show they are 'working,' a ceasefire that Putin turned to Russia's advantage.

Poroshenko never launched a full-scale war against the separatists and their Russian masters in the Donbas and it is therefore called an ATO. An ATO is usually of a short-term nature to combat a terrorist group or defeat a terrorist attack and is managed by the SBU and not the military. The Ukrainian forces

*Author with a Ukrainian sniper in a position west of Horlivka (May 2016)*

that were mobilised were limited in nature and only sufficient to halt Putin's strategy of taking control of eight *NovoRossiya oblasts* but they were insufficient to win the war by taking back all of the territory that had been lost to the separatists. Ukraine's 70,000 armed forces in the ATO are less than double the size of the Ukrainian Insurgent Army (UPA) during the 1940s and similar in size to the Ukrainian Galician Army in 1918-1919 and army of the Ukrainian Directorate in 1918-1919. They are far smaller than the 4.5 million Ukrainians mobilised into the Soviet armed forces during World War II. Ukraine would require a larger mobilisation of conscripts and reservists and the use of air power if it decided to launch a military operation to defeat the separatists.

Russian invasions of Ilovaysk, Debaltseve and Novoazovsk in August 2014 and February 2015 respectively were short-term incursions. Average Russian troops are not equipped in the same manner as the *spetsnaz*, marines and paratroopers who captured the Crimea. Such forces, whether 50,000 or even 100,000 in strength are insufficient to create a 'land bridge' to the Crimea, Galeotti writes.[1110] Russia's well equipped forces are sufficient for limited incursions using special forces and elite (airborne and marine) units which reinforce separatists and inflict humiliating defeats on the Ukrainians.[1111] Russia has the capacity to conduct low intensity conflicts and foreign interventions but not full-scale invasions which would require the use of conscripts and airpower, both of which could not be camouflaged within a hybrid war.[1112]

Russia has preferred to use hybrid warfare rather than contemplate a full-scale military invasion of a country far larger than Moldova and Georgia where more limited Russian forces inflicted defeats on central governments. South Ossetia is only 30 kilometres from Tbilisi whereas Donetsk is a seven-hour train journey on the inter-city train from Kyiv. Galeotti believes Russia's army remains a defensive force rather than one capable of foreign invasions.[1113] Russia's mobilisation of 90,000 armed forces in spring 2014 had to draw from 28 different military units. By February 2015, Russia's forces in eastern Ukraine drew on all but two of Russia's ten field armies based as far away as Vladivostok and the Kurile Islands. The shortage of manpower prevented the supply of manpower from entire units and units from the Buryat autonomous republic were transported thousands of miles with their tanks to fight in eastern Ukraine. Several fake 'separatists' had 'the wide Asian features typical of Russians from beyond the Urals, but not native to Ukraine.'[1114] It seems incredulous that the Russian leadership believed it could get away with Buryats, devoid of their Russian military patches, pretending to be local 'separatists.' Hutchings and Tolz write that the Buryats have considered their homeland to be the 'cradle of the Eurasian culture' and the Buryat region is 'being instrumental in revealing to the Russians their true identity.'[1115]

In Debaltseve, 5,000 of the 8,000 Russian forces were professional contract soldiers. But, it took many months for Russian professional forces to capture Donetsk Airport from Ukrainian Cyborgs. For a longer-term invasion and occupation of Ukraine, Putin would have to use half or more of his entire 800,000 armed forces because Ukraine is far bigger than Georgia or Moldova where Russian troops were in action in the early 1990s in the former and again in 2008 in Georgia.

An attempt to create a land bridge through Mariupol to Odesa would be an impossible feat as it would require an invasion army advancing over a large territory through four *oblasts* and inhospitable terrain. Hybrid war is only successful when 'little green men' can hide among local supporters which has proven difficult to find even in large areas of the Donbas. Putin's conundrum in Ukraine is that his *Russkiy Mir* is unpopular outside the DNR and LNR which

*View of the destroyed Donetsk Airport occupied by Russian and separatist forces which lies 1.5 kilometres from a Ukrainian base at the Butivka coal mine, Avdyivka (May 2016)*

would mean Russian occupation forces would face hostile local populations and a well organised guerrilla war. During World War II, Ukrainian nationalists and the Stalinist regime mobilised a combined 300,000 partisans. A Russian Nazi volunteer who fought alongside the separatists said 'You start to explain that you're a Russian nationalist who came here to fight for *NovoRossiya*, for Russian people' and 'They say: 'What Russians? We're Ukrainians. What *NovoRossiya*? We want to live autonomously from both Russia and Ukraine.'[1116]

In the first phase of the conflict a major part of the fighting was undertaken by Ukrainian volunteer battalions. Although Western media focused on the nationalist and oligarch-funded volunteer battalions these represented only a minority of the 50 formations and, more interestingly, a large proportion of the volunteers in the nationalist battalions were Russian speakers. Andriy Biletskiy, commander of the *Azov* battalion and himself from Kharkiv, pointed out that 'Half of the Azov speaks in the Russian language. But they die and kill for Ukraine.'[1117] One hundred ethnic Russians from Ukraine and Russia have fought in both *Pravyy Sektor* and *Azov* who justify their support for Ukraine not in anti-Russian terms. 'Pomor' from Murmansk said 'This is not a Russian-Ukrainian war. This is a war between *vatniks* and *non-vatniks*, Putinists and anti-

*Ukrainian troops in a donated pick up (2015)*

Putinists.' Ilya Bogdanov, an anti-Putin activist, added that the Putinist regime is not really nationalist as it does not care for its people and blames all of society's problems on the West. 'A proper nationalist admits his nation's mistakes and tries to correct them,' she added. Bogdanov said that some Russian nationalists supported the Euromaidan but were seduced by Putin when he annexed the Crimea.[1118]

The volunteer battalions were not a 'ragtag of uncontrolled right-wing extremists' but had a 'high level of motivation and patriotic commitment.'[1119] The patriotism of Ukrainians was evident in Donetsk Airport where the defenders were nicknamed 'Cyborgs' who withstood separatists and professional Russian troops, including marines, for 242 days between May 2014 and January 2015. 'Cyborgs' and soldiers from Ukraine's airborne brigades in Zhytomyr and Mykolayiv, two regions which suffered disproportionately higher military casualties, are strongly motivated and well-trained and they inflicted high casualties on Russian and separatist forces.

By the second phase of the conflict all of the volunteer battalions had been integrated into the armed forces and the National Guard and, despite predictions to the contrary, none had become private armies of oligarchs or had refused to submit to Kyiv's authority.[1120] Without a well organised civil society and military volunteers, Ukraine would have been defeated in 2014

*Author in Ukrainian trenches 500 metres from Russian lines in Horlivka (May 2016)*

and its statehood and sovereignty would have become insecure. Victories on the battlefield and halting Putin's aggression was largely thanks to these volunteer battalions, reservists and civil society, not to the General Staff which remains stuck in a Soviet mind-set.[1121] Mariupol would not have been retaken and southern Ukraine secured from the separatists without the formation of the highly motivated *Azov* battalion.[1122]

The Orange and Euromaidan Revolutions showed the resilience and fortitude of Ukrainians in their ability to adapt and utilise whatever was at their disposal. Ukraine, unlike the West, is not a throwaway society and 'things' are kept in storage just in case they may be needed in the future. As Ukrainians say: '*Mozhe prydastsya (maybe it will come in handy)*.' During the Euromaidan, activists built homemade bazookas and catapults while volunteer battalions transformed

*Ukrainian forward trenches west of Horlivka (May 2016)*

everyday vehicles into APCs. Many of these skills of foraging, building from old spare parts, and organising collections of donations were transferred to civil society volunteer groups that continued to supply the armed forces and the National Guard.

Of all of Ukraine's oligarchs only Kolomoyskyy adopted a patriotic stance by agreeing to become governor of an *oblast* adjacent to the war and to fund volunteer battalions. Pinchuk and Akhmetov refused the offer to become governors of Zaporizhzhya and Donetsk respectively. Kolomoyskyy said 'When the revolution happened, I showed what I was made of' and he added 'I was on the side of the Ukrainian state in its darkest hour.'[1123] Kolomoyskyy financed two *Dnipro* battalions and the *Donbas* battalion and adopted a very tough stance in Dnipro against any manifestations of separatism, even offering a $10,000 reward for each captured Russian soldier. One report claimed,

'Kolomoyskyy took some separatist leaders trained by the GRU for a walk in the woods where explanatory work was conducted to explain how exactly to love Ukraine. And the separatist threat just vanished.'[1124]

The Ukrainian authorities became concerned at the independence of the volunteer battalions and their threat to political stability. But, a coup d'état was unlikely and even nationalists disgruntled at Poroshenko understood that political instability would only benefit Putin. There were though limits to nationalist patience, as seen in the riots outside parliament in September 2015 over the issue of giving a 'special status' to the separatist enclaves during which three National Guard soldiers were killed. The proliferation of weapons in private hands will remain a concern to the authorities. Tension between Ukrainian patriots and the authorities should not be surprising as soldiers, National Guard and volunteers fought for Ukraine - not for Poroshenko – who has been a disappointment in not pursuing justice for those murdered on the Euromaidan, punishing leaders of the former regime for bankrupting Ukraine and committing treason. Patriotic Ukrainians volunteering and fighting in the ATO want to know their efforts are 'not being wasted to defend vested interests or to preserve a dysfunctional system.'[1125]

There are six factors worth considering when analysing Ukraine's security forces during the Russia-Ukraine war:

1.  Ukraine's armed forces declined in number and quality over the entire course of Ukrainian independence. But, the deterioration of Ukraine's armed forces was a deliberate, calculated and treasonous policy undertaken by President Yanukovych and the Party of Regions and in spring 2014, Ukraine had only 6,000 operational troops it could use. Although Yanukovych and his allies have fled to Russia, others are living in Monaco, Austria and the UK, where they have purchased real estate, while others have been elected to parliament within the Opposition Bloc. It is not credible that Chief of Staff Lyovochkin, a financier of the Opposition Bloc, did not know about Yanukovych's treason. Ukraine's gas lobby remains untouchable because of its long-standing relations with Poroshenko that were finalised during a meeting in March 2014 in Vienna.[1126]

2.  President Kuchma disbanded the National Guard in 2000 because he did not support it coming under the joint control of the president and parliament. The National Guard was revived in 2014 when it replaced the Ministry of Interior Internal Troops inherited from the USSR.

3.  Civil society continues to provide resources in the form of foodstuffs, transportation, medical supplies, uniforms, warm bedding and military equipment such as night and heat vision binoculars for the military and National Guard in the ATO. Ukrainian volunteers for the army and National Guard had to spend thousands of dollars of their own money to equip themselves. The equipment for 'Denys,' a volunteer 'Cyborg' who fought at Donetsk Airport, was paid for by the private company he worked for in Kyiv.[1127] Often the equipment that has been supplied by the Ministry of Defence has been of poor quality and volunteers have had to resort to foraging, buying and accepting donations. The cost of $2-2,500 for body armour, weapons, gun, night vision and uniform is a large sum for any Ukrainian. [1128]In Volnovakha in April 2015, I witnessed a Ukrainian military officer collecting US military fatigue trousers from a civil society group because the ones they had been supplied with were of such bad quality. A year later I travelled with civil society volunteers to the Donbas conflict front line where they distributed former British army uniforms that were of better quality and importantly fire proof and yet cost half that of Ukrainian uniforms (800 compared to 1,500 *hryvnya*). A major problem for the Ukrainian state arising from Ukrainian volunteers buying equipment or receiving donations is that it remained their personal property after they returned from the frontline. The increased circulation of weapons on the black market has led to the cost of a Kalashnikov rifle dropping fourfold from $800 to only $200. As I was told, bullets can be obtained for the price of a bottle of vodka.

4.  Weak presidential political will to fight corruption has meant the continuation of corruption in the Ministry of Defence where equipment is sold through intermediaries rather than supplied directly to military units. Civil society groups and private volunteer charities have had to purchase equipment using cash for military and National Guard units. Volunteers and supporters of the *Azov* battalion raised 1 million *hryvnya* to purchase equipment for a unit that is officially part of the Ministry of Interior's National Guard. The general prosecutor's office has never responded to this kind of corruption in the Ministry of Defence and it is 'Difficult to believe the government is not aware of this.' If Ukrainian army uniforms cost twice that of British uniforms and yet

are of worse quality and not fire proof, there must be corruption involved. Indeed, 'Why must troops purchase for cash from the state that what the state should be supplying free of charge?'[1129]

5. Poroshenko's reliance on the old guard and oligarchs in eastern and southern Ukraine and in the military stymies reform and the fight for justice and ends in military disasters. Ukraine's army requires a complete overhaul, not a little tinkering, as seen in the huge turnover of Ministers of Defence since the Euromaidan. Nepotism and corruption are rife at the senior levels of the military where Ukraine had an incredible 400 generals compared to the US which has only 40! 75 percent of the problems of Ukraine's military lie at the senior levels. Other problem areas include poor communications, rudderless military units on the frontline, and incompetent and infiltrated intelligence services. The Donbas conflict has shown weak coordination between units, lack of shared radio frequencies, security breaches through the continued use of mobile telephones, and confusion of tactics with strategy. At the Ilovaysk 'cauldron,' Ukrainian military intelligence declared the opposite to be true to the reality on the ground leading to 'Ukraine's Stalingrad.' Not only were Ukrainian generals cut off from reality on the frontline in Debaltseve but so was President Poroshenko whose repeated denials of a 'cauldron' (where Ukrainians troops were surrounded) was 'idiotic,' in the words of a Western diplomat.[1130]

6. Although Ukraine has sought defensive military equipment from the West, it has never had plans to purchase equipment. Supplying military equipment is pointless if it is not introduced alongside training and reform of Ukraine's General Staff and senior officers. During the chaotic rout at Debaltseve, Ukrainian forces left behind two US counter-mortar radars. Ukraine could buy weapons as Ukraine is not included on any international arms embargo and Russia's invasions and annexation of the Crimea have been condemned by the UN, OSCE, NATO and EU.

## RUSSIAN FORCES AND HYBRID WAR

In winter and spring 2014, Russian security forces in Ukraine consisted of the following units:

1. Black Sea Fleet marines and naval intelligence forces stationed since the Soviet era in the port of Sevastopol and the Crimea. These units

assisted Russian GRU 'little green men' in annexing the Crimea in spring 2014.

2. Since 2010, Russian intelligence and military intelligence ensconced inside the SBU and Ukrainian military intelligence who had been training, financing and equipping anti-Euromaidan vigilantes, pro-Russian groups and separatists in eastern and southern Ukraine and the Crimea.

3. Russian 'little green men' *spetsnaz* who invaded mainland Ukraine from the Crimea in April 2014. These were highly trained in urban warfare, constructing fortifications and providing covert support to unorganised protesters. They led the assault on state and government buildings and then passed control over them to local separatists.1131

4. From August 2014, larger Russian military units stationed inside the Donbas and on the Ukrainian-Russian border.

One of the most well-known Russian units was led by Girkin who took credit for 'pulling the trigger of war.' He claimed that pro-Russian leaders from the Donbas, Kharkiv, Odesa and Mykolayiv travelled to the Crimea to seek support for their uprisings. They, and Girkin, were convinced that Putin would order Russian forces to invade eastern Ukraine in 'defence of Russian speakers' and then annex *NovoRossiya*, as he had the Crimea. This though did not happen and large numbers of Russian forces only came to the rescue of the separatists in August 2014 when they were on the verge of being defeated. Since then, Putin has admitted that the separatists would not survive without massive Russian military assistance.[1132] By summer 2014, Putin could no longer hide 'the fact that Russian money, weapons and quite likely fighters were flowing across the border.'[1133] A DNR *spetsnaz* fighter admitted that Russian support was crucial and that Russia provided 'well disciplined and well-trained troops' while Russian generals ran 'large-scale operations.'[1134]

Although Putin and other Russian leaders continued to deny the presence of Russian forces evidence of their presence was available from independent Russian media, social media, Western reporters in eastern Ukraine, the Ukrainian media, satellite imagery and US and NATO sources. Ukraine's military intelligence released a detailed list of Russian officers who control the separatist units.[1135] Bellingcat provided a thorough analysis of medals awarded to Russian soldiers who had fought in Ukraine.[1136] Human rights NGOs provided

*Commander of the 15th battalion, 128th brigade with author (Butivka coal mine, Avdyivka, May 2016)*

irrefutable evidence of shelling from Russia into Ukraine in summer and autumn 2014.[1137]

By spring 2015, Russian soldiers in eastern Ukraine no longer sought to hide their presence. In March 2016, OSCE Deputy Head of Mission in Ukraine Alexander Hug admitted that the OSCE had for two years observed evidence of Russian troops and weapons in Ukraine.[1138] Putin may have continued the charade of denying the presence of his troops in eastern Ukraine, but Russian and separatist leaders on the ground were no longer in denial. Dmitriy Sapozhnikov, originally from St. Petersburg and a nationalist volunteer, said that it's no longer a secret that Russian officers lead the separatist forces: 'Everyone admits it, and the Russians admit it…Thanks to the Russian forces, we're able to take positions quickly.' He added that all large operations are directed by Russian officers: 'They make plans together with our commanders.'[1139]

A Russian nationalist volunteer confirmed that all the high-level officers who were 'active military officers' from brigade to battalion level were Russian and the military equipment was Russian. 'Russian advisers are the direct commanders on the ground and create the military rhythm of the whole machine,' a Russian Nazi volunteer said. 'Maybe in local conflicts [separatists] participate directly and give orders, but in general the battalions are tracked, controlled, and given orders by Russian military advisers, who in turn get their orders, of course, from Moscow.'[1140] Russia has supplied hardware since May 2014 and some of this, such as T-72 133 tanks, were only delivered to its army in 2013.[1141]

Deputy Commander of Moscow ground forces Lt. General Aleksandr Lentsov was in overall command of coordinating separatist forces. Russian Major Generals Vitaliy Sukuyev, Igor Tymofeyev and Valeriy Osiapov have been identified as commanders of units of separatist forces.[1142] The Russian high command was especially important during punishment incursions, such as at Ilovaysk and Debaltseve. In the latter, the battle was won by three Russian battle groups, 90 percent of who were troops and the remainder separatists and Cossacks. The Russian army is 'bearing the brunt of the fighting' and evidence, of this is 'now coming from Russian reporters or the mothers of dead soldiers.'[1143] Russian security forces in Ukraine and on its borders were not constituted as an invasion force but for the purpose of training and equipping separatists and Russian nationalist volunteers.

Three important aspects should be borne in mind when analysing Putin's hybrid war and Russian military options:

1. Hybrid war is only successful when there is local support, which exists in only in a small proportion of the Donbas in eastern Donetsk and southern Luhansk *oblasts*. Girkin had to withdraw from western Donetsk, pro-Russian forces were routed in Mariupol and they failed to establish bases in northern Luhansk. In these three regions, local support for Russia's hybrid war was weak. If this was true of these three areas of the Donbas it is even more the case for the other six *oblasts* of *NovoRossiya* where hybrid war could not have been successful because of low levels of local support.[1144]

2. The separatists operating on their own without Russian support would have been defeated in August 2014 and they would be defeated today if Russia did not provide a security guarantee. For them 'The Donbas on its own cannot provide resources for the continuation of war at the present level of hostilities' and without Russian support 'it would be doomed.'[1145]

3. A separatist defeat would mean the end of Putin's leverage over Ukraine.

Ukrainian 'Cyborgs' in Donetsk Airport mainly fought against Russian soldiers,[1146] including marines whose arm patches were shown mistakenly on

*Trenches manned by Ukrainian marines on the beach near Mariupol (April 2015)*

the *Russia Today* channel. The language they spoke, the accents, the jargon, the vocabulary – all was Russian. Russian, not even Ukrainian Russian.'[1147] Putin has stated that he would not allow a separatist defeat and Russian policy was described by one official as 'Whatever needs to be done will be done, right up to direct military intervention, if that is what it takes.'[1148] Ukraine is also constrained by the reaction of the West to any Ukrainian military attack. Talk about having your cake and eating it: Putin's multi-vector approach to the conflict involves participating in the peace negotiations on the one hand and supplying arms, training and leadership that fuels the conflict.

Ukrainian forces put up a determined fight in 2014-2015 and 'If armed and organised, they will put up a big fight. They have deep conviction.'[1149] Putin highly 'underestimated Ukraine's resilience.'[1150] A full scale Russian invasion of Ukraine would require the following:

1.  A willingness to accept tougher sanctions at a time when the Russian economy and financial system is in dire straits. Russia's military support for Syrian President Bashar al-Assad has inflamed the Sunni Muslim world which rules out Saudi Arabia agreeing to increase oil prices.

2. Willingness to withdraw Russian forces from strategic locations on the Chinese border, Central Asia, Kaliningrad and the Caucasus.

3. Provide resources to support a long-term occupation regime.

4. Ensure large amounts of financial means to buy local complicity.

5. Possess the means to fight a large-scale counter insurgency over a big territory where three quarters of the population blame Russia for the Donbas conflict.

Russian forces provide a command and control function, operate advanced military equipment (such as the surface to air *Buk* missile system), and form 'a sort of parallel command structure answerable to Moscow.'[1151] Lt. General Ben Hodges, US Commander-in-Chief of NATO, said 'There is direct Russian military intervention…these are not separatists, they are proxies for President Putin.'[1152] The separatists are 'boosted by (nationalist) Russian fighters, directed by Russian intelligence and armed with modern Russian weapons that roll across the border with impunity.'[1153] A separatist leader told the Russian assistant of *The Times* journalist 'There are a lot of your compatriots here.'[1154] The Russian Ministry of Interior's *Dzerzhinsky* Division has been seen behind Russian and separatist lines because of the unreliability and at times cowardice of separatists, as attested to by Russian forces, and to prevent Russian desertions. Not all Russian soldiers were happy at being used as 'cannon fodder.'

Russia's hybrid war integrated political subversion, trade war, territorial destabilisation, political propaganda and deceit. Wilson describes hybrid war as the foreign extension of domestic practices; that is, foreign policy as *reyderstvo*.'[1155] This type of Russian foreign policy is a form of corporate raiding that steals territory and assets from neighbouring countries using a militarised form of political technology that combines deniability, cynicism and doublespeak.

Military equipment and other supplies were delivered by 'humanitarian convoys' where the system worked as follows: 'Okay, you will get humanitarian goods, but it is not all humanitarian. You will take your part, and the military will take their part.'[1156] The US Mission to the OSCE (i.e. the US government) said in February 2015:

'The separatist movement at this point is a de facto extension of the Russian military and an instrument of Russian national power. The Russian military has put in place a robust command structure in eastern Ukraine, ranging from Russian General Staff Officers overseeing operations down to junior officers. Russian personnel conduct communications, intelligence gathering, direct military operations, and help correct artillery fire. Separatist fighters have publicly acknowledged that they are operating under instructions from Moscow.'[1157]

The camouflaging of Russian forces without country insignia or as local separatists is not a new strategy and was used by the NKVD in the 1940s to fight the UPA in western Ukraine. NKVD troops would wear UPA uniforms and massacre villagers and these graphic images were then used by Soviet propaganda to highlight the atrocities of 'Ukrainian fascists.' *Maskirovka* was the Soviet art of denial, disinformation and deception that accompanied invasion by stealth, deniability and confusion where the line dividing truth from illusion was blurred. In the post-Soviet era, Ukraine's first taste of such activities was in the 2004 elections when Russian political technologists working for the Yanukovych campaign used the concept of 'directed chaos.'[1158] Hybrid war is a militarised form of 'directed chaos' that includes agitation and propaganda, seizure of state institutions, insurgency and proxy war. In both cases, 'directed chaos' and hybrid war have concrete political objectives, whether the discrediting of Yushchenko and his electoral defeat in 2004 or the bigger goal of halting Ukraine's European integration and punishing Euromaidan leaders for overthrowing Yanukovych.

Russian forces brought from the Buryat autonomous republic to attack Debaltseve and 'bomb the *khokhols*' painted over the markings on their tanks and tore off patches and chevrons on their uniforms. All forms of ID (e.g. civilian passports and military service cards) and mobile phones were taken from the troops at the Rostov training base on the Ukrainian border.[1159] A wounded Russian Buryat told the independent *Novaya Gazeta* newspaper:

'We were told we were going on manoeuvres but we knew where we were going. All of us knew where we were going. I was morally and mentally ready to go to Ukraine...All of us knew we were crossing the frontier.'[1160]

An important aspect of Russia's hybrid war is serial lying which Putin is well versed in undertaking. Putin denied during the Crimean invasion that the 'little green men' were Russian troops and when asked replied 'There are many military uniforms. You can find them in any shop.' A month later he admitted they had been Russian active service troops. Lavrov responded in the same manner at the February 2016 Munich Security conference when Poroshenko showed Russian passports of dead and captured soldiers. The blueprints for the takeover of the Crimea had actually existed for many years but at least since

2008, Trenin writes.[1161] Pomerantsev described Putin's and Lavrov's wholesale deception as following in the Soviet tradition of *maskirovka* where 'Life is just one glittering masquerade, where every role and any position or belief is mutable.'[1162]

Putin and other Russian leaders have always lied about the presence of Russian forces in the Donbas and continue to brazenly lie. 'There are no armed Russian soldiers or Russian advisers in eastern Ukraine,' Putin said. 'There aren't any now and there were never any.'[1163] Russian military spokesmen denied there were manoeuvres on the Ukrainian border, that they were shelling Ukraine from inside Russia, [1164]or that there were Russian troops inside Ukraine.[1165] While such categorical lies could have worked decades ago this is not the case today in the age of satellites and social media when Russia's repeated denials have become a source of irritation to Western leaders. The denial of Russian troops in Ukraine was of course disingenuous Kurkov reminded his fellow Russians: 'Really? – and what about in Crimea?'[1166] A major source of open intelligence on Russian troops and casualties in eastern Ukraine is found on *VKontakte* and *Facebook* where Russian soldiers inside Ukraine post photographs.

One aspect of Russia's hybrid war is Putin's desire to punish Ukraine for its betrayal of 'Holy Rus' and the *Russkiy Mir*. He poured scorn on the fighting abilities of Ukrainian forces for being allegedly defeated by 'yesterday's coalminers or yesterday's tractor drivers.' Ensuring there were large numbers of Ukrainian casualties was a form of personal revenge by Putin against the Ukrainian revolutionaries who had twice embarrassed him in a decade. Leon Aron writes that 'Putin's goal was to punish, destabilise, dismember, and ultimately subvert and derail the new nation.'[1167]

Ukrainian forces who escaped from encirclements at Ilovaysk and Debaltseve have talked of the shock at the 'aggressiveness and harshness' of their Russian and separatist foes. In both encirclements, the aim was to kill as many Ukrainians as possible. Russian and separatist forces were ordered to shoot to kill Ukrainian combatants during the Debaltseve offensive and not to disarm or take them prisoner.[1168] Some of this venom came from Russia but it was also locally present and a Donbas resident said 'Deep down many people hated Ukraine.'[1169] In Ilovaysk the promise of a safe corridor for Ukrainian forces to withdraw was a brazen and calculated lie to lure Ukrainians into an ambush where they were slaughtered. In Ilovaysk and Debaltseve: 'The rebels would attack the first vehicle in the convoy and also the last one so that the convoy was blocked, and they would attack and kill every vehicle and person in it in between.'[1170]

The deep level of hostility among Russian nationalists for pro-Western Ukrainians could be seen in the chilling warning by RNE leader Barkashov:[1171]

'All (Ukrainian) military officers who gave orders will be eliminated without a court trial and investigation. All Kyiv-*Ukrop* politicians will be eliminated. All *RightSex (a pun on Right Sector)* and homosexuals will be eliminated. We will locate and find all those who are in their forest bunkers. We will find those who are abroad. Even if this takes us two to four years they will all die.

We will not leave anybody alive. Thinking about their families we believe them to be enemies of the people with all of the resultant consequences. We will hang all of them, even underage pro-Western football hooligans who are paid by oligarch finances to beat up (Soviet) veterans. We are not scaremongering and want everybody to know about our plans.

For every one of our comrades killed in combat in Donetsk, Luhansk, Kharkiv, and Slovyansk we will eliminate 100 (Ukrainian) soldiers. Not those who died in battle, but those who remain alive. We will hang them all.'

## RUSSIAN NATIONALIST VOLUNTEERS
## GIRKIN'S 'LITTLE GREEN MEN'

In early April 2014, Girkin invaded Ukraine with 52 GRU *spetsnaz* 'little green men' and chose Slovyansk as his first target. His unit was backed by 150-200 local recruits who were given weapons that were captured from Ministry of Interior and SBU arsenals. The force captured neighbouring Kramatorsk the next day. By the end of May, Girkin had collected 28,000 local volunteers after dismissing a large number, he claimed, because they had criminal backgrounds. The remainder became his personal Slavic battalion.[1172]

Girkin boasted 'If our squad had not crossed the border, everything would have come to an end like in Kharkiv, like in Odesa.' This was only true up to a point as the FSB and GRU had been active for a long time in recruiting, training and financing pro-Russian vigilante groups loyal to Moscow. On the other hand, Girkin and his 52 'little green men' blazed a path in the Donbas in providing 'muscle' and organisational expertise for local separatists enabling them to take control of Ukrainian state buildings (i.e. state administration, government, councils, Ministry of Interior, and SBU).

Girkin planned to hold on to the Donbas and await a Russian invasion that would have annexed *NovoRossiya*, repeating what Putin had undertaken in the Crimea. But, he was confronted by a fierce Ukrainian assault and had limited numbers of local separatist forces. In the absence of a Russian invasion, separatists were defeated in Mariupol by the *Azov* battalion[1173] and Girkin's forces retreated from western Donetsk in July 2014. While downplaying local support as inadequate, Girkin had respect for the motivation of the 'nationalist' Ukrainian National Guard and volunteer battalions who did much of the fighting.

The Russian authorities have always claimed that volunteers who have travelled to Ukraine have done so of their own accord. But, in authoritarian Russia where telephones, the Internet and social media are completely monitored it would be impossible for them to host websites recruiting volunteers, running training camps and equipping and transporting them to the border without the FSB's knowledge. 'Perhaps, secretly, it even encourages such activities' a *BBC* report on pro-Tsarist volunteers said.[1174]

Russian volunteers who fought in the Donbas came from military reconstruction groups, Cossacks, Hells Angels, neo-Nazis, Abkhaz and Chechen war veterans. They had many things in common that included being anti-Roma, anti-Semitic and Ukrainianophobes who travelled to Ukraine to fight 'fascists' and NATO. Girkin claimed his volunteers had not been sent to the Donbas which is difficult to believe as he already was in the Crimea on 21 February 2014,[1175] a day before Yanukovych fled from Kyiv. Girkin is a Russian intelligence service officer who has had a long career fighting in foreign and domestic wars; after all, there is no such thing as a 'former spook.' Girkin was a white army military enactor who used the Donbas to implement his White Guard fantasies to 'Restore the traditions of the Russian imperial army'[1176] into real life. Russian nationalist battalions sympathetic to Girkin included the Russian Orthodox Army and Imperial Legion whose flag carried the slogan 'God, Tsar, Nation.'[1177] A nationalist volunteer who supported the White monarchists explained that in creating these battalions 'our ambition was to create an orthodox al-Qaeda.'[1178]

Russian neo-Nazi and fascist groups had emerged in the 1980s and had always condoned the use of violence, as seen in their support for the Russian parliament's military standoff with President Yeltsin in 1993.[1179] Other neo-Nazis came from extreme right-wing groups in St. Petersburg, including 'Batman' Aleksandr Bednov, Aleksey Milchakov and Kiril Rimkus. One of these activists said he made up his mind to volunteer after the 2 May 2014 fire in the Trade Union building in Odesa and he joined the Dawn separatist battalion.

Other Russian neo-Nazi and fascist groups who sent volunteers included Ravil Khalikov, Rostoslav Zhuravlev and Eduard Limonov from Other Russia, the DNR's Deputy Foreign Minister Aleksandr Proselkov (assassinated in July 2015) from the Eurasian Youth Union, Alexey Khudyakov, leader of the anti-immigrant Shield of Moscow, and Aleksandr Boroday, editor of the extreme nationalist *Zavtra* newspaper which recruits mercenaries for the separatists, the National Bolshevik Party and the Black Hundred organisation. Brian Whitmore writes that although Russia cut off its gas supplies to Ukraine it remains 'busy exporting its mafia and neo-Nazis to its southern neighbour.'[1180]

Donbas separatists have received support from Russian nationalists groups, such as the Nazi RNE, Russia's oldest Nazi organisation that has been active since 1990 whose members wear black uniforms and use swastika-like symbols, espouse anti-Semitism and have a paramilitary force.[1181] The RNE is unabashedly Nazi, chauvinistic and imperialist and supports a unitary state for the *Rossiyany* and *Russki* who are defined as including the Great, Little and White Russians.

The RNE quickly took the initiative in the Russian Spring by taking control of the separatist protests. RNE member Gubarev led crowds that stormed the Donetsk *oblast* state administration where he hung a Russian flag and proclaimed himself the 'People's Governor' of Donetsk. His fellow RNE party member Aleksandr Boroday became DNR prime minister. Speaking about Gubarev, Donetsk businessperson Enrique Menendez said 'He just happens to have always been a Russian fascist.'[1182] One of the publicly available photographs of Gubarev clearly shows him in the black uniform of the Nazi RNE.[1183] A Ukrainian blogger writing about Russian neo-Nazi volunteers said 'The skinheads dressed uniformly were clearly not local, their shaved heads and bomber jackets have long gone out of fashion with those on the right.'[1184] RNE paramilitaries are fighting in the Donbas alongside the separatists.[1185]

Other Russian volunteers also upheld neo-Nazi and fascist ideologies and had provided paramilitary training to Ukrainian separatists, such as the Donetsk Republic. First Deputy Prime Minster of the DNR Purgin, Oleksandr Tsurkan, head of the Information Centre of the South-Eastern Front (a branch of the International Eurasian Movement) Kostyantyn Knyrik, Matyushkin and DNR parliamentary deputy Oleh Frolov received training in these Russian camps.

Nazi tattoos on separatists were either from their membership of neo-Nazi organisations or from criminal gangs when they had served time in prison.

Roman Tolstokorov who defected from Russian forces to *Pravyy Sektor* had a massive Nazi tattoo on his back from prison where he had been incarcerated for theft and narcotics.[1186] A journalist writing for *The New Republic* confronted a separatist with a swastika on his forearm. He replied 'This isn't a swastika. This is an ancient Slavic symbol. Swa is the God of the sky' and continued 'It's our Slavic heritage. It's not a swastika.'[1187] The *Azov* battalion also claim that their symbol is not a neo-Nazi *Wolfsangel (Wolf's Hook)* but the letters *SN (Slava Natsiyi – Glory to the Nation).*

Russian nationalist volunteers were drawn from the large skinhead groups in Russia which had long cooperated with pro-Russian and Pan-Slavic skinheads in the Crimea and eastern Ukraine. Hard-line, masculine, racist, anti-Western, hostile to immigrants and anti-Semitic they view the Donbas conflict as 'part of the bonding mechanism' with other skinheads through the gaining of experience of violence. Although Russian skinheads believe Putin is not nationalistic enough it is worth recalling that 'Skinheads did not emerge as a counterpoint to the political atmosphere of the 1990s but as a result of it.' Skinheads had hijacked Putin's Unity Day holiday as the 'Russian March' where they flaunted party and organisational flags and banners as 'integral to their process of identity formation and a tool by which they can promote their agenda in the general public through spectacle.'[1188] These fascist thugs were on display in Europe during the Euro-2016 football championship when many of them, including their leader Aleksandr Shprygin, were arrested and deported from France for organised violence. Shprygin's 'All-Russia Supporters Union is backed by the Kremlin. He is reported to hold far-right views and has been photographed giving a Nazi salute.'[1189] He demanded 'the Russian squad should be represented by "Slavic faces" at the World Cup due to be hosted by the country in 2018.' Shprygin said he was '100% anti-fascist' and that he didn't have 'anything against Jews.'[1190]

Hells Angels were another group of extremists who flocked to Ukraine. The Night Wolves came from Moscow 'to defend my motherland' and they travelled to the Donbas 'to take back the Russian lands.' A *Guardian* newspaper video report of the Night Wolves chapter in the LNR showed portraits of Stalin in their barracks.[1191] The Night Wolves, like their official financiers, view the Donbas as a 'religious and spiritual war' and believe the *NovoRossiya* project is not dead.

## SEPARATIST AND COSSACK FORCES

In the early part of the conflict in 2014, Russian commanders complained at the weak support given to them by locals and the difficulties they faced in recruiting fighters. Russian forces in Slovyansk had limited success in recruiting locals and of those who volunteered many were 'marginal people, commoners (lower class) *lumpen*, and some of them Orthodox priests.'[1192] The DNR and LNR battalions were as motley as the political, religious and criminal groups that created them:

- *Donbas Rus* was backed by the *Russkiy Bloc*, an ally of the Party of Regions in the Crimea.
- Donetsk Republic, led by Purgin, had been banned by Ukraine and its members had trained in Russian camps since summer 2006.
- *Narodnoe Opolcheniye* was linked to the RNE and Gubarev.
- *Oplot*, one of a number of separatist organisations sanctioned by the US government, originated within organised crime in Kharkiv where it had been allied to Mayor Kernes. DNR Prime Minister Zakharchenko was the head of the Donetsk branch of *Oplot*.[1193]
- *Vostok* was the reincarnation of a Russian *spetsnaz* unit that had been militarily active in the Caucasus and South Ossetia in the 1990s and 2000s but had been disbanded in 2008. Its reincarnation in the DNR is led by former SBU *Alpha* officer Khodakovskyy. *Vostok* and *Zapad* battalions are under the control of the GRU and in 2014 included pro-Putin Chechens loyal to President Kadyrov.[1194]
- Don Cossacks based in the LNR are led by Nikolay Kozitsyn.
- The Ghost battalion was led by Mozgovoy who was assassinated in May 2015.
- Sparta was led by Arseniy ('Motorola') Pavlov who had one of the worst reputations in the Donbas for human rights abuses. He was assassinated in October 2016.

Don and Kuban history represents cases of extreme Stockholm Syndrome. One million Cossacks were murdered during the Soviet regime's collectivisation, artificial famine, Great Terror and deportations. The Kuban, a region populated by Cossacks from Ukraine, was Ukrainian speaking until the 1930s when the region and Soviet Ukraine were devastated by the *holodomor* and subjected to high levels of Russification. By the 1980s and 1990s, Kuban Cossacks had joined their Don Cossack neighbours to become rabid Russian nationalists and imperialists in a region of Russia described as the 'Red Belt' because it gave high support to the KPRF. Russian Cossacks, murdered in huge numbers by the Communists had bizarrely become National Bolsheviks and were allied to their 'bitter enemies' in a 'strange but not altogether illogical coalition.'[1195] Cossacks opposed de-collectivisation of the farms that had been stolen from them decades before and they espoused extreme racism to non-Christian minorities in the Caucasus and towards pro-Western Georgians.

The Wolves Hundred Cossacks trace their founding to 1915 when Russian Colonel Andrey Shkuro established a Kuban Cossack unit. In World War II, Shkuro collaborated with the Nazis, he was captured by the British who returned him to the USSR where he was tried and executed in 1947. The Russian Supreme Court turned down a petition to overturn his conviction and clear his name. The Wolves Hundred, founded by a convicted Nazi collaborator, serves Russian imperialism in eastern Ukraine where they fight 'Ukrainian fascists.' Aleksandr Mozhaev, a Wolves Hundred Cossack, explained that 'We decided to go conquer some more historically Russian lands.' Referring to the land from where his ancestors had hailed, he said 'There is no such thing as Ukraine. There are only the Russian borderlands, and the fact they became known as Ukraine after the revolution, well, we intend to correct that mistake.'[1196] In the course of less than a century of denationalisation, the Kuban Cossacks had become not only imperialists but Ukrainophobic chauvinists. Other Russian Cossacks said 'Ukraine doesn't exist for us. There are no people called Ukraine.' Although they disliked Jews 'like Trotsky' for dividing the Slavic peoples, and were ardent anti-Semites, they were seemingly fighting 'fascism' in Ukraine.[1197]

Russian Cossacks are prominent in the LNR, rather than in the DNR where they have been implicated in various forms of criminal activities, including the theft of humanitarian assistance, and human rights abuses against Ukrainian and civilian captives. The Cossack battalion of the Great Don Army from Novocherkask are based in Stakhanov, west of Luhansk, and commanded by Pavel Dremov. Their base is an archetypical Donbas town where Soviet nostalgia is grounded in their local hero, Stakhanov, who became famous as a coal miner for exceeding production targets in 1935.

## RUSSIAN TERRORISM[1198]

Western focus on Russia's hybrid war in the Donbas has ignored Russia's promotion of terrorism throughout Ukraine. While the hybrid war in the Donbas was far away for most Ukrainians the terrorist campaign was closer as seen in explosions in Kharkiv, which injured 20 people, and Zaporizhzhya which derailed a train. On 20 January 2015, the RNBO introduced heightened security measures throughout the country because of the growing number of Russian-backed terrorist attacks.

Intelligence reports point to these terrorist attacks as not being the work of lone wolves, as in Boston and Ottawa, but a well-coordinated campaign orchestrated by Russian intelligence. Coordinating centre *'Novaya Rus' (New Russia)* trains groups of 3-5 Ukrainian and Russian citizens in the Russian cities of Belgorod, Tambov, Taganrog, and Rostov, the Crimea and the Trans-Dniestr. Training is provided by the GRU and the FSB.

The SBU and military intelligence have captured terrorists from the *Svat, Dzygit, Staryy, Pryzrak, Kharkov Partyzany, Kulykove Pole* and *Koban* groups. Captured terrorists from the *Svat* group who were active in the Mariupol region have testified to attending training camps in Sevastopol where they were taught how to build bombs and undertake urban guerrilla warfare, reconnaissance and intelligence operations behind enemy lines.[1199] Russian weapons and explosives have been intercepted being sent using private postal services. Roadblock checkpoints have also discovered explosives and weapons hidden in cars and trucks travelling to Kyiv from eastern Ukraine.

The greatest concentration of terrorist attacks took place in three strategic regions: (1) the capital city of Kyiv; (2) the two swing regions of Odesa and Kharkiv; and (3) the port city of Mariupol. Security expert Oleksiy Melnyk, from the Razumkov Centre, believed these four cities were 'where Russian-backed forces felt there was still a possibility to de-stabilise the situation.'

The SBU believe that *Oplot* members operating underground in Kharkiv are undertaking terrorist attacks in the city. Terrorists have targeted the city's prosecutor's office, military hospital, a furniture factory owned by a Euromaidan activist and the rock pub *Stina (Wall)* where Euromaidan activists gathered. An underground explosives and printing factory in Kharkiv was closed down in October 2014 and a number of separatist organisations were banned. In one anti-terrorist operation in Kharkiv, members of the *Iskhod* terrorist organisation were captured.[1200]

A group of five terrorists were detained in Odesa in September 2014 who had been trained in Russia and a second terrorist group had planned to copy the violent seizure of state buildings undertaken in the Donbas in spring 2015. A terrorist accidentally blew himself up in September 2014 while planting a bomb at a military academy in Odesa. Other targets have included terrorist attacks against Euromaidan civil society support groups who collect supplies for Ukraine's military, shops owned by these activists, train lines, and freight cars transporting oil. On 20 January 2015, three Ukrainian patriots were shot in Odesa, including a volunteer who had been collecting supplies for the Ukrainian army.

Terrorists have been captured by Ukraine's security forces throughout the country from Trans-Carpathia and Lviv in the west, Zhytomyr, Khmelnytskyy and Vinnytsa in central Ukraine and in the Kyiv metro and near Kyiv's Borispil airport. In eastern and southern Ukraine, terrorist groups have been captured in Zaporizhzhya, Odesa, Kherson, Mykolayiv, and Dnipro. Two terrorist attacks targeted the private home of popular Mayor of Lviv Andriy Sadovyy whose *Samopomich* party came third in the October 2014 Ukrainian parliamentary elections. The Dnipro region is on the frontline of the Donbas conflict and key to supplying Ukrainian army and National Guard units and treating wounded casualties. The SBU detained a group backed by the KPU that had planned to launch a series of terrorist attacks in Dnipro against banks and military bases. *Pryvat Bank*, owned by Kolomoyskyy and his business partners, has been nationalised in the Crimea and targeted by terrorists in Ukrainian cities.

Terrorist groups were trained by Russia to achieve five strategic goals in its hybrid war against Ukraine.

1.  Blow up train lines and key government buildings, launch small-scale hit and run attacks on military-industrial plants, bomb anniversaries of World War Two victory and Ukrainian Independence Day rallies, military recruiting centres and National Guard training facilities.
2.  De-stabilise and terrorise the population and provoke panic in the regions.
3.  Collect intelligence on movements of Ukrainian armed forces and National Guard forces. Terrorists mingle with the civilian population operating as spotters for separatist artillery and grad missile attacks against Ukrainian security forces. Terrorists have been captured with intelligence on key economic targets, such as the Mariupol port with the purpose of planning future terrorist attacks.

4. Establish underground print shops to publish pro-Russian separatist leaflets and newspapers propagating the ideology of *NovoRossiya* and hostility to pro-European 'fascists.'

5. Infiltrate Ukrainian National Guard battalions to collect intelligence about their locations, strengths, weaknesses and military plans. Russian and separatist forces hold extreme loathing for Ukrainian nationalist volunteers and the National Guard.

Former Prime Minister Yatsenyuk said that Ukraine is seeking compensation from Russia for its war of aggression and terrorism against Ukraine.[1201] In its operations in Ukraine, Russia has infringed the International Convention for the Suppression of the Financing of Terrorism adopted by the UN in December 1999.[1202] Russia has become what the US State Department defines as a 'state sponsor of terrorism according to Section 2656f(d) of Title 22 of the United States Code.' The US State Department determines countries to have provided support for terrorism pursuant to three laws: section 6(j) of the Export Administration Act, section 40 of the Arms Export Control Act, and section 620A of the Foreign Assistance Act.

Donbas separatist and terrorist groups fit the definition of 'international terrorism' and there are multiple sources that point to Russia providing training and military support to separatist and terrorist groups in Ukraine. Russia's use of *spetsnaz* in spring 2014 to back the initial separatist campaign, Moscow's extensive supply of high-tech weapons such as the *Buk* surface to air missile system that shot down Malaysian civilian airliner MH17 and training of separatist and terrorist groups classify Russia as a state sponsor of terrorism. Bellingcat, an independent British team of investigators, located the 'smoking gun' of MH17 being shot down by a *Buk* self-propelled missile launcher 332 from Russia's 53rd Antiaircraft Missile Brigade of Kursk.[1203] A *Buk* system is manned by a crew of four on a tank-like mobile vehicle (*Telar*) that includes a radar tracking system and a launcher with four missiles. *Buk* missiles could reach altitudes higher than the MH17 flight. The sophistication of a *Buk* system rules out its use by separatists meaning the missile that shot down MH17 had to have been shot by a Russian military crew.[1204] In May 2016, the families of those murdered on MH17 began a case at the ECHR against Russia and in September of that year the Dutch authorities released a report blaming Russia.

The *Buk* that shot down MH17 was driven from Kursk in late June 2014 to Donetsk and Snizhne and driven back to Russia through Luhansk, minus one of its four missiles. Bellingcat have identified the *Buk* as having been fired by Russian forces and they write: 'We want to say to the families of the victims that Russia was responsible, and we can say more, that these were the people in the unit that could be responsible.' Bellingcat lay the blame for the terrorist attack on Putin and Russian military officers who gave the order for the *Buk* to be transported to Ukraine. [1205]

There is no political will by the EU and US to declare Russia a state sponsor of terrorism and recognise the DNR and LNR as 'terrorist states,' a step that President Poroshenko requested during his October 2015 visit to Washington DC. If Russia were defined in such a manner, alongside Iran, Sudan and Syria, it could not be a party to peace negotiations in Minsk. Defining Russia as a state sponsor of terrorism would add to calls for Putin to be held accountable for war crimes at the ICC.

## CASUALTIES FROM RUSSIA'S UNDECLARED WAR

Before discussing casualties, we should take a sojourn into the cultural environment of Russia where human life has never traditionally been of much value to political rulers. In the USSR human beings were 'raw material' in the service of higher goals.[1206] Nothing has changed in post-communist Russia where 'The expendability of the individual was the dominant reality of post communist Russia, and it was reflected in individual fates.'[1207] The unhelpfulness of the Russian and to some degree the Ukrainian authorities when parents are seeking the fate of their family members, was as true of the war in Chechnya as it is of the Donbas conflict. Respect for the dead and honouring their patriotism has not been a priority for both Russian *and* Ukrainian politicians.[1208]

There are a number of problems in Ukraine when analysing the question of casualties. The first of these is a lack of dog tags and second the heavy use of Grad missiles, which destroys soldiers' bodies and makes them therefore difficult to recognise. A third factor is the lack of a database of Ukrainian soldiers, which is connected to the non-use of dog tags. A fourth factor until October 2014 was that DNA laboratories in different government ministries were not integrated into a national data base. A final factor is 'official indifference and incompetence' towards parents who are 'searching, suffering, given promises, excuses, and evasions.'[1209] 'The Ukrainian state had not allocated a single penny towards recovering the missing' and a mother of a son who died at the Ilovaysk 'cauldron' said 'Nothing changes, no one takes responsibility.'[1210]

Ukraine's Black Tulip NGO recovers the remains of dead soldiers without government assistance and raises the $3,000 each trip costs to battlefields from voluntary donations.

There are no figures for local separatists who up to summer 2014 suffered high levels of casualties because they were poorly trained and not well equipped. A similar situation existed for Russian nationalist volunteers whose casualty rates are also unknown. Unlike Russian military casualties transported in Cargo 200 trucks, the bodies of Russian nationalists are unlikely to have been transported to Russia and are buried in unmarked graves in the Donbas.[1211] With little respect for human life, very few of the Russian nationalist and separatist war dead have received an official burial or resting place in a cemetery.

**Table 9.1. Military and Civilian Casualties in Four Conflicts**

| USSR in Afghanistan, 1979-1989 | Ulster, UK, 1968-1998 | US in Iraq, 2003-2016 | Donbas, 2014-2016 |
|---|---|---|---|
| 14,500 | British troops and RUC 1,000. 530 terrorists. 2,000 civilians. Total military, police, terrorist and civilian 3,532. | 4,500 | 30,000 (estimate) 10,000 separatists, Russian nationalist volunteers and Russian soldiers. 10,000 Ukrainian troops and volunteers. 10,000 civilians |

Ukrainian security forces consist of armed forces, the National Guard, SBU and until 2015 (when they were integrated into the army and National Guard) volunteer battalions. Of these, the Ukrainian state provided casualty figures for the first three groups although they – similar to Russian armed forces – did not wear dog tags in 2014-2015 making personal identification of bodies and remains difficult. Six out of 10 Ukrainian casualties were due to friendly fire through an inability to use the weaponry, poor equipment and weak coordination between different security forces.[1212] The casualty rates for Ukrainian volunteer battalions, which were high in 2014 when they undertook

*Ukrainian spetsnaz at the destroyed Butivka coal mine (Avdiyivka, May 2016).*

the brunt of the fighting before Ukraine rebuilt its army, are not included in official figures.

The official Ukrainian casualty figures under-state the numbers, according to medical officers working with the troops. One of them said 'Take the official figure of dead and wounded and multiply it by three.'[1213] This would give a Ukrainian casualty figure of approximately 9,000 which is higher than the nearly 3,000 official figure. German intelligence estimated a combined total of 50, 000 civilian and military casualties, although there is no breakdown of the numbers in what was leaked to the media.[1214]

The Donbas conflict has produced in a short period of time proportionately higher casualties than the Soviet occupation of Afghanistan and US-led coalition intervention in Iraq. Table 1 compares Britain's Ulster and eastern Ukraine with the Donbas conflict. The three-decade long Ulster conflict took place between Irish nationalist and British loyalist terrorist groups on the one side and military and police forces that led to the deaths of 1,000 British soldiers and Royal Ulster Constabulary (RUC) officers and 530 Irish terrorists. In addition, 2,000 civilians were killed.

Casualty figures will continue to grow because the Donbas is an unresolved, rather than a frozen conflict, into which President-for-life Putin will continue to supply weaponry and soldiers and facilitate Russian nationalist volunteers joining the separatists. Since the Minsk-2 accords hundreds of Ukrainian soldiers have been killed in the Donbas. Proxy wars, such as the Donbas conflict, can last a long period of time.

The most intriguing casualty rate in the Donbas conflict is that of Russian armed forces. Russia is allegedly not fighting a war in the Donbas and yet its military casualties have been classified as a state secret. 'Russia's leaders are thus able to wage undeclared war on Ukraine, killing their own soldiers as well as thousands of Ukrainians, while calling this a 'special operation' hidden from the public eye as a 'state secret.'[1215]

Information about Russian and separatist casualties in the Donbas conflict are not readily available but the Russian NGO Convoy 200 has compiled a list of nearly 2, 000 killed Russian soldiers and nationalist volunteers,[1216] an estimate that they believe is too low because they believe the number of Russians killed is actually higher. A State Duma deputy revealed that 2, 000 families had received compensation for their family members killed in action in Ukraine and another 3,200 who were disabled and wounded.[1217] This information was leaked to the Russian news site *Delovaya Zhizn (Business Life)* which wrote 'as of 1 February 2015, monetary compensation had been paid to more than 2,000 families of fallen soldiers and to 3,200 military personnel suffering heavy wounds and recognised as invalids.'[1218]

Secret burials take place at night similar to during the Soviet occupation of Afghanistan. The parents and families of soldiers sent to Ukraine are 'ordered' to remain quiet. At the Russian-Ukrainian border, Russian soldiers 'were lined up and given the order to cross it' where they would become 'cattle to slaughter.'[1219] A Russian soldier explained how 'volunteering' for duty in Ukraine worked: 'Sure, we're volunteered. Nobody sent us there. They gave us an order; who wants to volunteer? And we put up our hands like this.'[1220]

The bodies of Russian casualties have been transported to Russia for burial or allegedly they have been disposed of in the Donbas by mobile incinerators used for stray dogs. Russian paratroopers are being sent to 'commit crimes on the territory of a neighbouring country.' But, on their death certificates there is complete deception and what is written is 'Died in a gas explosion, heart attack or stroke. The place of death is left empty,' said Lev Shlosberg, a provincial deputy from the opposition *Yabloko* party.'[1221] The mother of Russian soldier 'Sergey' said 'It's clear to me now that my son was killed, and no

one can explain anything to me.' 'We tried getting in touch with his commanders and fellow soldiers, but they refused to tell us anything.' In return for not
talking to journalists and staying quiet, families are awarded 100,000 *rubles*
($1,600).[1222]

Russian NGO activist Elena Vasilyeva launched a web site entitled
'Cargo 200 from Ukraine to Russia' (Cargo 200 is the Soviet/Russian euphe-
mism for the transportation of dead soldiers).[1223] After receiving information
from families in all corners of Russia, Cargo-200 prepared a list of the names
of nearly 2,000 Russian soldiers and mercenaries (i.e. volunteer nationalists)
killed in Ukraine.[1224] The number of wounded Russian soldiers (from elite
*spetsnaz*, paratrooper, air defence, motorised rifle brigade and armoured brigade
troops) and nationalist volunteers will be 2-3 times higher. Cargo-200's estimates are similar to those compiled by other Russian NGOs, such as los-
tivan.com.[1225] Committee of Soldiers Mothers and Inform Napalm website also
estimate Russian military casualties in eastern Ukraine to be in the thousands.
Vasilyeva is a veteran of such projects having earlier launched the Forgotten
Regiment NGO in 2007 to collect information on Russian veterans of Soviet
and post-Soviet conflicts. Vasilyeva lives in exile in Ukraine because it became
dangerous to collect and publicise Russian casualties in a war that Putin denies
he is undertaking.

There have been numerous reports from a variety of sources of Russian
casualties, especially when they are heavily used in decisive campaigns to secure
a separatist victory. The Pskov independent newspaper *Pskovskaya Guberniya*
published a transcript of conversations between two paratroopers that showed
almost all of the soldiers from the first regiment of the No. 76 Pskov airborne
paratrooper division were killed in action in eastern Ukraine. Of the unit, only
10 survived and there were casualties of 70 to 140 dead.[1226] Local Russian coun-
cillor Shlosberg was savagely beaten after attending funerals of 76th Airborne
Regiment's soldiers in Pskov who had been killed in battle in eastern Ukraine.
Shlosberg had been interviewed on Russian casualties by one of Russia's last
remaining independent television channels *Dozhd (Rain)* whose journalists were
also savagely attacked. In mid-November 2015 a Russian Missile battalion was
destroyed by Ukrainian forces with 150 confirmed Russian dead, including Russian General Sergey Chenko.

The estimates collected by Russian NGOs point to intense fighting and
casualties in 2014-2015. Very high Russian casualty rates reflect a full-blown
war between Ukraine and Russia rather an ATO.

Russia's denials of its invasion of eastern Ukraine resemble Soviet deception about its occupation of Afghanistan, although with two important caveats. First, under Soviet leader Gorbachev, there was greater media freedom and more opposition activity than in Putin's authoritarian Russia. Second, in a world of social media and the Internet it remains impossible to close all channels of information about Russia's invasion of the Donbas. Ukraine publishes the freest Russian-language media in the world and these publications are available online for Russian readers and civil society activists who have access to the Internet.

As Western sanctions, low oil prices and economic crisis become painful in Russia, support for Putin's nationalist militarism abroad is declining. In September 2015 in Moscow, 50,000 Russians marched for peace in Ukraine. Russian soldiers, in the view of Shlosberg, 'didn't die for Russia, but for Putin.' Russia's respected independent Levada Centre found as high as 65-70 percent of Russians oppose the sending of Russian troops into eastern Ukraine.[1227] In the USSR and today's Russia, soldiers undertook, and continue to undertake, horrific injuries to themselves to prevent being sent to Afghanistan and the Donbas. Vasilyeva said, 'One soldier told me how he broke his own leg. He thought up a special technique how to do it: he ties the leg around very tightly, applies ice to make it numb, and then you can hit it hard. Another guy told me how he gave himself a huge burn on the hip using liquid ammonia.[1228]

## HYBRID ANNEXATION

Putin adopted a two-track approach to his 'Ukrainian problem.' The first track of negotiations culminating in the Minsk-1 Accords aimed to present him as a peacemaker and to prevent the flow of Western defensive military equipment to Ukraine. The second track was described by the PACE as 'hybrid annexation.' 'After the illegal annexation of Crimea, the creeping hybrid annexation of the occupied areas in the Donbas region is unacceptable from the standpoint of international law,' PACE rapporteurs said after returning from a fact finding mission to eastern Ukraine.[1229] The goals of the two tracks were as contradictory as Russian goals pursued earlier by Presidents Yeltsin and Putin in the Trans-Dniestr, South Ossetia and Abkhazia frozen conflicts. Russian leaders while publicly declaring their intention to re-integrate these separatist enclaves into Moldova, Georgia (up to 2008) and Ukraine and restore their territorial integrity at the same time transformed these frozen conflicts into Russian satellite pseudo states.

*Ministry of Internal Affairs regional office damaged by fighting when the Azov battalion re-captured Mariupol in the first phase of the war (April 2015)*

Following the Minsk-1 Accords, Putin established Russia's complete dominance over the economic, financial and security aspects of the DNR and LNR in blatant violation of what he had signed. He emboldened and transformed the DNR and LNR into pseudo states dependent upon Russia for 70-90 percent of their financing. Putin's brazen double dealing could be seen in the chronology of developments when the Russian shadow government was formed only four months after the September 2014 Minsk-1 Accords and only two months after the signing of the Minsk-2 Accords Russia introduced *rubles* as the main currency of the DNR and LNR. The rubles are delivered to three key Donbas train station hubs in armoured trains each month.[1230] Confirmation of Russia's financing of pensions, welfare payments and state officials salaries was provided by former separatist leader Khodakovskyy who fell foul of the DNR-LNR leadership.[1231]

Surkov, the political *kurator*[1232] of the DNR and LNR, had earlier been Putin's go between to Yanukovych during the Euromaidan.[1233] A Russian shadow government runs the DNR-LNR and 'The regions are being treated as parts of Russia's sovereign territory' meaning the DNR and LNR have become a 'satellite state of Russia.' 'Rather than envisaging a reintegration of the regions in Ukraine over the medium term, this plan aims to secure its long-term existence under complete Russian control.'[1234] The shadow government is overseen by the FSB and operates through six working groups covering finance and taxation, wages and public service, industry, energy, electricity and transportation.[1235] The shadow government, formerly entitled the 'Inter-Ministerial Commission for the Provision of Humanitarian Aid for the Affected Areas in the South East of the Regions of Donetsk and Luhansk, Ukraine,' is headed by Deputy Prime Minister Kozak, well known for his memorandum on Trans-Dniestr, and Deputy Finance Minister Leonid Gorin. Kozak, as is true of many members of Russia's ruling elite, is directly linked to organised crime in Spain.[1236] The annual cost to Russia of subsidising the DNR and LNR satellite states is close to one billion euros or 0.6 percent of the Russian state budget on top of which should be added a large military outlay.

Putin's 'hybrid annexation' of the DNR and LNR between the Minsk-1 and Minsk-2 Accords also included the transformation of the rag tag separatist militias into a large and well equipped army. This took place at the same time when European governments and the US ruled out supplying defensive military equipment to Ukraine to allow 'the peace process a chance to work,' a process that Putin never intended to happen. Separatist militias were integrated under Russian command and control in the fields of formal military structures, military intelligence, planning and supplies of military equipment and fuel.

While Putin was negotiating Minsk-2, Russia was at the same time planning an offensive to capture Donetsk airport and Debaltseve. Investigations have conclusively proven that these operations were led by Russian military officers. Russian soldiers wounded in these two offensives were personally given watches on 21 February 2015 by Minister of Defence Sergey Shoygu, ten days after Minsk-2 was signed.[1237]

The Minsk Accords have not produced the peace process that the West hoped for or a Ukrainian leadership willing to play by Russia's rules. National Security adviser Horbulin explained that Ukraine would not reintegrate the DNR and LNR as Russian proxies.[1238] The Minsk Accords could never have worked because Russia, a party to the conflict, was invited to the negotiations and Putin had a two track policy of diplomacy *and* obfuscation and subterfuge. Only 16.6 percent of Ukrainians held a positive view of the Minsk Accords while 35.9 percent were negatively disposed towards it from a high of 47.9 in the west to 31.9, 31.1 and 30.2 percent in the south, east and Donbas respectively.

Only a minority of Ukrainians have ever supported their country transformed into a federal republic; in a 2016 opinion poll, 61 percent backed a unitary state and only eight percent federalism.[1239] Low support for federalism results in similarly low levels of public backing for a 'special status' or the DNR and LNR; the same poll gave only nine percent. 56.4 percent of Ukrainians are opposed, with only 23.8 percent agreeing, to give 'special status' to the DNR and LNR before they return to Kyiv's control, ranging from a very high 73.9 in the west to 44.2, 37.6 and 42.1 percent in the south, east and Donbas respectively. 42.3 percent of Ukrainians opposed the granting of amnesty to separatists while 31.2 percent are in favour.[1240]

## CONCLUSIONS

By the Euromaidan, Russia already had sufficient forces to overtly annex the Crimea and covertly assist local separatists in the Donbas. These included long-standing Black Sea Fleet forces which included marines, air defence troops and naval intelligence that could draw on Russian nationalist and Cossack paramilitaries and organised crime vigilantes (who were often one and the same) that had been training without hindrance from the SBU. During Yanukovych's presidency, the SBU had been infiltrated and co-opted by the FSB while the military was penetrated at the highest levels and degraded from the bottom up. Local Russian nationalist and Cossacks paramilitaries were supplemented by Russian Nazis, Eurasianists, White monarchists and zealot Orthodox who ostensibly travelled to the Donbas and other regions of what they termed *NovoRossiya* to fight 'Ukrainian fascists.'

Putin's hybrid war has remained covert and he has continued to deny the presence of Russian forces in Ukraine (outside the Crimea). Nevertheless, Russian military and nationalist volunteer casualties are higher proportionately than those suffered by the Soviet Union in Afghanistan and the US in Iraq. Greater numbers of Russian forces would be required for a transformation of Putin's tactics towards Ukraine from hybrid war to invasion, such as the goal of creating a 'land bridge' from the Russian-Ukrainian border east of Mariupol to the Crimea. Larger military operations of this nature would lead to even higher Russian military casualties and greater domestic opposition at a time of declining living standards. Russians of all political persuasions wholeheartedly support the annexation of the Crimea but have always been more cautious about an invasion of eastern Ukraine.

Another aspect of Russia's invasion and annexation of the Crimea and hybrid war in the Donbas has been accompanied by political, cultural and religious repression, human rights abuses and war crimes, which are the subject of the next chapter.

# CHAPTER 10

# HUMAN RIGHTS AND WAR CRIMES

*'The torture, ill-treatment and killing of captured, surrendered or wounded soldiers are war crimes. These claims must be promptly, thoroughly and impartially investigated, and the perpetrators prosecuted in fair trials by recognised authorities.'*

Amnesty International

Ukrainophobia in Russian television propaganda and public discourse by Russian politicians has contributed to a major deterioration of human rights for Ukrainians in Russia, Ukrainians and Tatars in the Crimea, and Ukrainian patriots in the separatist controlled Donbas as well as tolerance for human rights abuses and war crimes by Russian and separatist forces. The UNHCHR believe that 'Political leaders should refrain from using messages of intolerance or expressions which may incite violence, hostility or discrimination; but they also have a crucial role to play in speaking out firmly and promptly against intolerance, discrimination, stereotyping and instances of hate speech.'[1241] Putin's regime is guilty of all of the above through its massive use of Russian television propaganda and other forms of political technology, including blatant and crude lying. Inflammatory rhetoric and propaganda acerbates crises, such as in the Donbas, and contribute to making conflicts more vicious.

The Ukrainian authorities have reportedly raised the issue of war crimes committed in the Donbas and the Crimea with the ICC. Alex Whiting, a senior ICC prosecutor, believes 'there have been widespread allegations of war crimes and even crimes against humanity' in the Crimea and eastern Ukraine.[1242] An ICC ruling in November 2016, and growing Western claims Russia was committing war crimes in Syria, led Russia to withdraw from the ICC. The ICC reported 'the situation in the Crimea and Sevastopol is equivalent to the international armed conflict between Ukraine and the Russian Federation.' The ICC described the situation in Crimea an occupation by Russian forces and concluded that shelling by both sides in eastern Ukraine and Ukraine's detention of Russian military personnel there 'points to direct military engagement between Russian armed forces and Ukrainian government forces that would suggest the existence of an international armed conflict.'[1243]

The poor record of the Ukrainian authorities in pursuing domestic crimes by the ousted Yanukovych regime at home and through Interpol raises doubts they would be successful with the ICC. In addition, as Amnesty International pointed out in a September 2014 open letter to President Poroshenko, Ukraine has not ratified the Rome Statute of the ICC because of a 2001 ruling of its Constitutional Court that it is inconsistent with the constitution. In January 2007, Ukraine ratified the Agreement on the Privileges and Immunities of the Court (APIC) without ratifying the Rome Statute. Amnesty International argued that in ratifying the Rome Statute, the ICC would be given jurisdiction over genocide, war crimes and crimes against humanity when Ukrainian courts are unwilling or unable to investigate and prosecute crimes.[1244] In effect, President Poroshenko wants to have his cake and eat it by having the ICC pursue war crimes committed by separatist and Russian forces, while keeping other Ukrainian leaders and himself shielded from accusations by Ukraine not being a full member of the ICC.

Russian television in Russia and in the separatist enclaves broadcasts a very different view. Russia's Investigation Committee has laid charges against Ukraine for 'genocide' and its parliamentary human rights ombudsman (an oxymoron in authoritarian Russia) claimed that: 'mass political repression has become a reality in Ukraine. Large numbers of people who hold different political views, often on the basis of the language they use, their ethnic origin and on their residency in a particular area, have been subjected to arrests, torture and other infringements.'[1245]

Following Russia's annexation of the Crimea, General Prosecutor Natalya Poklonskaya demanded that all supporters of the Euromaidan leave the peninsula as they had ties to Ukrainian 'nationalists' and 'fascists.' Crimean Tatar *Mejlis (unofficial parliament)* head Refat Chubarov was banned from the Crimea and others were detained. Crimean Tatar and Ukrainian media have been closed down and Tatar and Ukrainian organisations banned. In spring 2015, the Russian occupation authorities banned Tatar TV channels and media outlets. ATR, the Crimean Tatar TV channel, radio station *Meydan* FM and even the children's TV channel, *Lale*, were closed. Young Tatars are warned not to wear any aspects of their national costume for fear of being attacked on the street. Crimean Tatars are banned from speaking their language at work.[1246]

After Turkey shot down a Russian fighter jet, Russian television fanned accusations that Crimean Tatar structures were controlled by Turkish intelligence. Crimea's prosecutor threatened reprisals against 50 Euromaidan activists and drew up a list of participants in 'pro-Ukrainian' meetings. 'Pro-Ukrainian' is a term which is as nebulous as that of 'bourgeois nationalist' in the Soviet Union. The Ukrainian flag and national symbols have been prohibited as 'extremist' in the Crimea following the March 2015 celebration of Taras Shevchenko's birthday. Poklonskaya said there is plenty of room in Crimean jails for 'Ukrainian nationalists and radicals' who support the 'fascism flourishing in Ukraine.' Prime Minister Aksyonov threatened a tribunal of Ukrainian Nazis, a rather curious threat by a leader of a political party that had cooperated with Russia's preeminent neo-Nazi RNE.

## POLITICAL REPRESSION AND ETHNIC CHAUVINISM

Soviet nationality policies promoted and thereby tolerated Russian chauvinism towards minority languages and cultures, especially Ukrainian and Belarusian who were slated for Russification because of the closeness of their languages to Russian. The three eastern Slavic peoples would become the core of the future Russian-speaking *Homo Sovieticus*. Russians and Russian-speakers looked down upon the Ukrainian and Belarusian languages as peasant dialects slated to disappear because Russian was the language of modernity. Similar condescending policies towards regional languages were evident in France, Great Britain and elsewhere in Europe until the 1960s and 1970s.

Resistance to affirmative support for the Ukrainian language since 1991 has arisen not because it constituted a threat to the Russian language *per se* but because a sizeable proportion of Russian speakers could not accept the change in language hierarchy in independent Ukraine where the former 'peasant dialect' (Ukrainian) had become a state language and Russian a national minority language. Ukrainians who hold to the Soviet myths of 'friendship of peoples' and eastern Slavic hierarchy of peoples will strongly object to Russians being

*Apartments destroyed by shelling in Slovyansk (December 2014)*

designated as a national minority. Since 1937, as the first among equals, Russians had no longer been defined in such a manner throughout the USSR.[1247] Fournier found that opposition to the growth of the Ukrainian language was correlated less to so-called threats to the Russian language than to the refusal to accept the designation of Russians and the Russian language with 'minority' status at the same time as the elevation of Ukrainian as the state language. [1248] Russians in the USSR and today, resented being told 'they were members of the former great power nationality who must make sacrifices on behalf of the formerly oppressed nations.'[1249]

Extreme left-wing political parties and the Party of Regions played on fears of threatened 'Ukrainianisation' during election campaigns and Russia and its separatist allies have exaggerated these to an even greater extent since the Euromaidan. A disparaging view of the Ukrainian language and culture was commonplace throughout Yanukovych's presidency heightening inter-regional tension and increasing electoral support for the *Svoboda* party. In February 2014, the overturning of the controversial July 2012 language law that elevated Russian to a regional language provided 'evidence' of the alleged Russophobic nature of the Euromaidan leaders.

Ukrainianophobia in Russia dramatically increased following the Orange Revolution and election of Yushchenko. The growth of nationalism, xenophobia and chauvinism from 2007-2008 when Putin turned to the right dramatically increased after 2010 when Yanukovych and Putin came to power.

The Ukrainian library in Moscow was raided by armed police and closed by the Ministry of Interior who took away 50 books for 'psychological-linguistic expertise.' Repression of its librarians has continued; Natalya Sharina, the head of the Ukrainian library in Moscow was arrested in October 2015 for allegedly stocking 'extremist' books and magazines. Sharina was detained on suspicion of 'inciting ethnic hatred,' and her home was searched and computers confiscated by 'not specialists in literature, but bone breakers.'[1250] Some of the literature confiscated included children's books with cartoons while other 'nationalist' books were planted by the police, according to the librarian. The Chair of Pen International's Writers in Prison condemned the raids: 'Whatever the content of the material alleged to have been in the library, the state response, to arrest a librarian, clearly seems disproportionate.'[1251]

Not all Russians have been sucked in by the massive television propaganda onslaught against Ukrainian 'fascists.' The Russian Sova Centre condemned the prosecution of Ukrainian librarians. Nevertheless, the majority of Russian public opinion has fallen in line with official propaganda and stereotypes about Ukrainians. In an outlandish protest at 'Ukrainian fascism,' Russian writers in Moscow severed ties with Kurkov, a well-known Russian-speaking writer living in Kyiv who sympathised with the Euromaidan and has been a staunch critic of Putin.[1252]

Throughout the DNR and LNR the separatist authorities pursued the same policies as in the Crimea of cleansing their regions of Euromaidan supporters and Ukrainian patriots whom they viewed as disloyal to Russia and their rule.[1253] While condemning the Euromaidan for pursuing discrimination against the Russian language, the DNR and LNR have ethnically cleansed Ukrainian culture, language and religion from territories they control. All traces of the Ukrainian language, culture, education, political and religious life have been eviscerated from the separatist enclaves of the DNR and LNR. 'There are no Ukrainian-language newspapers or (television) channels, any website of ours with a clearly pro-Ukrainian position is immediately blocked.'[1254]

In a replay of repression of mythical Ukrainian underground nationalist organisations last seen in the Stalinist Great Terror, Ukrainian and Tatar cultural and political activists and servicemen have been imprisoned on trumped-up charges in Russia and the Crimea.[1255] A total of 42 Ukrainian citizens have been illegally detained and imprisoned by Russia of whom six have been released.[1256]

Russian citizens opposed to Putin's aggression in Ukraine have also suffered from political repression. In Russia there has been a 300 percent increase in criminal charges for the catch-all criminal charge of 'extremism' and of these the fourth largest group who have been convicted are for condemning Russia's militaristic policies against Ukraine.[1257]

1. Poet and teacher **Aleksandr Byvshev** was sentenced for 'inciting enmity.' He had opposed Russia's annexation of the Crimea through a poem he had written which was entitled 'To Ukrainian Patriots.'

2. **Vladimir Podrezov** was sentenced to 2 year's imprisonment for painting the star on the spire of the Moscow skyscraper in Ukrainian national colours.

3. The spread of Ukrainophobia into Russia's Far East, thousands of miles from the Donbas, was evident in the repression faced by **Natalya Romanenko**, head of a Ukrainian choir in Khabarovsk who after returning from Ukraine was accused of 'nationalism' and doused in green paint as a *Banderite.*'[1258]

4. Chairman of the Tatar Public Centre NGO **Rafis Kashapov** was sentenced to three year's imprisonment for spreading ethnic enmity and 'separatism.' He had uploaded articles to web sites critical of Russia's policies in the Crimea and Donbas.

5. **Yekaterina Vologzheninova** was included in the official list of 'terrorists' and charged with 'inciting hatred' against 'militiamen-volunteers from Russia' who are fighting alongside separatists, inciting hatred and working 'against the authorities in modern day Russia.' She had circulated posts on the Donbas conflict through social media. Her laptop, tablet, digital camera and CD's were confiscated.

6. **Vladimir Kolesnykov** was expelled from school after he campaigned against Russian policies in the Crimea and Donbas. School officials and students were angered by his tee-shirt 'Return Crimea!' and his grandfather, a former KGB officer, told him 'You are my enemy. You betrayed your country…you don't understand that the United States used them (Ukrainians) as cannon fodder to bring down Putin.'[1259] Kolesnykov apparently committed 'suicide' in December 2015 - in Russia a murder can be made to look like 'suicide.' If his death was

really suicide the Russian authorities are guilty for having pressured him to take this tragic step.[1260]

7. **Viktor Shur**, a Russian national living permanently in Ukraine, was abducted and transported to Russia where he was sentenced to 12 years for 'espionage.'[1261]

The Crimea has long experienced tension between Russian speakers and Tatars who seek redress for their 1944 deportation to Soviet Central Asia when half of their population died. The Tatars define the 1944 deportations as 'genocide' because half of them died en route to Central Asia. Since returning to the Crimea in the late 1980s, they have commemorated the tragedy each year in May until 2014 when, following Russia's annexation, it was banned.[1262] Russian settlers were brought into the Crimea after World War II and occupied the empty properties of expelled Tatars. The Party of Regions, Russian and Ukrainian Communist Parties and Russian nationalists in the Crimea and Russia have supported Stalin's charges of 'Tatar collaboration' during the Nazi occupation as justification for their deportation. Crimean Prime Minister Anatoliy Mogilyov[1263] was typical of the xenophobic Tatarphobia espoused by the Party of Regions and Russian nationalists in his anti-Tatar diatribes written for the pages of *Krymskaya Pravda*, the peninsula's biggest selling newspaper.

The Russian occupation authorities have targeted Crimean Tatars in a region that traditionally had the highest levels of xenophobia in Ukraine.[1264] Anti-Tatar discourse and rhetoric had always been present in the Crimea but had exponentially grown during Yanukovych's presidency when the Party of Regions and their Crimean Russian nationalist allies tightened their grip on the Crimea. The European Commission against Racism and Intolerance (ECRI) reported the growth of anti-Tatar 'hate speech.'[1265] Many Crimean newspapers, including the largest circulation *Krymskaya Pravda*, had long published inflammatory and derogatory articles attacking Crimean Tatars and Ukrainians.[1266]

Although Russian television and inflammatory public statements claimed there was a serious threat to Russophones from the Euromaidan authorities the reality on the ground was very different. The Council of Europe found *no* threats to national minorities in Ukraine but they had 'urgent concerns' in the case of Russian policies towards Ukrainians, Tatars, Karaim and Krimchaks in the Crimea.[1267] Two years since the report was prepared the political atmosphere in the Crimea for Tatars and Ukrainians has become reminiscent of the darkest days of Soviet Union.

*Bridge destroyed near Slovyansk by Igor Girkin's Russian forces as they fled the Ukrainian advance (December 2014)*

Official attitudes to Crimean Tatars became evident almost immediately after Russian forces invaded and annexed the peninsula. On 3 March 2014, Crimean Tatar activist Reshat Ametov was kidnapped by Crimean paramilitaries and found tortured and murdered. Since then arrests, expulsions and imprisonments of Crimean Tatars have increased, Tatar schools and publications have been closed and Tatar monuments and graves desecrated. Crimean Tatar leaders have been banned from returning to the Crimea.[1268]

Since spring 2014, human and national rights have been under constant pressure in the Crimea in what Human Rights Watch describe as a 'pervasive climate of fear and repression.'[1269] During that time, the Russian occupation authorities 'failed to conduct meaningful investigations into actions of armed paramilitary groups, implicated in torture, extra-judicial killings, enforced disappearances, attacks and beatings of Crimean Tatar and pro-Ukraine activists and journalists.' In April 2016, the *Mejlis* was outlawed as 'extremist.'[1270] The authorities have 'harassed and intimidated' Crimean Tatar activists, conducted 'unwarranted searches at mosques, Islamic schools, and dozens of homes of

Crimean Tatars under the pretext of searching for drugs, weapons, and 'prohibited literature' and launched criminal proceedings on trumped up charges of 'rioting,' 'extremism' and 'terrorism.'[1271] There have been no investigations of the nine Crimean Tatar activists who were murdered or the 25 kidnapped and detained as political prisoners by Russian occupation authorities. In May 2016, one of the leaders of the World Congress of Crimean Tatars, Ervin Ibragimov, was abducted and is feared murdered.

The Ukrainian language, already weakly supported by the central government prior to Russia's annexation, has been eviscerated in the Crimea. The Council of Europe reported upon ethnic, religious and linguistic discrimination in the Crimea and the separatist enclaves but did not find similar policies in Ukraine.1272 Russian policies towards the Ukrainian language and education in the Crimea are an extension of their long-standing intolerance of Ukrainian inside the Russian Federation where Ukrainians are the one of the largest (but unrecognised) national minorities but have no cultural, educational and linguistic rights whatsoever. In April-May 2014, immediately after the annexation, the Crimean Department of Education downgraded the Ukrainian language and culture to voluntary subjects and at the same time greatly expanded instruction of the Russian language, literature, and history. By summer 2014, education policy in the Crimea resembled Russia where not a single one of its 600 schools included instruction in the Ukrainian language.[1273]

## RELIGIOUS PERSECUTION

Ukraine's first three presidents had sought to maintain a balance between pro-Ukrainian and pro-Russian Churches in Ukraine. Kravchuk, Kuchma and Yushchenko talked of a desire to create an autocephalous (independent) Ukrainian Orthodox Church but beyond empty rhetoric few steps in this direction were undertaken. Yanukovych ended this balancing act and openly sided with the Ukrainian (Russian) Orthodox Church. Yanukovych developed a close and personal relationship with Russian Orthodox Church Patriarch Kirill and was decorated with the highest award of the Church, the Order of the Holy Prince Vladimir. In January 2014, the head of the Ukrainian Greek Catholic Church Svyatoslav Shevchuk received a letter from the SBU through the Ministry of Culture that threatened its legal status if it continued to support the Euromaidan. The outlandish threat revealed the influence of the Russian intelligence services in the SBU and was evidence of traditional xenophobia among members of the Yanukovych cabal towards western Ukrainians that harked back to when the Greek-Catholic Church was banned in the Soviet Union.

Russian aggression against Ukraine, rather than the policies of the Ukrainian authorities, has become the most serious threat to the power and influence of the Ukrainian (Russian) Orthodox Church. Nevertheless, Russian television propaganda continues to spew untruths about Ukrainian pro-auto-cephalous Orthodox denominations. *Rossiya-1 channel* broadcast a major documentary *Persecution* that opened with a woman who claimed Patriarch Filaret was turning the Ukrainian Orthodox Church-Kyiv Patriarch into a 'Nazi spiritual centre where the chief saint will be Bandera.' Filaret was portrayed as a bloodthirsty fanatic seeking to exterminate the residents of the Donbas, the region where he was born. Meanwhile, the programme alleged that the Ukrainian Orthodox-Kyiv Patriarch was working on behalf of the US to destroy Orthodoxy in Ukraine.[1274]

In Ukraine there is religious pluralism and no state Church has been designated as the State Church. The DNR and LNR have replicated Putin's Russia where the Russian Orthodox Church is the State Church, as defined in the May 2014 'constitution' of the DNR.[1275] Other religious denominations have been hounded by Cossacks and Russian nationalist groups, such as the Russian Orthodox Army. Protests outside pro-autocephalous Ukrainian Churchs in the DNR and LNR and in Crimea have denounced them as funded by the West, linked to the CIA, supporters of the Ukrainian army and providing propaganda for an independent Ukrainian state.

Human rights abuses in the conflict have been committed by Russian Orthodox priests and Russian Orthodox extremists and fascists. 'Cyborgs' captured in Donetsk Airport were beaten by Russian Orthodox priests using wooden crosses over their heads. 'He just said that we were not human. It was by a priest in a cassock with a cross.' The wooden cross broke and he then used a metal crucifix. The 'Cyborg' said 'I've seen priests like that only in horror films.'[1276] Russian Orthodox Church priests, sometimes wearing Cossack hats and carrying Cossack swords, oversaw a punishment unit in the basement of a Church in Slovyansk where torture took place.[1277] In the 2014 movie *Leviathan* a Russian Orthodox priest advises the local mayor: 'Where there's power, there's might. If you hold power in your territory, solve your issues yourself, with your might.'[1278]

The Russian Orthodox Church has a close relationship with Cossack groups who have acted in some of the most brutal ways towards Ukrainian prisoners of war. Human rights abuses by the Most Glorious Legion of the Don Cossacks were 'some of the most vicious.' The Russian Orthodox Army, with its close ties to Girkin, has been involved in kidnapping, torture, murder, and ill-treatment.[1279]

Russian and separatist forces hold a burning hatred for Ukrainian Greek Catholics and 'schismatics' (supporters of Ukrainian Orthodox autocephaly) drawing on centuries of venom towards both religious denominations. Tsarist *and* Soviet armies destroyed the Greek Catholic Church in Galicia in World War 1 *and* World War 11 respectively. Religious denominations other than the Russian Orthodox Church have been 'subject to murder, torture, forcible transfers, imprisonment, and severe deprivation of liberty in violation of the fundamental rights set out in international law.'[1280] The Slovyansk city authorities rented the Villa Maria to the Ukrainan (Russian) Orthodox Church which used it for the 'collecting of humanitarian aid for the insurgents,' said Vira Kushnir, the museum guide. She added that Russian Orthodox priests were often seen on the separatists' barricades in Slovyansk.[1281] Rumours in the city talked of weapons delivered in coffins to Slovyansk ahead of the arrival of Girkin's 'little green men.' Russian Orthodox Church priests in Russia and eastern Ukraine have blessed separatist flags, joined road checkpoints, and participated in the torture of Ukrainian prisoners of war. A Russian Orthodox Church priest in the Urals blessed fighters travelling to the Donbas to fight 'fascist scum.'[1282] The Monarchist Party recruited volunteers in Russia to fight for the Donbas separatists. Russian Orthodox Church Father Oleg of the Cathedral of the Holy Spirit in Slovyansk became a chaplain to Girkin and he blessed separatist and Russian flags.

Paramilitary training camps were established in the Crimea in 2010 under the patronage of the Synodic Committee of the Russian Orthodox Church. Father Vitaliy Veseliy of the Church of Resurrection in Slovyansk and head of the Centre for Slavic Culture actively collaborated with Russian occupation forces. These Russian Orthodox Church priests hold the same views as Girkin and other Russian nationalists and imperialists; namely, that Ukraine does not exist and Ukrainians are a branch of the Russian people.

Protestants were additionally targeted by Russian and separatist forces because of their association with the US which is allegedly pushing non-indigenous religious confessions into what is 'Orthodox land.' The Russian Orthodox Church and its Cossack vigilantes described the Protestants as 'sects.' In April 2014, when the Russian-separatist forces captured western Donetsk *oblast*,

*Hospital near Slovyansk destroyed during heavy fighting in the first stages of the war (December, 2014)*

Russian Orthodox Church priests arrived with Cossacks and 'local thugs' and demanded other religious confessions turn over their buildings and Churches. In Slovyansk, Russian and separatist forces transferred Protestant Churches to the Russian Orthodox Church who permitted the grounds to be used for target practice and paramilitary training.[1283] The same priests had blessed the shelling of Ukrainian forces. Protestant Churches were often treated with contempt and used as storehouses for weapons.

During the brief Russian occupation of Slovyansk, four protestant leaders of the Evangelical Church of the Transfiguration were murdered: Pastor Oleksandr Pavenko's two adult sons Reuben and Albert as well as Church deacons Viktor Bradarskyy and Volodymyr Velychko.[1284] They were detained on 8 June 2014, brutally tortured, executed the following day and their bodies dumped in a mass grave along with others.[1285] The heads of the Evangelical Association Church Bishop Oleksiy Demidovych and Hennadiy Lysenko were detained, their hands and legs were bound and they were stabbed with bayonets and beaten, but fortunately they survived. Other protestant priests, such as Pastor Mykola Kalinichenko of the Word of Life Church in Shakhtarsk, were subjected to mock executions by firing squads.[1286] Some of the protestant leaders were murdered in Slovyansk by local criminals who had joined the separatists with the intention of taking control of their businesses.[1287]

Persecution of non-Russian Orthodox religious institutions in the separatist controlled regions has forced Jews, Protestants, Ukrainian Orthodox and Ukrainian Greek Catholics to flee to Ukrainian controlled territory. Separatists have destroyed or damaged Ukrainian Orthodox Church-Kyiv Patriarch and religious buildings of other denominations, repressed and murdered Ukrainian Orthodox and protestant priests and pastors. The 30-40 Ukrainian Orthodox Church-Kyiv Patriarch parishes in the DNR and LNR have been closed and the clergy have fled following the publication of their names on 'execution lists.' In Slovyansk and Novoazovsk, Ukrainian Orthodox Church-Kyiv Patriarch priests have been abducted, threatened, brutally beaten and their Churches shot at and vandalised. Protestant activists Alex Shumin, Valeriy Lotorev, Pavel Minkov and Yuriy Ivanov were kidnapped and made to undertake forced labour by separatist forces.[1288] In the Crimea, Ukrainian Orthodox-Kyiv Patriarch Church faithful have been attacked by Cossacks and vigilantes after being accused of being 'fascists' and 'Satanists.' Churches have been vandalised and picketed by protesters holding banners with provocative slogans such as 'No *Pravyy Sektor* in the Crimea!'[1289]

## RUSSIAN AND SEPARATIST HUMAN RIGHTS ABUSES AND WAR CRIMES

The brutal and inhumane treatment of Ukrainian prisoners of war is not surprising; after all, the Russian authorities have never expressed respect towards their own military casualties and captured soldiers. The treatment of Russian dead in two Chechen conflicts[1290] was symptomatic of a broader culture of disrespect for human life and human rights in Russian and Soviet history. The lack of respect for human life is 'traditional in Russia' where there has never been the rule of law and where human beings have no intrinsic value whatsoever. David Satter writes that, 'The expendability of the individual was the dominant reality of post communist Russia, and it was reflected in individual fates.'[1291] These human rights abuses and war crimes have included:[1292]

- Collective responsibility.
- Indiscriminate torture and inhumane treatment.

- Executions.
- Impunity for war crimes.
- Mass graves.
- Kidnappings for ransoms.
- Cruel interrogations.
- Looting.
- Mass aerial bombing of civilian residences in Grozny, Chechnya and Aleppo, Syria.

The UNHCHR and independent human rights groups in the West and Ukraine have systematically documented the appalling record of Russian and separatist forces involved in torture, ill treatment and summary executions. In an early report in spring 2014, the UNHCHR stated: 'Armed groups have increasingly committed human rights abuses, including abductions, torture/ill-treatment, unlawful detentions and killings as well as seizing and occupying of public buildings.'[1293] The UNHCHR documented the complicity of the *militia* in colluding with armed separatists. The OSCE reported on the rise of abductions and detentions by separatists. The UNHCHR recommended that 'Those found to be arming and inciting armed groups and transforming them into paramilitary forces must be held accountable under national and international law.'[1294] In late 2014, the UNHCHR reported that 'Armed groups continued to terrorise the population in areas under their control, pursuing killings, abductions, torture, ill-treatment, and other serious human rights abuses, including destruction of housing and seizure of property.'[1295]

Russian active duty troops and Russian nationalists such as Pavlov and pro-Kadyrov Chechen mercenaries have been guilty of undertaking the most human rights abuses and war crimes. Russian and separatist forces have been implicated in war crimes in Ukraine that have included human rights abuses, illegal detentions, looting, torture and killings. During the battle for Debaltseve, after the signing of the Minsk-2 agreement, Russian tank drivers admitted killing innocent civilians: 'I'm definitely not proud of this, that I shot and hit' civilians who were killed.'[1296] Ukrainian soldiers have witnessed human rights abuses committed by separatist forces who have torched tanks with men inside, killed by 'cutthroats who don't ever know against whom they are fighting.'[1297]

*SBU regional office in Slovyansk damaged by fighting when Igor Girkin's Russian forces captured the city (December, 2014)*

A large number of Ukrainian soldiers and volunteers have disappeared without trace some of who are being held prisoner in the regions the separatists control; the whereabouts of up to 1,500 remain unknown. Former President Kuchma believed that the majority of the known 133 Ukrainian prisoners in separatist hands were dead and the separatists admitted to holding only 30 who they claim are not prisoners of war but 'criminals' guilty of 'rape, murder and torture.'[1298]

In the 1940s and early 1950s, UPA partisans would shoot themselves or blow themselves up rather than be captured alive to avoid torture and executions. In March 1950, UPA Commander Roman Shukhevych shot himself when his hideout was surrounded by MGB (Ministry of State Security) Internal Troops. Some Ukrainian soldiers and volunteers have preferred to commit suicide because of the fear of being taken prisoner leading to torture and being used as slave labour. Ukrainian soldier Andriy Kozinchuk said 'The worst thing for us, worse than death, would be to be taken prisoner' and 'So the grenade was to take ourselves and hopefully a few of the enemy out.'[1299] A second reason to blow themselves up was if Ukrainian soldiers were outnumbered, as with two officers of the 51st brigade who used grenades to kill themselves and 12 Russian paratroopers.[1300]

The UN characterised the DNR-LNR treatment of prisoners-of-war as accompanied by 'killings, abductions, torture, ill-treatment, sexual violence, rape, forced labour, ransom and extortion.'[1301] Ukrainian soldiers released in spring 2016 provided harrowing accounts of long periods of imprisonment in isolation and torture by beatings and electrical shocks.[1302] Negotiations for their release have been conducted in a haphazard manner.[1303]

An NGO report entitled 'Those Who Survived Hell'[1304] reported harrowing details where 87 percent of Ukrainian soldiers and volunteers and half of civilians who had been taken prisoner or detained by Russian and separatist forces had been tortured through inhumane and brutal treatment, physical violence, deliberate maiming, and humiliation. Similar findings have been published by Human Rights Watch and Amnesty International.[1305] Nearly a quarter of Ukrainian prisoners of war have been beaten with rifles, given electric shocks, had their toes and fingers squeezed with pliers, wounded by shock pistols and in the case of women threatened with rape. Russian active duty soldiers and Russian nationalist volunteers participated in or oversaw 40 percent of these cases of torture. A third of Ukrainian military prisoners of war and 16 percent of civilian detainees had witnessed killings arising from torture.

These acts committed by Russian and separatist forces amount to war crimes. Amnesty International declared that the torture, ill-treatment and extrajudicial killings of 'captured, surrendered or wounded soldiers are war crimes.' 'Summary killings are a war crime, plain and simple,' Amnesty International Deputy Director for Europe and Central Asia Denis Krivosheev said.[1306]

Ukrainian patriots living in separatist controlled regions have been targeted for detention, torture and murder from the beginning of the armed revolt. Ukrainian patriots and religious leaders have been denounced as 'spies,' 'terrorists' and 'sectarians' working on behalf of Western intelligence agencies who should be driven out of the DNR and LNR.[1307] In Horlivka, *Batkivshchyna* local deputy Volodymyr Rybak who opposed the takeover of his town by Girkin's 'little green men' was detained by men in camouflage uniforms, brutally tortured, gutted like an animal in an abattoir and his body dumped in a river.[1308] When he was being taken away the local crowds hurled insults and jeered support for Russian 'little green men,' as they would on later occasions in Donetsk when Ukrainian prisoners were forcibly paraded. Two students and Euromaidan activists 19-year old Yuriy Popravko and 25-year old Yuriy Dyakovskyy

*Motorway bridge on the highway to Donetsk blown up by Russian and separatist forces as they fled advancing Ukrainian forces (Pisky, March 2016)*

– were also detained, tortured and executed in Horlivka. During my visit to Slovyansk, Ukrainian activists talked of the brief Russian occupation of Slo-vyansk when their homes were searched by armed men looking for them; most had gone into hiding.

Ukrainian prisoners-of-war and Ukrainian political and civic activists and religious leaders have been executed by Russian military and separatist forces. A military court created by the separatists has been given the right to impose the death penalty for alleged crimes of 'state treason,' 'spying,' 'desertion,' 'loot-ing' and 'propagation of fascism.'[1309] KHRPG analyst Halya Coynash points out that 'The 'law' banning 'propaganda of fascism' looks copy-pasted from the Russian equivalent which was probably sensible since any scrutiny would make it clear  how many of the militants and those in Russia involved in training them  have the far-right and neo-Nazi leanings the document purports to be prohibiting.' The courts are an outgrowth of growing insecurity in the separatist enclaves because of limited financial resources to pay pensions, wages and social benefits which is leading to desertions, protests and strikes. 'With rule already based on denunciations, violence, and intimidation, the military 'three-man courts' are another chilling reminder of the worst Soviet methods and clearly aimed at terrorising the population,' Coynash writes.[1310]

Torture by separatist and Russian forces has been widespread since the beginning of the conflict.[1311] Former Russian separatist commander Girkin admitted to ordering executions in territories his forces controlled, in some cases for looting. This should not be surprising in the light of accusations in the Bosnian-Herzegovina media by a retired Bosnian army officer that Girkin participated in massacres in Visegrad in which 3,000 Bosnian (Bosniak) Muslim civilians, including 600 women and 119 children according to documents in the hands of the ICC, were murdered in spring-summer 1992 during a campaign of ethnic cleansing by Serbian nationalists and paramilitary units. Girkin participated in the second Russian military campaign in Chechnya after 2000 where Russia committed numerous war crimes. Girkin's participation in both of these conflict and ethnic cleansings came ahead of his human rights violations and war crimes in Ukraine.

The DNR separatist authorities installed a military court and re-introduced 1941 military laws from Soviet dictator Stalin, itself an admission of the ideological leanings of Russian nationalists and separatists. DNR security forces exist somewhere 'between Soviet rule and vigilante justice.'[1312] 'Under this legislation we tried people and executed the convicted,' Girkin said,[1313] admitting to executing four people in Slovyansk, three for looting and a fourth for killing a Russian soldier. The 'crime' of one of those who was executed was that he was allegedly an 'ideological' supporter of *Pravyy Sektor*. Girkin's forces undertook far more executions than he has publicly admitted to, including Protestant religious leaders. Separatist leaders have admitted scorched earth tactics of razing villages as they retreated from Ukrainian forces in summer 2014.[1314]

Ukrainian prisoners-of-war, wounded and dead have been treated with little dignity. Separatists, such as Mikhail ('Givi') Tolstykh[1315] and Pavlov were filmed pulling out Ukrainian dead from vans and dumping them on the roadside where they were left unburied.[1316] 'Givi' tormented wounded and captured Ukrainian prisoners of war, throwing them on to the ground, slicing off their lapel badges and stuffing them in their mouths forcing them to eat them. A separatist commander commenting about the dead Ukrainian soldiers says they died because they refused to surrender; a hint they were executed after being captured.[1317] Of the 17 Ukrainian soldiers captured retreating from Ilovaysk, at least four were executed because they had not stripped fast enough when ordered to do so. Two of these included Artom Kalyberda who had become 'hysterical' and Lozinskyy who had requested to be able to ring home to his mother. A former Ukrainian prisoner-of-war confirmed to a mother searching for her son missing in action that the separatists had ordered wounded and injured prisoners to strip, and had then executed them.[1318]

Wounded Ukrainian prisoners of war with shrapnel in their legs were forced to march through central Donetsk taunted by jeers, spitting and the thumps of local residents fired up by Russian and local Ukrainophobic television propaganda. Oksana, who travelled to Donetsk to seek the release of her husband, Sergeant-Major Anatoliy Svirid, was herself beaten and electrocuted. She recalled that 'I was beaten just as hard as the men' because 'they wanted us to admit that we were spies.'[1319]

Following the battle of Debaltseve, 'dogs were gnawing those corpses' after which 'there was so little left of them you couldn't even bury them.' Separatist and Russian forces did not bother to bury Ukrainian military dead and left them rotting to become food for stray dogs.[1320] 'AP reporters who arrived in Debaltseve soon after it was captured by Russian and separatist forces witnessed uncovered bodies of Ukrainian solders lying on the roads and the front gardens of people's homes.'[1321] DNR Prime Minister Zakharchenko taunted Ukrainian prisoners of war captured at Debaltseve shivering and kneeling in the snow with the words that President Poroshenko had 'betrayed them' because to him 'you are nothing but a piece of meat.'[1322]

The decline in law and order in the separatist enclaves fuelled such acts of lawlessness such as looting and summary executions of Ukrainian prisoners of war. Zakharchenko publicly lamented he could not shoot all the prisoners of war he had paraded in Donetsk.[1323] Olekandr Mashonkin, a wounded Ukrainian 'Cyborg' captured at Donetsk airport recalled that their separatist captors 'beat everyone with pipes, stools, and table legs. They beat us all over on the head, all over the body and in the groin.' 'Sever,' another 'Cyborg,' recalled: 'They beat us for six or seven hours with pipes, automatic rifles, bats and anything they could lay their hands on.'

Amnesty International has documented the numerous war crimes committed by separatist and Russian forces against Ukrainian activists, journalists and combatants. These have included executions of captured wounded prisoners and execution of nationalist prisoners. As Ukrainian forces advanced in summer 2014, LNR separatists executed their Ukrainian prisoners by shooting them in the head and neck before fleeing. These executions resembled the murderous actions of fleeing NKVD troops against Ukrainian prisoners in western Ukraine in September 1939.[1324]

Of the separatist and Russian forces that have committed the most fragrant abuses of human rights, *Sparta* and *Prizrak* battalions which are based respectively in Donetsk and Alchevsk, have been accused of committing numerous crimes against humanity. These have included undertaking the following executions of Ukrainian soldiers:

1. Ihor Branovytskyy (90th battalion, 81st brigade) was wounded and captured at Donetsk airport. 'Sever' witnessed how Pavlov executed Branovytskyy with two bullets shot into his head after he admitted to being the machine gunner among the 'Cyborgs' who had been captured.[1325] 'Sever' believes he could have survived his wounds if he had been evacuated to a hospital but 'Motorola' did not want to be burdened looking after wounded Ukrainian prisoners.[1326] The group of 'Cyborgs' were then tortured by 'Givi,' two Chechens known as 'Tanchik' and 'Stalin' and 'an (Russian) Orthodox priest who used his cross as a means of torture.'[1327]

2. Andriy ('Bur') Havrilyuk (95th airborne brigade) was wounded and captured at Donetsk airport and was shot three times in his head.

3. Four Ukrainian prisoners of war from the Donetsk territorial battalion were executed at Krasnyy Partyzan: Andriy Kolesnik, Albert Sarukhanyan, Serhiy Sliesarenko, and a soldier identified as 'Romchik' (a diminutive form of 'Roma'). Sarukhanyan was executed with two shots because he was Armenian, after he was asked what he was doing and replying he was 'fighting for Ukraine.' Video evidence shows bullet holes in the wall behind prisoners lined up, four of who are dead and crumpled on the floor. A female sniper 'did as she pleased' and was the most vicious of the separatists who were present, wanting to execute all of them and shooting at their knees and lungs.[1328]

4. Three soldiers from the 30th Mechanised Corps were captured and their bodies found executed the following day: Oleksandr Berdes, Vasiliy Demchuk and Pavlo Plotsinskiy.

In contravention of the Geneva Convention, Ukrainian prisoners-of-war have been treated as slave labourers: 'They told us we were 'Ukrainian slaves' Mashonkin recalled.[1329] Reports have surfaced of Ukrainian prisoners of war who have been listed as 'missing in action' being forced to work in illegal coal mines.[1330] Amnesty International reported that separatist forces 'disrupted medical services, unlawfully detained people, ill-treated detainees and subjected them to forced labour, and kidnapped civilians for ransom and used them as hostages.'[1331] A major report published by the Eastern Human Rights Group revealed the existence of 5,000 'slave labourers' in 15 correctional colonies in the LNR who were forced to work twelve hour days with porridge their only food and provided with no medical facilities. They were beaten, starved and tortured if they refused to carry out their unpaid work or protested their conditions. The profits from the goods they produced were taken by the LNR leadership.[1332]

One of the most brutal acts of torture has been the castration of Ukrainian prisoners of war:

'There are situations when men come back disabled after being held captive,' Alyona Zubchenko, the spokeswoman for the Kyiv-based International Women's Rights Centre La Strada said. She found that 'We have cases where men were castrated. This is a massive blow for men. We have calls from parents whose 20-year-old sons committed suicide after being held captive and castrated, because they could no longer live with this. But there are other situations when men who have lost their sexuality try to compensate by being violent.'[1333]

## UKRAINIAN HUMAN RIGHTS ABUSES

International human rights organisations have to check the veracity of allegations made against Ukrainian forces which often turn out to be lies or exaggerations. Typical of this highly biased reporting has been Sakwa who, using mainly official Russian sources, when discussing human rights abuses only writes about those committed by Ukrainian nationalist battalions who he alleges are 'shocking in its brutality,' 'infamous' for 'indiscipline and cruelty' and 'regularly commit atrocities against civilians and captured territory.'[1334] To back up his obsession with Ukrainian nationlists, Sakwa cites Russian disinformation by Russian Foreign Minister Lavrov and DNR Prime Minister Zakharchenko of 'mass graves' of victims murdered by Ukrainian forces in Komunar and Nyzhnya Krynka. The graves have never existed. Fake news and 'alternative facts' should have no place in work purporting to be scholarly.

Both parties to the Donbas conflict have been condemned for indiscriminately firing artillery shells and Grad rockets into areas where civilians live.[1335] Indiscriminate shelling and rocket attacks cannot distinguish between civilian and military targets. Russian state television has inadvertently shown separatists firing from residential buildings with the purpose of attracting return Ukrainian fire that would damage the buildings and kill civilians. 'Ukrainian and rebel forces are violating international humanitarian law by endangering civilians with indiscriminate attacks, despite the fact that attacks may only be directed against combatants,' Amnesty International said. 'These attacks are unlawful because Ukrainian forces are using weapons in populated areas that cannot be targeted with sufficient accuracy to distinguish between civilian objects and military objectives.'[1336] Amnesty International criticised the basing of military targets in residential areas when 'rebel forces have failed to take all feasible precautions to protect civilians and have endangered civilians in violation of the laws of war.'[1337]

Both sides have also been accused of mistreating prisoners of war. Nevertheless, there have been fewer documented cases of Ukrainian abuses and Amnesty International has reported that the worst abuses are in areas controlled by separatist and Russian forces. PACE has pointed out that human rights abuse and war crimes in the Crimea and the DNR-LNR are the responsibility of Russia because the former has been annexed and the latter is occupied by Russian military personnel and dependent upon Russian financial, logistical and administrative support.

Former separatist prisoners have reported beatings, torture using electrical shocks, and denial of medical attention by volunteers in *Pravyy Sektor* and *Aydar* battalions and the Luhansk-based Ministry of Interior *Tornado* battalions. Amnesty International documented abuses by the *Aydar* battalion in northern Luhansk in 2014.[1338] Accusations made against the *Tornado* battalion led to its disbandment and the sentencing of one officer to a term of six years in prison.[1339] Another 12 of its members were arrested and went on trial behind closed doors in Kyiv. The defendants include Ruslan Onyshchenko, leader of the disbanded *Tornado* unit. 12 more of *Tornado's* 170 former members are on a wanted list for serious crimes.

Amnesty International made an important distinction between captivity by Ukrainian and Russian and separatist forces. In the former, 'most prisoners in Ukrainian custody were eventually brought before a judge, given a lawyer, and placed in the formal legal proceedings.'[1340] PACE commended the Ukrainian authorities for cooperating with international organisations and for beginning 'prosecutions of alleged perpetrators of war crimes and other human rights violations on the sides of pro—government forces.'[1341] Ukrainian forces have not instituted long detentions, torture and murder of activists and journalists that are commonplace in the DNR and LNR. Ukrainian journalist Mariya Var-folomeyeva was illegally held in captivity by separatists for 419 days. [1342]

## CONCLUSIONS

Russian chauvinism through television propaganda and the public rhetoric of officials and Russian nationalists directed at ethnic Ukrainian and Crimean Ta-tar identity, language and religion created the charged atmosphere within which the conflict became more vicious, human rights were flouted and war crimes would be tolerated. While demanding rights for Russian speakers in the Don-bas, the DNR and LNR, Crimean and Russian authorities have removed all vestiges of Ukrainian and Tatar language, culture and religion from their terri-tories. Jews have fled from the DNR and LNR to Ukraine when faced with a return to Soviet era anti-Zionist (i.e. anti-Semitic) rhetoric.

The greatest number of human rights abuses and war crimes has been committed by Russian active duty soldiers and Russian nationalist volunteers and separatists. This should come as no surprise for four reasons. The first is Russian and Soviet history where human life never had any value. The second is that active duty soldiers and nationalists had committed war crimes in Bosnia, Chechnya and elsewhere prior to those they undertook in the Donbas. The third is the permissive atmosphere created by Russian propaganda and public discourse describing all Ukrainians who are opposed to Putin's *Russkiy Mir* as 'fascists' towards who any manner of human rights abuses and war crimes are permissible. The fourth factor is the lack of accountability for crimes commit-ted whether earlier in Chechnya and Georgia or since 2014 in the Donbas. There is a large volume of evidence of the inhumane treatment of Ukrainian prisoners of war, their torture and use as slave labour and most troubling of all executions of wounded prisoners. Ukrainian soldiers were treated with utter contempt when they were captured during the battles at Ilovaysk, Donetsk Air-port and Debaltseve.

Ukrainian forces have been implicated in far fewer human rights abuses by international organisations and human rights NGOs. All parties to the con-flict have used artillery and surface to surface missiles in residential areas that have caused destruction and civilian casualties. Human rights abuses ended af-ter volunteer battalions were integrated into the army and the National Guard.

The persecution of the Ukrainian language, cultural and religious iden-tity, the 'stab in the back' annexation of the Crimea, and the ferociousness, human rights abuses and war crimes by Russian and separatist forces against Ukrainian civic activists, journalists, and security forces (irrespective of whether they were Ukrainian or Russian language speakers) has led to rapid changes in Ukrainian national identity. Russian presidents have failed to learn from their own history when in the 1990s, the contempt with which Kuchma was treated by Yeltsin led him to turn away from Russia to NATO and the US. Putin's support for Yanukovych in 2004 and 2013 culminated in two popular uprisings. Similarly, today where instead of subduing Ukrainians, Russia's aggression has irrevocably transformed the identity of Ukrainian people, which is the subject of Chapter 11.

# CHAPTER 11

# UKRAINE'S NATIONAL IDENTITY AND PUTIN'S WAR

*Perhaps no one in Russia has done so much to ensure victory for Viktor Yush-*
*chenko as Putin.*
Nikolay Petrov (2004)[1343]

*Putin is both the man who most wants change stopped and the one who has created*
*the best opportunity for it.*
Sabrina Tavernise (2015)[1344]

Russian politicians, particularly émigrés from Ukraine such as Glazyev, senior adviser to President Putin, have always believed they are very knowledgeable about Ukraine even though they have repeatedly reached wrong and often incomprehensible conclusions. During the height of the Ukraine-Russia crisis, Russians were prone to telephoning their friends and business acquaintances in Ukraine to ask them how they could live in a country over-run by 'fascists.'[1345] Russians adamantly believe they know Ukraine better than the Ukrainians who live there.

Ultimately, the major reasons why these Russian 'experts' always get Ukraine wrong is four-fold. Firstly, they purport to analyse a country that only exists in their mind-sets and stereotypes but not in reality. Secondly, they refuse to see Ukrainians as a separate people or Ukraine as a sovereign country and therefore their 'analysis' is highly subjective. Thirdly, Russians have never undergone a process of de-Sovietisation similar to de-Nazification in post-war

Germany and unlike Poland have never come to terms with their imperial past. Poland and Ukraine have undergone a decades-long process of historical reconciliation that has not yet begun in the case of Russia-Ukraine and Russians do not therefore understand Ukrainian grievances. Fourthly and importantly in the context of the analysis in this chapter, 'separatist and Russian forces are facing people who speak the same language and share the same cultural background (which) neutralises all these attempts at presenting them (Ukrainian forces) as Galician Ukrainian nationalists or neo-Nazis.'[1346]

Russian politicians and 'experts' on Ukraine have never understood the genuine and local roots of the Orange and Euromaidan Revolutions and made the wrong predictions about Russian speakers during the so-called Russian Spring of 2014. Solzhenitsyn, similar to the majority of Russians, could not fathom how there could be hostility between Ukrainians and Russians because 'there isn't even a hint of intolerance' he wrote in his 1990 essay *How to Rebuild Russia*. Glazyev wanted to believe, similar to the majority of Russians, that Ukrainians are striving for union with Russia:

'Most people living in Ukraine, the overwhelming majority – I was born there and know the situation well – want to live with Russia in one country. Ukraine, Russia and Belarus are one country except that state borders now come between us, so we should do everything possible to remove these borders and reunite.'[1347] Glazyev's desire to present the Ukraine that Russia wants to see ultimately clouds his 'analysis.'

Putin and other Russian leaders have repeatedly described Ukrainians and Russians as one people. These chauvinistic views ignore the Soviet experience which culminated in nation building for many nationalities, albeit in a socialised format, when Ukrainians and Belarusians came to associate their identities with their republican borders. Belarusian President Lukashenka, although very much a leader in the Soviet mould, is nevertheless also a Soviet Belarusian nationalist who has turned down Russian proposals for the merger of their two countries. The Russian view of Ukrainians as 'Little Russians' also comes up against the obstacle of western Ukrainians who undertook nation building outside the Russian Empire and the USSR. Russian nationalists have dealt with this issue by artificially dividing western and eastern Ukrainians into 'fascist Russophobes' and 'Little Russians' respectively. Sakwa likewise simplistically divides Ukrainians into supporters of *'maloros' (Little Russian)* and Ukrainian identities.

*Volunteers Natali Prylutska (Dzi-uba) and Dr. Ev-dokiya Stepanivna Vepryk (Pisky, March 2016). 'Stepanivna,' as she is affectionately known to soldiers, came out of retire-ment to provide medical services to wounded Ukrain-ian soldiers*

Russia experienced a different trajectory to Ukraine and Belarus in the USSR and never underwent nation building within its republican borders. The Soviet Union and Russian SFSR were integrated for all but two of the Soviet Union's 69 years of existence and therefore Russian and Soviet great power and imperial identity was one and the same. The Russian population has therefore never viewed the borders of the Russian Federation in the same holistic manner as Ukrainians and Belarusians. The Russian Orthodox Church continues to view the entire former USSR as its canonical territory.

Russian misconceptions of Ukraine have wanted to believe that there has been a strong latent desire in Ukraine for union and towards this end Russian speakers were conflated with 'Russians' who were, in turn, assumed to be pro-Putin. This ignored surveys and public opinion polls in Ukraine. A 2007 survey found that the majority of Ukraine's Russian speakers were not separatists and similar to Hispanics in the US they were not a homogenous group on language and foreign policy questions.[1348] This should not be surprising when one compares and contrasts Russian speakers in for example Donetsk, Odesa, Kyiv and Lviv.

Ukrainian identity has changed over the quarter of a century of independence and this process underwent a faster trajectory after the Orange and Euromaidan Revolutions; in the latter case followed by Russia's annexation of the Crimea and hybrid invasion of the Donbas. Ukrainian patriotism has grown throughout the country and 78 percent of Ukrainians described themselves as 'patriotic,' a rise of 12 percent on 2005, with 17 percent who did not. This has been most noticeable in eastern and southern Ukraine where Ukrainians with mixed identities and Russian speakers had to make a choice during the Ukraine-Russia crisis. In the Ukrainian-controlled Donbas, support for separatism has declined. There has been a shift from regional to Ukrainian identity and a decline in pro-Russian orientation. By the time of the Orange Revolution, Ukrainian civic national identity had moved eastwards to central Ukraine and a decade later it has moved further east and south to encompass the remainder of the country.[1349] Bekeshkina concluded that attitudes towards identity and foreign orientation in Ukraine's east and south are moving towards the views of centre, and Ukraine's east-west fault line is moving from the Dnipro river to the boundary between Donetsk and Dnipro *oblasts*.[1350]

This chapter begins with an analysis of weak support for separatism throughout Ukraine, including in the Crimea. The next three sections discuss the reconfiguration of Ukraine's 'east' in term of its changing identity, the sources of exceptionalism in the Donbas and the two swing regions of Kharkiv and Odesa. The next three sections analyse the impact of Russian policies towards Ukraine that is leading to a divorce of the two countries and the ending of their 'fraternal brotherly' relationship, how Ukrainians view Russian leaders and Russians and the impact of the conflict upon Ukrainian attitudes towards history, religion and foreign policy.

## WEAK SUPPORT FOR SEPARATISM

Until the Ukraine-Russia crisis support for separatism was limited to 30 percent in the Donbas and 40 percent in the Crimea[1351] and in both regions it never constituted a majority of the population. An April 2014 survey by the Kyiv International Institute for Sociology (KIIS) found 27 and 30 percent supported

*Greetings sent by young school children to Ukrainian soldiers and delivered by volunteers (2015)*

separatism in Donetsk and Luhansk respectively with 52 percent opposed in both regions. In comparison, separatism was supported by only 7 percent in Dnipro and Odesa.[1352] Eleanor Knott found Crimean identity to be 'complex, fractured and contested' and she divides Crimeans into five groups: (1) discriminated Russians; (2) ethnic Russians; (3) Crimeans; (4) political Ukrainians; and (5) ethnic Ukrainians. She found only the first group, often members of Russian nationalist groups, to be ardently pro-Russian and identifying wholeheartedly with Russia, partly out of a sense of being losers in the post-Soviet transition. Ethnic Russians did not feel discriminated against or feel uncomfortable living in Ukraine, while those who identified as Crimeans were bi-ethnically Ukrainian-Russian. Political Ukrainians identified in a civic manner with Ukraine while ethnic Ukrainians were born in Ukraine but outside the Crimea.[1353] There was unlikely therefore to be support for 'reunion' with Russia in the Crimea and Sevastopol respectively at the levels of 95.6 and 96.77 percent respectively that were officially declared in the March 2014 referendum.

In a poll conducted in late 2014, 50 percent of the Donbas supported Ukrainian territorial integrity and 35 percent separatism, of who 20 backed an independent Donbas and 15 were in favour of a union of their region with

Russia.[1354] Separatists represented an aggressive third of the Donbas who believed it is important to 'struggle against nationalistic tendencies.'[1355] They were strongly supported by Russian television propaganda, weapons and *spetsnaz* 'little green men' who side-lined and violently subdued a largely passive pro-Ukrainian patriotic majority. Official results in separatist referendums in the Donbas and Crimea should be therefore taken with a big pinch of salt. In Donetsk, the 89 percent in favour of a separatist republic was pre-calculated as the desired result by the neo-Nazi RNE, as recorded in a telephone conversation that was intercepted by the SBU between RNE activist and DNR leader Dmytro Boytsov and RNE leader Barkashov.[1356] In the Crimea, the official 97 percent result (with a turnout of 83) in favour of union with Russia was far more than the real vote of 15-30 percent (turnout of 30-50) which was leaked by a member of Putin's Council on Civil Society and Human Rights.[1357]

In 2001, 71.3 percent of Crimeans (80 percent of Tatars and Ukrainians, 66.8 percent of Russians) had viewed Ukraine as their homeland. Meanwhile, in Ukraine as a whole, only 5 percent had supported the Crimea joining Russia and 85 percent opposed this step, with the highest opposition in the south and Donbas (19 and 8 percent respectively). 77 percent of Ukrainians supported Crimea remaining an autonomous republic in Ukraine, with the highest again being 89 percent in the east and the lowest 65 percent in the west.[1358] Russian public opinion was – and remains - diametrically different with a Levada[1359] poll finding 84-88 percent supporting and 'mainly' supporting the union of Crimea with Russia. Such views are not confined to pro-Putin nationalists but are also to be found among opposition leaders such as Aleksey Navalny and Mikhail Khodorokovsky. Talking about Ukrainians, Navalny said 'I don't see any kind of difference at all between Russians and Ukrainians.'[1360]

Opinion polls have on occasion produced contradictory results. The question 'Do you support Ukrainian and Russian 'unity'' is abstract and could be understood in different ways, ranging from a union of both countries to maintaining a closeness in the cultural, linguistic and religious fields. Supporting Russian-Ukrainian 'unity' does not therefore necessarily equate to support for separatism. In February 2014, on the eve of Russia's annexation of the Crimea, 41 percent backed Ukrainian-Russian 'unity' but only 10 percent supported an independent Crimea and the Crimea 'reuniting' with Russia.[1361] A second factor is that support for separatism is calculated by combining support for independent statehood for the Crimea and the Donbas with those who support a union of both regions with Russia, which reflects an ambiguity in the identities of the peoples living in these two regions. In a 2011 poll, 71 percent of Crimeans viewed their autonomous republic as a part of the 'Ukrainian homeland' with only 17 percent disagreeing. 80 percent of Crimean Tatars and ethnic Ukrainians and 67 percent of ethnic Russians supported the Crimea remaining a part of Ukraine.[1362]

The majority of Ukrainians have traditionally supported their country's territorial integrity and only 5 percent supported Crimea's annexation by Russia with a far higher 77 percent believing the peninsula should remain a part of Ukraine. In a jointly conducted poll by Russia's Levada Centre and KIIS, 88 percent of Russians supported and 80 percent of Ukrainians opposed the Crimea's annexation. An equal number (10 percent) of Russians and Ukrainians opposed and supported the annexation.[1363] In the Donbas only 8 percent backed the Crimea's annexation. 77 percent of Ukrainians supported the status quo of the Crimea as an autonomous republic within Ukraine while a minority of 11 percent (29 percent in western Ukraine) disagreed and believed the Crimea should be returned to the status of an *oblast* that existed in 1944-1990.[1364]

Why then did Ukrainian citizens, particularly in the Donbas, split into pro-separatist and pro-Ukrainian groups? This may be an impossible question to answer for political scientists as the decision is a personal one for each person that is difficult to quantify. 'Dushman,' when asked why he had become a separatist leader, answered that a person should only swear one oath to a homeland in their life time. 'I swore my oath to the Soviet Union. We have one land. To me, it is indivisible. That's why I'm here, in my homeland, in the Donbas.'[1365] 'Dushman,' in a similar manner to DNR Prime Minister Zakharchenko, views the Donbas in abstract terms as a synonym for the long disappeared Soviet Union which is a reflection of the lingering and deep Soviet identity in the region. Armenian volunteer Artur Gasparyan fighting for the separatists said he did not consider Russia to be a 'foreign country' and that he had 'the mentality of a Soviet person.' Like many on the separatist side, he equated 'Russia' with the USSR and said 'My grandfather fought for the Soviet Union and I am fighting for it'.[1366]

Another soldier, 'Spartanets,' agreed with 'Dushman' that 'We're all children of the Soviet Union. We were brought up on the patriotic feelings of the Afghan war.'[1367] But, although respectful of the Soviet legacy, 'Spartanets' nevertheless opted to join the Ukrainian side. The first protestor to be killed by a sniper on the Euromaidan was Armenian Serhiy Nigoyan, the son of refugees

*Greetings from young schoolchildren delivered by volunteer Natali Prylutska (Dziuba) to Ukrainian soldiers at a front line position west of Horlivka (May 2016)*

from Nagorno Karabakh who had moved to Ukraine. Sarukhanyan, an Armenian volunteer for the Ukrainian army who was captured was executed by the separatists because of his Ukrainian patriotism.

Separatism in the Donbas has never had a mass popular base or influenced the political agenda of mainstream regional political parties, such as the Labour Party, Liberal Party, Party of Regional Revival, and the Party of Regions. Nevertheless, relatively high levels of Soviet identity and stronger identification with the region than with Ukraine provided a basis for an aggressive pro-Russian minority who equated 'Russia' with the Soviet Union. 37.1 percent in Donetsk and 32.2 percent in the Crimea upheld Soviet cultural traditions, larger than the numbers of those holding Ukrainian and Russian identities. Donetsk was therefore more Soviet in its identity than the Crimea and within Ukraine had the largest number of streets named after Lenin (430). In Ukraine's south and east, 40.9 and 42 percent percent respectively identified with Ukrainian cultural traditions and 26.5 and 26.3 percent with Soviet.[1368] Eastern and southern Ukraine outside the Donbas and the Crimea therefore possessed higher levels of Ukrainian identity; albeit Russian speaking. 95 percent (53 of who very strongly) of the residents of the Donbas identified with the Russian state and 97 percent identified very closely with the Russian language and culture.[1369] Nostalgia for the USSR was also high in the Crimea where it was 'almost universal.'[1370] A vote for union with Russia was understood as far more than joining the Russian Federation; it was also a vote to return to the Soviet Union of which Putin's Russia proudly boasted it was the successor state.

States and peoples that are close in language and culture can be peaceful neighbours and at the same time 'can often produce more – not less – conflict over national identity.'[1371] Austria, although German-speaking, was at war with Germany in 1866, supported unification with Germany in 1938 and became a truly independent country only after World War II. The Ukraine-Russia crisis is playing a similar role in forging a new Ukrainian national identity independent of Russia, irrespective of the fact that a large proportion of Ukrainians will continue to remain Russian or Ukrainian-Russian bilingual speakers. Indeed, upwards of two thirds of Ukrainian forces in the ATO are Russian speakers,[1372] a figure which is readily borne out from the large amount of film footage available on YouTube and other Internet web sites. 'Sever,' himself a Russian speaker from Poltava, calculated that 80 percent of Ukrainian forces at Donetsk Airport and on the nearby front line were Russophones.

The majority of Ukraine's Russian speakers have shown themselves to be Ukrainian patriots who are opposed to Putin's policies towards Ukraine. Russia, which portrays all Ukrainians who support the Euromaidan and European integration as 'fascists,' finds it incomprehensible that separatists and Russian forces are fighting against Russian speaking Ukrainian citizens. Being a Russian speaker did not therefore predispose one to be unpatriotic in Ukraine. By 2016, 60 percent of Ukrainians gave Ukrainian as their native language, 22 percent said both Ukrainian and Russian and 15 percent Russian. For participants in the ATO, the figures were higher and 73 percent declared Ukrainian to be their native language, with 19 percent both and only 6 percent Russian.[1373]

The native language that is declared in a census and the language used on a daily basis can often be different. The populations of the city of Kyiv (65 percent), Podilya (65), Volyn (53),Trans-Carpathia (67) and Chernivtsi (67) identified with Russian language and culture.[1374] 57 percent of Ukrainians feel close to the Russian language and culture (the equivalent for Polish is 19 percent).[1375] But, on the whole, these regions voted for what Moscow defined as 'fascist' and Russophobe parties and large numbers of them participated in the Orange and Euromaidan Revolutions.

In Ukraine, the country with the largest proportion of independent Russian-speaking media in the world, Ukrainians do not believe language is a major concern showing how completely misplaced is Sakwa's analysis of the causes of the Ukraine-Russia crisis.[1376] 82 percent of Ukraine's Russian speakers do not feel their language is threatened.[1377] The Donbas (97 percent), Kharkiv (89 percent), Dnipro and Zaporizhzhya (84 percent) and Odesa, Mykolayiv and Kherson (67 percent) have high levels of identification with the Russian language and culture but violent separatism emerged in only the first of these regions. 67 percent of people in Trans-Carpathia, a region that has supported both pro-Western forces and pro-Russian forces, feel an affinity to the Russian language and culture. The only Ukrainian region which does not have an affinity is Galicia.[1378]

A paltry one percent of Ukrainians believe the status of the Russian language is an important question, a viewpoint borne out by countless polls over the last two decades which has shown that socio-economic questions are a priority for eastern and western Ukrainians, but especially for the residents of the Donbas. When asked if the status of the Russian language had changed since the Euromaidan, 65 percent of Ukrainians believed nothing had happened while 10 percent were convinced the status had actually improved. Nevertheless, 18 percent believed there had been a deterioration and undoubtedly among this group would be supporters of Donbas and Crimean separatism.[1379] When asked if Russian speakers are under pressure or threatened since the Euromaidan because of their language only one percent said definitely 'yes' while another 10 percent said 'somewhat,' giving a total of 11 which still remains low. When this response is broken down by ethnic group not surprisingly more ethnic Russians (23 percent) than ethnic Ukrainians (8 percent) feel that the Russian language is more threatened since the Euromaidan.[1380] In Canada, a far larger group of French speakers feel their language and culture is threatened by Anglophone Canada and the US.

The influence of Russian television propaganda about developments in Euromaidan Ukraine is clearly visible in the Donbas where 40 and 30 percent of Donetsk and Luhansk respectively believe there is oppression of the rights of Russian speakers in Ukraine in general, which is different to attitudes found elsewhere in the east and south. At the same time, only 5 and 3.5 percent of Donetsk and Luhansk respectively believed such oppression existed in their regions.[1381]

*Ukrainian soldiers receiving deliveries from volunteer Natali Prylutska (Dziuba) (May 2016)*

Ukrainians do not feel their patriotism is compromised by using both languages and only 11 percent of Ukrainians view Russian-Ukrainian bilingualism as a barrier to Ukraine's development.[1382] The Ukraine-Russia crisis has led to the Ukrainian language becoming more popular.[1383] Ukrainians who support official recognition of Russian as a state language has declined from 27 to 19 percent, although in the east and south this is higher at 50 percent. A larger group of 52 percent of Ukrainians prefer Russian to be recognised at the local level in regions where it is used by a large proportion of people.[1384]

Russia's aggression in Ukraine has influenced Ukrainian national identity in four different ways. These include: (1) reconfiguration of the political spectrum; (2) expansion of Ukrainian national identity from the centre to the east and south of the country; (3) promotion of Ukraine's national integration; and (4) growing patriotism among Ukrainians of all generations.

Firstly, the pro-Russian and Sovietophile Party of Regions and KPU no longer command electoral support following their disintegration and marginalisation in elections held in 2014-2015. Since the October 2014 elections, Ukraine has for the first time a constitutional majority of deputies who support European integration and a far smaller pro-Russian group. On 21 April 2015, the Ukrainian parliament adopted a resolution by 250 votes (with none opposed) 'On countering Russian Federation military aggression and dealing with its consequences.'[1385]

Secondly, pro-Ukrainian civic and state identity is spreading eastwards across the country. In the late 1980s, western Ukrainians were the driving force for *perestroika* and independence and by the 2004 Orange Revolution, Ukrainian ethnic and civic identity had spread to central Ukraine which a decade earlier had voted with the east to elect Kuchma.

Thirdly, the crisis and Russia's policies are promoting Ukrainian national integration. Until the 2014-2015 crisis, Ukrainian speakers would often identify with Ukraine while Russian speakers could identify sometimes with their region and city. Since 2014 there has been a growth of Ukrainian patriotism among Russian speakers and for the first time more people in the (Ukrainian controlled) Donbas hold a Ukrainian over a regional identity.[1386]

Fourthly, there has been a growth of patriotism, rather than ethnic nationalism which is being driven by civic rather than ethnic, cultural and linguistic factors.[1387] The growth in Ukrainian identity is compatible with and sufficiently inclusive to accommodate the Russian language. Ukraine's civic identity, similar to that commonly found in most Western states, has a strong ethnocultural basis. With Ukrainians comfortable in both Ukrainian and Russian, Wanner writes that 'non-accommodation has become a norm.'[1388]

Ukrainians are negatively disposed towards the Russian state and leader rather than the Russian people.[1389] A majority of Ukrainians have negative views of Putin, the State Duma and Russian government. 68 percent of Ukrainians are neutral or positively inclined towards Russian citizens while a minority (23 percent) hold negative views.[1390]

The war has increased symbolic support for Ukrainian nationalism without a growth of electoral support for nationalist parties. Nationalist leaders, including the controversial Bandera, are perceived as agents of Ukraine's national liberation struggle against Russia's unfair treatment of their country. Nearly half of Ukrainians believe they have from ancient times fought for freedom from Russian oppression (with 29 percent disagreeing). Nationalism is understood not as a means to construct the Ukrainian state but as integral to their national liberation.[1391]

Electoral support for nationalism has remained low. Political parties such as *Pravyy Sektor* and *Svoboda* espousing ethnic Ukrainian nationalism received very low results in the three elections held in 2014-2015. The majority

*Armenian-Ukrainian local deputy Armen Shakharyanets collecting and preparing support for Ukrainian soldiers (Yahotyn, near Kyiv, March 2016)*

of Russian speakers in Ukraine identify with the Ukrainian state where language is not the main or sole determinant of their identity. Jews in Ukraine are largely Russian speakers and have supported the Euromaidan and the Ukrainian state in its war with Russia. The opposite process is taking place in Russia with the growth of a *Russkiy* identity at the expense of a *Rossiyskiy* identity[1392] (the closest analogy would be English and British).

When asked which population groups they did not like to be with in close circles, only 9 percent of young Ukrainians said Russians and even fewer, 3 percent, of Russian-speakers held such views.[1393] 82 percent of Ukrainians consider themselves to be patriots with a high of 92-94 percent in the west and Kyiv and 88-89 percent in the centre and north. 79 and 56 percent of Ukrainians respectively view themselves as patriots in the south and the east.[1394] 59, 71 and 80 percent respectively of southern, central and western Ukrainians feel good about being citizens of Ukraine.[1395] 93-95 percent of Ukrainians have pride in the Ukrainian flag, national symbols and the Ukrainian language.[1396]

Ukrainian opinion polls show very high levels of negative feeling towards Russian political and government leaders but not to the Russian people in the Russian Federation. Many Ukrainians were psychologically unprepared, Denis Gavrilov, deputy head of Civil Defence in Mariupol, said to 'accept that a brotherly neighbour would attack us' and they view the annexation of the Crimea as a stab in the back when Ukraine was down.[1397] In April 2014, this author was asked by an elderly taxi driver in Kyiv 'Will there be war' to which I replied 'Yes.' His answer was typical of the older generation when he said 'How can brothers fight against brothers?' In spring 2014, the shock of Russian 'brothers' shooting Ukrainians had to be quickly overcome and Lozhkin writes 'Today, our fighters are ready to kill and to die for their country.'[1398]

Following two years of annexation, war and destruction the Russians are no longer viewed as Ukraine's 'brothers.' A military intelligence officer recounted to this author how he had lost two men in his unit in summer 2014 when he had not believed Russians he witnessed crossing the border would shoot at Ukrainians. After this incident the soldiers under his command and he quickly adapted to the new reality.

Conflict and war in the Donbas has cardinally changed the Soviet stereotype about the 'friendship of peoples' and Ukrainians and Russians as 'brothers.'[1399] Nearly two thirds of Ukrainians, but only a quarter of Russian citizens, are convinced that Ukraine and Russia are at war, ranging from a high of 87.5 percent in the west to 41.1 and 45.4 percent in the east and south respectively. A similar number, 65 percent of Ukrainians but only 27 percent of Russian citizens, believe Russian troops are stationed and fighting inside Ukraine, ranging from a high of 89.3 percent in the west to 36.6 and 57.2 percent in the east and south respectively.

Ukrainians and Russians also radically differ on attitudes to Putin's annexation of the Crimea with 80 percent of Ukrainians but only 13 percent of Russian citizens opposing the annexation while 10 and 83 percent respectively support it. While it is not surprising that very high majorities in the west and centre of Ukraine oppose the annexation of the Crimea, 79.8 and 62.9 percent in the Russian-speaking south and east respectively also adopt this tough stance. The Crimea is adjacent to southern Ukraine and for those living in that region the possibility of becoming a future conflict zone is too close for comfort.

*Ukrainian pensioners and farmers Lyudmilla and Petro Luchinskyy who prepare food for delivery to Ukrainian soldiers (near Poltava, March 2016)*

## RECONFIGURATION OF UKRAINE'S 'EAST'

Tatyana Zhurzhenko has written that the 'east' has shrunk to the two separatist enclaves while Kharkiv, Dnipro and Zaporizhzhya are in a process of reinvention of their identities. Nostalgia for the Soviet Union is dissipating in the face of a Russian aggressor which views itself as the reincarnation of the USSR.[1400] Some of these changes in identity had been gradually taking place since 1991, particularly among young people and middle class businesspersons and professionals, but have speeded up since 2014.

The Euromaidan Revolution received a mixed reception in eastern and southern Ukraine. The greatest antagonism to the Euromaidan was to be found in the Donbas where only 12 percent held positive views and 69 percent were negative, views that are not surprising because 'their lad' (Yanukovych) was the target of Euromaidan revolutionaries incensed at his policies. But, high levels of negativity were to be also found in Kharkiv (55 negative to 36 percent positive) and Zaporizhzhya and Dnipro where views were more polarised (47 negative to 44 percent positive).[1401]

Unlike during the Orange Revolution, the Euromaidan Revolution received varying levels of support in eastern and southern Ukraine (outside the Donbas) and a large proportion of these supporters became military volunteers in the ATO or unpaid volunteers in civil society support groups. In a region with low levels of efficacy many of them, particularly the older generation, stood up for their rights for the first time in their lives. The majority of the women who dominate civil society support groups for the military are middle aged and pensioners who had become volunteers for the first time. In Kyiv, Poltava, Kharkiv, Kherson, Mykolayiv, and Odesa the overwhelming majority of civil society volunteers met by this author were Russian-speaking women. Of young Ukrainians, 49 percent of them participated in support groups to the army and volunteer battalions.[1402] The Euromaidan, and subsequent Ukraine-Russia crisis, contributed to enhancing the individual as the carrier of civic rights and pressuring Ukrainians with bi-ethnic (Russian/Soviet-Ukrainian) identities to choose one side of the fence.

Tolerant attitudes towards the Ukrainian language had been spreading to eastern Ukraine prior to the crisis. Wanner writes that in the early 1990s, heads would turn around when one would speak Ukrainian in Kharkiv but by 2010 there was no reaction. Wanner describes language in Ukraine as fluid and 'non-accommodating bilingualism.' This presented challenges to political scientists and sociologists 'who rely on fixed, unambiguous categories to conduct survey research.'[1403] Zhurzhenko writes that 'the era of post-Soviet ambiguity and tolerance of blurred identities and multiple loyalties has ended.'[1404] This process has been accentuated by Russia's policies towards Ukraine that removed large numbers of traditionally pro-Russian voters in the Crimea and the Donbas.[1405] Official Ukrainian policies have blocked the transmission of television from Russia over cable television networks, although some channels could still be available through the installation of a satellite dish and on the Internet. 63 and 43 percent respectively in eastern and southern Ukraine believe Russian television circulates untruths about Ukraine.[1406]

Identities in Ukraine can be 'situational and contextual and can rapidly change, especially under conditions of territorial secession, external aggression, and military conflict.'[1407] Natalya Zubchenko, a resident of Dnipro, said 'the Maidan roused people's sense of national identity.' Kharkiv resident Volodymyr Ohloblyn pointed to how the Euromaidan showed Ukrainians and Russians to be very different because in Russia they could not comprehend that

*Volunteers showing sniper's costumes they had sown from old clothes for Ukrainian soldiers (Mariupol, April 2015)*

'Ukrainians on the Maidan were ready to die for their country.' This was because, he believes, 'We (Ukrainians) are spiritually free. And they aren't. They love to say Russia is a great country. I always tell them it's not great – it's just big.'[1408]

Zhurzhenko's analysis points to Ukraine's 'east' changing in two ways. Firstly, in conflicts and wars people have to choose which side of the fence they stand on and in Ukraine this inevitably is reducing the number of people holding bi-ethnic and multiple identities. Secondly, growth of a primary identification with Ukraine over region: 57.5 percent identify with Ukraine and 29 percent with their region, town and village, with the highest proportions in the latter three categories to be found in eastern (where it is a combined 32 percent compared to 54 percent Ukrainian) and southern (42.5 percent compared to 45 percent Ukrainian). These figures are not much higher than those found in western and central Ukraine where a 23-24 percent combined support for local identity is 8-9 percent lower than in eastern Ukraine. The Donbas was unique in being the only Ukrainian region where identification with town and region (combined 59.5 percent) was far higher than the 25 percent who identified with Ukraine, but this has changed since 2015.[1409]

Zhurzhenko believes the Donbas 'turned out to be an extreme case' that differentiated the region from the remainder of Russian-speaking Ukraine outside the Crimea. She believes the 'rhetoric of the Kremlin was more or less congruent with the identity politics of the Party of Regions' and the formulation of the anti-Western *Russkiy Mir* civilisation project. The Party of Regions was in turn supported by the KPU, the Progressive Socialist party, Soviet veteran's associations, Russian Cossacks and Russian Orthodox Brotherhoods who 'created a heterogeneous yet active, even aggressive milieu. In 2014 this became the breeding ground for pro-Russian separatism.'

## DONBAS EXCEPTIONALISM

Donbas exceptionalism includes the following 10 attributes of identity:

1. 55 percent of the Donbas positively view the formation of the Russian Empire in 1721.[1410]

2. It had the lowest levels of support for Ukrainian independence of any region and was the only Ukrainian region with a higher identification of the population with the Donbas than with Ukraine. 40 percent of the Donbas viewed Ukrainian independence in positive terms while 32 percent viewed it negatively.[1411]

3. Anti-Kyiv feelings have translated into 'anti-fascist' and 'anti-nationalist' rhetoric.

4. The region has a 'negative identity' which was mobilised by the Party of Regions during election campaigns against pro-western political forces and western Ukraine more generally.

5. Defence of Soviet values, such as protecting monuments of Lenin, mobilised the local population against 'nationalist' Kyiv and the Euromaidan.

6. Widely circulated and accepted myths of the Great Patriotic War and hostility to the rehabilitation and glorification of Ukrainian nationalist leaders and groups. Of Ukraine's regions, 96 percent of the Donbas view the defeat of Nazi Germany in the Great Patriotic War as their most popular historical event, the highest of any Ukrainian region.[1412]

7. Conservative Russian Orthodox Church values that exist in a region where there are fewer believers and religious parishes than in western and central Ukraine.

*Professor Mariya Podybaylo, head of the Novyy Mariupol (New Mariupol) NGO that assists Ukrainian soldiers (April 2015)*

8. The myth of Donbas industry 'feeding' the remainder of Ukraine.
9. Russian language and culture need to be defended against 'Ukrainian nationalists.'
10. Soviet style opposition to NATO membership coupled with anti-Americanism.[1413]

Public attitudes towards the disintegration of the USSR are a relatively good barometer of Soviet nostalgia and pro-Russian feelings in Ukraine. The highest levels of negative feelings that lament the passing away of the Soviet superpower were to be found in the Donbas (70 percent), Kharkiv (52 percent) and Dnipro-Zaporizhzhya (49 percent). But, these figures also reveal a stark difference between these regions because in the Donbas there were only 12 percent who held positive feelings about the disintegration of the USSR whereas in Kharkiv and Dnipro-Zaporizhzhya these were higher at 31 and 39 percent respectively. The latter figure is especially interesting because it was not much lower than the number of those who were nostalgic about the USSR's demise (49). Lower levels of Soviet nostalgia and higher levels of Ukrainian patriotism enabled pro-Ukrainian forces to defeat pro-Russian sentiment in spring 2014 in Kharkiv and Dnipro.[1414] Language never became a dividing line between opposing groups because Russian speakers predominated among both pro-Russian and pro-Ukrainian protesters. Odesa self-defence units visited by this author in June 2015 were all Russian speakers.[1415]

## SWING REGIONS: ODESA AND KHARKIV

In more middle class Odesa and Kharkiv, with large student populations and small and medium businesses, the mentality is very different to the more working class Donbas. In Odesa, political apathy has always been high and political parties are weak with most people focused on making money.[1416] Economics and business always trumped politics in Odesa and pro-Russian groups found it difficult to mobilise supporters, particularly after the 2 May 2014 clashes between pro-Russian and pro-Ukrainian forces. With its numerous coffee bars, restaurants and night life, Odesa resembles Kyiv and Lviv rather than towns in the Donbas where atomised people socialised, as in Soviet times, at home or in private venues. The working classes of the Donbas rarely travelled outside their city, never mind their *oblast*, and if they had travelled it had only been to Russia.[1417] In Odesa this was very different: 'We Odessites know better, having been long connected to the rest of the world through our sailors and trading. We are 'internationals,' liberal in mind and business-oriented.'[1418]

Conflict in Odesa, far from the Russian border, was less discernable than in Kharkiv but nevertheless, culminated in 48 deaths on 2 May 2014. Some weapons were smuggled into the city from the Trans-Dniestr frozen conflict in Moldova. Separatism was also feared among the Bulgarian population in the southern part of Odesa *oblast* which had traditionally voted for the Party of Regions and KPU. There were fewer political tourists from Russia than had been bussed into Kharkiv. What turned the tide in Kharkiv and Odesa was a combination of the mobilisation of Russian speaking Ukrainian patriots and the continued loyalty of the bulk of the local security forces.

Russia nevertheless attempted to create an Odesa People's Republic (ONR). The Glazyev tape recordings and an investigation by *Dumskaya* TV journalists provide evidence of Moscow's ties to local Russian nationalists and neo-Nazis who formed the Odesa *Dryzhyna* in late February 2014. Odesa *Druzhyna*, whose most prominent leader was Denys Yatsyuk, began the day's carnage on 2 May with the shooting of pro-Ukrainian marchers. Another active organisation in Odesa was the Union of Orthodox Citizens of Ukraine. Odesa Russian nationalists were promised intervention by Russian 'little green men' by Glazyev and Crimean Prime Minister Aksyonov if the state administration and Odesa *oblast* council denounced the regime that had emerged from the Euromaidan Revolution, then declared a ONR and called for Russian assistance.[1419] But, Moscow's plans were thwarted by the Odesa *oblast* council vote to denounce Russian aggression and by the mobilisation of Ukrainian patriots.

The Council of Europe reported that four of the five fires in the Trade Union building were begun by Russian nationalists because 'other than the fire in the lobby, the fires could only have been started by those inside the building.' The fire spread in the building after the barricade in the front entrance caught fire from an exchange of Molotov cocktails thrown by both sides.[1420]

**Table 11.1. The Odesa Conflict on 2 May 2014: A Chronology of What Took Place**

| Event | Analysis | Outcome |
|---|---|---|
| Odesa and Kharkiv football fans and Ukrainian patriots led a peaceful march for a United Ukraine from central *Soborna* square to the football stadium for a game beginning at 17.00 | 1,000 fans and marchers were mainly civilians, including parents with children protected by 100 *Samoborona* stewards. A dozen *Pravyy Sektor* supporters joined them | Ukrainian fans and marchers were unarmed, peaceful and did not commit violence or hooliganism |
| Anti-*Maidan*, Russian nationalist activists mobilised supporters against the march | 300-400 anti-*Maidan* supporters attacked far larger numbers of pro-Ukrainian activists | 150-200 anti-*Maidan* activists arrived with weapons, helmets and baseball bats 'ready for clashes' |
| Odesa Squad activist 'Denys' fired the first shots of an air gun | Increased the tension | Detained by the *militia* |
| Anti-*Maidan* activists were given weapons as they assembled at the pro-Russian Public Security Council NGO | Odesa Squad activists moved towards the marchers | Violent clashes began with firecrackers, explosives (with screws and nails fixed to them) and paving stones thrown. 40 *Samoborona* members |

| Event | Analysis | Outcome |
| --- | --- | --- |
| | | are wounded; only their body armour prevented some of them from being killed |
| Odesa *militia*, led by former Yanukovych and new appointees, were unprepared and the bulk of them were based at the stadium. In some cases they were in cahoots with anti-*Maidan* activists | *Militia* officers are shown on video footage standing in front of anti-*Maidan* activists shooting at pro-Ukrainian supporters | Odesa *militia* permitted the use of weapons and assisted in the escape of key anti-*Maidan* leaders |
| The anti-*Maidan* at *Kulikova* Field Trade Union building, announce a full mobilisation of activists. | Divided over whether to stay and defend the tent camp at Kulikova or to go and assist the anti-*Maidan* activists fighting pro-Ukrainian marchers | Poor and disorganised leadership leads to chaos and lack of co-ordination between rival groups |
| At 16.00 a white ford transit van with pro-Russian activists armed with *kalashnikovs* arrives at the clashes | Led by 'Votsman' they began shooting at pro-Ukrainian marchers | Pro-Ukrainian marchers were killed, the first being leader of Odesa *Pravyy Sektor* Ihor Ivanov and Euromaidan activist Andriy Bilikov |
| Pro-Ukrainian marchers fight back and surround smaller numbers of pro-Russian activists. Odesa fans leave the stadium and smash Party of Regions billboards on the way to *Kulikova*. Pro-Russian | Pro-Russian activists begin bringing their tents and the gasoline generator inside the Trade Union building. The generator was left in the lobby and became a major source later for the fire and | Tension was heightened throughout Odesa as the news spread of killings on social media, ending the possibility for a peaceful outcome. This led to a greater use of rocks, paving |

| Event | Analysis | Outcome |
|---|---|---|
| activists begin building barricades in the lobby of the Trade Union building | carbon monoxide fumes | stones, firecrackers and weapons. Pro-Russian activist Yevhen Losynskyy is killed |
| *Pravyy Sektor* activists wearing captured helmets and shields enter the rear of the Trade Union building. What is left of the tent city is destroyed | Pro-Russian activists were vastly outnumbered, with many more women than men, but refused to retreat | Molotov cocktails begin to be thrown by both sides, first from inside the building after which pro-Ukrainian activists reply with their own |
| *Militia* were ordered not to intervene and fire services were very late to arrive | Fire and combustion spreads quickly because of the large lobby, big doors and wide staircases and corridors | Fire spreads to the 5th floor where many anti-*Maidan* activists had retreated to 15 bodies were found who had been poisoned by carbon monoxide. Some anti-*Maidan* activists are afraid to come outside because of the large group of pro-Ukrainian supporters |
| The appearance of Ukrainian flags in the windows of the Trade Union building was met with cries of 'Glory to Ukraine!' by the pro-Ukrainian crowd outside | As captured by photographer Oleh Kutskiy, wounded anti-Maidan activists are assisted and taken to ambulances using doors as stretchers. Scaffolding from the tent camp is pushed to the Trade Union building to assist anti-*Maidan* activists to escape | Some anti-*Maidan* activists moved to the roof. Others begin jumping from windows or tried to hold on to the outside of the building. An anti-*Maidan* sniper shooting from the third floor of the Trade Union building wounds Kyiv Euromaidan activist |

| Event | Analysis | Outcome |
|-------|----------|---------|
| | | and ethnic Russian Euromaidan activist Andriy Krasilnikov |
| Chaos, fire, weak presence and late intervention by *militia*, ambulance and emergency services | Volodymyr Sarkisyan said there would have been fewer casualties if the fire services had arrived earlier and not until 40 minutes after they were telephoned. Firemen entered the Trade Union building at 20.31 and the last person was rescued at 5am | 'Both sides of the conflict used weapons' (Captain 'Mykola'). Sarkisyan helped save an anti-*Maidan* activist saying to him 'Remember it was a Banderite who saved your life.' |
| The use of weapons from inside the Trade Union building led to searches and checks of anti-*Maidan* activists as they were brought outside | Anti-*Maidan* activists who survived had 20-30 percent severe burns. None had gunshot wounds | 6 pro-Ukrainian and 42 anti-*Maidan* activists died from gunshot, fire and carbon monoxide smoke. 300 activists and 70 *militia* were injured |

**Analysis:** The film is an objective portrayal of the conflicts on 2 May 2014 in Odesa drawing upon interviews with 257 eyewitnesses (local activists on both sides of the clashes, journalists, veterans and *militia*), video evidence, fire engineering tests, inspections of the Trade Union building site and analysis of the criminal case files with the events chronologically detailed. Key people who were interviewed included the head of Odesa *Samoborona* Vitaliy Svychinskiy, deputy head of Odesa *Samoborona* Vitaliy Kozhuhar, (pro-Russian) Odesa Squad leader Serhiy Rudych, Captain of *Samoborona* Vitaliy Ustymenko, First Commander of the Kulikova tent camp Serhiy Dmytriev, anti-*Maidan* activists Oleksandr Herasymov and Artem Davydchenko, deputy head of the Odesa *oblast* council and leader of the Odesa branch of the Party of Regions Vyacheslav Markin.

*Volunteer painting road blocks in Ukrainian national colours on the road to the Russian occupied zone east of Mariupol (April 2015)*

**Source:** Yelyzaveta Tatarynova (Author) and Serhiy Polishchuk (Film Editor), *Odesa. May 2 – What Really Happened?* http://uatoday.tv/society/odesa-may-2-watch-on-ukraine-today-424573.html

As is evident from the chronology of events of the conflict on 2 May 2014 in Odesa which is laid out in detail in Table 11.1, the description of the Odesa conflict given by Sakwa is premised on highly prejudiced views of 'Ukrainian nationalists.'[1421] Sakwa's book does not cite any interviews with local politicians, activists and journalists (unlike the documentary film used as the basis for Table11.1). His main source for the tragedy that he covers in less than three pages of his book is the highly biased Russian Ministry of Foreign Affairs White Book on discrimination of Russian speakers in Ukraine. Two other sources are the *New York Times* and the tabloid *Daily Mail* (the latter a British newspaper that Wikipedia has banned because it is an 'unreliable source'[1422]).

That day's confrontation is described as taking place between 'patriots' and 'nationalists' with the derogatory term of 'nationalist' only reserved for the Ukrainian side. Shooting by anti-Maidan activists at Ukrainians is described as 'allegedly' when video footage of this is available on YouTube and in the video documentary that was drawn upon for Table 11.1. Sakwa draws on the Russian

Ministry of Foreign Affairs White Book to describe 'Ukrainian nationalists' as in effect evil monsters who were burning tents, throwing Molotov cocktails at pro-Russian activists and 'beating back protestors with clubs and knives,' adding that these activists were in addition 'raped and killed before the fire took hold…' Those who jumped from the windows of the burning building were allegedly 'clubbed to death' by 'chants of 'Glory to Ukraine!' and 'Death to enemies!' He never mentions the use of weapons by pro-Russian nationalists prior to and when they were inside the Trade Union building, that both sides were throwing Molotov cocktails and the bravery and decency of Euromaidan activists who were assisting anti-*Maidan* activists escaping from the fire. Sakwa believes that 'several hundred' were killed, not 48, but cites no sources whatsoever to back up this inflated number. His entire presentation of the Odesa tragedy is based on Russian official sources and Putin's hybrid war propaganda which is unsuited for publication in a book that purports to be a scholarly study of the Ukraine-Russia crisis.

On 2 May 2014, a deliberate provocation in Odesa by a small group of Russian nationalist anti-*Maidan* activists inflamed a peaceful march by a larger number of peaceful and unarmed pro-Ukrainian Euromaidan marchers and football fans from Kharkiv and Odesa whose teams were playing that day in the city. A total of 48 died, six from gunshot wounds, 34 from smoke inhalation and burns and eight from jumping to their deaths. Video footage clearly showed how pro-Russian vigilantes shot at the peaceful *ultras* from behind police lines.[1423] The organisers of the provocation wanted pro-Russian vigilantes to retreat to their base in the Trade Union building. [1424] Pro-Ukrainian and pro-Russian supporters *both* threw Molotov cocktails and it is impossible to know which set the building on fire. Ultimately, the decision by the pro-Russians to barricade themselves in the Trade Union building and bring inside the gasoline generator was a major mistake. The building was not set alight intentionally by pro-Ukrainian activists.[1425]

Four questions remain unclear:

1. Who made the decision to bring the gasoline generator inside the building which contributed to a bigger fire, its more rapid spread and denser fumes from which 36 of the 48 died?

2. Who tipped off Russian television that there would be carnage producing great television footage at the Trade Union building? This television coverage would proceed to inflame Russian citizens and Ukrainians with pro-Russian separatist sympathies.

3. Pro-Ukrainians providing aid to victims and rescuing pro-Russian supporters trapped inside the building were shot at from the inside of the building. Vitaliy Hdenisku, a member of the Brighter Future for Ukraine NGO, was shot in the leg as he was seeking to assist pro-Russian activists fleeing from the building.[1426] Euromaidan activist Krasilnikov was shot in the arm from inside the building. Shooting from inside the Trade Union building were not covered in television broadcasts.

4. Did the release of most of the pro-Russian culprits by the *militia* indicate there had been collusion between some pro-Russian *siloviki*, Russian intelligence and anti-Maidan activists to stage a provocation?

It is highly unlikely that the answers to these and other questions will be found because too much time has been lost since the clashes during which Ukraine has not undertaken a thorough investigation of that day's tragedy. This factor was condemned by the International Advisory Group of the Council of Europe but it should not come as a surprise; after all, no political leaders or *Berkut* riot police had been criminally charged either.[1427] Ukraine's general prosecutor's office was highly efficient at covering up crimes and protecting ruling elites but unwilling and unable to provide the justice that Ukrainians had demanded in two democratic revolutions.[1428] The blame for the day turning violent should be laid at the door of pro-Russian groups who with police complicity began shooting at peaceful fans and marchers.[1429] Moscow, on the one hand, and pro-Putin scholars such as Sakwa, on the other, politicise the tragedy by transforming it into a 'massacre,' inflaming the number of casualties from 48 into the hundreds and describing it as a clash between (pro-Russian) 'patriots' and 'barbaric (Ukrainian) nationalists.'[1430]

In Odesa and Kharkiv support for separatism ranged between 10-15 percent; that is, more than half less than that found in the Donbas. Large pro-Ukrainian patriotic majorities existed in both regions and important sections of the security forces remained loyal to Kyiv. Kharkiv, only 38 kilometres from the Russian border, experienced an influx of what were termed 'political tourists' who cooperated with *Oplot* vigilantes to seize the State Administration building. But, quick intervention by Kyiv using police *spetsnaz* ejected them and 70 out of 300 of them were detained. A particularly humorous episode showed

*Olena Mokrynchuk, head of Soldatska Poshta (Soldiers Post Office)
NGO that assists Ukrainian soldiers (Volnovakha, April 2015)*

Russian 'political tourists' did not know the city of Kharkiv when they proclaimed they had occupied the city hall but in fact had taken control of the Opera House.

Kharkiv city Mayor Kernes, who had been a staunch supporter of Yanukovych and the Party of Regions, initially flirted with the separatists through *Oplot* who had operated as an organised crime vigilante force for his business interests. Kernes had begun his career in the 1990s in the Kharkiv underworld and black markets where he had needed the services of vigilante sportsmen. In the 2010 elections, Kernes was elected mayor in a fraudulent election forcing his rival Arsen Avakov (supported by BYuT) to flee abroad. Relations between Kernes and his vigilantes became strained in March 2014 after *Pravyy Sektor* shot dead two *Oplot* members and were allowed by the mayor to flee in the hope that this would deescalate tension. Kernes visiting the scene of the shooting shouted at *Oplot* members standing outside 'Don't fucking wind up the crowds.'[1431] Pro-Russian vigilantes roamed the city the following day attacking Euromaidan and pro-Ukrainian supporters and the following month *Oplot* attempted to assassinate Kernes, but he survived.

By April 2014, the tide had begun turning in favour of pro-Ukrainian groups because 'Separatists in Kharkiv are not numerous illegal groups who do

*Women volunteers collecting and preparing donations for Ukrainian soldiers (Kherson, May 2015)*

not have real power and mass support of the people.'[1432] A crucial role in defeating the separatists was played by young citizens of Kharkiv, particularly 'ultra' football supporters, who held protests and wrote imaginative and humorous new songs such as *Putin Khuylo! (Putin is a dickhead!)* which became a nationwide hit.[1433] These young football fans were not your typical Euromaidan protesters as they were unafraid of fighting pro-Russian vigilantes and the *militia*. The support of football fans, students and later *Azov* battalion nationalists (their leader Andriy Biletskyy is from Kharkiv) gave confidence to a broader cross-generational group of pro-Ukrainians to come on to the streets in opposition to Russian nationalists. Self defence units were established with the assistance of retired military officers in each district of the city and many of these street activists later joined volunteer battalions in the ATO. By May 2014, pro-Ukrainian groups had come out on top in Odesa and other key cities in eastern and southern Ukraine pushing the pro-Russian *Oplot*, *Rodina*, the Russia Bloc, and the KPU's *Borotba (Struggle)* into the underground or forcing them to flee to the separatist controlled DNR and LNR.

The aggressive behaviour of pro-Russian vigilantes and groups, many of who were financed and trained by Russian intelligence,[1434] 'became increasingly incompatible with the moderate, cautious, intelligent ways of Kharkiv.'[1435] To middle class and educated citizens of Kharkiv, the intellectual capital of eastern Ukraine, the vigilantes and 'political tourists' were looked down upon as the 'marginalised,' unemployed, and uneducated. Middle class citizens of Kharkiv largely viewed the Euromaidan positively associating it with the growth of Ukrainian patriotism and many become emotional for the first time in their lives. When they heard the national anthem 'Tanya' said 'I feel my heart stop' and 'Lena' added that 'My heart stops and I have to catch my breath and I get goose bumps down my neck.'[1436] A CBC reporter, who had grown up in Kharkiv and had emigrated to Canada, asked if this emotion was real to which 'Lena' replied 'It's real, very real' and 'When the anthem starts I feel the urge to stand up and sing.' When she heard it on television, 'Lena' said 'I have an involuntary urge to sing along.' 'Lena' and 'Tanya' both replied that before the Euromaidan they did not feel so emotional about the Ukrainian national anthem.[1437]

## RUSSIAN 'BROTHERS' NO MORE

Similar changes in identity are manifesting themselves throughout eastern and southern Ukraine. Ukrainian flags are quite prominent in areas of the Donbas controlled by Kyiv and Viktor Alanov, an ethnic Russian resident of the Donbas, said 'I feel a lot more emotional than before' when he sees them.[1438] Flags represent what has been described by Michael Billig as 'banal nationalism'[1439] that we take for granted because we see them on a daily basis when we ignore them but they become symbolically important when identities are in a process of change and challenged by external threats. Aleksey Ryabchyn, another ethnic Russian and Ukrainian citizen said, 'The Russian part of me died on 1 March when I saw the Russian senate allowed Putin to send troops into Ukraine: It was the biggest shock of my life.'[1440] Another Russian speaker who used to be pro-Russian said 'I don't feel like that any more. Russians are a bunch of mercenaries and cutthroats. They came to Ukraine; we didn't go to them.'[1441] Ruslan Onishchenko, an officer in the *Tornado* battalion, said 'We always wonder why Russia started hating us; Ukrainians are Slavs just like them and their brothers' and he asked 'Why are they killing us, why are they destroying our cities?'[1442]

Alanov 'always took Ukraine for granted' and admits that he was 'never a fervent Ukrainian patriot.' He continues: 'I never felt any particular emotion when I saw a Ukrainian flag. I did not like the anthem much and I definitely never liked nationalists.' But, spring 2014 was a 'time of unabashed idiocy and

*'Undeclared War' banner denouncing Russian aggression against Ukraine in a park in central Odesa (May 2015)*

surrealism' when 'defenders of the Donbas' used 'antifascist slogans to attack peaceful demonstrations by pro-Ukrainian Donbas residents.' He recalled the calls for violence to be unleashed against 'fascists' and asks 'What is this, if not fascism?' The thousands who rallied in support of Ukrainian territorial integrity were attacked by 'defenders of the Donbas' who beat, maimed and murdered them. Pro-Russian backers of the *Russkiy Mir* confronted pro-Ukrainian sympathisers with 'Russian nationalism, monarchical bells and whistles, and a boorish rejection of all things progressive. For some reason this was called 'antifascism.'[1443] Russian writer Kurkov, who lives in Kyiv, points out that protests in the Donbas 'can be much more violent and chaotic than those in the West' and writing in spring 2014 he said 'Hatred is overflowing.'[1444]

In the early 1990s in independent Ukraine, Konstantyn Morozov, Ukraine's first defence minister who was born in the Donbas and Kuchma became Ukrainians after previously being defined by themselves, their families and the Soviet state as 'Russians.' Journalist Pomerantsev follows in a long line of Ukrainians whose identities have changed at critical periods of contemporary Ukrainian history. Pomerantsev was nine months old when his family emigrated from Soviet Ukraine and they never identified with the Ukrainian national liberation movement. His parents were Russian speakers, he was brought up on Russian literature and he was viewed in London as a 'Russian.' But the Euromaidan opened the door to his identity change and, he writes, 'I suddenly felt very sharply that my mother was from Kyiv, my father grew up in Chernivtsi, my grandparents are from Odesa and Kharkiv.' It felt 'strange' to feel Ukrainian and 'The Physical sensation of saying the words is revolutionary: like a new planet in the mouth.'[1445]

Although an ethnic Ukrainian, 'Oleksandr' voted againstl Ukrainian independence in 1991 and participated in Russian nationalist groups where he took part in violent attacks against 'Ukrainian nationalists' in Kharkiv. But, 'Oleksandr' joined a volunteer battalion because 'My views completely changed during the Revolution of Dignity: I came to Kyiv to fight with Banderites, but when I saw with my own eyes what was taking place I stood on that side of the barricades.' 'Oleksandr' recognised a will to liberty during the Euromaidan and in the ATO.[1446]

Ukrainians with mixed families have opted for Ukraine and some have fought for their country in the ATO. Serhiy Halyan, whose father lives in Russia and is a colonel in the Russian army, was one of the 'Cyborgs' who fought at Donetsk airport.[1447] Andriy Romaniy, an actor by profession who had lived all of his life in Donetsk, has a Ukrainian father while his mother's family is Russian and Jewish. Meanwhile, he viewed himself as 'ethnic Soviet;' in other words, he was a typical resident of the Donbas who until 2013 held multiple identities. At school he, in principle, never learnt the Ukrainian language, held up Soviet myths and opposed Ukraine's independence in 1991. After he moved to Kyiv as an IDP he read books on Ukrainian history and culture and his feelings for Ukraine became more positive and patriotic.[1448] Volodymyr Kachmar, whose family suffered in the 1930s and 1940s from political repression and deportations to Siberia, said 'I can't say I have hatred towards Russia, but they never saw us as a real nation. They stole our history, and now they're trying to steal it again.'[1449]

Russian volunteers fighting in Luhansk upon returning home revealed that the 'local population in some places call us occupiers.' Vladimir Yefimov, who brought over 100 volunteers from Russia, was disappointed at the coolness that he found among some local Ukrainians in the Luhansk region, the people he was supposedly protecting from 'fascists' and NATO, and for this he blamed the 'duplicitous (separatist) leaders.'[1450] In more rural northern Luhansk bordering Kharkiv a higher share of Ukrainian-language speakers made the separatists unpopular and the local self-defence units made them un-welcome.[1451]

Re-identification would inevitably take place during conflicts especially among young people. In some cases this has led to families dividing in their loyalties with the older generation remaining opponents of the Euromaidan and the children its supporters, as in the case of Oleksandr Makarov and his daughter Katerina in Mariupol.[1452] The older generation and the less educated, who are the least mobile and least likely to travel within the country and abroad, are the most likely to be nostalgic for the USSR, oppose the dismantling of Soviet monuments, support Ukraine's organic participation in the *Russkiy Mir* because they identify with Russia, do not see much difference between Ukrainian and Russian culture, and sympathise with the separatists.[1453] In contrast, young Ukrainians, some of who have already travelled or desire to travel, look to the future which they associate with Europe rather than the past which they associate with the USSR, Russia and in some cases their parents. Of the countries where young Ukrainians would like to study, 43 percent would choose the UK, 38 percent the US and 33 percent Germany; Russia is not popular among them.[1454] Young Ukrainians are optimistic about the future and they identify themselves as Ukrainian patriots in every region of Ukraine. 58 percent of young Ukrainians believe democracy is better than dictatorship although 26 percent agree that dictatorship can in some cases be advantageous over democracy.[1455] Young Ukrainians believe in the need for a political opposition, citizens have a right to express their views through protests, and are tolerant towards other groups.[1456]

Young Ukrainians through their participation in the Euromaidan, as civil society and military volunteers or through being conscripted into the army have undergone a process of a deepening of their Ukrainian identity and patriotism. One aspect of this is the growing use of the Ukrainian language as a marker of identification with the Ukrainian state and opposition to Putin's aggression. A Ukrainian said 'My kid brother and all his friends used to speak Russian. It was just normal for them. They watched Russian movies, they read Russian magazines, and the language of their pop culture just seeped into their daily interaction.' He continued, 'It used to be cool to speak Russian. Now it's cool to speak Ukrainian.'[1457] In comparison to 2006, the number of Ukrainians who said their native language was Russian has dropped by half from 31 to 15 percent. This was a reflection of the growth of Ukrainian-Russian bilingualism from 16 to 22

*'Eternal Memory to the Heroes of the Ukrainian-Russian War' bill-board in a park in central Odesa (May 2015)*

percent and those who gave Ukrainian as their native language rising from 52 to 60 percent.[1458]

The majority of Ukrainians are patriots, not ethnic nationalists and differentiate between Russian political leaders and Russian citizens. In Ukraine, there is no state-directed anti-Russian propaganda in the Ukrainian media and no state-led campaign to depict 'Moskali' (Muscovites – a derogatory name for Russians) as 'imperialists.' This is very different to authoritarian Russia where the state has mobilised vitriolic and chauvinistic television propaganda against 'Ukrainian fascists' and 'Banderites' who are in the pay of NATO and the West. Under this barrage of Russian television propaganda during the Yushchenko presidency and during and since the Euromaidan, Russians who hold positive attitudes to Ukrainians slumped from 66 to 35 percent while negative views increased from 26 to nearly half of Russian citizens.

In 2008-2014, following Russia's invasion of Georgia and leading up to the Ukraine-Russia crisis, a large majority of Ukrainians held positive attitudes towards Russia. From a high of 83 percent of Ukrainians who held positive views of Russia in 2011-2012 this plummeted by half in 2014 to 37-41 percent when for the first time more Ukrainians (47 percent) held negative views, ranging from a high of 70 percent in the west to 46 and 33 percent respectively in the south and east.[1459] By 2015, those Ukrainians who harboured cold and very cold feelings about Russia had grown to 51 percent compared to only 16 percent who had very warm and warm feelings.[1460] By 2015, a two thirds majority (67 percent) of Ukrainians held negative views of Russia and the CIS Customs Union (61 percent).[1461] Ukrainian attitudes towards the US and Russia fundamentally differ. Only 15 percent of Ukrainians harbour cold and very cold attitudes to the US whereas 41 percent hold very warm and warm views, feelings which are very different to high levels of anti-Americanism in Russia.

A major shock to Ukrainians, which was widely viewed as a 'stab in the back,' was Russia's rapid annexation of the Crimea which 59 percent of ethnic Ukrainians (but only 28 percent of ethnic Russians) viewed negatively. A very high 83 percent of Ukrainians (combining those holding 'definitely no' and 'somewhat no' views) did not support the 'decision of the Russian Federation to send the Army to protect Russian speaking citizens of Ukraine.'[1462] A whopping 92 percent (categorically and mainly) of Ukrainians do not support Russia sending troops into Ukraine to protect Russian language speakers with only eight percent disagreeing. Similarly, only 9 percent view Russia's actions in the Crimea positively with 63 percent viewing it as an illegal invasion and occupation of Ukrainian territory. [1463]It has not gone unnoticed by Ukrainians that 90 percent of Russian citizens supported the annexation of the Crimea and similarly high numbers back Putin. [1464]

In Ukraine there are very high levels of negative views of Putin across all of Ukraine's regions, although only by a modest majority in the east. 79 percent of Ukrainians do not approve of Putin's role in the crisis (compared to 6 percent who do) ranging from a very high of 94 in the west and north to 72 and 53 percent respectively in the south and east. The only region with high approval rates were the two Donbas separatist enclaves where 58 percent approved of Putin's actions. Fundamentally, a very large majority of Ukrainians reject the right of Russia to intervene in Ukraine's domestic affairs.[1465] Very high negative feelings for Putin in the west and centre of Ukraine of 96 and 93 percent respectively were matched by high negativity in the east (59 percent) and south (52 percent). 73 percent of Ukrainians hold negative views of Putin and 69 percent of the State Duma and Russian government.[1466] The Donbas is an outlier although 26 percent negativity towards Putin remains relatively high. Similar levels of negative views towards the Russian government and State Duma can be found in the east (54 and 54 percent respectively) and south (49 and 46 percent).[1467] When asked which leader they had confidence in to do the right thing in world affairs, 51 and 56 percent of Ukrainians respectively backed President Obama and Chancellor Merkel but only 10 percent believed this to be the case for Putin.[1468] 75.5, 72 and 70 percent of Ukrainians hold negative views of Putin, the Russian government and the State Duma, respectively.

These views were a reflection of the growth of Ukrainian patriotism rather than a narrow ethnic nationalism. Support for a civic identity where all of the people in Ukraine are treated as citizens has similar levels of support in western Ukraine (50 percent) to the Donbas (58 percent).[1469] There are more Ukrainians holding positive views of Russian citizens (29 percent) than negative views of them (26 percent) which in of itself is a lot lower than negativity towards Russian politicians and the Russian state. [1470] The highest negativity towards Russian citizens is not surprisingly to be found in western Ukraine (37 percent), 11 percent more than in central Ukraine, with far lower levels of negativity (ranging from 10-14 percent) in eastern and southern Ukraine and the Donbas.[1471]

Another survey found that whereas 69-73 percent of Ukrainians held negative views of Putin, the State Duma and Russian government, only 23 percent were negatively disposed towards Russian citizens while 30 and 38 percent were positive or neutral respectively.[1472] Indeed, fewer Russians (27 percent) hold positive views of Ukrainians than Ukrainians hold of Russians (30 percent).[1473] Nevertheless, there had been nearly a halving in positive Ukrainian views of Russian citizens from 45 to 29 percent. Russians and Ukrainians are no longer viewed as 'brothers' in the sense understood by Soviet nationalities policies because, as a Donetsk Airport 'Cyborg' told me in late 2015, 'brothers' do not invade your land and act as enemies and aggressors.' The 'Cyborg' viewed himself as a soldier defending his land from an invasion by a foreign power.[1474]"Sova,' another Donetsk Airport 'Cyborg,' explained in the Russian language that 'Yes, I wanted to fight. I wanted to fight for my loved ones and for my beloved Ukraine.'[1475]

## UKRAINIAN VIEWS OF THE 'CRISIS'

How then do Ukrainians characterise the Ukraine-Russia crisis? A very high 85 percent believe relations with Russia are difficult and even hostile and 80 percent believe they are at war with Russia.[1476] These figures and other sociological data led Julie Ray and Neli Esipova to believe that what was happening was a complete divorce between Ukraine and Russia across the entire breadth of their

*Volunteer who collects and distributes clothes and other items for IDP's (Odesa, May 2015)*

relationship. Ray and Esipova conclude that, 'Any kinship Ukrainians used to feel with Moscow's leadership is gone after Russia's annexation of Ukraine's Crimea region in March.'[1477]

There are nuances in Ukrainian attitudes to Ukrainians with the Donbas showing far less critical attitudes to Russia than the remainder of eastern and southern Ukraine. In the east, 48 percent of Ukrainians but only 26 percent in the Donbas believe that Russia is pursuing 'unfriendly policies' towards Ukraine. When asked who should be blamed for the crisis, 54 percent of Ukrainians pointed to Russia and 11 percent to Ukraine, with a regional breakdown of 36, 27 and 11 percent respectively in the east, south and the Donbas.[1478] 68 and 60 percent respectively of western and central Ukrainians, between 33-36 percent of eastern and southern Ukrainians and 24 percent in the Donbas blamed Russia for the war. 22 percent of western Ukrainians and 42 percent in the Donbas blamed both sides.[1479]

Fundamental changes in national identity have consequences for the foreign orientation of a people; this is particularly the case when three quarters of Ukrainians are unhappy at Russia refusing to recognise Ukraine as a sovereign country. 85 percent of Ukrainians seek to therefore leave the Russian sphere of influence, signalling a rejection of the *Russkiy Mir* and the CIS Customs Union and Eurasian Union. Russian and Ukrainian citizens view Ukraine in starkly different ways with the former seeing an inherently hostile, Russophobic 'fascist' Ukraine in cahoots with the West while the latter feel a strong sense of injustice and betrayal at the hands of Russian policies. Russian speaking Ukrainian poetess Anastasiya Dmytruk was typical of those feeling betrayed by the 'Russian brother' and she explained her feelings in a poem entitled 'We will never be brothers!' that has been viewed millions of times on You Tube.[1480] Indeed, it is far more likely that Russian speakers in Ukraine feel more betrayed than Ukrainian speakers because the latter were less likely to have bought into Tsarist and Soviet nationalities policies of Russians as 'brothers' and especially 'elder brothers.'

Dmytruk's poem was expressing something more profound than simply a sense of betrayal. She was also saying there was no going back to the Soviet friendship of people's doctrine and Russians would no longer be viewed as close and practically the same people. Russia's annexation and aggression had brought about an irreversible identity cleavage between both countries and peoples. Putin's annexation of the Crimea, hybrid war and hostile economic, financial and energy policies have set in motion a fundamental reappraisal of Ukrainian identity and attitudes towards Russia. The Crimea was symbolically transferred to Ukraine in 1954 on the 300th anniversary of the Treaty of Peryaslav which was touted in Soviet propaganda as the 'reunion' of two 'fraternal peoples,' Ukraine and Russia. Logically therefore, Putin's invasion and annexation has overturned this decision, destroyed the Russian-Ukraine union and irrevocably shattered the myth of 'fraternal' Ukrainians and Russian 'brothers.'

Russian citizens see swarms of 'Ukrainian fascists' which Ukrainian citizens are at pains to find. When asked how best to categorise the Donbas conflict, 42 percent described it as a war between Ukraine and Russia and 23 percent as a separatist revolt supported by Russia, amounting to two thirds of Ukrainians believing the war is a product of Russian intervention.[1481] The Ukrainian public through a free and independent media is well aware of the factors behind Russia's actions; 46 percent are convinced Russia is opposed to Ukraine's European integration and the same figure believes Russia is seeking to prevent Ukraine breaking out of Russia's sphere of influence. 42 percent of Ukrainians feel that Russia does not recognise Ukraine as a separate country, an important bone of contention and only 12 percent of Ukrainians believe Russia's justification for intervening was to protect Russian speakers.[1482]

## CHANGING VIEWS OF UKRAINIAN HISTORY, RELIGION
## AND FOREIGN POLICY

Russian Orthodoxy is in irreversible decline in Ukraine, a country which is central to the influence the Russian Church has in international Orthodox affairs and vis-à-vis the Patriarch of Constantinople. On the eve of the disintegration of the USSR, 6,000 of the 12,000 parishes of the Russian Orthodox Church were in Soviet Ukraine of which two thirds were in western and central Ukraine. Of the 12,000 Russian Orthodox Church parishes in the USSR only a quarter were in the Russian SFSR, belying the claim that Russians are highly religious. Three years into the Ukraine-Russia crisis, 15 million Ukrainians identified with the Ukrainian Orthodox Church-Kyiv Patriarch and 10 million with the Ukrainian (Russian) Orthodox Church. Democratic Initiatives Foundation gave 44 percent of Ukrainians as supporters of the Ukrainian Orthodox Church-Kyiv Patriarch and 21 percent of its Russian competitor. A different survey gave 25 percent support for the Ukrainian Orthodox Church-Kyiv Patriarch and 15 percent for the Ukrainian (Russian) Orthodox Church, a lower figure because it asked respondents if they were just 'Orthodox' without declaring allegiance to either side (21 percent, down from 39 percent in 2000).[1483]

Although Ukraine's population is only a third of that of Russia's it had until the 2014 crisis a similar number of Russian Orthodox Church parishes. As the popularity of the Russian Orthodox Church is declining, the popularity of the Ukrainian Orthodox Church-Kyiv Patriarch is growing and Patriarch Filaret enjoys the highest popularity of any Church leader in all regions of Ukraine. Russian Orthodox religious leaders have the highest distrust of Church leaders in Ukraine.[1484] By 2016, more Ukrainians owed their allegiance to the two pro-autocephalous Orthodox Churches than to the Ukrainian (Russian) Orthodox Church.[1485] In the Donbas cities of Slovyansk and Kramatorsk, briefly occupied in spring 2014 by Russian and separatist forces, the Ukrainian Orthodox Church- Kyiv Patriarch is supported by growing numbers of Orthodox believers.[1486] These trends will increase pressure for recognition of autocephaly (i.e. independence) for Ukraine's Orthodox Church by the Orthodox Patriarch in Istanbul (Constantinople), a step that would dramatically reduce the worldwide influence of Russian Orthodoxy. Without Ukrainian Orthodox parishes, Russia will drop below Romania and Ukraine in the size of its Orthodox Church.

Changes in Ukrainian and Russian identities are most easily discernible in attitudes to their Soviet past. In Russia, re-Sovietisation (including protection of and re-building of Soviet monuments) has gone hand in hand with re-Stalinisation whereas in Ukraine the Euromaidan ushered in de-Sovietisation that has come on the back of a three decade-long de-Stalinisation. To those seeking to put the Soviet Union behind them and move on, Lenin is a symbol of authoritarianism in the USSR while he remains a hero to those who seek to wallow in Soviet nostalgia in contemporary Russia and the DNR and LNR. In Ukraine, a quarter of a century after the disintegration of the USSR, the country is burying its Soviet past and removing Soviet Communist monuments and symbols and changing hundreds of Soviet street names.1487 Since the Euromaidan, 1,400 monuments of Lenin (described as *Leninopad*) have been pulled down; the largest of which were in Kharkiv in September 2014 and Zaporizhzhya in March 2016.[1488] 55,000 streets have been renamed from their Communist names. Dnipropetrovsk was renamed Dnipro. [1489]

De-Stalinisation has been taking place in Ukraine for nearly three decades and a majority of Ukrainians view Soviet tyrant Stalin very negatively. Eighty percent of Ukrainians, including large majorities in its east (64 percent) and south (69 percent), view the 1933 holodomor as a 'genocide.'1490 54 percent of Ukrainians view the holodomor as a negative period of Ukrainian history, the highest of any Ukrainian event. The only other political figure a large proportion of Ukrainians also view in negative terms is Yanukovych with an average of 51 percent. 50-67 percent of Ukrainians hold negative views of Yanukovych in the the south, centre and west and even 32 percent hold negative views of him in the east with the lowest number being 20 percent in the Donbas. [1491]

In contrast to Ukraine, Putin's Russia is undergoing re-Stalinisation and re-Sovietisation where Stalin is praised as an economic 'moderniser,' and a great war time leader who transformed the USSR into a nuclear superpower. In militarily attacking Ukraine to keep the country within Russia's sphere of influence, President Putin is seeking to impose his subjective history of the Tsarist and Soviet past, including the glorification of Stalin and the obfuscation of his crimes. Russian leaders have vehemently opposed Ukraine's de-Stalinisation and depictions of the *holodomor* as a genocide and demanded that Kyiv follow Russian portrayals of the famine as engulfing the entire USSR. Large portraits of Stalin hang in Donetsk.

The national histories we chose to educate our children, the leaders that we praise and whether we denounce or hide their crimes against humanity reflect our political beliefs and our attitudes towards democracy and human rights. Stalin and Hitler are the antithesis of the European democracy that Ukraine is seeking to build. Meanwhile, Stalin is central to Putin's authoritarian political system, the mythology of the Great Patriotic War, justification of the Molotov-Ribbentrop pact, and his vision of a resurgent Great Russian power.

A major impact of Russian aggression against Ukraine has been on public attitudes to World War II whose victory day is celebrated by Europe and Ukraine on 8 May while Russia celebrates the Great Patriotic War a day later. A majority of Ukrainians for the first time are positively inclined towards the nationalist partisans who fought against Nazi and Soviet occupation forces for a decade in the 1940s.[1492] The OUN and UPA, vilified by both the Soviet Union and contemporary Russia, organised one of the largest partisan armies in World War II using the same self-organisation and creativity as was found during the Euromaidan and by civil society volunteers in the ATO.

At the same time, popular views of Bandera have yet to become more positive and only in the west do 36 percent view him positively. Negative views of Bandera are though declining and stand at 13 percent which is only one percent higher than positive views of the OUN leader.[1493]

A majority of Ukrainians for the first time support NATO membership which had stood at a third under Kuchma but declined to twenty percent under Yanukovych.[1494] Between 2015 and 2016, support for NATO membership increased from 43 to 48 percent with some opinion polls giving over half of Ukrainians in support.[1495] Support for NATO membership is higher than opposition to it in every region of Ukraine except the east where 15 percent are in favour and the same are opposed.[1496] Democratic Initiatives Foundation found that support for NATO membership between 2013-2015 had grown from 7 to 33.5 percent in the south and 2 to 32 percent in the east.[1497]

49 percent of Ukrainians support closer ties to Europe and only 8 percent with Russia,[1498] while 64, 50 and 45 percent of Ukrainians respectively hold positive views of the EU, US and NATO. This represents a profound and lasting change in Ukrainian attitudes to the outside world.

Public support for Ukrainian integration into the Russian-led Customs Union has collapsed from a high of 40 percent in 2011, when Yanukovych was Ukrainian president, to 13 percent and lower today.[1499] 57 percent of Ukrainians would support a policy of reducing cooperation and Russian influence in Ukraine, which in fact is what has been taking place since 2014 in the fields of energy, trade and the military-industrial complex, while 23 percent back increased cooperation. Even in Ukraine's east, 43 percent support reducing cooperation and Russian influence while 33 percent oppose this step.[1500] Another opinion poll in September 2015, eighteen months after the Ukraine-Russia crisis began, found 48-49 percent of Ukrainians backing closer ties to the EU and NATO and only 8 percent to Russia. 64 and 50 percent of Ukrainians respectively held positive views of the EU and NATO and only 12 percent of Russia.[1501] When choosing foreign policy orientations, Ukraine's west (83 percent), centre (58 percent) and south (48 percent) gave high support to the EU and low backing for the CIS Customs Union of between 4-18 percent. In Ukraine's east, public opinion remained evenly split with 26 and 28 percent respectively backing the EU and CIS Customs Union.[1502]

## CONCLUSIONS

Asked if there could be a return to 'brotherly' relations, former Ukrainian President Kravchuk replied 'we will never (again) be brothers. It's for good.' Kravchuk cited a new poem by the well-known poet and writer Lina Kostenko that described changing attitudes towards Russia: 'Terror and blood and death and despair. The road of voracious waters. The little grey man has caused dark tribulation. He is a beast of a disgusting kind. The Loch Ness Monster of the Neva.'[1503] By the third year of the Ukrainian-Russian war, a striking 71.8 percent of Ukrainians describe Russia as an 'aggressor state' and 'party to the conflict' in the Donbas with only between 8.4-12.2 percent of Ukrainians disagreeing.[1504]

Conflicts change the national identities of countries, relations between the dominant nationality and minority groups and their attitudes towards their neighbours. Russia's annexation of the Crimea and hybrid war in the Donbas has changed, and will continue to transform, Ukrainian national identity in three ways.

Firstly, Yanukovych's violent kleptocracy and Putin's annexation of the Crimea and hybrid annexation of the Donbas has led to an implosion of the pro-Russian political camp. Ukraine's three pro-Russian political forces became marginalised (Party of Regions), lost their parliamentary representation (KPU) or are no longer based inside Ukraine (Crimean Russian nationalists). The 2014 parliamentary elections, which were held in all areas outside the Crimea and the DNR and LNR, produced a pro-European constitutional majority. The Party of Regions switched its allegiance to Putin's Unified Russia party in the September 2014 Crimean elections and a month later renamed itself the Opposition Bloc in the Ukrainian elections when it received nine percent, a dramatic decline from the 30-33 percent it received in 2006, 2007 and 2012. The KPU, which had become a Party of Regions satellite, failed to enter parliament for the first time since Ukraine became an independent state.

Secondly, growth in Ukrainian and Russian-speaking Ukrainian patriotism in central and eastern Ukraine. The number of Russian-speaking eastern Ukrainians who hold a bifurcated Russian-Ukrainian identity (with Soviet and Pan-Slavic overtones) has sharply declined. Two thirds or more of Ukrainian security forces in the ATO are Russian-speakers and they receive a large proportion of their supplies from Russian speaking civil society volunteer groups. Some volunteer battalions and *Pravy Sektor* received funding from Jewish-Ukrainian community leader, oligarch and Dnipro Governor Kolomoyskyy, and Ukraine's Russian-speaking Jewish community has repeatedly condemned Putin's misuse of the term 'fascist' to describe Euromaidan leaders.[1505]

Thirdly, divorce of Ukraine's relations with, and attitudes towards Russia. Until the 2014 crisis, anti-Russian sentiments were confined to western Ukraine but since have spread into other regions of Ukraine. A September 2014 poll found that 75 percent of Ukrainians held negative views of President Putin, the highest negative rating of any foreign politician, with only 16 percent holding a positive view.[1506] Russia's imperialistic policies towards Ukraine have negatively affected their trade and energy relations forcing Ukraine to move from a decade-long rhetoric of achieving energy independence to taking action to achieve it.

Although the Ukraine-Russia crisis is transforming Ukrainian identity, there remain two main caveats. The first is that weak Ukrainian political parties have not reached out to the population in eastern and southern Ukraine or to the large number of IDP's, leaving a political vacuum that continues to be filled by the old guard reconstituted as the Opposition Bloc, *Vidrodzhennya* and other virtual election projects established by oligarchs. The second is that Putin and other Russian nationalists will continue to harbour chauvinistic views of Ukrainians as a branch of the Russian people irrespective of what Ukrainians think. Putin believes that 'No matter what happens, or where Ukraine goes, anyway, someday we will be together (as one nation) because we are one people.'[1507] Such views of Ukrainians are not confined to Putin and it would be therefore a mistake to believe that a new Russian leader from any part of the political spectrum would change Moscow's inability to treat Ukrainian sovereignty with the equality that Russia so vehemently demands the US treats it with. The Ukrainian-Russian divorce will continue in parallel with a long-term Ukraine-Russia crisis.

The roots of Putin's war against Ukraine, Europe's biggest crisis since World War II, lie in Russia's inability to come to terms with losing an empire and its prioritisation of building supra-national structures rather than focusing on creating a Russian nation state. No Russian leader has shaped up to Ataturk who transformed the Ottoman empire into a new Turkish nation-state. Russia is the only country of the four BRIC members, the others being China, India and Brazil, that is a great power in decline and this will inevitably create future crises for the West and Europe and continued confrontation with NATO. Following Russia's aggression and hyperbole in 2014-2015, and continued confrontation beyond the Minsk accords, Ukraine's relations with Russia will never be the same again.

# INTERVIEWS CONDUCTED IN UKRAINE

## KYIV (2013-2016)

Iryna Bekeshkina, president, Democratic Initiatives Fundation

Anatoliy Rachok, director, Razumkov Ukrainian Centre for Economic and Political Studies

Yuriy Pavlenko, Razumkov Ukrainian Centre for Economic and Political Studies

Mykola Senhurovskyy, Razumkov Ukrainian Centre for Economic and Political Studies

Vitaliy Sych, editor, *Novoye Vremya*

Yuriy Lutsenko, NGO activist and General Prosecutor

Tatyana Chornovol, journalist and parliamentary deputy

Oleh Medvedev, political technologist, Petro Poroshenko bloc

Hryhoriy Nemyrya, parliamentary deputy, *Batkivshchyna* party and chairman of the parliamentary committee on human rights

Rostyslav Pavlenko, deputy head, presidential administration

Wlliam Risch, professor, Department of History, University of Georgia

Borys Tarasyuk, parliamentary deputy, *Batkivshchyna* party

Joseph Zisels, Association of Jewish Organisations and Communities of Ukraine (VAAD)

Tanya Bezruk, Association of Jewish Organisations and Communities of Ukraine (VAAD)

Valeriy Khmelko, Kyiv International Institute of Sociology (KIIS)

Yuriy Lukanov, Independent Journalists Trade Union

Andriy Kormenivskyy, Euromaidan self defence forces
Ihor Koliushko, president, Centre for Policy and Legal Reform
Volodymyr Vyatrovych, head, Ukrainian Institute of National Remembrance
Andriy Kohut, director, State Archives, Security Service of Ukraine
Vitaliy Shabunin, head, Anti-Corruption Centre NGO
Hryhoriy Perepylytsya, professor, Diplomatic Academy
Bohdan Kryklyvenko, deputy head, Ukrainian Parliamentary Commission for Human Rights

## DONETSK, DONETSK OBLAST (DECEMBER 2013)

Ihor Todorov, professor, Donetsk National University
Kyryll Cherkashyn, professor, Donetsk National University
Eugene Tarasov, head, Centre for Political Studies
Serhiy Tkachenko, head of regional branch, Committee of Voters
Tetyana Durnyeva, Committee of Voters
Serhiy Harmash, editor, *Ostrov*

## SLOVYANSK, KRAMATORSK AND MYKOLAYIVKA, DONETSK OBLAST (DECEMBER 2014)

Oksana Mikitenko, International Relief and Development
Mykhaylo Nechiporenko, head, *Khurtom Slovyansk* NGO
Alya Bytalvna, teacher, Slovyansk School
Tatyana Pavlovna, teacher, Slovyansk school
Zoya Nikolovna, headmistress, Slovyansk school
Martyros Grigorian, local activist, *Batkivshchyna* party
Denys Bihunov, head of political analysis, Slovyansk Town Council
Artur Nasibyan, Slovyansk Rotary Club
Ihor Rybalchenko, officer in charge of a *rayon* district, Slovyansk *militia*
Father Serhiy Demydovych, Christians of the Evangelical Church (Church of God)
Volodymyr Serhiyenko, director, Donmet private company, Kramatorsk
Serhiy Borozentsev, NGO activist, Kramatorsk
Olha Vychyslavivna, teacher, Kramatorsk school

## MARIUPOL AND VOLNOVAKHA, DONETSK OBLAST (APRIL 2015)

Mariya Podybaylo, head, *Novyy Mariupol* NGO and professor, Mariupol University

Vadym Dzhuvaha, *Novyy Mariupol* NGO
Ivan Kharkiv, press officer, Azov battalion
Ruslan Hanushchak, officer, Azov battalion
Olena Mokrynchuk, head, *Soldatska Poshta* NGO, Volnovakha,

## ATO, DONETSK OBLAST (MARCH and MAY 2016)

Natali Prylutska (Dziuba), ATO volunteer, Kyiv
Armen Shakharyanets, Armenian-Ukrainian local deputy, Yahotyn, and ATO volunteer
Officers and soldiers at the 93rd Guards Mechanised Brigade base, Cherkaske *rayon*, Dnipro
Ukrainian troops in the 81st, 95th, and 128th brigades, Kyiv Rus battalion and 122nd battalion (81st brigade), near Donetsk Airport, Pisky, Novhorodske, 'Promzone' (Industrial Zone), and Butivka, Avdyivka

## KHARKIV (MARCH AND OCTOBER 2014)

Oleksandr Kravchenko, professor, Kharkiv State University
Olekandr Fisun, professor, Kharkiv State University
Yulya Bidenko, professor, Kharkiv State University
Olexiy Krysenko, professor, Kharkiv State University
Viktor Kovalenko, Regional State Administration
Viktor Rud, deputy, Kharkiv City Council
Volodymyr Chystylin, deputy, Kharkiv City Council
Valeriy Dudko, political technologist, *Slobozhanshyna* Regional Centre
Iryna Abramova, Kharkiv Invest
Iryna Sklokina, NGO activist
Viktor Harbar, NGO activist
Viktoriya Sybir, NGO activist

## DNIPRO (MAY 2014)

Denis Semenov, political technologist
Oleksandr Vysotskyy, professor, National Metallurgical Academy
Volodymyr Ryzhkov, NGO activist
Volodymyr Vashchenko, NGO activist
Natalya Mykytchuk, NGO activist
Artem Ivantsiv, professor, Dnipro State University
Serhiy Shulyk, professor, Dnipro State University

Oleh Dyachok, professor, Dnipro State University
Vadym Osyn

## ZAPORIZHZHYA (DECEMBER 2015)

Volodymyr Milchev, professor, Zaporizhzhya State University
Serhiy Bilivnenko, professor, Zaporizhzhya State University
Oleksiy Shteinle, professor, Zaporizhzhya State University
Fedir Turchenko, professor, Zaporizhzhya State University
Oleksandr Dablehov, professor, Zaporizhzhya State University

## POLTAVA (DECEMBER 2015)

Oksana Kravchenko, NGO activist
Yuriy Voloshyn, professor, Poltava State University
Olha Rupnytska, journalist and ATO volunteer

## ODESA (OCTOBER 2014 and MAY 2015)

Olexiy Honcharenko, head, *oblast* council
Hennadiy Trukhanov, mayor, city council
Dmytro Spivak, deputy, city council
Inna Starchikova, head, *Moloda Hromada* NGO
Tetyana Semikop, head, Trust. Hope. Love NGO
Denys Kuzmin, professor, Odesa State University
Volodymyr Dubovyk, professor, Odesa State University
Alla Ponomarenko, head, *Alta Krayna* NGO
Mykola Shmushkovych, deputy, *oblast* council
Serhiy Nazarov, head of Odesa branch, *Hromadske* television
Vyacheslav Kasim, journalist, 7 channel
Denys Korhushev, journalist, 368 media
Anatoliy Boyko, head of regional branch, Committee of Voters
Denys Yakovlev, Dean, National University 'Odesa Law Academy'
Hryhoriy Hrinshpun, deputy, *Batkivshchyna* party
*Samoborona* volunteers
Dina Kazatsker, NGO activist
Kateryna Nozhevnikova, NGO activist

## KHERSON (MAY 2015)

Stanislav Troshin, mayor, city council

Volodymyr Mykolaenko, deputy mayor, city council
Ihor Pastukh, deputy, People's Front, city council
Mykhaylo Linetskyy, entrepreneur
Maksym Emihulaylidi, head, Civic Fund Kherson "Defence"
Dementiy Bilyy, head of local branch, Committee of Voters
Oleksandr Tokalenko, legal adviser, Committee of Voters
Ivan Antypenko, local correspondent, *Den* newspaper
Irina Snihur, editor, *Kherson Visnyk*
Olha Samolenko, journalist, *Kherson Visnyk*
Vyacheslav Gusakov, local correspondent, *Radio Svoboda*
Women volunteers, head, *Oblast* Centre for Support of the Military
Angela Lytvinenko, head, *Uspishna Zhinka* NGO
Olena Mykytas, deputy head, *Uspishna Zhinka* NGO
Kateryna Handzyuk, UN High Commissioner for Refugees (UNHCR)
Valentyna Sichova, deputy head, *oblast* state administration
Max Ieligulashvily, head, *Zahyst i Diya* NGO
Artem Kiyanovskyy, professor, School of Humanitarian Labour and deputy in the city council

## MYKOLAYIV (MAY 2015)

Oksana Yanishevska, deputy head, *oblast* state administration
Mykola Dmytriyev, *oblast* state administration
Denys Barashkovskyy, head, Centre for Anti-Corruption Research NGO
Mykhaylo Zolotukhin, head, Fund for City Development
Antonina Galkins, head, Open Platform 'New Mykolayiv'
Vik Tonkovid, journalist, *Inshe* TV
Oleksiy Omelchyk, head of the Opposition Bloc, city council
Tatyana Polishchuk, ATO volunteer
Olha Dotsenko, ATO volunteer
Inna Tokareva, ATO volunteer
Yaroslav Zakharenko, head of local branch, Democratic Alliance
Denys Plishko, Democratic Alliance activist
Svitlana Andryeyeva, Democratic Alliance activist

# FURTHER READING

## 1. EUROMAIDAN REVOLUTION

Bezruk, Tatiana, 'On the Same Side of the Barricades. Observations Concerning Radical Rightists and Leftists on Kiev's Euromaidan,' *Russian Politics and Law*, vol. 53, no. 3 (May-June 2015), pp. 97–104.

Blacker, Uilleam, 'Martyrdom, Spectacle, and Public Space in Ukraine: Ukraine's National Martyrology from Shevchenko to the Maidan,' *Journal of Soviet and Post-Soviet Politics and Society*, vol.2, no.2 (2016), pp. 257-292.

Chupyra, Olga, 'Civic Protest. Version 2.0. Maidan 2013 –2014 as a Catalyst of Russian-Speaking Ukrainian Patriotism,' *Russian Politics and Law*, vol. 53, no. 3 (May-June 2015), pp. 86–96.

Cybriwsky, Roman, 'Kyiv's Maidan: from Duma Square to sacred space,' *Eurasian Geography and Economics*, vol. 55, no. 3 (May 2015), pp.270–285.

Erpyleva, Svetlana, 'Freedom's children in protest movements: Private and public in the socialization of young Russian and Ukrainian activists,' *Current Sociology* (2017).

Gruzd, Anatoliy and Tsyganova, Ksenia, 'Information Wars and Online Activism During the 2013/2014 Crisis in Ukraine: Examining the Social Structures of Pro- and Anti-Maidan Groups,' *Policy and Internet*, vol.7, no.2 (June 2015), pp.121-158.

Khmelko, Irina and Pereguda, Yevgen, 'An Anatomy of Mass Protests: The Orange Revolution and Euromaydan Compared,' *Communist and Post-Communist Studies*, vol.47, no.2 (June 2014) pp.227-236.

Khromeychuk, Olesya, 'Negotiating Protest Spaces on the Maidan: A Gender Perspective,' *Journal of Soviet and Post-Soviet Politics and Society*, vol.2, no.1 (2015), pp.9-48.

Kurkov, Andrey, *Ukraine Diaries. Dispatches from Kiev* (London: Harvill Secker, 2014).

Kuzio, Taras, 'The Orange and Euromaidan Revolutions: Theoretical and Comparative Perspectives,' *Kyiv-Mohyla Law and Politics Journal*, no.2 (2016), pp.91-115. http://kmlpj.ukma.edu.ua/article/view/88183/83977

Kuzio, T., 'Ukraine's Other War: The Rule of Law and Siloviki After the Euromaidan Revolution,' *Journal of Slavic Military Studies*, vol.30, no.1 (December 2016), pp. 681-706.

Macdonald, Euan, Bonner, Brian, Shevchenko, Daryna, Grytsenko, Oksana, Quinn, Allison, Sukhov, Oleh, Lavrov, Vlad, *Ukraine: Witness to Revolution: How Kyiv Post journalists saw EuroMaidan* (Kyiv: Kyiv Post, March 2016).

Metzger, M. Megan, Bonneaub, Richard, Nagler, Jonathan, and Tucker, A. Joshua, 'Tweeting identity? Ukrainian, Russian, and #Euromaidan,' *Journal of Comparative Economics*, vol.44, no.1 (February 2016), pp.16–40.

Marples, David, and Mills V. Frederick eds., *Ukraine's Euromaidan. Analyses of a Civil Revolution* (Stuttgart: Ibidem Verlag and Columbia University Press, 2015).

Martsenyuk, Tamara, 'Sexuality and Revolution in Post-Soviet Ukraine: LGBT Rights and the Euromaidan Protests of 2013–2014,' *Journal of Soviet and Post-Soviet Politics and Society*, vol.2, no.1 (2016), pp.49-74.

Minakov, Mikhail, 'Utopian Images of the West and Russia Among Supporters and Opponents of the Euromaidan. Elements of Ideological Framing of the Conflict in Ukraine in 2013 –2014,' *Russian Politics and Law*, vol. 53, no. 3 (May-June 2015), pp. 68–85.

Moussienko, Natalia, 'Art and Revolution: Kyiv Maidan of 2013-2014' in Viktor Stepanenko and Yaroslav Pylynskyi eds., *Ukraine after the Euromaidan. Challenges and Hopes* (Bern: Peter Lang, 2015), pp.257-264.

http://commonweb.unifr.ch/artsdean/pub/gestens/f/as/files/4760/39746_152121.pdf

Onuch, Olga, 'Who were the Protesters?' *Journal of Democracy*, vol.25, no.3 (July 2014), pp.44-51.

Onuch, O., 'EuroMaidan Protests in Ukraine: Social Media Versus Social Networks,' *Problems of Post-Communism*, vol.62, no.4 (July 2015), pp.217-235.

Onuch, O., 'Facebook Helped Me Do It': Understanding the Euromaidan Protestor Tool-Kit,' *Studies in Ethnicity and Nationalism*, vol.15, no.1 (April 2015), pp.170-184.

Onuch, O. & Sasse, Gwendolyn, 'The Maidan in Movement: Diversity and the Cycles of Protest,' *Europe-Asia Studies*, vol. 68, no. 4 (June 2016), pp.556-587.

Philips, D. Sarah, 'The Women's Squad in Ukraine's protests: Feminism, nationalism, and militarism on the Maidan,' *American Ethnologist*, vol. 41, no. 3 (August 2014), pp. 414–426.

Poltorakov, Aleksey, 'The Functional Dynamic of Ukraine's "Maidan" (November 2013 – January 2014),' *Russian Politics and Law*, vol. 53, no. 3 (May-June 2015), pp. 28–36.

Popova, Maria, 'Why the Orange Revolution Was Short and Peaceful and Euromaidan Long and Violent,' *Problems of Post-Communism*, vol.61, no.6 (November 2015), pp.64-70.

Pop-Eleches, Grigore and Robertson, Graeme, 'After the Revolution,' *Problems of Post Communism*, vol.61, no.4 (July 2014), pp.2-22.

Portnov, Andriy and Portnova, Tetiana, 'The Ukrainian "Eurorevolution": Dynamics and Meaning' in V. Stepanenko and Y. Pylynskyi eds., *Ukraine after the Euromaidan*, pp.59-72.

Reznik, Oleksandr, 'From the Orange Revolution to the Revolution of Dignity: Dynamics of the Protest Actions in Ukraine,' *East European Politics and Societies and Cultures*, vol. 30, no.4 (November 2016), pp. 750–765.

Riabova, Tatiana, "Gayromaidan": Gendered Aspects of the Hegemonic Russian Media Discourse on the Ukrainian Crisis,' *Journal of Soviet and Post-Soviet Politics and Society*, vol.1, no.1 (2015), pp.83-108.

Shestakovskii, Aleksey, 'Radicalized Europeans? The Values of Euromaidan Participants and Prospects for the Development of Society,' *Russian Politics and Law*, vol. 53, no. 3 (May-June 2015), pp. 37–67.

Shulga, Olexander, 'Consequences of the Maidan: War of Symbols, Real War and Nation Building' in V. Stepanenko and Y. Pylynskyi eds., *Ukraine after the Euromaidan*, pp.231-241.

Shveda, Yuriy and Park, Ho Joung, 'Ukraine's revolution of dignity: The dynamics of Euromaidan,' *Journal of Eurasian Studies*, vol. 5, no.2 (July 2014), pp.107-115.

Shveda, Y., 'The Revolution of Dignity in the Context of Theory of Social Revolutions' in V. Stepanenko and Y. Pylynskyi eds., *Ukraine after the Euromaidan*, pp.83-96.

Sklokina, Iryna, 'Veterans of the Soviet–Afghan War and the Ukrainian Nation-Building Project: From Perestroika to the Maidan and the War in the Donbas,' *Journal of Soviet and Post-Soviet Politics and Society*, vol.2, no.2 (2016), pp.133-168.

Stepanenko, V., 'Ukraine's Revolution as De-Institutionalisation of the Post-Soviet Order' in V. Stepanenko and Y. Pylynskyi eds., *Ukraine after the Euromaidan*, pp.29-46.

Stepanenko, V. and Pylynskyi, Y., 'Ukraine's Revolution: The National Historical Context and the New Challenges for the Country and the World' in V. Stepanenko and Y. Pylynskyi eds., *Ukraine after the Euromaidan*, pp.11-28.

Stepanenko, V. and Pylynskyi, Y. eds., *Ukraine after the Euromaidan*.

Umland, Andreas and Shekhovtsov, Anton, 'Ukraine's Radical Right,' *Journal of Democracy*, vol. 25, no. 3 (July 2014), pp. 58 – 63.

Mierzejewski-Voznyak, Melanie G., 'Party politics after the colour revolutions: party institutionalisation and democratisation in Ukraine and Georgia,' *East European Politics*, vol.30, no.1 (January 2014), pp.86-104.

Way, Lucan, 'Civil Society and Democratization,' *Journal of Democracy*, vol.25, no.3 (July 2014), pp.35-43.

Wilson, Andrew, *Ukraine Crisis. What it Means for the West* (New Haven, CT: Yale University Press, 2015).

## 2. RUSSIA AS THE VICTIM: EU AND NATO ENLARGEMENT AND REALISM

Becker, E. Michael, Cohen, S. Matthew, Kushi, Sidita and McManus, P. Ian, 'Reviving the Russian empire: The Crimean intervention through a neo-classical realist lens,' *European Security*, vol.25, no.1 (January 2015), pp.112-133.

Bennett, Kirk, 'The Realist Case for Arming Ukraine,' *The American Interest*, 20 February 2015. http://www.the-american-interest.com/2015/02/20/the-realist-case-for-arming-ukraine/

Bennett, K., 'Condemned to Frustration. What Russia wants, the West simply cannot deliver,' *The American Interest*, 1 April 2016. http://www.the-american-interest.com/2016/04/01/condemned-to-frustration/

Boyd-Barrett, Oliver, *Western Mainstream Media and the Ukraine Crisis. A Study in Conflict Propaganda* (London: Routledge, 2017).

Charap, Samuel and Troitskiy, Mikhail, 'Russia, the West and the Integration Dilemma,' *Survival*, vol.55, no.6 (December 2013), pp.49-62.

Charap, S., 'The Ukraine Impasse,' *Survival*, vol.56, no.5 (September 2014), pp.225-232.

Charap, S. and Darden, Keith, 'Russia and Ukraine,' *Survival*, vol.56, no.2 (March 2014), pp.7-14.

Götz, Elias, 'Neorealism and Russia's Ukraine policy, 1991–present,' *Contemporary Politics*, vol.22, no.3 (July 2016), pp.301-323.

Kanet E. Roger and Sussex, Matthew eds., *Power, politics and confrontation in Eurasia: Foreign policy in a contested region* (New York: Palgrave Macmillan, 2015).

Larson, W. Deborah and Shevchenko, Alexei, 'Russia Says No: Power, Status and Emotions in Foreign Policy,' *Communist and Post-Communist Studies*, vol.11, nos.3-4 (September 2014), pp.269-279.

Lucas, Edward, 'The Realism We need. The Cold War is Not Over,' *First Things*, 4 October 2016. https://www.firstthings.com/web-exclusives/2016/10/the-realism-we-need

MacFarlane, S. Neil, 'Kto Vinovat? Why is there a crisis in Russia's relations with the West?' *Contemporary Politics*, vol.22, no.3 (July 2016), pp.342-358.

McFaul, Michael, 'Moscow's Choice,' *Foreign Affairs*, vol.93, no.6 (November-December 2014), pp.167-171.

Motyl, J. Alexander, 'The surrealism of realism: Misreading the war in Ukraine,' *World Affairs*, vol.177, no.5 (January-February 2015), pp.75–84. http://www.worldaffairsjournal.org/article/surrealism-realism-misreading-war-ukraine

Mearsheimer, J. John, 'Why the Ukraine Crisis is the West's Fault,' *Foreign Affairs*, vol.93, no.5 (September-October 2014), pp.77-89.

Menon, Rajan, and Rumer, Eugene, *Conflict in Ukraine. The Unwinding of the Post-Cold War Order* (Cambridge, MA: MIT Press, 2015).

Nimmo, Ben, *Backdating the Blame. How Russia Made NATO a Party to the Ukraine Conflict*, (Riga: NATO Strategic Communications, Centre of Excellence, 2016). http://www.stratcomcoe.org/backdating-blame-how-russia-made-nato-party-ukraine-conflict-author-ben-nimmo

Owen M. John and Inboden, William, 'Putin, Ukraine and the Question of Realism,' *The Hedgehog Review* (Spring 2015), pp.87-96. http://iasc-culture.org/THR/channels/THR/2015/03/putin-ukraine-and-the-question-of-realism/

Pänke, Julian, 'The Fallout of the EU's Normative Imperialism in the Eastern Neighbourhood,' *Problems of Post-Communism*, vol.62, no.6 (November 2015), pp.350-363.

Robertshaw, Sam, 'Why the EU got the Ukraine crisis wrong,' *Global Affairs*, vol.1, no.3 (2015), pp.335-343.

Rynning, Sten, 'The false promise of continental concert: Russia, the West and the necessary balance of power,' *International Affairs* vol.91, no.3 (May 2015), pp. 539-552.

Sakwa, Richard, *Frontline Ukraine. Crisis in the Borderlands* (London: I. B. Tauris, 2016).

## 3. RUSSIA IN GEOPOLITICAL COMPETITION: EU, SANCTIONS, INTERNATIONAL LAW AND NON-PROLIFERATION

Allison, Roy, 'Russian 'deniable' intervention in Ukraine: how and why Russia broke the rules,' *International Affairs,* vol. 90, no.6 (November 2014), pp. 1255-1297.

Auer, Stefan, 'Carl Schmitt in the Kremlin: The Ukraine crisis and the return of geopolitics,' *International Affairs*, vol. 91, no. 5 (September 2015), pp.953–968.

Averre, Derek, 'The Ukraine Conflict: Russia's Challenge to European Security Governance,' *Europe-Asia Studies*, vol. 68, no. 4 (June 2016), pp. 699–725.

Bechev, Dimitar, 'Understanding the Contest Between the EU and Russia in Their Shared Neighbourhood,' *Problems of Post-Communism*, vol. 62, no.6 (December 2015), pp.340–349.

Braun, Aurel, 'Tougher sanctions now: Putin's delusional quest for empire,' *World Affairs*, vol.177, no.2, (July-August 2014), pp.34–42. http://www.worldaffairsjournal.org/article/tougher-sanctions-now-putin%E2%80%99s-delusional-quest-empire

Burke-White, W. William, *Crimea and the International Legal Order* (Penn Law: University of Pennsylvania Law School, Legal Scholarship Repository, 2014). http://scholarship.law.upenn.edu/cgi/viewcontent.cgi?article=2360&context=faculty_scholarship

Burlyuk, Olga, 'Same End, Different Means: The Evolution of Poland's Support for Ukraine at the European Level,' *East European Politics and Societies and Cultures*, (2017).

Cadier, David, 'Eastern Partnership vs Eurasian Union? The EU–Russia Competition in the Shared Neighbourhood and the Ukraine Crisis,' *Global Policy*, vol. 5, Supplement 1 (October 2014), pp.76-85.

Casier, Tom, 'From logic of competition to conflict: understanding the dynamics of EU–Russia relations,' *Contemporary Politics*, vol.22, no.3 (July 2016), pp.376-394.

Cross, Sharyl, 'NATO–Russia security challenges in the aftermath of Ukraine conflict: managing Black Sea security and beyond,' *Southeast European and Black Sea Studies*, vol. 15, no. 2 (April 2015), pp.151–177.

Cross, K.D. Mai'a, and Korolewski, P. Ireneusz, 'What Type of Power has the EU Exercised in the Ukraine-Russia Crisis? A Framework of Analysis,' *Journal of Common Market Studies*, vol.55, no.1 (January 2017), pp.3-19.

Daalder, Ivo, Flournoy, Michele, Herbst, John, Lodal, Jan, Pifer, Steve, Stavridis, James, Talbott, Strobe, Wald, Charles, *Preserving Ukraine's Independence, Resisting Russian Aggression: What the United States and NATO Must Do* (Washington DC: Brookings Institution and Atlantic Council of the US, 2015). http://www.brookings.edu/research/reports/2015/02/ukraine-independence-russian-aggression

D'Anieri, Paul, 'Democracy and Geopolitics: Understanding Ukraine's Threat to Russia' in Agnieszka Pikulicka-Wilczewska and R. Sakwa eds., *Ukraine and Russia: People, Politics, Propaganda and Perspectives* (Bristol: E-International Relations, March 2015), pp.233-241. http://www.e-ir.info/wp-content/uploads/2015/03/Ukraine-and-Russia-E-IR.pdf

Davies, Lance, 'Russia's 'Governance' Approach: Intervention and the Conflict in the Donbas,' *Europe-Asia Studies*, vol. 68, no. 4 (June 2016), pp. 726–749.

Delcour, Laure, 'Between the Eastern Partnership and Eurasian Integration: Explaining Post-Soviet Countries' Engagement in (Competing) Region-Building Projects,' *Problems of Post-Communism*, vol.62, no.6 (November 2015), pp.316-327.

Ditrych, Ondrej, 'Bracing for Cold Peace. US-Russia Relations after Ukraine,' *The International Spectator*, vol.49, no.4 (December 2014), pp.76-96.

Dragneva, Rilka and Wolczuk, Kataryna, *Ukraine Between the EU and Russia. The Integration Challenge* (London: Palgrave Macmillan, 2015).

Dragneva, R. and Wolczuk, K., Between Dependence and Integration: Ukraine's Relations with Russia,' *Europe-Asia Studies*, vol. 68, no. 4 (June 2016), pp. 678-698.

Dreyer, Iana, and Popescu, Nicu, *Do sanctions against Russia work?*, Brief 35, (Paris: European Union Institute for Security Studies, 2014). http://www.iss.europa.eu/uploads/media/Brief_35_Russia_sanctions.pdf.

Einhorn, Robert, 'Ukraine, Security Assurances, and Non-Proliferation,' *The Washington Quarterly*, vol.38, no.1 (January 2015), pp.47-72.

Fitzpatrick, Mark, 'The Ukraine Crisis and Nuclear Order,' *Survival*, vol. 56, no. 4 (August–September 2014), pp. 81–90.

Freedman, Lawrence, 'Ukraine and the Art of Crisis Management,' *Survival*, vol. 56, no. 3 (June–July 2014), pp. 7–42

Fursov, Andrey, 'Thirty Days That Changed the World,' *Russian Politics and Law*, vol. 53, no. 1 (January-February 2015), pp. 47–72.

Giles, Keir, Hanson, Philip, Lyne, Roderic, Nixey, James, Sherr, James, and Wood, Andrew, eds., *The Russian Challenge, Chatham House Report* (London: Royal Institute for International Affairs, June 2015). https://www.chathamhouse.org/sites/files/chatham-house/field/field_document/20150605RussianChallengeGilesHanson-LyneNixeySherrWood.pdf

Götz, E., 'It's Geopolitics, stupid: explaining Russia's Ukraine policy,' *Global Affairs*, vol.1, no.1 (2015), pp.3-10.

Götz, E., 'Russia, the west, and the Ukraine crisis: three contending perspectives,' *Contemporary Politics*, vol.22, no.3 (July 2016), pp.249-266.

Götz, E., 'Putin, the State, and War: The Causes of Russia's Near Abroad Assertion Revisited,' *International Studies Review*, vol.18, no.4 (December 2016).

Grant, D. Thomas, *Aggression against Ukraine Territory, Responsibility, and International Law* (London: Palgrave Macmillan, 2015).

Grant, T.D., 'International Dispute Settlement in Response to an Unlawful Seizure of Territory: Three Mechanisms,' *Chicago Journal of International Law*, vol.16, no.1 (Summer 2015), pp.1-42.

Gretskiy, Igor, Treshchenkov, Evgeny and Golubev, Konstantin, 'Russia's perceptions and misperceptions of the EU Eastern Partnership,' *Communist and Post-Communist Studies*, vol.47, nos.3-4 (September 2014), pp.375-383.

Hamilton, S. Daniel and Meister, Stefan eds., *The Eastern Question. Russia, the West, and Europe's Grey Zone* (Washington DC: Center for Transatlantic Relations, Johns Hopkins University, 2016). http://www.bosch-stiftung.de/content/language1/downloads/The_Eastern_Question.pdf

Haukkala, Hiski, 'From Cooperative to Contested Europe? The Conflict in Ukraine as a Culmination of a Long- Term Crisis in EU–Russia Relations,' *Journal of Contemporary European Studies*, vol. 23, no. 1 (January 2015), pp.25–40.

Haukkala, H., 'A Perfect Storm; Or What Went Wrong and What Went Right for the EU in Ukraine,' *Europe-Asia Studies,* vol. 68, no. 4 (June 2016), pp.653-664.

Howorth, Jolyon, 'Stability on the Borders': The Ukraine Crisis and the EU's Constrained Policy Towards the Eastern Neighbourhood,' *Journal of Common Market Studies*, vol.55, no.1 (January 2017), pp.121-136.

Hansen, S. Flemming, 'Russia's relations with the West: ontological security through conflict,' *Contemporary Politics*, vol.22, no.3 (July 2016), pp.359-375.

Kagan, Robert, *Backing Into World War III, Foreign Policy*, 6 February 2017. http://foreignpolicy.com/2017/02/06/backing-into-world-war-iii-russia-china-trump-obama/

Kazharski, Aliaksei and Makarychev, Andrey, 'Suturing the Neighbourhood? Russia and the EU in Conflictual Intersubjectivity,' *Problems of Post-Communism*, vol. 62, no.6 (December 2015), pp. 328–339.

Korolewski, I.P., and Cross, M. K. D., 'The EU's Power in the Russia-Ukraine Crisis: Enabled or Constrained?' *Journal of Common Market Studies*, vol.55, no.1 (January 2017), pp.137-152.

Kostanyan, Hrant and Meister, S., *Ukraine, Russia and the EU. Breaking the deadlock in the Minsk process*, CEPS Working Document 423 (Brussels, Centre for European Policy Reform, 9 June 2016). https://www.ceps.eu/publications/ukraine-russia-and-eu-breaking-deadlock-minsk-process

Krastev, Ivan and Leonard, Mark, *The new European disorder* (London: European Council on Foreign Relations, November 2014). http://www.ecfr.eu/page/-/ECFR117_TheNewEuropeanDisorder_ESSAY.pdf

Kriskovic, Andrej, 'Imperial Nostalgia or Prudent Geopolitics? Russia's Efforts to Reintegrate the Post-Soviet Space in Geopolitical Perspective,' *Post-Soviet Affairs*, vol.30, no.6 (November 2014), pp.503-528.

Kundnani, Hans, 'Germany Looks East,' *Foreign Affairs,* vol.94, no.1 (January-February 2015), pp. 108-116.

Kuzio, T., 'Ukraine between a Constrained EU and Assertive Russia,' *Journal of Common Market Studies*, vol.55, no.1 (January 2017), pp.103-120.

Latynina, Yulia, 'A New World Order,' *Russian Politics and Law*, vol. 53, no. 1 (January-February 2015), pp. 73–80.

Makarychev, A., 'A New European Disunity: EU-Russia Ruptures and the Crisis in the Common Neighbourhood,' *Problems of Post-Communism*, vol.62, no.6 (November 2015), pp.313-315.

Makarychev, A., and Yatsyk, Alexandra, eds., *Vocabularies of International Relations after the Crisis in Ukraine* (London: Routledge, 2017).

Marinov, Nikolay, 'Sanctions and Democracy,' *International Interactions*, vol.41 no.4 (August 2015), pp.765-778.

Mead, R. Walter, 'Geopolitics are back. The revenge of the revisionist powers,' *Foreign Affairs*, vol.93, no.3 (May-June 2014), pp.69-79.

Middelaar, van Luuk, 'The Return of Politics – The European Union after the crises in the eurozone and Ukraine,' *Journal of Common Market Studies*, vol.54, no.3 (May 2016), pp. 495–507.

Natorski, Michal, and Pomorska, Karolina, 'Trust and Decision-Making in Times of Crisis: The EU's Response to the Events in Ukraine,' *Journal of Common Market Studies*, vol.55, no.1 (January 2017), pp.54-70.

Neuwirth, J. Rostam and Svetlicinii, Alexandr, 'The current EU/US–Russia conflict over Ukraine and the WTO: a preliminary note on (trade) restrictive measures,' *Post-Soviet Affairs*, vol.32, no.3 (May 2015), pp. 237-271.

Nitoiu, Cristian and Sus, Monika, 'The EP's Diplomacy – a Tool for Projecting EU Power in Times of Crisis? The Case of the Cox–Kwasniewski

Mission,' *Journal of Common Market Studies*, vol.55, no.1 (January 2017), pp.71-86.

Novaky, I.M. Niklas, 'Why so Soft? The European Union in Ukraine,' *Contemporary Security Policy*, vol.36, no.2 (May 2015), pp.244–266.

Orenstein, A. Mitchell, and Kelemen R. Daniel, 'Trojan Horses in EU Foreign Policy,' *Journal of Common Market Studies*, vol.55, no.1 (January 2017), pp.87-102.

Orlov, Vladimir, 'Security Assurances to Ukraine and the 1994 Budapest Memorandum: from the 1990s to the Crimea Crisis,' *Security Index*, vol.20, no.2 (April 2014), pp.133-140.

Pond, Elizabeth, 'Will Ukraine snatch defeat from the jaws of victory?' *Survival*, vol.57, no.6 (November 2015), pp.59–68.

Romanova, Tatiana, 'Sanctions and the Future of EU–Russian Economic Relations,' *Europe-Asia Studies*, vol. 68, no. 4 (June 2016), pp.774-796.

Rutland, Peter, 'An Unnecessary War: The Geopolitical Roots of the Ukrainian Crisis' in A. Pikulicka-Wilczewska and R. Sakwa eds., *Ukraine and Russia: People, Politics, Propaganda and Perspectives*, pp.129-140.

Schilde, Kaija, 'European Military Capabilities: Enablers and Constraints on EU Power?' *Journal of Common Market Studies*, vol.55, no.1 (January 2017), pp.37-53.

Sherr, J., *The New East-West Discord. Russian Objectives, Western Interests, Clingendael Report* (The Hague: Netherlands Institute of International Relations, December 2015). https://www.clingendael.nl/sites/default/files/The_New_East-West_Discord_JSherr.pdf

Siddi, Marco, 'German Foreign Policy towards Russia in the Aftermath of the Ukraine Crisis: A New Ostpolitik?' *Europe-Asia Studies*, vol. 68, no. 4 (June 2016), pp. 665–677.

Sjursen, Helene, and Rosen, Guri, 'Arguing Sanctions. On the EU's Response to the Crisis in Ukraine,' *Journal of Common Market Studies*, vol.55, no.1 (January 2017), pp.20-36.

Smith, R., Nicholas, 'The EU and Russia's conflicting regime preferences in Ukraine: assessing regime promotion strategies in the scope of the Ukraine crisis,' *European Security*, vol.24, no.4 (October 2015, pp.525-540.

Stulberg, N. Adam, 'Out of Gas? Russia, Ukraine, Europe and the Changing Geopolitics of Natural Gas,' *Problems of Post-Communism*, vol.62, no.2 (March 2015), pp.112-130.

Wolff, T., Andrew, 'The future of NATO enlargement after the Ukraine crisis,' *International Affairs*, vol.91, no.5 (September 2015), pp.1103–1121.

Vysotskaya, Alena and Vieira, Guedes, 'Ukraine's Crisis and Russia's Closest Allies: A Reinforced Intra-Alliance Security Dilemma at Work,' *The International Spectator*, vol.49, no.4 (December 2014), pp.97-111.

Yost, S. David., 'The Budapest Memorandum and Russia's intervention in Ukraine,' *The International Spectator*, vol.49, no.4 (December 2014), pp.62-75.

## 4. RUSSIA THE TROUBLEMAKER: FROZEN CONFLICTS, THE CRIMEA, IMPERIALISM AND EMPIRE

*A Brief History of the Ukrainian Conflict from the Sky: Using historical satellite imagery to understand the war in the Donbas, pre-Minsk I* (Washington DC: Digital Forensic Research Lab, 24 January 2017). https://medium.com/@DFRLab/a-brief-history-of-the-ukrainian-conflict-from-the-sky-part-i-381d229018af#.zazhzq2yy

Astapenia, Ryhor and Balkunets, Dzmitry, *Belarus-Russia Relations after the Ukraine Conflict*, Analytical Paper 5 (Minsk-London: Ostrogorski Centre, 1 August 2016). http://belarusdigest.com/papers/belarus-russia-relations.pdf

Bacon, Edwin, 'Putin's Crimea Speech, 18 March 2014: Russia's Changing Public Political Narrative,' *Journal of Soviet and Post-Soviet Politics and Society*, vol.1, no.1 (2015), pp.13-36.

Bari Urcosta, Ridvan, and Abalkin, Lev, *Crimea: Russia's stronghold in the Black Sea* (London: European Council on Foreign Relations, 1 September 2016). http://www.ecfr.eu/article/essay_crimea_russias_stronghold_in_the_black_sea

Biersack, John, & O'Lear, Shannon, 'The geopolitics of Russia's annexation of Crimea: narratives, identity, silences, and energy,' *Eurasian Geography and Economics*, vol. 55, no.3 (May 2014), pp.247-269.

Bugajski, Janusz, and Assenova, Margarita, *Eurasian Disunion. Russia's Vulnerable Flanks* (Washington DC: Jamestown Foundation, June 2016). https://jamestown.org/wp-content/uploads/2016/06/Eurasian-Disunion2.pdf

Byzov, L. Leontii, 'National Consensus or Social Anomaly?' On the Peculiarities of Mass Consciousness in "Post-Crimean" Russia,' *Russian Politics and Law*, vol. 54, no. 1 (January-February 2016), pp. 55–73.

Connolly, Richard, 'The Empire Strikes Back: Economic Statecraft and the Securitisation of Political Economy in Russia,' *Europe-Asia Studies*, vol. 68, no. 4 (June 2016), pp.750-773.

*Crimea in the Dark. The Silencing of Dissent.* EUR 50/5330/2016 (London: Amnesty International, 15 December 2016). https://www.amnesty.org/en/documents/eur50/5330/2016/en/

Danylov, Sergey, 'Crimean Tatar's National Institutes under the Occupation: The Case of the Muftiyat of Crimea' in V. Stepanenko and Y. Pylynskyi eds., *Ukraine after the Euromaidan*, pp.193-202.

Delcour, L. and Wolczuk, K., 'Spoiler or facilitator of democratization? Russia's role in Georgia and Ukraine,' *Democratization*, vol. 22, no. 3 (April 2015), pp.459–478.

Grigas, Agnia, *Beyond Crimea: The New Russian Empire* (New Haven, CT: Yale University Press, 2016).

Grigas, A. *Frozen Conflicts. A Tool Kit for US Policymakers* (Washington DC: Atlantic Council of the US, July 2016). http://www.atlanticcouncil.org/images/publications/Frozen_Conflicts_web_0715.pdf

Flemming Splidsboel, Hansen, 'Framing yourself into a corner: Russia, Crimea, and the minimal action space,' *European Security*, vol.24, no.1 (January 2015), pp.141-158.

Karagiannis, Emmanuel, 'The Russian Interventions in South Ossetia and Crimea Compared: Military Performance, Legitimacy and Goals,' *Contemporary Security Policy*, vol.35, no.3 (September 2014), pp.400–420.

Klymenko, Andriy, *The Militarization of Crimea under Russian Occupation* (Washington DC: Atlantic Council of the US, October 2015). http://www.atlanticcouncil.org/images/publications/The_Militarization_of_Crimea_under_Russian_Occupation.pdf

Krastev, I. 'Russian revisionism: Putin's plan for overturning the European order,' *Foreign Affairs*, 3 March 2014. https://www.foreignaffairs.com/articles/russia-fsu/2014-03-03/russian-revisionism

Krastev, I. and Leonard, M. 'Europe's Shattered Dream of Order. How Putin is Disrupting the Atlantic Alliance,' *Foreign Affairs*, vol.94, no.3, (May-June 2015), pp. 48-58.

Kuzio, T., *Ukraine-Crimea-Russia: Triangle of Conflict, Soviet and Post-Soviet Politics and Society series* (Hannover: Ibidem-Verlag, 2007).

Kuzio, T. *The Crimea: Europe's Next Flashpoint?* (Washington DC: The Jamestown Foundation, November 2010).

Lukanov, Fyodor, 'Putin's Foreign Policy. The Quest to Restore Russia's Rightful Place,' *Foreign Affairs*, vol.95, no.3 (May-June 2016), pp.30-37.

Magocsi, R. Paul, *This Blessed Land: Crimea and the Crimean Tatars* (Toronto: University of Toronto Press 2014).

Malinova, Olga, 'Obsession with status and resentment: Historical backgrounds of the Russian discursive identity construction,' *Communist and Post-Communist Studies*, vol.47, nos. 3-4, (September 2014), pp.291-303.

Malyarenko, Tetyana and Galbreath, J. David, 'Crimea: Competing Self-Determination Movements and the Politics at the Centre,' *Europe-Asia Studies*, vol.65, no.5 (July 2013), pp.912-928.

Matsuzato, Kimitaka 'Domestic Politics in Crimea, 2009-2015,' *Demokratizatsiya*, vol. 24, no. 2 (Spring 2016), pp.225-256.

*Ongoing Human Rights and Security Violations in Russian-Occupied Crimea* (Washington DC: Commission on Security and Cooperation in Europe, 10 November 2016). https://www.csce.gov/sites/helsinkicommission.house.gov/files/Crimea%20Briefing%20Transcript%202016.pdf

Petrov, Nikolai. 'Chronology of the Transformation of the Crimean Peninsula into a Russian Region,' *Russian Politics and Law*, vol. 54, no. 1 (2016), pp.96-105.

Petrov, N. 'Crimea Transforming the Ukrainian Peninsula into a Russian Island,' *Russian Politics and Law*, vol.54, no.1 (January-February 2016), pp.74-95.

Plokhy, Serhiy, 'The City of Glory: Sevastopol in Russian Historical Mythology,' *Journal of Contemporary History*, vol.35, no.3 (July 2000), pp.369-384.

Rácz, András and Moshes, Arkady, *Not Another Transnistria. How sustainable is separatism in Eastern Ukraine?* FIIA Analysis 4 (Helsinki: Finnish Institute of International Affairs, 1 December 2014). http://www.fiia.fi/en/publication/456/not_another_transnistria/

Rácz, A. *Russia's Hybrid War in Ukraine: Breaking the Enemy's Ability to Resist*, FIIA Report 43 (Helsinki: Finnish Institute of International Affairs, 16 June 2015). http://www.fiia.fi/en/publication/514/russia_s_hybrid_war_in_ukraine/

Rogov, Kirill, 'Crimean Syndrome" Mechanisms of Authoritarian Mobilization,' *Russian Politics and Law*, vol. 54, no. 1 (January-February 2016), pp. 28–54.

Sasse, G., *The Crimea Question. Identity, Transition, and Conflict* (Cambridge, MA: Harvard University Press, 2007).

Smirnov, Mikhail, 'Like a Sack of Potatoes: Who Transferred the Crimean Oblast to the Ukrainian SSR in 1952– 54 and How It Was Done,' *Russian Politics and Law*, vol. 53, no. 2 (March-April 2015), pp. 32–46.

Suslov, D. Mikhail, '"Crimea Is Ours!" Russian popular geopolitics in the new media age,' *Eurasian Geography and Economics*, vol.55, no.6 (November 2014), pp.588-609.

Teper, Yuri, 'Official Russian identity discourse in the light of the annexation of the Crimea: national or imperial?' *Post Soviet Affairs*, vol. 32, no.4 (July 2016), pp. 378-396.

Tsygankov, Andrey, 'Assessing Cultural and Regime-Based Explanations of Russian Foreign Policy: Authoritarian at Heart and Expansionist by Nature?' *Europe-Asia Studies*, vol.64, no.4 (June 2012), pp.695-713.

Tsygankov, A. *Russia and the West from Alexander to Putin: Honor in International Relations* (Cambridge: Cambridge University Press, 2012).

Tsygankov, A. 'Vladimir Putin's last stand: the sources of Russia's Ukraine Policy, *Post-Soviet Affairs*, vol.31, no.4 (July 2015), pp. 279-303.

Uehling, Greta, 'Everyday Life After Annexation: The Autonomous Republic of Crimea' in A. Pikulicka-Wilczewska and R. Sakwa eds., *Ukraine and Russia: People, Politics, Propaganda and Perspectives*, pp.69-79.

Urnov, Mark, 'Greatpowerness' as the key element of Russian self-consciousness under erosion,' *Communist and Post-Communist Studies*, vol.47, nos.3-4 (September 2014), pp.305-322.

## 5. RUSSIA AS THE AGGRESSOR: MILITARY, HYBRID AND INFORMATION WAR

*APT28: A Window into Russia's Cyber Espionage Operations?* (Milpitas, CA: Fire Eye, December 2016). https://www2.fireeye.com/rs/fireye/images/rpt-apt28.pdf

Artillerymen of Russia's 136th Motorized Infantry Brigade in the Donbass, *Report by Bellingcat*, 13 November 2015. https://www.bellingcat.com/news/uk-and-europe/2015/11/13/136-brigade-in-donbass/

Bonch-Osmolovskaya, Tatiana, 'Combating the Russian State Propaganda Machine: Strategies of Information Resistance,' *Journal of Soviet and Post-Soviet Politics and Society*, vol.1, no.1 (2015), pp.175-218.

Case, Sean, Putin's Undeclared War: Summer 2014 – Russian Artillery Strikes against Ukraine, *Report by Bellingcat*, 21 December 2016. https://www.bellingcat.com/news/uk-and-europe/2016/12/21/russian-artillery-strikes-against-ukraine/

Chunan, L. Anne, 'Historical aspirations and the domestic politics of Russia's pursuit of international status,' *Communist and Post-Communist Studies*, vol.47, nos.3-4 (September 2014), pp.281-290.

Cimbala, J. Stephen, 'Sun Tzu and Salami Tactics? Vladimir Putin and Military Persuasion in Ukraine, 21 February–18 March 2014,' *Journal of Slavic Military Studies*, vol.27, no.3 (July 2014), pp.359–379.

Coupé, Tom and Obrizan, Maksym, 'Violence and political outcomes in Ukraine—Evidence from Sloviansk and Kramatorsk,' *Journal of Comparative Economics*, vol.44, no.1 (February 2016), pp.201–212.

Czuperski, Maksymilian, Herbst, J., Higgins, Eliot, Polyakova, Alina, and Wilson, Damon, *Hiding in Plain Sight: Putin's War in Ukraine* (Washington DC: Atlantic Council of the US, 13 July 2015). http://www.atlanticcouncil.org/publications/reports/hiding-in-plain-sight-putin-s-war-in-ukraine-and-boris-nemtsov-s-putin-war

Darczewska, Jolanta, and Piotr Zochowski, Piotr, *Russophobia in the Kremlin's Strategy. A Weapon of Mass Destruction,* Point of View 56 (Warsaw: Centre for Eastern Studies, October 2015). http://www.osw.waw.pl/sites/default/files/pw_56_ang_russophobia_net.pdf

Darczewska, J. *Russia's Armed Forces on the Information War Front. Strategic Documents,* no.57 (Warsaw: Centre for Eastern Studies, June 2016). http://www.osw.waw.pl/en/publikacje/osw-studies/2016-06-27/russias-armed-forces-information-war-front-strategic-documents

Demidov, Andrey, and Kurdalanova, Margarita, *Online Russia, today. How is Russia Today framing the events of the Ukrainian crisis of 2013 and what this framing says about the Russian regime's legitimation strategies? The case of the Russian-language online platform of RT* (Amsterdam: Graduate School of Social Sciences, Authoritarianism in a Global Age, University of Amsterdam, 24 June 2016). http://scriptiesonline.uba.uva.nl/document/638768

Doran, Peter B., *Land Warfare in Europe. Lessons and Recommendations from the War in Ukraine* (Washington DC: Center for European Policy Analysis, November 2016). https://cepa.ecms.pl/files/?id_plik=2991

Duvanovaa, Dinissa and Nikolaev, Alexander, Nikolsko-Rzhevskyyc, Alex and Semenov, Alexander, 'Violent conflict and online segregation: An analysis of social network communication across Ukraine's regions,' *Journal of Comparative Economics,* vol.44, no.1 (February 2016), pp.163–181.

Galeotti, Mark, 'Hybrid War' and 'Little Green Men': How It Works, and How It Doesn't' in A. Pikulicka-Wilczewska and R. Sakwa eds., *Ukraine and Russia: People, Politics, Propaganda and Perspectives,* pp.156-164.

Galeotti, M., *Hybrid War or Gibridnaya Voina? Getting Russia's non-linear military challenge right* (Lulu: 27 November 2016).

http://www.lulu.com/shop/mark-galeotti/hybrid-war-or-gibridnaya-voina-getting-russias-non-linear-military-challenge-right/paperback/product-22962814.html

Geers, Kenneth ed., *Cyber War in Perspective: Russian Aggression against Ukraine* (Tallinn: NATO Cooperative Cyber Defence Centre of Excellence Publications, 2015). https://ccdcoe.org/sites/default/files/multimedia/pdf/CyberWarinPerspective_full_book.pdf

Giles, K. *Handbook of Russian Information Warfare*. Fellowship Monograph (Rome: NATO Defence College, November 2016). http://www.ndc.nato.int/download/downloads.php?icode=506

Goldsmith, Jett, Were Chemical Weapons Used in Donetsk Airport's Last Stand? *Report by Bellingcat*, 23 January 2015. https://www.bellingcat.com/news/uk-and-europe/2015/01/23/were-chemical-weapons-used-in-donetsk-airports-last-stand/

Gressel, Gustav, *Russia's quiet military revolution, and what it means for Europe* (London: European Council on Foreign Relations, 2015). http://www.ecfr.eu/publications/summary/russias_quiet_military_revolution_and_what_it_means_for_europe4045

Horner, Will, Who Exactly Are the Terek Wolf Sotnia? *Report by Bellingcat*, 27 August 2014. https://www.bellingcat.com/news/uk-and-europe/2014/08/27/who-exactly-are-the-terek-wolf-sotnia/

Human Shields in Donetsk: Launching Grads near a Residential Area, *Bellingcat and Conflict Intelligence Team Report*, 2 February 2017. https://www.bellingcat.com/news/uk-and-europe/2017/02/02/human-shields-in-donetsk-launching-grads-near-a-residential-area/

Hutchings, Stephen and Szostek, Joanna, 'Dominant Narratives in Russian Political and Media Discourse During the Ukraine Crisis' in A. Pikulicka-Wilczewska and R. Sakwa eds., *Ukraine and Russia: People, Politics, Propaganda and Perspectives*, pp.183-196.

Hutchings, S. and Tolz, Vera, *Nation, Ethnicity and Race on Russian Television. Mediating post-Soviet difference* (London and New York: Routledge, 2015).

How to Locate a "Secret" Pro-Russian Training Camp, *Report by Bellingcat*, 15 August 2014. https://www.bellingcat.com/resources/case-studies/2014/08/15/how-to-locate-a-secret-pro-russian-training-camp/

Jonsson, Oscar and Seely, Robert, 'Russian Full-Spectrum Conflict: An Appraisal After Ukraine,' *Journal of Slavic Military Studies*, vol.28, no.1 (January 2015), pp.1–22.

Judah, Tim, *In Wartime. Stories from Ukraine* (New York: Tim Duggan Books, 2015).

Presentation preliminary results criminal investigation MH-17, *Joint Investigation Team*, 28 September 2016. https://www.om.nl/onderwerpen/mh17-vliegramp/presentaties/presentation-joint/

Karber, A. Philip, *Russia's Hybrid War Campaign. Implications for Ukraine and Beyond* (Washington DC: The Potomac Foundation and Center for Strategic and International Studies, Russia and Eurasia Program, 10 March 2015). http://www.thepotomacfoundation.org/russias-hybrid-war-campaign-implications-for-ukraine-and-beyond/

Kropatcheva, Elena, 'The Evolution of Russia's OSCE Policy: From the Promises of the Helsinki Final Act to the Ukrainian Crisis,' *Journal of Contemporary European Studies*, vol. 23, no. 1 (January 2015), pp.6–24.

Kuzio, T. 'Russianization of Ukrainian National Security Policy under Viktor Yanukovych,' *Journal of Slavic Military Studies*, vol.25, no.4 (December 2012), pp.558-581.

Kuzio, T., *Why Vladimir Putin is Angry with the West. Understanding the Drivers of Russia's Information, Cyber and Hybrid War*, Security Policy Working Paper No.7 (Berlin: Federal Academy for Security Policy, February 2017). https://www.baks.bund.de/en/newsletter/archive/view/971

Leviev, Ruslan, Three Graves: Russian Investigation Team Uncovers Spetsnaz Brigade in Ukraine, *Report by Bellingcat*, 22 May 2015. https://www.bellingcat.com/news/uk-and-europe/2015/05/22/three-graves/

"Little Green Men": a primer on Modern Russian Unconventional Warfare (Fort Bragg, North Carolina, United States Army Special Operations Command, 2015). http://www.jhuapl.edu/ourwork/nsa/papers/ARIS_LittleGreenMen.pdf

Lucas, E. and Nimmo, B. *Information Warfare. What Is It and How to Win It?* CEPA Infowar Paper No.1 (Washington DC: Center for European Policy Analysis, November 2015). http://www.cepa.org/sites/default/files/Infowar%20Report.pdf

Lucas, E. and Pomerantzev, Peter, *Winning the Information War Techniques and Counter-strategies to Russian Propaganda in Central and Eastern Europe, A Report by CEPA's Information Warfare Project in Partnership with the Legatum Institute* (London: Legatum Institute, August 2016). https://cepa.ecms.pl/files/?id_plik=2706

Lutsevych, Orysia, *Agents of the Russian World: Proxy Groups in the Contested Neighbourhood* (London: Royal Institute of International Affairs, April 2016). https://www.chathamhouse.org/publication/agents-russian-world-proxy-groups-contested-neighbourhood

Malyarenko, Tetyana, 'Playing a Give-Away Game? The Undeclared Russian-Ukrainian War in Donbas,' *Small Wars Journal* (23 December 2015). http://smallwarsjournal.com/jrnl/art/playing-a-give-away-game-the-undeclared-russian-ukrainian-war-in-donbas

McIntosh, E. Scott, 'Kyiv, International Institutions, and the Russian People: Three Aspects of Russia's Current Information Campaign in Ukraine,' *Journal of Slavic Military Studies*, vol.28, no. 2 (April 2015), pp.299–306.

Miazhevich, Galina, 'Russia Today's coverage of Euromaidan,' *Journal of Communication*, vol.6, no.2 (May 2014), pp.186-191.

Miller, James, Vaux, Pierre, Fitzpatrick, A. Catherine, and Weiss, Michael, *An Invasion by Any Other Name. The Kremlin's Dirty War in Ukraine* (New York: The Interpreter, Institute of Modern Russia, 17 September 2015). http://www.interpretermag.com/wp-content/uploads/2015/11/IMR_Ukraine_final_links_updt_02_corr.pdf

Mitrokhin, Nikolay, 'Infiltration, Instruction, Invasion: Russia's War in the Donbass,' *Journal of Soviet and Post-Soviet Politics and Society*, vol.1, no.1 (2015), pp.219-249.

http://spps-jspps.autorenbetreuung.de/files/07-mitrokhin.pdf

Motyl, A. J., 'The west should arm Ukraine,' *Foreign Affairs*, 10 February 2015. https://www.foreignaffairs.com/articles/russia-fsu/2015-02-10/west-should-arm-ukraine

Murphy, N. Martin, *Understanding Russia's Concept for Total War in Europe,* Special Report No.184 (Washington DC: Heritage Foundation, September 2016). http://www.heritage.org/research/reports/2016/09/understanding-russias-concept-for-total-war-in-europe

Oliker, Olga, Davis, E. Lynn, Crane, Keith, Radin, Andrew, Gventer, W. Celeste, Sondergaard, Susanne, Quinlivan, T. James, Seabrook, B. Stephan, Bellasio, Jacopo, Frederick, Bryan, Bega, Andriy, and Hlavka, Jakub, *Security Sector Reform in Ukraine* (Santa Monica, CA: Rand, 2016). http://www.rand.org/pubs/research_reports/RR1475-1.html

*Operation Armageddon: Cyber Espionage as a Strategic Component of Russian Modern Warfare* (n.p.: Looking Glass Cyber Threat Intelligence Group [CTIG], 28 April 2015). https://www.lookingglasscyber.com/webinar-operation-armageddon/

Origin of Artillery Attacks on Ukrainian Military Positions in Eastern Europe Between 14 July 2014 and 8 August 2014, *Report by Bellingcat*, 17 February 2015. https://www.bellingcat.com/news/uk-and-europe/2015/02/17/origin-of-artillery-attacks/

Origins of the Separatists Buk, *Report by Bellingcat*, 8 November 2014. https://www.bellingcat.com/news/uk-and-europe/2014/11/08/origin-of-the-separatists-buk-a-bellingcat-investigation/

Paul, Christopher, and Mathews, Miriam, *The Russian "Firehose of Falsehood" Propaganda Model. Why It Might Work and Options to Counter It,* Rand Perspective (Santa Monica, CA: Rand Corporation, 2016). http://www.rand.org/pubs/perspectives/PE198.html

Perry, Bret, 'Non-Linear Warfare in Ukraine: The Critical Role of Information Operations and Special Operations,' *Small Wars Journal,* (14 August 2015). http://smallwarsjournal.com/jrnl/art/non-linear-warfare-in-ukraine-the-critical-role-of-information-operations-and-special-opera

Political Capital Institute, *The Russian Connection. The Spread of Pro-Russian Policies on Europe's Far Right* (Budapest: Political Capital Institute, 14 March 2014). http://www.riskandforecast.com/useruploads/files/pc_flash_report_russian_connection.pdf

Pesenti, Marina, and Pomerantsev, P., *Beyond Propaganda. How to Stop Disinformation. Lessons from Ukraine for the Wider World* (London: Legatum Institute,

August 2016). http://www.li.com/activities/publications/how-to-stop-disinformation-lessons-from-ukraine-for-the-wider-world

Polyakova, A., Laruelle, Marlene, Meister, Stefan and Barnett, Neil, *The Kremlin Trojan Horses* (Washington DC: Atlantic Council of the US, 15 November 2016).

http://www.atlanticcouncil.org/images/publications/The_Kremlins_Trojan_Horses_web_1213_second_edition.pdf

Pomerantsev, P. *Nothing Is True and Everything Is Possible: The Surreal Heart of the New Russia* (London: Faver and Faver, 2015).

Pomerantsev, P. and Weiss, M., *The Menace of Unreality: How the Kremlin Weaponizes Information, Culture and Money, A Special Report presented by The Interpreter* (New York: The Institute of Modern Russia, 2014). http://www.interpretermag.com/wp-content/uploads/2015/07/PW-31.pdf

Pomerantsev, P., *Russia: A Postmodern Dictatorship* (London: Legatum Institute and Institute of Modern Russia, October 2013). http://www.li.com/docs/default-source/publications/pomeransev1_russia_imr_web_final.pdf?sfvrsn=4Pridham, Geoffrey, 'EU-Ukraine Relations and the Crisis with Russia, 2013-2014: A Turning Point,' The International Spectator, vol.49, no.4 (December 2014), pp.53-61.

Pynnöniemi, Katri and Rácz, A. eds., *Fog of Falsehood: Russian Strategy of Deception and the Conflict in Ukraine* (Helsinki: Finnish Institute of International Affairs, 5 October 2016).

http://www.fiia.fi/en/publication/588/fog_of_falsehood/

Renz, Bettina, 'Russia and 'hybrid warfare,' *Contemporary Politics*, vol.22, no.3 (July 2016), pp. 283-300.

Revealed: Around 40 Russian Troops from Pskov Died in Ukraine, Reinforcement Sent In, *Report by Bellingcat*, 27 August 2014. https://www.bellingcat.com/news/mena/2014/08/27/revealed-around-40-russian-troops-from-pskov-died-in-the-ukraine-reinforcement-sent-in/

Romein, Daniel, MH17 - Potential Suspects and Witnesses from the 53rd Anti-Aircraft Missile Brigade, *Report by Bellingcat*, February 2016.

https://www.bellingcat.com/wp-content/uploads/2016/02/53rd-report-public.pdf

Russia's Path(s) to War, *Report by Bellingcat*, 21 September 2015. https://www.bellingcat.com/news/uk-and-europe/2015/09/21/belling-cat-investigation-russias-paths-to-war/

Russia's Version of the Navy SEAL's May be Fighting in Ukraine, *Report by Bellingcat*, 28 August 2014. https://www.belling-cat.com/news/mena/2014/08/28/russias-version-of-the-navy-seals-may-be-fighting-in-ukraine/

Russia's War in Ukraine: The Medals and Treacherous Numbers, *Report by Bellingcat*, 31 August 2016. https://www.bellingcat.com/news/uk-and-europe/2016/08/31/russias-war-ukraine-medals-treacherous-numbers/

Shekhovtsov, A. 'The spectre of Ukrainian fascism: Information wars, political manipulation, and reality,' in A. Wilson ed., *What does Ukraine think?* (London: European Council on Foreign Relations, 18 May 2015), pp.80-88. http://www.ecfr.eu/publications/summary/what_does_ukraine_think3026

Snegovaya, Maria, *Putin's Information warfare in Ukraine. Soviet Origins of Russia's hybrid Warfare* (Washington DC: Institute for the Study of War, September 2015). http://understandingwar.org/report/putins-information-warfare-ukraine-soviet-origins-russias-hybrid-warfare

Spiessens, Anneleen and Poucke, van Piet, 'Translating news discourse on the Crimean crisis: patterns of reframing on the Russian website InoSMI,' *Translator*, vol.22, no.3 (September 2016), pp.319-339.

Stępniewski, Tomasz and Hajduk, Jurij, 'Russia's Hybrid War with Ukraine. Determinants, Instruments, Accomplishments and Challenges,' *Studia Europejskie*, no.2 (2016), pp.37-51.

http://www.ce.uw.edu.pl/pliki/pw/2-2016_hajduk.pdf

Stratfor, *Wargaming Ukraine*. https://www.stratfor.com/video/wargaming-russias-military-options-ukraine and http://www.slideshare.net/Stratfor/wargaming-ukraine

Sutyagin, Igor, *Russian Forces in Ukraine*, RUSI Briefing Paper (London: Royal United Services Institute, 9 March 2015). https://rusi.org/publication/briefing-papers/russian-forces-ukraine

Szostek, J., 'Russia and the News Media in Ukraine: A Case of "Soft Power"?' *East European Politics and Societies and Cultures*, vol.28, no.3 (August 2014), pp.463–486.

Three Graves: Russian Investigation Team Uncovers Spetsnaz Brigade in Ukraine, *Report by Bellingcat*, 22 May 2015. https://www.bellingcat.com/news/uk-and-europe/2015/05/22/three-graves/

Thomas, Timothy, 'Russia's Military Strategy and Ukraine: Indirect, Asymmetric—and Putin-Led,' *The Journal of Slavic Military Studies*, vol.28, no.3 (July 2015), pp.445-461.

Toler, Aric, As Eastern Ukraine Heads Towards the Ceasefire, Russian Armour Heads Towards Ukraine, *Report by Bellingcat*, 13 February 2015.

https://www.bellingcat.com/news/uk-and-europe/2015/02/13/as-eastern-ukraine-heads-towards-the-ceasefire-russian-armour-heads-towards-ukraine/

Vanderhill, Rachel, 'Active resistance to democratic diffusion,' *Communist and Post-Communist Studies* (2017).

Vojtíšková, Vladislava, Novotný, Vít, Schmid-Schmidsfelden, Hubertus and Potapov, Kristina, *The Bear in Sheep's Clothing. Russia's Government-Funded Organisations in the EU* (Brussels: Wilfried Martens Centre for European Studies, July 2016). http://www.martenscentre.eu/publications/bear-sheeps-clothing-russias-government-funded-organisations-eu

Yermolenko, Volodymyr, 'Russia, Zoopolitics, and Information Bombs,' in A. Wilson ed., *What does Ukraine think?* pp.72-79.

Way, Lucan, 'The Limits of Autocracy Promotion: The Case of Russia in the 'Near Abroad," *European Journal of Political Research*, vol.54, no.4 (November 2015), pp.691-706.

Wilson, L. Jeane, 'The Legacy of the Color Revolutions for Russian Politics and Foreign Policy,' *Problems of Post-Communism*. vol.57, no.2 (March-April 2010), pp.21-36.

Žielys, Povilas and Rudinskaitė, Rūta, 'US democracy assistance programs in Ukraine after the Orange Revolution,' *Communist and Post-Communist Studies*, vol.47, no.1 (March 2014), pp.81-91.

## 6. DOMESTIC RUSSIA: PUTIN'S REGIME, MILITOCRACY, KLEPTOCRACY AND NATIONALISM

Bateman, Aaron, 'The Political Influence of the Russian Security Services,' *Journal of Slavic Military Studies*, vol.27, no.3 (September 2014), pp.380-403.

Bukkvoll, Tor, 'Why Putin went to war: ideology, interests and decision-making in the Russian use of force in Crimea and Donbas,' *Contemporary Politics*, vol.22, no.3 (July 2016), pp.267-282.

Cameron, R. David, and Orenstein, A. M., 'Post-Soviet Authoritarianism: The Influence of Russia in its 'Near Abroad,'' *Post-Soviet Affairs*, vol.28, no.1 (January 2012), pp.1-44.

Clover, Charles, *Black Wind, White Snow. The Rise of Russia's New Nationalism* (New Haven, CT: Yale University Press, 2016).

Dawisha, Karen, 'Is Russia's foreign policy that of a corporatist-Kleptocratic regime?' *Post-Soviet Affairs*, vol.27, no.4 (October 2011), pp.331–365.

Dawisha, K., *Putin's Kleptocracy. Who Owns Russia?* (New York: Simon & Schuster, 2015).

Francis, Diane, *Stolen Future* (Washington DC: Dinu Patriciu Eurasia Center, Atlantic Council, May 2016). http://www.atlanticcouncil.org/images/publications/Stolen_Future_web_0509.pdf

Galeotti, M. and Bowen, S. Andrew, 'Putin's Empire of the Mind,' *Foreign Policy*, 21 April 2014. http://foreignpolicy.com/2014/04/21/putins-empire-of-the-mind/

Gaufman, Elizaveta, 'World War II 2.o: Digital Memory of Fascism in Russia in the Aftermath of Euromaidan in Ukraine,' *Journal of Regional Security*, vol.10, no.1 (2015), pp.17-36.

Gaufman, E., 'Memory, Media, and Securitization: Russian Media Framing of the Ukrainian Crisis,' *Journal of Soviet and Post-Soviet Politics and Society*, vol.1, no.1 (2015), pp.141-174.

Joo, Hyung-min, 'The Soviet Origin of Russian Chauvinism: Voices from below,' *Communist and Post-Communist Studies*, vol.41, no.2 (June 2008), pp.217-242.

Kryshtanovskaya, Olga, and White, Stephen, 'Putin's Militocracy,' *Post-Soviet Affairs*, vol.19, no.4 (January 2003), pp.289-306.

Kupatadze, Alexander, *Organized Crime, Transitions and State Formation in Post-Soviet Eurasia* (London: Palgrave Macmillan UK, 2012).

Laruelle, M., 'The Ukrainian Crisis and Its Impact on Transforming Russian Nationalism Landscape,' in A. Pikulicka-Wilczewska and R. Sakwa eds., *Ukraine and Russia: People, Politics, Propaganda and Perspectives,* pp.123-128.

Laruelle, M. 'Russia as a "Divided Nation," from Compatriots to Crimea: A Contribution to the Discussion on Nationalism and Foreign Policy,' *Problems of Post Communism*, vol.62, no.2 (March 2015), pp.88-97.

Laruelle, M. 'The three colors of Novorossiya, or the Russian nationalist mythmaking of the Ukrainian crisis,' *Post-Soviet Affairs*, vol.32, no.1 (January 2016), pp.55-74.

Makarychev, A. and Yatsyk, Alexandra, 'The Four Pillars of Russia's Power Narrative,' *The International Spectator*, vol.49, no.4 (October 2014), pp.62-75.

Motyl, A.J., 'The Myth of Russian Nationalism' in *Sovietology, Rationality, Nationality. Coming to Grips with Nationalism in the USSR* (New York: Columbia University Press, 1990), pp.161-173.

Motyl, A.J., 'Fascistoid Russia: Putin's Political System in Comparative Context,' in Susan Stewart, Margarete Klein, Andrea Schmitz, and Hans-Henning Schröder, eds., *Presidents, Oligarchs and Bureaucrats: Forms of Rule in the Post-Soviet Space* (Farnham, UK: Ashgate, 2012), pp.107-124.

Motyl, A.J., 'Putin's Russia as a Fascist Political System,' *Communist and Post-Communist Studies*, vol. 49, no. 1 (March 2016), pp.25-36.

Ostrovsky, Arkady, *The Invention of Russia. The Journey from Gorbachev's Freedom to Putin's War* (London: Atlantic Books, 2015).

Riley, Alan, *Ukraine v Russia and the Kleptocrats. The Legal Route to Recover Russia's Losses* (Washington DC: Dinu Patriciu Eurasia Center, Atlantic Council,

April 2016). http://www.atlanticcouncil.org/images/publications/Ukraine_v_Russia_and_the_Kleptocrats_web_0404.pdf

Shevtsova, Lilia, 'The Russian Factor,' *Journal of Democracy*, vol.25, no.3 (July 2014), pp.74-82.

Shlapentokh, V. Dmitry, 'Implementation of an Ideological Paradigm: Early Duginian Eurasianism and Russia's Post-Crimean Discourse,' *Contemporary Security Policy*, vol.35, no.3 (September 2014), pp.380–399.

Skak, Mette, 'Russian strategic culture: the role of today's chekisty,' *Contemporary Politics*, vol.22, no.3 (July 2016), pp.324-341.

Strasheim, Julia, 'Power-sharing, commitment problems, and armed conflict in Ukraine,' *Civil Wars*, vol.18, no.1 (January 2016), pp.25-44.

Svarin, David, 'The construction of 'geopolitical spaces' in Russian foreign policy discourse before and after the Ukraine crisis,' *Journal of Eurasian Studies*, vol.7, no.2 (July 2016), pp.111-222.

Umland, A. 'Aleksandr Dugin's Transformation from a Lunatic Fringe Figure into a Mainstream Political Publicist, 1980-1998: A Case Study in the Rise of Late and Post-Soviet Russian Fascism,' *Journal of Eurasian Studies*, vol.1, no,2. (July 2010), pp.144-152.

Wood, A. Elizabeth, 'Performing Memory: Vladimir Putin and the Celebration of World War II in Russia,' *The Soviet and Post-Soviet Review*, vol. 38, no.2 (September 2011), pp.172–200.

Wood, E.A., Pomerantz, E. William E., Merry, Wayne, E. and Trudolyubov, Maxim, *Roots of Russia's War in Ukraine* (Washington DC: Woodrow Wilson Center Press, 2016).

## 7. EXTERNAL RUSSIA: UKRAINE, IDENTITY AND CHAUVINISM

Brudny, M. Yitzhak and Finkel, Evgeny, 'Why Ukraine is not Russia. Hegemonic National Identities and Democracy in Russia and Ukraine,' *East European Politics and Societies*, vol.25, no.4 (November 2011), pp.813-833.

Bukkvoll, T., 'Off the Cuff Politics—Explaining Russia's Lack of a Ukraine Strategy,' *Europe-Asia Studies*. vol.53, no.8 (December 2001), pp.1141-57.

Chebankova, Elena, 'Contemporary Russian conservatism,' *Post-Soviet Affairs*, vol. 32, no. 1 (January 2016), pp.28–54.

Goble, Paul, 'Russian National Identity and the Ukraine Crisis,' *Communist and Post-Communist Studies*, vol. 49, no.1 (March 2016), pp.37-43.

Giuliano, Elise, 'The Social Bases of Support for Self-determination in East Ukraine,' *Ethnopolitics*, vol.14, no.5 (October 2015), pp.513-522.

Horvath, Robert, 'The Euromaidan and the crisis of Russian nationalism,' *Nationalities Papers*, vol.43, no.6 (November 2015), pp.819-839.

Kappeler, Andreas, 'Ukraine and Russia: Legacies of the imperial past and competing memories,' *Journal of Eurasian Studies*, vol. 5, no. 2 (July 2014), pp.107-115.

Kuzio, T., 'Soviet conspiracy theories and political culture in Ukraine. Understanding Viktor Yanukovych and the Party of Regions,' *Communist and Post-Communist Studies*, vol.44, no.3 (September 2011), pp.221-232,

Kuzio, T., 'Competing Nationalisms, Euromaidan and the Russian-Ukrainian Conflict,' *Studies in Ethnicity and Nationalism*, vol.15, no.1 (April 2015), pp. 158-169.

Kuzio, T., 'Soviet and Russian Anti(Ukrainian)Nationalism and Restalinization,' *Communist and Post Communist Studies*, vol.49, no. 1 (March 2016), pp.87-99.

Kuzio, T., *Russian National Identity and the Russia-Ukraine Crisis*, Security Policy Working Paper No.20 (Berlin: Federal Academy for Security Policy, September 2016). https://www.baks.bund.de/sites/baks010/files/working_paper_2016_20.pdf

Mills, F.V., 'Understanding the Euromaidan: The View from the Kremlin,' in D. Marples and F.V. Mills eds., *Ukraine's Euromaidan*, pp.239-260.

Motyl, A.J., 'Putin's Zugzwang: The Russia–Ukraine standoff,' *World Affairs*, vol.177, no.2 (July-August 2014), pp.58–65. http://www.worldaffairsjournal.org/article/putin%E2%80%99s-zugzwang-russia-ukraine-standoff

Motyl, A.J., 'Ukraine's Next 25 Years. Moving Forward under a Permanent Russian Threat,' *Foreign Affairs*, 25 September 2016. https://www.foreignaffairs.com/articles/ukraine/2016-09-25/ukraines-next-25-years

Onuch, O., 'Brothers Grimm or Brothers Karamazov: The Myth and the Reality of How Russians and Ukrainians View the Other' in A. Pikulicka-Wilczewska and R. Sakwa eds., *Ukraine and Russia: People, Politics, Propaganda and Perspectives*, pp.36-58.

Riabchuk, Mykola, 'The Ukrainian 'Friday' and the Russian 'Robinson': The Uneasy Advent of Postcoloniality' in S. Yekelchyk (Guest Editor), *Ukrainian Culture after Communism, a special issue of Canadian American Slavic Studies*, vol. 44, nos. 1-2 (2010), pp. 5-20.

Riabchuk, M., 'The 'New Eastern Europe' and East Slavonic 'Umma': Uneasy Emancipation' in Jan Malicki ed., *Russia of the Tsars, of the Bolsheviks, and of the New Times* (Warsaw: Center for East European Studies, 2012), pp. 151-162.

Riabchuk, M., 'Ukrainian Culture after Communism: Between Post-Colonial Liberation and Neo-Colonial Subjugation' in Dobrota Pucherova and Robert Gafrik eds., *Postcolonial East-Central Europe: Essays on Literature and Culture* (Amsterdam: Rodopi, 2015), pp. 337-355.

Riabchuk, M., 'Two Ukraine's' Reconsidered: The End of Ukrainian Ambivalence? *Studies in Ethnicity and Nationalism*, vol. 15, no. 1 (April 2015), pp. 138–156.

Riabchuk, M., 'Ukrainians as Russia's Negative 'Other': History Comes Full Circle,' *Communist and Post-Communist Studies*, vol.49, no. 1 (March 2016), pp.75-86.

Shkandrij, Myroslav, *Ukrainian Nationalism: Politics, Ideology, and Literature, 1929–1956* (New Haven, CT: Yale University Press, 2015).

Shulman, Stephan, 'National Identity and Public Support for Political and Economic Reform in Ukraine,' *Slavic Review*, vol.64, no.1 (Spring 2005), pp.59-87.

Wanner, Catherine, '"Fraternal" nations and challenges to sovereignty in Ukraine: The politics of linguistic and religious ties,' *American Ethnologist*, vol. 41, no. 3 (August 2014), pp. 427–439.

Wawrzonek, Michał, 'Ukraine in the "Gray Zone": Between the "Russkiy Mir" and Europe,' *East European Politics and Societies*, vol. 28, no.4 (November 2014), pp.758–780.

Zevelev, Igor, *The Russian World in Moscow's Strategy* (Washington DC: Center for Strategic and International Studies, 22 August 2016). https://www.csis.org/analysis/russian-world-moscows-strategy

## 8. UKRAINE: WAR, NATIONAL MINORITIES, REGIONALISM, AND ECONOMICS

Aslund, Anders, 'Oligarchs, Corruption, and European Integration,' *Journal of Democracy*, vol.25, no.3 (July 2014), pp.74-82.

Buzgalin, Alexander, 'Ukraine: Anatomy of a Civil War,' *International Critical Thought*, vol.5, no.3 (July 2015), pp.327-347.

Clem, S. Ralph, 'Dynamics of the Ukrainian state-territory nexus,' *Eurasian Geography and Economics*, vol. 55, no. 3 (May 2015), pp.219–235.

Esch, Christian, *"Banderites" vs. "New Russia." The Battle Field of History in the Ukraine Conflict*, Reuters Institute Fellowship Paper (Oxford: Reuters Institute for the Study of Journalism, 2015).

https://reutersinstitute.politics.ox.ac.uk/sites/default/files/Banderites%20vs%20New%20Russia%20The%20Battlefield%20of%20History%20in%20the%20Ukraine%20Conflict.pdf

Feferman, Kiril, 'The Crisis in Ukraine: Attitudes of the Russian and Ukrainian Jewish Communities,' *Israel Journal of Foreign Affairs*, vol.9, no.2 (May 2015), pp.227-236.Michael

Fournier, Anna, 'Mapping Identities: Russian Resistance to Linguistic Ukrainianisation in Central and Eastern Ukraine,' *Europe-Asia Studies*, vol.54, no.3 (May 2002), pp.415–33.

Fredheim, Rolf, Howanitz, Gernot, and Makhortykh, Mykola, 'Scraping the Monumental: Stepan Bandera Through the Lens of Quantitative Memory Studies,' *Digital Icons: Studies in Russian, Eurasian and Central European New Media*, no.12 (2014), pp.25-33. http://www.digitalicons.org/wpcontent/uploads/issue12/files/2014/11/DI12_2_Fredheim.pdf

Klymenko, Lina, 'World War II or Great Patriotic War remembrance? Crafting the nation in commemorative speeches of Ukrainian presidents,' *National Identities*, vol.17, no.4 (October 2015), pp.387–403.

Kulyk, Volodymyr, 'The Media, History and Identity: Competing Narratives of the Past in the Ukrainian Popular Press,' *National Identities*, vol.13, no.3 (June 2011), pp.287-303.

Kulyk, V., 'What is Russian in Ukraine? Popular Beliefs Regarding the Social Roles of the Language' in Lara Ryazanova-Clarke ed., *The Russian Language Outside the Nation: Speakers and Identities* (Edinburgh: Edinburgh University Press, 2014), pp.117-140.

Kulyk, V., 'National Identity in Ukraine: Impact of Euromaidan and the War,' *Europe-Asia Studies*, vol. 68, no. 4 (June 2016), pp. 588–608.

Kuzio, T., 'Nationalism, Identity and Civil Society in Ukraine: Understanding the Orange Revolution', *Communist and Post-Communist Studies,* vol.43, no.3 (September 2010), pp. 285-296.

Kuzio, T., 'Vigilantes, Organized Crime and Russian and Eurasian Nationalism: The Case of Ukraine,' in D. Marples and F. V. Mills eds., *Ukraine's Euromaidan*, pp.57-76.

Kuzio, T., 'A New Framework for Understanding Nationalisms in Ukraine: Democratic Revolutions, Separatism and Russian Hybrid War,' *Geopolitics, History, and International Relations*, vol. 7, no.1 (2015), pp.30-51. http://www.addletonacademicpublishers.com/contents-ghir#catid358

Lozhkin, Borys, *The Fourth Republic. Why Europe Needs Ukraine and Why Ukraine Needs Europe* (Kyiv: Novyj Druk, 2016).

Marples, D.R., 'Stepan Bandera: The Resurrection of a Ukrainian National Hero,' *Europe-Asia Studies*, vol.58, no.4 (June 2006), pp.555-566.

Motyl, A.J., *Ukraine, Europe, and Bandera*, Cicero Foundation Great Debate Paper No.10/05 (Maastricht: The Cicero Foundation, March 2010). http://www.cicerofoundation.org/lectures/Alexander_J_Motyl_UKRAINE_EUROPE_AND_BANDERA.pdf

Narvselius, Eleonora, 'The 'Bandera Debate': The Contentious Legacy of World War II and Liberalization of Collective Memory in Western Ukraine,' *Canadian Slavonic Papers*, vol.54, nos.3-4 (September 2012), pp.469-490.

Olszanski, Tadeusz, *Ukraine's Wartime Nationalism,* OSW Commentary, no.179 (Warsaw: Centre for Eastern Studies, 28 August 2015).

http://www.osw.waw.pl/en/publikacje/osw-commentary/2015-08-19/ukraines-wartime-nationalism

Pavlyuk, Lyudmyla, 'Vocabularies of Colliding Realities: A Report of Conflict and War in the Ukrainian Media' in V. Stepanenko and Y. Pylynskyi eds., *Ukraine after the Euromaidan*, pp.241-256.

Puglisi, Rosaria, *Heroes or Villains? Volunteer Battalions in Post-Maidan Ukraine*, IAI Working Paper, no.15 (Rome: Instituto Affari Internazionali, 8 March 2015). http://www.iai.it/sites/default/files/iaiwp1508.pdf

Razumkov Ukrainian Centre for Economic and Political Studies, 'Ukrainian-Russian Relations, Current Situation, Consequences, Prospects.' *National Security and Defence*, nos.5-6, 2014. http://www.uceps.org/eng/journal.php?y=2014&cat=206

Tumarkin, Nina, 'The Great Patriotic War as Myth and Memory,' *European Review*, vol.1, no.4 (October 2003), pp.595-611.

Yekelchyk, Serhy, The Conflict in Ukraine. What *Everyone Needs to Know* (Oxford: Oxford University Press, 2015).

Wilson, ed., A., *What does Ukraine think?*

Zhukov, M. Yuri, 'Trading hard hats for combat helmets: The economics of rebellion in eastern Ukraine,' *Journal of Comparative Economics*, vol..44, no.1 (February 2016), pp.1-15.

## 9. THE DONBAS AND EASTERN UKRAINE

Friedgut, H. Theodore, *Life and Work in Russia's Donbass, 1869-1924*, vol.1, *and Politics and Revolution in Russia's Donbass, 1869-1924*, vol.2 (Princeton, NJ: Princeton University Press, 1989 and 1994).

Gentile, Michael, 'The Post-Soviet urban poor and where they live: Khrushchev-era blocks, "bad" areas, and the vertical dimension in Luhansk, Ukraine,' *Annals of the Association of American Geographers*, vol.105, no.3 (May 2015), pp.583-603.

Gentile, M., 'West oriented in the east-oriented Donbas: a political stratigraphy of geopolitical identity in Luhansk, Ukraine,' *Post-Soviet Affairs*, vol.31, no.3 (May 2015), pp.201-223.

Klymovskyi, Sergiy, 'The Donbas: An Uprising of the People or a Putsch by Slaveholders' in V. Stepanenko and Y. Pylynskyi eds., *Ukraine after the Euromaidan*, pp.203-218.

Kononov, Ilya and Khobta, Svitlana, 'Public Opinion in the Donbas and Halychyna on the Ukraine's Upheavals of Winter 2013-Summer 2014' in V. Stepanenko and Y. Pylynskyi eds., *Ukraine after the Euromaidan*, pp.181-192.

Kudelia, Serhiy, 'Domestic Sources of the Donbas Insurgency,' *Ponars*, 29 September 2014. http://www.ponarseurasia.org/article/new-policy-memo-domestic-sources-donbas-insurgency

Kudelia, S., 'The House That Yanukovych Built,' *Journal of Democracy*, vol.25, no.3 (July 2014), pp.19-34.

Kudelia, S., and Kuzio, T., 'Nothing personal: explaining the rise and decline of political machines in Ukraine,' *Post-Soviet Affairs*, vol.31, no.3 (May 2015), pp.250-278.

Kudelia, S., 'The Donbas Rift,' *Russian Politics and Law*, vol.54, no.1 (January-February 2016), pp.5-27.

Kuromiya, Hiroaki, *Freedom and Terror in the Donbas. A Ukrainian-Russian Borderland, 1870s to 1990s* (Cambridge: Cambridge University Press, 1998).

Kuzio, T., 'Crime, Politics and Business in 1990s Ukraine,' *Communist and Post-Communist Politics*, vol.47, no.2 (July 2014), pp.195-210.

Kuzio, T., 'The Rise and Fall of the Party of Regions Political Machine,' *Problems of Post-Communism*, vol.62, no.3 (May-June 2015), pp. 174-186.

Moser, Michael, *Language Policy and the Discourse on Languages in Ukraine under President Viktor Yanukovych* (25 February 2010-28 October 2012) (Stuttgart: Ibidem Press, 2013).

Osipan, L. Ararat and Osipan, L. Alex, 'Why Donbas Votes for Yanukovych: Confronting the Ukrainian Orange Revolution,' *Demokratizatsiya*, vol.14, no.4 (Fall 2006), pp.495-517.

Osipian, A.L. and Osipian, A.L., 'Regional Diversity and Divided Memories in Ukraine: Contested Past as Electoral Resource, 2004–2010,' *East European Politics and Societies*, vol.26, no.3 (August 2012), pp.616-642.

Osipian, A., 'Historical Myths, Enemy Images, and Regional Identity in the Donbass Insurgency (Spring 2014),' *Journal of Soviet and Post-Soviet Politics and Society*, vol.1, no.1 (2015), pp.109-140.

Peshkov, Vladimir, *The Donbas: Back in the USSR* (London: European Council on Foreign Relations, 1 September 2016). http://www.ecfr.eu/article/essay_the_donbas_back_in_the_ussr

Portnov, Andriy, 'The Heart of Ukraine: Dnipropetrovsk and the Ukrainian Revolution,' in A. Wilson, ed., *What does Ukraine think?* pp.62-71.

Rodgers, Peter, *Nation, Region and History in Post-Communist Transitions: Identity Politics in Ukraine, 1991-2006* (Stuttgart: Ibidem Press, 2008).

Shukan, Ioulia, 'Intentional disruptions and violence in Ukraine's Supreme Rada: political competition, order, and disorder in a post-Soviet chamber, 2006–2012,' *Post-Soviet Affairs*, vol.29, no.5 (September 2013), pp. 439-456.

Smith, Graham, and Wilson, A., 'Rethinking Russia's Post-Soviet Diaspora: The Potential for Political Mobilisation in Eastern Ukraine and North-East Estonia,' *Europe-Asia Studies*, vol.49, no.5 (July 1997), pp.845-864.

Swain, Adam, ed., Re-*Constructing the Post-Soviet Industrial Region. The Donbas in Transition* (London: Routledge 2007).

Vyshniak, Olexander, 'The Maidan and Post-Maidan Ukraine: Public Attitudes in Regional Dimension' in V. Stepanenko and Y. Pylynskyi eds., *Ukraine after the Euromaidan*, pp.171-180.

Wilson, A., 'The Donbas between Ukraine and Russia: The use of history in political disputes,' *Journal of Contemporary History*, vol.30, no.2 (April 1995), pp. 265-289.

Wilson, A., 'The Donbas in 2014: Explaining Civil Conflict Perhaps, but not Civil War,' *Europe-Asia Studies*, vol. 68, no. 4 (June 2016), pp. 631–652.

Zakem, Vera, Saunders, Paul, and Antoun, Daniel, *Mobilizing Compatriots: Russia's Strategy, Tactics, and Influence in the Former Soviet Union*, Center for Strategic Studies Occasional Paper (Washington DC: CAN Analysis and Solutions, November 2015). https://www.cna.org/CNA_files/PDF/DOP-2015-U-011689-1Rev.pdf

Zakharchenko, Tanya, 'East Ukraine beyond pro and anti: monochrome prefixes and their discontents' in A. Wilson ed., *What does Ukraine think?* pp.53-61.

Zhurzhenko, Tatiana, '"Capital of Despair": Holodomor Memory and Political Conflicts in Kharkiv after the Orange Revolution,' *East European Politics and Societies*, vol.25, no.3 (August 2011), pp.597-639.

Zhurzhenko, T., 'Ukraine's Eastern Borderlands: The End of Ambiguity?' in A. Wilson ed., *What does Ukraine think?* pp.45-52.

Zimmer, Kirsten, 'The Comparative Failure of Machine Politics, Administrative Resources and Fraud,' *Canadian Slavonic Papers*, vol.47, nos.3-4 (September 2005), pp.361-384.

Zon, van Hans, *The Political Economy of Independent Ukraine, Captured by the Past* (London: Palgrave Macmillan, 2000).

Zon, van H., 'Neo-Patrimonialism as an Impediment to Economic Development: The Case of Ukraine,' *Journal of Communist Studies and Transition Politics*, vol.17, no.3 (September 2001), pp.71-95.

Zon, van H., 'The Rise of the Conglomerates in Ukraine' in Alex E. Fernandez Jilberto and Barbara Hogenboom eds., *Big Business and Economic Development. Conglomerates and economic groups in developing countries and transition economies under globalization* (London: Routledge, 2007), pp.378-397. http://www.taraskuzio.net/researchdocs/vanZon_Donetsk.pdf

# INDEX

Oplot, 55, 87, 98, 139, 147, 174, 175, 198, 201, 247, 249, 296, 299, 365-367

Orange Revolution, 5, 10, 28, 35, 40, 53, 71, 75, 77, 111, 117, 118, 140, 172, 183, 196, 198, 216, 220, 225, 231, 232, 233, 234, 248, 253, 258, 316, 340, 348, 352, 391, 392, 415, 421, 424, 425

OUN, 99, 106, 123, 142, 149, 379, 380

PACE, 265, 307, 334, 335

Party of Regions, 5, 21, 23, 27, 28, 29, 34, 35, 70, 71, 76, 77, 78, 79, 80, 87, 89, 92, 95, 101, 104, 110-124, 136, 137, 145, 147, 153, 157, 159, 161, 163, 166, 167, 168, 170, 171, 172, 173, 174, 179, 181, 187, 188, 190-193, 197-225, 240, 241, 247, 250-253, 260, 269, 281, 296, 315, 319, 344, 347, 354, 357, 359, 362, 365, 381, 418, 424

Party of Slavic Unity, 75, 77, 136, 191, 219, 221

Pavlov, Arseniy ('Motorola'), 297, 326, 330, 332

Pavlovsky, Gleb, 71, 81, 231, 233

Plotnitsky, Igor, 138, 266

Pomerantsev, Peter, 100, 178, 188, 290, 369, 412

Poroshenko, Petro,, 11, 19, 32, 89, 97, 105, 114, 116, 119, 136, 138, 139, 140, 145, 169, 193, 196, 211, 252, 265, 266, 272, 274, 281, 283, 290, 301, 313, 331, 384

Pravyy Sektor, 19, 33, 97, 103, 105, 114, 121, 142, 144, 145, 146, 175, 277, 295, 325, 330, 334, 349, 358, 359, 360, 366

Progressive Socialist Party, 77, 191, 215, 247

Pshonka, Viktor ,158, 168, 171

Putin, Vladimir, 1-22, 26-36, 40, 42, 45, 46, 49, 50, 52-59, 61-117, 121, 123-125, 129-136, 161, 162, 174, 176, 177, 180, 183, 193, 195, 196, 198, 202, 203, 204, 206, 207, 208, 215, 216, 220, 221, 223, 226, 227, 228, 229, 230, 231, 232, 233, 234, 236, 237, 238, 241, 242, 243, 244, 245, 246, 247, 255, 256, 257, 258, 259, 261, 262, 263, 264, 266, 267, 268, 269, 272, 273, 274, 275, 276, 277, 278, 281, 284, 285, 287, 288, 289, 290, 291, 293, 295, 296, 301, 304, 306, 307, 308, 309, 310, 312, 316, 317, 318, 322, 335, 336, 337, 338, 339, 342, 345, 348, 350, 363, 365, 366, 368, 371, 373, 374, 377, 379, 381, 382, 395, 396, 398, 403-406, 407, 413-419

Tymoshenko, Yulia, 3, 118, 119, 138, 145, 148, 169, 171, 173, 193, 211, 214, 224, 242

UDAR, 119, 121, 147, 179

Ukrainian Front, 79, 82, 246, 255, 256, 257, 259

United Russia, 3, 6, 49, 50, 71, 92, 180, 206, 215, 224, 241, 242, 260

Vigilantes, 171, 172, 173, 174, 422

Vostok, 55, 140, 175, 198, 296

Yanukovych, Viktor, 3, 5, 11, 13, 17, 22-31, 34, 35, 45, 65, 71, 77, 78, 79, 81, 83, 87, 89, 90, 92, 95, 100, 104, 105, 107, 111, 113, 115, 117, 118, 119, 122, 123, 138, 141, 143, 151, 152, 153, 156, 158-173, 175, 176, 179, 181, 183, 192, 193, 194, 195, 196, 197, 198, 199, 200, 204, 206, 207, 208, 212, 213, 214, 215, 216, 217, 219-226, 232, 233, 239, 240, 241, 242, 243, 244, 245, 246, 247, 248, 249, 250, 251, 252, 253, 254, 255, 256, 257, 258, 259, 260, 268, 281, 290, 293, 308, 310, 313, 315, 316, 319, 321, 336, 352, 359, 365, 379, 380, 381, 410, 418, 424

Yeltsin, Boris, 25, 40, 42, 44, 48, 51, 54, 59, 74, 182, 230, 231, 236, 293, 307, 336

Yushchenko, Viktor, 6, 12, 29, 45, 50, 71, 76, 83, 89, 105, 114, 115, 116, 117, 118, 145, 146, 148, 154, 168, 171, 193, 195, 196, 214, 216, 233, 237, 241, 242, 248, 249, 250, 252, 254, 290, 316, 321, 337, 372

Zakharchenko, Aleksandr, 78, 84, 86, 87, 120, 122, 138, 173, 175, 201, 222, 255, 266, 296, 331, 333, 343, 425

Zakharchenko, Vitaliy, 181, 227, 257

Zhirinovsky, Vladimir, 50, 51, 144, 262

# NOTES

[1] Germany and the EU now view Russia as a security threat: http://www.new-york-un.diplo.de/contentblob/4847754/Daten/6718448/160713weibuchEN.pdf and https://eeas.europa.eu/top_stories/pdf/eugs_review_web.pdf

[2] http://www.rferl.org/a/us-russia-new-sanctions-over-hacking/28204378.html

[3] https://www.theguardian.com/commentisfree/2016/dec/30/first-world-cyberwar-historians?utm_source=esp&utm_medium=Email&utm_campaign=The+Best+of+CiF+base&utm_term=206398&subid=13203085&CMP=ema_1364

[4] https://www.lookingglasscyber.com/webinar-operation-armageddon and /https://www2.fireeye.com/rs/fireye/images/rpt-apt28.pdf

[5] https://www.washingtonpost.com/opinions/global-opinions/beware-the-russian-bear-is-getting-bolder/2016/12/01/5f8535ae-b738-11e6-a677-b608fbb3aaf6_story.html?utm_term=.3f1550254582

[6] http://www.rferl.org/a/us-russia-new-sanctions-over-hacking/28204378.html

[7] http://www.rferl.org/a/balkans-russias-friends-form-new-cossack-army/28061110.html

[8] http://www.rferl.org/a/montenegro-coup-plot-suspect-instagram-lavrov-ristic/28176472.html

[9] http://www.thetimes.co.uk/edition/world/kremlin-supports-kissinger-93-as-americas-go-between-jrhvtm0bt

[10] Leonid Kravchuk, *Ostanni Dovira* (Kyiv: Dovira, 1994), p.162.

[11] Mikhail Zygar, *All the Kremlin's Men: Inside the Court of Vladimir Putin* (New York: Public Affairs, 2016).

[12] Elias Götz, 'Putin, the State and War: The Causes of Russia's Near Abroad Assertion Revisited,' *International Studies Review*, vol.18, no.4 (December 2016).

[13] Borys Lozhkin, *The Fourth Republic, Why Europe Needs Ukraine and Ukraine Needs Europe* (Kyiv: Novyj Druk, 2016), p.23.

[14] Mark Galeotti and Andrew Bowen, 'Putin's Empire of the Mind,' *Foreign Policy*, 21 April 2014. http://foreignpolicy.com/2014/04/21/putins-empire-of-the-mind/

[15] Brandon Valeriano and Ryan C. Maness, 'Paper Tiger Putin. The Failure of Russia's Anachronistic Antagonism,' *Foreign Affairs*, 30 April 2015. https://www.foreignaffairs.com/articles/russia-fsu/2015-04-30/paper-tiger-putin

[16] Richard H. Shultz and Roy Godson, *Dezinformatsia: Active Measures in Soviet Strategy* (McLean, Virginia: Pergamon-Brasseys International Defense Publishers, 1984) and Max Holland, 'The Propagation and Power of Communist Security Services *Dezinformatsiya*,' *International Journal of Intelligence and CounterIntelligence*, vol.19, no.1 (January 2006), pp.1-31.

[17] Stephen Hutchings and Vera Tolz, *Nation, Ethnicity and Race on Russian Television. Mediating post-Soviet difference* (London and New York: Routledge, 2015), p.258.

[18] 'The fog of wars,' *The Economist*, 22 October 2016. http://www.economist.com/news/special-report/21708880-adventures-abroad-boost-public-support-home-fog-wars

[19] Dominic Sandbrook, *State of Emergency. The Way We Were. Britain 1970-1974* (London: Penguin, 2011), p.492.

[20] See the list of books on Putin reviewed by Bnjamin Nathans in 'The Real Power of Putin,' *The New York Review of Books*, 29 September 2016. http://www.nybooks.com/articles/2016/09/29/real-power-vladimir-putin/

[21] Robert Horvath, 'The Euromaidan and the crisis of Russian nationalism,' *Nationalities Papers*, vol.43, no.6 (November 2015), pp.819-839.

[22] Hyung-min Joo, 'The Soviet Origin of Russian Chauvinism: Voices from below,' *Communist and Post-Communist Studies*, vol.41, no.2 (June 2008), p.223.

[23] Ivan Krastev, 'What does Russia want and why?' *Prospect*, 6 March 2014. http://www.prospect-magazine.co.uk/politics/what-does-russia-want-and-why. Ronald D. Asmus writes that the 2008 Georgia-Russia war was not over territory but a geopolitical contest with Russia refusing to countenance Georgia moving out of its sphere of influence. See *A Little War That Shook the World: Georgia, Russia and The Future of the West* (New York: Macmillan, 2010), pp.8-14.

[24] https://www.ndi.org/publications/ndi-research-opportunities-and-challenges-facing-ukraine%E2%80%99s-democratic-transition

[25] *Interfax-Ukraine*, 7 June 2016.

[26] http://www.danyliwseminar.com/#!serhiy-kudelia/cfss

[27] Hiroaki Kuromiya, 'Political Leadership and Ukrainian Nationalism, 1938-1989. The Burden of History,' *Problems of Post-Communism*, vol.52, no.1 (January-February 2005), p.42.

[28] H. Kuromiya, 'Political Leadership and Ukrainian Nationalism, 1938-1989,' p.43.

[29] T. Kuzio, 'Two myths about nationalism and anti-Semitism in Ukraine,' *The Washington Post*, 1 August 2016. https://www.washingtonpost.com/news/monkey-cage/wp/2016/08/01/ukraine-is-seeing-nationalism-and-anti-semitism-from-both-right-and-left-wing-forces/

[30] 'Fascism: Russian Media's Favourite Label,' *RFERL*, 6 October 2016. http://www.rferl.org/a/fascism-russian-medias-new-favorite-label/28035946.html

[31] Richard Sakwa, *Frontline Ukraine. Crisis on the Borderlands* (London: I. B .Tauris, 2016), p.257.

[32] Ibid., p.14.

[33] *Natsionalna Bezpeka i Oborona*, nos.3-4 (2016), p.57. http://www.razumkov.org.ua/ukr/journal.php?y=2016&cat=242

[34] http://m.nv.ua/publications/v-donbasse-protestanty-okazalis-odnoj-iz-naibolee-patriotichnyh-sotsialnyh-grupp-104809.html

[35] Paul S. Pirie, 'National Identity and Politics in Southern and Eastern Ukraine,' *Europe-Asia Studies*, vol.48 no.7 (November 1996), pp.1088-1089.

[36] Andrew Wilson, 'The Donbas in 2014: Explaining Civil Conflict Perhaps, but not Civil War,' *Europe-Asia Studies*, vol.68, no.4 (June 2015), pp.637 and 641.

[37] http://www.theguardian.com/world/2016/jun/05/russias-valiant-hero-in-ukraine-turns-his-fire-on-vladimir-putin

[38] Orysia Lutsevych, *Agents of the Russian World: Proxy Groups in the Contested Neighbourhood* (London: Royal Institute of International Affairs, April 2016). https://www.chathamhouse.org/publication/agents-russian-world-proxy-groups-contested-neighbourhood

[39] A. Wilson, 'The Donbas in 2014,' pp. 631-652.

[40] Nikolay Mitrokhin, 'Infiltration, Instruction, Invasion: Russia's War in the Donbass,' *Journal of Soviet and Post-Soviet Politics and Society*, vol.1, no.1 (2015), pp.219-249. http://spps-jspps.autorenbetreuung.de/files/07-mitrokhin.pdf

[41] My *Eurasia Daily Monitor* articles on the Yanukovych presidency and the Party of Regions are available at http://www.jamestown.org/articles-by author/?no_cache=1&tx_cablanttnewsstaffrelation_pi1%5Bauthor%5D=126

[42] Yuri M. Zhukov, 'Trading hard hats for combat helmets: The economics of rebellion in eastern Ukraine,' *Journal of Comparative Economics*, vol..44, no.1 (February 2016), pp.1-15.

[43] *Russia and the Separatists in Eastern Ukraine*, Briefing No. 79 (Brussels: International Crisis Group, 5 February 2016), p.9. http://www.crisisgroup.org/en/regions/europe/ukraine/b079-russia-and-the-separatists-in-eastern-ukraine.aspx

[44] *Dynamics of Soviet Nostalgia*, Rating Sociological Group, September 2016. http://rating-group.ua/en/research/ukraine/c910ad1d40079f7a2a28377c27494738.html

[45] H. Kuromiya, *Freedom and Terror in the Donbas. A Ukrainian-Russian Borderland, 1870s to 1990s* (Cambridge: Cambridge University Press, 1998), pp.334-335.

[46] Ibid., p.337.

[47] Ibid., p.337.

[48] Andras Racz and Arkady Moshes, *Not Another Transnistria. How sustainable is separatism in Eastern Ukraine?* FIIA Analysis 4 (Helsinki: Finnish Institute for International Affairs, 1 December 2014). http://www.fiia.fi/en/publication/456/not_another_transnistria/

[49] Michael Vickery, 'Ukraine's other Russians. Meet the Russians fighting for Ukraine,' *Aljazeera*, 25 September 2015. http://www.aljazeera.com/indepth/features/2015/09/ukraine-russians-150924155813472.html

[50] Paul DAnieri, 'Ethnic Tensions and State Strategies: Understanding the Survival of the Ukrainian State,' *Journal of Communist Studies and Transition Politics*, vol.23, no.1 (March 2007), p.20.

[51] http://www.pewglobal.org/2015/08/05/russia-putin-held-in-low-regard-around-the-world/

[52] Maria Savchyn Pyskir, *Thousands of Roads. A Memoir of a Young Woman's Life in the Ukrainian Underground During and After World War II* (Jefferson, NC and London: McFarland and co, 2001), p.203.

[53] *Hazeta po-Ukrayinski*, 16 December 2010.

[54] Anna Procyk, *Russian nationalism and Ukraine: the nationality policy of the volunteer army during the Civil War* (Toronto: Canadian Institute of Ukrainian Studies Press, 1995).

[55] S. Hutchings and V. Tolz, *Nation, Ethnicity and Race on Russian Television*, p.162.

[56] T. Kuzio, 'The Myth of the Civic State: A Critical Survey of Hans Kohn's Framework for Understanding Nationalism,' *Ethnic and Racial Studies*, vol.25, no.1 (January 2002), pp.20-39.

[57] Terry Martin, *The Affirmative Action Empire. Nations and Nationalism in the Soviet Union* (Ithaca, NY: Cornell University Press, 2001), p.112.

[58] Ralph S. Clem, 'The Integration of Ukraine into Modernized Society in the Ukrainian SSR,' in R.S. Clem, *The Soviet West. Interplay Between Nationality and Social Organisations* (New York and London: Praeger, 1975), p.63.

[59] Martin Aberg, 'Putnam's Social Capital Theory Goes East: A Case Study of western Ukraine and L'viv,' *Europe-Asia Studies*, vol.52, no.2 (March 2000), pp.295-317 and Mark R. Beissinger, *Nationalist Mobilization and the Collapse of the Soviet State* (Cambridge: Cambridge University Press, 2002).

[60] Lowell Barrington, 'Russian Speakers in Ukraine and Kazakhstan: 'Nationality,' 'Population' or Neither,' *Post-Soviet Affairs*, vol.17, no.2 (2001), pp.129-158 and Pal Kolsto, 'The New Russian Diaspora – An Identity of Its Own? *Ethnic and Racial Studies*, vol.19, no.3 (July 1996), pp.608-639.

[61] 'Russians and Russophones in the Former USSR and Serbs in Yugoslavia: A Comparative Study of Passivity and Mobilisation' in T. Kuzio, *Theoretical and Comparative Perspectives on Nationalism: New Directions in Cross-Cultural and Post-Communist Studies* (Hannover: Ibidem-Verlag, 2007), pp.177-217.

[62] Geoffrey Hosking, 'Can Russia become a Nation-State?' *Nations and Nationalism*, vol.4, no.4 (1998), pp. 449-46.

[63] Serhiy Plokhy, 'The City of Glory: Sevastopol in Russian Historical Mythology,' *Journal of Contemporary History*, vol.35, no.3 (2000), pp.369-384.

[64] 'Common identity of the citizens of Ukraine,' *National Security and Defence*, no.9 (2007). http://www.uceps.org/eng/journal.php?y=2007&cat=37

[65] David G. Rowley, 'Imperial versus national discourse: the case of Russia,' *Nations and Nationalism*, vol.6, no.1 (January 2000), p.34.

[66] V. Tolz, 'Conflicting "Homeland Myths" and Nation-State Building in Postcommunist Russia,' *Slavic Review*, vol.57, no.2 (Summer 1998), pp.267-294 and 'Forging the Nation: National Identity and Nation Building in Post-Communist Russia,' *Europe-Asia Studies*, vol.50, no.6 (September 1998), p.993-1022.

[67] T. Martin, *The Affirmative Action Empire*, p.395.

[68] Rogers Brubaker, 'Nationhood and the national question in the Soviet Union and post-Soviet Eurasia: An institutionalist account,' *Theory and Society*, vol.23, no.1 (February 1994), p.70.

[69] T. Martin, *The Affirmative Action Empire*, p.460.

[70] Ibid., p.457.

[71] Cheng Chen, *The Prospects for Liberal Nationalism in Post-Leninist States* (University Park, PA: Penn State University Press, 2007), p.76.

[72] Aleksei M. Salmin, 'Russia's emerging statehood in the national security content' in Vladimir Baranovsky ed., *Russia and Europe. The Emerging Security Agenda* (Oxford: Oxford University Press and SIPRI, 1997), pp.104-134.

[73] Catherine Andreyev, *Vlasov and the Russian Liberation Movement. Soviet reality and émigré theories* (Cambridge: Cambridge University Press, 1989), pp.131-132, 170, 187,189, 191.

[74] Ibid., p.132.

[75] Bohdan Krawchenko, *Social Change and National Consciousness in Twentieth Century Ukraine* (Oxford: St. Anthony's College and London: Macmillan, 1985), p.251.

[76] 'The Myth of Russian Nationalism,' in Alexander J. Motyl, *Sovietology, Rationality, Nationality. Coming to Grips with Nationalism in the USSR* (New York: Columbia University Press, 1990), p.165.

[77] D. G. Rowley, 'Imperial versus national discourse,' p.36.

[78] Mikhail Gorbachev cited by *Reuters*, 16 December 1996.

[79] Yitzhak Brudny, *Reinventing Russia. Russian Nationalism and the Soviet State, 1953-1991* (Cambridge, MA: Harvard University Press, 1998), p.262.

[80] G. Hoskings, 'Can Russia become a nation-state?' p.457.

[81] James P. Scanlan, 'The Russian Idea from Dostoevskii to Ziuganov,' *Problems of Post-Communism*, vol.43, no.4 (July-August 1995), p.40.

[82] V. Tolz, *Russia. Inventing the Nation* (London: Arnold Press, 2001).

[83] C. Chen, *The Prospects for Liberal Nationalism in Post-Leninist States*, p.92.

[84] Ibid., p.76.

[85] Russians are prone to the 'conviction of moral superiority' and 'moral chauvinism' and see the world revolving around Russia. Hedrick Smith, *The Russians* (New York: Quadrangle, 1976), pp.307 and 311.

[86] Victor Zaslavsky, *The Neo-Stalinist State. Class, Ethnicity, and Consensus in Soviet Society* (Armonk, NY: M. E. Sharpe, 1982), p.128.

[87] Ibid., p.128.

[88] *Russian Federation: Violent Racism Out of Control*, EUR 46/022/2006 (London: Amnesty International, 3 May 2006). https://www.amnesty.org/en/documents/EUR46/022/2006/en/

[89] Liah Greenfeld, *Nationalism. Five Roads to Modernity* (Cambridge, MA: Harvard University Press, 1993), pp.254 and 270.

[90] M. Francetti, 'Putin boosted by Orthodox 'inquisition.'

[91] Y. M. Brudny, *Reinventing Russia*, p.16.

[92] Marlene Laruelle, 'The "Russian Idea" on the Small Screen: Staging National Identity on Russia's TV,' *Demokratizatsiya*, vol.22, no.2 (Spring 2014), p.332.

[93] Walter Laqueur, *Black Hundred. The Rise of the Extreme Right in Russia* (New York: Harper Collins, 1993), p.15, C. Andreyev, *Vlasov and the Russian Liberation Movement*, pp.175-177 and Anton Barbashin and Hannah Thoburn, 'Putin's Philosopher. Ivan Ilyin and the Ideology of Moscow's Rule,' *Foreign Affairs*, 20 September 2015. https://www.foreignaffairs.com/articles/russian-federation/2015-09-20/putins-philosopher

[94] Nikolai Petrushev interviewed by *Moskovskii Komsomolets*, 26 January 2016. http://www.mk.ru/politics/2016/01/26/nikolay-patrushev-mirovoe-soobshhestvo-dolzhno-skazat-nam-spasibo-za-krym.html

[95] Joseph Parent and Joseph Uscinski, 'People who believe in conspiracy theories are more likely to endorse violence,' *The Washington Post*, 5 February 2016. https://www.washingtonpost.com/news/monkey-cage/wp/2016/02/05/are-conspiracy-theorists-plotting-to-blow-up-the-u-s/?wpmm=1&wpisrc=nl_cage

[96] W. Laqueur, *Black Hundred*, p.95.

[97] H-m. Joo, 'The Soviet Origin of Russian Chauvinism,' p.233.

[98] J. Wishnevsky, 'Soviet Newspaper Expresses Concern Over Russian Nationalist Gathering in Leningrad,' *Radio Liberty*, RL 485/87 (2 December 1987).

[99] John J. Stephan, *The Russian Fascists. Tragedy and Farce in Exile, 1925-1945* (Hamish Hamilton, 1978), p.373.

[100] Ibid., pp.16-30 and W. Laqueur, *Black Hundred*, p.74.

[101] W. Laqueur, *Black Hundred*, p.84.

[102] Victor Yasmann, 'Red Religion: An Ideology of Neo-Messianic Russian Fundamentalism,' *Demokratizatsiya*, vol. 1, no.2 (Spring 1992), p.26.

[103] 'The Russian National Movement' in Ludmilla Alexeyeva, *Soviet Dissent: Contemporary Movements for National, Religious, and Human Rights* (Middletown, Conn.: Wesleyan University Press, 1985), p.434.

[103] Ibid., pp.431-449.

[104] Charles Clover, *Black Wind, White Snow. The Rise of Russia's New Nationalism* (New Haven, CT: Yale University Press, 2016), pp.20 and 65.

[105] Ibid., p.174.

[106] Robert Zubrin, 'Dugin's Evil Theology,' *National Review*, 18 June 2014. http://www.nationalreview.com/article/380614/dugins-evil-theology-robert-zubrin

[107] C. Clover, *Black Wind, White Snow*, p.260.

[108] Ibid., p.205.

[109] Ibid., p.206.

[110] Ibid., pp.225-226.

[111] Ibid, pp.241, 271, 275, 278.

[112] Ibid., p.280.

[113] W. Laqueur, *Black Hundred*, p.146.

[114] A. Umland, 'Who is Alexander Dugin?' *Open Democracy*, 26 September 2008. https://www.opendemocracy.net/article/russia-theme/who-is-alexander-dugin

[115] Ibid.,

[116] 'Russia Hews Closer to Zhirinovsky's Wacky Vision Than You Might Have Expected,' *RFERL*, 25 April 2016. http://www.rferl.org/content/russia-zhirinovsky-no-longer-so-wacky/27696519.html

[117] http://news.bbc.co.uk/1/hi/world/europe/1446759.stm

[118] Anton Shekhovtsov, 'The Palingenetic Thrust of Russian Neo-Eurasianism: Ideas of Rebirth in Aleksandr Dugin's Worldview,' *Totalitarian Movements and Political Religions*, vol.9, no.4 (December 2008), pp. 492.

[119] Pavel Felgenhauer, 'Russian military weakness could delay conflict with Ukraine,' *Eurasia Daily Monitor*, vol.6, no. 156 (13 August 2009). http://www.jamestown.org/single/?tx_ttnews%5Btt_news%5D=35404&no_cache=1#.Vr9JaZMrKt8

[120] A. Shekhovtsov, 'How Alex Dugin's Neo-Eurasianists geared up for the Russian-Ukrainian War in 2005-2013,' *Anton Shekhovtsov blog*, 25 January 2015. http://anton-shekhovtsov.blogspot.com/2016/01/how-alexander-dugins-neo-eurasianists.html

[121] A. Dugin, 'Putin's Advisor Dugin says Ukrainians must be "killed, killed, killed"' https://www.youtube.com/watch?v=MQ-uqmnwKF8

[122] W. Laqueur, *Black Hundred*, p.213.

[123] An FSB Lieutenant Colonel described oligarch Boris Berezovsky as a 'filthy Jew.' Luke Harding, *A Very Expensive Poison. The Definitive Story of the Murder of Litvinenko and Russia's War with the West* (London: Guardian Books, 2016), p.28.

[124] C. Clover, *Black Wind, White Snow*, p.165.

[125] Julia Wishnevsky, 'The Emergence of "Pamyat" and "Otechestvo," *Radio Liberty*, RL 342/87 (26 August 1987).

[126] C. Clover, *Black Wind, White Snow*, pp.162-163.

[127] *Samizdat* document 'Fascism in the USSR: A Spontaneous Protest or an Inspired Movement?'

[128] J. Wishnevsky, 'Neo-Nazis in the Soviet Union,' *Radio Liberty*, RL 226/85 (11 July 1985), 'Soviet Neo-Nazis in the Official Press,' *Radio Liberty*, RL 40/86 (23 January 1986), 'Soviet Weekly Publishes Letter from Neo-Fascists', *Radio Liberty*, RL 219/86 (4 June 1986), and 'More About Neo-Nazis in Leningrad,' *Radio Liberty*, RL 312/87 (29 July 1987).

[129] W. Laqueur, *Black Hundred*, p.294.

[130] Ibid., p.295.

[131] M. Laruelle, 'The three colors of Novorossiya, or the Russian nationalist mythmaking of the Ukrainian crisis,' *Post-Soviet Affairs*, vol.32, no.1 (January 2016), pp.55-74.

[132] Ibid.,

[133] Yuri Teper, 'Official Russian identity discourse in the light of the annexation of the Crimea: national or imperial?' *Post Soviet Affairs*, vol. 32, no.4 (July 2016), pp. 378-396.

[134] M. Laruelle, 'The three colors of Novorosiya,' p.67.

[135] Chris de Pleg, 'In Ukraine Europe is collaborating with oligarchs and fascists,' *Spectrezone*, 29 February 2016. http://www.spectrezine.org/ukraine-europe-collaborating-oligarchs-and-fascists

[136] S. Walker, 'We are preventing a third world war: the foreigners fighting with Ukrainian rebels,' *The Guardian*, 24 September 2015. http://www.theguardian.com/world/2015/sep/24/ukraine-conflict-donbass-russia-rebels-foreigners-fighting

[137] Ibid.,

[138] P. Jackson, 'Ukraine war pulls in foreign fighters,' *BBC*, 31 August 2014. http://www.bbc.com/news/world-europe-28951324

[139] Ukrainian hacker's groups leaked emails that showed Russia had issued visas to foreigner mercenaries who wanted to fight for pro-Russian separatists in the Donbas. https://informnapalm.org/en/russia-opens-visas-terrorists-operating-ukraine/

[140] A. J. Motyl, 'Is Putin's Russia Fascist?' *The National Interest*, 3 December 2007, 'Russia's Systemic Transformations since Perestroika: From Totalitarianism to Authoritarianism to Democracy—to Fascism?' *The Harriman Review*, vol.17, no.2, (March 2010), pp.1-14 and 'Putin's Russia as a fascist political system,' *Communist and Post-Communist Studies*, vol.49, no. 1 (March 2016), pp.25-36.

http://nationalinterest.org/commentary/inside-track-is-putins-russia-fascist-1888
and
http://harriman.columbia.edu/files/harriman/newsletter/Harriman%20Review%20vol%2017%20no%202%20to%20post%20on%20web.pdf

[141] A. J. Motyl, 'Putin's Russia as a fascist political system' and Valerie Sperling, 'Putin's Macho Personality Cult.' *Communist and Post-Communist Studies*, vol. 49, no. 1 (March 2016), pp.13-24.

[142] Ben Judah, *Fragile Empire. How Russia Fell in and Out of Love with Vladimir Putin* (New Haven, CO: Yale University Press, 2013), p.179.

[143] Ibid., p,196.

[144] Hutchings and Tolz believe that Putin's turn to the right came after the 2003-2004 Rose and Orange Revolutions and Beslan school siege by Chechen terrorists. These events led to growing xenophobia against the West, claims the West is set on destroying Russia, Russia championed as the protector of compatriots abroad and demands for recognition of Russian primacy in Eurasia. See their *Nation, Ethnicity and Race on Russian Television*, pp.176, 257-258.

[145] C. Clover, *Black Wind, White Snow*, p.315.

[146] Lilia Shevtsova, 'The Putin Doctrine: Myth, Provocation, Blackmail, or the Real Deal,' *The American Interest*, 14 April 2014. http://www.the-american-interest.com/2014/04/14/the-putin-doctrine-myth-provocation-blackmail-or-the-real-deal/

[147] A. Wilson, *Belarus. The Last European Dictatorship* (New Haven, CT: Yale University Press, 2011), p.259.

[148] Sven G. Simonsen, 'Alexander Barkashov and RNE: Blackshirt Friends of the Nation,' *Nationalities Papers*, vol.24, no.4 (December 1996), p.632.

[149] Simon Shuster, 'Meet the Cossack 'Wolves' Doing Russia's Dirty Work in Ukraine,' *Time*, 12 May 2014. http://time.com/95898/wolves-hundred-ukraine-russia-cossack/

[150] M. Laruelle, 'The three colors of Novorossiya.'

[151] Photographs of RNE neo-Nazi paramilitaries in the Donbas can be viewed at 'Neo-Nazi Russian National Unity in Eastern Ukraine,' *Anton Shekhovtsov's blog*, 14 August 2014. http://anton-shekhovtsov.blogspot.com/2014/08/neo-nazi-russian-national-unity-in.html

[152] Richard Arnold, 'The Involvement of Russian Ultra-Nationalists in the Donbas Conflict,' *Eurasia Daily Monitor*, vol.11, no.105 (11 June 2014). http://www.jamestown.org/programs/edm/single/?tx_ttnews%5btt_news%5d=42481&tx_ttnews%5bbackPid%5d=756&no_cache=1#.VsQpwZMrKCR

[153] Russia and the Separatists in Eastern Ukraine, *International Crisis Group, Briefing no. 79* (5 February 2016), p.10. http://www.crisisgroup.org/en/regions/europe/ukraine/b079-russia-and-the-separatists-in-eastern-ukraine.aspx

[154] http://ukraineatwar.blogspot.nl/2015/06/nazis-are-core-of-russias-hybrid-army.html

[155] Yuri Slezkine, 'The USSR as a Communal Apartment, or How a Socialist State Promoted Ethnic Particularism,' *Slavic Review*, vol..53, no.2 (Summer 1994), p.443.

[156] David Brandenberger, 'It is Imperative to Advance Russian Nationalism as the First Priority: Debates Within the Stalinist Ideological Establishment, 1941-1945' in Ronald G. Suny and T. Martin eds., *A State of Nations. Empire and Nation-Making in the Age of Lenin and Stalin* (Oxford: Oxford University Press, 2001), p.280 and D. L. Brandenberger and A.M. Dubrovsky, "The People Needs a Tsar': The Emergence of National Bolshevism in Stalinist Ideology, 1931-1941,' *Europe-Asia Studies*, vo.50, no.5 (July 1998), p.878.

[157] J. Wishnevsky, 'Dissidence under Andropov: A Return to Stalinist Methods,' *Radio Liberty*, RL 411/83 (28 October 1983).

[158] The conference adopted 'Measures to Further Improve the Study and Teaching of the Russian Language in the Union Republics.' See V. Zaslavsky, *The Neo-Stalinist State*, pp.102-103.

[159] W. Laquer, *Black Hundred*, p.66.

[160] Teresa Rakowska-Harmstone, 'The study of ethnic politics in the USSR' in George W. Simmons ed., *Nationalism in the USSR and Eastern Europe in the era of Brezhnev and Kosygin* (Detroit: University of Detroit Press, 1977), p.22.

[161] Andrei Amalrik, *Will the Soviet Union Survive until 1984?* (London: Allen Lane, The Penguin Press, 1971).

[162] D. L. Brandenberger and A.M. Dubrovsky, 'The People Needs a Tsar,' pp.873-892.

[163] Serhy Yekelchyk, *Stalin's Empire of Memory. Russian-Ukrainian Relations in the Soviet Historical Imagination* (Toronto: University of Toronto Press, 2004), p.88.

[164] T. Martin, *The Affirmative Action Empire*, pp.270 and 272.

[165] Ibid., p.453.

[166] Russian Consul in the Crimea cited by *Istorychna Pravda*, 18 January 2011.

[167] V. Tolz, 'The Lay of the Host of Igor in the Service of Ideology,' *Radio Liberty*, RL 390/85 (22 November 1985).

[168] S. Yekelchyk, *Stalin's Empire of Memory*, p.97.

[169] M. Vickery, 'Ukraine's other Russians. Meet the Russians fighting for Ukraine.'

[170] J. Wishnevsky, 'Molodaya Gvardiya: A Leading Voice of Opposition to Restructuring,' *Radio Liberty*, RL 1/88 (5 January 1988) and Y. M. Brudny, *Reinventing Russia*, p.57.

[171] Y. M. Brudny, *Reinventing Russia*, p.102.

[172] Ibid., pp.15 and 21.

[173] V. Tolz, 'Russian Nationalism in the 1980s: Echoes of Stalinist Policy,' *Radio Liberty*, RL 370/85 (7 November 1985).

[174] John T. Ishiyana, 'Strange bedfellows: explaining political cooperation between communist successor parties and nationalists in Eastern Europe,' *Nations and Nationalism*, vol.4, no.1 (January 1998), pp. 61-85.

[175] The election platform of the KPRF can be found in *Rossiyskaya Gazeta*, 23 November 1999.

[176] D. L. Brandenberger and A. M. Dubrovsky, 'The People Need a Tsar,' p.875.

[177] Y. M. Brudny, *Reinventing Russia*, p.254.

[178] L. Greenfeld, *Nationalism*, p.261.

[179] L. Alexeyeva, 'The Russian National Movement,' p.439.

[180] Ibid., pp.431-449.

[181] Jonathan Frankel, *The Soviet Regime and Anti-Zionism: An Analysis*, Research Paper no.55 (Jerusalem: Hebrew University of Jerusalem, The Soviet and East European Research Centre, May 1984). pp.21 and 58.

[182] Prince A. Wolkonsky, *The Ukraine Question*, pp.169, 190.

[183] J. J. Stephan, *The Russian Fascists,* p.373.

[184] W. Laquer, *Black Hundred*, p.63.

[185] Yulia Voznesenskaya, 'Transformation of the Image of the White Guard Officer in Soviet Cinema,' *Radio Liberty*, no.409/84 (23 October 1984).

[186] Clifford G. Gaddy and Fiona Hill, *Mr. Putin. Operative in the Kremlin* (Washington DC; Brookings Institution Press, 2015), pp.101-103.

[187] Gregory Feifer, 'Putin's White Guard. Why Russia's Former Nobility is Supporting the Kremlin,' *Foreign Affairs*, 23 March 2015. https://www.foreignaffairs.com/articles/russian-federation/2015-03-23/putins-white-guard

[188] M. Gessen, 'The Dearly Departed Return to Russia,' *The New Yorker*, 21 August 2015. http://www.newyorker.com/news/news-desk/the-dearly-departed-return-to-russia

[189] A. Barbashin and H. Thoburn, 'Putin's Philosopher.'

[190] Ibid.,

[191] Carl Schreck and Dmitriy Volchek, 'Russian 'Former Fascist' Who Fought with Separatists Says Moscow Unleashed, Orchestrated Ukraine War.' *RFERL*, 8 March 2016.

http://www.rferl.mobi/a/ukraine-russia-neo-nazi-fought-with-separatists-says-kremlin-behind-war/27598825.html

[192] Mark Franchetti, 'Russian nationalist warns Putin risks being toppled 'like the tsar,'' *The Sunday Times*, 22 March 2015. http://www.the-sundaytimes.co.uk/sto/news/world_news/Europe/article1534275.ece

[193] Sonya Koshkina, *Maidan. Nerasskazannya Istoriya* (Kyiv: Bright Star Publishing, 2015), p.360.

[194] M. Laruelle, 'The three colors of Novorossiya.'

[195] Arne Delfs and Henry Meyer, 'Putin's Propaganda Machine Is Meddling with European Elections,' *Bloomberg*, 20 April 2016. http://www.bloomberg.com/news/articles/2016-04-20/from-rape-claim-to-brexit-putin-machine-tears-at-europe-s-seams

[196] Maria Engstrom, 'Contemporary Russian Messianism and New Russian Foreign Policy,' *Contemporary Security Policy*, vol.35, no.3 (September 2014), pp.356-279.

[197] M. Laruelle, 'The three colors of Novorossiya.'

[198] R. Zubrin, 'Moscow's Mad Philosopher's,' *National Review*, 18 February 2015. http://www.nationalreview.com/article/398811/moscows-mad-philosophers-robert-zubrin.'

[199] M. Laruelle, 'The three colors of Novorossiya.'

[200] M. Engstrom, 'Contemporary Russian Messianism and New Russian Foreign Policy.'

[201] 'New Stalin Monument Attracts Flowers, Vandals,' *RFERL*, 26 August 2015. http://www.rferl.org/media/video/russia-stalin-history/27210078.html

[202] Nikolas K. Gvosdev, 'The New Party Card? Orthodoxy and the Search for Post-Soviet Russian Identity,' *Problem of Post-Communism*, vol.47, no.6 (November-December 2000), pp.29-38.

[203] 'Putin's people,' *The Economist*, 13 December 2014. http://www.economist.com/news/europe/21636047-president-remains-popular-his-ukrainian-adventure-could-change-faster-many

[204] Maksym Bugriy, 'The War and the Orthodox Churches in Ukraine,' *Eurasia Daily Monitor*, vol.12, no. 30 (18 February 2015). http://www.jamestown.org/programs/edm/single/?tx_ttnews%5Btt_news%5D=43548&cHash=3dc1a85482a515406a43403429694d66#.VrxxeZMrLR0

[205] 'Thousands Parade on Russia's National Unity Day,' *RFERL*, 4 November 2015. http://www.rferl.org/media/video/russia-moscow-march-unity-putin-/27345263.html

[206] Michal Wawrzonek, 'Ukraine in the "Gray Zone": Between the "Russkiy Mir" and Europe,' *East European Politics and Societies*, vol.28, no.4 (November 2014), p.766.

[207] Alexander Verkhovsky, 'The Role of the Russian Orthodox Church in Nationalist, Xenophobic and antiwestern Tendencies in Russia Today: Not Nationalism, but Fundamentalism,' *Religion, Sate and Society*, vol.30, no.4 (December 2002), pp.333-345.

[208] Andrew Higginssept, 'Evidence Grows of Russian Orthodox Clergy's Aiding Ukraine Rebels,' *New York Times*, 6 September 2014. http://www.nytimes.com/2014/09/07/world/europe/evidence-grows-of-russian-orthodox-clergys-aiding-ukraine-rebels.html?_r=0

[209] M. Laruelle, 'The three colors of Novorossiya,' p.62.

[210] *Novaya Gazeta*, 24 February 2015.

[211] Aleksandr Sytyn, 'Anatomiya provala: O mekhanizme prynytya vneshnepoliticheskykh resheniy Kremlya,' *Bramaby*, 5 January 2015. http://www.bramaby.com/ls/blog/rus/1841.html

212 C. Clover, *Black Wind, White Snow*, pp.325-326.

213 http://www.themoscowtimes.com/news/article/russian-prime-minister-ukraine-has-no-industry-or-state/564756.html

214 Olga Malinova, 'Obsession with status and resentment: Historical backgrounds of the Russian discursive identity construction,' *Communist and Post-Communist Studies*, vol.47, nos. 3-4, (September 2014), pp.291-303.

215 Olga Kryshtanovskaya and Stephen White, 2003. 'Putin's Militocracy,' *Post-Soviet Affairs*, vol.19, no.4 (October 2003), pp.289-306.

216 B. Judah, 'Putin's Coup.'

217 M. Engstrom, 'Contemporary Russian Messianism and New Russian Foreign Policy.'

218 Y. Teper, 'Official Russian identity discourse in the light of the annexation of the Crimea: national or imperial?'

219 Ibid.,

220 Chapter 3, 'The Kosovo Precedent' in R. D. Asmus, *A Little War That Shook the World*, pp.87-109.

221 M. Wawrzonek, 'Ukraine in the "Gray Zone."'

222 Andrei Kozyrev is cited by C. G. Gaddy and F. Hill, *Mr. Putin*, pp.34-35. On Dmitrii Medvedev see Roger McDermott, 'Russia Promotes its "Sphere of Privileged Interests" in Kyrgyzstan,' *Eurasia Daily Monitor*, vol. 6, no.144 (28 July 2009). http://www.jamestown.org/single/?tx_ttnews%5Btt_news%5D=35330#.Vrxh0pMrLR0

223 Stephen Blank, 'Putin and Lavrov Again Play the Ethnic Compatriot Card,' *Eurasian Daily Monitor*, vol.12, no.207, 13 November 2015. http://www.jamestown.org/programs/edm/single/?tx_ttnews%5Btt_news%5D=44596&cHash=019d56a714ac7ddc7f619df330dd3237#.Vl3dgN-rTVo

224 Sergei Lavrov, 'Support of Russian world is priority for Russia's foreign policy,' *Tass*, 2 November 2015. http://tass.ru/en/politics/833358

225 Catherine Wanner, '"Fraternal" nations and challenges to sovereignty in Ukraine: The politics of linguistic and religious ties,' *American Ethnologist*, vol.41, no.3 (August 2014), p.432.

226 S. Blank, 'Putin and Lavrov Again Play the Ethnic Compatriot Card.'

227 Ibid.,

228 S. Hutchings and V. Tolz, *Nation, Ethnicity and Race on Russian Television*, p.257.

229 P. Tolstoy, *Politika, Russian Channel One*, 28 October 2015.

230 www.politcom.ru, 29 November 2004 and 27 December 2004, www.gazeta.ru, *Komsomolskaya Pravda*, 28 December 2004.

231 Vladimir Socor, 'Putin Outlines Current Policy Toward Ukraine,' *Eurasia Daily Monitor*, vol.12, no.77 (23 April 2015). http://www.jamestown.org/programs/edm/single/?tx_ttnews%5Btt_news%5D=43829&cHash=5689d3204bb4744030391e198737760d#.VrxtGpMrLR0

232 N. Petrushev interviewed by *Moskovskii Komsomolets*, 26 January 2016.

233 Sergei Ivanov interviewed by http://tass.ru/opinions/top-officials/2356242?page=2

234 'Ukraine in the Russian National Consciousness,' in V. Tolz, *Russia: Inventing the Nation*, pp.227-228 and 230.

235 Russian Patriots, 'A Nation Speaks,' *Survey*, vol.17, no.3 (Autumn 1971), pp.191-199. The original *Radio Liberty Arkhiv Samizdata* document is in the hands of the author and an excerpt is cited at the beginning of the book.

236 Alexander Solzhenitsyn, 'Rebuilding Russia,' 1990. http://www.solzhenitsyn.ru/pro-izvedeniya/publizistika/stati_i_rechi/v_izgnanii/kak_nam_obustroit_rossiyu.pdf. For a comparison of Putin's and Solzhenitsyn's views see Robert Coalson, 'Is Putin 'Rebuilding Russia' According to Solzhenitsyn's Design?' *RFERL*, 1 September 2014. http://www.rferl.org/content/russia-putin-solzhenitsyn-1990-essay/26561244.html

237 Robert Horvath, 'Apologist of Putinism? Solzhenitsyn, the Oligarchs, and the Specter of Orange Revolution,' *The Russian Review*, vol.70, no.1 (April 2011), p.312.

238 B. Judah, *Fragile Empire*, p.57.

239 R. Horvath, 'Apologist of Putinism?' p.318.

240 M. Laruelle, 'The three colors of Novorossiya.'

241 V. Putin, 'Speech to NATO Summit in Bucharest.'

242 Oleksandr Bazylyuk believes Russian and Ukrainian culture 'represents a single whole.' See also Stephen Shulman, 'Nationalist Sources of International Economic Integration,' *International Studies Quarterly*, vol.44, no.3 (September 2000), p.386.

243 Anatol Lieven, 'The Weakness of Russian Nationalism,' *Survival*, vol.41, no.2 (Summer 1999), pp.53-70.

244 Yuriy Boldyrev cited by *Reuters*, 28 March 1994.

245 http://www.cvk.gov.ua/pls/vd2002/webproc0v?kodvib=1&rejim=0

246 Oleksandr Mayboroda, *Rosiyskiy Natsionalizm v Ukrayini (1991-1998rr.)* (Kyiv: Kyiv Mohyla Academy, 1999), p.27.

247 Stephen Crowley, 'Between Class and Nation. Worker Politics in the New Ukraine,' *Communist and Post-Communist Studies*, vol.28, no.1 (March 1995), p.64.

248 Nikolai Levchenko, 'Sekretar miskrady Donetska: rosiyska stane yedynoyu derzhavnoyu movoyu' (The Secretary of the Donetsk City Council: Russian Will become the Only State Language), *Hazeta po-ukrayinsky*, 25 February, 2007
http://gazeta.ua/articles/politics/_sekretar-miskradi-donecka-rosijska-stane-yedinoyu-derzhavnoyu-movoyu/151649

249 T. Martin, *The Affirmative Action Empire*, p.363.

250 A. Wilson, *The Ukrainians. Unexpected Nation* (New Haven, CT: Yale University Press, 2000), p.309.

251 Interview with Civic Congress leader Oleksandr Bazylyuk, Donetsk, 30 August 1996.

252 O. Mayboroda, *Rosiyskiy Natsionalizm v Ukrayini*, p.25.

253 A. Shekhovtsov, 'How Alexandr Dugin's Neo-Eurasianists geared up for the Russia-Ukraine war in 2005-2013.'

254 Vladimir Peshkov, *The Donbas: Back in the USSR* (London: European Council on Foreign Relations, 1 September 2016). http://www.ecfr.eu/article/essay_the_donbas_back_in_the_ussr

255 Halya Coynash, 'Selective Anti-Fascism,' *KHRPG*, 17 July 2013. http://khpg.org/en/index.php?id=1373836134

256 Olena Matusova, 'Belkovskyy: Na Donbasi zbyrayutsya marginaly i vbyvtsi, yakyh vykorystovuvav Kreml v ostanni roky,' *Radio Svoboda*, 24 November 2014. http://www.radiosvoboda.org/content/article/26707140.html

[257] Richard Arnold, 'Surveys show Russian nationalism is on the rise. This explains a lot about the country's foreign and domestic politics,' *The Washington Post*, 30 May 2016. https://www.washingtonpost.com/news/monkey-cage/wp/2016/05/30/surveys-show-russian-nationalism-is-on-the-rise-this-explains-a-lot-about-the-countrys-foreign-and-domestic-politics/

[258] H. Coynash, 'BORN in the Kremlin? Russian ultranationalist trial and links with Ukraine,' *KHRPG*, 12 June 2015. http://khpg.org/en/index.php?id=1433976348

[259] C. Clover, *Black Wind, White Snow*, p.291.

[260] Ibid., p.287.

[261] O. Matusova, 'Belkovskyy: Na Donbasi zbyrayutsya marginaly i vbyvtsi, yakyh vykorystovuvav Kreml v ostanni roky.'

[262] V. Nalyvaychenko interviewed by *Den*, 1 April 2015.

[263] Valentyn Landyk interviewed in http://news.online.ua/743660/vladimir-landik/

[264] N. Mitrokhin, 'Ukraine's Separatists and Their Dubious Leaders,' *Searchlight*, 18 April 2014. http://www.searchlightmagazine.com/news/featured-news/ukraines-separatists-and-their-dubious-leaders

[265] Mykola Riabchuk, 'Ukrainians as Russia's Negative 'Other': History Comes Full Circle,' *Communist and Post-Communist Studies*, vol.49, no. 1 (March 2016), pp.75-86.

[266] V. Tolz, *Russia. Inventing the Nation*, pp.216, 218.

[267] http://flot2017.com/ru/opinions/ 4398

[268] Ibid.,

[269] Igor Zhadan, 'Operatsiya "Mekhanycheskyy apelsyn. Khochesh mira?' *Russkii Zhurnal*, 21 April 2008. Translation at Falcon Bjorn, 'Operation Clockwork Orange. Si vis pacem?' *Inform Napalm*, 6 January 2015.
http://www.russ.ru/pole/Operaciya-Mehanicheskij-apel-sin; https://informna-palm.org/en/operation-clockwork-orange-si-vis-pacem/

[270] Greg Austin, 'President Putin of Ukraine? Is it only a question of time before Russia will annex parts of Ukraine?' *The Diplomat*, 29 January 2015. http://thediplo-mat.com/2015/01/president-putin-of-ukraine/

[271] 'Vladimir Putin, Is That You?' *RFERL*, 7 April 2015. http://www.rferl.org/content/vladi-mir-putin-defends-ukraine-borders/26942991.html

[272] Y. M. Brudny, 'Soviet and Post-Soviet Remembrances of World War II and Its Aftermath,'

[273] Dmitriy Bykov, 'Voina Pisatelei,' *Novya Gazeta*, 9 July 2014. www.novayaga-zeta.ru/socity/64337.html. On Berezin see Jack Hitt, 'The Russian Tom Clancy is on the Front Line for Real,' *The New Yorker*, 7 January 2016. http://www.newyorker.com/books/page-turner/the-russian-tom-clancy-is-on-the-front-lines-for-real

[274] 'U Rossii prodayut knyhy pro viynu z Ukrayinoyu,' *Ukrayinska Pravda*, 2 March 2009. http://www.pravda.com.ua/news/2009/03/2/3772247/

[275] *Ukrayinska Pravda*, 2 March 2009.

[276] Ibid.,

[277] H. Smith, *The Russians*, p.123.

[278] Leonid Plyushch, *History's Carnival. A Dissident Autobiography* (Harcourt Brace Jovanovich, 1977), p.8.

[279] Sergei Karaganov, 'Nobody needs a monster. Desovereignisation of Ukraine,' *Russskii Zhur-nal*, 20 March 2009.

www.russ.ru/Mirovaya-povestka/Nikomu-ne-nuzhnye-chudischa

[280] A. Kulakov, 'Failed state, abo Ukrayina ochyma Rossii.'

[281] *Komsomolskaya Pravda v Ukrainy,* 11 February 2009. http://kp.ua/interview/72530-vyktor-chernomyrdyn-ukrayna-ot-rossyy-nykuda-ne-denetsia-denetsia-esche-kak-polnyi-tekst-skandalnoho-yntervui

[282] Ibid.,

[283] *Ukrayinska Pravda,* 18 February 2009.

[284] Aleksandr Zakharchenko cited by *Bloomberg,* 16 April 2015.

[285] S. Hutchings and V. Tolz, *Nation, Ethnicity and Race on Russian Television,* pp.24, 26, 29.

[286] Interview with Democratic Initiatives Foundation President, Iryna Bekeshkina, Kyiv, 18 May 2016.

[287] A. Wilson, 'The Donbas in 2014,' p.636.

[288] *Natsionalna Bezpeka i Oborona,* nos.3-4 (2016), pp.9 and 36.

[289] 'What unites and divides Ukrainians,' Democratic Initiatives Foundation, 22 January 2015. http://dif.org.ua/ua/publications/press-relizy/sho-obednue-ta-rozednue-ukrain-civ.htm

[290] 'The Battle for Ukraine,' *PBS Frontline,* 27 May 2014. http://www.pbs.org/wgbh/pages/frontline/battle-for-ukraine/

[291] Lozhkin says his home town of Kharkiv was 'never a city of crime.' See his *The Fourth Republic,* p.51.

[292] Yuras Karmanau, 'Ukraine's rebels center in limbo as fighting dies down,' *AP,* 5 November 2015. http://bigstory.ap.org/article/22e8c00482b5470ab67263efb6400c2c/ukraines-rebel-center-limbo-fighting-dies-down

[293] Jack Losh, 'Rebel-held Ukraine overhauls education system as it aligns itself with Russia,' *The Guardian,* 16 August 2015. http://www.theguardian.com/world/2015/aug/16/ukraine-rebel-territories-education-system-overhaul-russia

[294] Andrew E. Kramer, 'Ukrainian Separatists Rewrite History of 1930s Famine,' *New York Times,* 29 April 2015. http://www.nytimes.com/2015/04/30/world/europe/ukraine-separatists-rewrite-history-of-1930s-famine.html

[295] Zakharchenko cited by *Interfax,* 27 January 2016.

[296] Tom Balmforth, 'Fascists and Evil Americans: Ukrainian Separatists Launch Magazine For Kids,' *RFERL,* 18 February 2016. and http://www.rferl.org/content/ukraine-separatists-magazine-kids-fascists-propaganda/27560436.html and http://life.pravda.com.ua/society/2016/02/25/208667/

[297] Peter Pomerantsev, 'Propagandalands,' *Granta,* no.134, 2016. http://granta.com/propagandalands/

[298] Mikhail Nikanorov, 'Inside rebel-held Ukraine, where a small pocket of nationalists hope of a life without Russian interference,' *The Independent,* 2 September 2015. http://www.independent.co.uk/news/world/europe/inside-rebel-held-ukraine-where-a-small-pocket-of-nationalists-hope-of-a-life-without-russian-10475513.html

[299] 'Stalin's portraits emerge in heart of Ukraine's Rebel-held territory,' *The Guardian,* 19 October 2015 and Roman Olearchyk, 'Donetsk faces a creeping Russification,' *Financial Times,* 5 June 2016.

http://www.theguardian.com/world/2015/oct/19/stalin-portraits-ukraine-rebel-territory

[300] 'Ukraine's Fragile Ceasefire,' *BBC Our World,* 11 April 2015.

301 http://dnr-online.ru/

302 Zakharchenko cited by *Interfax*, 27 January 2016.

303 See for example, A. Shekhovtsov and A. Umland 'Ukraine's Radical Right,' *Journal of Democracy*, vol. 25, no. 3 (July 2014), pp. 58 – 63.

304 M. Franchetti, 'Russian nationalist warns Putin risks being toppled 'like the tsar'.'

305 Benjamin Bidder, 'Russian Far-Right Idol. The man Who Started the War in Ukraine,' *Spiegel Online*, 18 March 2015. http://www.spiegel.de/international/europe/the-ukraine-war-from-perspective-of-russian-nationalists-a-1023801.html

306 M. Franchetti, 'Ukraine licks wounds as guns go quiet,' *The Sunday Times*, 7 September 2014. http://www.thesundaytimes.co.uk/sto/news/world_news/Ukraine/article1455859.ece

307 Courtney Weaver, 'Café encounter exposes realty of Russian soldiers in Ukraine,' *Financial Times*, 22 October 2014.

308 *Disinformation Review*, European External Action Service, no.29 (7 June 2016). http://us11.campaign-archive1.com/?u=cd23226ada1699a77000eb60b&id=17e3fdd693

309 R. Olearchyk, 'Donetsk faces a creeping Russification.'

310 Tim Whewell, 'The Russians fighting a 'holy war' in Ukraine.' *BBC News magazine*, 17 December 2014. http://www.bbc.co.uk/news/magazine-30518054

311 Ibid.,

312 T. Whewell, 'Russia's Imperialist Warriors,' *BBC*, 11 January 2015. http://www.bbc.co.uk/programmes/n3csxl5s

313 Y. M. Brudny and Evgeny Finkel, 'Why Ukraine is not Russia. Hegemonic National Identities and Democracy in Russia and Ukraine,' *East European Politics and Societies*, vol.25, no.4 (November 2011), pp.813-833.

314 'Independent Ukraine between Two Viktors (2004–2014)' in T. Kuzio, *Ukraine. Democratization, Corruption and the New Russian Imperialism* (Santa Barbara, CA: Praeger), pp.77-116.

315 http://flot2017.com/ru/opinions/4398

316 https://wikileaks.org/gifiles/docs/25/2555041_ukraine-russia-wikileaks-gryshchenko-says-putin-has-low.html

317 http://tass.ru/en/russia/807578

318 R. Olearchyk, 'Donetsk faces a creeping Russification.'

319 M. Wawrzonek, 'Ukraine in the "Gray Zone.'

320 Yuriy Lukanov, then president of the Independent Trade Union of Journalists, found during his visit to the Crimea in Spring 2014 very high levels of xenophobia, Ukrainophobia, unfriendliness to outsiders and disrespect to visitors (interview with the author, Kyiv, 16 April 2014).

321 Andrey Kurkov, *Ukraine Diaries. Dispatches from Kiev* (London: Harvill-Secker, 2014), p.210.

322 Prince A. Wolkonsky, *The Ukrainian Question* and Par Perre Bregy and Serge Obolensky, *The Ukraine. A Russian Land* (London: Selwyn and Blount, 1940).

323 Thomas Ambrosio, 'Insulating Russia from a Color Revolution: How the Kremlin Resists Regional Democratic Trends,' *Demokratization*, vol.14, no.2, April 2007), pp.232-252 and Vitali Silitski, 'Preempting Democracy: The Case of Belarus,' *Journal of Democracy*, vol.16, no.4, October 2005), pp.83-97.

324 V. Putin, Speech to the United Nations, 28 September 2015. https://www.washingtonpost.com/news/worldviews/wp/2015/09/28/read-putins-u-n-general-assembly-speech/

[325] The *BBC* (24 November 2004) quoted Russian government newspaper *Izvestia* as writing 'Ukraine faces the threat of a civil war between its two regions. A disintegration of the country is more likely than ever before.'

[326] M. Riabchuk, 'Ukrainians as Russia's Negative 'Other.'

[327] Ivan Dzyuba, *Internationalism or Russification?* (New York: Pathfinder Press, 1974), p.99.

[328] Y. Teper, 'Official Russian identity discourse in light of the annexation of the Crimea: national or imperial?'

[329] Elizaveta Gaufman, 'World War II 2.0: Digital Memory of Fascism in Russia in the Aftermath of Euromaidan in Ukraine,' *Journal of Regional Security*, vol.10, no.1 (2015), p.28.

[330] S. Hutchings and V. Tolz, *Nation, Ethnicity and Race on Russian Television.*

[331] Paul Goble, 'Propaganda, Mass Manipulation, and Russian National Identity,' *Communist and Post-Communist Studies*, vol.49, no. 1 (March 2016), pp.37-44.

[332] P. Goble, 'Lies, Damned Lies and Russian Disinformation,' *Eurasia Daily Monitor*, 13 August 2014 and O. Sukhov, 'Propaganda Army Speaks Fluent Kremlin,' *Kyiv Post*, 11 September 2014. http://www.jamestown.org/single/?tx_ttnews%5Btt_news%5D=42745#.VCQA6StdVIU and http://www.kyivpost.com/content/ukraine/putins-propagandists-not-known-for-ethics-364352.html

[333] Ben Hoyle, 'Putin tightens his grip on dissenting media,' *The Times*, 25 September 2014.

[334] 'A Comprehensive Threat,' *The Daily Vertical, RFERL*, 28 January 2016. http://www.rferl.org/content/daily-vertical-comprehensive-threat/27516531.html

[335] C. Clover, *Black Wind, White Snow*, p.259. Dugin did not see this as out of the ordinary and accepted funding from organised crime and a South Ossetia 'banker' for his Eurasia party project. Ibid., p.241.

[336] T. Kuzio, 'Ukrainian Nationalism Again under Attack in Ukraine,' *Eurasia Daily Monitor*, vol.7, no.138 (19 July 2010). http://jamestownfoundation.blogspot.ca/2010/09/orange-revolution-erased-from-ukrainian.html

[337] *Ukrayinska Pravda*, 29 January 2012.

[338] V. Putin, Address to State Duma deputies, Federation Council members, heads of Russian regions and civil society representatives in the Kremlin, 18 March 2014.
http://en.kremlin.ru/events/president/news/20603

[339] Olga Bertelsen and M. Shkandrij, 'The secret police and the campaign against Galicians in Soviet Ukraine, 1929-1934,' *Nationalities Papers*, vol.42, no.1 (January 2014), p.53.

[340] Ibid., p.53.

[341] Yaroslav Bilinsky, 'Shcherbytskyi, Ukraine and Kremlin Politics,' *Problems of Communism*, vol. 32, no.4 (July-August 1983), p.10.

[342] H. Coynash, 'Russia's Sentsov – Kolchenko case – "an absolutely Stalinist trial" and 'Nadiya Savchenko: "You can call me the artillery spotter,"' *KHRPG*, 21 August and 30 September 2015.
http://khpg.org/en/index.php?id=1440076117 and http://khpg.org/en/index.php?id=1443558682

[343] Andrei Soldatov and Irina Borogan, *The New Nobility. The Restoration of Russia's Secret State and the Enduring Legacy of the KGB* (New York: Public Affairs, 2010), p.73.

[344] A. Wilson, *Ukraine Crisis. What it Means for the West* (New Haven, CT: Yale University Press, 2015).

[345] C. G. Gaddy and F. Hill, *Mr. Putin*, p.391.

346 D. Volchek and Claire Bigg, 'Volunteers, Cutthroats and Bandits. Volunteers Stint with Ukrainian Rebels Turns to Nightmare,' *RFERL*, 25 April 2015. http://www.rferl.org/content/ukraine-war-russian-volunteer-interview/26976499.html

347 Ilya Kazakov, 'Mstnye nazyvaly okkupantamy: bolshe sotny uraskykh dobrovoltsev vernulys s Ukrayiny v Ekaterynburg,' www.E1.ru, 15 April 2015. http://www.e1.ru/news/spool/news_id-422297.html

348 *Ukrayinska Pravda*, 29 July 2014.

349 *Rossiya-1*, 4 March 2015.

350 James J. Coyle, 'Russian Disinformation Alienates the West from Russia's Periphery,' *New Atlanticist, Atlantic Council of the US*, 20 July 2015. http://www.atlantic-council.org/blogs/new-atlanticist/russian-disinformation-alienates-the-west-from-russian-periphery

351 *Disinformation Review*, European External Action Service, no.29 (7 June 2016). http://us11.campaign-achive1.com/?u=cd23226ada1699a77000eb60b&id=17e3fdd693

352 Joshua Yaffa, 'The Search for Petr Khokhlov,' *New York Times*, 7 January 2015. http://www.nytimes.com/2015/01/11/magazine/a-russian-soldier-vanishes-in-ukraine.html?_r=1

353 'Propaganda 'Scares the Kids' in Russian Schools,' *RFERL*, 29 January 2016. http://www.rferl.org/media/video/russia-schools-propaganda/27518589.html

354 Lucy Ash, 'How Russia outfoxes its enemies,' *BBC Magazine*, 29 January 2015. http://www.bbc.com/news/magazine-31020283

355 Shaun Walker, 'Komunar, east Ukraine: "Nothing to eat, nothing to do, no point in life",' *The Guardian*, 6 February 2015. http://www.theguardian.com/world/2015/sep/24/ukraine-conflict-donbass-russia-rebels-foreigners-fighting

356 Natalia Antelava, 'Russia's Invasion Uncorks Ethnic Strife in Crimea,' The New Yorker, 3 March 2014.

357 M. Franchetti, 'Putin boosted by Orthodox 'inquisition,' The Sunday Times, 5 April 2015. http://www.thesundaytimes.co.uk/sto/news/world_news/Europe/article1539859.ece

358 Halyna Tereshchuk and R. Coalson, 'Ukrainian 'Cyborg': They Tried to Break Me, But It Didn't Work,' *RFERL*, 19 August 2015. http://www.rferl.org/content/ukrainian-cyborg-prisoner-of-war-torture-beating-donetsk/27197605.html. A Russian Orthodox priest pictured with armed separatists was denied entry to Ukraine in October 2016: https://ssu.gov.ua/ua/news/1/category/2/view/2089#sthash.5BZqcbu6.OPWS-BSmy.dpbs.

359 S. Walker, 'Komunar, east Ukraine: "Nothing to eat, nothing to do, no point in life."'

360 'Sever' is interviewed in the documentary film 'Donetsk Airport,' December 2015. http://www.currenttime.tv/fullinfographics/infographics/aiportdo-netsk/27255834.html# and https://www.youtube.com/watch?v=2gmYVryLPow

361 M. Franchetti, 'Ukraine licks wounds as guns go quiet.'

362 Noah Sneider, *The Empire Strikes Back. A journey through Russia and Ukraine, where the deep past shapes the future* (The Open Rehearsal Project with the Big Roundtable, 6 November 2014). https://medium.com/the-empire-strikes-back/the-empire-strikes-back-c6e51efe9973

363 Alex Shprintsen, 'CBC producer revisits Ukraine to explore conflict,' *CBC*, 22 February 2015. http://www.cbc.ca/player/News/TV%20Shows/The%20National/ID/2487330867/htt

364 'The Battle for Ukraine.'

365 'Crimea Welcomes Riot Cops After Murdering Euromaidan Protesters in Kiev Ukraine,' https://www.youtube.com/watch?v=efii3FK9W7A

366 Letters from Donbas, Part 3: 'Dirt, Tears, and Blood', *RFERL*, 8 February 2015. http://www.rferl.org/content/ukraine-letters-from-donbas-situation-fighting-day-to-day-life/26836295.html

367 Ibid.,

368 A. Wilson, 'Is Russian Politics Still Virtual?' *Aspen Review*, no.2 (2015). http://www.aspeninstitute.cz/en/article/2-2015-is-russian-politics-still-virtual/

369 Ibid.,

370 'Russia: Kremlin's 'hate TV' compares West to Nazis,' *BBC*, 3 October 2013. http://www.bbc.com/news/blogs-news-from-elsewhere-24383550

371 B. Whitmore, 'Is the Kremlin Drinking Its Own Kool-Aid?' *RFE-RL*, 3 July 2015. http://www.rferl.org/content/podcast-is-the-kremlin-drinking-its-own-cool-aid/27108528.html

372 Vitaliy Sych, 'The moment of truth,' *Novoye Vremya*, 4 April 2015. http://nv.ua/opinion/sych/the-moment-of-truth-42442.html

373 Ibid.,

374 A. Wilson, 'Is Russian Politics Still Virtual?'

375 Anders Aslund, *Ukraine. What Went Wrong and How to Fix It* (Washington DC: Petersen International Institute of Economics, 2015), p.106.

376 'Breaking down the Surkov leaks,' *Digital Forensic Research Laboratory*, 26 October 2016. https://medium.com/dfrlab/breaking-down-the-surkov-leaks-b2feec1423cb#.w52irqfsc

377 Elizabeth A. Wood, 'Introduction,' in E. A. Wood, William E. Pomerantz, E. Wayne Merry and Maxim Trudolyubov, *Roots of Russia's War in Ukraine* (Washington DC: Woodrow Wilson Center Press, 2016), p.14.

378 *The Ukraine Crisis: Risks of Renewed Military Conflict after Minsk II* (Brussels: International Crisis Group, 1 April 2015). http://www.crisisgroup.org/~/media/Files/europe/ukraine/b073-the-ukraine-crisis-risks-of-renewed-military-conflict-after-minsk-ii.pdf

379 P. Pomerantsev, *Nothing is True and Everything is Possible. The Surreal Heart of the New Russia* (New York: Public Affairs, 2014).

380 Joshua Yaffa, 'Putin's Hard Turn. Ruling Russia in Leaner Times,' *Foreign Affairs*, vol.94, no.3 (May-June, 2015), pp.128-135.

381 E. A. Wood, 'A Small, Victorious War? The Symbolic Politics of Vladimir Putin' in E. A. Wood, W.E. Pomerantz, E. W. Merry and M. Trudolyubov, *Roots of Russia's War in Ukraine*, pp.116 and 118.

382 Glenn Kates, 'Sevastopol's Olympic-Sized Take On Ukraine: Bikers, Ballet, and Swastikas, *RFERL*, 11 August 2014 and Max Seddon, 'This Pro-Putin Bike Show Is a Trashy Neo-Soviet "Triumph Of The Will" Remake,' *Buzzfeed*, 11 August 2014. http://www.rferl.org/content/feature/26525150.html and http://www.buzzfeed.com/maxseddon/russian-motorbike-gang-tells-the-conflict-in-ukraine#1dopuge. The show can be watched at https://www.youtube.com/watch?v=NPnb97ybtiU

[383] *Russian War Crimes in Eastern Ukraine in 2014.* The report was prepared by Polish and Ukrainian volunteers and commissioned by Polish MP Malgorzata Gosiewska. http://3millionpage.com/index.php/web-digest/329-russian-war-crimes

[384] Putin used the explosive term 'ethnic cleansing' to describe Ukrainian military actions. *AP*, 17 November 2014.

[385] *Den*, 21 July 2000.

[386] H. Coynash, 'Arrest a Ukrainian – Russia's Investigative Committee will do the rest,' *KHRPG*, 14 July 2015. http://khpg.org/index.php?id=1436827549

[387] Anna Shamanska, 'Russia Ridiculed on Internet Over Claim Ukrainian Prime Minister Fought in Chechnya,' *RFERL*, 30 September 2015. http://www.rferl.org/content/ukraine-yatsenyuk-chechen-war-claims-internet-ridicule-memes/27235710.html

[388] 'Russian media recycle fake Ukrainian claim over Mongol invasion,' *BBC Monitoring*, 4 March 2016.

[389] R. Sakwa, *Frontline Ukraine.*

[390] Ibid., p.290.

[391] Will Stewart, 'Inside Putin's secret 'troll factory:' How Mother turned whistle-blower to reveal the secrets of shadowy propaganda unit where staff were told to call Obama a 'monkey' and Ukraine 'Nazis' on line,' *The Daily Mail*, 26 June 2015. http://www.dailymail.co.uk/news/article-3138847/Putin-s-secret-troll-factory-branded-Barack-Obama-monkey-Ukraine-Nazis-mum-went-undercover-expose-dirty-tricks.html

[392] The interview with a Buryat-Russian tank driver wounded in Debaltseve was the basis for Elena Kostychenko, 'Myi vse znaly, na chto idyem i chto mozhet byt,' *Novaya Gazeta*, 13 March 2015. http://en.nvayagazeta.ru/politics/67620.html

[393] Stefan Huijboom, 'Journalism hardships and hazards in Russian-controlled Donetsk,' *Kyiv Post*, 14 March 2015. http://www.kyivpost.com/opinion/op-ed/stefan-huijboom-journalism-hardships-and-hazards-in-russian-controlled-donetsk-384316.html

[394] *Ukrayinska Pravda*, 4 August 2015.

[395] 'Russian TV shows choreographed interrogation to drive home key Ukrainian messages,' *BBC Monitoring*, 19 February 2015.

[396] D. Brandenburger, 'It is Imperative to Advance Russian Nationalism as the First Priority,' p. 280.

[397] Ibid., p. 287

[398] S. Yekelchyk, *Stalin's Empire of Memory*, p.16.

[399] Ibid., p. 39

[400] Ibid., pp. 31, 50, 54, 56-57.

[401] Ibd., p.71.

[402] M. Shkandrij, 'Colonial, Anti-Colonial and Postcolonial in Ukrainian Literature' in Jaroslaw Rozumnyj ed., *Incomplete Nation. Twentieth Century Ukrainian Literature. Essays in honor of Dmytro Shtohryn* (Kyiv: Kyiv Mohyla Academy Publishing House, 2011), p.284.

[403] O. Bertelsen and M. Shkandrij, 'The secret police and the campaign against Galicians in Soviet Ukraine, 1929-1934.'

[404] H. Kuromiya, *Freedom and Terror in the Donbas*, p.247.

[405] Y. Boldyrev, interviewed by censor, www.censor.net.ua, 16 March 2012. http://censor.net.ua/resonance/200314/regional_boldyrev_galichane_doljny_znat_svoe_mesto_v_ukraine_oni_prijivalschiki

[406] Ibid.,

[407] Mustafa Nayem and Serhiy Leshchenko, 'Restorannye posydelky Herman, Kolesnykova i Arfusha s inostrannymy zhurnalystamy,' *Ukrayinska Pravda*, 27 May 2010. http://www.pravda.com.ua/articles/2010/05/27/5081646/

[408] S. Yekelchyk, *Stalin's Empire of Memory*, p.78.

[409] Zhores A. Medvedev and Roy A. Medvedev eds, *Nikita S. Khrushchev, The Secret Speech* (Nottingham: Spokesman Books and Russsell Press, 1976), p.58.

[410] Jeffrey Burds, 'Agentura: Soviet Informant's Networks and the Ukrainian Underground in Galicia, 1944-48,' *East European Politics and Societies*, vol.11, no.1 (December 1996), p.112 and Alexander Statiev, *The Soviet Counterinsurgency in the Western Borderlands* (Cambridge and New York: Cambridge University Press, 2010), pp.44, 106.

[411] Mark Beissinger, 'Ethnicity, the Personnel Weapon, and Neo-Imperial Integration: Ukrainian and RSFSR Provincial Party Officials Compared,' *Studies in Comparative Communism*, vol.XXI, no.1 (Spring 1988), p.84.

[412] John Kolasky, *Education in Soviet Ukraine. A Study in Discrimination and Russification* (Toronto: Peter Martins Association, 1968), p.XIII.

[413] Heorhii Kasyanov, *Teorii Natsii ta Natsionalizm* (Kyiv: Lybid, 1999) and A. Wilson, *Ukraine Crisis*, p.126.

[414] Todd H. Nelson, 'History as ideology: the portrayal of Stalin and the Great Patriotic War in contemporary Russian high school textbooks,' *Post-Soviet Affairs*, vol.31, no.1 (January 2015), p.61.

[415] Dina Khapaeva, 'Historical Memory in Post-Soviet Gothic Society,' *Social Research*, vol.76, no.1 (Spring 2009), p.369.

[416] 'Take care of Russia,' *The Economist*, 22 October 2016. http://www.economist.com/news/special-report/21708881-mr-putin-not-setting-about-it-best-way-take-care-russia

[417] Alyona Zhuk, 'Russia retains Soviet propaganda tools in its war against Ukraine,' *Kyiv Post*, 5 June 2015. http://www.kyivpost.com/content/kyiv-post-plus/russia-retains-soviet-propaganda-tools-in-its-war-against-ukraine-390320.html

[418] 'Russian TV News: Anti-Maydan vs "fascists," "peace returning" to Debaltseve,' *BBC Monitoring*, 23 February 2015.

[419] Christian Neef, 'Fortress of Nationalism: Russia is Losing Its Political Morals,' *Spiegel on line*, 31 March 2015. http://www.spiegel.de/international/world/russia-recedes-into-nationalism-and-political-immorality-a-1026259.html

[420] Sarah E. Mendelson and Theodore P. Gerber, 'Soviet Nostalgia: An Impediment to Russian Democratization,' *The Washington Quarterly*, vol.29, no.1 (Winter 2005-2006), pp.83-96.

[421] C. G. Gaddy and F. Hill, *Mr. Putin*, pp.366-367.

[422] Ibid., p.369.

[423] T. Kuzio, 'History and National Identity Among the Eastern Slavs. Towards a New Framework,' *National Identities*, vol.3, no.2 (July 2001), pp.109-132 and 'Nation-State Building and the Re-Writing of History in Ukraine: The Legacy of Kyiv Rus,' *Nationalities Papers*, vol.33, no.1 (March 2005), pp.30-58.

[424] D. Khapaeva, 'Historic Memory in Post-Soviet Gothic Society,' p.369.

[425] Nina Tumarkin, *The living and the dead: the rise and fall of the cult of World War II in Russia* (New York: Basic Books, 1994), pp.197-198.

[426] Ibid., p. 130.

[427] Ibid., p.133.

[428] 'World War II Was Only Yesterday' in H. Smith, *The Russians*, pp.302-325.

[429] Ibid., 134.

[430] Ibid., p.152.

[431] Ibid., p.155.

[432]'Put in more flags,' *The Economist*, 14 May 2009. http://www.economist.com/node/13653939

[433] Lesya Jones and Bohdan Yasen eds., *Dissent in Ukraine. The Ukrainian Herald, Issue 6. An Underground Journal from Soviet Ukraine* (Baltimore: Smoloskyp Publishers, 1977), p.129.

[434] 'Ti, Shcho Perezhyly Peklo' (Kyiv: Coalition Justice for Donbas, November 2015). https://drive.google.com/file/d/0B6aQraZ4SSM9UmpLWVVVMXQ5VGM/view?pli=1

[435] A. J. Motyl, 'Do Animals Speak Ukrainian?' *World Affairs blog*, 11 February 2011. http://worldaffairsjournal.org/blog/alexander-j-motyl/do-animals-speak-ukrainian

[436] Personal recollections from a journalist at the time.

[437] Roman Szporluk, 'Valentyn Moroz: His Political Ideas in Historical Perspective,' *Canadian Slavonic Papers*, vol.18, no.1 (March 1976), p.84.

[438] Olga Rudenko, 'Ethnic Russians in Ukraine's Luhansk also want closer ties with Moscow,' *Kyiv Post*, 16 March 2014. http://www.kyivpost.com/content/ukraine/ethnic-russians-in-ukraines-luhansk-also-want-closer-ties-with-moscow-339683.html

[439] Anna Fournier, *Forging Rights in a New Democracy. Ukrainian Students Between Freedom and Justice* (Philadelphia: University of Pennsylvania Press, 2012).

[440] On 12 June 1990, the Russian Congress of People's Deputies, which was then headed by Boris Yeltsin, adopted the Declaration of the State Sovereignty. A similar Declaration of Sovereignty was adopted by the Ukrainian parliament a month later. The following year in August 1991, the Ukrainian parliament adopted a Declaration of Independence that was confirmed by a referendum in December which received over 90 percent backing. The Russian SFSR never took these last two steps in 1991 and therefore celebrates 'Russia Day' on 12 June based on its 1990 Declaration of Sovereignty.

[441] V. Socor, 'Putin Outlines Current Policy to Ukraine,' *Eurasia Daily Monitor*, vol.12, no.77, (23 April 2015).

[442] T. Martin, 'An Affirmative Action Empire' in Ronald G. Suny and T. Martin eds., *A State of Nations*, p.81.

[443] O. Jonsson and R. Seely, 'Russia's Full-Spectrum Conflict: An Appraisal After Ukraine,' *Journal of Slavic Military Studies*, vol.28, no.1 (January 2015), p.13.

[444] *Pravyy Sektor* and *Svoboda* received 1.8 and 4.73 percent respectively. A small number of nationalists were elected in single mandate districts.

[445] A. Shekhovtsov, 'Neo-Nazi Russian National Unity in Eastern Ukraine.'

[446] Ibid.,

[447] Julia Ioffe, 'My Mind-Melting Week on the Battlefields of Ukraine,' *New Republic*, 16 June 2014. http://www.newrepublic.com/article/118131/week-battlefields-ukraine

[448] C. Schreck and D. Volchek, 'Russian 'Former Fascist' Who Fought with Separatists Says Moscow Unleashed, Orchestrated Ukraine War.'

[449] N. Mitrokhin, 'Ukraine's Separatists and Their Dubious Leaders.'

[450] H. Coynash, 'Russia bans Mejlis, declares war on Crimean Tatar people while the West watches,' *KHRPG*, 27 April 2016. http://khpg.org/en/index.php?id=1461673479

451 V. Putin, Speech to the NATO Summit in Bucharest, *UNIAN*, 18 April 2008. http://www.unian.info/world/111033-text-of-putins-speech-at-nato-summit-bucha-rest-april-2-2008.html

452 L. Harding, *A Very Expensive Poison*, pp.304-305 and p.314.

453 M. Wawrzonek, 'Ukraine in the "Gray Zone."'

454 S. Shulman, 'National Identity and Public Support for Political and Economic Reform in Ukraine,' *Slavic Review*, vol.64, no.1 (Spring 2005), pp.59-87.

455 Andrei Tsygankov views the Ukraine-Russia crisis as a clash of identities between the pro-European Euromaidan Revolution and 'eastern Slavic Orthodox civilization.' See his 'Vladimir Putin's last stand: the sources of Russia's Ukraine Policy, *Post-Soviet Affairs*, vol.31, no.4 (July 2015), p.296.

456 Mark Mackinnon, 'We have no homeland': Ukraine dissolves as exiles flee,' *The Globe and Mail*, 28 November 2014. http://www.theglobeandmail.com/news/world/we-have-no-homeland-ukraine-dissolves-as-exiles-flee/article21832829/

457 A. J. Motyl, 'Facing the Past: In Defense of Ukraine's New Laws, *World Affairs* (Fall 2015), pp.58-66. http://www.worldaffairsjournal.org/article/facing-past-defense-ukraine%E2%80%99s-new-laws

458 The Commission was established by presidential decree on 15 May 2009 and closed on 14 February 2012.

459 Dmitri Medvedev, Address to the President of Ukraine Viktor Yushchenko, 11 August 2009. http://archive.kremlin.ru/eng/text/docs/2009/08/220759.shtml

460 'Great patriotic war, again,' *Economist*, 2 May 2015. http://www.economist.com/news/europe/21650177-vladimir-putin-twists-memory-soviet-unions-victory-over-nazism-justify-his-struggle

461 T. Kuzio, 'Antinationalist Campaign to Discredit Our Ukraine,' *RFERL Poland, Belarus and Ukraine Report*, 9 April 2002. http://www.rferl.org/content/article/1344071.html

462 T. Kuzio, 'Large Scale Anti-American Campaign Planned in Ukraine,' *Eurasian Daily Monitor*, vol.1, no.102 (8 October 2004).

http://www.jamestown.org/articles-by-author/?no_cache=1&tx_cablanttnewsstaffrelation_pi1%5Bauthor%5D=126

463 Sergei Glazyev interviewed by *Radio Russia*, 5 March 2004.

464 Secret Instructions of the Yanukovych Election Campaign, *Ukrayinska Pravda*, 12 November 2004. http://www.pravda.com.ua/news/2004/11/12/3004124/

465 *Itar-Tass*, 14 July 2002.

466 Neil Barnett, 'Backing the bad guy?' *National Post*, 4 December 2004.

467 *RTR Planeta*, 26 September 2007.

468 Tatiana Zhurzhenko, 'From borderlands to bloodlands,' *Eurozine*, 19 September 2014. http://www.eurozine.com/articles/2014-09-19-zhurzhenko-en.html

469 Vadym Kolesnichenko is one of the authors of Russian-style legislation in the Ukrainian parliament discriminating against gays.

470 V. Kolesnichenko, *Ukrayinska Pravda blog*, 3 January 2014. http://blogs.pravda.com.ua/authors/kolesnichenko/52c6bc1fee67a/

471 Heorhii Kryuchkov and Dmytro Tabachnyk, *Fashizm v Ukraine: ugroza ili realnost* (Kharkiv: Folio, 2008).

472 D. Tabachnyk, 'Kakim dolzhen byt uchebnyk istorii,' http://www.partyofregions.org.ua/pr-east-west/4c08a20a530d1 (the Party of Regions website has been closed down).

473 H. Coynash, 'Dangerous "antifascist" card,' *Kyiv Post*, 20 May 2013. http://www.kyivpost.com/opinion/op-ed/a-dangerous-antifascist-card-324525.html

474 Anatoliy Grytsenko, *Ukrayinska Pravda blog*, 20 May 2013. http://blogs.pravda.com.ua/authors/grytsenko/5199dee053209/

475 Volodymyr Shklar, 'Who is against us is a fascist!' *Ukrayinska Pravda*, 21 May 2013. http://www.pravda.com.ua/columns/2013/05/21/6990349/

476 R. Olearchyk, 'Bitter residents of Slovyansk pick up pieces of shattered city,' *Financial Times*, 13 July 2014. http://www.ft.com/cms/s/0/4fc63f78-0a92-11e4-be06-00144feabdc0.html#axzz3yvsmMP9o

477 Maxim Tucker and B. Hoyle, 'Ukrainian ceasefire ends in Donetsk bloodbath,' *The Times*, 23 January 2015. http://www.thetimes.co.uk/tto/news/world/europe/article4331736.ece

478 A copy of the statement is in the author's possession.

479 Human Rights Assessment Mission in Ukraine, Human Rights and Minority Rights Situation, Office for Democratic Institutions and and Human Rights and High Commissioner for National Minorities, Organisation for Security and Cooperation in Europe, 6 March-17 April 2014. http://www.osce.org/odihr/118454

480 Oksana Grytsenko, 'Pro-Ukrainian activists in Luhansk go into hiding, wait for help from Kyiv,' *Kyiv Post*, 21 May 2014. http://test.kyivpost.com/article/content/ukraine-politics/pro-ukrainian-activists-in-luhansk-go-into-hiding-wait-for-help-from-kyiv-348683.html

481 *Ukrayinska Pravda*, 20 May 2013.

482 *Ukrayinska Pravda*, 18 April 2014.

483 'New wave of 'arrests' & attack on Ukrainian churches in militant controlled Donetsk,' *KHRPG*, 30 January 2016. http://khpg.org/en/index.php?id=1454112238

484 Vyacheslav Likhachev and Tetyana Bezruk, 'Two Years of War: Xenophobia in Ukraine in 2015,' Congress of National Communities of Ukraine, National Minority Rights Monitoring Group, January 2016. http://www.vaadua.org/sites/default/files/files/Xenophobia_in_Ukraine_2015.pdf

485 Ukraine was to have held presidential elections in January 2015 but these never took place because Yanukovych fled from Ukraine and political leaders who had backed the Euromaidan Revolution came to power. Presidential elections were held in May 2014 and won by Poroshenko. If there had been no Euromaidan and elections had gone ahead as planned in 2015, the likelihood of a popular revolt would have been high as Yanukovych, who was unpopular, would have been forced to use greater fraud than he used in the 2004 elections to remain in power.

486 Photographs can be viewed on *Ukrayinska Pravda*, 9 May 2011.

487 Tetiana Nikolayenko and Serhiy Shcherbyna, 'Zakhid stavyt na Klychka, Rosiya shukaye opozytsiynoho kandydata,' *Ukrayinska Pravda*, 13 June 2013. http://www.pravda.com.ua/articles/2013/06/13/6992155/.

488 *Ukrayinska Pravda*, 6 February 2014.

489 *Ukrayinska Pravda*, 5 December 2013.

490 Ukrayinska Pravda, 19 May 2013.

491 H. Coynash, 'Politics and human rights. Dangerous "antifascist" card,' *KHRPG*, 20 May 2013. http://khpg.org.index.php?id=1368921089

[492] Ludmilla Parasivka, 'If the discourse about fascism will continue then everything will end very badly,' *Hazeta po-Ukrayinski*, 21 May 2013. http://gazeta.ua/ru/articles/yurij-romanenko/_akscho-diskurs-z-fashizmom-bude-prodovzhuvatis-to-vse-zakinchitsya-duzhe-sumno/498189

[493] 'Masovo Nyshchyty Pamyatnyky v Ukrayini Pochaly Tsyoho Roku,' *Istorychnya Pravda*, 1 April 2013. http://www.istpravda.com.ua/short/2013/04/1/118931/

[494] Aleksandr Dugin interviewed in the wide circulation *Krymskaya Pravda*, 29 May 2014.

[495] Robert Conquest, *We and They. Civic and Despotic Cultures* (London: Temple Smith, 1980), pp.83-84.

[496] W. Laqueur, *Black Hundred*, p.110.

[497] T. Kuzio, "Anti-Semitism as an Integral Component of Soviet Belarusian Nationalism and Pan Eastern Slavism," *RFERL Poland, Belarus, Ukraine Report*, August 20, 2002, http://www.rferl.org/content/article/1344088.html.

[498] V. Zaslavsky, *The Neo-Stalinist State*, p.17.

[499] N. Tumarkin, *The Living and the Dead*, p.115.

[500] Mikhail Agursky, *The Third Rome. National Bolshevism in the USSR* (Boulder, Co: Westview, 1987), pp.318-327.

[501] J. Wishnevsky, 'Glasnost on Anti-Semitism in the Soviet Union,' *Radio Liberty*, RL 254/87 (6 July 1987).

[502] Timothy Johnston, *Being Soviet. Identity, Rumour, and Everyday Life Under Stalin, 1939-1953* (New York: Oxford University Press, 2011), pp.78-79.

[503] Leon Fram, 'Commentary: Antisemitism as a government policy in Soviet Russia' in G. W. Simmons, ed., *Nationalism in the USSR and Eastern Europe in the era of Brezhnev and Kosygin*, pp.346-347.

[504] Howard Spier, 'Zionist Masonic Theme Fashionable in Soviet Publications,' *Radio Liberty*, RL 75/84 (15 February 1984).

[505] W. Laqueur, *Black Hundred*, p.107.

[506] J. Wishnevsky, 'Neo-Nazis in the Soviet Union,' *Radio Liberty*, RL 226/85 (11 July 1985).

[507] David Greenberg, 'A Step Forward for the Anti-Zionist Committee,' *Radio Liberty*, RL 107/85 (9 April 1985).

[508] Howard Spier, 'Soviet Authorities Exclude Emigration Option for Jews,' *Radio Liberty*, RL 233/84 (14 June 1984).

[509] A. J. Motyl, 'Putin's Russia as a fascist political system.'

[510] A. I. Filatova ed., Soviet Public Anti-Zionist Committee and Association of Soviet Lawyers, *Belaya kniga: Novye fakty, svidetelistva, dokumenty (White Book: New Facts, Testimonies and Documents)* (Moscow: Yuridicheskaya Literatura, 1985).

[511] D. Greenberg, 'Anti-Zionist "White Book" Given Wide Publicity,' *Radio Liberty*, RL 327/85 (30 September 1985).

[512] A. Shprintsen, 'CBC producer revisits Ukraine to explore conflict.'

[513] W. Laqueur, *Black Hundred*, pp.107-108.

[514] http://www.rferl.org/content/russia-putin-us-wants-to-dominate-world/26835291.html

[515] Director of the Union of Councils of Jews of the Former Soviet Union Meylakh Sheykhet interviewed by *The Ukrainian Weekly*, 20 May 2012. http://ukrweekly.com/archive/2012/The_Ukrainian_Weekly_2012-21.pdf

[516] N. Tumarkin, *The Living and the Dead*, pp.119-121.

[517] Ibid., pp.185-186.

[518] Ibid., p.124.

[519] W. Laqueur, *Black Hundred,* p.110.

[520] J. Wishnevsky, 'Glasnost on Anti-Semitism in the Soviet Union.'

[521] See the notorious Valery I. Skurlatov, *Zionism and Apartheid* (Kyiv: Politizadat, 1975) which was described as 'anti-Semitic in substance and tone' by Ben Cohen, American Jewish Committee, 'The Ideological Foundations of the Boycott Campaign Against Israel,' *Frontpagemag*, 18 September 2007. http://archive.frontpagemag.com/readArticle.aspx?ARTID=28117

[522] D. Greenberg, 'Soviet Publication Attacks Moscow and Odessa Synagogues,' *Radio Liberty*, RL 116/85 (15 April 1985).

[523] Howard Spier, 'Article by Anti-Semitic Author Stirs up Protests,' *Radio Liberty*, RL 53/84 (2 February 1984).

[524] H. Spier, 'Soviet Brochure Says Jews are Responsible for Deterioration in East-West Relations,' *Radio Liberty*, RL 303/84 (9 August 1984).

[525] H. Spier, 'An Ominous Development in Soviet and Anti-Semitic Propaganda,' *Radio Liberty*, RL 345/83 (15 September 1983).

[526] A. Z. Romanenko, *O klassovoi suchchasnosti sionizma. Istoriografichesky obzor literatury* (Leningrad: Leninzdat, 1986).

[527] D. Greenberg, 'Anti-Semitism Proves Deep-Seated Despite Official Discouragement,' *Radio Liberty*, RL 239/87 (26 June 1987).

[528] P. Goble, 'Moscow Moves to Close Ukrainian Institutions in Russia,' *Window on Eurasia*, 17 January 2011. http://windowoneurasia.blogspot.com/2011/01/window-on-eurasia-moscow-moves-to-close.html

[529] D. Greenberg, 'Vladimir Begun – A Doughty Fighter Against "The Zionist Conspiracy,"' *Radio Liberty*, RL 458/87 (17 November 1987).

[530] W. Laqueur, *Black Hundred*, p.169.

[531] Ibid., p.168.

[532] J. Wishnevsky, 'Glasnost on Anti-Semitism in the Soviet Union.'

[533] M. Laruelle, 'The three colors of Novorossiya,' p.67.

[534] C. G. Gaddy and F. Hill, *Mr. Putin*, pp.374-375.

[535] M. Laruelle, 'The three colors of Novorossiya,' p.67.

[536] N. Mitrokhin, 'Aspects of the Religious Situation in Ukraine,' *Religion, State and Society*, vol.29, no.3 (September 2001), p.188.

[537] Theodore H. Friedgut, *Life and Work in Russia's Donbas, 1869-1924*, vol.1 (Princeton, NJ: Princeton University Press, 1989), p.199.

[538] H. Kuromiya, *Freedom and Terror in the Donbas*, p.135.

[539] Ibid., pp.247 and 302.

[540] Ibid., pp.322-323.

[541] C. Clover, *Black Wind, White Snow*, p.273.

[542] 'Ukrainian Jews rally to nations cause in conflict with Russia,' *BBC Monitoring*, 11 November 2014.

[543] Sam Sokol, 'Ukraine rebels shoot Jewish man,' *Jerusalem Post*, 2 September 2014. http://www.jpost.com/Diaspora/Jewish-man-reported-shot-by-Ukrainian-rebels-374236

[544] 'Anti-Xenophobia Unit: Off to a Slow Start,' *US Embassy Kyiv*, 13 November 2008. https://wikileaks.org/plusd/cables/08KYIV2243_a.html

545 A. Shekhovtsov 'Extremism in South-Eastern Ukraine,' *Open Democracy*, 7 May 2014. https://www.opendemocracy.net/od-russia/anton-shekhovtsov/dangers-of-extremism-in-southeastern-ukraine-far-right-eurasianism-slavic-unity

546 Vyacheslav Lykhachov and Tetyana Bezruk eds., Ksenofobiya v Ukrayni v 2014 r. v konteksti revolyutsii ta interventsii: Informatsiyno-analitychna dopovid za rezultatamy monitorynhu (Kyiv: Congress of National Communities of Ukraine), pp.41-42. http://eajc.org/data//file/Xenophobia_in_Ukraine_2014.pdf

547 H. Coynash, 'Kremlin's anti-Semitic proxies in Donbas turn on each other,' *KHRPG*, 17 July 2015. http://www.khpg.org/pda/index.php?id=1436541311

548 http://paulocanning.blogspot.nl/2015/08/the-fascists-in-russias-hybrid-army.html

549 W. Stewart, 'Inside Putin's secret 'troll factory' and D. Volchek and Daisy Sindelar, 'One Professional Russian Troll Tells All,' *RFERL*, 25 March 2015. http://www.rferl.org/content/how-to-guide-russian-trolling-trolls/26919999.html

550 V. Lykhachov and T. Bezruk eds., Ksenofobiya v Ukrayni v 2014 r. v konteksti revolyutsii ta interventsii.

551 'Comparison of xenophobia in Ukraine and in Russia,' *KHRPG*, 1 May 2015. http://khpg.org/en/index.php?id=1398892043

552 H. Coynash, 'Neo-Nazis in Moscow's Service,' *KHRPG*, 8 May 2014. http://khpg.org/en/index.php?id=1399501345

553 Vicki L. Hesli, Arthur H. Miller, William M. Reisinger and Kevin L. Morgan, 'Social Distance from Jews in Russia and Ukraine,' *Slavic Review*, vol.53, no.3 (Fall 1994), p.824.

554 H. Coynash, '"Jewish pogroms in Ukraine" that we all missed,' *KHRPG*, 25 June 2015. http://khpg.org/index.php?id=1435154461

555 B. Hoyle, David Taylor and M. Tucker, 'Ukraine rebels promise army of 100, 000,' *The Times*, 3 February 2015. http://www.thetimes.co.uk/tto/news/world/europe/article4342379.ece

556 A. Kurkov, *Ukraine Diaries*, p.232.

557 Olga Irisova 'Manageable anti-Semitism. The Kremlin is keeping anti-Semitism "under control,"' *Intersection*, 19 May 2016. http://intersectionproject.eu/article/politics/manageable-anti-semitism

558 A. Shekhovtsov, 'Extremism in South-Eastern Ukraine.'

559 S. Sokol, 'Top Rebel Leader Accuses Jews of Masterminding Ukrainian Revolution,' *Jerusalem Post*, 22 June 2015. http://www.jpost.com/Diaspora/Top-rebel-leader-accuses-Jews-of-masterminding-Ukrainian-revolution-406729

560 Cathy Young, 'Fascism Comes to Ukraine – From Russia,' *Real Clear Politics*, 21 May 2014. http://www.realclearpolitics.com/articles/2014/05/21/fascism_comes_to_ukraine_--_from_russia_122700.html

561 A. Shekhovtsov, 'Extremism in South-Eastern Ukraine.'

562 C. Schreck and D. Volchek, 'Russian 'Former Fascist' Who Fought with Separatists Says Moscow Unleashed, Orchestrated Ukraine War.'

563 S. Shuster, 'Meet the Pro-Russian 'Partisans' Waging a Bombing Campaign in Ukraine.'

564 H. Coynash, 'Kremlin Proxies call 'Kyiv Junta' "miserable Jews,"' *KHRPG*, 3 February 2015. http://khpg.org/index.php?id=1422974633

565 A. Shekhovtsov, 'Extremism in South-Eastern Ukraine.'

566 Allison Quinn, 'Foreigners Who Fight and Die for Ukraine: Even Those killed get no recognition.' *Kyiv Post*, 24 April 2015. http://www.kyivpost.com/article/content/kyiv-post-

plus/foreigners-who-fight-and-die-for-ukraine-even-those-killed-get-no-recognition-387000.html

[567] V. Lykhachev ed., *Anti-Semitism in the FSU in 2014* (Kyiv-Jerusalem: Eurasian Jewish Congress, 2015), pp.11-15. V. Lykhachev, *Antysemytyzm v Ukraine, 2015* (Kyiv-Jerusalem: Eurasian Jewish Congress, 2015), pp. 12-17. http://www.eajc.org/data/file/AntisemitismReport2014engl.pdf and http://eajc.org/data//file/Antisemitism_in_Ukraine_2015.pdf

[568] H. Coynash, 'Kremlin's anti-Semitic proxies in Donbas turn on each other.'

[569] V. Likhachev ed., *Anti-Semitism in the FSU in 2014*, p.13.

[570] The official name of OUNb was OUN revolutionaries (OUNr).

[571] OUNm was officially called OUN Solidarists (OUNs).

[572] T. Kuzio, 'The U.S. Support for Ukraine's Liberation during the Cold War: A Study of Prolog Research and Publishing Corporation,' *Communist and Post-Communist Studies,* vol.45, nos.1-2 (March-June 2012), pp.51-64.

[573] Interview with Joseph Zisels Kyiv, 11 December 2014.

[574] Hannah Rosenthal, special envoy to monitor and combat anti-Semitism, 'Anti-Semitism in the Former Soviet Union,' Annual Board of Governors of the NCSJ (Advocates on behalf of Jews in Russia, Ukraine, the Baltic States & Eurasia), Washington, DC, 28 June 2011. http://www.state.gov/j/drl/rls/rm/2011/167738.htm.

[575] O. Irisova 'Manageable anti-Semitism.

[576] T. Kuzio, 'Gender bias, anti-Semitism contributed to Yanukovych's victory', *Kyiv Post*, 19 March 2010. http://www.kyivpost.com/opinion/op-ed/gender-bias-anti-semitism-contributed-to-yanukovyc-62040.html

[577] H. Coynash, 'Debunking Russia's Narrative of Rampant Anti-Semitism in Ukraine Again,' *Atlantic Council of the US*, 4 August 2015. http://www.atlanticcouncil.org/blogs/new-atlanticist/debunking-russia-s-narrative-of-rampant-anti-semitism-in-ukraine-again

[578] Aleksandr Burakovskiy, 'Key Characteristics and Transformation of Jewish-Ukrainian Relations During the Period of Ukraine's Independence,' *Nationalism and Ethnic Politics*, vol.15, no.1 (January 2009), p.126.

[579] T. Kuzio, 'Tatars Fear a Future Under Russia. Putin's anti-Semitism claims in Ukraine are overblown,' *Al Jazeera America*, 2 April 2014. http://america.aljazeera.com/opinions/2014/4/ukraine-crimean-tatarsinputinsrussia.html

[580] T. Kuzio, *Democratization, Corruption and the New Russian Imperialism*, pp.276-282.

[581] Gideon Rachman, 'Ukraine's revolution still deserves our support,' *Financial Times*, 5 May 2014.

[582] http://vaadua.org/news/doklad-o-proyavleniyah-antisemitizma-v-ukraine-v-2012-godu

[583] *Segodnya*, 3 June 2002 cited from 'Skinheads in Ukraine: First Symptoms?' *Ukrainian Centre for Independent Political Research, Research Update*, no.264 (22 April 2002). https://core.ac.uk/download/files/415/11871621.pdf

[584] A. Shekhovtsov, 'Extremism in South-Eastern Ukraine.'

[585] T. Kuzio, 'Gender bias, anti-Semitism contributed to Yanukovych's victory.'

[586] The publications and letter are in the possession of the author.

[587] J.V. Koshiw, *Abuse of Power. Corruption in the Office of the President* (Reading: Artemia Press, 2013), p.134 and p.75.

[588] Open letter of Ukrainian Jews to Russian Federation President Vladimir Putin, 5 March 2014. http://eajc.org/page32/news43672.html

589 H. Coynash, 'Anti-Semitism is no vote-winner even for Ukraine's far-right,' *KHRPG*, 30 September 2015. http://khpg.org/index.php?id=1443479556

590 T. Martin, *The Affirmative Action Empire*, p.354.

591 M. Galeotti, 'How the Invasion of Ukraine is Shaking up the Global Crime Scene,' *Vice News*, 6 November 2014. http://www.vice.com/read/how-the-invasion-of-ukraine-is-shaking-up-the-global-crime-scene-1106

592 H. Kuromiya, *Freedom and Terror in the Donbas*, p.32.

593 Louise Shelley, 'Internal Migration and Crime in the Soviet Union,' *Canadian Slavonic Papers*, vol. XXIII, no.1 (March 1981), pp.77-85.

594 Ibid., pp.246 and 336.

595 Ibid., p.301.

596 Ibid., p.301.

597 Interview with Mykhaylo Pozhivanov, University of Birmingham, 2 March 1996.

598 *Kozly* were both collaborators with the camp guards, such as Yanukovych, and 'bitches' who were used for, or sold their sexual services to criminals incarcerated in prisons and camps. Yanukovych described the opposition as *kozly* meaning he understood them as a force that required physically subduing similar to the violent encounters and rapes he had witnessed in prison (A. Fournier, *Forging Rights in a New Democracy*, p.125). Active homosexuality was permitted by the criminal world in prisons and camps but passive homosexuality and permitting oneself to be raped was viewed very negatively. Men who had been raped were regarded as outcasts and honour dictated they murder the rapists. Yuri Glazov, 'Thieves in the USSR – a Social Phenomenon,' in M. Galeottti ed., *Russian and Post-Soviet Organized Crime* (Dartmouth: Ashgate, 2002), pp.11 and 36.

599 A. Fournier, *Forging Rights in a New Democracy*, p.120.

600 Y. Glazov, '"Thieves" in the USSR: A Social Phenomenon' in M. Galeotti ed., *Russian and Post-Soviet Organized Crime*, pp.31-46.

601 Interview with J. Zisels.

602 Joseph D. Serio and Vyacheslav Razinkin, 'Thieves Professing the Code' in M. Galeotti ed., *Russian and Post-Soviet Organized Crime*, pp.90-91.

603 Interview with J. Zisels.

604 Ararat L. Osipan and Alex L. Osipan, 'Why Donbas Votes for Yanukovych: Confronting the Ukrainian Orange Revolution,' *Demokratizatsiya*, vol.14, no.4 (Fall 2006), p.498.

605 Frederico Varese, 'The Society of the Vory 1930s-1950s' and J. D. Serio and V. Razinkin, 'Thieves Professing the Code: Traditional Role of Vory v Zakone in Russia's Criminal World and Adaptations to a New Social Reality' in M. Galeotti ed., *Russian and Post-Soviet Organized Crime*, p.9 and p.95.

606 Yulia Mostova, 'Nakazano: vyzhaty,' *Tserkalo Tyzhnya*, 25 January 2013. http://gazeta.dt.ua/internal/nakazano-vizhati.html

607 Polls cited by *Ukrayinska Pravda*, 3 June 2004, *Tserkalo Tyzhnya*, 3 September 2004 and L. Kuchma, *Posle Maydana, Zapysky prezydenta 2005- 2006* (Vremya, Moscow and Dovira, Kyiv, 2007), p.507.

608 Poll cited by *Tserkalo Tyzhnya*, 5 June 2004.

609 John A. Armstrong, *The Soviet Bureaucratic Elite. A Case Study of the Ukrainian Apparatus* (New York: Frederick A. Praeger, 1959), pp.129-130.

610 Zenon Zawada, 'Yevhen Stakhiv returns to Donetsk, where he once led nationalist underground,' *The Ukrainian Weekly*, 10 July 2005. http://www.ukrweekly.com/old/archive/2005/280510.shtml. After World War II, Stakhiv aligned with the more democratic zpUHVR (external representation of the Ukrainian Supreme Liberation Council) in the Ukrainian diaspora. See T. Kuzio, 'The U.S. Support for Ukraine's Liberation during the Cold War.'

611 H. Kuromiya, Freedom and Terror in the Donbas, p.328.

612 Y. Bilinsky, 'The Communist Party of Ukraine After 1966' in Peter J. Potichnyj ed., *Ukraine in the Seventies* (Oakville: Mosaic Press, 1975), p.245.

613 Olga Medvedkov, *Soviet Urbanization* (London and New York: Routledge, 1990), pp.104 and 148.

614 J. A. Armstrong, *The Soviet Bureaucratic Elite*, p.145.

615 L. Shelley, 'Internal Migration and Crime in the Soviet Union', p.85.

616 R. Szporluk, 'Urbanization in Ukraine Since the Second World War' in Ivan L. Rudnytsky ed., *Rethinking Ukrainian History* (Edmonton: Canadian Institute of Ukrainian Studies, 1981), pp. 185 and 190-193.

617 T. H. Friedgut, 'Perestroika in the Provinces: The Politics of Transition in Donetsk' in T.H. Friedgut and W. Hahn eds., *Local Power and Post-Soviet Politics* (Armonk, NY: M.E. Sharpe, 1994), p.163.

618 Ibid., p.164.

619 Interview with Yuriy Lutsenko, Kyiv, 1 November 2013.

620 Interview with Ukrainian Parliamentary Commission for Human Rights deputy head Bohdan Kryklyvenko, Kyiv, 17 December 2015.

621 H. Kuromiya, *Freedom and Terror in the Donbas*, p.306.

622 Volodymyr Shcherban interviewed by *Kievski Vedomosti*, 21 October 1997.

623 *Ukrayinska Pravda*, 18 October 2005.

624 L. I. Shelley, 'Russia and Ukraine: Transition or Tragedy?' in Roy Godson ed., *Menace to Society. Political-Criminal Collaboration Around the World* (New Brunswick, NJ and London: Transaction Publishers, 2003), p. 206.

625 http://ord-ua.com/2011/03/10/ukrainian-nepotism-in-persons-pshonka-dynasty/

626 http://www.cpj.org/killed/2001/igor-aleksandrov.php

627 T. Kuzio, 'Donetsk Becomes the Most Dangerous Place in Ukraine for Journalists,' *RFERL Media Matters*, 19 September 2003. http://www.rferl.org/content/article/1343765.html

628 'Ukraine: Engaging Yanukovych, The Man of the Moment,' *US Embassy Kyiv*, 20 November 2006. https://wikileaks.org/plusd/cables/06KYIV4313_a.html

629 Moises Naim, 'Mafia States,' *Foreign Affairs*, vol.91, no.3 (May-June 2012), pp.100-111.

630 Quoted from Timothy Garten Ash, 'Cameron mustn't visit Ukraine while Tymoshenko remains imprisoned,' *The Guardian*, 30 May 2012. http://www.theguardian.com/commentisfree/2012/may/30/ukraine-euro-2012-cameron-tymoshenko.

631 Oliver Bullough, *Looting Ukraine: The East, the West, and the Corruption of a Country* (London: Legatum Institute, 17 July 2014). http://li.com/events/looting-ukraine-the-east-the-west-and-the-corruption-of-a-country

632 A. Wilson, *Ukraine Crisis*, p.126.

633 Ibid., p.127.

634 W. F. Butler, 'Crime in the Soviet Union. Early Glimpses of the True Story' in M. Galeotti ed., *Russian and Post-Soviet Organized Crime*, p.77.

635 Yevhen Shyvalov, 'Donbaske identity: ne ukrayinska Ukrayina,' *Tserkalo Tyzhnya*, 22-28 December 2007.

636 Karen Dawisha, *Putin's Kleptocracy. Who Owns Russia?* (New York: Simon and Schuster, 2014), p.31.

637 A. Fournier, *Forging Rights in a New Democracy*, pp.27-28.

638 Ibid., pp.101-201.

639 Piotr H. Kosicki and Oksana Nesterenko, 'Eastern Ukraine Has Been a Mafia State for Years. Can Kiev Break the Cycle of Violence?' *New Republic*, 5 June 2014. https://newrepublic.com/article/118010/eastern-ukraine-mafia-state-can-kiev-impose-rule-law

640 Interview with Democratic Initiatives Foundation President, I. Bekeshkina.

641 S. Walker, 'Komunar, east Ukraine: 'Nothing to eat, nothing to do, no point in life,' *The Guardian*, 6 February 2015. http://www.theguardian.com/world/2015/feb/06/ukraine-life-hard-horrors-war-kommunar-food-medicine-russian

642 Denys Kazansky and Serhiy Harmash, 'Ukraine's illegal coal mines are dirty, dangerous and deadly,' *Kyiv Post*, 27 May 2014. http://www.kyivpost.com/article/content/ukraine/ukraines-illegal-coal-mines-are-dirty-dangerous-and-deadly-349592.html

643 M. Mackinnon, 'We have no homeland.'

644 Jakob Preuss, *The Other Chelsea. A Story from Donetsk*, 2010. https://www.youtube.com/watch?v=VZx_NulsQVU

645 Tom Coupe and Maksym Obrizan, 'Violence and political outcomes in Ukraine – Evidence from Sloviansk and Kramatorsk,' *Journal of Comparative Economics*, vol.44, no.1 (February 2016), pp.201-212.

646 I. Bekeshkina, 'Donbas yak Osoblyvyy Rehion Ukrayiny' (Kyiv: Kyiv International Institute for Sociology, 9 March 2015). http://www.public-consultation.org/studies/Ukraine_0315.pdf

647 *Natsionalna Bezpeka i Oborona*, nos.3-4, 2016, pp.61-65.

648 Anna Fournier, *Forging Rights in a New Democracy*, p.68.

649 Ibid., pp.85-88 and H. Kuromiya, *Freedom and Terror in the Donbas*, pp.246, 336.

650 O. Bullough, *Looting Ukraine*.

651 *Ukrayinska Pravda*, 11 October 2012.

652 T. Kuzio, 'Viktor Yanukovych – Mr 50 Percent,' *Financial Times*, 24 March 2014. http://blogs.ft.com/beyond-brics/2014/03/24/guest-post-viktor-yanukovich-mr-50-per-cent/

653 'Ukraine: IUD's Taruta on Regions, Elections, and Gas Deals,' *US Embassy Kyiv*, 13 September 2007. https://wikileaks.org/plusd/cables/07KYIV2286_a.html

654 Hans van Zon, 'The Rise of the Conglomerates in Ukraine' in Alex E. Fernandez Jilberto and Barbara Hogenboom eds., *Big Business and Economic Development. Conglomerates and economic groups in developing countries and transition economies under globalization* (London: Routledge, 2007), pp.386-387 and Roman Kupchinsky, 'The Clan from Donetsk,' *RFERL Poland, Belarus and Ukraine Report*, 26 November and 10 December 2002. http://www.rferl.org/content/article/1344102.html, http://www.rferl.org/content/article/1344104.html

655 Interview with Tatyana Chornovol, Kyiv, 31 October 2013.

656 J.V. Koshiw, *Abuse of Power*, p.202.

657 In 2013, Akin Gump Strauss Hauer & Feld, a US law firm working on behalf of Akhmetov, threatened the University of Toronto Press with a libel case if they published my book *Ukraine. Democratization, Corruption and the New Russian Imperialism* leading them to cancel my contract. The book was published in the US where libel laws work for the benefit of authors.

658 http://reportingproject.net/new/REPORTS/Document%20about%20Donetsk%20crime%20group.pdf

659 Alexander Kupatadze, *Transitions After Transitions: Coloured Revolutions and Organized Crime in Georgia, Ukraine and Kyrgyzstan*. A Thesis Submitted for the Degree of PhD at the University of St. Andrews, 2010, p.143. http://research-repository.st-andrews.ac.uk/handle/10023/1320

660 Interview with T. Chornovol.

661 Y. Mostova, 'Nakazano: vyzhaty,' *Tserkalo Tyzhnya*, 25 January 2013. http://gazeta.dt.ua/internal/nakazano-vizhati.html

662 See the photographs in T. Chornovil, 'Donetska vendetta.' http://tabloid.pravda.com.ua/photos/4f63197aba18d/, and http://tabloid.pravda.com.ua/news/51076ecbd0e33/

663 A. Kupatadze, *Organized Crime, Transitions and State Formation in Post-Soviet Eurasia* (London: Palgrave Macmillan UK, 2012), pp.74-75.

664 K. Dawisha, *Putin's Kleptocracy*, p.25.

665 Ibid., p.33.

666 D. Kazansky, 'The Myth of Rinat Akhmetov,' *Ukrainian Week*, no.10 (October 2015). http://i.tyzhden.ua/content/photoalbum/2015/10_2015/09/Book10.pdf

667 A. Kupatadze, Organized Crime, Political Transitions and State Formation in Post-Soviet Eurasia, p.74.

668 K. Dawisha, *Putin's Kleptocracy*, p.25.

669 Ukrayinska Pravda, 14 May 2005.

670 Taras Chornovil interviewed by *Hazeta po-Ukrayinski*, 2 March 2012. www.gazeta.ua/articles/425098

671 'Ukraine: IUD's Taruta on Regions, Elections, and Gas Deals.'

672 Ibid.,

673 S. Leshchenko, *Mezhyhirskyy Syndrom. Diahnoz Vladi: Viktora Yanukovycha* (Kyiv: Bright Star Publishing, 2014), p.23.

674 Ibid., p.24.

675 Matthew A. Rojansky, 'Corporate Raiding in Ukraine. Causes, Methods and Consequences,' *Demokratizatsiya*, vol.22, no.3 (Fall 2014), p.427.

676 Harriet Salem, 'Ukraine's Oligarchs: A Who's Who Guide,' *Vice News*, 13 October 2014. https://news.vice.com/article/ukraines-oligarchs-a-whos-who-guide

677 A. Wilson, *Ukraine's Orange Revolution* (New Haven, CT: Yale University Press, 2005), p.13 and A. Wilson, *Ukraine Crisis*, p.122.

678 Hennadiy Moskal interviewed by *Ukrayinska Pravda*, 21 March 2013. http://www.pravda.com.ua/articles/2013/03/21/6986155/

679 The bodies were found in the village of Novyy Svit, Donetsk *oblast*.

680 T. Chornovol, 'Kinets donetskoi mafii,' *Levyi Bereg*, 28 December 2010.

681 Y. Lutsenko interviewed by *Ukrayinska Pravda*, 11 November 2010.

682 Givi Nemsadze was employed by Akhmetov. See A. Kupatadze, *Transitions After Transitions: Coloured Revolutions and Organized Crime in Georgia, Ukraine and Kyrgyzstan*, p.133.

683 Interview with T. Chornovol.

684 Vlad Lavrov, 'Ivaniushchenko works to clean up reputation,' *Kyiv Post*, 29 April 2011. http://www.kyivpost.com/content/ukraine/ivaniushchenko-works-to-clean-up-reputation-103198.html

685 T. Chornovol interviewed by *Hazeta po-Ukrayinski*, http://gazeta.ua/articles/politics/_nayanukovicha-povisili-vbivstvo-scherbanya/480045

686 Serhiy Kuzin, 'Aktualni spravy mynulykh dniv,' *Dserkalo Tyzhnya*, 6 April 2012. http://gazeta.dt.ua/POLITICS/aktualni_spravi_minulih_dniv.html

687 See the table in J.V. Koshiw, *Abuse of Power,* p.208.

688 J.V. Koshiw, *Abuse of Power*, p.218.

689 Photographic and video footage of Akhmetov and Brahin at the funeral of Aleksandr Krantz in 1992 and at other similar events have been published after they were leaked by the Ministry of Interior. T. Chornovol, 'Donetska vendetta,' *Ukrayinska Pravda blogs*, 28 January 2013 and http://blogs.pravda.com.ua/authors/chornovol/5106584eed6da/ and 'Donetskaya mafiya. Chast pervaya: pryshestviye Akhmetova,' http://www.youtube.com/watch?v=dA29BDRfCEA

690 http://glavcom.ua/articles/9889.html and http://www.faz.net/aktuell/politik/ausland/europa/julija-timoschenko-die-dunkle-seite-der-macht-12117180.html

691 http://www.bloomberg.com/news/2012-11-01/the-world-s-200-richest-people.html

692 Interview with Lutsenko. The initial sources of their capital were theft, racketeering, currency operations and bribes. On this see A. Kupatadze, *Organized Crime, Transitions and State Formation in Post-Soviet Eurasia*, p.95.

693 'Ukraine: IUD's Taruta on Regions, Elections, and Gas Deals.

694 'Ukraine: Presidential Adviser Sees Possibilities in Party of Regions,' *US Embassy Kyiv*, 31 January 2006. https://wikileaks.org/plusd/cables/06KIEV400_a.html

695 'Ukraine: Extreme Makeover for the Party of Regions?' *US Embassy Kyiv*, 3 February 2006. https://wikileaks.org/plusd/cables/06KIEV473_a.html

696 L. I. Shelley, 'Russia and Ukraine: Transition or Tragedy?' p.213.

697 J. V. Koshiw, *Abuse of Power*, pp.216-217.

698 Ioulia Shukan, 'Intentional disruptions and violence in Ukraine's Supreme Rada: political competition, order, and disorder in a post-Soviet chamber, 2006–2012,' *Post-Soviet Affairs*, vol.29, no.5 (September 2013), p.448.

699 Ibid., p.449.

700 *Ukrayina Moloda*, 8 October 2004.

701 See the photographs of corporate raiding by Volodymyr Boyko, https://ord.ua, 20 June 2013 and https://ord-ua.com/2013/06/20/prokurorski-zhniva/ 20 June 2013

702 *Ukrayina Moloda*, 2 November 2004 and *Ukrayinska Pravda*, 19 November 2004.

703 *Nichna Varta* (organised by Our Ukraine) leader Oleksandr Popov interviewed by *Ukrayinska Pravda*, 27 January 2006. http://www.pravda.com.ua/articles/2006/01/27/3057173/

704 Mykola Tomenko cited by *Ukrayinska Pravda*, 26 October 2004.

705 A. Wilson, *The Ukraine Crisis*, p.49.

706 S. Koshkina, *Maidan*, p.155.

[707] On 9 December 2013, the SBU raided the headquarters of the *Batkivshchyna* party and confiscated servers and computers. No other opposition parties were raided.

[708] A. Wilson, *Ukraine Crisis*, pp.78-79.

[709] General's prosecutor's office cited by *Ukrayinska Pravda*, 17 November 2015.

[710] General's prosecutor's office cited by *Ukrayinska Pravda*, 18 November 2015.

[711] https://www.treasury.gov/press-center/press-releases/Pages/jl9729.aspx

[712] Oliver Carroll, 'Why Ukraine's Separatist Movement Failed in Kharkiv,' *New Republic*, 22 June 2014. https://newrepublic.com/article/118301/kharkivs-kernes-returns-different-city-after-being-shot

[713] H. Coynash, 'Another person charged with Euromaidan crimes allowed to escape?' *KHRPG*, 9 September 2015.

[714] *Ukrayinska Pravda*, 17 November 2015.

[715] 'The Battle for Ukraine.'

[716] O. Carroll, 'Star Wars in Ukraine: Poroshenko vs Kolomoisky,' *Politico*, 21 December 2015. http://www.politico.eu/article/star-wars-in-ukraine-poroshenko-vs-kolomoisky/

[717] R. Olearchyk, 'Life in Ukraine's grey zone: Dangerous and desperate,' *Financial Times*, 7 June 2015.

[718] http://uawire.org/news/igor-strelkov-pro-russian-separatists-have-brought-poverty-and-ruin-to-the-donbas

[719] 'Debaltseve – Gunmen, Looting and Bread Queues,' *RFERL*, 19 April 2015. http://www.rferl.org/media/video/ukraine-debaltseve-civilians/26956743.html

[720] Sheren Khalel and Matthew Vickery, 'Donetsk has become eastern Ukraine's lawless city,' *USA Today*, 18 May 2015. http://www.usatoday.com/story/news/world/2015/05/17/donetsk-ukraine-separatists-marauding-militias/27190647/

[721] D. Volchek and Claire Bigg, 'Cutthroats and Bandits: Volunteers Stint with Ukrainian Rebels Turns to Nightmare,' *RFERL*, 25 April 2015. http://www.rferl.org/content/ukraine-war-russian-volunteer-interview/26976499.html

[722] James Sherr, 'A War of Narratives and Arms' in Keir Giles, Philip Hanson, Roderic Lyne, James Nixey, J. Sherr and Andrew Wood eds., *The Russian Challenge, Chatham House Report* (London: Royal Institute for International Affairs, June 2015), p.27. https://www.chathamhouse.org/sites/files/chathamhouse/field/field_document/20150605RussianChallengeGilesHansonLyneNixeySherrWood.pdf

[723] B. Judah, *Fragile Empire*, pp.51, 262.

[724] Ibid., p.86.

[725] Ibid., pp.109, 111-112, 114.

[726] B. Bidder, 'Russian Far-Right Idol.'

[727] Paul Kubicek, 'Regional Polarization in Ukraine: Public Opinion, Voting, and Legislative Behaviour,' *Europe-Asia Studies*, vol.52, no.2 (March 2000), p.282.

[728] Michael Gentile, 'West oriented in the east-oriented Donbas: a political stratigraphy of geopolitical identity in Luhansk, Ukraine,' *Post-Soviet Affairs*, vol.31, no.3 (May 2015), p.219.

[729] Tim Judah, 'Ukraine: Two Poets in the war,' *New York Review of Books*, 6 April 2015. http://www.nybooks.com/daily/2015/04/06/ukraine-two-poets/

[730] John Simpson, 'Vladimir Putin is fighting for his political survival by provoking unrest in Ukraine,' *New Statesman*, 30 March 2015. http://www.newstatesman.com/politics/2015/03/vladimir-putin-fighting-political-survival-provoking-unrest-ukraine

731 'Letters from Donbas, Part 3.'

732 T. Judah, 'Ukraine: Divided and Bitter,' *New York Review of Books*, 23 March 2015. http://www.nybooks.com/daily/2015/03/23/two-ukraine-towns-divided-bitter/

733 P. Pomerantsev, 'Propagandalands.'

734 A. Wilson, *Ukraine Crisis*, p.135.

735 Sergei Loiko, 'The Unravelling of Moscow's 'Novorossia' Dream,' *RFERL*, 1 June 2016. http://www.rferl.org/content/unraveling-moscow-novorossia-dream/27772641.html

736 Devin Ackles, Maxim Eristavi and Randy R. Potts, 'A Guide to the Warlords of Ukraine's Separatist Republic,' *Hromadske International*, 13 November 2014. https://medium.com/@Hromadske/a-guide-to-warlords-of-the-ukraine-separatist-republics-2be78dfc7a5e

737 David Satter, *Darkness at Dawn. The Rise of the Russian Criminal State* (New Haven, Conn: Yale University Press, 2003), pp.133-134 and M. Galeotti, 'The Mafia and the New Russia' in M. Galeotti ed., *Russian and Post-Soviet Organized Crime*, p.295.

738 A. Shprintsen, 'CBC producer revisits Ukraine to explore conflict.'

739 Noah Sneider, 'The Empire Strikes Back,' *The Open Rehearsal Project with the Big Roundtable*, 5 November 2014. https://medium.com/the-empire-strikes-back/the-empire-strikes-back-c6e51efe9973#.fnl2hesmd

740 Scott Peterson, 'At key Ukrainian flashpoint, both rebels and loyalists wait and worry,' *Christian Science Monitor*, 5 March 2015. http://www.csmonitor.com/World/Europe/2015/0305/At-key-Ukraine-flashpoint-both-rebels-and-loyalists-wait-and-worry

741 'Letters from Donbas, Part 2: 'Do You Understand What is Going on Here?' *RFERL*, 2 January 2015. http://www.rferl.org/content/letters-from-donbas-day-to-day-life-in-eastern-ukraine/26773671.html

742 B. Hoyle, 'Cheating mars poll that threatens Europe,' *The Times*, 3 November 2014. http://www.thetimes.co.uk/tto/news/world/europe/article4255618.ece

743 *Summary Killings During the Conflict in Eastern Ukraine*. Eur50/042/2014 (London: Amnesty International, 20 October 2014). https://www.amnesty.org/en/latest/news/2014/10/eastern-ukraine-conflict-summary-killings-misrecorded-and-misreported/

744 'Ukraine: Land, Power, and Criminality in Crimea,' *US Embassy Kyiv*, 14 December 2006. https://wikileaks.org/plusd/cables/06KYIV4558_a.html

745 A. Wilson, *Ukraine Crisis*, p.109.

746 N. Mitrokhin, 'Ukraine's Separatists and Their Dubious Leaders.'

747 http://www.pravda.com.ua/articles/2010/02/19/4788595/

748 A. Kupatadze, *Transitions After Transitions: Coloured Revolutions and Organized Crime in Georgia, Ukraine and Kyrgyzstan*, p.133.

749 Sydorenko and Kurishko, 'Vspomnil Vse.'

750 A. Wilson, *Ukraine Crisis*, p.126.

751 Ibid., p.128.

752 B. Whitmore, 'Russia's Spooks and Crooks,' *RFERL*, 24 February 2016. http://www.rferl.org/content/daily-vertical-estonia-border-russia-spooks-crooks-kohver/27571143.html

753 Paul Stronski, 'Broken Ukraine,' *Foreign Affairs*, 17 March 2015. https://www.foreignaffairs.com/articles/eastern-europe-caucasus/2015-03-17/broken-ukraine

754 'Ukraine: The Russia Factor in Crimea – Ukraine's "Soft Underbelly?"' *US Embassy Kyiv*, 17 December 2006 and 'Ukraine: Crimea Update – Less Tense Than in 2006: Interethnic, Russia, Land Factors Remain Central,' *US Embassy Kyiv*, 8 June 2007. http://wikileaks.org/cable/2006/12/06KYIV4489.html

and http://wikileaks.org/cable/2007/06/07KYIV1418.html

755 Alex Luhn, 'Separatist Leader with Murky Past Cements Control of Crimea,' *Vice News*, 11 October 2014. https://news.vice.com/article/separatist-leader-with-murky-past-cements-control-of-crimea

756 Neil MacFarquhar, 'Seizing Assets in the Crimea, From Shipyard to Film Studio,' *New York Times*, 10 January 2015. http://www.nytimes.com/2015/01/11/world/seizing-assets-in-crimea-from-shipyard-to-film-studio.html?_r=0

757 L. Kravchuk, *Ostanni Dni Imperii*, p.21.

758 Viktor Byichkov cited by *The Independent*, 7 December 1991.

759 T. H. Friedgut, *Politics and Revolution in Russia's Donbass, vol.2* (Princeton, NJ: Princeton University Press, 1994), p.309.

760 'Vladimir Putin accuses Lenin of placing a 'time bomb' under Russia,' *The Guardian*, 25 January 2016.

http://www.theguardian.com/world/2016/jan/25/vladimir-putin-accuses-lenin-of-placing-a-time-bomb-under-russia

761 pp.193-194.

762 T. H. Friedgut, *Politics and Revolution in Russia's Donbass*, p.163.

763 Ibid., p.164.

764 Stephen Velychenko, *Shaping Identity in Eastern European, Russian, Soviet Russian and Polish Accounts of Ukrainian History, 1914-1991* (New York: St. Martin's Press, 1993), p.14.

765 Steven L. Guthier, 'Ukrainian Cities during the Revolution and the Interwar War Era,' in Ivan L. Rudnytsky ed., *Rethinking Ukrainian History* (Edmonton: Canadian Institute of Ukrainian Studies, 1981), p.168.

766 T. H. Friedgut, *Politics and Revolution in Russia's Donbass*, p.207.

767 Ibid., p.214.

768 Ibid., pp.193-198.

769 T. H. Friedgut, *Politics and Revolution in Russia's Donbass*, p.208.

770 T. Martin, *The Affirmative Action Empire*, pp.84 and 92.

771 H. Kuromiya, *Freedom and Terror in the Donbas*, p.198.

772 Ibid., p.201

773 Ibid., p.245.

774 Ibid., p.234.

775 B. Krawchenko, 'Ethno-Demographic Trends in Ukraine' in B. Krawchenko ed., *Ukraine after Shelest* (Edmonton: Canadian Institute of Ukrainian Studies, 1983), p.113.

776 T. Martin, *The Affirmative Action Empire*, p.355.

777 R. Szporluk, 'Urbanization in Ukraine Since the Second World War,' p.193.

778 Ibid, p.104.

779 O. Medvedkov, *Soviet Urbanization*, p.104.

780 Y. Bilinsky, 'The Communist Party of Ukraine After 1966,' p.245.

781 Volodymyr Kipen, 'Donetsk Regional Identity: Some Dimensions of Analysis,' *National Security and Defence*, no.1 (2006), p.58. http://www.razumkov.org.ua/eng/journal.php?y=2006&cat=15

[782] Kirstin Zimmer, 'Trapped in Past Glory. Self-Identification and Self-Symbolisation in the Donbas' in Adam Swain ed., *Re-Constructing the Post-Soviet Industrial Region, The Donbas in Transition* (London: Routledge 2007), p.115.

[783] Borys Lewytzkyj, 'The Ruling Party Organs of Ukraine' in P. J. Potichnyj ed., *Ukraine in the Seventies*, p.273.

[784] B. Krawchenko, 'Ethno-Demographic Trends in Ukraine,' p.108.

[785] *Samvydav* newspaper *Dosvitni Vohni*, no.3 (November 1989).

[786] Mykhaylo Pleshanov (UNIAR), Ukraine Press Agency press release no.260, 11 October 1990.

[787] 'Formation of a Common Identity of the Citizens of Ukraine.'

[788] K. Zimmer, 'Trapped in Past Glory,' p.105.

[789] Interview with two representatives of the independent miner's trade union, Ukraine Press Agency press release, 22 December 1990.

[790] H. van Zon, *The Political Economy of Independent Ukraine, Captured by the Past* (London: Palgrave Macmillan, 2000), p.141.

[791] H. van Zon, 'Neo-Patrimonialism as an Impediment to Economic Development: The Case of Ukraine,' *Journal of Communist Studies and Transition Politics*, vol.17, no.3 (September 2001), p.77.

[792] 'Ukraine's troubles. Into battle,' *Economist*, 17 May 2014. http://www.economist.com/news/europe/21602289-despite-all-fighting-country-could-just-hold-together-after-may-25th-battle

[793] P, Pomerantsev, 'Propagadalands.'

[794] Interview with Donetsk State University Professor Ihor Todorov, Donetsk, 18 December 2013.

[795] H. van Zon, 'Neo-Patrimonialism as an Impediment to Economic Development: The Case of Ukraine,' p.89.

[796] S. Yekelchyk, *Stalin's Empire of Memory*, p.64.

[797] H. van Zon, *The Political Economy of Independent Ukraine*, p.141.

[798] S. Yekelchuk, *Stalin's Empire of Memory*, p.64.

[799] See comments by then leader of the Party of Slavic Unity Bazylyuk in *Holos Ukrayiny*, 4 March 1999.

[800] M. Pozhivanov, Mayor of Maryupol, speaking to the Future of Europe Trust Young Leaders Forum III, University of Birmingham, 2 March 1996.

[801] Interview with Donetsk State University Professor Ihor Todorov.

[802] H. Moskal interviewed by *The Ukrainian Week*, no.3 (March 2015). http://i.tyzhden.ua/content/photoalbum/2015/03_2015/16/Book3.pdf

[803] M. Gentile, 'The Post-Soviet urban poor and where they live: Khrushchev-era blocks, "bad" areas, and the vertical dimension in Luhansk, Ukraine,' *Annals of the Association of America Geographers*, vol.105, no.3 (May 2015), p.18.

[804] Aleksandra Vagner, 'Freed Ukrainian journalist says rebels 'being trained for an offensive,' *RFERL*, 6 January 2015. http://www.rferl.org/a/ukraine-journalist-cheremskiy-separatists/26779805.html

[805] Daniel J. Walkowitz, '"Normal Life": The Crisis of Identity Among Donetsk's Miners' in Lewis H. Siegelbaum and D. J. Walkowitz eds., *Workers of the Donbass Speak. Survival and Identity in the New Ukraine, 1989-1992* (Albany, NY: State University of New York Press, 1995), p.180.

806 P. S. Pirie, 'National Identity and Politics in Southern and Eastern Ukraine,' p.1086 and M. Aberg, 'Paradox of Change: Soviet Modernisation and Ethno-Linguistic Modernisation in Lviv, 1945-1989,' *Harvard Ukrainian Studies*, vol. XXIV, nos. 1-4 (u2000), p.295.

807 P.S. Pirie, 'National Identity and Politics in Southern and Eastern Ukraine.'

808 Graham Smith and A. Wilson were mistaken to believe there was no defined community in the Donbas where polls have shown a strong attachment to regional identity. See their, 'Rethinking Russia's Post-Soviet Diaspora. The Potential for Political mobilisation in east Ukraine and north-east Estonia,' *Europe-Asia Studies*, vol.49, no.5 (July 1997), pp.845-864.

809 I. Bekeshkina, 'Donbas yak Osoblyvyy Rehion Ukrayiny.'

810 J. Hitt, 'The Russian Tom Clancy is on the Front Lines for Real.'

811 'Public opinion in liberated areas of Kramatorsk and Slovyansk,' Democratic Initiatives Foundation, November 2014. http://dif.org.ua/en/polls/2014_polls/obshestven-navjansk.htm

812 'Common Identity of the Citizens of Ukraine.'

813 *Ukrayinska Pravda*, 25 April 2006.

814 *Ukrayinska Pravda*, 19 December 2005.

815 Fournier described this as de-modernisation and a return to feudalism. See her *Forging Rights in a New Democracy*, p.28.

816 H. van Zon, 'Neo-Patrimonialism as an Impediment to Economic Development,' pp.74-75.

817 J. V. Koshiw, *Abuse of Power*, p.242.

818 In December 1998, the Ukrainian parliament adopted a law on Special Economic Zones and the Special Investment Regions.'

819 Interview with the head of the Donetsk *oblast* Committee of Voters Serhiy Tkachenko, Donetsk, 19 December 2013.

820 Ibid.,

821 Joel S. Hellman. 'Winners Take All: The Politics of Partial Reform in Postcommunist Transitions,' *World Politics* vol.50, no. 2 (January1998), pp. 203-234.

822 E. Kovaleva, 'Regional Politics in Ukraine's Transition: The Donetsk Elite,' p.72.

823 H. van Zon, 'The Rise of Conglomerates in Ukraine: The Donetsk Case,' p.384.

824 'Social foundation of the middle class formation in Ukraine: identification criteria, structure, key features,'
*National Security and Defence*, nos.1-2 (2014). http://www.razumkov.org.ua/eng/journal.php?y=2014&cat=201

825 http://www.artukraine.com/famineart/fam_hearing6.htm

826 Viktor Yanukovych cited by *Den*, 7 August 2004.

827 'U pidruchnykakh z istorii znykly rozdily "Rusyfikatsiya' ta "UPA,' *Ukrayinska Pravda Zhyttya*, 31 March 2011. http://life.pravda.com.ua/society/2011/03/31/76082/

828 'What unites and divides Ukrainians.'

829 V. Landyk cited by *Den*, 19 August 1997.

830 'Common Identity of the Citizens of Ukraine: Prospects and Challenges.'

831 T. Kuzio, 'Party of Regions Splits over Georgia and NATO,' *Eurasia Daily Monitor*, vol.5, no.167 (2 September 2008). http://www.jamestown.org/single/?tx_ttnews%5Btt_news%5D=33911&no_cache=1#.Vsc1J5MrKt8

832 https://www.rt.com/news/putin-address-parliament-crimea-562/

833 Vitaliy Pyrovych, 'Yanukovych khochet stat poslednym prezydentom,' *Komentarii*, 2 April 2010. http://gazeta.comments.ua/?art=1270140253

834 *Ukrayinska Pravda*, 28 February 2006.

835 G. Smith and A. Wilson, 'Rethinking Russia's Post-Soviet Diaspora,' p.849.

836 On Russia's takeover of Ukrainian *siloviki* under Yanukovych see T. Kuzio, 'Russianization of Ukrainian National Security Policy under Viktor Yanukovych,' *Journal of Slavic Military Studies*, vol.25, no.4 (December 2012), pp.558-581.

837 S. Koshkina, *Maidan*, p.402.

838 http://www.pbs.org/wgbh/frontline/film/battle-for-ukraine/

839 S. Koshkina, *Maidan*, p.399.

840 Editor of *Ostrov* Serhiy Harmash interviewed by *Krayina*, 22 May 2014, pp.7-8.

841 V. Pyrovych, 'Yanukovych khochet stat poslednym prezydentom.'

842 R. Olearchyk, 'Ukraine's oligarchs accused of double dealing over separatism,' *Financial Times*, 15 April 2014.

843 A. Wilson, 'The Donbas in 2014,' p.644.

844 Serhiy Kudelia, 'The Donbas Rift,' *Russian Politics and Law*, vol.54, no.1 (January-February 2016), pp.12 and 13.

845 http://www.pravda.com.ua/news/2016/04/18/7105953/ and http://novosti.dn.ua/details/273084/

846 A. Wilson, *Ukraine Crisis*, p.130.

847 H. Salem, 'Ukraine's Oligarchs.'

848 A. Wilson, *Ukraine Crisis*, pp.130-131.

849 *Rossiyskaya Gazeta*, 12 May 2014. Keith Gessen reaches the same conclusions about Akhmetov providing resources to the separatists. See Keith Gessen, 'Why not kill them all?' *London Review of Books*, vol.36, no.17 (11 September 2014). http://www.lrb.co.uk/v36/n17/keith-gessen/why-not-kill-them-all

850 A. Wilson, *Ukraine Crisis*, p.126.

851 S. Leshchenko, 'The Kings of the Donbas. Where are they now?' *New Eastern Europe*, no.4, (XIII) (2014), pp.103-110.

852 Hanna Soderbaum, 'Parallel Worlds in Ukraine,' *Baltic Worlds*, vol.VII, no.1 (24 April 2014).

853 D. Kazanskyy, 'The Myth of Rinat Akhmetov.'

854 Pavel Kangyn, 'Upravlayemaya Vesna,' *Novaya Gazeta*, 8 December 2014. http://www.novayagazeta.ru/politics/66411.html

855 P. Kangyn, 'Upravlayemaya Vesna.'

856 A. Kurkov, *Ukraine Diaries*, p.215.

857 Dmitri Trenin, 'The Revival of the Russian Military,' *Foreign Affairs*, vol.95, no.3 (May-June 2016), p.12.

858 T. Chornovol, 'Terorysty Donbasu (poimenno),' *Ukrayinska Pravda blog*, 22 April 2014. http://blogs.pravda.com.ua/authors/chornovol/5356b7e3e741d/

859 Stanislav Kmet, 'Tin Yefremova nad "LNR,"' *Ukrayinska Pravda*, 24 December 2014. http://www.pravda.com.ua/articles/2014/12/24/7053114/

860 V. Landyk interviewed by http://news.online.ua/743660/vladimir-landik/. A video of Yefremov giving a speech to Luhansk separatists can be seen here: https://www.youtube.com/watch?v=hFx3Yw0PlMw

[861] Tomasz Piechal, *The War Republics in the Donbas One Year After the Outbreak of the Conflict*, OSW Commentary, no.174 (Warsaw: Centre for Eastern Studies, 17 June 2015). http://www.osw.waw.pl/sites/default/files/commentary_174.pdf

[862] S. Yekelchyk, *The Conflict in Ukraine. What Everyone Needs to Know* (New York: Oxford University Press, 2015), p.118.

[863] M. Laruelle, 'The three colours of Novorossiya.'

[864] Owen Matthews, 'Russia's Ukraine Retreat,' *Newsweek*, 8 June 2015.

[865] 'Project Novorossiya – game over?' *BBC Monitoring*, 2 June 2015.

[866] Igor Girkin interviewed by *Komersant*, 14 November 2014. www.komersant.ru/doc/2611911

[867] Ironically, the Ukrainian diaspora has also found it difficult to see Russian speaking Ukrainians as Ukrainian patriots.

[868] Hannah Thoburn, 'Mykolayiv Makes a Surprising Turn Toward the West,' *Atlantic Council of the US*, 1 December 2015. http://www.atlanticcouncil.org/blogs/new-atlanticist/mykolayiv-makes-a-surprising-turn-toward-the-west

[869] http://assembly.coe.int/nw/xml/News/News-View-EN.asp?newsid=6124&lang=2&cat=137

[870] R. Olearchyk, 'Donetsk faces a creeping Russification.'

[871] S. Leshchenko, *Mezhyhirskyy Syndrom*, p.97.

[872] I. Krastev, 'Paradoxes of the New Authoritarianism,' *Journal of Democracy*, vol.22, no.2 (April 2011), p.11.

[873] K. Zimmer, 'The comparative failure of machine politics, administrative resources and fraud,' *Canadian Slavonic Papers*, vol.47, nos. 3-4 (September 2005), p.374.

[874] H. van Zon, 'The Rise of Conglomerates in Ukraine: The Donetsk Case,' pp.390 and 394.

[875] Rinat Akhmetov cited by *Ukrayinska Pravda*, 20 February 2006.

[876] H. Salem, 'Ukraine's Oligarchs.'

[877] 'Ukraine: Engaging Yanukovych, The Man of the Moment.'

[878] Lyudmilla Pavlyuk, 'Extreme Rhetoric in the 2004 Presidential Campaign: Images of Geopolitical and Regional Divisions,' *Canadian Slavonic Papers*, vol. XLVII, nos.3-4 (September-December 2005), p.308.

[879] H. van Zon, 'Alternative Scenarios for Ukraine,' *Futures*, vol.34, no.5 (June 2002), p.408.

[880] H. van Zon, 'Neo-Patrimonialism as an Impediment to Economic Development,' p.77.

[881] http://forbes.ua/business/1340389-rassledovanie-obogashchenie-aleksandra-yanukovicha

[882] Ihor Zhdanov, 'Peremozhna komanda Yushchenka vs peremozhenoyi komandy Yanukovycha abo koho obyrayemo u 2006 rotsi,' *Ukrayinska Pravda*, 8 December 2005. http://www.pravda.com.ua/articles/2005/12/8/3030470/

[883] http://glavred.info, 5 and 7 April 2005.

[884] T. Chornovil interviewed by *Ukrayinska Pravda*, May 29, 2012. http://www.pravda.com.ua/articles/2012/05/29/6965540/

[885] H. Van Zon, *The Political Economy of Independent Ukraine*, p.39.

[886] Oleksandr Sushko, 'The 2002 Parliament Elections as an Indicator of the Sociopolitical Development of Ukraine,' *Demokratizatsiya*, vol.10, no.4 (Fall 2002), p.572. See A. Aslund, 'Is Viktor Yanukovych Ukraine's Putin?' *The Washington Post*, 7 May 2011. https://www.washingtonpost.com/opinions/is-viktor-yanukovych-ukraines-putin/2011/04/27/AFVH3sUF_story.html

[887] E. Kovaleva, 'Regional Politics in Ukraine's Transition' in A. Swain ed., *Re-Constructing the Post-Soviet Industrial Region*, p.66.

[888] Ivan Sokolovskyy, 'Elektoralni prykhylnosti hromadayan Ukrayiny ta yikh zvyazok iz sotsialno-strukturnymy kharakteristykamy pid chas prezydentskykh vyboriv 2004 roku,' *Politychnyy Portret*, no.33 (2005), pp.79-84.

[889] A. L. Osipan and A. L. Osipan, 'Why Donbass Votes for Yanukovych, p.502.

[890] Viktor Tikhonov is cited by *Ukrayinska Pravda*, 10 October 2011.

[891] A. Fournier, *Forging Rights in a New Democracy*, 118. 97, 114-115, 118 and 121.

[892] K. Zimmer points out that there is admiration for a good master in Donetsk. 'The Comparative Failure of Machine Politics.'

[893] S. Leshchenko, Tetyana Nikolayenko and M. Nayem, 'Mashyna chasu Viktora Yanukovycha – nazad u "sovok," *Ukrayinska Pravda*, 25 April 2010. http://www.pravda.com.ua/articles/2010/04/25/4969640/

[894] Stefan Wagstyl and R. Olearchyk, 'Their Ukraine,' *Financial Times*, 15 June 2007.

[895] See the documents published at http://www.pravda.com.ua/cdn/graphics/2016/05/black-pr/index.html

[896] H. Kryuchkov and D. Tabachnyk, *Fashizm v Ukraine*.

[897] Z. Zawada, 'Party of Regions wages aggressive campaign for power,' *The Ukrainian Weekly*, 24 December 2006.

[898] A. Fournier, *Forging Rights in a New Democracy*, p.118.

[899] J. Yaffa, 'The Search for Petr Khokhlov.'

[900] 'Ukraine: Yanukovych Suggests Won't Accept Orange; Wants Yushchenko to Agree to Broad Coalition,' *US Embassy Kyiv*, 4 October 2007. http://wikileaks.org/cable/2007/10/07KYIV2522.html

[901] Yanukovych was for a 'strong and flowering Ukraine' and 'My goal is to ensure economic growth throughout the country' (*Ukrayinska Pravda*, 19 October 2004, Ukrainian State Channel One, 24 February 2006). Akhmetov said 'our main goal is to ensure economic growth' and 'happiness' in the Donbas 'is when we have a strong economy, new jobs, good employment, good salary and good life.' Cited from *AFP*, 2 April 2006 and Irena Chalupa and James Rupert, 'In Ukraine's East, the Cautionary Middle Path of Oligarch-in-Chief Rinat Akhmetov', *New Atlanticist, Atlantic Council of the US*, 15 May 2014.

[902] S. Shulman, 'National Identity and Public Support for Political and Economic Reform in Ukraine.'

[903] *Natsionalna Bezpeka i Oborona*, nos.3-4 (2016), p.31.

[904] Survey by the Razumkov Ukrainian Centre for Economic and Political Studies in *National Security and Defence*, nos.7-8 (2011), p.8. http://www.razumkov.org.ua/eng/files/category_journal/NSD125-126_eng_1.pdf p.8

[905] Vybory-2012: politychne strukturvannya suspilstva ta perspektyvy bahatopartiynosti v Ukrayini, Democratic Initiatives Foundation and Razumkov Ukrainian Centre for Economic and Political Studies, 1 October 2012 and *Public Opinion in Ukraine. Key findings from an IFES July 2011 Survey* (Washington DC: International Foundation for Electoral Systems, 2011). http://dif.org.ua/ua/publications/press-relizy/politichne-strukturuvannja.html and http://www.ifes.org/Content/Publications/Press-Release/2011/Ukrainians-Pessimistic-about-Countrys-Future-Confidence-in-Political-Leaders-Falling.aspx

[906] http://dif.org.ua/ua/publications/press-relizy/ukraini---22-dumka-gromadjan.htm

[907] K. Zimmer, 'The Comparative Failure of Machine Politics,' 361-384.

908 A. Wilson, 'Ukraine's crisis of governance,' www.opendemocracy.net, 30 April 2007. http://www.opendemocracy.net/democracy-ukraine/crisis_governance_4581.jsp

909 H. van Zon, 'The Rise of Conglomerates in Ukraine: The Donetsk Case' in Alex E. Fernandez Tilberto and Barbara Hogenboom eds., *Big Business and Economic Development. Conglomerates and economic groups in developed countries and transition economies under globalization* (London: Routledge, 2007), p.384.

910 E. Kovaleva, 'Regional Politics in Ukraine's transition: The Donetsk Elite. p.69

911 H. van Zon, 'The Rise of Conglomerates in Ukraine: The Donetsk Case,' p.381.

912 This was heard on the tapes made illicitly in President Kuchma's office by presidential guard Mykola Melnychenko and made public by Socialist Party leader Oleksandr Moroz. See J. Koshiw, *Abuse of Power*, p.212.

913 Cited from Melnychenko recording. http://www.pravda.com.ua/news/2004/07/14/3001142/

914 Our Ukraine and the KPU won first place plurality in all other Ukrainian *oblasts* and cities.

915 Yevhen Marchuk interviewed by *Den*, 19 February 2005. http://www.day.kiev.ua/uk/article/podrobici/ievgen-marchuk-rushiiem-politiki-ie-ne-ideologiya-principi

916 V. Yanukovych interviewed by *Inter*, ICTV and Channel 1 channels, February 27, 2012. www.president.gov.ua/news/23133.html

917 'Ukraine: The Russia Factor in Crimea – Ukraine's "Soft Underbelly?"'

918 'Ukraine: Crimea Update – Less Tense Than in 2006.'

919 'What factors unite and divide Ukrainians,' Democratic Initiatives Foundation, 22 January 2015 and 'Do Dnya Nezalezhnosti: Shcho ukrayintsi dumayut pro Ukrayinu?' Democratic Initiatives Foundation, 21 August 2015. http://dif.org.ua/ua/polls/2015a/do-dnja-nezalezhnosti-sho-ukrainci-dumayut-pro-ukrainu__1440150573.htm

920 A. L. Osipan and A. L. Osipan, 'Why Donbass Votes for Yanukovych.'

921 http://partyofregions.ua/news/5306776bf620d2320c00000c

922 K. Zimmer, 'Donetsk in Kyiv and Kyiv in Donetsk: Centre-Periphery Linkages in the Post-Soviet Context,' Association for the Study of Nationalities Convention, Columbia University, 3-5 April 2003.

923 http://zn.ua/POLITICS/frakciyu-partii-regionov-pokinuli-esche-dva-deputata-143022_.html

924 Yevhen Shybalov, "'DNR" z seredyny, Korotkyy Liknep,' *Tserkalo Tyzhnya*, 27 September 2014. http://gazeta.dt.ua/internal/dnr-zseredini-korotkiy-liknep-_.html

925 Oleh Tsaryov offered to be leader of the separatists. http://www.pravda.com.ua/news/2014/04/11/7022153/

926 The seven candidates included Mykhaylo Dobkin, Tsaryov (who was banned from standing), Boyko, Natalia Korolevska (who dropped out), former First Deputy General Prosecutor Renat Kuzmin, Serhiy Tihipko and Valeriy Konovalyuk. The other three candidates included KPU leader Symonenko, Socialist Party member and former Interior Minister Vasyl Tsushko and Jewish-Ukrainian oligarch Vadym Rabinovich. http://www.cvk.gov.ua/pls/vp2014/WP001

927 http://static.partyofregions.ua/uploads/presentation.pdf

928 T. Kuzio, 'Yanukovych Awaits a Third Term or a Third Sentence,' *Eurasia Daily Monitor*, vol.9, no.25 (6 February 2012). http://www.jamestown.org/single/?no_cache=1&tx_ttnews|tt_news|=38977#.Uhu1yRB0ySo

929 T. Kuzio, 'Ukraine Continues to Play with the Rules, Not by the Rules,' *Eurasia Daily Monitor*, vol.10, no.72 (17 April 2013). http://www.jamestown.org/single/?no_cache=1&tx_ttnews[tt_news]=40742

930 Putin quoted by *Itar-Tass*, 9 October 1999.

931 Mykhaylo Pashkov and Valeriy Chalyy, 'Mizhnarodnyy Imidzh Ukrayiny: pohlyad iz Rosii,' *Natsionalna Bezpeka i Oborona*, no.3, 2000, p.65. http://razumkov.org.ua/additional/article_pashkov_chaly2_NSD3_ukr.pdf

932 Stephen Kotkin, 'Russia's Perpetual Geopolitics,' *Foreign Affairs*, vol.95, no.3 (May-June 2016), p.4.

933 S. Kotkin, 'Russia's Perpetual Geopolitics,' p.4.

934 E. W. Merry, 'The Origins of Russia's War in Ukraine: The Clash of Russian and European "Civilizational Choices" for Ukraine,' in E. A. Wood, W. E. Pomerantz, E. W. Merry and M. Trudolyubov, *Roots of Russia's War in Ukraine*, pp.29-31.

935 Ibid., pp.37-38.

936 R. D. Asmus, *A Little War That Shook the World*, p.193.

937 'Inside the bear,' *The Economist*, 22 October 2016. http://www.economist.com/news/special-report/21708879-when-soviet-union-collapsed-25-years-ago-russia-looked-set-become-free-market

938 Edward Lucas, 'Now that Litvinenko's murder 'probably' points to Putin, what's next for British relations with Russia?' *The Daily Telegraph*, 24 January 2016.
http://www.telegraph.co.uk/news/worldnews/europe/russia/12115968/Now-that-Litvinenkos-murder-probably-points-to-Putin-whats-next-for-British-relations-with-Russia.html

939 'The EU and Russia: before and beyond the crisis in Ukraine,' European Union Committee, 6th Report of Session 2014-2015. HL Paper 115 (20 February). http://www.publications.parliament.uk/pa/ld201415/ldselect/ldeucom/115/11502.htm

940 K. Giles, P. Hanson, R. Lyne, J. Nixey, J. Sherr, and A. Wood, *The Russian Challenge*, p.VII.

941 O. Malinova, 'Obsession with status and resentment,' p.291.

942 K. Giles, P. Hanson, R. Lyne, J. Nixey, J. Sherr, and A. Wood, *The Russian Challenge*, p.VII.

943 I. Krastev and Mark Leonard, 'Europe's Shattered Dream of Order. How Putin is Disrupting the Atlantic Alliance,' *Foreign Affairs*, vol.94, no.3, (May-June 2015), pp. 48-58.

944 L. Kuchma, *Posle Maydana*, p. 472.

945 'Russia and Me: Leonid Kravchuk,' *RFERL*, 22 February 2016. http://www.rferl.org/media/video/ukraine-kravchuk-russia-leonid/27566961.html

946 V. Putin, 'Prepared Remarks at 43rd Munich Conference on Security Policy,' *The Washington Post*, 12 February 2007 and 'Speech to NATO Summit in Bucharest,' *UNIAN*, 18 April 2008. http://www.washingtonpost.com/wpdyn/content/article/2007/02/12/AR2007021200555.html
and http://www.unian.info/world/111033-text-of-putins-speech-at-nato-summit-bucharest-april-2-2008.html

947 Y. M. Brudny, 'Soviet and Post-Soviet Remembrances of World War II and Its Aftermath,' conference 'Contested Ground: The Legacy of the Second World War for Eastern Europe,' Canadian Institute for Ukrainian Studies, University of Alberta, 23-24 October 2015.

948 B. Judah, *Fragile Empire*, p.164.

949 Ibid., p.84.

950 C. G. Gaddy and F. Hill, *Mr. Putin*, pp. 379-381.

[951] https://www.litvinenkoinquiry.org/.

[952] B. Whitmore, 'It All Began with Litvinenko,' *RFERL, The Daily Vertical*, 21 January 2016. http://www.rferl.org/content/daily-vertical-it-all-began-with-litvinenko/27501234.html. This was not the first assassination carried out by Russia; in February 2004, Chechen leader Zelimkhan Yandarbiyev was assassinated in Qatar and Anna Politkovskaya was murdered in Moscow on 7 October 2006 (the latter on the same day as Putin's birthday).

[953] Boris Reitschuster, 'Vladimir Putin's formative German years' cited by Chris Bowlby in the *BBC Magazine*, 27 March 2015.

[954] F. Stephan Larrabee, Peter A. Wilson and John Gordon, *The Ukrainian Crisis and European Security. Implications for the United States and U.S. Army* (Santa Monica, CA: Rand Corporation, 2015), p.25.

[955] A. Tsygankov, 'Vladimir Putin's last stand,' p.280.

[956] See the comments by Fyodor Lukyanov, editor of *Russia in Global Affairs*, in the *Financial Times*, 16 December 2004.

[957] Gleb Pavlovsky is cited by *Ukrayinska Pravda*. Interview with Volodymyr Lytvyn in Tserkalo Tyzhnya, 26 June-2 July 2004.

[958] Eduard Glezin, 'Eyewitness notes or the 'Russian Maidan' in Kyiv,' *The Day*, 1 March 2005.

[959] T. Ambrosio, 'Insulating Russia from a Color Revolution,' p.236.

[960] Ibid, p.239.

[961] Vitali Silitski, 'Pre-empting Democracy: The Case of Belarus,' *Journal of Democracy*, vol.16, no.4 (October 2005), pp.83-97.

[962] Robert Parsons, 'Russia: Putin Backtracks on NGO Bill,' *RFERL*, 6 December 2005. http://www.rferl.org/content/article/1063570.html

[963] Sinikukka Saari, 'Russia's Post-Orange Revolutionary Strategies to Increase Its Influence in Former Soviet Republics: Public Diplomacy Po russkii,' *Europe-Asia Studies*, vol.66, no.1 (January 2014), p.61.

[964] A. Shekhovtsov, 'How Alexander Dugin's Neo-Eurasianists geared up for the Russian-Ukrainian War in 2005-2013.' See also Ekaterina Levintova and Jim Butterfield, 'Historical education and historical remembrance in contemporary Russia: Sources of political attitudes of pro-Kremlin youth,' *Communist and Post-Communist Studies*, vol.43, no.3 (September 2010), pp.139-166.

[965] P. Pomerantsev, 'Propagandalands.'

[966] Evgeny Feldman and Christopher Miller, 'One year later, Kiev and Moscow remember Ukrainian uprising in very different ways,' *Mashable*, 21 February 2015. http://mashable.com/2015/02/21/ukraine-euromaidan-killings-anniversary/#BQ6FnlIkcGqU

[967] B. Judah, *Fragile Empire*, p.164.

[968] C. Gaddy and F. Hill, *Mr. Putin*, pp.263 and 390.

[969] T. Kuzio, *The Crimea: Europe's Next Flashpoint?* (Washington DC: The Jamestown Foundation, November 2015).

[970] 'The Battle for Ukraine' and M. Galeotti, 'Moscow's Spy Game. Why Russia is Winning the Intelligence War in Ukraine,' *Foreign Affairs*, 30 October 2014. https://www.foreignaffairs.com/articles/russia-fsu/2014-10-30/moscows-spy-game

[971] C. G. Gaddy and F. Hill, *Mr. Putin*, p.341.

972 Konstantyn Mashovets, 'Rossiyskyy spetsnaz na Donbasse: dyversanty, reydery, "turysty",' *News Resistance*, 31 July 2015. Informationhttp://ru.espreso.tv/article/2015/07/31/rossyyskyy_specnaz_na_donbasse_dyversanty__reydery__quotturystyquot

973 Josh Rogin, 'Germany Helped Prep Russia for War, U.S. Sources Say,' *The Daily Beast*, 22 April 2014. http://www.thedailybeast.com/articles/2014/04/22/germany-helped-prep-russia-for-war-u-s-sources-say.html

974 MH17 Crash, Dutch Safety Board, 2015. http://www2.onderzoeksraad.nl/uploads/phase-docs/1006/debcd724fe7breport-mh17-crash.pdf

975 'Situation in Ukraine,' Report on the Advisory Committee of the Framework Convention for the Protection of National Minorities. Ad Hoc Visit to Ukraine, Council of Europe, 21-26 March 2014. https://search.coe.int/cm/Pages/result_details.aspx?ObjectID=09000016805c6161

976 L. Harding, A Very Expensive Poison, p.310.

977 Charles T. Baroch, *The Soviet Doctrine of Sovereignty. The So-Called Brezhnev Doctrine* (n.p.: American Bar Association, 1970), Tor Bukkvoll, 'Why Putin went to war: ideology, interests and decision-making in the Russian use of force in the Crimea and the Donbas,' *Contemporary Politics*, vol. 22, no.3 (July 2016), p.273, E. Wayne Merry, 'The Origins of Russia's War in Ukraine: The Clash of Russian and European "Civilizational" Choices for Ukraine' and Elizabeth A. Wood, 'A Small Victorious War? The Symbolic Politics of Vladimir Putin' in E. A. Wood, William E. Pomerantz, E. W. Merry and Maxim Trudolyubov, *Roots of Russia's War in Ukraine* (Washington DC; Woodrow Wilson Center, 2016), pp.30 and 98.

978 L. Harding, *A Very Expensive Poison*, p.317.

979 *Public Opinion Survey. Residents of Ukraine*, (Washington DC: International Republican Institute, 28 May-14 June 2016). http://www.iri.org/sites/default/files/wysiwyg/2016-07-08_ukraine_poll_shows_skepticism_glimmer_of_hope.pdf

980 Ibid.

981 Ibid.

982 Interview with Vitaliy Sych, Kyiv, 29 July 2016.

983 T. Bukkvoll, 'Why Putin went to war,' p.278.

984 K. Giles, P. Hanson, R. Lyne, J. Nixey, J. Sherr, and A. Wood, *The Russian Challenge*, p.2.

985 V. Yanukovych interviewed by *Moskovski Komsomolets*, 5 November 2004.

986 'National Security Adviser Jone's Attendance at Yanukovych Inauguration,' *US Embassy Kyiv*, 10 February 2000. https://wikileaks.org/plusd/cables/10KYIV275_a.html

987 'Ukraine: Regions Party Congress: A Handshake, a Communist, and the Russians,' *US Embassy Kyiv*, 8 August 2007. https://wikileaks.org/plusd/cables/07KYIV1940_a.html

988 A. Wilson, *Ukraine Crisis*, p.148.

989 In *Frontline Ukraine*, Sakwa completely ignores Russian pressure upon Yanukovych laying all blame for the crisis upon the EU.

990 Vitaliy Melnychuk and Lyubomyr Shavalyuk, 'Putin on the squeeze: The Yanukovych debt,' *The Ukrainian Week*, no.7 (July 2016). http://ukrainianweek.com/Politics/170081

991 'A short history of the world's wackiest bond,' *The Economist*, 8 September 2015. http://www.economist.com/blogs/freeexchange/2015/09/what-ukraine-owes-russia

992 S. Leshchenko, *Mezhyhirskyy Syndrome*, p.215.

[993] Lukashenka's and Sikorski's revelations were confirmed four years later by the Ukrainian Ministry of Justice. https://www.unian.info/politics/1769481-russia-was-preparing-to-annex-crimea-in-2013-justice-ministry-says-has-enough-evidence.html

[994] B. Judah, 'Putin's Coup.'

[995] *Novaya Gazeta*, 24 February 2015 and B. Judah, 'Putin's Coup'.

[996] B. Judah, 'Putin's Coup. How the Russian leader used the Ukraine crisis to consolidate his dictatorship,' *Politico*, 19 October 2014. http://www.politico.com/magazine/story/2014/10/vladimir-putins-coup-112025_Page3.html#.VsQ4v5MrLR0

[997] B. Judah, 'Putin's Coup.'

[998] Valery Dzutsati, 'Terek Cossacks Reveal Their Extensive Participation in the Annexation of Crimea,' *Eurasia Daily Monitor*, vol.13, no.191 (6 December 2016). https://jamestown.org/program/terek-cossacks-reveal-extensive-participation-annexation-crimea/

[999] S. Shuster, 'Meet the Cossack 'Wolves' Doing Russia's Dirty Work in Ukraine.'

[1000] Nikolay Mitrokhin, 'Ukraine's Separatists and Their Dubious Leaders,' *Searchlight*, 18 April 2014. http://www.searchlightmagazine.com/news/featured-news/ukraines-separatists-and-their-dubious-leaders

[1001] http://euromaidanpress.com/2014/07/30/pre-history-of-the-donetsk-republic-goes-back-almost-a-decade/

[1002] 'Intelligence Chief: 100 Russian Officers Are Leading Ukraine's Uprisings,' *Atlantic Council of the US*, 22 April 2014. http://www.atlanticcouncil.org/blogs/new-atlanticist/intelligence-chief-100-russian-officers-are-in-ukraine-directing-uprisings

[1003] E. A. Wood, 'Introduction' in E.A. Wood, W. E. Pomerantz, E. W. Merry and M. Trudolyubov, *Roots of Russia's War in Ukraine*, pp.8-9.

[1004] N. Mitrokhin, 'Ukraine's Separatists and Their Dubious Leaders.'

[1004] http://www.pravda.com.ua/articles/2010/02/19/4788595/

[1005] S. Shuster, 'Moscow's Man in Crimea is Ukraine's Worst Nightmare,' *Time*, 24 March 2014. http://time.com/19097/putin-crimea-russia-ukraine-aksyonov/

[1006] N. Mitrokhin, 'Ukraine's Separatists and Their Dubious Leaders.'

[1006] http://www.pravda.com.ua/articles/2010/02/19/4788595/

[1007] 'Russian GRU military spy chief Igor Sergun dies,' *BBC*, 5 January 2016.

[1008] 'Battle for Ukraine.'

[1009] Aleksandr Mishchenko, 'Donetskyi boomerang. Separatyzma dlia Yanukovycha,' *Kommenatarii*, 9 April 2010.

[1010] A. Kurkov, *Ukraine Diaries*, p.171.

[1011] T. Kuzio, 'Russia's Ideological Crusade Against Ukraine,' *Eurasia Daily Monitor*, vol.6, no. 113 (12 June 2009), 'SBU Challenges the FSB in Crimea,' *Eurasia Daily Monitor*, volume 6, no. 134 (14 July 2009), 'Ukraine Tightens the Screw in Sevastopol,' *Eurasia Daily Monitor*, vol. 6, no. 141 (23 July, 2009), 'Russia-Ukraine Diplomatic War,' *Eurasia Daily Monitor*, vol. 6, no. 147 (31 July 2009), and 'Ukrainian-Russian Diplomatic War Intensifies,' *Eurasia Daily Monitor*, vol.6, no. 158 (17 August 2009). http://www.jamestown.org/single/?tx_ttnews%5Btt_news%5D=35123&no_cache=1#.Vr3A55MrJsM; http://www.jamestown.org/single/?tx_ttnews%5Btt_news%5D=35261&no_cache=1#.Vr3BO5MrJsM

http://www.jamestown.org/sin-
gle/?tx_ttnews%5Btt_news%5D=35304&no_cache=1#.Vr3Az5MrJsM;
http://www.jamestown.org/sin-
gle/?tx_ttnews%5Btt_news%5D=35347&no_cache=1#.Vr3BAZMrJsM; and
http://www.jamestown.org/sin-
gle/?tx_ttnews%5Btt_news%5D=35420&no_cache=1#.Vr3BFZMrJsM

[1012] V. Nalyvaychenko interviewed by *Den*, 1 April 2015.

[1013] The distribution of Russian passports and Tuzla clash are recalled by L. Kuchma in *Posle Maydana*, pp.399-340.

[1014] T. Chornovil interviewed by *Radio Svoboda*, 16 October 2011.

[1015] T. Chornovil interviewed by *Liga Novosti*, www.newsliga.net, 24 December 2010.

[1016] T. Kuzio, 'Russianization of Ukrainian National Security Policy under Viktor Yanukovych.'

[1017] A. Wilson, *Ukraine Crisis*, p.142. T. Kuzio, 'Gas Lobby Takes Control of Ukraine's Security Service,' *Eurasia Daily Monitor*, vol.7, no.53 (18 March 2010) and 'Pro-Russian Old Guard, returns to Run Ukrainian Security Forces,' *Eurasia Daily Monitor*, vol.7, no.59 (26 March 2010). http://www.jamestown.org/sin-
gle/?tx_ttnews%5Btt_news%5D=36172&no_cache=1#.Vr0nHZMrL-Y and
http://www.jamestown.org/sin-
gle/?tx_ttnews%5Btt_news%5D=36200&no_cache=1#.Vr0nSpMrL-Y

[1018] B. Hoyle, 'Divisions leave Ukraine troops in despair,' *The Times*, 26 March 2014.

[1019] S. Leshchenko, *Mezhyhirskyy Syndrom*, p.146.

[1020] http://gordonua.com/publications/stenogramma-sekretnogo-zasedaniya-snbo-vo-vremya-anneksii-kryma-v-2014-godu-polnyy-tekst-na-russkom-yazyke-121122.html

[1021] S. Walker, 'Crimea still erasing its Ukrainian past a year after Russia's takeover,' *The Guardian*, 13 March 2015. http://www.theguardian.com/world/2015/mar/13/crimea-still-erasing-its-ukrainian-past-a-year-after-russias-takeover

[1022] http://www.pravda.com.ua/news/2016/02/29/7100681/

[1023] Russian presidential representative in the Crimea Oleg Belaventsev interviewed by *NTV*: http://www.ntv.ru/novosti/1613061/?fb#ixzz42mrilC1p

[1024] 'Vony zdaly Krym. Poimennyy spysok. Khto byvsya za "Kharkivski uhody," yaki dozvolyly Rosii pochaty okupatsiyu,' www.teksty.org.ua, 1 March 2016. http://texty.org.ua/pg/article/editorial/read/65730/

[1025] 160 out of 161 Party of Regions, all 27 KPU and all 20 Lytvyn bloc deputies voted for the Kharkiv Accords. 9 (out of 154) BYuT and 7 (out of 72) NU-NS (Our Ukraine-People's Self Defence) deputies supported them.

[1026] The key actors who railroaded through the Kharkiv Accords were Lytvyn, Andriy Kluyev, Volodymyr Sivkovych, Vladyslav Lukyanov, Tsaryov, Kolesnichenko, Volodymyr Oliynyk, Salamatin, Lebyedev, (Medvedchuk ally) Nestor Shufrych, Vasyl Stelmashchenko and Elbrus Tedeyev (two organised crime leaders elected within the Akhmetov quota by the Party of Regions). 'Vony zdaly Krym. Poimennyy spysok.'

[1027] T. Kuzio, 'Crimean separatists buoyed by the election of Yanukovych', *Eurasia Daily Monitor*, vol.7, no.41 (2 March 2010), 'Yanukovych Will Ignore Russian Espionage Against Ukraine', *Eurasia Daily Monitor*, vol.7, no.49 (12 March 2010), and 'The FSB Returns to Ukraine', *Eurasia Daily Monitor*, vol.7, no.100, 24 May 2010.

http://www.jamestown.org/sin-
gle/?tx_ttnews%5Btt_news%5D=36104&no_cache=1#.VugLmZMrKt8;

http://www.jamestown.org/sin-
gle/?tx_ttnews%5Btt_news%5D=36151&no_cache=1#.VugLQ5MrKt8 and
http://www.jamestown.org/sin-
gle/?tx_ttnews%5Btt_news%5D=36411&no_cache=1#.VugMRZMrKt8

[1028] T. Kuzio, 'Terrorist Bombings in Ukraine Resolved, but Are Likely to Continue to Grow,' *Jamestown Foundation blog*, June 5, 2012.
http://jamestownfoundation.blogspot.ca/2012/06/terrorist-bombings-in-ukraine-re-
solved.html

[1029] 'On the decision of the RNBO on 25 May 2012 'On steps towards strengthening steps in the struggle against terrorism in Ukraine.' Decree no. 388/2012. http://www.presi-
dent.gov.ua/documents/14822.html

[1030] 'On information and explanatory measures in the fight against terrorism,' Cabinet of Ministers Resolution, 12 September 2012. http://www.kmu.gov.ua/control/newsnpd. During the 2004 elections, NGO's were also accused of 'extremism' and 'terrorism' and
this tactic re-surfaced in summer 2013 with accusations against the Femen gender
movement whose offices were raided in a search for 'weapons and explosives'
(http://www.pravda.com.ua/news/2013/08/27/6996736/. T. Kuzio, 'Ukrainian Officials Increasingly Denounce Opposition as "Extremists" and "Terrorists", *Eurasian
Daily Monitor*, vol.1, no.96 (30 September 2004) and 'Ukrainian Authorities Target Student and Youth Election-Monitoring Groups', *Eurasian Daily Monitor*, vol.1, no.104 (13
October 2004).
http://www.jamestown.org/single/?no_cache=1&tx_ttnews[tt_news]=26923#.UhyhvRB0ySo
and http://www.jamestown.org/sin-
gle/?no_cache=1&tx_ttnews[tt_news]=26981#.Uhyh8BB0ySo

[1031] Anton Herashchenko, adviser to Minister of Interior Arsen Avakov, interviewed by
*Ukrayinska Pravda*, 30 September 2014 and S. Shuster, 'Ukraine Powerless to Act as
East Slips under Russian Control,' *Time*, 14 April 2014. http://www.pravda.com.ua/ar-
ticles/2014/09/30/7039343/ and http://time.com/61971/ukraine-powerless-to-act-
as-east-slips-under-russian-control/

[1032] http://www.novayagazeta.ru/inquests/72830.html

[1033] Poroshenko talking to students at Kharkiv University, 26 March 2015.

[1034] T. Kuzio, 'Russianization of Ukrainian National Security Policy under Viktor Yanukovych.'

[1035] http://www.pravda.com.ua/news/2016/04/24/7106600/ and
http://www.pravda.com.ua/news/2016/04/16/7105759/

[1036] http://dumskaya.net/news/komissiya-minoborony-komanduyushchiy-vmsu-razvel-
056067/

[1037] S. Leshchenko, *Mezhyhirskyy Syndrom*, pp.56-57.

[1038] T. Kuzio, 'Yanukovych's Assassination-Phobia Deepens,' *Jamestown Foundation blog*, 28 October 2010, 'Russians control Yanukovych,' *Jamestown Foundation blog*, 13 October 2010,
'Assassination Phobia Spreads in Ukraine', *Eurasia Daily Monitor*, vol.7, no. 124 (28 June
2010). http://jamestownfoundation.blogspot.com/2010/10/yanukovychs-assassina-
tion-phobia.html; http://jamestownfoundation.blogspot.com/2010/10/russians-con-
trol-yanukovych.html and http://www.jamestown.org/sin-
gle/?tx_ttnews%5Btt_news%5D=36540&no_cache=1#.Vr0mSpMrKCQ

[1039] Veronika Melkozerova, 'Ukraine tries to catch up to Russia in intelligence war,' *Kyiv Post*, 19
August 2015. See also L. Harding, *A Very Expensive Poison*, p.381.

[1040] T. Kuzio, 'Yanukovych Will Ignore Russian Espionage Against Ukraine' and 'The FSB Returns to Ukraine.

[1041] V. Nalyvaychenko interviewed by *Den*, 1 April 2015. http://www.jamestown.org/single/?tx_ttnews%5Btt_news%5D=36151&no_cache=1#.Vr0lt5MrL-Y

[1042] V. Nalyvaychenko cited by Christopher Miller, 'Ukraine's top intelligence agency deeply infiltrated by Russian spies,' www.mashable.com, 30 July 2014.

[1043] An SBU source confided this to an informant of the author's, Kyiv, 16 December 2014.

[1044] The separatists captured three SBU *Alpha* officers because of leaked intelligence, tortured them and placed them on public display.
https://www.youtube.com/watch?v=vqaSakthib0&feature=em-subs_digest-vrecs

[1045] http://www.sbu.gov.ua/sbu/control/uk/publish/article?art_id=178743&cat_id=39574 and https://psb4ukr.org/532062-spisok-kolishnix-spivrobitnikiv-sb-ukra%D1%97ni-yaki-zradili-prisyazi-i-perejshli-na-bik-voroga/#more-532062. See also the video film showing the faces of Crimean SBU officers who betrayed Ukraine and agreed to work in the Crimean branch of the FSB: https://www.youtube.com/watch?v=QaM-ZWyDW3q0

[1046] http://tsn.ua/ato/zastupnik-nachalnika-shtabu-ato-viyavivsya-rosiyskim-shpigunom-sbu-674237.html

[1047] A. Kurkov, *Ukraine Diaries*, p.210.

[1048] Sonya Koshkina, *Maidan*, p.254.

[1049] M. Galeotti, 'Moscow's Spy Game.

[1050] Vitaly Churkin, 'Ukraine's Yanukovych asked for troops, Russia tells UN,' *BBC*, 4 March 2014. The documents showing Yanukovych's treason were made public by General Prosecutor Lutsenko in January 2017.
(http://www.pravda.com.ua/news/2017/01/17/7132676/)

[1051] http://gazeta.ua/articles/politics/_azarov-zayaviv-scho-krim-nikoli-ne-vhodiv-do-skladu-ukrayini/679052

[1052] Kimitaka Matsuzato, 'Domestic Politics in Crimea, 2009-2015,' *Demokratizatsiya*, vol. 24, no. 2 (Spring 2016), p.244.

[1053] This episode is recounted by S. Koshkina, *Maidan*, pp.312, 321, 323-332.

[1054] R. Zubrin, 'Putin Adviser Publishes Plan for Domination of Europe,' *National Review*, 10 March 2014. http://www.nationalreview.com/corner/373064/putin-adviser-publishes-plan-domination-europe-robert-zubrin

[1055] S. Leshchenko, *Mezhyhirskyy Syndrome*, p.214.

[1056] A. Shekhovtsov, 'The "Ukraine Crisis" is a long planned operation,' *Anton Shekhovtsov blog*, 29 August 2014. http://anton-shekhovtsov.blogspot.com/2014/08/the-ukraine-crisis-is-long-planned.html

[1057] 'The Ukrainian People on the Current Crisis,' KIIS and Program for Public Consultation, University of Maryland, 9 March 2015. http://www.public-consultation.org/studies/Ukraine_0315.pdf and I. Bekeshkina, 'Donbas yak Osoblyvyy Rehion Ukrayiny.'

[1058] C. G. Gaddy and F. Hill, *Mr. Putin*, p.361.

[1059] Ibid., p.362.

[1060] Ukrainian political technologist Mykhaylo Pogrebynskyy described this as a 'pure lie' in *The Washington Post*, 31 October 2004.

[1061] V. Lytvyn interviewed by *Tserkalo Tyzhnya*, 26 June-2 July 2004. http://gazeta.dt.ua/AR-CHIVE/volodimir_litvin_verhovna_rada_mae_stati_garantom_vidkritosti_y_demo-kratichnosti_prezidentskih_vibor.html

[1062] *Novaya Gazeta*, 24 February 2015 and translated by *UNIAN*, 25 February 2015. http://www.novayagazeta.ru/politics/67389.html and http://www.unian.info/politics/1048525-novaya-gazetas-kremlin-papers-article-full-text-in-english.html

[1063] R. D. Asmus, *A Little War That Shook the World*, pp.166, 172-173, 179-181, 187, 193, 201-202, 206-207.

[1064] Rajan Menon and Eugene Rumer, *Conflict in Ukraine. The Unwinding of the Post-Cold War Order* (Cambridge, MA; MIT Press, 2015), p.98.

[1065] R. Sakwa, *Frontline Ukraine*, p.52 and R. Menon and E. Rumer, *Conflict in Ukraine*, p.98.

[1066] On 21 March 2014, Putin signed the law on 'Admitting to the Russian Federation the Republic of Crimea and Establishing within the Russian Federation the new Constituent Entities of the Republic of Crimea and the city of Federal Importance Sevastopol.'

[1067] http://ratinggroup.ua/en/research/ukraine/obschestvenno-politicheskie_nastroeniya_naseleniya_oktyabr_2016.html

[1068] Vladimir Voronov, 'Crimea and the Kremlin: From Plan "A" to Plan "B",' *RFERL and Russia Studies Centre, Henry Jackson Society*, March 2015. http://henryjacksonsociety.org/wp-content/uploads/2015/03/Crimea-and-the-Kremlin.pdf

[1069] *Berkut* officers returning to the Crimea from the Euromaidan on 22 February 2014 were greeted with cries of 'Well done lads!', 'There should have been more (dead)!', 'Heroes!' and 'Glory to the *Berkut*!'
https://www.youtube.com/watch?v=6QKbVNQCFOo;
https://www.youtube.com/watch?v=efii3FK9W7A and
https://www.youtube.com/watch?v=bUWOZwT46wk

[1070] S. Koshkina, *Maidan*, p.353-354.

[1071] K. Matsuzato, 'Domestic Politics in Crimea, 2009-2015,' p.251.

[1072] S. Loiko, 'The Unravelling of Moscow's 'Novorossia' Dream.'

[1073] Timothy Snyder, 'Putin's New Nostalgia,' *New York Review of Books*, 10 November 2014. http://www.nybooks.com/daily/2014/11/10/putin-nostalgia-stalin-hitler/

[1074] John J. Mearsheimer, 'Why the Ukraine Crisis is the West's Fault,' *Foreign Affairs*, vol.93, no.5 (September-October 2014), pp.77-89 and R. Menon and E. Rumer, *Conflict in Ukraine.*

[1075] A.J. Motyl, 'Kissinger's Vapid Vision Thing,' *New Atlanticist*, Atlantic Council of the US, 15 February 2016.
http://www.atlanticcouncil.org/blogs/new-atlanticist/kissinger-s-vapid-vision-thing

[1076] R. Sakwa, Frontline Ukraine.

[1077] S. Kotkin, 'The Resistible Rise of Vladimir Putin,' *Foreign Affairs*, vol. 94 no2 (March-April 2015), p. 151.

[1078] P. Felgenhauer, 'Russia Proposes a Yalta-2 Geopolitical Tradeoff to Solve the Ukraine Crisis,' *Eurasia Daily Monitor*, vol.12, no.36 (26 February 2015) and 'Putin Calls on Germany to Mend Fences by Recognizing Russian 'National' Interests,' *Eurasian Daily Monitor*, vol.13, no.9 (14 January 2016). http://www.jamestown.org/single/?tx_ttnews%5Btt_news%5D=43586&no_cache=1#.VsWNapMrKt8 and https://jamestown.org/program/putin-calls-on-germany-to-mend-fences-by-recognizing-russian-national-interests/

[1079] P. Felgenhauer interviewed by the *Kyiv Post*, 25 January 2015.

[1080] B. Judah, 'Putin's Coup.'

[1081] C. G. Gaddy and F. Hill, *Mr. Putin*, pp.394-396.

[1082] F. Hill, 'This is What Putin Really Wants,' *The National Interest*, 24 February 2015. http://www.nationalinterest.org/feature/what-putin-really-wants-12311

[1083] Yuval Weber, 'Why the U.S. does nothing in Ukraine,' *The Washington Post*, 18 March 2015. https://www.washingtonpost.com/blogs/monkey-cage/wp/2015/03/18/why-the-u-s-does-nothing-in-ukraine/ and and https://www.youtube.com/watch?v=l6K1_vHrJPU

[1084] English translation and audio links can be found at: http://uaposition.com/analysis-opinion/english-translation-audio-evidence-putins-adviser-glazyev-russian-politicians-involvement-war-ukraine/. Also available here: https://www.youtube.com/watch?v=l6K1_vHrJPU

[1085] *Tserkalo Tyzhnya*, 4 January 2015. T. Kuzio, 'Farewell, Crimea. Why Ukrainians Don't Mind Losing the Territory to Russia,' *Foreign Affairs*, 13 March 2014. https://www.foreignaffairs.com/articles/russia-fsu/2014-03-13/farewell-crimea

[1086] *Political Consequences of the Russian Aggression in Ukraine*, Resolution 2132 (Strasbourg: PACE, 12 October 2016). http://assembly.coe.int/nw/xml/XRef/Xref-XML2HTML-EN.asp?fileid=23166&lang=en

[1087] Hrant Kostanyan and Stefan Meister, *Ukraine, Russsia and the EU. Breaking the deadlock in the Minsk process*, CEPS Working Document 423 (Brussels: Centre for European Policy Studies, 9 June 2016). https://www.ceps.eu/publications/ukraine-russia-and-eu-breaking-deadlock-minsk-process. Krastev makes a similar analogy of Russia seeking 'Bosnianisation' where the DNR and LNR would resemble Respublika Sprska, the Serbian separatist enclave in Bosnia-Herzegovina. See I. Krastev, 'What does Russia want and why?'

[1088] L. Kuchma interviewed by *Holos Ukrayiny*, 26 February 2015.

[1089] Oleg Varfolomeyev, 'Ukrainian Media Speculate That Akhmetov, Boyko May Head Rebel-Occupied Provinces,' *Eurasia Daily Monitor*, vol.13, no.55 (21 March 2016). http://www.jamestown.org/single/?tx_ttnews%5Btt_news%5D=45225&tx_ttnews%5BbackPid%5D=7&cHash=341c9e0f5c9d4553bcc8f8e69f28466b#.VvOrU5N95sM

[1090] Andrew E. Kramer, 'Ex-Professor Upsets Ukraine Politics, and Russia Peace Accord,' *New York Times*, 18 March 2016. http://www.nytimes.com/2016/03/19/world/europe/ukraine-oksana-syroyid.html

[1091] *Razumkov Centre Newsletter*, no.40 (13 October 2016).

[1092] A. J. Motyl, 'Time for Ukraine to Take the Initiative,' *World Affairs blog*, 23 March 2016. http://www.worldaffairsjournal.org/blog/alexander-j-motyl/time-ukraine-take-initiative

[1093] A. J. Motyl, 'Why Reintegrating the Donbas Is Suicide for Ukraine,' *World Affairs*, 25 February 2016. http://www.worldaffairsjournal.org/blog/alexander-j-motyl/why-reintegrating-donbas-suicide-ukraine

[1094] http://www.economist.com/news/europe/21716632-reintegrating-donbas-starting-look-russian-trap-ukraines-leaders-may-be-giving-up?frsc=dg%7Cd

[1095] http://ba.org.ua/zayava-frakci%D1%97-batkivshhina-shhodo-pidsumkiv-minskix-domovlenostej/

[1096] Sergei Tsekov cited by *Istorychna Pravda*, 18 January 2011.

[1097] B. Hoyle, Maximilian Clarke, and Tom Coghlan, 'Truce at breaking point as rebel's march on,' *The Times*, 21 February 2015.

[1098] P. Felgenhauer, 'Minsk Ceasefire Agreements Are Dead, but the Russian Offensive is Faltering,' *Eurasia Daily Monitor*, vol.12, no.18 (29 January 2015). http://www.jamestown.org/programs/edm/single/?tx_ttnews%5Btt_news%5D=43467&cHash=473ef3e152a20900cb88c9bdd1e982b9#.Vr-HF5MrKt8

[1099] B. Hoyle, 'Russian tanks spotted as ceasefire unravels,' *The Times*, 17 February 2015.

[1100] S. Koshkina, *Maidan*, p.403.

[1101] Boris Nemtsov, 'Why does Putin wage war with Ukraine?' *Kyiv Post*, 1 September 2014. http://www.kyivpost.com/opinion/op-ed/why-does-putin-wage-war-on-ukraine-362884.html

[1102] A. Shprintsen, 'CBC producer revisits Ukraine to explore conflict.'

[1103] P. Felgenhauer, 'Fortress Russia: Pushing Foreigners Back,' *Eurasian Daily Monitor*, vol.13, no. 83 (28 April 2016).http://www.jamestown.org/programs/edm/single/?tx_ttnews%5Btt_news%5D=45367&tx_ttnews%5BbackPid%5D=827&no_cache=1#.Vy125qN97Jw

[1104] M. Laruelle, 'The three colors of Novorossiya.'

[1105] S. Sokol, 'Top Rebel Leader Accuses Jews of Masterminding Ukrainian Revolution.'

[1106] B. Whitmore, 'Gangsters and Fascists and Separatists – Oh My!' *RFERL*, 5 June 2014. http://www.rferl.org/content/gangsters-and-fascists-and-separatists----oh-my/25411895.html

[1107] 'Russia's Ghost Army in Ukraine (Part 3)' *Vice News*, 6 March 2015. https://news.vice.com/video/russias-ghost-army-in-ukraine-full-length

[1108] Lucian Kim, 'The Battle of Ilovaysk: Details of a Massacre Inside Rebel-Held Eastern Ukraine,' *Newsweek*, 4 November 2014. For video imagery of the Ilovaysk battle see 'Weltspiegel extra: Mörderischer Ukraine Krieg – Flucht aus Ilowajsk (with subtitles),' https://www.youtube.com/watch?v=hF_RguYpBnU. The figures are taken from the August 2015 official parliamentary enquiry and published in Lily Hyde, 'The Missing: What have they done with our sons? *The Guardian*, 3 February 2016. http://europe.newsweek.com/battle-ilovaisk-details-massacre-inside-rebel-held-eastern-ukraine-282003?rm=eu and http://www.theguardian.com/world/2016/feb/03/the-missing-what-have-they-done-with-our-sons

[1109] 'Russia Ante Portas: Updated Satellite Imagery,' *Report by Bellingcat*, 15 June 2016. https://www.bellingcat.com/news/uk-and-europe/2016/06/15/9629/

[1110] M. Galeotti, 'Putin's Countermove,' *Foreign Policy*, 11 February 2015. http://foreignpolicy.com/2015/02/11/putin-ukraine-russia-kiev/

[1111] M. Galeotti, 'Don't buy the hype: Russia's military is much weaker than Putin wants us to think,' *Vox*, 23 February 2016. http://www.vox.com/2016/2/23/11092614/putin-army-threat

[1112] Ryan Faith, 'Why Russia Spent 2015 Half-Assing it in Ukraine,' *Vice News*, 31 December 2015. https://news.vice.com/article/why-russia-spent-2015-half-assing-it-in-ukraine1

[1113] Interview with M. Galeotti, 'The West and Russia are already at war,' *Meduza*, 13 February 2015. https://meduza.io/en/feature/2015/02/13/the-west-and-russia-are-already-at-war

[1114] B. Hoyle, 'Rebels 'will fight to end' despite peace plan,' *The Times*, 10 February 2015.

[1115] S. Hutchings and V. Tolz, *Nation, Ethnicity and Race on Russian Television.*

[1116] C. Schreck and Dmitry Volchek, 'Russian 'Former Fascist' Who Fought with Separatists Says Moscow Unleashed, Orchestrated Ukraine War.'

[1117] Andrei Biletskyy interviewed by *Levy Bereg*, 10 December 2014. http://lb.ua/news/2014/12/10/288683__biletskiy_polovina_azova.html

[1118] A. Quinn, 'Foreigners Who Fight and Die for Ukraine.'

[1119] Rosaria Puglisi, *Heroes or Villains? Volunteer Battalions in Post-Maidan Ukraine.* IAI Working Paper no.15 (Rome: Instituto Affari Internazionali, 8 March 2015). http://www.iai.it/sites/default/files/iaiwp1508.pdf

[1120] Realists use these two arguments. See R. Menon and E. Rumer, *Conflict in Ukraine*, p.149.

[1121] R. Puglisi, *Heroes or Villains?*

[1122] A. Herashchenko interviewed by *Ukrayinska Pravda.*

[1123] Guy Chazan and R. Olearchyk, 'Ukraine: An oligarch brought to heel,' *Financial Times*, 25 March 2015.

[1124] Katya Gorchinskaya, 'Poroshenko sends a shot across oligarchs bow by sacking Kolomoysky,' *Kyiv Post*, 25 March 2015. http://www.kyivpost.com/article/content/kyiv-post-plus/poroshenko-sends-shot-across-oligarchs-bow-by-sacking-kolomoisky-384407.html

[1125] R. Puglisi, *Heroes or Villains?*

[1126] A. Wilson, *Ukraine Crisis*, p.158.

[1127] Interviews with Ukrainian 'Cyborgs' 'Denys,' 'Vanya' and 'Sever.'

[1128] Aleksandr Lapko, 'Ukraine's Own Worst Enemy. In War Time, Corruption in Ukraine Can Be Deadly,' *New York Times*, 7 October 2014. http://www.nytimes.com/2014/10/08/opinion/in-war-time-corruption-in-ukraine-can-be-deadly.html

[1129] Dmytro Mendelyeyev, '"Tin" Viyny,' *Tserkalo Tyzhnya*, 5 September 2014.

[1130] Max Seddon, 'Ukrainian Troops Withdraw from Key Town in Humiliating Defeat,' *Buzzfeed*, 18 February 2015. http://www.buzzfeed.com/maxseddon/ukrainian-troops-withdraw-from-key-town-in-humiliating-defea

[1131] S. Peterson, 'In Slaviansk, rebels leave a trail of Russian expertise - and Ukrainian ruin,' *Christian Science Monitor*, 30 July 2014. http://www.csmonitor.com/World/Europe/2014/0730/In-Slaviansk-rebels-leave-a-trail-of-Russian-expertise-and-Ukrainian-ruin

[1132] *The Ukraine Crisis: Risks of Renewed Military Conflict after Minsk II.*

[1133] J. Yaffa, 'The Search for Petr Khokhlov.'

[1134] Goryanov and Olga Ivshina, 'Boyets "spetsnaza DNR": pomoshch Rossii byla reshayushey,' *BBC Russian Service*, 31 March 2015. http://www.bbc.com/russian/international/2015/03/150325_donetsk_rebel_interview

[1135] http://gur-mou.gov.ua/content/viiskovi-zlochyntsi-ofitsery-5-ombr-1-ak-tstv-pivdennoho-vo-zs-rf.html

[1136] 'Russia's War in Ukraine: The Medals and Treacherous Numbers,' *Report by Bellingcat*, 31 August 2016. https://www.bellingcat.com/news/uk-and-europe/2016/08/31/russias-war-ukraine-medals-treacherous-numbers/

[1137] *Where did the shells come from? investigation of cross-border attacks in eastern Ukraine* (Brussels: International Partnership for Human Rights together with Norwegian Helsinki Committee and Ukrainian Helsinki Human Rights Union, 2016). http://iphronline.org/wp-content/uploads/2016/07/Joint-report-on-cross-border-shelling-June-2016.pdf

1138 http://www.kyivpost.com/article/content/ukraine-politics/osce-sees-russian-soldiers-weapons-in-ukraine-for-two-years-410764.html

1139 A. Luhn, 'Russian Soldiers Have Given Up Pretending They Are Not Fighting in Ukraine,' *Vice News*, 31 March 2015. https://news.vice.com/article/russian-soldiers-have-given-up-pretending-they-are-not-fighting-in-ukraine

1140 C. Schreck and D. Volchek, 'Russian 'Former Fascist' Who Fought with Separatists Says Moscow Unleashed, Orchestrated Ukraine War.'

1141 B. Hoyle, 'Russian tanks spotted as ceasefire unravels.'

1142 Their photographs can be found in *Ukrayinska Pravda*, 4, 6 and 14 March 2016.

1143 Mark Urban, 'How many Russians are fighting in Ukraine? *BBC*, 10 March 2015 and Igor Sutyagin, *Russian Forces in Ukraine*, RUSI Briefing Paper (London: Royal United Services Institute, 9 March 2015). http://www.bbc.co.uk/news/world-europe-31794523 and https://rusi.org/publication/briefing-papers/russian-forces-ukraine

1144 Sten Rynning, 'The false promise of continental concert: Russia, the West and the necessary balance of power,' *International Affairs*, vol.91, no.3 (May 2015), pp.539-552.

1145 P. Felgenhauer interviewed by the *Kyiv Post*, 25 January 2015.

1146 Interview with Ukrainian 'Cyborgs' 'Denys,' 'Vanya' and 'Sever.'

1147 Z. Zawada, 'Russia escalates war, dispatches new forces,' *Ukrainian Weekly*, 8 February 2015.

1148 S. Walker, 'Ukraine Ceasefire: 'There is shooting all the time,' *The Guardian*, 30 June 2015.

1149 Alan Chin, 'Ukraine's military is stronger than believed. Here's what it needs to win,' *Reuters*, 16 December 2015.

1150 Gustav Gressel, 'Russia's military options in Ukraine,' *European Council on Foreign Relations*, 27 April 2015. http://www.ecfr.eu/article/commentary_russias_military_options_in_ukraine3010

1151 'The fire that did not cease,' *Economist*, 21 February 2015. http://www.economist.com/news/europe/21644241-fall-debaltseve-underlines-cynicism-minsk-ceasefire-fire-did-not-cease

1152 Ben Macintyre, 'Putin's bodyguard of lies has taken over Russia,' *The Times*, 13 February 2015.

1153 Richard Balmforth, 'Options narrow for Ukraine's Poroshenko after Debaltseve defeat,' *Reuters*, 20 February 2015.

1154 B. Hoyle, 'Rebels 'will fight to end' despite peace plan,' *The Times*, 10 February 2015.

1155 A. Wilson, *Ukraine Crisis*, p.192.

1156 S. Peterson, 'In Slaviansk, rebels leave a trail of Russian expertise – and Ukrainian ruin.'

1157 Kate Byrnes, US Charge d'Affaires, OSCE Permanent Council, Vienna, 26 February 2015.

1158 T. Kuzio, 'State-Led Violence in Ukraine's 2004 Elections and Orange Revolution', *Communist and Post-Communist Studies*, vol.43, no.4 (December 2010), pp. 383-395.

1159 E. Kostyuchenko, *Novaya Gazeta*, 4 March 2015.

1160 Ibid.,

1161 D. Trenin, 'The Revival of the Russian Military,' p.25.

1162 B. Macintyre, 'Putin's bodyguard of lies has taken over.'

1163 'Russia's Ghost Army in Ukraine,' Part 1, *Vice News*, 3 March 2015.

1164 https://www.bellingcat.com/news/uk-and-europe/2015/02/17/origin-of-artillery-attacks/

[1165] Tom Parfitt, 'Russian dead being removed from Ukraine,' *The Daily Telegraph*, 13 November 2014. http://www.telegraph.co.uk/news/worldnews/europe/ukraine/11229643/Russian-dead-being-removed-from-Ukraine.html

[1166] A. Kurkov, *Ukraine Diaries*, p.228.

[1167] Leon Aron, 'A Premature Party for Poroshenko,' *Foreign Policy*, 18 September 2014. http://foreignpolicy.com/2014/09/18/a-premature-party-for-poroshenko/

[1168] *Watching the Watchman: Russia's top brass linked to war in Ukraine*, Conflict Intelligence Team, 8 February 2016. https://citeam.org/russia-s-top-brass-linked-to-war-in-ukraine/

[1169] P. Pomerantsev,' Propagandalands.'

[1170] Zhanna Byezpyatchuk and Luke Johnson, 'Lawmaker Tells of Shelling and 'Chaotic Retreat' After Eastern Ukraine Cease-Fire,' *RFERL*, 27 February 2015. http://www.rferl.org/content/ukraine-withdraw-eyewitness-debaltseve-russia/26873579.html

[1171] V. Lykhachov and T. Bezruk eds., Ksenofobiya v Ukrayni v 2014 r. v konteksti revolyutsii ta interventsii.

[1172] I. Girkin interviewed by *Zavtra*, 20 November 2014. http://zavtra.ru/content/view/kto-tyi-strelok/

[1173] https://www.youtube.com/watch?v=j_qqR4Up0vw

[1174] T. Whewell, 'The Russians fighting a 'holy war' in Ukraine.'

[1175] B. Bidder, 'Russian Far-Right Idol.'

[1176] T. Whewell, 'Russia's Imperialist Warriors.'

[1177] 'Russian Nationalists Prepare for New Battles in Ukraine,' *RFERL*, 5 March 2015. http://www.rferl.org/media/video/russia-ukraine-nationalists/26882025.html

[1178] T. Whewell, 'The Russians fighting a 'holy war' in Ukraine.'

[1179] See the special issue of *Transition*, vol.1, no.10 (23 June 1995) 'Taken to Extremes: Confronting the Fascist Threat in Russia.'

[1180] 'B. Whitmore, 'Gangsters and Fascists and Separatists – Oh My!'

[1181] K. Malfliet and R. Laenen, Current Developments in Russian State Identities and Institutional Reforms under President Putin (Leuven: Leuven University, 2007), p.41.

[1182] K. Gessen, 'Why not kill them all?'

[1183] https://pressimus.com/Interpreter_Mag/press/3654

[1184] H. Coynash, 'Putin's Neo-Nazi Helpers,' *KHRPG*, 10 March 2014. http://khpg.org/en/index.php?id=1394442656

[1185] A. Shekhovtsov, 'Neo-Nazi Russian National Unity in Eastern Ukraine.'

[1186] *Ukrayinska Pravda*, 15 June 2015.

[1187] J. Ioffe, 'My Mind-Melting Week on the Battlefields of Ukraine.'

[1188] Peter Worger, 'A mad crowd: Skinhead youth and the rise of nationalism in post-communist Russia,' *Communist and Post-Communist Studies*, vol.45, no.3 (September 2012), p.276.

[1189] 'Euro 2016: France expels Russia far-right fan chief Shprygin,' *BBC*, 16 June 2016. http://www.bbc.com/news/world-europe-36546183

[1190] 'Russia's Shprygin, supporters' leader at centre of French spat,' *BBC*, 15 June 2016. http://www.bbc.com/news/world-europe-36539018

[1191] Sebastien Rabas and Jack Lush, 'The Night Wolves: Putin's motorbiking militia of Luhansk,' *The Guardian*, 30 January 2016. http://www.theguardian.com/news/video/2016/jan/29/the-night-wolves-putins-motorbiking-militia-of-luhansk-video

[1192] S. Peterson, 'In Slaviansk, rebels leave a trail of Russian expertise - and Ukrainian ruin.'

[1193] http://www.treasury.gov/press-center/press-releases/Pages/jl9729.aspx

[1194] Emil Souleimanov, 'An ethnography of counterinsurgency: kadyrovtsy and Russia's policy of Chechenization,' *Post Soviet Affairs*, vol.31, no.2 (March 2015), p.103.

[1195] W. Laqueur, *Black Hundred*, p.20.

[1196] S. Shuster, 'Meet the Cossack 'Wolves' Doing Russia's Dirty Work in Ukraine.'

[1197] L. Harding, A Very Expensive Poison, p.301.

[1198] T. Kuzio, 'Is Russia a State Sponsor of Terrorism?' *New Eastern Europe*, 22 January 2015. http://neweasterneurope.eu/interviews/1461-is-russia-a-state-sponsor-of-terrorism

[1199] https://www.youtube.com/watch?v=BB8aicOTXss

[1200] http://www.pravda.com.ua/news/2015/01/20/7055767/

[1201] http://www.pravda.com.ua/news/2014/12/5/7046577/

[1202] T. Kuzio, 'Ukraine Ignites. Why Russia Should Be Added to the State Sponsors of Terrorism List,' *Foreign Affairs*, 25 January 2015. https://www.foreignaffairs.com/articles/russian-federation/2015-01-25/ukraine-reignites

[1203] https://www.bellingcat.com/wp-content/uploads/2016/05/The-lost-digit-BUK-3x2_EN_final-1.pdf

[1204] Amy Knight, 'Flight MH17: Will Russia Get Away with It?' *New York Review of Books*, 19 November 2014. http://www.nybooks.com/daily/2014/11/19/flight-mh-17-will-russia-get-away-it/

[1205] 'Origins of the Separatists' Buk,' *Report by Bellingcat*, 8 November 2014. https://www.bellingcat.com/news/uk-and-europe/2014/11/08/origin-of-the-separatists-buk-a-bellingcat-investigation/

[1206] D. Satter, *Darkness at Dawn*, p.204.

[1207] Ibid., p.204.

[1208] Ibid., pp.210-218.

[1209] L. Hyde, 'The missing: What have they done with our sons?'

[1210] Ibid.,

[1211] H. Coynash, 'Unmarked Graves of Russia's Undeclared War,' *KHRPG*, 5 February 2016. http://khpg.org/en/index.php?id=1454596666

[1212] Bojan Pancevski, 'Half of Ukrainian fighters killed by poor kit and friendly fire,' *The Sunday Times*, 22 February 2015.

[1213] M. Tucker and B. Hoyle, 'Rebels make fresh advance in east Ukraine,' *The Times*, 2 February 2015.

[1214] Figure cited by Frankfurter Allgemeine Sonntagszeitung and taken from Ukrayinska Pravda, 8 February 2015.

[1215] H. Coynash, 'Russia refuses to probe sharp rise in soldiers' deaths during war in Donbas,' *KHRPG*, 8 February 2016. http://www.khpg.org/en/pda/index.php?id=1453857209

[1216] http://www.slideshare.net/tsnua/ss-59145514

[1217] Paul Roderick Gregory, 'Russia May Have Inadvertently Posted Its Casualties In Ukraine: 2,000 Deaths, 3,200 Disabled,' *Forbes*, 25 August 2015.

http://www.forbes.com/sites/paulroderickgregory/2015/08/25/kremlin-censors-rush-to-erase-inadvertent-release-of-russian-casualties-in-east-ukraine/#17c67f125b26

1218 'Russia 'accidentally reveals' number of its soldiers killed in eastern Ukraine,' *The Independent*, 26 August 2015. http://www.independent.co.uk/news/world/europe/the-number-of-russian-troops-killed-or-injured-fighting-in-ukraine-seems-to-have-been-accidentally-10472603.html

1219 'Russia's Ghost Army in Ukraine (Part 3)' *Vice News*, 6 March 2015. https://news.vice.com/video/russias-ghost-army-in-ukraine-full-length

1220 Courtney Weaver, 'Cafe encounter exposes reality of Russian soldiers in Ukraine,' *Financial Times*, 22 October 2014.

1221 I. Chalupa, 'In Russia, Speaking Power to Truth,' *New Atlanticist, Atlantic Council of the US*, 4 September 2014. http://www.atlanticcouncil.org/blogs/new-atlanticist/in-russia-speaking-power-to-truth

1222 'Russia's Ghost Army in Ukraine (Part 2)' *Vice News*, 4 March 2015. https://news.vice.com/video/russias-ghost-army-in-ukraine-part-2

1223 http://www.kyivpost.com/content/kyiv-post-plus/elena-Vasilyeva-soldiers-in-russia-break-their-own-legs-to-avoid-going-to-donbas-373015.html

1224 Cargo-200 NGO estimates can be viewed at https://www.facebook.com/groups/gruz200/ and the list of dead soldiers and mercenary volunteers is provided at

https://d23ya87silh7sb.cloudfront.net/pdf/000/001/454/888_929835154.pdf

1225 www.lostivan.com and www.polk.ru. David M. Herszenhorn and Alexandra Odynova, 'Soldiers Graves Bear Witness to Russia's Role in Ukraine,' *New York Times*, 21 September 2014. http://www.nytimes.com/2014/09/22/world/europe/soldiers-graves-bear-witness-to-russias-role-in-ukraine.html

1226 H. Coynash, 'Entire Pskov paratrooper regiment killed in Ukraine?' *KHRPG*, 3 September 2014. http://khpg.org/en/index.php?id=1409690121 and the original article, since deleted from the newspaper web site,

http://web.archive.org/web/20140902154652/ and http:/gubernia.pskovregion.org/number_706/00.php

1227 http://www.levada.ru/25-11-2014/sobytiya-na-vostoke-ukrainy-vybory-v-dnr-i-lnr-peremirie

1228 http://www.kyivpost.com/content/kyiv-post-plus/elena-Vasilyeva-soldiers-in-russia-break-their-own-legs-to-avoid-going-to-donbas-373015.html

1229 http://assembly.coe.int/nw/xml/News/News-View-en.asp?newsid=6100&lang=2

1230 Julian Ropcke, 'Putin's shadow government for Donbass exposed,' *Bild*, 29 March 2016. http://www.bild.de/politik/ausland/ukraine-konflikt/donbass-shadow-government-45102202.bild.html

1231 'Moscow's bankrolling Ukraine rebels: Ex-Separatist Official,' *Reuters*, 5 October 2016. http://www.reuters.com/article/us-ukraine-crisis-separatists-idUSKCN1251UQ. V. Peshkov writes, 'The banking sector is virtually non-existent. Russia supplies the physical cash on a special train that also carries weapons, ammunition, and cartridges – products that the DNR and LNR cannot manufacture themselves' (*The Donbas: Back in the USSR*).

[1232] A *kurator* is a 'political bureaucrat, a project manager authorised by the Kremlin to operate through personal agents.' Gleb Pawlowsky, 'Russian Politics Under the System Will Outlast the Master,' *Foreign Affairs*, vol.95, no.3 (May-June 2016), p.13.

[1233] Russia and the Separatists in Eastern Ukraine.

[1234] J. Ropcke, 'How Russia Finances the Ukrainian rebel territories,' *Bild*, 16 January 2016. http://www.bild.de/politik/ausland/ukraine-konflikt/russia-finances-donbass-44151166.bild.html

[1235] Ibid.,

[1236] L. Harding, *A Very Expensive Poison*, p.71.

[1237] *Watching the Watchman.*

[1238] See two articles by senior national security adviser Volodymyr Horbulin on Russia's hybrid war against Ukraine: 'Hibrydna viyna yak klyuchovyy instrument rosiyskoi heostratehii revanshu,' and 'Hibrydna viyna: vse tilky pochynayetsya,' *Tserkalo Tyzhnya*, 23 January 2015 and 25 March 2016. http://gazeta.dt.ua/internal/gibridna-viyna-yak-klyuchoviy-instrument-rosiyskoyi-geostrategiyi-revanshu-_.html and http://gazeta.dt.ua/internal/gibridna-viyna-vse-tilki-pochinayetsya-_.html

[1239] http://ratinggroup.ua/en/research/ukraine/obschestvenno-politicheskie_nastroeniya_naseleniya_oktyabr_2016.html

[1240] http://www.uceps.org/upload/1461830509_file.pdf

[1241] Report on the human rights situation in Ukraine, Office of the United Nations High Commissioner for Human Rights (UNHCHR), 15 May 2014, p.33.
http://www.ohchr.org/Documents/Countries/UA/HRMMUReport15May2014.pdf

[1242] 'Ukraine Wants Global Court to Investigate Crimes in Crimea and East,' *New York Times*, 17 April 2015.

[1243] http://reliefweb.int/report/world/report-preliminary-examination-activities-2016

[1244] https://www.amnesty.org/download/Documents/96000/eur500022004en.pdf

[1245] H. Coynash, 'The Kremlin's New Project on 'Ukraine's political prisoners,' *KHRPG*, 31 July 2015. http://khpg.org/en/index.php?id=1438114915

[1246] Ayder Muzhdabaev, 'Putin's new ghetto has no barbed-wire fence – just surveillance and harassment,' *The Guardian*, 12 December 2016. https://www.theguardian.com/world/commentisfree/2016/dec/12/putins-new-ghetto-has-no-barbed-wire-fence-just-surveillance-and-harassment

[1247] T. Martin, *The Affirmative Action Empire*, p.460.

[1248] A. Fournier, 'Mapping Identities: Russian Resistance to Linguistic Ukrainianisation in Central and Eastern Ukraine,' *Europe-Asia Studies*, vol.54, no.3 (2002), pp.415–33.

[1249] T. Martin, *The Affirmative Action Empire*, p.351.

[1250] T. Balmforth, 'Russia Arrests Ukrainian Library Director,' *RFERL*, 29 October 2015. http://www.rferl.org/content/russia-ukrainian-literature-library-extremist-books-director-arrested/27333929.html

[1251] A. Luhn, 'Moscow library of Ukrainian literature raided by 'anti-extremist' police,' *The Guardian*, 3 November 2015. http://www.theguardian.com/books/2015/nov/03/ukrainian-literature-library-moscow-raided-anti-extremist-police

[1252] A. Kurkov, *Ukraine Diaries*, p.132.

[1253] M. Mackinnon, 'We have no homeland.'

[1254] 'Short guide to separatist media in east Ukraine,' *BBC Monitoring*, 16 November 2014.

[1255] 'Portraits Unveiled of Ukrainians Detained in Russia,' *RFERL*, 29 January 2016. http://www.rferl.org/media/video/ukraine-russia-portraits/27519347.html

[1256] See the interactive graphic at: http://euromaidanpress.com/2016/12/24/there-are-36-ukrainian-hostages-of-the-kremlin-send-them-a-christmas-postcard-letmypeoplego/

[1257] http://www.gazeta.ru/politics/2016/05/04_a_8211929.shtml

[1258] Andriy Sharyi, and Olga Rasskazova, 'Eto tebe za Novorossiyu, banderovka!' *Radio Svoboda*, 26 March 2015. http://www.svoboda.org/content/article/26915369.html

[1259] D. Volchek and R. Coalson, 'Russian Youth Pays Price for Speaking Out Over Ukraine,' *RFERL*, 12 June 2015. http://www.rferl.org/content/russia-youth-antiwar-ukraine-persecution/27069023.html

[1260] Claire Bigg, 'Death of a Russian teenager who opposed the war in Ukraine,' *The Guardian*, 14 January 2016. http://www.theguardian.com/world/2016/jan/14/death-russian-teenager-who-opposed-war-ukraine

[1261] H. Coynash, 'Russian jailed for 12 years for mystery 'spying for Ukraine," *KHRPG*, 9 October 2015. http://khpg.org/en/index.php?id=1444305679

[1262] 'Crimean Tatar National Movement,' in L. Alexeyeva, *Soviet Dissent*, pp.137-159.

[1263] 'A. Mogilyov's Krymskaya Pravda article,' *T. Kuzio Ukrayinska Pravda blog*, 4 December 2011. http://blogs.pravda.com.ua/authors/kuzyo/4edabbffaa116/

[1264] Andrii Klymenko, *Human Rights Abuses in Russian-Occupied Crimea* (Washington DC: Freedom House and Atlantic Council, March 2015), H. Coynash, 'Targeting the Crimean Tatar Mejlis as pro-Russian euphoria fades in Crimea,' *KHRPG*, 19 September 2014, 'Crimean Tatar TV channel ATR accused of 'extremism,' *KHRPG*, 25 September 2014 and 'Moscow endorses offensive against Crimean Tatar Mejlis,' *KHRPG*, 26 September 2014.

https://freedomhouse.org/report/special-reports/human-rights-abuses-russian-occupied-crimea#.Vq9c3jYrKt8, http://khpg.org/en/index.php?id=1411135890; http://khpg.org/en/index.php?id=1411646632, and http://khpg.org/index.php?do=print&id=1411739009

[1265] Report on Ukraine, European Commission against Racism and Intolerance (ECRI), 21 February 2012. https://www.coe.int/t/dghl/monitoring/ecri/Country-by-country/Ukraine/Ukraine_CBC_en.asp

[1266] Serhiy Bahrianyy, 'Ukrayinophobia – ne ratsyzm?' *Ukrayinska Pravda*, 5 February 2009. http://www.pravda.com.ua/articles/2009/02/5/3712373/

[1267] 'Situation in Ukraine.'

[1268] Report on the human rights situation in Ukraine, 15 May 2014. Office of the UNHCHR. http://www.ohchr.org/Documents/Countries/UA/HRMMUReport15May2014.pdf. A similar conclusion was reached by the Human Rights Assessment Mission in Ukraine.

[1269] *Ukraine: Fear, Repression in Crimea. Rapid Rights Deterioration in 2 Years of Russian Rule* (New York: Human Rights Watch, 18 March 2016). https://www.hrw.org/news/2016/03/18/ukraine-fear-repression-crimea

[1270] Idil P. Izmirli, 'Crimea's Supreme Court Bans Crimean Tatar Mejlis Based on Fictitious Claims,' *Eurasia Daily Monitor*, vol. 13, no.87 (4 May 2016). http://www.jamestown.org/single/?tx_ttnews%5Btt_news%5D=45401&tx_ttnews%5Bback-Pid%5D=7&cHash=f078ac3f4aaad04fabeae6410430f30f#.Vyr7DaN97Vo

[1271] Ibid.,

1272 Ukraine, Human Rights Assessment Mission.

1273 A. Klymenko, *Human Rights Abuses in Russian-Occupied Crimea.*

1274 'Russian TV Rounds on Ukrainian Church,' *BBC Monitoring*, 9 April 2015.

1275 H. Coynash, 'New wave of 'arrests' & attack on Ukrainian churches in militant controlled Donetsk.'

1276 H. Tereshchuk and R. Coalson, 'Ukrainian 'Cyborg.''

1277 'When God becomes the weapon. Persecution based on religious beliefs in the armed conflict in eastern Ukraine,' Centre for Civil Liberties, Civic Solidarity, and International Partnership for Human Rights, April 2015. http://iphronline.org/wp-content/up-loads/2015/07/when_god_becomes_the_weapon_may2015.pdf

1278 http://www.imdb.com/title/tt2802154/

1279 'When God becomes the weapon.'

1280 Ibid.,

1281 'Sloviansk remembers, recovers two years after ending occupation by Kremlin-backed separatists,' *Kyiv Post*, 13 July 2016.

1282 M. Franchetti, 'Putin boosted by Orthodox 'inquisition.''

1283 T. Whewell, 'Russia's Imperialist Warriors.'

1284 An analysis of their murders can be found in Alexei Gordeyev, 'Chysto "novorossiyskoe" ubiystvo. Kak i pochemu adepty "DNR" rasstrelyaly 4 protestantov,' *Ukrayinska Pravda Life*, 13 June 2016.
http://life.pravda.com.ua/society/2016/06/13/213618/

1285 'Summary Killings During the Conflict in Eastern Ukraine.'

1286 'When God becomes the weapon,' pp.19-20.

1287 Al Jazeera International, 15 August 2014.

1288 'When God becomes the weapon.'

1289 H. Coynash, 'Crimean Church of the Kyiv Patriarch and its believers attacked,' *KHRPG*, 2 June 2014. http://www.khpg.org/en/index.php?id=1401631140

1290 D. Satter, *Darkness at Dawn,* pp.210-218.

1291 Ibid., p.204.

1292 E. Souleimanov, 'An ethnography of counterinsurgency,' pp.100-101.

1293 *Report on the Human Rights Situation in Ukraine*, Office of the UNHCHR, 15 May 2014. p.21. http://www.ohchr.org/Documents/Countries/UA/HRMMUReport15May2014.pdf

1294 Report on the Human Rights Situation in Ukraine, 15 May 2014. p.32.

1295 *Report on the human rights situation in Ukraine*, Office of the UNHCHR, 16 September 2014. http://www.ohchr.org/Documents/Countries/UA/OHCHR_sixth_re-port_on_Ukraine.pdf

1296 Elena Kostyuchenko, 'Myi vse znaly, na chto idiom i chto mozhet byt,' *Novaya Gazeta*, 4 March 2015. http://en.novayagazeta.ru/politics/67620.html

1297 Dmitry Volchek and Claire Bigg, 'Cutthroats and Bandits: Volunteers Stint with Ukraine Rebels Turns to Nightmare,' *RFERL*, 25 April 2015. http://www.rferl.org/con-tent/ukraine-war-russian-volunteer-interview/26976499.html

1298 Pierre Vaux, 'The War in Ukraine Is Back—So Why Won't Anyone Say So?', *The Daily Beast*, 3 February 2016 and H. Coynash, 'Kremlin-backed Donbas militants threaten to execute Ukrainian prisoners,' *KHRPG*, 9 February 2016. http://www.thedailybeast.com/articles/2016/02/03/the-war-in-ukraine-is-back-so-why-won-t-anyone-say-so.html and http://khpg.org/en/index.php?id=1454895232

[1299] Nolan Petersen, 'Is this Real Life? Inside the Ukraine War's Gray Zone,' *Daily Signal*, 18 March 2016. http://dailysignal.com/2016/03/18/is-this-real-life-inside-the-ukraine-wars-gray-zone/

[1300] James Miller, Pierre Vaux, Catherine A. Fitzpatrick, and Michael Weiss, *An Invasion by Any Other Name. The Kremlin's Dirty War in Ukraine* (New York: The Interpreter, Institute of Modern Russia, 17 September 2015). p.29. http://www.interpretermag.com/wp-content/uploads/2015/11/IMR_Ukraine_final_links_updt_02_corr.pdf

[1301] Gianni Magazzeni, head of the division of the UN human rights office that deals with Europe and Central Asia, is cited by Nick Cumming-Bruce, 'Hardships Grow in Ukraine, UN says,' *New York Times*, 15 December 2014. http://www.nytimes.com/2014/12/16/world/europe/hardships-grow-for-millions-in-eastern-ukraine-un-report-says.html

[1302] Nolan Peterson, 'Putin's Prisoners: Kiev Forces Are Routinely Tortured,' *Newsweek*, 28 February 2016. http://europe.newsweek.com/putins-prisoners-kiev-forces-are-routinely-tortured-430936?rm=eu

[1303] Paul Stronski and Isaac Webb, 'Prisoners Dilemma in Ukraine,' Carnegie Endowment, 23 June 2015. http://carnegieendowment.org/2015/06/23/prisoners-dilemma-in-ukraine/iay3

[1304] 'Ti, Shcho Perezhyly Peklo,' Małgorzata Gosiewska, *Russian War Crimes in Eastern Ukraine in 2014*, 1 January 2016 and 'Compelling proof: Polish parliamentarians published report on Russian war crimes in Ukraine, 19 December 2015. http://www.donbasswarcrimes.org/report/
and http://euromaidanpress.com/2015/12/19/86992/

[1305] *Ukraine: Mounting evidence of abduction and torture* (London: Amnesty International, 10 July 2014) and *Ukraine: Rebel Forces Detain, Torture Civilians* (New York: Human Rights Watch, 28 August 2014). http://www.amnesty.ca/news/news-releases/ukraine-mounting-evidence-of-abduction-and-torture and http://www.hrw.org/news/2014/08/28/ukraine-rebel-forces-detain-torture-civilians

[1306] *New evidence of summary killings of Ukrainian soldiers must spark urgent investigations*, (London: Amnesty International, 9 April 2015). https://www.amnesty.org/en/latest/news/2015/04/ukraine-new-evidence-of-summary-killings-of-captured-soldiers-must-spark-urgent-investigations/

[1307] H. Coynash, 'New wave of 'arrests' & attack on Ukrainian churches in militant controlled Donetsk,' *KHRPG*, 30 January 2016. http://khpg.org/en/index.php?id=1454112238

[1308] A photograph of his detention just prior to his brutal ordeal is to be found in 'Murdered' Ukraine politician faced hostile mob, video shows,' *Reuters*, 23 April 2014. http://uk.reuters.com/article/us-ukraine-crisis-politician-video-idUSBREA3M0EX20140423

[1309] The 'DNR' introduced its own 'criminal code' in August 2014, with the death penalty for grave crimes. H. Coynash, 'Execution for 'Spying', 'Desertion' or for a Ukrainian Flag?' *KHRPG*, 24 November 2015. http://khpg.org/index.php?id=1416534347

[1310] H. Coynash, 'Execution for 'Spying', 'Desertion' or for a Ukrainian Flag.'

[1311] H, Coynash, 'Tortured by Kremlin-backed militants,' *KHRPG*, 15 September 2014. http://khpg.org/index.php?do=print&id=1410645361

[1312] Kristina Jovanovski, 'The Corrupt Cops of Rebel-Held East Ukraine,' *The Daily Beast*, 11 December 2014. http://www.thedailybeast.com/articles/2014/12/11/the-corrupt-cops-of-rebel-held-east-ukraine.html

[1313] Anna Shamanska, 'Former Commander of Pro-Russian Separatists Says He Executed People Based On Stalin-Era Laws,' *RFERL*, 19 January 2016. http://www.rferl.org/content/ukraine-girkin-strelkov-executions-stalin-era/27497491.html

[1314] A. Zakharchenko cited by *Interfax*, 27 January 2016.

[1315] 'Givi' was wanted by the Ukrainian police for participating in violent separatism and committing human rights abuses against Ukrainian prisoners of war. He was assassinated in February 2017.

[1316] https://www.youtube.com/watch?v=o7r6rbvLWF

[1317] Nick Cohen, 'Do these grotesque pictures show that Putin wants Europe as his prisoner?' *The Spectator*, 7 February 2015. http://blogs.spectator.co.uk/2015/02/do-these-grotesque-pictures-show-that-putin-wants-europe-as-his-bitch/

[1318] L. Hyde, 'The missing: what have they done with our sons?'

[1319] Tom Burridge, 'Ukraine crisis: A family's story after 'hell' of Donetsk airport battle,' *BBC*, 24 March 2015. http://www.bbc.com/news/world-europe-32028959

[1320] See the amazing photographs in Max Avdeev and Max Seddon, 'Horrific Images Capture the Sheer Brutality of War in Ukraine,' *Buzzfeed News*, 17 February 2015. http://www.buzzfeed.com/avdeev/horrific-images-capture-the-sheer-brutality-of-ukraine-war#.lv4Rx93w1

[1321] Kiran Moodley, 'Dogs ate bodies in the aftermath of the battle for Debaltseve in Ukraine,' *The Independent*, 11 March 2015. http://www.independent.co.uk/news/world/europe/dogs-ate-bodies-in-the-aftermath-of-the-battle-for-debaltseve-in-ukraine-10099960.html

[1322] M. Tucker and B. Hoyle, 'Battle for key town leaves Ukraine ceasefire in tatters,' *The Times*, 18 February 2015.

[1323] M.Tucker and B. Hoyle, 'Ukrainian ceasefire ends in Donetsk bloodbath,' *The Times*, 23 January 2015.

[1324] 'Summary Killings During the Conflict in Eastern Ukraine.'

[1325] *Breaking Bodies. Torture and Summary Killings in Eastern Ukraine* EUR 50/1683/2015 (London: Amnesty International, May 2015). https://www.amnesty.org/en/documents/eur50/1683/2015/en/

[1326] http://www.kyivpost.com/article/content/kyiv-post-plus/murder-of-ukrainian-prisoner-by-russian-backed-separatists-investigated-videos-385322.html

[1327] H. Coynash, 'Interpol refuses to search for Russian militant suspected of war crimes in Donbas,' *KHRPG*, 15 June 2016. http://khpg.org/en/index.php?id=1465857439

[1328] *Breaking Bodies. Torture and Summary Killings in Eastern Ukraine.*

[1329] H. Tereshchuk and R. Coalson, 'Ukrainian 'Cyborg.''

[1330] L. Hyde, 'The missing: what have they done with our sons?'

[1331] Denis Krivosheev, Amnesty International, commenting about the report *New evidence of summary killings of Ukrainian soldiers must spark urgent investigations.*

[1332] Patrick Evans, 'Slave Labour' in the prisons of eastern Ukraine,' *BBC Magazine*, 3 October 2016. http://www.bbc.com/news/magazine-37512356. The Russian-language report can be found here: https://drive.google.com/file/d/0B7oLXom125V-am1ZZ3pvU2hkRDg/view

1333 'Men Return Completely Changed': Ukraine Conflict Fuelling Surge in Domestic Violence,' *RFERL*, 26 April 2015. http://www.rferl.org/content/ukraine-conflict-domestic-violence/26979064.html

1334 R. Sakwa, *Frontline Ukraine*, pp.152, 159 and 160.

1335 'Ukraine: Unguided Rockets Killing Civilians,' *Human Rights Watch*, 24 July 2014. https://www.hrw.org/news/2014/07/24/ukraine-unguided-rockets-killing-civilians

1336 https://www.amnesty.org/en/latest/news/2014/10/ukraine-forces-must-stop-firing-civilians-after-nine-killed-donetsk/

1337 https://www.amnesty.org/en/latest/news/2014/10/ukraine-forces-must-stop-firing-civilians-after-nine-killed-donetsk/

1338 Lyudmila Klochko, 'Report on the Human Rights mission to the Donetsk and Luhansk oblasts,' *KHRPG*, 1 January 2015. http://www.epde.org/tl_files/European-Exchange/Statements/Report_EN_fin.pdf

1339 Alexander Rychkov and Oleg Sukhov, 'Torture, rape and murder accusations swirl around Luhansk volunteer unit,' *Kyiv Post*, 26 June 2015. http://www.kyivpost.com/multimedia/photo/gbcnbvbnvbn-392002.html

1340 'Breaking Bodies. Torture and Summary Killings in Eastern Ukraine.'

1341 'Legal Remedies for human rights violations on the territories outside the control of the Ukrainian authorities,' PACE, Resolution 2133 (12 October 2016). https://assembly.coe.int/nw/xml/XRef/Xref-XML2HTML-EN.asp?fileid=23167&lang=en

1342 Anna Shamanska, 'Ukrainian journalist Details Her 419 Days in Separatist Captivity,' *RFERL*, 7 March 2016. http://www.rferl.org/content/ukraine-journalist-talks-419-days-separatist-captivity/27595944.html

1343 Nikolai Petrov, 'A Major Setback for Putin,' *Moscow Times*, 29 November 2004.

1344 Sabrina Tavernise, 'The Next Battle for Ukraine,' *New York Times*, 3 January 2015. http://www.nytimes.com/2015/01/04/sunday-review/the-next-battle-for-ukraine.html

1345 I heard this in many places in Kyiv and was told this in October 2014 on the overnight train from Kyiv to Odesa by a businesswoman who is from Odesa and was travelling from Moscow. When visiting Russia, she would be told by her business partners that she did not understand Ukrainian situation and should listen to them who did.

1346 Andriy Zayarnyuk, 'A Revolution's History, A Historians War, *Ab Imperio*, no.1, 205, p.471. http://abimperio.net/cgi-bin/aishow.pl?idlang=2&state=shown&idnumb=123

1347 *Radio Russia*, 5 March 2004.

1348 'Common Identity of the Citizens of Ukraine.'

1349 I. Bekeshkina, 'Viyna zhurtuvala natsiyu,' *Novoye Vremya*, 9 June 2013. http://nv.ua/ukr/opinion/bekeshkina/vijna-zgurtuvala-natsiju-144094.html

1350 I. Bekeshkina, 'Donbas yak Osoblyvyy Rehion Ukrayiny.'

1351 In February 2014, less than half, or 41 percent, of Crimean's supported Ukraine-Russia unity. S. Yekelchyk, *The Conflict in Ukraine*, p.129.

1352 I. Bekeshkina, 'Donbas yak Osoblyvyy Rehion Ukrayiny.'

1353 Eleanor Knott, 'Do Crimean's see themselves as Russian or Ukraine? It's complicated,' *The Washington Post*, 3 December 2015. https://www.washingtonpost.com/news/monkey-cage/wp/2015/12/03/do-crimeans-see-themselves-as-russian-or-ukrainian-its-complicated/

1354 'Public opinion liberated areas - Kramatorsk, Slovyansk,' Democratic Initiatives, November 2015.

http://dif.org.ua/ua/polls/2014_polls/obshestvennavjansk.htm

1355 'What factors unite and divide Ukrainians.'

1356 C. J. Chivers and David M. Herszenhorn, 'Separatists Defy Kiev and Putin on Referendum,' *New York Times*, 8 May 2014. http://www.nytimes.com/2014/05/09/world/europe/ukraine.html?_r=0.

1357 http://www.forbes.com/sites/paulroderickgregory/2014/05/05/putins-human-rights-council-accidentally-posts-real-crimean-election-results-only-15-voted-for-annexation/#2f5f1fb110ff

1358 A. Klymenko, *Human Rights Abuses in Russian-occupied Crimea*, pp.4-5, *The Attitude to the State System and Status of Crimea*, Rating Sociological Group, 14 March 2014. http://ratinggroup.ua/en/research/ukraine/otnoshenie_ukraincev_k_territorialnomu_ustroystvu_strany_i_statusu_kryma.html

1359 Levada Centre poll, 22-26 January 2015.

1360 T. Bukkvoll, 'Why Putin went to war,' p.270.

1361 S. Yekelchyk, *The Conflict in Ukraine*, p.129.

1362 A. Klymenko, Human Rights Abuses in Russian-Occupied Crimea.

1363 http://www.levada.ru/en/2016/06/22/russia-ukraine-relations-2/

1364 'Stavlennya Ukrayintsiv do Terytorialnoho Ustroyu Krayiny ta Statusu Kryma,' Rating Sociological Group, 14 March 2014.

http://ratinggroup.ua/research/ukraine/otnoshenie_ukraincev_k_territorialnomu_ustroystvu_strany_i_statusu_kryma.html

1365 Documentary film 'Donetsk Airport,' December 2015: http://www.currenttime.tv/fullinfographics/infographics/aiportdonetsk/27255834.html#

1366 'Interview with a separatist fighter,' *RFERL*, 13 July 2014. http://www.rferl.org/content/ukraine-i-was-a-separatist-fighter/25455466.html

1367 Documentary film 'Donetsk Airport.'

1368 'Common Identity of the Citizens of Ukraine.'

1369 'What unites and divide Ukrainians.'

1370 L. Harding, *Mafia State. How one reporter became an enemy of the brutal new Russia* (London: Guardian Books, 2011) p.202.

1371 L. Barrington, 'Views of the 'Ethnic Other' in Ukraine,' *Nationalism and Ethnic Politics*, vol.8, no.2 (June 2002) p.361. See also T. Kuzio, 'Identity and Nation Building in Ukraine. Defining the 'Other'', *Ethnicities*, vol.1, no.3 (December 2001), pp.343-366.

1372 President Poroshenko gave a figure of 62 percent of Ukrainian forces in the ATO who are Russian speakers. http://ukraineunderattack.org/4338-prezident-62-bijtsiv-ato-rosijskomovni.html

1373 'Identychnist Hromadyan Ukrayiny v Novykh Umovakh: Stan, Tendentsii, Rehionalni Osoblyvosti,' Razumkov Centre, 7 June 2016. http://www.razumkov.org.ua/upload/Identi-2016.pdf

1374 'What unites and divides Ukrainians.'

1375 Ibid.,

1376 Kharkiv-born Russian speaking Lozhkin, Poroshenko's Chief of Staff in 2014-2016, called into question Sakwa's division of Ukraine into those supporting monistic and pluralistic approaches to language policies. B. Lozhkin, *The Fourth Republic*, pp.77-78.

1377 *Public Opinion Survey. Residents of Ukraine*, 16-30 June 2015, IRI. http://www.iri.org/sites/default/files/wysiwyg/2015-08-24_survey_of_residents_of_ukraine_july_16-30_2015.pdf

1378 Ibid.,

1379 Ibid.,

1380 Ibid.,

1381 I. Bekeshkina, 'Donbas-2015: deyaki problemy reintehratsii rehiony,' *Ukrayinske Suspilstvo: Monitorynh Sotsialnykh Zmin* (Kyiv: Institute of Sociology, National Academy of Sciences, 2015), pp.40-50.

1382 Martin Dowle, Natasha Vasylyuk, and Mona Lotten, *Hopes, Fears and Dreams. The Views of Ukraine's next generation*, British Council, 2015. https://www.britishcouncil.org/organisation/policy-insight-research/research/hopes-fears-and-dreams

1383 Ievgen Vorobiov, 'Why Ukrainians are Speaking More Ukrainian,' *Foreign Policy*, 26 June 2015. http://foreignpolicy.com/2015/06/26/why-ukrainians-are-speaking-more-ukrainian/

1384 'Yak zminylosya stavlennya naselennya Ukrayiny do Rosii ta Naselennya Rosii do Ukrayiny,' KIIS, 6 February 2015.
http://www.kiis.com.ua/?lang=ukr&cat=reports&id=502&page=1

1385 http://w1.c1.rada.gov.ua/pls/zweb2/webproc4_2?id=&pf3516=2332&skl=9

1386 'Public opinion liberated areas - Kramatorsk, Slovyansk.'

1387 M. Riabchuk, 'Two Ukraine's' Reconsidered: The End of Ukrainian Ambivalence?' *Studies in Ethnicity and Nationalism*, vol.15, no.1 (April 2015), p.152.

1388 C.Wanner, '"Fraternal" nations and challenges to sovereignty in Ukraine,' p.432.

1389 Volodymyr Kulyk, 'National Identity in Ukraine: Impact of Euromaidan and the War,' *Europe-Asia Studies*, vol.68, no.4 (June 2016), p.601.

1390 Maksym Bugriy, 'Ukraine's Resilience Strengthens, Though Regional Cohesion Risks Remain,' *Eurasia Daily Monitor*, vol. 13, no.126 (13 July 2016). https://jamestown.org/program/ukraines-resilience-strengthens-though-regional-cohesion-risks-remain/

1391 V. Kulyk, 'National Identity in Ukraine,' pp.604-606.

1392 Tadeusz Olszanski, *Ukraine's Wartime Nationalism*, OSW Commentary, no.179 (Warsaw: Centre for Eastern Studies, 28 August 2015). http://www.osw.waw.pl/en/publikacje/osw-commentary/2015-08-19/ukraines-wartime-nationalism

1393 M. Dowle, N. Vasylyuk, and M. Lotten, *Hopes, Fears and Dreams*.

1394 Ibid.,

1395 'Do Dnya Nezalezhnosti: Shcho Ukrayintsi dumayut pro Ukrayinu?' Democratic Initiatives Foundation, 21 August 2015. http://www.dif.org.ua/ua/polls/2015a/do-dnja-nezalezhnosti-sho-ukrainci-dumayut-pro-ukrainu__1440150573.htm

1396 Deutsche Welle, 'Sotsiolohy: Ukrayintsi staly pyshatyshya svoyeyu krayinoyu,' *Ukrayinska Pravda*, 23 August 2015. http://www.pravda.com.ua/inozmi/deutsche-welle/2015/08/23/7078759/

1397 Scott Peterson, 'At key Ukrainian flashpoint, both rebels and loyalists wait and worry,' *Christian Science Monitor*, 5 March 2015. http://www.csmonitor.com/World/Europe/2015/0305/At-key-Ukraine-flashpoint-both-rebels-and-loyalists-wait-and-worry

1398 B. Lozhkin, *The Fourth Republic*, p.67.

1399 The Levada Centre in Russia and KIIS in Ukraine conducted simultaneous polls.
http://www.levada.ru/2016/02/03/majdan-ukraina-krym/
and http://kiis.com.ua/?lang=ukr&cat=reports&id=609&page=1

1400 T. Zhurzhenko, 'Ukraine's Eastern Borderlands: The end of ambiguity?' in A. Wilson ed., *What Does Ukraine Think?* (London: European Council on Foreign Relations, 18 May 2015), pp.45-52. http://www.ecfr.eu/publications/summary/what_does_ukraine_think3026

1401 'What unites and divides Ukrainians.'

1402 M. Dowle, N. Vasylyuk, and M. Lotten, *Hopes, Fears and Dreams.*

1403 C. Wanner, 'Fraternal" nations and challenges to sovereignty in Ukraine,' pp.431-432.

1404 T. Zhurzhenko, 'From Borderlands to Bloodlands,' conference 'Negotiating Borders: Comparing the Experience of Canada, Europe and Ukraine,' Canadian Institute of Ukrainian Studies, University of Alberta, 16-17 October 2014.

1405 All 12 Crimean, 9 out of 21 Donetsk and 6 out of 11 Luhansk election districts did not participate in the October 2014 parliamentary elections.

1406 In western and central Ukraine, 86 percent believed Russian television spread falsehoods. *Ukrayinska Pravda,* 24 December 2014.

1407 T. Zhurzhenko, 'From Borderlands to Bloodlands, conference.'

1408 Daisy Sindelar, 'We're nothing more than bargaining chips,' *The Guardian,* 23 January 2015. http://www.theguardian.com/world/2015/jan/23/-sp-ukraine-russia-identity-wartime

1409 'Do Dnya Nezalezhnosti: Shcho Ukrayintsi dumayut pro Ukrayinu?'

1410 'What unites and divides Ukrainians.'

1411 Ibid.,

1412 Ibid.,

1413 T. Zhurzhenko, 'From Borderlands to Bloodlands, conference.'

1414 'What unites and divides Ukrainians.'

1415 Peter Leonard, 'Ukraine's Self-Defense Units Look for the Enemy Within,' *Associated Press,* 11 July 2015. http://bigstory.ap.org/article/d483d91ae1104902b731fe9c15061838/ukraines-self-defense-units-look-enemy-within

1416 See Alla Chernova ed., *Ukrayinskyy Seredenyy Klas Ochyma Yoho Predstavnykiv* (Kyiv: Razumkov Centre, 2014), pp. 62 and 67. http://www.razumkov.org.ua/ukr/news.php?news_id=536

1417 P. Pomerantsev, 'Propagandalands.'

1418 R. Olearchyk, 'Former Georgian president shakes up Odesa,' *Financial Times,* 8 July 2015.

1419 H. Coynash, 'Odesa Smoking Gun Leads Directly to Moscow, *KHRPG,* 29 September 2016. 'http://khpg.org/en/index.php?id=1473972066&w=odesa

1420 Report of the International Advisory Panel on its Review of the Investigation into the Events in Odesa on 2 May 2014, Council of Europe, 4 November 2015. https://www.coe.int/en/web/kyiv/report-on-investigations-of-odesa-events

1421 R. Sakwa, *Frontline Ukraine,* pp.97-99.

1422 https://www.theguardian.com/technology/2017/feb/08/wikipedia-bans-daily-mail-as-unreliable-source-for-website

1423 'Odesa. May 2: What Really Happened,' http://uatoday.tv/society/odesa-may-2-watch-on-ukraine-today-424573.html and https://www.youtube.com/watch?v=fG-21ChuofA

1424 R. Zubrin, 'Did Putin Plan the Odesa Massacre?' *National Review,* 13 May 2014. http://www.nationalreview.com/article/377818/did-putin-plan-odessa-massacre-robert-zubrin

[1425] H. Coynash, 'Russia's New Odesa File. Manufacturing international outrage over an Odesa Massacre that never was,' *KHRPG*, 4 November 2014. http://khpg.org/en/index.php?id=1415072123

[1426] James Kirchick, 'Ukraine's Vigilante Peacemakers,' *The Daily Beast*, 17 May 2014. http://www.thedailybeast.com/articles/2014/05/17/ukraine-s-vigilante-peacemakers.html

[1427] https://rm.coe.int/CoERMPublicCommonSearchServices/DisplayDCTMContent?documentId=090000168048851b

[1428] H. Coynash, 'Clear Signs of Sabotage' in Odesa 2 May Investigation,' *KHRPG*, 15 January 2016. http://khpg.org/en/pda/index.php?do=print&id=1452811753

[1429] http://2maygroup.blogspot.com/2016/01/20.html?spref=fb

[1430] Sakwa's account includes no references to Ukrainian sources, such as the numerous reports by the *KHRPG* and analyses by local NGO's and journalists, one of which I have used in Table 11.1. Sakwa (*Frontline Ukraine*, p.137) describes Odesa oligarch Serhiy Kivalov as a 'long-time voice of moderation and inclusivity.' Kivalov has no credibility as he was the disgraced Chairman of the Central Election Commission at the centre of massive election fraud in the 2004 elections.

[1431] 'The Battle for Ukraine.' See also Linda Kinstler, 'A Ukrainian City Holds Its Breath,' *Foreign Policy*, 20 February 2015. http://foreignpolicy.com/2015/02/20/the-ukrainian-separatists-next-target-kharkiv-ukraine-donbass-russia-war/

[1432] Denys Kazanskyy, 'Pryvid 'KNR'' z pidvalu na bazar,' *Ukrayinsky Tyzhden*, 26 Sptember-2 October 2014.

[1433] See a video clip from Kharkiv in Spring 2014 at https://www.youtube.com/watch?v=ApNCSQpYxAc. A documentary entitled 'Khchorobri sertse. Ultras,' was shown on 2+2 channel on 24 December 2015: https://www.youtube.com/watch?v=op5WNrViP2s

[1434] 'The Battle for Ukraine.'

[1435] O. Carroll, 'Why Ukraine's Separatist Movement Failed in Kharkiv.'

[1436] A. Shprintsen, 'CBC producer revisits Ukraine to explore conflict.'

[1437] Ibid.,

[1438] 'Letters from Donbas, Part 3.'

[1439] Michael Billig, *Banal Nationalism* (London: Sage, 1995).

[1440] Neil MacFarquhar, 'Conflict Uncovers a Ukrainian Identity Crisis Over Deep Russian Roots,' *New York Times*, 18 October 2014. http://www.nytimes.com/2014/10/19/world/europe/conflict-uncovers-a-ukrainian-identity-crisis-over-deep-russian-roots-.html?_r=0

[1441] 'Ukraine crisis: Mariupol preparing for attack,' *BBC*, 26 February 2015. http://www.bbc.com/news/world-europe-31636492

[1442] Alexander Rychkov, 'Convicts-turned-cops on forefront of Ukraine's battle against Russia,' *Kyiv Post*, 18 February 2015. http://www.kyivpost.com/content/kyiv-post-plus/convicts-turned-cops-on-forefront-of-ukraines-battle-against-russia-381135.html

[1443] 'Letters from Donbas, Part 3.'

[1444] A. Kurkov, *Ukraine Diaries,* p.103.

[1445] P. Pomerantsev, 'Diary.'

[1446] Deutsche Welle, 'Sotsiolohy: Ukrayintsi staly pyshatyshya svoyeyu krayinoyu.'

[1447] 'Ukrainian 'Cyborg' Describes Nine Days Defending Donetsk Airport,' *RFERL*, 15 November 2014. http://www.rferl.org/content/donetsk-fighters-ukraine/26693593.html

[1448] Deutsche Welle, 'Sotsiolohy: Ukrayintsi staly pyshatyshya svoyeyu krayinoyu.'

[1449] 'We're nothing more than bargaining chips.'

[1450] *Novosti Ekaterynberg*, 15 April 2015. http://www.e1.ru/news/spool/news_id-422297.html

[1451] S. Kudelia, 'Domestic Sources of the Donbas Insurgency.'

[1452] Marc Champion, 'Putin's big mistake,' *Bloomberg*, 19 November 2014. http://www.bloombergview.com/articles/2014-11-19/putins-big-mistake

[1453] Oksana Malanchuk, 'Social Identification versus Regionalism in Contemporary Ukraine,' *Nationalities Papers*, vol. 33, no.3 (September 2005), pp.345-368.

[1454] M. Dowle, N. Vasylyuk, and M. Lotten, *Hopes, Fears and Dreams.*

[1455] Ibid.,

[1456] Ibid.,

[1457] Yaroslav Baran, 'Ukraine One Year After the Euromaidan: Amid an Undeclared War, Deep Social Change,' *Policy Magazine*, January-February 2015. http://policymagazine.ca/pdf/11/PolicyMagazineJanuaryFebruary-2015-Baran.pdf

[1458] *Natsionalna Bezpeka i Oborona*, nos.3-4 (2016), p.33.

[1459] 'The Ukrainian People on the Current Crisis.'

[1460] Public Opinion Survey. Residents of Ukraine, IRI, June 2015.

[1461] Razumkov Centre poll, 6-12 March 2015. http://www.razumkov.org.ua/ukr/socpolls.php?cat_id=51

[1462] Public Opinion Survey. Residents of Ukraine, IRI, June 2015.

[1463] http://ratinggroup.ua/en/research/ukraine/obschestvenno-politicheskie_nastroeniya_naseleniya_oktyabr_2016.html

[1464] 'Pivtora roky pislya pochatku Yevromaydanu: dynamika stavlennya ukrayintsiv i rosiyan odne do odnoho,' KIIS, *Ukrinform*, 21 May 2014. http://presscenter.ukrinform.com/ukr/news/2055534

[1465] 'The Ukrainian People on the Current Crisis.'

[1466] 'Identychnist Hromadyan Ukrayiny v Novykh Umovakh.'

[1467] 'The Ukrainian-Russian Conflict: current state, implications, scenarios.' *National Security and Defence*, no.5 (2014). http://www.razumkov.org.ua/eng/journal.php?y=2014&cat=206

[1468] NATO Publics Blame Russia for Crisis, But Reluctant to Provide Aid, Pew Research Center, 10 June 2015. http://www.pewglobal.org/2015/06/10/nato-publics-blame-russia-for-ukrainian-crisis-but-reluctant-to-provide-military-aid/

[1469] *Natsionalna Bezpeka i Oborona*, nos.3-4 (2016), p.39.

[1470] Razumkov Centre poll, 6-12 March 2015.

[1471] *Natsionalna Bezpeka i Oborona*, nos.3-4 (2016), p.47.

[1472] 'Identychnist Hromadyan Ukrayiny v Novykh Umovakh.'

[1473] 'Public opinion liberated areas - Kramatorsk, Slovyansk.'

[1474] Interview with Ukrainian 'Cyborgs' 'Denys,' 'Vanya' and 'Sever.'

[1475] Documentary film 'Donetsk Airport.'

[1476] Julie Ray and Neli Esipova, 'Ukrainian Approval of Russia's Leadership Dives Almost 90%,' *Gallup*, 15 December 2014. http://www.gallup.com/poll/180110/ukrainian-approval-russia-leadership-dives-almost.aspx?utm_source=alert&utm_medium=email&utm_content=morelink&utm_campaign=syndication

[1477] Gallup poll cited by Joel Weickgenant, 'Even 'Novorossiya' Isn't that into Russia Anymore,' *RCW Blog*, 16 December 2014. http://www.realclearworld.com/blog/2014/12/even_novorossiya_isnt_that_into_russia_anymore.html

[1478] Special issue on 'The Ukrainian-Russian Conflict: current state, implications, scenarios.'

[1479] *Natsionalna Bezpeka i Oborona*, nos.3-4 (2016), p.51.

[1480] Anastasia Dmitruk, 'We will never be brothers!' April 2014. https://www.youtube.com/watch?v=Qv97YeC563Y and https://www.youtube.com/watch?v=jj1MTTArzPI

[1481] 'The Ukrainian-Russian Conflict: current state, implications, scenarios,' p.73.

[1482] Ibid., p.72.

[1483] James J. Coyle, 'Thanks to Russia, Ukrainians Swell Ranks of Kyiv Patriarch,' *New Atlanticist*, *Atlantic Council of the US*, 22 June 2016 and Alexandra Markovich, 'As more Ukrainians choose Kyiv Patriarchate, push intensifies for unified national Orthodox church,' *Kyiv Post*, 23 June 2016. http://www.atlanticcouncil.org/blogs/new-atlanticist/thanks-to-russia-ukrainians-swell-ranks-of-kyiv-patriarchate and https://www.kyivpost.com/article/content/ukraine-politics/divided-by-politics-orthodox-church-fails-to-unite-ukrainian-people-417077.html

[1484] http://ratinggroup.ua/en/research/ukraine/otnoshenie_k_lideram_religioznyh_konfessiy.html

[1485] Razumkov Centre, 'To which Orthodox Church do you owe your allegiance?' http://www.uceps.org/ukr/poll.php?poll_id=883

[1486] Vitaliy Chervonenko, 'Sotsiolohichne doslidzhennya: paradoksy Slovyanska ta Kramatorska,' *BBC Ukrainian Service*, 19 December 2014. http://www.bbc.com/ukrainian/politics/2014/12/141219_donbas_pools_vc

[1487] S. Yekelchyk, 'In Ukraine, Lenin finally falls,' *The Washington Post*, 28 February 2014. https://www.washingtonpost.com/opinions/in-ukraine-lenin-finally-falls/2014/02/28/a6ab2a8e-9f0c-11e3-9ba6-800d1192d08b_story.html

[1488] Liza Premiyak and Niels Ackermann, 'Looking for Lenin. Hunting down banned Soviet statues in Ukraine,' http://calvertjournal.com/features/show/5790/lenin-soviet-monument-ukraine

[1489] Ibid.,

[1490] Only 12 percent of Ukrainians disagree with the designation of the *holodomor* as a 'genocide.' http://www.istpravda.com.ua/short/2015/11/24/148747/. The full survey can be found at http://ratinggroup.ua/research/ukraine/dinamika_otnosheniya_k_golodomoru_noyabr_2015.html

[1491] 'Do Dnya Nezalezhnosti: Shcho Ukrayintsi dumayut pro Ukrayinu?'

[1492] 'Dynamika Stavlennya do Vyznannya OUN-UPA,' Rating Sociological Group, 12 October 2015. http://ratinggroup.ua/en/research/ukraine/dinamika_otnosheniya_k_priznaniyu_oun-upa.html

[1493] 'Do Dnya Nezalezhnosti: Shcho Ukrayintsi dumayut pro Ukrayinu?'

[1494] http://ratinggroup.ua/en/research/ukraine/dinamika_obschestvenno-politicheskih_nastroeniy_v_ukraine.html

[1495] Ievgen Vorobiov, 'Surprise! Ukraine Loves NATO,' *Foreign Policy*, 13 August 2015. http://foreignpolicy.com/2015/08/13/surprise-ukraine-loves-nato/

[1496] Razumkov Centre poll cited by *Den*, 13 January 2016. http://www.day.kiev.ua/uk/news/130116-48-ukrayinciv-za-vstup-do-pivnichnoatlantychnogo-alyansu

[1497] I. Bekeshkina, 'Donbas yak Osoblyvyy Rehion Ukrayiny.'

[1498] *Public Opinion Survey, Residents of Ukraine*, IRI 7-21 September 2015,
http://www.iri.org/sites/default/files/wysiwyg/2014-10-14_survey_of_ukrain-ian_public_opinion_september_7-21_2015.pdf

[1499] http://www.razumkov.org.ua/eng/socpolls.php?cat_id=46 and
http://www.razumkov.org.ua/eng/socpolls.php?cat_id=139

[1500] 'The Ukrainian-Russian Conflict: current state, implications, scenarios.'

[1501] Public Opinion Survey, Residents of Ukraine, IRI, September 2015.

[1502] Ibid.,

[1503] 'Russia and me: Leonid Kravchuk.'

[1504] *Razumkov Centre Newsletter*, no.1 (15 February 2016).

[1505] T. Kuzio, 'Tatars Fear a Future Under Russia.'

[1506] Poll of foreign leaders, *Ukrayinska Pravda*, 23 September 2014.
http://www.pravda.com.ua/news/2014/09/23/7038653/

[1507] V. Putin cited by www.kremlin.ru, 4 September 2013.